THE AMERICAN
FILM
INDUSTRY

THE AMERICAN FILM INDUSTRY

A HISTORICAL DICTIONARY

Anthony Slide

RESEARCH ASSOCIATES ————————————————————

Val Almendarez
Rudy Behlmer
John Belton
Alan Gevinson
Robert Gitt
Thomas W. Hoffer
Richard Alan Nelson
Susan Perez Prichard ————————————————————

GREENWOOD PRESS
NEW YORK
WESTPORT, CONNECTICUT
LONDON

Library of Congress Cataloging-in-Publication Data

Slide, Anthony.
   The American film industry.
   Bibliography: p.
   Includes index.
   1. Moving-picture industry—United States—
Dictionaries. I. Title.
PN1993.5.U6S539   1986   384′ .8′0973   85-27260
ISBN 0–313–24693–9 (lib. bdg. : alk. paper)

Library of Congress Catalog Card Number: 85–27260
ISBN: 0–313–24693–9

First published in 1986

Greenwood Press, Inc.
88 Post Road West, Westport, Connecticut 06881

Printed in the United States of America

∞™

The paper used in this book complies with the
Permanent Paper Standard issued by the National
Information Standards Organization (Z39.48–1984).

10 9 8 7 6 5 4 3 2 1

For Andre de Toth
whose films and attitude
represent what I like best
about the American Film Industry

Contents

Preface   ix

Entries   1

Resource Libraries and Institutions   405

Bibliography   407

Index   409

Preface

There have been many "Who's Who" of the American film industry, but this is the first "What's What," a dictionary of American producing and releasing companies, technological innovations, film series, industry terms, studios, genres, and organizations. Included here are more than 600 entries on everything from the Academy of Motion Picture Arts and Sciences to the Zoom Lens, from Astoria Studios to Zoetrope. There are entries on more than 100 companies active in the teens, as well as all the major studios, such as Metro-Goldwyn-Mayer and 20th Century-Fox. The various color systems, such as Technicolor, Kinemacolor, Prizma Color, and Eastman Color, are described in this volume, as are CinemaScope, Todd-AO, Dolby Sound, and Panavision.

Following many of the entries, which vary in length according to the importance of the subject matter, will be an address (if the company or organization is still active), a short bibliography, and, where appropriate, information—under the heading "Resources"—as to institutional holdings of the subject's films, papers, or still photographs. A general bibliography appears at the end of the book. An asterisk (*) following a name in any of the entries indicates that there is a separate entry for that subject.

Headings are based on the best-known name of a company, studio, or technical innovation and are not necessarily the final name by which the subject was known. However, cross-references within the text will immediately indicate the heading used. Cross-references have also been used to refer researchers to a studio or a company outside of a major film community, where the researcher is familiar only with the town or city in which the company was located but is not aware of its name. Thus, under Lake Placid, New York, will be found a cross-reference to Excelsior Feature Film Company, Inc., and under Providence, Rhode Island, will be found a cross-reference to Eastern Film Company. The index includes the names of all individuals associated with a particular company, thus enabling a researcher, yet again, to track down a company without prior knowledge of its name.

Aside from my research associates, I would like to thank the following individuals, organizations, and companies for their cooperation: the Margaret Herrick Library of the Academy of Motion Picture Arts and Sciences; the Cannon Group, Inc.; DeLuxe Laboratories, Inc.; Du Art Film Laboratories, Inc.; Eastman Kodak Company; Films Incorporated; Jeff Goodman; Sherman Grinberg Film Libraries, Inc.; Harold E. Guthrie; Hanna-Barbera Productions; Vernon Harbin; Anne Kail; Doug Lemza; Andrew C. McKay; Newhall Land and Farming Company; Walter O'Connor; Trans-Lux Corporation; The Doheny Memorial Library of the University of Southern California; Laura Voisin; and Marc Wanamaker.

The following periodicals were of particular value for research purposes: *Boxoffice*, *Daily Variety*, *Motion Picture Herald*, *Motion Picture News*, *The Moving Picture World*, *The New York Dramatic Mirror*, and *Variety*.

The essay on Animation is the work of Thomas W. Hoffer, the essay on Costume Design the work of Susan Perez Prichard, the essay on Florida the work of Richard Alan Nelson, and the essays on Sound and the Zoom Lens the work of John Belton. Special thanks are due Alan Gevinson for his exemplary research on pre–1920 American companies.

THE AMERICAN FILM INDUSTRY

A

AA FINANCE CORPORATION. See ART CINEMA CORPORATION

ABC MOTION PICTURES, INC. Formed in May 1979 by the American Broadcasting Company, ABC Motion Pictures, Inc. was the network's second attempt to become involved in feature film production. Under Brandon Stoddard's presidency, the company waited almost two years before commencing production on its first feature, *Young Doctors in Love* (1982). The best known of ABC Motion Pictures productions, all of which were released by 20th Century-Fox*, is *Silkwood* (1983). The American Broadcasting Company closed down its Motion Picture division in October 1985.

BIBLIOGRAPHY

Kilday, Gregg, "ABC Motion Pictures Comes of Age," *Los Angeles Herald-Examiner*, July 16, 1982, p. D4.

ACADEMY FOUNDATION. See ACADEMY OF MOTION PICTURE ARTS AND SCIENCES

ACADEMY OF MOTION PICTURE ARTS AND SCIENCES. The concept for the Academy of Motion Picture Arts and Sciences was first discussed at a dinner hosted in January 1927 by M-G-M* production head, Louis B. Mayer. On January 11, 1927, a meeting was held at the Ambassador Hotel in Los Angeles, and the Academy of Motion Picture Arts and Sciences was officially formed. Among its founders were Louis B. Mayer, Mary Pickford, Douglas Fairbanks (who became the first president), Frank Lloyd, Joseph M. Schenck, Fred Niblo, and Cedric Gibbons. It was granted a charter as a nonprofit California organization on May 4, 1927, and an organizational banquet was held at the Biltmore Hotel, Los Angeles, on May 11, 1927.

The Academy was formed to fend off attacks against the industry, to promote unity among the various groups of workers within the industry, to advance the power and influence of the motion picture, and—for what it is best known—to "encourage the improvement and advancement of the arts and sciences of the profession by the interchange of constructive ideas and by awards of merit for distinctive achievement."

To this end the Academy gives annual awards of merit—first presented at the Hollywood Roosevelt Hotel on May 16, 1929, for the year August 1, 1927–July 31, 1928—which became known by the late thirties as "Oscars." The Oscar statuette, which has never changed (except for the height of its base) stands 13.5 inches tall and weighs 8.5 pounds. It is manufactured from Britannium and is gold-plated. Conrad Nagel, one of the Academy's founders, urged that the award be a "symbol of continuing progress—militant, dynamic." Art director Cedric Gibbons sketched a knight, holding a crusader's sword and standing on a reel of film, and the figure was molded by sculptor George Stanley. The name "Oscar," according to the Academy, was given to the statuette by the organization's first librarian, Margaret Herrick (then Margaret Gledhill), who claimed it looked like her Uncle Oscar. Other stories have the name originating with Bette Davis.

Awards for Best Actor, Actress, Art Direction, Picture, Cinematography, Directing, and Writing have been given since the first year. Special Awards—from 1950 onward called Honorary Awards—have also been part of the Academy Awards ceremony since its conception. Sound was added to the Awards schedule in 1929/1930; Scientific or Technical Awards were added in 1930/1931; Short Subjects were added in 1931/1932; Assistant Director Awards were given from 1932/1933 to 1937; Music and Film Editing were added in 1934; Dance Direction was given from 1935 to 1937; Best Supporting Actor and Actress were introduced in 1936; the Irving G. Thalberg Memorial Award was introduced in 1937; Special Effects was first given an Award in 1939; Documentary Awards were first given in 1942; Costume Design was added in 1948, and that same year the Foreign Language Film Award was given as a Special Award—it did not become a regular category until 1956; the Jean Hersholt Humanitarian Award was introduced in 1956.

Initially the Academy was heavily involved in labor relations and disputes within the industry. Because it was quickly branded as a producers' tool, it lost much of its membership, and the March 5, 1936, Awards Banquet was boycotted by the majority of filmmakers; at that ceremony Dudley Nichols became the first man to refuse an Oscar—for Best Screenplay. The following year, the Academy completely removed itself from the area of labor relations responsibilities and, today, has no concern with either economic or political matters.

Another area in which the Academy immediately became involved was that of technical research, about which it remained concerned until its Research Council went under the aegis of the Association of Motion Picture Producers in January 1948.

It has always been concerned with educational and cultural matters, co-sponsoring, with the University of Southern California, a 1928 course on "Introduction to the Photoplay." On January 31, 1944, the Academy Foundation was incorporated, and under its aegis the Academy has presented major retrospective film screenings and tributes, as well as lectures and seminars. Its Student Film Awards have been an annual event since 1973. It provides scholarships and grants and regularly sends members to talk on college campuses. The Academy's Margaret Herrick Library, named for its first librarian and one-time executive director (1943–1970), is considered one of the finest film-related research libraries in the country, with access by mail available through the National Film Information Service.

Through the *Screen Achievement Records Bulletin*, first published in 1933, the Academy provides valuable documentation on screen credits. The *Academy Players Directory*, first published as the *Players Directory Bulletin* in 1937, is considered the casting director's bible, with its photographs of players, broken down by category, and with the agents' names and telephone numbers.

During the Second World War, the Academy administered a War Film Library, securing prints of documentaries produced by the Allies and making them available to studios and for nontheatrical screenings. The Academy has also maintained a regular film library, consisting chiefly of films nominated for Academy Awards but also including 16mm* copies of Paper Prints* from the Library of Congress.

The Academy moved to its present, seven-story office building in the fall of 1975. Here are housed the library, players directory, and its Samuel Goldwyn Theatre, at which new films are screened for members each Sunday.

The activities of the Academy of Motion Picture Arts and Sciences are almost exclusively funded by membership subscriptions—membership is by invitation only and remains constant at around 4,000—and through revenues from the Academy Awards presentations.

Address: 8949 Wilshire Boulevard, Beverly Hills, Calif. 90211.

BIBLIOGRAPHY

Brown, Peter H. *The Real Oscar*. Westport, Connecticut: Arlington House, 1981.

Champlin, Charles, "The Academy at Fifty," *American Film*, March 1978, pp. 16–19.

Osborne, Robert. *50 Golden Years of Oscar*. La Habra, California: ESE California, 1979.

Sands, Pierre Norman. *A Historical Study of the Academy of Motion Picture Arts and Sciences*. New York: Arno Press, 1973.

Shale, Richard. *Academy Awards*. New York: Frederick Ungar, 1978 (revised 1982).

Slide, Anthony, "Academy of Motion Picture Arts and Sciences," *Films in Review*, May 1976, pp. 289–293.

ACADEMY OF SCIENCE FICTION, FANTASY & HORROR FILMS. A nonprofit organization, founded by Dr. Donald Reed (who remains president of the Academy) in 1972, the Academy of Science Fiction, Fantasy & Horror Films consists, according to its prospectus, "of dedicated individuals devoted to presenting awards of merit and recognition for science fiction films, fantasy films and horror films, and to promoting the arts and sciences of science fiction, fantasy and horror films." Membership is open to anyone, and all members are eligible to vote in the Academy's annual selection of the best films in the genres which it promotes. Apart from its annual awards ceremony, the Academy publishes a newsletter titled *Saturn*, arranges screenings for its members, and in 1980 established the George Pal Memorial Award, "given for outstanding achievement by an individual in science fiction, fantasy or horror in film, television, literature or other arts."

Address: 334 West 54 Street, Los Angeles, Calif. 90037.

ACADEMY WAR FILM LIBRARY. See ACADEMY OF MOTION PICTURE ARTS AND SCIENCES

ACE. See COMPO

"ACE" BRAND. See DAVID HORSLEY PRODUCTIONS

ACETATE FILM. Although it is really a misnomer, as film today is generally triacetate, acetate film is the term used to describe safety or noninflammable filmstock, which has an estimated life span of 200 years or more. Eastman Kodak* first introduced acetate film in 1908, and, although it was crucial in the development of 16mm* and 8mm* film, it was not generally used for 35mm* film production by the industry. However, in the late forties, Eastman Kodak introduced an improved safety-base motion picture film—for which in 1949 the company received a Class I (Oscar statuette) Scientific or Technical Award; this new safety film superseded nitrate film*, and from 1950/1951 all film has been shot and processed on safety stock.

ACME VIDEOTAPE AND FILM LABORATORIES. See CONSOLIDATED FILM INDUSTRIES

ACTOPHONE COMPANY. The Actophone Company was an early independent manufacturing company formed by Mark M. Dintenfass, who earlier was involved in the installation of the Cameraphone, a talking picture device, in New York. Actophone released its first film, *The Third Degree*, on February 23, 1910. It produced weekly one-reel comedies and dramas. William Rising, formerly with the Edison Manufacturing Company*, was the director, and Harry Ferrini, also from Edison, was the cameraman. Actophone ceased production when it was sued by the Motion Picture Patents Company*, and its last film was *Love's Great Tragedy*, released on May 25, 1910.

Dintenfass next began the Champion Film Company, which released its first film, *Abernathy Kids to the Rescue*, on July 13, 1910. Champion later became part of Universal Pictures*, in 1912.

THE ACTORS STUDIO, INC. The home of a style known as "method acting," which had its origins in the Russian theatre at the turn of the century and in the work of Constantin Stanislavski, the Actors Studio, Inc., was opened in September 1947 by Cheryl Crawford and Elia Kazan, with classes taught by Kazan and

Robert Lewis. The Actors Studio is "a workshop for professional actors," and among its "graduates" are Paul Newman, Joanne Woodward, Karl Malden, Lee Grant, Raymond St. Jacques, Kim Hunter, and Marlon Brando. Lee Strasberg became involved with the Studio in 1949 and, in 1952, was named its artistic director, a title he held until his death in 1982. Strasberg was succeeded by Ellen Burstyn and Al Pacino as artistic co-directors. A West Coast operation, Actors Studio West, was formed in Los Angeles in 1966.

Address: 432 West 44 Street, New York, N.Y. 10036.

BIBLIOGRAPHY

Adams, Cindy. *Lee Strasberg: The Imperfect Genius*. New York: Doubleday, 1980.

Garfield, David. *A Player's Place: The Story of the Actors Studio*. New York: Macmillan, 1980.

Hethman, Robert H., editor. *Strasberg at the Actors Studio*. New York: Viking Press, 1965.

Hirsch, Foster. *A Method in Their Madness*. New York: W. W. Norton, 1984.

THE ADULT FILM ASSOCIATION OF AMERICA. Founded in Kansas City on January 14, 1969, the Adult Film Association of America is a nonprofit corporation set up to protect and promote the interests of its member producers, distributors, and exhibitors, all of whom are involved with what they describe as "sexually explicit" films. On July 14, 1977, the Association presented the first of what has become its annual Erotic Film Awards, and, since 1971, the Association has published *The AFAA Bulletin*.

Address: 5445 Sunset Boulevard, Hollywood, Calif. 90027.

BIBLIOGRAPHY

Friedman, David, "A History of the AFAA," *Boxoffice*, March 1982, pp. 20, 22, 24, 26.

Knight, Arthur, "Adult Film Group in Quest to Gain Respect," *Los Angeles Times*, Calendar Section, February 17, 1974, pp. 14, 17.

" 'Sexploitation' Filmmakers, Showmen Form Adult Motion Picture Ass'n," *Boxoffice*, January 20, 1969, p. 8.

AFFILIATED DISTRIBUTORS' CORPORATION. Affiliated Distributors' Corporation, incorporated in May 1918, was formed to serve exhibitors as a national clearinghouse to ensure that the various exhibitor booking associations in different states would get a consistent supply of high-quality films. The exhibitor-controlled organization was led by Frank Rembusch, Sydney Cohen, and general counsel Charles C. Pettijohn. In September 1918, it distributed Leonce Perret's *Lafayette, We Come*. In November 1918, Affiliated acquired 51 percent of the Mutual Film Corporation*. With headquarters established in Grand Rapids, Michigan, the exhibitors planned to divide the country into five sections and cooperatively book films directly from the producer to the exhibitor. The plan took effect on November 20, 1918, when the Robertson-Cole Company* made a long-term contract to furnish all films for the new organization, which had changed its name to Exhibitors' Mutual Distributing Corporation.

BIBLIOGRAPHY
"Affiliated Distributors Are Incorporated," *The Moving Picture World*, May 11, 1918,
    p. 1003.
"Affiliated Takes Over Mutual Film," *The Moving Picture World*, November 23, 1918,
    p. 809.

AIP. See AMERICAN INTERNATIONAL PICTURES

ALBUQUERQUE FILM MANUFACTURING COMPANY, INC. The Albuquerque Film Manufacturing Company, Inc., organized in the fall of 1913 with G. P. Hamilton as its president and general manager, specialized in the production of three-reel Westerns, written by and starring Dot Farley. Milton H. Fahrney directed at the company's inception and his wife appeared in the films. The company used the studios at the J.A.C. plant on Broadway in downtown Los Angeles and released its product through Warners Features, Inc. By August 1914, Archer McMackin, a comedy director from the Essanay Film Manufacturing Company*, had been hired, and in October of that year the company was re-incorporated as the Albuquerque Film Company of Los Angeles with a capitalization of $200,000. At this point the company began releasing one-reel comedies and comedy dramas with United Film Service* under the brand name of Luna Films and starring Dot Farley. Augustus Carney, known as "Alkali Ike," appeared in Albuquerque productions at this time. In July 1915, the company occupied temporary studios on Allesandro Street in Los Angeles and produced two reels a week, the one being a comedy-drama written by Dot Farley and supervised by Hamilton and the other a comedy directed by Nick Cogley. In early 1918, Hamilton declared bankruptcy.

BIBLIOGRAPHY
"New Western Film Company," *The New York Dramatic Mirror*, November 12, 1913,
    p. 27.

ALCO FILM CORPORATION. Al Lichtman, former sales manager for Famous Players Film Company, who lost his job when Paramount Pictures Corporation* was formed to distribute the Famous Players product, formed the Alco Film Corporation in August 1914 with newspaperman Walter Hoff Seeley to distribute films to their own exchanges* throughout the country. Lichtman's idea was to organize a circuit of the largest theatres in the country, one in each city of over 200,000 people, which would book through Alco at the highest justifiable price in return for exclusive rights in that city for a certain period. The system would enable exhibitors to charge higher admissions without the fear of competition. After a week's run, the film would not be shown again in that city for six months, then it would play in smaller towns, distributed through Alco exchanges. Lichtman, by engaging the feature film companies of All-Star Feature Company*, California Motion Picture Corporation*, Popular Plays and Players, Inc.*, Favorite Players Film Co.*, Excelsior Feature Film Co.*, Tiffany Film Corporation*, B. A.

Rolfe*, and Life Photo*, set up distribution centers in twenty cities to take their entire output for five years. Alco executives were to approve all scenarios and casts and all production plans. On October 1, 1914, Alco began to issue one film per week. Lichtman left the corporation in November 1914. Bankruptcy proceedings were initiated early in 1915 because of internal dissension. Richard Rowland, one of the lessees, formed Metro Pictures Corporation* in 1915.

BIBLIOGRAPHY

"Alco Another Big Combine," *The Moving Picture World*, September 5, 1914, p. 1383.
"For Film Distribution," *The New York Dramatic Mirror*, July 22, 1914, p. 24.

ALDRICH STUDIOS. Built in 1913, consisting of two sound stages and production offices, and formerly known as the Sutherland and Occidental Studios, the Aldrich Studios were located at 201–225 North Occidental Boulevard, Los Angeles. Director Robert Aldrich acquired the complex in January of 1968 for a reported $1,150,000, using profits from his feature *The Dirty Dozen*. The studios became the headquarters for the director's company, Associates & Aldrich (formed in 1954). The first three features filmed by Aldrich at his new studios were *The Killing of Sister George* (1968), *Whatever Happened to Aunt Alice* (1969), and *Too Late the Hero* (1970). The studios were sold to Video Cassette Industries (VCI) in July 1973.

ALHAMBRA MOTION PICTURE COMPANY. The Alhambra Motion Picture Company was formed in November 1914 to produce comedies and dramas written by and starring Betty Harte. In January 1915, it commenced releasing under the Kriterion* brand. Directors included L. B. Carleton and Sidney Debray, who also played starring roles. Actors included E. J. Peil, Master Edward Peil, and Etta Raynor. In September 1915, Alhambra joined the Associated Film Manufacturers, which consisted of eight West Coast producers.

AL JENNINGS PRODUCTION COMPANY. Al Jennings, once the leader of a band of outlaws known as "The Long Riders," formed the Al Jennings Production Company in July 1918 to make films about his exploits as an outlaw and his later struggles to become a respectable citizen after he joined the Baptist church. Both he and his brother, Frank, an attorney who also had been an outlaw, were to appear in the films. Jennings, the president and general manager of the company, promised that the films would contain real banditry and no idle sentimentality about the West. He hoped that by showing the outlaw's life realistically, and emphasizing the grimness, privation, and dangers, the films would teach audiences the futility of crime. The Jennings' company studios were in both Tucson and Los Angeles. W. S. Van Dyke was the director of productions, and the company's first film was *The Lady in the Dugout* with Corinne Grant. Jennings' films were distributed by Ernest Shipman.

BIBLIOGRAPHY
"Jennings Forms Company to Film His Experiences," *The Moving Picture World*, July
     13, 1918, p. 232.

ALL-AMERICAN NEWS. See NEWSREELS

ALL-CELTIC FILM COMPANY. The All-Celtic Film Company, incorporated
early in 1915, produced the "Peaceful Rafferty" series. Charles J. O'Hara wrote
and directed the series and also was the president of the company, which used
the Physioc Studios at 624 West 24 Street, New York.

ALLIANCE FILMS CORPORATION. Alliance Films Corporation was formed
in September 1914 as an organization of exchanges. A rotating committee
appointed by the exchange decided whether or not to purchase films from selected
manufacturers. The organization received its profits from a percentage of the
bookings of the films selected. Its goal was to eliminate states rights* buying
and to secure high-quality films. The first film to be released by Alliance was
At the Crossroads, produced by the Select Photoplay Producing Company. Andrew
J. Cobe, Hector J. Streyckmans and P. P. Craft were involved in the company.
BIBLIOGRAPHY
"The Alliance Program," *The Moving Picture World*, October 10, 1914, p. 166.

ALLIANCE OF MOTION PICTURE AND TELEVISION PRODUCERS.
In 1924, the Association of Motion Picture Producers was formed initially as a
public relations organization for the film industry and later as a contract negotiating
body with various guilds and unions. It became the Association of Motion Picture
& Television Producers in 1964 when it merged with the Alliance of Television
Film Producers. Internal bickering among the various producer-members in 1975
led to the breakup of the Association and Universal's and Paramount's forming
a new negotiating body, The Alliance. The Association continued in existence
until 1982 when it merged with The Alliance to form the new organization.
   The member companies of the Alliance as of 1984 were Aaron Spelling
Productions, Inc.; Columbia Pictures*; Embassy* Productions, Inc.; The Ladd
Company*; Leonard Goldberg Co.; Lorimar Productions*; Metro-Goldwyn-
Mayer*; Metromedia Producers Corp.; MTM Enterprises; Orion TV Productions,
Inc.; Paramount Pictures Corporation*; Tandem/Embassy Television; 20th
Century-Fox Film Corporation*; Universal Pictures*; Viacom*; Walt Disney*;
Warner Bros.*; and Witt/Thomas/Harris Productions.
   Address: 14144 Ventura Boulevard, 3rd Floor, Sherman Oaks, Calif. 91423.
BIBLIOGRAPHY
Robb, David, "How and Why the ASSOCIATION Became The ALLIANCE of Motion
     Picture & Television Producers," *Daily Variety*, October 26, 1982, pp. 34, 50.

ALLIED ARTISTS. Formerly Monogram Productions, Inc.*, Allied Artists came into being in September 1952. Despite ambitious plans, it was in poor financial shape until 1965, when it released the Elvis Presley vehicle, *Tickle Me*. By the mid-sixties, Allied Artists was renting out its studio, which it sold eventually in 1967 (and which is now KCET). After sale of the studio the company concentrated on releasing foreign films, such as *A Man and a Woman* (1966) and *Belle de Jour* (1968), but it returned to active film production in the seventies, under Emanuel L. Wolf (who took over the company in 1967), with its best-known films including *Cabaret* (1972), *Papillon* (1973), *The Man Who Would Be King* (1975), and *Conduct Unbecoming* (1975).

In January 1976, Allied Artists Industries, Inc., was formed by the merger of Allied Artists Pictures Corporation; Kalvex Inc.; and PSP, Inc. The consumer products group of Allied Artists Industries was concerned with motor homes, men's sportswear, imported consumer goods, and drug distribution. Financial problems continued to plague the company, and, in May 1979, it filed for reorganization under Chapter XI of the bankruptcy laws. The reorganization proved unsuccessful, and in 1980 Allied Artists—with a library of 450 films—was sold for a reported $7 million to television producer Lorimar Productions*.

BIBLIOGRAPHY

"Allied Artists Is New Company Name, Plan 33," *Motion Picture Herald*, September 27, 1952, p. 22.

Lubasch, Arnold H., "Allied Artists Seeks Help under Chapter XI Filing," *The New York Times*, April 5, 1979, pp. D1, D5.

Penn, Stanley, "How 'Little Guy' Allied Artists Tumbled from Moviemaking Role into Chapter 11," *The Wall Street Journal*, May 4, 1979, p. 40.

"Success Story: The New Allied Artists," *Motion Picture Herald*, February 25, 1970, pp. 6–7.

ALLIED STATES ASSOCIATION OF MOTION PICTURE EXHIBITORS. See NATIONAL ASSOCIATION OF THEATRE OWNERS, INC.

ALL-STAR FEATURE COMPANY. Incorporated in Albany, New York, in 1913, All-Star Feature Company had Harry Raver as its president, Archibald Selwyn as vice-president and Augustus Thomas as director-general. Its first production was *Arizona*, a six-reel feature version of Thomas' play. Its studio was on Fox Hill, near Fort Wadsworth, Staten Island. Lawrence Gill assisted Thomas in directing. Other films that followed include *Checkers*, with Thomas W. Ross, and *Soldiers of Fortune*, with Dustin Farnum. All-Star also used the old Lee Lash scenic studio in Mount Vernon, New York. Among the performers who made their screen debuts with All-Star are Ethel Barrymore, William Faversham, and Lew Dockstader. Burr McIntosh was also in some of its films. Irvin Willat was a cameraman for the production of *America*, filmed on the New York Hippodrome stage, where it was produced as a play. Sol Lesser was the president and general manager of All-Star Feature Distributors of San Francisco,

Los Angeles, Denver, Seattle, and Portland. The Exclusive Supply Corporation* distributed All-Star's product from its inception, as Raver was president and general manager of that concern. As of August 25, 1914, Alco Film Corporation* distributed the All-Star product. In December 1914, Harry Raver and Augustus Thomas withdrew, and John Dunlap became head. Alco secured the complete control of All-Star, and George Foster Platt became the company's new director-general. Like Alco, All-Star went bankrupt in early 1915. Among the more important All-Star features were *The Nightingale* (1914), starring Ethel Barrymore, and *The Jungle* (1914), based on the novel by Upton Sinclair.

BIBLIOGRAPHY

"Alco Absorbs All-Star," *The Moving Picture World*, December 19, 1914, p. 1699.
"All-Star Feature Company," *The New York Dramatic Mirror*, July 9, 1913, p. 25.

AMERICAN CINEMA EDITORS, INC. American Cinema Editors, Inc., is a professional group of film editors from Los Angeles Local 776 and New York Local 551. The group's stated objectives and purposes are "to advance the art and science of the film editing profession; to increase the entertainment value of motion pictures by attaining pre-eminence and scientific achievement in the creative art of film editing; to bring into close alliance those Film Editors who desire to advance the prestige and dignity of the film editing profession." Members are permitted to use the initials "A.C.E." after their names for screen credit purposes.

The society was first discussed by a small group of editors on October 26, 1950, formal plans for its creation were made on November 28, 1950, and the first general membership meeting took place on January 9, 1951. American Cinema Editors publishes a newsletter, *Cinemeditor*, and presents annual awards, Eddies, for best-edited features, documentaries, television episodes, and television specials.

Address: 4416 1/2 Finley Avenue, Los Angeles, Calif. 90027.

BIBLIOGRAPHY

First Decade Anniversary Book. Hollywood, California: American Cinema Editors, Inc., 1961.
ACE Second Decade Anniversary Book. Los Angeles: American Cinema Editors, Inc., 1971.

AMERICAN CONGRESS OF EXHIBITORS. See COMPO

AMERICAN CORRESPONDENT FILM COMPANY, INC. The American Correspondent Film Company, Inc., was formed in mid–1915 to produce films of the war in Europe. President M. B. Clausson planned to arrange for his newspapers to hire halls in various cities in which to screen the films. He had cameramen and correspondents at the German-Austrian war fronts, the Italian frontier, and the German front. The company's "factory" was located in Stamford, Connecticut, and it had offices in the Candler Building at 222 West 42 Street,

New York. Its first film, *The Battle and Fall of Przemsyl*, was released in August 1915. According to Terry Ramsaye, in *A Million and One Nights* (p. 690), the company later admitted having made an arrangement to propagandize for Germany and Austria, and after the United States entered the war, some officials of the company were sentenced to prison terms for violation of war laws.

BIBLIOGRAPHY

"American Correspondent Film Company, Inc.," *The Moving Picture World*, July 3, 1915, p. 67.

AMERICAN DOCUMENTARY FILMS. See FRONTIER FILMS

AMERICAN EXHIBITORS' ASSOCIATION. The American Exhibitors' Association (AEA) was a short-lived offshoot of the Motion Picture Exhibitors League of America (MPELA)*, formed in August 1917 by eighty-five delegates to the MPELA's convention when they felt they were not getting a fair deal from president Lee Ochs. The president of the AEA was Jack Wells and general manager was Charles Pettijohn. The AEA fought to end the system whereby exhibitors were required to make an advance deposit for films which they wished to screen.

BIBLIOGRAPHY

"Exhibitors Form New Association," *The Moving Picture World*, August 21, 1917, p. 798.

AMERICAN FILM INSTITUTE. On September 29, 1965, President Lyndon B. Johnson signed the National Arts and Humanities Act, at which time he announced plans for the creation of an American Film Institute. However, it was not until June 5, 1967, that the Institute was founded as a nonprofit, nongovernmental corporation, with headquarters in Washington, D.C. The Institute's basic premise was "to advance and preserve the art of the moving image."

With establishing grants from the National Council of the Arts, the Ford Foundation, and the Motion Picture Association of America, the Institute allocated (on December 11, 1967) $1.2 million for a nitrate film rescue program, established (on January 23, 1968) a $500,000 production fund for student and independent filmmakers, announced (on April 3, 1968) the commencement of a National Film Catalog project, and financed (on June 15, 1968) an oral history program in film begun by UCLA.

The most promoted of the Institute's activities is its film preservation program, whereby films are preserved in the National Film Collection at the Library of Congress. The Institute has no film archives itself and, in recent years, only a minute portion of its budget has actually been spent on film preservation. In reality, it siphons money received from the National Endowment for the Arts to the various American organizations active in film preservation.

In September 1969, the Institute's Center for Advanced Film Studies, located at the Greystone Mansion in Beverly Hills, became operational. The Center initially accepted both filmmaking and research fellows, but for more than a decade now has limited its activities to working with independent and young filmmakers. A Directing Workshop for Women was created in 1974, and the Center also receives funding from the Academy of Motion Picture Arts and Sciences* for a chair in screenwriting. In August 1980, the Institute purchased the former Immaculate Heart College campus in Hollywood, and, on October 3, 1980, it was opened as the new headquarters for the Center, officially known as the American Film Institute-West.

The National Film Catalog project has as its aim the documentation of all American films from the 1890s onward. Two catalogs covering feature films from 1921 to 1930 and 1961 to 1970 have been published, and work is proceeding on the volume for feature films from 1911 to 1920.

The oral history program continued for a number of years, with funding from the Louis B. Mayer Foundation, but is no longer pursued by the Institute.

On March 3, 1973, the American Film Institute presented the first of its Life Achievement Awards to John Ford, at a ceremony attended by President Richard Nixon, a presence which resulted in much negative comment and picketing. Thanks to its television coverage, the Life Achievement Award has become the best known of the Institute's activities. Second in importance to the Award is the Institute's journal, *American Film*, first published in 1975.

George Stevens, Jr., was the founding director of the Institute. He resigned in 1979 to become its co-chairman with Charlton Heston—Gregory Peck was the Institute's first chairman of the Board of Trustees—and on January 1, 1980, Jean Firstenberg became the Institute's new director.

The American Film Institute has long been the subject of much controversy and adverse publicity. There have been frequent complaints that it is too much concerned with self-promotion and little interested in performing any of the functions—particularly film preservation—for which it actively seeks funding. Its Education Department has repeatedly been closed down and its staff fired. George Stevens, Jr., was severely criticized in 1972 for utilizing $300,000 of the Center's production budget for an unreleased feature film titled *In Pursuit of Treasure*. Stevens came under even stronger fire in 1973 when he cancelled one of the opening films at the Institute's new AFI Theatre at the Kennedy Center. The film was *State of Siege*, which Stevens denounced as rationalizing assassination. As a result of Stevens' action, many filmmakers withdrew their films from the opening program.

National Film Day, first held on October 23, 1973, was organized to raise funds for the Institute's activities, but it proved to be a disastrous failure and was cancelled after a few years. The Institute has repeatedly had problems in funding its various programs. Sustaining grants from both the Ford Foundation and the Motion Picture Association of America ended in 1974, and in December of that year Congress voted against direct federal funding, forcing the Institute to apply, as must other organizations, for funds from the National Endowment for the Arts.

According to its various publicity brochures, "The American Film Institute is concerned with the motion picture in American life—in theatres, homes, libraries, classrooms and wherever films are found. To bring cinema to its fullest stature in the country of its birth, to preserve, stimulate, enrich and nurture the art of film in America—these are the Institute's goals." There are many who would question if the American Film Institute has achieved much progress toward such goals.

Addresses: John F. Kennedy Center for the Performing Arts, Washington, D.C. 20566; 2021 North Western Avenue, Hollywood, Calif. 90027.

BIBLIOGRAPHY

The American Film Institute. *The First Ten Years*. Washington, D.C.: The Author, 1977.

Farber, Stephen, "Alienation and Success for AFI," *Los Angeles Times*, Calendar Section, September 2, 1973, pp. 1, 16, 22–23.

Gold, Ronald, "Rundown of Issues under Dispute, American Film Institute vs. Dissenters," *Variety*, July 7, 1971, pp. 13, 21.

Harmetz, Aljean, "Custodian for Cinema Culture," *Show*, August 20, 1970, pp. 16–19.

"The Journal Looks at AFI and other Film Institutes," *Journal of the Producers Guild of America*, September 1967, entire issue.

McBride, Joseph, editor. *Filmmakers on Filmmaking: The American Film Institute Seminars on Motion Pictures and Television*. Los Angeles: J. P. Tarcher, 1983.

McCarty, Todd, "George Stevens Jr. Reviews 12 Years of AFI Progress," *Daily Variety*, January 22, 1980, pp. 12, 15.

Shales, Tom, editor. *The American Film Heritage: Impressions from the American Film Institute Archives*. Washington, D.C.: Acropolis Books, 1972.

Stevens, George, Jr., "About the American Film Institute," *Film Quarterly*, Winter 1971–72, pp. 36–42.

Yoffe, Emily, "Popcorn Politics," *Harper's*, December 1983, pp. 17–22.

AMERICAN FILM MANUFACTURING COMPANY. The announcement of the formation of the American Film Manufacturing Company appeared in the October 8, 1910, edition of *The Moving Picture World*. Organized by exchangemen John R. Freuler, Harry E. Aitken, Charles J. Hite, and Samuel S. Hutchinson to furnish their exchanges* with films after the Motion Picture Patents Company* cut off their supply, American—with headquarters in Chicago—succeeded in snatching players and staff of the nearest member of the Patents Company, Essanay Film Manufacturing Company*, thus acquiring such players as J. Warren Kerrigan and Dot Farley; scenarist Allan Dwan; directors Thomas Ricketts, Sam Morris, and Frank Beal; technical expert Charles Ziebath; and executives Aubrey M. Kennedy and Gilbert P. Hamilton. With a "Flying A" as its symbol and nickname, American copied Essanay's product and established three companies making comedies, dramas, and Westerns*. Frank Beal took a company West in the spring of 1911. Dwan followed and relieved Beal of directorial duties, as it located in San Juan Capistrano, later in La Mesa, California, and, finally, in June 1912, in an abandoned ostrich farm in Santa Barbara. American made two reels per week at this time.

In June 1912, American joined Harry Aitken's newly formed Mutual Film Corporation* and began producing its entire output in Santa Barbara. Roy O. Overbaugh became an American cameraman in 1912. Early in 1913 American built a well-equipped studio on Mission and Chapala streets in Santa Barbara, and according to Overbaugh this was the first time a glass stage was used on the West Coast for staging interior scenes. Wallace Reid began directing society dramas in 1913, and, when Dwan left in May 1913, Lorimer Johnston became the leading director. In January 1914, American began releasing the weekly "Beauty" brand of comedies. When the Santa Barbara Motion Picture Company*, a neighbor newly formed by Aubrey M. Kennedy and former Santa Barbara mayor Elmer J. Boeseke, hired away Johnston, Overbaugh, and assistant cameraman Victor Fleming in mid–1914, Sydney Ayres became American's chief director.

American made its first feature film, *The Quest*, with Margarita Fischer, directed by her husband Harry Pollard, in 1915, and it was soon followed by its first serial, *The Diamond from the Sky*, with Lottie Pickford, directed by Jacques Jaccard and William Desmond Taylor. In the next year, American added more brands, including "Vogue" comedies, "Mustang" Westerns and "Clipper" dramas, starring Harold Lockwood and May Allison. In 1917, American began producing features exclusively and became Mutual's chief producer, with its stars Mary Miles Minter, William Russell, and Margarita Fisher (who dropped the Germanic "c" after the United States entered the First World War).

When Mutual ended in mid–1918, American began distributing through Pathé.* The number of its productions decreased until Fisher left the company in 1921, after which it soon disbanded.

Other directors of note with American were Lloyd Ingraham, Henry King, Frank Borzage, and Edward Sloman.

BIBLIOGRAPHY

"The American Studio," *The Moving Picture World*, July 10, 1915, p. 255.

"American's Santa Barbara Plant," *The Moving Picture World*, February 8, 1913, p. 559.

Birchard, Robert S., "Roy Overbaugh, ASC," *American Cinematographer*, May 1984, pp. 34–38.

Lyons, Timothy J. *The Silent Partner: The History of the American Film Manufacturing Company 1910–1921*. New York: Arno Press, 1974.

AMERICAN FILM MARKET. The American Film Market is sponsored by the American Film Marketing Association as a showcase and sales market for primarily English-language films. Each year more than 1,000 distributors from over 60 countries participate. The *Los Angeles Herald-Examiner* (March 24, 1981) described the American Film Market as "a kind of Cannes Film Festival, minus the topless sunbathers and the histrionics of an international awards ceremony." First held March 21–31, 1981, the American Film Market is not open to the public and takes place each March (dates vary) in Los Angeles.

Address: American Film Marketing Association, 9000 Sunset Boulevard, Suite 420, Los Angeles, Calif. 90069.

AMERICAN FILM THEATRE. The American Film Theatre project was conceived in 1972 by Ely A. Landau, working in association with American Express Films and the Ely Landau Organization. Landau's idea was to provide "a national theatre on film," offering screen versions of major contemporary stage classics to film audiences on a subscription basis. Each film would be produced at a minimal cost of $750,000, with directors, stars, and production staff working at minimum rates. Four hundred and fifty American theatres were signed to participate in the first season of films, 1973/1974, which consisted of *The Iceman Cometh, Rhinoceros, The Homecoming, A Delicate Balance, Luther, Butley, Lost in the Stars,* and *Three Sisters.*

Unfortunately, the concept was not successful. Critics considered the idea neither film nor theatre and were basically negative in their comments. Further, the subscription idea meant that theatres were required to set aside one or two days a month for the American Film Theatre productions, and the major film distributors made it very clear that they would boycott those theatres which elected to interrupt the run of one of their films for an American Film Theatre presentation.

Despite problems and the loss of 35 percent of participating theatres, a second season was presented for 1974/1975, consisting of *The Maids, The Man in the Glass Booth, Galileo, Jacques Brel Is Alive and Well and Living in Paris,* and *In Celebration.* In June 1975, Landau announced a year's intermission for the American Film Theatre, and the concept was never revived. Worldwide distribution rights to the features were subsequently acquired by Telepictures Corporation.

BIBLIOGRAPHY

Kerr, Walter, "The Score is Theatre 7, Movies 1," *The New York Times,* April 7, 1974, Section 2, pp. 1, 15.

McKee, Allen, "Will These 'New Era' Movies Bring Out the Snob in You?" *The New York Times,* October 28, 1973, p. D13.

Pennington, Ron, "Ely Landau Reveals Details of American Film Theatre," *The Hollywood Reporter,* April 21, 1972, pp. 1, 3.

Rich, Frank, "A Discouraging Word or Two about the American Film Theatre," *New Times,* December 14, 1975, pp. 60–61.

AMERICAN FOTOFONE COMPANY. See POWERS COMPANY

AMERICAN INTERNATIONAL PICTURES. American International Pictures (AIP) began as American Releasing Corporation in 1954, founded by James H. Nicholson and Samuel Z. Arkoff with $3,000. Their announced plans were to release eight films in 1955, to be sold either as a block or film by film. In March 1956, American Releasing changed its name to American International Pictures and announced a schedule of fourteen films to be delivered by five independent producers, among whom was Roger Corman.

AIP's films were sold for flat fees to exhibitors since they were invariably relegated to the bottom half of double bills. In order to combat this problem and to increase its rentals, AIP decided to send its films out as paired double bills. The company started this policy in 1956 with *The Day the World Ended* and *The Phantom from 10,000 Leagues*. The success of the idea led other companies to copy AIP; as a result, it was in danger of losing its share of the market. In 1959 the company decided it would have to distribute more expensive films if it was to compete with other releasing organizations and so decided to make its films in color and CinemaScope*. *The House of Usher* (1960) was the first film to be made after this change in policy, and it was the first AIP film to play by itself at most theatres and to be booked on a percentage basis.

The cycle of horror films based on the Edgar Allen Poe stories was a success for the company and was followed in 1963 by a cycle of teen films beginning with *Beach Party*. The company was successful enough that, in February 1964, it was planning to produce a television series based on *Beach Party* and was also thinking of purchasing theatres around the country. The latter did not happen, but in November 1965 AIP did set up Trans American Films to distribute its foreign and art features.

In 1966, thanks to the success of *The Wild Angels* (1966), it started a cycle of protest films. Business was going so well that, in March 1966, AIP purchased an office building in Beverly Hills, which became its corporate headquarters. In June 1969, after many years of refusing to consider the idea, Nicholson and Arkoff took the company public.

In January 1972 Nicholson resigned as president to become an independent producer. In June of that same year, Arkoff became president as well as chairman of the board. The company continued to be profitable, and in 1974 it took over distributing the films of Cinerama*.

In 1975, Arkoff announced plans to change the philosophy of AIP and to begin the production of big-budget films costing between $3 and $4 million each. In that same year the company reported profits of $3.5 million, the best ever.

Plans were announced for a merger with Filmways, the reasons having to do with the need for more money to fund the big-budget films which AIP was making and wished to make. The merger was called off in December 1978, but talks began again in March 1979. In May 1979, AIP announced the first loss—$1.5 million—in its history, and, in July 1979, it merged with Filmways.

BIBLIOGRAPHY

American International Pictures: Twenty-Five Years. New York: Museum of Modern Art, 1979.

Harmetz, Aljean. *Rolling Breaks and Other Movie Breaks.* New York: Alfred A. Knopf, 1983.

McGee, Mark Thomas. *Fast and Furious: The Story of American International Pictures*. Jefferson, North Carolina: McFarland, 1984.

Ottoson, Robert, L. *American International Pictures: A Filmography*. New York: Garland, 1985.

AMERICAN MUTOSCOPE AND BIOGRAPH COMPANY. See BIOGRAPH COMPANY

AMERICAN MUTOSCOPE COMPANY. See BIOGRAPH COMPANY

AMERICAN NATIONAL ENTERPRISES. See JENSEN-FARLEY PICTURES, INC.

AMERICAN RELEASING CORPORATION. See AMERICAN INTERNATIONAL PICTURES

AMERICAN SOCIETY OF CINEMATOGRAPHERS. In 1913, a group of West Coast cameramen formed a group called The Static Club of America*, which published a newspaper-style journal, titled *Static Flashes*, and which served as a meeting place for the exchange of ideas. The Static Club was disbanded in 1918, and a group of its members—Charles Rosher, Arthur Edeson, Victor Milner, L. Guy Wilky, Philip Rosen, Homer Scott, William Foster, Del Clawson, Eugene Gaudio, Walter Griffin, Roy Klaffki, Joseph August, Fred Granville, Deveral Jennings, and Robert Newhard—founded a new organization, the American Society of Cinematographers, which was incorporated on January 18, 1919.

The Society's motto, "Loyalty, Progress, and Artistry," sums up the aims and ideals of the organization, membership in which is by invitation only. The initials "ASC" after a cinematographer's name indicates that he or she is a member of the Society; it is generally considered a mark of quality. Since November 1, 1920, the Society has published *American Cinematographer*; it maintains a museum in its clubhouse (located since 1937 at the corner of Franklin Avenue and Orange Drive in Hollywood) and, in recent years, has embarked on a publication program. The American Society of Cinematographers provides monthly meetings for its members, at which the latest developments in all aspects of film and television production are discussed. It is the oldest extant motion picture organization in Los Angeles.

Address: 1782 North Orange Drive, Hollywood, Calif. 90028.

BIBLIOGRAPHY

Broening, H. Lyman, "How It All Happened," *American Cinematographer*, November 1, 1921, p. 13.

Mitchell, George, "The ASC Is an Honor Society, Not a Trade Union, of Cinematographers," *Films in Review*, August-September 1967, pp. 385–397.

"Six Decades of 'Loyalty, Progress, Artistry,' " *American Cinematographer*, June 1979, pp. 576–577, 580–581, 600–601.

Williams, Whitney, "Society of Cinematographers Marks 50 Years of Achievement," *Daily Variety*, January 17, 1969, pp. 10, 16.

AMERICAN TALKING-PICTURE COMPANY. See KINETOPHONE

AMERICAN WOMAN FILM COMPANY. Financially backed almost entirely by wealthy society women of Los Angeles, the American Woman Film Company was formed in May 1916 to produce ten-reel features. Mrs. May Whitney Emerson was president. J. Farrell MacDonald was to be in charge of production at a studio located at 1339 Gordon Street in Hollywood, with the first film to be *Saul of Tarsus*. As far as can be ascertained, the company did not actually produce any films.

BIBLIOGRAPHY

"Women Start Something," *The Moving Picture World*, May 27, 1916, p. 1515.

AMERICAN ZOETROPE. See ZOETROPE

AMKINO CORPORATION. See ARTKINO PICTURES, INC.

ANAGLYPHIC PROCESS. See THREE-DIMENSIONAL FILMS

ANAMORPHIC LENS. The most important element in widescreen photography and projection, the anamorphic lens compresses the width, but not the height, of the image in the camera. When the image is projected the picture is "unsqueezed" by use of a deanamorphic lens. Thus a widescreen effect can be obtained by use of an anamorphic lens with standard camera or projection equipment.

ANCHORS AWEIGH. See HOLLYWOOD VICTORY COMMITTEE

"ANDY HARDY" SERIES. Arguably the most popular, the most commercially successful, and the most wholesome group of films ever produced in the history of the American motion picture, the "Andy Hardy" series began in 1937 with *A Family Affair*, based on the 1928 play, *Skidding*, by Mrs. Aurania Rouverol. In that first film, Andy Hardy's father, Judge Hardy, was played by Lionel Barrymore, his mother by Spring Byington, Andy Hardy by Mickey Rooney, Aunt Milly by Sara Haden, and Marian Hardy by Cecilia Parker. Only the last three continued in the series, with Judge Hardy subsequently played by Lewis Stone and Mrs. Hardy by Fay Holden. George Seitz directed all but three films in the series, and the scripts were generally by Kay Van Riper, William Ludwig, and Agnes Christine Johnston.

Set in Carvel, Idaho, the films were concerned with Andy Hardy's exploits.

Judy Garland was featured in three of the films, *Love Finds Andy Hardy*, *Andy Hardy Meets a Debutante*, and *Life Begins for Andy Hardy*. Lana Turner was featured in *Love Finds Andy Hardy*. Ostensibly the series ended in 1946 with *Love Laughs at Andy Hardy*, but a final film, *Andy Hardy Comes Home*, was released in 1958, with Mickey Rooney, Fay Holden, Sara Haden, and Cecilia Parker essaying their former roles. The following is a complete list of all the films in the series, all of which were produced and released by M-G-M*: *A Family Affair* (1937), *You're Only Young Once* (1937), *Judge Hardy's Children* (1938), *Love Finds Andy Hardy* (1938), *Out West with the Hardys* (1938), *The Hardys Ride High* (1939), *Andy Hardy Gets Spring Fever* (1939), *Judge Hardy and Son* (1939), *Andy Hardy Meets a Debutante* (1940), *Andy Hardy's Private Secretary* (1941), *Life Begins for Andy Hardy* (1941), *Courtship of Andy Hardy* (1942), *Andy Hardy's Double Life* (1942), *Andy Hardy's Blonde Trouble* (1944), *Love Laughs at Andy Hardy* (1946), and *Andy Hardy Comes Home* (1958).
BIBLIOGRAPHY

Jordan, Don, and Edward Connor, "Judge Hardy and Family," *Films in Review*, January 1974, pp. 1–10.

ANIMATION. There are many definitions of animation but not one has universal acceptance among filmmakers, critics, or viewers. All moving pictures are literally created frame by frame, photographed on a strip of chemical compounds, sensitized to light so they will develop into a series of successive still pictures, and, when projected, these pictures become fused together in our mind's eye as moving pictures. Typically, animation has been defined as the process of exposing film by individual frames, with some change introduced in the photographed object or drawing, following each exposure. After the photography of hundreds of frames of objects or drawings, the materials become animated; they move in line with the absolute intention of the person creating the animation. Many of these films have been cartoons, but other animated films are created by single frame exposures of objects, models, miniatures, or photographs. Still other forms of animation eliminate the camera altogether by drawing directly on the film, or the soundtrack, or both. Newer technologies have now made possible machine-created images, having the potential for lower production costs while providing television viewers flashy and stylized commercials and program openings and theatrical film audiences an array of dazzling special effects and simulations of reality.

Since the beginning of moving pictures in the United States, there have evolved numerous kinds of animation. These can be classified by their technologies and techniques and include the cel drawings of Winsor McCay, Raoul Barré, or John Bray; the stop-action tricks of Georges Méliès or Edwin S. Porter; the silhouette cutouts of Lotte Reiniger; the object or dimensional animation of Willis O'Brien, Will Vinton, or George Pal; the animated collages of Bob Godfrey or Terry Gilliam; the abstract drawings on film and soundtracks of Len Lye, Norman

McLaren, or Oskar Fischinger; and the computer-generated images orchestrated by John and Michael Whitney, Larry Cuba, or John Halas.

Definitions of animation that limit the subject to either photography shot a frame at a time or to movements created frame by frame do not have sufficient breadth to accommodate all the varied forms just identified. Animation technologies share a common element, and that is the manipulation imposed between the frames, whether these are drawn, photographed individually, or generated by a machine. Norman McLaren, of the National Film Board of Canada, defined the process in this way:

> Animation is not the art of drawings that move, but the art of movements that are drawn. What happens between each frame is more important than what exists on each frame. Animation is therefore the art of manipulating the invisible interstices that lie between the frames. The interstices are the bones, flesh and blood of the movie, what is on each frame, merely the clothing.

As the innovation of live-action movies spread across America before the twentieth century, early animated films exploited both the "camera tricks" of stop-action and, a bit later, cel technology. The stop-action trick in the 1895 Edison film *The Execution of Mary, Queen of Scots* was a typical novelty. In chopping off the Queen's head, Alfred Clark stopped the camera just before the axe fell and substituted a dummy for the actress stretched across the block. When the cranking resumed, the dummy's head fell to the ground. After processing, the two shots were edited together to give a smoother continuity, with the movement of the axe and other action occurring so rapidly that the audience did not notice the substitution across the two shots. In a few short years, Georges Méliès exploited stop-action and other trick effects by incorporating stop-action, fast and slow motion, dissolves, and split screens into his fantasy films. As a "lightning cartoonist" he drew film caricatures of various personalities accelerating the drawings by undercranking the camera. By 1902, Edwin S. Porter, J. Stuart Blackton, Oscar B. Dupe, and, in Europe, Segundo de Chomon, had used similar techniques, some discovered by accident. Winsor McCay and Emile Cohl were among the earliest to use cels in their animation, drawing moving characters on separate sheets of paper, or celluloid, and photographing them in succession. Cel technology vastly improved through the second decade of the new century, enabling artists to create animated cartoons for a growing mass market. The work of Max and Dave Fleischer, Raoul Barré, Earl Hurd, John R. Bray, Walter Lantz, Walt Disney, and many others resulted in more than movement of simple drawings. They created characters, told stories, used and exploited stereotypes, and caricatured life and personalities.

Object animation, or the manipulation of static materials or three-dimensional objects, such as puppets, also evolved into many diverse forms after 1895. There are the early puppet and single-frame films of Emile Cohl; the "monstrous miniature" films of Willis O'Brien and Ray Harryhausen; cutout silhouette films of Lotte Reiniger, Sid Marcus, or Larry Jordan; pixilated films of Bernard

Longpre and André Leduc; kinestasis animation by Charles Braverman and Dan McLaughlin; clay-animated films of Will Vinton; pinscreen films of Alexandre Alexeieff and Claire Parker; stills-in-motion films of Al Stahl and many television documentary filmmakers; and the abstractions of Oskar Fischinger, Viking Eggeling, Hans Richter, and Mary Ellen Bute. The abstractionists incorporated many technologies and techniques into their experimental works, including object animation.

During the first twenty years of the American film industry, up to 1915, cel and object animations were the two principal approaches used. While object animation expanded with different techniques, cel technology changed markedly with the inventions and innovations by John Bray, Raoul Barré, and Earl Hurd. For example, Barré divided up the labor in cartoon production, assigning various tasks to his staff, spending much of his time supervising their work. His "slash system" of redrawing only the moving parts of characters in each frame, a uniform peg or registration system, coupled with Bray's "inbetweening" system, the Bray-Hurd celluloid system, and Bill Nolan's moving background system, were examples of the refinements in the cel process that made possible mass production of cartoons. There were no similar solutions for cutting the time to produce stop-action films as indicated in Willis O'Brien's *The Dinosaur and the Missing Link* (1914), taking two months to photograph. Cel animations were soon released at the rate of one split reel a week. The Barré organizational "model" was refined and carried forward by Walt Disney in the early thirties, supplemented with model charts, training sessions, pencil tests, storyboards, script conferences, and other devices which helped his group produce a single, cel-animated style.

The formation of cartoon studios such as Bray* or the Fleischers after 1912 eventually brought forward the first generation of cel-animating artists, many of whom moved into the studio system or became closely aligned with it. Shortcuts and labor-saving devices brought artistic compromises to cel animation. Gone were the fully animated, fluid movements typical in the Winsor McCay animation. These movements were replaced with simple backgrounds, staid characters moving in limited, sometimes jerky, fashion, with cycles of movements and lots of holds. Most theatrical cartoons were based on comic strips, but Otto Messmer's animation of Felix the Cat was one character which expressed more individuality and personality by the late twenties. Out of failure and trial and error, Walt Disney* formed his West Coast organization in 1923, and within ten years he became the first to exploit successfully sound and color in the cel form, providing him with a competitive edge in the marketplace. The technologies of sound and color resuscitated the cel form, nearly artistically moribund and suffering from exhibitor and audience apathy. In the Disney organization, a new emphasis was placed on character, storyline, full animation, technical development, merchandising, and organization, enabling Disney to outdistance his competition, at least in terms of mass appeal, to the present day.

In Europe, from the teens through the twenties, there was a greater emphasis on abstractions, turning away from mass appeals and characters. Hans Richter soon joined with Viking Eggeling in making films that explored rhythm in painting. Oskar Fischinger experimented with silhouettes, wax, and patterns created by multiple exposures. The Dadaists created photomontage resulting in a provocative dismembering of reality, eventually amalgamating into animated collage and kinestasis such as Frank Mouris' *Frank Film* (1973). The line of influence from the photomontage experimenters, montage and constructive-editing techniques, and the abstractionists is not easily drawn, but manifestations of their visual style are evident in many of today's television commercials and film and television program titles.

Up through the mid-thirties, object animation has been exploited in landmark theatrical films such as *The Lost World* (1925) and *King Kong* (1933). Early examples also demonstrated a mix of media technologies such as transparency projection, glass and traveling mattes, miniatures, and slow motion. Animation used in support of special photographic effects would continue to be exploited in contemporary films such as *The Empire Strikes Back* (1980).

Cameraless animation, created by drawing on the film or soundtrack, emerged in the works of Len Lye, Oskar Fischinger, and Norman McLaren in the thirties.

With the rise of cel animation within the American studio system, including the organizations of Disney, Walter Lantz, Warner Bros.*, Terrytoons*, Metro-Goldwyn-Mayer*, and Screen Gems, two developments had considerable influence on American theatrical animation. The formation of United Productions of America (UPA)* brought a departure from the realistic, full animation typical of Disney, toward greater abstractions, as in Mr. Magoo (1949) or Gerald McBoing Boing (1951), a clever little fellow who spoke in sound effects. At UPA, another generation of animators emerged including John Hubley, Peter Burness, Bill Littlejohn, Bill Melendez, and Jules Engel, whose style would eventually appeal to television advertisers for reasons of economy and clarity. The UPA style—abstract, two-dimensional (flat) but embellished with personality through voice characterization and sound effects—brought new economies for television animation. The second development was the divestment of theatres from distribution and production by the major studios, along with the dissolution of discriminatory and anticompetitive booking practices and price-fixing. Without guaranteed access to a diminishing number of theatre screens, and rising labor costs, the studios could no longer afford to produce cel- and object-animated cartoons in the same numbers as before the Second World War. Removing block booking practices gave greater access to theatrical screens for the foreign film. Concurrently, network television was growing, opening up a new demand for films of all types and, by 1960, the electronic medium had devoured both the mundane and classic animated short films formerly seen only in theatres. The new medium, after the mid-sixties, stimulated the growth of animation production both in children's programming and commercials. With the adoption of limited cel techniques, and later the introduction of computer-assisted technologies, animated programming increased sharply. Television's programming demands also brought new markets for object or dimensional animation and other forms of stop-action photo animation. For example, the NBC-TV *Project Twenty* documentary series, using stills-in-motion techniques, revived old photographs, embellishing them with sound effects, music, reenacted dialogue, and tied them together with the omniscient narrator.

Scientists at Bell Laboratories made the first computer-animated films in 1963. Others developed and exploited theory, hardware, and software to evolve computer graphics, first used in auto and aircraft industries as an aid to design. The theory and applications from numerical control in engineering had direct implications for computer-assisted animation. Experimentalists such as Stan Vanderbeek and John Whitney connected with programmers and the new technology. After 1969, Scanimate, Animac, Caesar, Video Cel, and Antics offered computer graphics for television commercial production. With the invention of computer-assisted animation, or motion control, it was possible to incorporate efficiently streaks and slit-scan techniques as those used in the titles for *Superman: The Movie* (1983) or the stargate sequence in *2001: A Space Odyssey* (1968).

In 1985, computer animation had three forms: motion control, analogue systems, and digital systems. Motion control involves the use of a computer to control the operation of an animation stand for special effects such as streaking. The computer also controls the motion of the miniature or artwork during a single frame exposure. Analogue systems manipulate artwork on videotape by stretching, flipping, distorting, and colorizing the material in real time. Digital systems, however, generate their own images and animate them, using either vector or raster graphics. In raster graphics, the image is created by thousands of dots, called pixels. The chief difference from the analogue system is that the digital image is based on mathematically derived information while the analogue image is based on a televised image. Digital systems, however, give the animator the largest degree of control over the final form and color. Landmark films incorporating these technologies include *Tron* (1982) and *The Last Starfighter* (1984), with the computer used to generate images that simulate reality.

The new generation of machine-created images is considered by some as too cold, hard, and "unfeeling." Computer images lack movements which give a weight to a moving figure, the prime ingredient that makes any action convincing, said Frank Thomas, a retired Disney cel animator. Others like the steel quality of brand names, show titles, or television station logos tumbling through space, glittering in a systematic manner. Perhaps the preferred union between computers and the artist in this television age of animation is at the Hanna-Barbera* studios, where a number of series such as *The Flintstones* have been produced. While computers are not considered suitable for character animation, they are used to automate or speed up inking, painting, inbetweening, and some special effects such as dissolves and wipes. There are, however, greater expectations that the computer will retrace one function of the very early American motion picture in future years, and that is the goal to develop a technology that will create (or simulate) a reality with such resolution as to make the difference between machine-created images and live-action film virtually indistinguishable.

BIBLIOGRAPHY

Canemaker, John. *Winsor McKay*. New York: Abbeville Press, 1986.

Crafton, Donald. *Before Mickey: The Animated Film 1896–1928*. Cambridge, Massachusetts: MIT Press, 1982.

Heraldson, Donald. *Creators of Life*. New York: Drake, 1975.

Hoffer, Thomas W. *Animation: A Reference Guide*. Westport, Connecticut: Greenwood Press, 1981.

Imes, Jack. *Special Visual Effects: A Guide to Special Effects Cinematography*. New York: Van Nostrand Reinhold, 1984.

Lenberg, Jeff. *The Great Cartoon Directors*. Jefferson, North Carolina: McFarland, 1983.

Maltin, Leonard. *Of Mice and Magic: A History of American Animated Cartoons*. New York: McGraw-Hill, 1980.

Peary, Gerald, and Danny Peary, editors. *The American Animated Cartoon*. New York: E. P. Dutton, 1980.

Rubin, Susan. *Animation: The Art and the Industry*. Englewood Cliffs, New Jersey: Prentice-Hall, 1984.

Russett, Robert, and Cecile Starr, editors. *Experimental Animation*. New York: Van Nostrand Reinhold, 1976.

APOGEE, INC. Apogee, Inc., was formed in September 1978 by a group of nine special effects* experts who had first come together to work for George Lucas on *Star Wars*: John Dykstra, Robert Shepherd, Alvah Miller, Grant McCune, Don Trumbull, William Shourt, Richard Alexander, Douglas Smith, and Roger Dorney. The first major project on which Apogee worked was *Battlestar Galactica* (1979); the group has also worked on *Star Trek—The Motion Picture*, *Caddyshack*, and *Firefox*. Located originally in San Francisco, the company now maintains its headquarters in the San Fernando Valley area of Los Angeles.

Address: 6842 Valjean Avenue, Van Nuys, Calif. 91406.

BIBLIOGRAPHY

Lightman, Herb A., "Apogee, Inc.: 'Starflight' and Beyond," *On Location*, January 1983, pp. 122–129, 132.

APOLLO PICTURES, INC. Apollo Pictures, Inc., was incorporated late in 1916. Harry R. Raver was its president. It was affiliated with Art Dramas, Inc.*, a combination of independent producers modeled on Metro Pictures Corporation's* system of distribution. Apollo's first film, *The God of Little Children* (1917), starred Alma Hanlon and was directed by Richard Ridgley. In 1917, Apollo leased the Solax* plant at Fort Lee*, New Jersey. Stars appearing in Apollo productions included Bigelow Cooper and Viola Dana, who made *Rosie O'Grady* in 1917 under the direction of John H. Collins.

ARGOSY PICTURES CORPORATION. Argosy Pictures Corporation was John Ford's production company—he was its chairman of the board and Merian C. Cooper was its president—during the late forties and early fifties. Argosy produced *Mighty Joe Young* (1949), directed by Ernest B. Schoedsack, and seven John Ford features: *The Fugitive* (1947), *Fort Apache* (1948), *3 Godfathers* (1948), *She Wore a Yellow Ribbon* (1949), *Wagon Master* (1949), *Rio Grande* (1950), and *The Quiet Man* (1952).

ARMY-NAVY SCREEN MAGAZINE. See "WHY WE FIGHT" SERIES

ARMY PICTORIAL CENTER. See ASTORIA STUDIOS

ARMY PICTORIAL SERVICE. See ASTORIA STUDIOS

AROMARAMA AND SMELL-O-VISION. AromaRama and Smell-o-Vision were two systems introduced in the 1959–1960 period, whereby theatre patrons could smell a film as well as see and hear it. AromaRama basically utilized a theatre's existing air-conditioning system to filter smells to the audience, while Smell-o-Vision required the installation of piping to bring the smells to individual seats.

AromaRama was invented by Charles Weiss in 1958 and the system cost between $3,500 and $7,500 to install in individual theatres. Its scents were developed by Rhodia, Inc., and the air purification system necessary to remove each odor was created by American Statronic Corporation. The first, and last, feature in AromaRama was *Behind the Great Wall*, a documentary on China, which received its New York premiere at the Mayfair Theatre on December 2, 1959.

Smell-o-Vision, initially called Scentovision, was created by a Swiss osmologist, Professor Hans Laube, who demonstrated it to showman Mike Todd in 1954. The system was explained in the February 1960 issue of *American Cinematographer*:

> The heart of the process is an electrically controlled dispensing machine which acts as the "smell-brain." Made of stainless steel, specially treated rubber, and glass, it looks like something out of an Atomic plant. Installed in the depths of the theatre, this mechanical monster is equipped with a series of metal vials containing essences of every aroma to be projected during the run of the film. It also has a central panel with a bank of dials for regulating the concentration of odors.
>
> The machine begins to operate as soon as the projectionist starts the 70mm* picture print running through the projector. A precisely synchronized separate track cued with electronic signals for each odor triggers the smell mechanism and the almost-human machine moves into action selecting in order and dispensing over 30 different scents from the circular tray of vials.

The process was utilized for only one feature, *Scent of Mystery*, first screened at the Cinestage, Chicago, on January 12, 1960, and which was subsequently released, without Smell-o-Vision, as *Holiday in Spain*.

Neither process was greeted with much enthusiasm by the general public, and contemporary reports indicate that the major problem was disposing of one smell from the auditorium before the arrival of the next.

BIBLIOGRAPHY
Alpert, Hollis. "Aromatics," in *The Dreams and the Dreamers*. New York: Macmillan, 1962, pp. 178–181.
Lightman, Herb A., "The Movie Has Scents!" *American Cinematographer*, February 1960, pp. 92–93, 120.
"Nose Opera," *Time*, February 29, 1960, p. 98.

ARROW FILM CORPORATION. Arrow Film Corporation began its existence in July 1915 as a producer for the Pathé* Exchange. It made the *Who Is Guilty?* series, featuring Emmy Wehlen, and a five-reel feature with baseball star Mike Donlin titled *Right Off the Bat*. In late 1915 it reorganized and incorporated in Virginia with a capitalization of $350,000. Arrow contracted with Pathé to produce ten five-reel Gold Rooster features a year. W. E. Shallenberger was the president and Albert S. Le Vino was the head of the scenario department. In 1916, it was producing five-reel features, seven- and eight-reel specials, and serials. Henry Cronjager was the chief cameraman at this time.

By the late teens, Arrow was a distributor of films for the states rights* market. It remained active through the mid-twenties.

ART CINEMA CORPORATION. Art Cinema Corporation was formed by Joseph M. Schenck in July 1926 to take over his earlier Art Finance Corporation, a financial entity which in turn had organized Feature Productions, Inc. (Both Art Finance and Feature Productions were created in 1925 and were responsible for three features, *The Eagle* [1925], *The Bat* [1926], and *The Son of the Sheik* [1926].) In existence through 1933, Art Cinema Corporation produced a number of features at what became known as the Samuel Goldwyn Studios in Hollywood, among which were *Topsy and Eva* (1927), *The Beloved Rogue* (1927), *Lady of the Pavements* (1929), *Lummox* (1930), *Be Yourself* (1930), *Abraham Lincoln* (1930), *The Bat Whispers* (1931), *Kiki* (1931), *Street Scene* (1931), *Rain* (1932), and *Hallelujah, I'm a Bum* (1933).

BIBLIOGRAPHY
Balio, Tino. *United Artists*. Madison, Wisconsin: University of Wisconsin Press, 1976.

ARTCOLOR PICTURES COMPANY. Artcolor Pictures Company was formed in April 1918 to market and produce films by L. J. Dittmar, the president of the Majestic Amusement Company of Louisville, who earlier was active in the Kinemacolor* Company and was one of the incorporators of the Natural Color Picture Company. With offices at 1600 Broadway in New York, the company planned to build a manufacturing plant at Whitestone, Long Island, to produce its own features and educational shorts or to cooperate in the production of other manufacturers' films. The company claimed to use a new color process, perfected by W. Francis Fox and A. G. Waddington of England, based on the Kinemacolor process. It would use no dyes or coloring matters but rather would involve chemical action on the film's emulsion. The projection of the color films could be accomplished using standard equipment.

BIBLIOGRAPHY

"L. J. Dittmar Forming New Company," *The Moving Picture World*, April 13, 1918, p. 227.

"New Color Concern Starts Work on Commercial Lines," *The Moving Picture World*, January 25, 1919, p. 481.

ARTCO PRODUCTIONS, INC. Artco Productions, Inc., entered the producing field in February 1919 after producer Harry Raver received an option from author Augustus Thomas for the rights to some of his old plays and a contract for Thomas to write a series of original screenplays. Raver called the resulting films "Four Star Productions," to emphasize the four essential production elements: author, star, director, and producer. Artco's first production, *As a Man Thinks*, was directed by George Irving and starred Leah Baird, whose husband, Arthur Beck, was an executive with the company. When Raver left the company in August 1919, four old plays by Thomas stayed with Artco, while Raver kept the rights to one new play. In September 1919, Artco took out a long lease on the Kalem* studios.

BIBLIOGRAPHY

"Four Star Combination Enters Field," *The Moving Picture World*, February 15, 1919, p. 874.

ART DIRECTION. The art director, along with the director of photography and the director, is ultimately responsible for the "look" of the film on which he is working, be it naturalistic or imaginative. He must have a basic understanding of the principles of architecture and painting and of cinematography. As Leo K. Kuter wrote in 1957, "An art director conceives, designs, and completes a film's settings with no thought other than to help tell the story in every way commensurate with the production values indicated in the budget." The art director's department will include set dressers and designers and scenic artists. The costume designer also works closely with the art director, and, indeed, during the silent era, many art directors were also responsible for the costume design on the film.

Wilfred Buckland is generally considered to have been America's first art director, having started his film career with the Jesse L. Lasky Feature Play Company in the early teens. Previous to Buckland's hiring, the "look" of the film was haphazardly decided by the director, the cinematographer, and the propman, taking into account whatever furnishings might be available. During the silent era, the art director was often referred to as the technical director. In the thirties, William Cameron Menzies or David O. Selznick introduced the title of production designer implying that the art director's work in certain cases was on a par with that of the director, which in the case of William Cameron Menzies and director Sam Wood was undoubtedly true.

It was customary for the head of the art department to take credit for all of a studio's films, no matter which individual actually happened to be responsible for the art direction. Thus, the art director on M-G-M* films for almost three decades was always Cedric Gibbons, just as the art director on all Fox* and 20th Century-Fox* features was William Darling. In the fifties, there was a unique journal, *Production Design*, devoted to the art and craft of art direction and published by the Society of Motion Picture and Television Art Directors*.

Academy Awards have been given for art direction since their inception in 1927–1928, with the first award going to William Cameron Menzies for his work on *The Dove* and *Tempest*. From 1941 onward, the Art Direction Award has gone both to the art director and the set decorator (initially called the interior decorator).

BIBLIOGRAPHY

Barsacq, Leon, and Elliot Stein. *Caligari's Cabinet and Other Grand Illusions*. Boston: New York Graphic Society, 1976.

Kuter, Leo K., "Art Direction," *Films in Review*, June-July 1957, pp. 248–258.

Larson, Orville, editor. *Scene Design for Stage and Screen*. East Lansing, Michigan: Michigan State University Press, 1961.

Marner, Terence St. John. *Film Design*. New York: A. S. Barnes, 1974.

Thames Television Ltd. *The Art of Hollywood*. London: Thames Television, 1979.

ART DRAMAS, INC. Art Dramas, Inc., was a grouping of independent manufacturers formed in late 1916 to distribute fifty-two five-reel features a year. The production companies associated with Art Dramas included Apollo*, Van Dyke Film Productions Company, Erbograph*, and William L. Sherrill Feature Corporation. Sherrill was the company's first president, with Herbert Blaché its treasurer. Art Dramas announced it was not going to emphasize stars and that its chief concern would be with the stories of its films. Its distribution system was patterned after that of Metro Pictures Corporation* in that there was to be direct cooperation between the producers and the exchange men. Harry R. Raver became president of Art Dramas in 1917, resigning later that same year.

BIBLIOGRAPHY

"New Group of Independent Manufacturers," *The Moving Picture World*, October 7, 1916, p. 60.

ART FILM COMPANY. The Art Film Company, whose offices and studio were located at 25 and Lehigh avenues in Philadelphia, was formed in April 1915 to release to states rights* buyers one five-reel film a month, based on a popular book or play and with a well-known star. Broadway star Laura Nelson

Hall appeared in the first film, *The Stubbornness of Geraldine*, with Marie Empress and Vernon Steele. Gaston Mervale was the general manager for all productions and William S. Forsythe was the chief cameraman.

ART HOUSES. Although the art house or "little cinema" movement is said to have originated in France, there were art houses specializing in critically acclaimed films of an artistic or noncommercial nature as early as 1925 in the United States.

Symon Gould (who died in 1963 at the age of seventy) founded the International Film Arts Guild in October 1925 and organized screenings on Sundays at the George M. Cohan and Central Theatres in New York City. In 1926, the International Film Arts Guild inaugurated regular screenings at the Cameo Theatre on 42 Street. The Guild presented an Ernst Lubitsch retrospective, and, during 1926, screened *The Birth of a Nation*, *Intolerance*, *The Last Laugh*, and other classics. The last film to be screened at the Cameo under the sponsorship of the International Film Arts Guild was *Stark Love* on February 28, 1927. In 1927, Symon Gould founded the Film Guild Cinema at 52 West 8 Street in New York (now the 8th Street Playhouse) and two years later opened the Film Art Cinema (formerly the Regent Theatre) at 16 and Market streets in Philadelphia.

Michael Mindlin (who died in 1946 at the age of fifty-four) was founder of the 5th Avenue Playhouse Group, nicknamed "The Aristocrats of the Cinema." He was managing director and founder of the 5th Avenue Playhouse at 66 Fifth Avenue, New York, which was designed by his wife, Betty. The theatre opened on October 9, 1926, with *The Cabinet of Dr. Caligari*. Mindlin also opened the 55th Street Playhouse in New York, on May 20, 1927 (and which changed its name in the early thirties to the Europa), and the Little Carnegie Playhouse on 57 Street in New York, which opened on November 2, 1928, with *Ten Days That Shook the World*. Mindlin also operated the St. George Theatre in Brooklyn, the Chicago Playhouse, the Buffalo Playhouse, and the Rochester Playhouse.

Nathan Machet's Motion Picture Guild opened the first art house in Washington, D.C., the Wardman Park Theatre, which was active from 1926 to 1929. The Film Mutual Benefit Bureau opened the Little Picture House, at 151 East 50 Street in New York, on December 23, 1929, with the British feature, *The Unwritten Law*. The Film Mutual Benefit Bureau also published *The Film Bulletin* from 1923 to 1929. Another organization of the art house movement was Film Associates, founded in 1925, which sponsored screenings at the Klaw Theatre in New York in the mid-twenties.

Art houses survive through the present, but they are as much concerned with the screening of popular revivals as with what may be classified as "art" films. Landmark Theatres of Southern California and Laemmle Theatres* are two circuits which operate a number of art houses. In more recent years, the best-known art houses in New York have been the Bleeker Street Theatre, the Carnegie Hall Cinema, the New Yorker, and the Thalia; in Chicago, the Walnut Street Theatre; and in Washington, D.C., the Biograph, the Circle, and the Key theatres.

BIBLIOGRAPHY
Larkin, John, Jr., "The Guild Movie Is Here," *Theatre*, May 1926, pp. 32, 62.
Mindlin, Michael, "The Little Cinema Movement," *Theatre*, July 1928, pp. 18, 62.
Weinberg, Herman G., "The Fallacy of the 'Art' Theatre," *Motion Picture Herald*,
        March 30, 1935, pp. 75–76.

ARTHUR MAYER & JOSEPH BURSTYN, INC. See JOSEPH BURSTYN, INC.

ARTKINO PICTURES, INC. Artkino Pictures, Inc., was the official distributor of Soviet features, shorts, documentaries, and newsreels in both North and South America from 1940 to 1980. It was a successor to Amkino Corporation, formed in the late twenties, which had been the exclusive distributor of Soviet films in North and South America. Amkino had come into being with the increased interest in the artistic aspects of Soviet cinema in the twenties. Artkino ceased operations because there was sufficient interest in Soviet films to warrant their release by any number of commercial American distributors.

ARTLEE. See LEE-BRADFORD CORPORATION

ASBURY PARK, NEW JERSEY. See SAWYER, INC.

ASC. See AMERICAN SOCIETY OF CINEMATOGRAPHERS

ASIFA. ASIFA (Association International du Film d'Animation or the International Animated Film Association) was formed in 1960 to promote the art and craft of animation. Through more than 1,000 members in 33 countries, it organizes festivals, sponsors books on animation, and, since October/December 1978, publishes a quarterly, *Animafilm*. The Hollywood branch of ASIFA presents annual "Annie" awards and publishes a newsletter.
   Addresses: 5301 Laurel Canyon Boulevard, Suite 219, North Hollywood, Calif. 91607; 25 West 43 Street, Room 1018, New York, N.Y. 10036.

ASPECT RATIOS. The aspect ratio is the ratio of the width to the height of the image as projected on a screen or printed on the film. The standard aspect ratio is 1.33:1, with the 1.33 indicating the horizontal dimension and the 1 signifying the vertical. Widescreen aspect ratios can vary from 1.65:1 to 2.55:1. The aspect ratio of the original CinemaScope* productions was 2.55:1, but it was later modified to 2.35:1.

ASSOCIATED CINEMA STARS. Associated Cinema Stars was a short-lived organization of early film personalities formed by pioneer J. Stuart Blackton in 1936. The group organized a dinner dance at the Los Angeles Biltmore Hotel in the summer of 1936, which was attended by D. W. Griffith, Clara Kimball Young, Agnes Ayres, Maurice Costello, Mrs. Wallace Reid, Florence Lawrence, and others.

BIBLIOGRAPHY

"Blackton Founds Organization of Screen Pioneers," *Motion Picture Herald*, September 5, 1936, p. 36.

ASSOCIATED FILM SALES CORPORATION. A group of eight West Coast manufacturers combined in mid–1915 under the name of "The Associated Service" (more formally known as Associated Film Sales Corporation) to distribute their own product. The companies involved were the Empire Film Manufacturing Company, Santa Barbara Motion Picture Company*, Liberty Film Company, Burke Film Manufacturing Company, Navajo Film Manufacturing Company*, Federal Film Company, and Alhambra Motion Picture Company*.

BIBLIOGRAPHY

"Associated Service Enters Field," *The Moving Picture World*, June 5, 1915, p. 1590.

ASSOCIATED FIRST NATIONAL PICTURES INCORPORATED. See FIRST NATIONAL PICTURES, INC.

ASSOCIATED INDEPENDENT MANUFACTURERS. See MOTION PICTURE DISTRIBUTING AND SALES COMPANY.

ASSOCIATED MOTION PICTURE ADVERTISERS, INC. Active in the teens and twenties, Associated Motion Picture Advertisers, Inc., was formed August 2, 1916, at a meeting in the Hotel Claridge, New York. Its purposes as stated in contemporary publicity were "to voluntarily foster the interests of motion picture advertisers and to promote a more enlarged and friendly intercourse between persons connected with the business of advertising motion pictures and general motion picture advertisers and to reform abuses relative thereto; and to voluntarily diffuse accurate and reliable information affecting the standing of persons engaged in, and with reference to the conditions, customs and usages of the trade or business of motion picture advertising, as well as affecting and relating to the motion picture industry."

ASSOCIATED PICTURES, INC. Associated Pictures, Inc., was formed in June 1918 to produce, market, and exploit Ralph Ince Film Attractions, a series of "big" features based on stage successes and books by famous authors. Along with Ince, Arthur H. Sawyer, Herbert Lubin, and Louis Joseph Vance (who functioned as production analyst and writer) were involved.

BIBLIOGRAPHY
"Ralph Ince at Head of New Company," *The Moving Picture World*, June 8, 1918,
    p. 1417.

ASSOCIATED PRODUCERS, INC. On November 8, 1919, Thomas H. Ince announced the formation of Associated Producers, Inc., to organize a distribution chain of offices to handle the films made by himself, Maurice Tourneur, Allan Dwan, Mack Sennett, Marshall Neilan, and George Loane Tucker. The organization planned to take effect September 1920 when all the above producers would have been free of their present contracts. Ince was the president and Sennett was the treasurer. B. P. Schulberg and Walter Greene were rumored to have been involved with the formation of the company. All films were to be rented on an open-booking plan. The organization remained active through 1921.

ASSOCIATES & ALDRICH. See ALDRICH STUDIOS

ASSOCIATION INTERNATIONAL DU FILM D'ANIMATION. See ASIFA

ASSOCIATION OF MOTION PICTURE & TELEVISION PRODUCERS.
See ALLIANCE OF MOTION PICTURE AND TELEVISION PRODUCERS

ASSOCIATION OF MOTION PICTURE PRODUCERS. See ALLIANCE
OF MOTION PICTURE AND TELEVISION PRODUCERS

ASTORIA STUDIOS. Located in the Astoria Section of the Queens Borough of New York, on Long Island, the Astoria Studios opened on September 20, 1920, as the new East Coast production center for Famous Players-Lasky (better known as Paramount*). More than 100 silent features were shot there—including all the Paramount films of D. W. Griffith and many of Gloria Swanson's productions—and the studio was also utilized for the testing of potential film personalities from the New York stage. In 1925, Jesse L. Lasky opened on the lot the Paramount Acting School, whose members included Charles "Buddy" Rogers and Thelma Todd, and the school's pupils were featured in a 1926 feature, *Fascinating Youth*, directed by Sam Wood and also filmed at Astoria.

Astoria closed briefly in 1927 but was reopened a year later, and among the Paramount early sound features filmed on the lot were *The Letter*, *Glorifying the American Girl*, *The Cocoanuts*, and *Applause*, all released in 1929. In the thirties, the studio was utilized as an independent production center, and among the films shot there were *The Emperor Jones* (1933) and the Ben Hecht–Charles MacArthur features of 1934–1936. The last two features of the thirties to be filmed at Astoria were *Backdoor to Heaven* and *One Third of a Nation* (both released by Paramount in 1939).

Between 1940 and 1946, Astoria was taken over by the War Department and became the U.S. Army Pictorial Center, at which worked directors such as Frank

Capra, George Cukor, and John Huston and at which such mundane series as the *Army-Navy Screen Magazine* were produced. The U.S. Army Pictorial Service continued to utilize Astoria through 1970, although from 1946 onward it was also available as a rental facility.

In 1976, a nonprofit organization, the Astoria Motion Picture and Television Center Foundation, was created to take over the studio, and *Thieves* (1977) became the first commercial feature to be made at Astoria since before the Second World War. Among other films shot at Astoria were *The Wiz* (1977), *Hair* (1979), *All That Jazz* (1979), *Eyewitness* (1981), *Arthur* (1981), *Author, Author* (1982), *The World According to Garp* (1982), and *Daniel* (1983).

In addition to operating as a major East Coast studio facility, Astoria also offers a regular screening program of classic and important new films and has announced plans for the opening of a museum devoted to East Coast motion picture and television production.

The studios are also known as the Kaufman Astoria Studios, after its chairman of the board, George S. Kaufman.

Address: 34–31 35 Street, Astoria, N.Y. 11106.

BIBLIOGRAPHY

Brady, Frank, "Astoria Lives Again," *American Film*, December 1979, pp. 42–48.

Koszarski, Richard. *The Astoria Studio and Its Fabulous Films*. New York: Dover, 1983.

Krista, Charlene, "Kaufman Astoria Studios," *Films in Review*, August/September 1985, pp. 398–403.

Reilly, Charles Phillips, "Astoria Film Studio," *Films in Review*, January 1976, pp. 59–60.

ASTOR PICTURES CORPORATION. Astor Pictures Corporation advertised itself as "where all the big major company releases go for reissue," and it is for its reissue of such classic films as *Tumbleweeds* (1925, reissued 1939), *Hell's Angels* (1930), *The Bat Whispers* (1931), *Front Page* (1931), *Street Scene* (1931), *Scarface* (1932), and *Rain* (1932) that the company is best remembered. Formed in 1925, Astor also released many new features and short subjects. In the thirties, it operated three subsidiary companies, Vigilant Pictures Corporation, B 'n' B Film Corporation, and Promotional Films, Inc., and in 1936 formed a Hollywood production company, Astor Productions, Inc. In the fifties, Astor formed Atlantic Television Corporation to sell its product to television. The New York–based corporation was headed by Robert M. Savini, until his death at the age of seventy-one in 1956. Astor Pictures filed for bankruptcy on January 31, 1963.

ASTRA FILM CORPORATION. Louis J. Gasnier, former vice-president and general manager of Pathé*, formed Astra Film Corporation in March 1916 and became its president. George Baker was vice-president and George B. Seitz was secretary. Astra's productions were released through Pathé, and the company leased the Pathé Studios in Jersey City, New Jersey. In 1919, it purchased a studio on Verdugo Road in Glendale, California, which had formerly been occupied by the Diando Film Company*. The company produced serials and comedies; its directors included George Fitzmaurice, Donald Mackenzie, William C. Parke, and George B. Seitz; and its stars included Pearl White, Grace Darmond, Mollie King, Creighton Hale, Helene Chadwick, and Warner Oland.

BIBLIOGRAPHY

"Gasnier Forms Producing Company," *The Moving Picture World*, March 18, 1916, p. 834.

ATLANTIC TELEVISION CORPORATION. See ASTOR PICTURES CORPORATION

AUDIO BRANDON. See FILMS INCORPORATED

AUDIO FILM CENTER. See FILMS INCORPORATED

AVCO EMBASSY PICTURES CORPORATION. See EMBASSY COMMUNICATIONS

AYWON FILM CORPORATION. Nathan Hirsch, former general manager and president of Pioneer Film Corporation, formed Aywon Film Corporation in early 1919. He purchased sixteen negatives of five-reel features, each of which he planned to distribute to states rights* exchanges after they were retitled and re-edited, sometimes with new material shot and added. Its first film to be released was *The Eternal Penalty*, which was a re-edited version of the 1915 Triumph Film Corporation production of *The Warning*, although Aywon in releasing the film made no mention of the earlier title. Aywon's offices were located at 729 Seventh Avenue in New York, and the company remained in existence through 1929. It is probably best remembered for its reissue of the D. W. Griffith Biograph* short subjects, many of which it managed to change from one- to two-reelers by the addition of lengthy and often unnecessary subtitles*.

AZTECA FILMS. The leading American distributor of Mexican films since 1932, Azteca Films is chiefly concerned with supplying Spanish-language theatres with product. In the sixties, some 90 percent of all Hispanic theatres in the United States were supplied by Azteca Films, but by 1985 the number had dropped to between 40 and 60 percent. In 1984, Azteca reported that it controlled the rights to more than 5,000 Spanish-language films.

Addresses: 555 N. La Brea Avenue, P.O. Box 36095, Los Angeles, Calif. 90036; also offices in New York, Chicago, Denver, and San Antonio.

B

BACON-BACKER FILM CORPORATION. The Bacon-Backer Film Corporation, owned by George Backer, who supervised productions, and Gerald F. Bacon began production on February 17, 1918. *The Havoc*, directed by Perry Vekroff, was its first production. The films were made for the states rights* market. The company's three-story studio was located at 230 West 38 Street, New York.

BALBOA AMUSEMENT PRODUCING COMPANY. The Balboa Amusement Producing Company, with capital of $7,000, began work on May 23, 1913, at its studio located at 6th and Alamitos streets in Long Beach, California, a studio formerly utilized by J. Searle Dawley of the Edison Manufacturing Company*. H. M. Horkheimer, a former ticket seller for a circus, was president and general manager, while his brother, Elwood, was secretary and treasurer. In 1914, Balboa contracted to release all its films through Box Office Attractions Company*. In 1917, it claimed to have the largest glass studio in the industry.

William Desmond Taylor was with Balboa until November 1914. Henry B. Walthall and Ruth Roland made films for the company, some of which were released under the "Panama" brand. In 1917, it contracted with the General Film Company to produce Knickerbocker Star Features*. The Balboa studios were turned over to creditors on March 25, 1918, for liquidation, and early in 1919 the Master Pictures Corporation purchased the real estate, studio, and other company property.

BIBLIOGRAPHY
"Balboa Continues to Grow," *The Moving Picture World*, September 4, 1915, p. 1653.
"The Balboa Enterprise," *The Moving Picture World*, July 10, 1915, p. 245.
"Balboa's Plant Growing Steadily," *The Moving Picture World*, September 23, 1916, p. 1977.
Fernett, Gene, "Balboa Studios Brought Fame to Long Beach," *Classic Images*, no. 82, April 1982, pp. 50–51.
RESOURCES
Papers: Historical Society of Long Beach (scrapbook for 1913 and 1914).

BANK NIGHTS. Bank nights were introduced as a box office stimulant by theatres in the depression era of the late twenties and early thirties. On these nights, patrons had the opportunity to win prizes for the price of an admission ticket. The concept of bank nights fell foul of the law in the mid-thirties, with many states declaring them nothing more than illegal lotteries.

BANNER FILM COMPANY. Formed in 1915 and located in San Mateo, California, the Banner Film Company made "Banner" brand comedies starring Bill Stinger, who was the president of the company. It banded together with seven other companies to form the Associated Service in mid–1915. In October 1915, its president was Miss Sadie Lindblom.

BANTHA MUSIC. See LUCASFILM, LTD.

B. A. ROLFE PHOTOPLAYS, INC. Benjamin A. Rolfe, Charles B. Maddox, and Maxwell Karger were directors of the B. A. Rolfe Photoplays, Inc., which was incorporated in New York in July 1914 with offices at 1493 Broadway. Its first production, *Satan Sanderson*, was released by the Alco Film Corporation*. In December 1914, the company changed its name to simply Rolfe Photoplays, Inc. It soon dropped Alco because of doubts concerning the regularity of Alco's releases and began to release with the newly formed Metro Pictures Corporation*, which owned part of Rolfe. Edwin Carewe and John H. Collins were among Rolfe's directors, and its players included Ethel Barrymore, William Faversham, and Viola Dana. In June 1915, Rolfe bought the Dyreda Art Film Company* and occupied its studio at 3 West 61 Street, New York. On May 25, 1917, Rolfe was completely absorbed by Metro, along with Columbia and Popular Plays and Players*, with B. A. Rolfe becoming the general manager of the three producers. Maxwell Karger, previously Rolfe's general manager, left to oversee special productions at another of Metro's studios. B. A. Rolfe left the Metro organization in April 1918 to form Rolfe Productions, Inc., which made a Houdini serial and films starring Marguerite Marsh and directed by Burton King. In August 1919, Rolfe signed a contract to make films exclusively for A. H. Features, Inc., and occupied the Thanhouser* studios in New Rochelle, New York.
BIBLIOGRAPHY
"B.A. Rolfe Company Incorporated," *The New York Dramatic Mirror*, July 22, 1914, p. 24.

BATJAC PRODUCTIONS, INC. Batjac Productions, Inc., was formed in 1951 by John Wayne and Robert Fellows as Wayne-Fellows Productions. Batjac was the name of the trading company owned by Luther Adler in *Wake of the Red Witch* (1948). It produced the following John Wayne features: *Blood Alley* (1955), *Legend of the Lost* (1957), *The Alamo* (1960), *McLintock!* (1963), *Cast a Giant Shadow* (1966), *War Wagon* (1967), and *The Green Berets* (1968). The company which remains in existence under the presidency of Wayne's son,

Michael, also produced some non-Wayne features such as *Track of the Cat* (1954).

Address: 9570 Wilshire Boulevard, Suite 400, Beverly Hills, Calif. 90212.

BIBLIOGRAPHY

Zolotow, Maurice. *Shooting Star*. New York: Simon and Schuster, 1974.

BAYONNE, NEW JERSEY. See CENTAUR FILM COMPANY and DAVID HORSLEY PRODUCTIONS

BB FEATURES. See ROBERTSON-COLE COMPANY

BBS PRODUCTIONS. BBS Productions was formed in 1969 by Berton J. Schneider, Robert J. Rafelson, and J. Stephen Blauner. The most prominent member of the trio was Bert Schneider, a former Columbia Pictures–Screen Gems executive, who had earlier—in 1975—formed, with Robert Rafelson, the television production company of Raybert, which was responsible for the popular series *The Monkees*. BBS produced five features, which were all released by Columbia: *Easy Rider* (1969), *Five Easy Pieces* (1970), *The Last Picture Show* (1971), *Drive, He Said* (1971), and *A Safe Place* (1971). Columbia refused to release BBS's controversial feature-length documentary on the Vietnam war, *Hearts and Minds* (1974), and this led, indirectly, to the breakup of the company. All BBS stock was purchased in December 1971 by Columbia Pictures*. "There was no corporate ideology," Schneider told *The New York Times* (May 4, 1975), "The only philosophy we had was backing particular people." The result was BBS's producing the most important independent American feature films from 1969 to 1971.

BEACH MOVIES. Although beach movies are commonly thought to have begun with *Beach Party* (1963), the roots of the cycle are in *Gidget* (1959) and *Where the Boys Are* (1960). These two films set out the basic situation of teenagers on vacation falling in love away from adult supervision. With *Beach Party*, however, American International Pictures* pushed the basic situation to an extreme: the vacation became permanent, falling in love did not mean marriage but permanent courtship, any problems from real life were banished, and adults had no power. As William Asher, the director of most of the films in the cycle remarked, "There was no real fruition of sex. There was no booze. No cigarettes. The nucleus of the beach gang just weren't in trouble. . . . The theme was almost like a Doris Day picture I guess."

This formula of pretty girls, no problems, music, and broad comedy proved very popular, and it led to a series which includes *Bikini Beach* (1964), *Muscle Beach Party* (1964), *Pajama Party* (1964), *Beach Blanket Bingo* (1965), and *How to Stuff a Wild Bikini* (1965). The cycle proved popular enough that another studio, aside from American International Pictures, made a beach film, but when Paramount* produced *Beach Ball* in 1965 it met without much success. This was an indication that the formula was beginning to erode, as was the fact that American International Pictures began attempting variations on the formula with *Dr. Goldfoot and the Bikini Machine* (1965), *Ski Party* (1965), and *The Ghost in the Invisible Bikini* (1966). Consequently, in 1966, American International Pictures announced it would commence producing a new cycle of films which it dubbed "protest" films. As Sam Arkoff said, "If our public wants more serious subjects, we'll supply them."

The beach film was not entirely dead, for it enjoyed a slight comeback with *Malibu Beach* (1978) and *The Beach Girls* (1982). Despite the interest of the genre's best-known stars, Frankie Avalon and Annette Funicello, in making a comeback, it is doubtful that the cycle will return.

BIBLIOGRAPHY

"AIP: Action, Youth, Older O'Seas Fans; Let TV Gravy Bubble Up by Itself," *Variety*, June 22, 1966, p. 24.

Ehrlich, Henry, "Hollywood's Teen-Age Gold Mine," *Look*, November 3, 1964, pp. 59–66.

Levy, Alan, "Peekaboo Sex, or How to Fill a Drive-In," *Life*, July 16, 1965, pp. 81–88.

Lewis, Richard Warren, "Those Swinging Beach Movies," *The Saturday Evening Post*, July 31, 1965, pp. 83–87.

McGee, Mark Thomas. *Fast and Furious: The Story of American International Pictures*. Jefferson, North Carolina: McFarland, 1984.

Penn, Jean Cox, " 'Hey, Annette . . . Those Surfers Are Actually Getting into the Water," *Los Angeles*, March 1978, pp. 78–88.

BELL & HOWELL. It has been Bell & Howell's boast that it is "the largest manufacturer of professional motion picture equipment for Hollywood and the world." In fact, by 1948, only 5 percent of the company's sales was to professionals, with Bell & Howell's chief interest being in the area of 16mm* and 8mm* projectors and cameras for the amateur enthusiast. The company entered the amateur movie field in 1922, after agreeing with Eastman Kodak* that 16mm should be the standard for amateurs. (That same year, Charles H. Percy, who was to become president in 1949, joined the company.) It introduced its popular Filmosound 16mm projector in 1932 and its first double-run 8mm camera in 1936.

Bell & Howell was founded by projectionist Donald H. Bell and camera repairman Albert S. Howell in 1907, with a reported initial investment of $5,000. Their precision-built cameras and projectors soon became well known in the film industry, with the company's claiming it had taken "the flick out of flickers." Bell sold out in 1921 to Joe Hector McNabb, who became the head of the company and the man largely responsible for Bell & Howell's ongoing success. Howell retired from active duty in 1940 but continued to maintain an interest in the company until his death.

Address: 7100 McCormick Boulevard, Chicago, Ill. 60645.

BIBLIOGRAPHY
"Elegant Bell & Howell," *Fortune*, July 1948, pp. 92–95, 150, 153–155.
"Half-a-Hundred . . . The Bell & Howell Story," *Film News*, Summer 1957, pp. 7, 11.

BETZWOOD FILM COMPANY. Early in 1918, the Betzwood Film Company bought the 400-acre Lubin plant in Betzwood, Pennsylvania, on the Schuylkill River, one mile from Valley Forge and twenty miles from Philadelphia. Clarence Wolf was the president and Ira M. Lowry was the general manager of the plant. The company's first two stars were Louis Bennison and Tsen Mei. J. Allen Dunn was the scenarist. The banking establishment of Wolf Brothers and Company backed Betzwood, whose first film was *For the Freedom of the East* (1918).

THE BIG BROADCAST SERIES. The Big Broadcast series consists of four features produced by Paramount* between 1932 and 1938, each with a radio background. The first, titled simply *The Big Broadcast* (1932), featured a number of popular radio personalities of the day: Bing Crosby, Arthur Tracy ("The Street Singer"), Kate Smith, George Burns and Gracie Allen, Cab Calloway, Vincent Lopez and His Orchestra, the Mills Brothers, and the Boswell Sisters. It was followed by *The Big Broadcast of 1936*, *The Big Broadcast of 1937*, and *The Big Broadcast of 1938*. In the last, Bob Hope and Shirley Ross introduced what was to become Hope's signature tune, "Thanks for the Memory."

BIOGRAPH COMPANY. There can be little argument that the Biograph Company is the best known of all early American production companies, thanks entirely to its being the studio where D. W. Griffith (1875–1948) began his directorial career (with *The Adventures of Dollie* in 1908) and where he remained through 1913 creating the entire grammar and syntax of filmmaking. At Biograph, Griffith built up a stock company of players, including Mary Pickford, Blanche Sweet, Lillian and Dorothy Gish, Mae Marsh, Henry B. Walthall, and Robert Harron, all of whom enjoyed major success after leaving the company.

The Biograph Company was founded in 1895 by Henry Norton Marvin as the American Mutoscope Company, with financial backing from Abner McKinley and the New York Security and Trust Company. Its initial purpose was to manufacture a peep-show machine, the Mutoscope, along with a series of flipped photographs for use therein. With the help of Edison associate, W. K. L. Dickson, the company manufactured a camera that did not infringe upon Thomas Edison's patents and presented its first film program, on October 12, 1896, at Hammerstein's Olympia Music Hall, New York. At that time, the company became the American Mutoscope and Biograph Company and by 1909 had shortened its name simply to the Biograph Company. In 1908, with Edison, it helped set up the Motion Picture Patents Company and released its films through that organization's General Film Company.

The best-known studio of the Biograph Company was a brownstone mansion at 11 East 14 Street in New York, where the company made the bulk of its films from 1908 to 1912. In 1913, it moved to a new studio in the Bronx, at 807 East 175 Street, where it remained until 1917. Additionally, Biograph operated two studios in Los Angeles; the first (from January to April 1910) was located at Grand Avenue and Washington Street, and the second (from 1911 to 1915) was at Georgia Street and Girard Street.

In 1913, Biograph signed a contract with the theatrical firm of Klaw & Erlanger (K & E), to produce five-reel features, based on its plays, with such films being screened at K & E theatres. The venture was not particularly successful.

When D. W. Griffith left Biograph in 1913, largely out of frustration at the company's refusal to allow him to direct feature-length productions, not to mention its attitude regarding the nonpublicity of either himself as director or the names of his players, Biograph lost its importance. It remained active through 1917, producing new films for a short period, but basically reissuing its old Griffith productions. One of the last releases from Biograph was a six-reel version of D. W. Griffith's only Biograph feature, *Judith of Bethulia*, retitled by the company in 1917, *Her Condoned Sin*.

BIBLIOGRAPHY

Bowser, Eileen, editor. *Biograph Bulletins: 1908–1912*. New York: Octagon Books, 1973.

Dickson, W.K.L. *The Biograph in Battle*. London: T. Unwin Fisher, 1901.

Graham Cooper C., Steven Higgins, Elaine Mancini, and João Luiz Vieira. *D. W. Griffith and the Biograph Company*. Metuchen, New Jersey: Scarecrow Press, 1985.

Henderson, Robert M. *D. W. Griffith: The Years at Biograph*. New York: Farrar, Straus and Giroux, 1970.

Niver, Kemp R. *Mary Pickford, Comedienne*. Los Angeles: Locare Research Group, 1969.

———, editor. *Biograph Bulletins: 1898–1908*. Los Angeles: Locare Research Group, 1971.

———. *D. W. Griffith: His Biograph Films in Perspective*. Los Angeles: n.p., 1974.

Stern, Seymour, "11 East 14 Street," *Films in Review*, October 1952, pp. 399–406.

RESOURCES

Films: Library of Congress; Museum of Modern Art.

Papers: Museum of Modern Art.

BIRNS & SAWYER, INC. Founded in 1954, by Jack Birns and Cliff Sawyer, Birns & Sawyer, Inc., is Hollywood's leading rental agency for anything relating to cinematography, including cameras, dollies, grip equipment, lenses, blimps, batteries, and lights.

Address: 1026 North Highland Avenue, Hollywood, Calif. 90038.

BLACK AMERICAN CINEMA SOCIETY. The Black American Cinema Society is a division of the Western States Black Research Center, founded in 1972 by Mrs. Mayme Agnew Clayton, which "exists to preserve and disseminate the unique history and cultural heritage of the American of African descent." The Society presents an annual program in Los Angeles, titled "Black Talkies on Parade." Each year, it honors a black American who has made considerable contributions to the motion picture. The first honoree was Lena Horne in 1983; Bill "Bojangles" Robinson was honored in 1984, and Dorothy Dandridge in 1985.

Address: 3617 Montclair Street, Los Angeles, Calif. 90018.

BLACK FILMMAKERS HALL OF FAME, INCORPORATED. A nonprofit California corporation, the Black Filmmakers Hall of Fame, Incorporated, organizes an annual tribute to black filmmakers each February in Oakland, California, consisting of special screenings and the Oscar Micheaux Awards Ceremony. Founded in 1974 under the sponsorship of the Cultural and Ethnic Affairs Guild of the Oakland Museum Association, the organization has been an independent corporation since 1977.

Among the inductees into the Hall of Fame are Ossie Davis, Sammy Davis, Jr., Clarence Muse, Gordon Parks, Sr., Stepin Fetchit, and Paul Robeson (all 1974); Eddie "Rochester" Anderson, Ruby Dee, Rex Ingram, Quincy Jones, Butterfly McQueen, Hattie McDaniel, Sidney Poitier (all 1975); Josephine Baker, Louise Beavers, Harry Belafonte, Eubie Blake, the Nicholas Brothers, Ethel Waters (all 1976); Dorothy Dandridge, James Earl Jones, Cicely Tyson (all 1977); William "Count" Basie, Nat "King" Cole, Ella Fitzgerald, Nina Mae McKinney, Bill "Bojangles" Robinson (all 1978); Paul Winfield (1979); Woody Strode (1980); Maya Angelou, Lou Gossett, Jr. (both 1981); and Cab Calloway (1982).

Addresses: 477 15 Street, Suite 200, Oakland, Calif. 94612; P.O. Box 28055, Oakland, Calif. 94604.

BLACKLISTING. See COMMUNISM and THE HOLLYWOOD TEN

BLACK MARIA. See KINETOGRAPH AND KINETOSCOPE

BLACKS IN AMERICAN FILM. Black Americans have been appearing in films from the 1890s, generally in the capacity of servants or as comic relief. In the silent era, it was not uncommon to have a white actor portray a Negro in blackface, as in *The Birth of a Nation* (1915). When the great black vaudeville performer Bert Williams appeared in a 1916 one-reel short, *A Natural Born Gambler*, he was also required to don blackface makeup. Black Americans were seldom permitted major roles in white-produced American films of the silent era, one exception being James E. Lowe, who was featured as Uncle Tom in Universal's 1927 production of *Uncle Tom's Cabin*.

In the thirties, a number of black actors and actresses were featured in Hollywood productions, and notable among them were Bill "Bojangles" Robinson, Clarence Muse, Stepin Fetchit, Nina Mae McKinney, Willie Best, Louise Beavers, and Hattie McDaniel (who was the first black performer to receive an Academy Award, for Best Supporting Actress for her work in the 1939 feature *Gone with*

the Wind). Paul Robeson, who had been seen in the 1924 Oscar Micheaux*
production of *Body and Soul*, as well as *The Emperor Jones* (1933) and *Show
Boat* (1937), achieved greater fame in European films, beginning with *Borderline*
(1928) and including *King Solomon's Mines* (1937), *Song of Freedom* (1938),
and *The Proud Valley* (1941).

There were two all-black features produced in Hollywood in the forties—
Cabin in the Sky (1942) and *Stormy Weather* (1943)—but outside of these films,
blacks still found themselves relegated to supporting roles of a menial nature
or, as with Lena Horne and similar performers, to cameo parts which could
easily be cut from films for consumption by southern audiences.

A new black image began to be projected in American films of the fifties,
such as *Carmen Jones* (1954), *Island in the Sun* (1957), and *Take a Giant Step*
(1958). The new "look" continued into the sixties with *Lillies of the Field*
(1967), *Guess Who's Coming to Dinner* (1968), and *In the Heat of the Night*
(1968), among other features. At the same time producers began to realize the
box office potential of black heroes, such as Jim Brown, Calvin Lockhart,
Godfrey Cambridge, Pamela Grier, and Richard Roundtree, who introduced the
black private detective, Shaft, in the 1971 feature of the same name. Black
heroes came of age with *Superfly* (1972), directed by Gordon Parks, Jr., one of
America's few black directors. There were new black stars, including Ossie
Davis, Ruby Dee, Brock Peters, Beah Richards, and, most important of all,
Sidney Poitier.

Blacks have starred in *Lady Sings the Blues* (1972), *Sounder* (1972), *Claudine*
(1972), and *The Wiz* (1978). A new market has opened up for black exploitation
films, such as *Blacula* (1972) and *Super Fly T.N.T.* (1973).

Independent black films produced for and by black Americans date back to
the teens. They include films produced by the Lincoln Motion Picture Company*
and the Micheaux Film Corporation* and features such as *The Scar of Shame*
(1927), produced by the Colored Players Film Corporation of Philadelphia;
Chicago after Dark (1946), *Boarding House Blues* (1948), and *Killer Diller*
(1948), all produced by the All American News, Inc.; *Go Down, Death!* (1944)
and *Juke Joint* (1947), from Sack Amusement Enterprises*; *Harlem on the
Prairie*, an all-black musical Western; and Clarence Muse's *Broken Strings*
(1940).

Hattie McDaniel was the first black to receive an Academy Award. She was
followed by James Baskett (who received a Special Award in 1947 "for his able
and heart-warming characterization of Uncle Remus, friend and story teller to
the children of the world" in *Song of the South*), Sidney Poitier (who received
the 1963 Academy Award for Best Actor for his work in *Lillies of the Field*),
and Isaac Hayes (who received the 1971 Academy Award for Best Music—Song
for "Theme from *Shaft*").

BIBLIOGRAPHY

Bogle, Donald. *Toms, Coons, Mulattoes, Mammies, and Bucks*. New York: Viking Press,
    1973.
Cripps, Thomas. *Slow Fade to Black*. New York: Oxford University Press, 1977.

———. *Black Films as Genre*. Bloomington, Indiana: Indiana University Press, 1978.

Landay, Eileen. *Black Film Stars*. New York: Drake, 1973.

Leab, Daniel J. *From Sambo to Superspade*. Boston: Houghton Mifflin, 1975.

Mapp, Edward. *Blacks in American Films: Today and Yesterday*. Metuchen, New Jersey: Scarecrow Press, 1972.

Noble, Peter. *The Negro in Films*. London: Skelton Robinson, 1948.

Patterson, Lindsay, editor. *Black Films and Film-Makers*. New York: Dodd, Mead, 1975.

Powers, Ann, compiler. *Blacks in American Movies: A Selected Bibliography*. Metuchen, New Jersey: Scarecrow Press, 1974.

Sampson, Henry T. *Blacks in Black and White*. Metuchen, New Jersey: Scarecrow Press, 1977.

BLANEY-SPOONER FEATURE FILM COMPANY. Established in mid–1913, the Blaney-Spooner Feature Film Company produced films starring Cecil Spooner, based on her highly successful plays. In October 1914, the company, which had changed its name to the Charles E. Blaney Feature Play Company, was purchased by Lewis J. Selznick for the World Film Corporation*. The Blaney studio, for the short time that it existed, was located between Clason's Point and Throgg's Neck. The films which it produced, along with the other Blaney plays, became the property of World.

BLAZED TRAIL PRODUCTIONS, INC. Blazed Trail Productions, Inc., began in 1919 to produce a series of films with subjects set in the Canadian North Woods. The films, distributed by Arrow Film Corporation*, were written by L. Case Russell, directed by Joseph J. Barry, photographed by Joseph Settle, starred John Lowell, and were shot in the Adirondacks. The Blazed Trail studio was located in Gloversville, New York.

BLIND BIDDING. Blind bidding or selling is the practice by which distributors rent a group of films to exhibitors before the majority of the films have been produced. Thus, the exhibitors are renting a block of films about which they know next to nothing—not the stars, the story, the title, or the release date.

This practice, a necessary complement to block booking*, was prohibited by the 1940 consent decree*. The major distributors agreed to trade show their completed films in each exchange district so that an exhibitor had the opportunity to see the film and decide whether to rent it.

The distributors continued to trade show their films even after the terms of the consent decree had expired. Since the trade shows were so poorly attended by exhibitors, the 1946 court decision which forced divestiture of theatres and banned block booking did not prohibit blind bidding or selling, so that it is legal to this day. However, there have been attempts by individual states to outlaw the practice.

BIBLIOGRAPHY
"Court Decision in the New York Equity Suit," *Film Daily Year Book, 1947*, pp. 848–863.
Machetti, Roger. *Law of the Stage, Screen and Radio*. San Francisco: Suttonhouse, 1936.
"A Review of the New York Equity Suit and the Consent Decree," *Film Daily Year Book, 1941*, pp. 636–649.
Valenti, Jack, and A. Alan Friedberg, "Blind Bidding: Two Sides of the Box Office Dollar," *Premiere*, vol. II, no. 1, July 15, 1980, pp. 16–19, 26.

BLOCK BOOKING. Block booking is the practice of renting one group of films on the condition that the exhibitor, during the same period, also rents another group of films. The second group was usually designated "B" movies*, as it would not feature the stars and production values of the films in the first group. Though not called such, the practice of block booking was common from the early history of the American film industry as exhibitors would contract for the total output from the General Film Company, Universal*, or Mutual*.

It was only with the dominance of feature films and the attempt by Paramount's Adolph Zukor to control the industry that block booking became a problem for the independent exhibitor. In 1921, the Federal Trade Commission filed suit against Famous Players-Lasky (Paramount*) charging restraint of trade and unfair methods of competition. Block booking was one of the methods prohibited, but this ban was overturned by a court of appeals in 1932.

In July 1938, the federal government filed suit against Paramount and the other major producers and distributors. Under the consent decree* of November 1940, the government agreed not to press for the divorcement of theatres from producers for three years, and in return the studios agreed to modify their trade practices, including block booking. Instead of selling a year's worth of films, the distributors agreed to sell films in blocks of five or less.

In August 1944, the government reactivated the case and, in June 1946, a court ruled a large number of distribution practices illegal, including block booking. On appeal, the Supreme Court, in 1948, affirmed the lower court ruling and thus signalled the end of block booking. Unofficially, however, the practice still survives as was seen when 20th Century-Fox* was fined in 1978 for forcing exhibitors to take *The Other Side of Midnight* in order to show *Star Wars*. *See also* Blind Bidding.

BIBLIOGRAPHY
Conant, Michael. *Antitrust in the Motion Picture Industry*. Berkeley: University of California Press, 1960.
"Fed Grand Jury Indicts, 20th Pleads No Contest, Is Fined 25G, Costs of Investigation," *Variety*, September 13, 1978, pp. 1, 19.

"BLONDIE" SERIES. Based on the King Features newspaper comic strip, created by Chic Young, the "Blondie" series was filmed by Columbia Pictures* between 1938 and 1950 with Peggy Singleton as Blondie and Arthur Lake as her husband Dagwood. (The couple also appeared as Blondie and Dagwood on radio from 1939 to 1950, although Singleton's role was later taken over by other actresses.) The following is a complete list of the "Blondie" features: *Blondie* (1938), *Blondie Meets the Boss* (1939), *Blondie Takes a Vacation* (1939), *Blondie Brings Up Baby* (1939), *Blondie on a Budget* (1940), *Blondie Has Servant Trouble* (1940), *Blondie Plays Cupid* (1940), *Blondie Goes Latin* (1941), *Blondie in Society* (1941), *Blondie Goes to College* (1942), *Blondie's Blessed Event* (1942), *Blondie for Victory* (1942), *It's a Great Life* (1943), *Footlight Glamor* (1943), *Leave It to Blondie* (1945), *Blondie Knows Best* (1946), *Life with Blondie* (1946), *Blondie's Lucky Day* (1946), *Blondie's Big Moment* (1947), *Blondie's Holiday* (1947), *Blondie in the Dough* (1947), *Blondie's Anniversary* (1947), *Blondie's Reward* (1948), *Blondie's Secret* (1949), *Blondie's Big Deal* (1949), *Blondie Hits the Jackpot* (1949), *Blondie's Hero* (1950), and *Beware of Blondie* (1950).

BIBLIOGRAPHY

Cornes, Judith, "Living with Father," *American Classic Screen*, vol. VI, no. 1 (1982), pp. 25–28.

Zinman, David. *Saturday Afternoon at the Bijou*. New Rochelle, New York: Arlington House, 1973.

"B" MOVIES. "B" movies is a term used to describe films of a secondary or lesser nature, usually produced to fill the second half of a double bill. The features of many of the so-called poverty row studios, such as Monogram*, Republic*, Mascot*, and Grand National*, were always—often quite erroneously—described as "B" movies. Some of the smaller of the major studios, notably Columbia* and Universal*, operated production units exclusively involved in the making of "B" movies as did the major studios starting around 1935. With the demise of the two-feature program at most theatres in the fifties, the "B" movie ceased to be produced, and although there are many films today of a minor nature, none can be legitimately referred to as "B" movies. Among the best-known producers of "B" movies are Sam Katzman, Nat Levine, Herbert J. Yates, Trem Carr, Bryan E. Foy, Sol Wurtzel, Albert Zugsmith, and Val Lewton.

BIBLIOGRAPHY

McCarthy, Todd, and Charles Flynn, editors. *King of the Bs*. New York: E. P. Dutton, 1975.

Miller, Don. *"B" Movies*. New York: Curtis Books, 1973.

B 'n' B FILM CORPORATION. See ASTOR PICTURES CORPORATION

BOARD OF CENSORSHIP. See NATIONAL BOARD OF CENSORSHIP OF MOTION PICTURES

BOOTS AND SADDLES PICTURES, INC. See CALIFORNIA STUDIOS

BORDER FEATURE FILM CORPORATION. Based in Bisbee, Arizona, and with studios in Bisbee and Tombstone, the Border Feature Film Corporation was active early in the twenties, producing two-reel Westerns. Its leading man was Grant Merrill, its leading lady Peggy Parkan, and the two directors under contract were Therdo Joos and Harry Moody.

BORIS THOMASHEFSKY FILM COMPANY. Boris Thomashefsky, a leading Yiddish actor who opened the first Yiddish theatre in America on the Bowery some thirty years previous, formed the Boris Thomashefsky Film Company early in 1915 to produce film versions of modern Yiddish stage successes. Sidney M. Goldin was engaged to direct the films, which starred Thomashefsky, among which were *The Jewish Crown*, *The Period of the Jew*, and *Hear Ye, Israel*.
BIBLIOGRAPHY
"Producing Primarily for the Jews," *The Moving Picture World*, February 6, 1913,
    p. 809.

BOSTOCK JUNGLE AND FILM COMPANY. In July 1915, David Horsley formed the Bostock Jungle and Film Company after having bought the entire Bostock collection of animals and transported them to a five-acre site he secured in Los Angeles. Horsley had six stages erected and proceeded to produce two reels per week of animal films which were released through Mutual Film Corporation*.

BOSTON. See HOLLAND FILM MANUFACTURING COMPANY, MASTERCRAFT PHOTO-PLAY CORPORATION, and PURITAN SPECIAL FEATURES COMPANY

BOSWORTH, INC. In August 1913, Hobart Bosworth (1867–1943), an actor who had previously worked with the Selig Polyscope Company*, encouraged by W. W. Hodkinson, formed Bosworth, Inc., with H. T. Rudisill and a California capitalist and sportsman, Frank A. Garbutt. The primary object of the new company was to produce films based on the Jack London stories, after the author had declared that an earlier contract with Balboa* was nullified by reason of that company's failure to produce any films by a specified date. The first Bosworth film was *The Sea Wolf*, which featured Hobart Bosworth and was filmed, in seven reels, at Truckee, California, and at the J.A.C. Studios in Los Angeles. It was followed by film versions of other Jack London stories: *John Barleycorn*, *The Valley of the Moon*, and *Martin Eden*.
    Phillips Smalley and Lois Weber joined Bosworth as actor-directors in June 1914, and Oscar Apfel was added to the directorial staff early in 1915. Among the stars who appeared in Bosworth productions were Myrtle Stedman, Elsie Janis, Owen Moore, and Fritzi Scheff. When Paramount Pictures* was formed

in May 1914, it distributed the Bosworth films. In November 1914, Bosworth became associated with the Oliver Morosco Photoplay Company*, and both companies shared a studio at 201 North Occidental Boulevard in Los Angeles. Hobart Bosworth left the company in March 1915, and, by October 1916, Bosworth, Inc., was no longer part of the Paramount program, its productions having been taken over by Morosco and Pallas Pictures.

BIBLIOGRAPHY

"Bosworth, Inc.," *The Moving Picture World*, August 13, 1913, p. 848.
"Morosco-Bosworth," *The Moving Picture World*, July 10, 1915, p. 242.

BOUND BROOK, NEW JERSEY. See PATHÉ

BOX OFFICE ATTRACTIONS COMPANY. In January 1914, William Fox formed Box Office Attraction Film Rental Company, which owned the exclusive exhibition rights in New York City, New York State, and New England of the films produced by Solax*, Blaché, American Film Manufacturing Company*, Film Releases of America, Ramo*, Electric, Great Northern Special Features, and Great Northern Preferred Features. In May 1914, the name was shortened to the Box Office Attractions Company, and it began distributing films nationally on a states rights* basis. At the time, an arrangement was made with Balboa* to have Box Office Attractions sell all of Balboa's features to exchanges.

The company was located at 130 West 46 Street in New York, with Fox as president and Winfield R. Sheehan as general manager. By mid–1914, Box Office Attractions was offering at least four features a week selected from twenty-one manufacturers. In September 1914, Frank Powell and Edgar Lewis were hired to direct films for the company, the first of which was Powell's *The Children of the Ghetto*. Other directors were to include J. Gordon Edwards and Lloyd B. Carleton, and the company's stars included Theda Bara and Betty Nansen. Box Office Attractions was replaced by the Fox Film Corporation* when the latter was incorporated in February 1915.

BIBLIOGRAPHY

"Fox Starts Feature Exchange," *The Moving Picture World*, January 10, 1914, p. 182.
"Fox to Sell State Rights," *The Moving Picture World*, May 16, 1914, p. 977.

BOY CITY FILM CORPORATION. Judge Willis Brown, who presided over a juvenile court in Salt Lake City, and established a boys' city, dramatized typical problems of the boys in half-hour films produced by his company, Boy City Film Corporation. Brown hired King Vidor, who had earlier worked with Brown when he was a newsreel cameraman, to direct the films, which were made at a Culver City, California, studio and a self-governed boys' town that was set up. The company produced some ten to twelve films in 1918 before it stopped production because of financial problems. General Film Company released the films.

BIBLIOGRAPHY
"Judge Says His Stories Are Designed for Adult Appeal," *The Moving Picture World*,
    June 1, 1918, p. 1304.

BRANDON FILMS, INC. See FILMS INCORPORATED

BRAY STUDIOS, INC. J. R. Bray, formerly a newspaper and journal cartoonist,
spent six years studying animal movements at the Bronx Zoo and experimenting
with animation* processes before he signed a contract with Pathé* Freres in
1912 to release his animated cartoons on its program. Bray Studios, Inc., produced
the popular "Colonel Heeza Liar" and "Police Dog" series for Pathé in its
New York studios before Bray signed with Paramount* to produce one reel of
animated cartoons per week as well as cartoons to be included in Paramount's
news weekly, to begin in January 1916. Bray patented his work-saving methods
in 1914 and 1915, involving the use of backgrounds on translucent paper which
could be laid over the paper on which the part of the picture that would appear
to move would be drawn. Later, Bray formed the Bray-Hurd Patent Trust with
Earl Hurd, a holder of a patent for the use of cels in animation, and studios
using cels had to pay license fees to the Trust.

Bray sold his cartoons in 1916 for $2 a foot. The Paramount-Bray Pictograph
screen magazine began in 1916 and incorporated live action with the animation.
Max Fleischer created his "Out of the Inkwell" series for these pictographs.
During the First World War, the Bray Studios produced training films for the
military. In June 1919, the company enlarged to become a million-dollar
corporation, the Bray Pictures Corporation, and began production of its "Greater
Bray Pictographs." In September 1919, it produced color-animated cartoons,
which were released by the Goldwyn Distributing Corporation. Bray closed his
animation studio in 1927, but his company continued producing documentaries
and educational filmstrips. In addition to Max Fleischer, Paul Terry and Walter
Lantz also worked at Bray early in their careers.

BIBLIOGRAPHY
"Animated Cartoons in Motion Pictures," *The Moving Picture World*, April 3, 1915,
    p. 54.
"Bray Studios, Inc. to Reorganize," *The Moving Picture World*, June 21, 1919, p. 1784.
"Cartoonist Bray with Paramount," *The Moving Picture World*, December 11, 1915,
    p. 1988.
Crafton, Donald. *Before Mickey*. Cambridge, Massachusetts: MIT Press, 1982.

BRENTWOOD FILM CORPORATION. The Brentwood Film Corporation
was formed in 1918 by nine doctors in the Los Angeles area to produce feature-
length films directed by King Vidor "that will stir the emotions with stories of
every-day life and its problems, every-day drama and every-day comedy."
Brentwood leased a studio, located at 4811 Fountain Street in Hollywood, formerly
occupied by the Mena Film Corporation, whose plans to produce biblical stories
shot both in Hollywood and Palestine were interrupted by the First World War.

Later, Brentwood purchased outright the three-and-one-half acres fronting Fountain Street, between Berendo and Catalina streets. Lloyd C. Hughes was Brentwood's first president.

Brentwood's first production, *The Turn in the Road*, with Helen Jerome Eddy, Ben Alexander, and George Nichols, opened at a small theatre in Los Angeles and attracted overflow crowds for eleven weeks until Brentwood contracted with the Robertson-Cole Company* to distribute it nationally. The film, a critical and financial success, launched Vidor's career and made him a much sought-after director, but he felt obligated to remain with Brentwood for a year, with his second film being *Better Times*, with ZaSu Pitts in her first starring role.

When Vidor signed with the First National* Exhibitors Circuit in September 1919, after writing, producing, and directing four films for Brentwood, the company hired Henry Kolker to replace him as director but planned to keep the basic Christian Science philosophy which Vidor's films exemplified. Although Kolker made *Bright Skies*, with ZaSu Pitts, Brentwood soon disbanded.

BIBLIOGRAPHY
Vidor, King. *A Tree Is a Tree*. New York: Harcourt, Brace, 1952.

BRIDGEPORT, CONNECTICUT. See NATIONAL CAMERAPHONE COMPANY

"BROADWAY FAVORITES." See KALEM COMPANY, INC.

THE BRYNA COMPANY. The Bryna Company, also known as Bryna Productions, was formed in 1955 by Kirk Douglas—Bryna is his mother's name—to produce *Spartacus*, which was not completed until 1960. Bryna has produced or co-produced the following Kirk Douglas features: *The Indian Fighter* (1955), *The Vikings* (1958), *The Devil's Disciple* (1959), *Strangers When We Meet* (1960), *Spartacus* (1960), *The Last Sunset* (1961), *Cast a Giant Shadow* (1966), *A Gunfight* (1971), *The Light at the Edge of the World* (1971), *Catch Me a Spy* (1971), *Scalawag* (1973), and *Posse* (1975). During the sixties, Douglas also owned Joel Productions.

Address: 141 El Camino Drive, Beverly Hills, Calif. 90212.

B. S. MOSS MOTION PICTURE COMPANY. The B. S. Moss Motion Picture Company was incorporated in New York in mid–1915 to maintain a theatrical and vaudeville agency and to engage in motion picture business. Benjamin S. Moss, a manager of theatres in New York, had been president of an earlier production company, the Reliance Feature Film Corporation, formed late in 1914, which produced the five-reel *Three Weeks* from Elinor Glyn's novel. The Moss Company did not begin production until September 1916, at which time it released, on the states rights* market, George Bronson Howard's *The Power of Evil*. The company gave first-run privilege to the Moss theatre chain. It practiced block booking* arrangements but allowed purchasers to see at least four of its features before they agreed to purchase up to twelve. Other Moss productions included *In the Hands of the Law* and *Boots and Saddles*. The company ceased operations in 1918.

BIBLIOGRAPHY

"B. S. Moss Enters the Production Field," *The Moving Picture World*, July 29, 1916, p. 771.

BUENA VISTA DISTRIBUTION COMPANY, LTD. Buena Vista Distribution Company, Ltd., was formed in 1953 as a wholly owned subsidiary of Walt Disney Productions* to distribute the company's films theatrically. It took its name from the street upon which the studios were built. From 1930 to 1932, all Walt Disney films had been distributed theatrically in the United States by Columbia Pictures*. From 1932 to 1937, distribution was handled by United Artists Corporation*, but with the release of Disney's first feature-length cartoon, *Snow White and the Seven Dwarfs*, in 1937, distribution of all films was taken over by RKO Radio Pictures* (except *Victory through Air Power* in 1942, which was released by United Artists). The first Disney film to be released by Buena Vista was *The Living Desert* in 1953. The next Disney release, *Rob Roy, the Highland Rogue* (1954), was distributed by RKO, but from the following production, *20,000 Leagues under the Sea* (1954), onward, all films were Buena Vista releases.

Address: 350 South Buena Vista Street, Burbank, Calif. 91521.

BULLS EYE FILM CORPORATION. The Bulls Eye Film Corporation, formed in 1918, was a producer of short comedies for the states rights* market. Billy West was Bulls Eye's first star, and he was supported by Ethel Gibson. Gale Henry, formerly with Universal*, began starring in Bulls Eye comedies in February 1919. The company's offices were located in New York, but its studio was in Hollywood. Charles Parrot was the company's director and Milton L. Cohen its president. Bulls Eye ceased production in 1920.

THE BURBANK STUDIOS. The Burbank Studios (generally referred to simply as TBS) was created in 1972, when Warner Bros.* invited Columbia Pictures* to share its studio production facilities in Burbank. Aside from serving as a joint home for the two major companies, the Burbank Studio has served, and serves, as headquarters for a number of independent producers, including The Ladd Company*, Orion Pictures*, Rastar* Films, Inc., Wildwood Enterprises, and Clint Eastwood's Malpaso Productions.

Address: 4000 Warner Boulevard, Burbank, Calif. 91522.

BURTON HOLMES TRAVELOGUES. The best known of all travelogues—indeed, Burton Holmes is credited with coining the word in 1904—the Burton Holmes Travelogues began with the use of projected slide photographs in 1891. Holmes made his first motion pictures in 1897, forming the Burton Holmes

Corporation, with Oscar DePue, a year later. Initially, Holmes would present his slides and films in person, but by the twenties he was producing travelogue shorts for release by Paramount*, and, in 1931, he produced a series of sound shorts for M-G-M*. Burton Holmes (1870–1958) said that his credo was "to satisfy that universal yearning to see and know the wonders and the beauty of that world of Otherwhere—the earth-wide realm of modern travel." In 1952, there were abortive plans for Sol Lesser to edit the Burton Holmes travelogues for a television series. Since Holmes' death, Burton Holmes Travelogues has remained in existence as a supplier of stock footage.

Address: 8853 Sunset Boulevard, Los Angeles, Calif. 90069.

BIBLIOGRAPHY

"And Now It's Travel Lecturer Burton Holmes in Film," *Motion Picture News*, January 8, 1916, p. 50.

Caldwell, Genoa, editor. *The Man Who Photographed the World*. New York: Harry N. Abrams, 1977.

Evans, Delight, "An Invincible Violet," *Photoplay*, July 1919, pp. 73–74.

Holmes, Burton. *The World Is Mine*. Culver City, California: Murray & Gee, 1953.

"Holmes's Happy Days," *Life*, August 11, 1958, pp. 8–9.

Scully, Sir Francis, "The Noble Neighbor," *Variety*, January 7, 1959, pp. 46, 86.

Stewart, Leslie, "The Roving Eye," *Westways*, November 1979, pp. 32–36.

C

THE CADDO COMPANY, INC. The Caddo Company, Inc., was Howard Hughes' production company, releasing through Paramount* or United Artists*, from 1927 to 1932; he was president and Noah Dietrich was vice-president. (Caddo was incorporated in Louisiana in 1912). Hughes (1905–1976) produced nine features with Caddo: *Two Arabian Knights* (1927), *The Racket* (1928), *The Mating Call* (1928), *Hell's Angels* (1930), *The Front Page* (1931), *This Age for Love* (1931), *Cock of the Air* (1932), *Scarface* (1932), and *Sky Devils* (1932). In 1932, he became bored with filmmaking, and Caddo became inoperative. Caddo had maintained headquarters in Hollywood at 1040 North Las Palmas Avenue, at the United Artists* Studios, and at 7000 Romaine Street.

CALIFORNIA MOTION PICTURE CORPORATION. Opera singer Beatriz Michelena (1890–1942) was the featured star of the California Motion Picture Corporation, which was formed early in 1914. Its offices were in San Francisco, while its studios were located near San Raphael, California. Some of the state's best-known businessmen and capitalists financed the new company, and among them were Charles Temple Crocker, the owner of the St. Francis Hotel in San Francisco, and Herbert Scott, president of the Mercantile Bank. Herbert Payne was president of the company, Alexander E. Beyfuss the vice-president and general manager, George E. Middleton (Michelena's husband) the production manager and director, and Louis Hutt the chief cameraman and head of its laboratory.

California's first release was *Salomy Jane*, based on the Bret Harte novel, and it was followed by other adaptations of books, plays, and operas, including *Mrs. Wiggs of the Cabbage Patch*, *Mignon*, and *The Lily of Poverty Flat*. Beginning August 25, 1914, California's productions were distributed by Alco Film Corporation*. In December 1914, the World Film Corporation* began distributing the films, and, in February 1916, California began selling to the states rights* market because it claimed it would not be hampered by set release dates or contracts. Michelena and Middleton left the company in November 1916 when, during the production of *Faust*, California asked Michelena to continue without compensation. She refused, she said, because the company already owed her $12,000. California went out of business soon thereafter.

BIBLIOGRAPHY

Bell, Geoffrey, "The Rise and Fall of the California Motion Picture Company," *American Classic Screen*, May/June 1981, pp. 16–24.

———. *The Golden Gate and the Silver Screen*. New York: Cornwall Books, 1984.

"California Motion Picture Company's First Release," *The Moving Picture World*, July 4, 1914, p. 68.

"California Motion Picture Corporation," *The Moving Picture World*, July 10, 1915, p. 252.

"A Prima Donna of the Screen," *The New York Dramatic Mirror*, July 1, 1914, p. 25.

CALIFORNIA PICTURES CORPORATION. See CALIFORNIA STUDIOS

CALIFORNIA STUDIOS. Formerly the Tec-Art Studio*, the California Studios were also known as the Prudential Studios (1933–1936) although they were the home of California Studio's owner, Harry Sherman from 1934 onward. Sherman utilized the studios, which he leased from the Clune Family, for the production of the Hopalong Cassidy Westerns, featuring William Boyd, and for the Edward Finney productions made under the Boots and Saddles Pictures, Inc., banner.

In 1944, California Pictures Corporation was formed on the lot by Howard Hughes, with Preston Sturges as president, for the production of Sturges' *Mad Wednesday* (1947), starring Harold Lloyd. Sherman leased the studios to Enterprise Productions, Inc.*, in 1946, and it was renamed Enterprise Studio through 1948. In the fifties, California Studios was the home of Albert Zugsmith Productions (from 1952), Horizon Productions (from 1952), Stanley Kramer Productions (from 1955), and utilized for many television series, notably *Superman*. In February 1961, the studio was acquired by Producers Studios Incorporated, which renamed it Producers Studios, and, as a rental lot, it was used by Jack Lemmon, Richard Quine, and American International Pictures*. In 1980, Raleigh Enterprises, Inc., purchased the studio and renamed it the Raleigh Studios. The studio has utilized three different postal addresses: 5360 Melrose Avenue, 650 Bronson Avenue, and 5255 Clinton Street, Los Angeles, Calif. 90004.

"CAMEO" COMEDIES. See COLONIAL MOTION PICTURE CORPORATION

CAMERAPHONE. See NATIONAL CAMERAPHONE COMPANY

THE CANNON GROUP, INC. The Cannon Group, Inc., has its origins in Cannon Films, formed in 1967 by Dennis Friedland and Chris Dewey. The company's earliest films were little more than sex exploitation subjects, but it gained a reputation in 1970 with the low-budget feature *Joe*. In 1979, a majority holding in the company was acquired by two Israelis, Menahem Golan (who serves as chairman of the board) and Yoram Globus (who serves as president). The two men began an aggressive policy of producing films for independent distribution throughout the world at a logical budget and with pre-licensing to ensure immediate profits. An Italian production arm, Cannon Italia, S.R.L., was formed in 1982, in which year London-Cannon Films, Ltd., was established in the United Kingdom, and the company acquired the Classic Cinema chain, with 130 screens in the British Isles.

By 1983, Cannon was California's fastest growing corporation, with more films in production than many of the major studios. *Forbes* (March 26, 1984) described Cannon as "one of Hollywood's more prolific and profitable film finance and production houses."

Among Cannon's productions were *That Championship Season* (1982), *Death Wish II* (1982), *Treasure of the Four Crowns* (1983), *The Wicked Lady* (1983), *Revenge of the Ninja* (1983), *Sahara* (1984), and *Bolero* (1984).

Address: 640 San Vicente Boulevard, Los Angeles, Calif. 90048.

BIBLIOGRAPHY

Barnett, Chris. "Israelis Invade Hollywood," *OTC Review*, July 1983, pp. 18–23.

Ilott, Terry, "Five Years On, Golan and Globus Make Cannon a Major Force," *Screen International*, March 10, 1984, pp. 61–62.

Malan, Rian, "Two Guys from Israel," *California Magazine*, November 1983, pp. 109–110.

Minard, Lawrence, "Givebacks, Hollywood Style," *Forbes*, March 26, 1984, pp. 182–183.

Murnane, Tom, "The Cannon Group, Inc." *California Business*, September 1983, pp. 79–80.

Rehfeld, Jerry, "Cannon Fathers," *Film Comment*, December 1983, pp. 20–24.

CANON CITY, COLORADO. See COLORADO MOTION PICTURE COMPANY

CAPITAL FILM COMPANY. The Capital Film Company, incorporated on February 27, 1918, with $2.5 million capital stock, was backed by bankers and financiers throughout the state of Indiana. With headquarters in the Merchants Building in Indianapolis, Capital planned to manufacture and distribute a regular program of twenty-one reels a week. Production began in mid-May 1918 in a studio on the outskirts of the city. Grain dealer William H. Miller, the first president, was soon succeeded by Ike Schlank of New York, who headed the company for a year. Other interested parties included a sheriff, a tobacco dealer, a newspaper president, and bankers. In June 1918, Capital began releasing a portion of the Selig* output. It ended operations in 1924.

BIBLIOGRAPHY

"Capital Film Incorporates in Indiana," *The Moving Picture World*, March 23, 1918, p. 1647.

CARDINAL FILM COMPANY. The Cardinal Film Company was formed by Paramount Pictures* in 1916 to handle the special release and exploitation of *Joan the Woman*, directed by Cecil B. DeMille and starring Geraldine Farrar as Joan of Arc, supported by Raymond Hatton, Hobart Bosworth, Theodore Roberts, and Wallace Reid.

CARTHAY CIRCLE THEATRE. Designed by architect Dwight Gibbs, the Carthay Circle Theatre combined both modern and Spanish styles to become one of the most impressive and important of Los Angeles theatres. It opened on May 18, 1926, with Cecil B. DeMille's *The Volga Boatman*, and was the site of many Los Angeles premieres, including *Sunrise*, *What Price Glory*, and *Gone with the Wind*; when *The Heiress* had its premiere there in 1949, a publicity stunt involved the invitation of stars from twenty-six earlier films which had received their premieres at the Carthay Circle. During the silent era and through the early thirties, Carli Elinor was conductor at the theatre, and he composed the scores for the silent features screened there. Also known as the Fox Carthay Circle Theatre and located at Wilshire Boulevard and Camarillo Drive, with a postal address of 6316 San Vicente Boulevard, the Carthay Circle closed in April 1969 following the West Coast premiere of *Shoes of the Fisherman* and was demolished shortly thereafter.

CASABLANCA FILM WORKS. See POLYGRAM PICTURES

CASINO STAR COMEDIES. See GAUMONT COMPANY

CASTLE FILMS. Castle Films was formed in 1924 by Eugene W. Castle (1897–1960), and, by the thirties, had become the leading distributor of 16mm* and 8mm* short films and condensations of features for sale to the home market. In the summer of 1937, it introduced a newsreel series titled *News Parade*. The company was sold to Universal* in 1947 for a reported $4 million and continued in existence for many more years as a division of Universal's 16mm subsidiary, United World Films*.

C.B.C. FILM SALES CORPORATION. See COLUMBIA PICTURES INDUSTRIES, INC.

CELEBRITY SERVICE. Celebrity Service came into being in 1940, after a failed actor named Earl Blackwell and his partner, Ted Strong, had served as heads of the celebrity department of the 1939 New York World's Fair. Blackwell's organization operates as a service to subscribers, providing information on the present whereabouts, telephone numbers, marital status, and so on, of world personalities. It publishes a *Celebrity Bulletin* and an annual *Contacts Book*.

Addresses: Celebrity Service, Inc., 171 West 57 Street, New York, N.Y. 10019; 8831 West Sunset Boulevard, Suite 303, Los Angeles, Calif. 90036; also offices in other major cities.

BIBLIOGRAPHY

Birmingham, Stephen, "Celebrity Service: The Antic Business of Star Watching," *Cosmopolitan*, April 1976, pp. 208–211, 236.

Blackwell, Earl, editor. *Celebrity Register*. New York: Simon and Schuster, 1973.

Jennings, Dean, "Man of a Thousand Secrets," *The Saturday Evening Post*, April 2, 1955, pp. 22–23, 78, 82–83.

Whitman, Howard, "They Sell Secrets," *Pageant*, vol. I, no. 11, December 1945, pp. 4–11.

CENSORSHIP. Unlike most countries, the United States of America has shied away from official censorship of motion pictures, relying on the film industry to regulate itself by way of the Production Code* or on private bodies, such as the National Board of Review of Motion Pictures*, to provide a seal of approval.

Although films were the subject of considerable complaint regarding moral content, theme, and lurid advertising from the turn of the century onward, the first film to experience widespread censorship was D. W. Griffith's *The Birth of a Nation* (1915), which has been the subject of at least 100 challenges as to its presentation and continues to arouse demands for censorship because of its depiction of blacks and of the Ku Klux Klan (curiously, not from conservative elements, but from liberals, those who historically have abhorred censorship and limitations on freedom of speech). D. W. Griffith was a staunch opponent of censorship, always available to speak in states considering censorship laws, and the author of a 1915 pamphlet, *The Rise and Fall of Free Speech in America*. Racial tension was also the reasoning behind a curious federal law which, from 1912 to 1940, banned the importation and transportation across state lines of any film picturing a prize fight, a law that had its origins in black-white violence created by the 1909 Jeffries-Johnson fight.

On November 4, 1907, Chicago passed the first local censorship ordinance, "prohibiting the exhibition of obscene and immoral pictures and regulating the exhibition of pictures of the classes and kinds commonly shown in mutoscope, kinetoscopes, cinematographs and penny arcades." Pennsylvania was the first state to approve a film censorship law (on July 19, 1911); it was followed by Kansas (1913), Ohio (1913), Maryland (1916), New York (1921), Florida (1921), Virginia (1922), Massachusetts (1922), Connecticut (1925), and Louisiana (1935). The film industry was very familiar with the workings of local censorship boards and tried to avoid the depiction of anything which might offend them. It knew that Ohio was opposed to brutality and it limited the number of punches in a fist fight accordingly. New York was strict on immorality.

The constitutionality of such state censorship laws was increasingly questioned, and gradually the states—as much on the grounds of cost as of legality—gave up their rights to censor. Despite the U.S. Supreme Court's quashing of the conviction of a Maryland exhibitor who, in 1964, screened *Revenge at Daybreak* without a state license, Maryland continued as the only state with local censorship laws until it finally closed down its Censor Board on June 30, 1981.

In 1915, the Supreme Court had ruled that films were not constitutionally protected from censorship—in the cases of *Mutual Film Corp. v. Industrial Commission of Ohio* and *Mutual Film Corp. of Missouri v. Hodges*—and it did not grant such protection until 1952, in a case involving the Italian film *The Miracle*, which was declared "officially and personally blasphemous" by the commissioner of licenses for New York City, following condemnation of the film by Cardinal Spellman. The Supreme Court ruled that "sacrilege was not a justifiable ground of censorship" and that motion pictures constituted a form of expression protected by the First Amendment.

The federal government has been able to prevent the import of foreign films into the United States if they are considered immoral, subversive, or obscene. In 1935, the Czech film, *Extase*, which featured a lengthy nude bathing scene with Hedy Lamarr, was refused entry by New York customs officials, as was a 1965 Swedish film, *491*. Generally, local antiobscenity and antipornography laws have offered the only opportunity for the continued censorship of motion pictures.

BIBLIOGRAPHY

Berman, Lamar Taney, editor. *Selected Articles on Censorship of the Theatre and Moving Pictures*. New York: H. W. Wilson Company, 1931.

Carmen, Ira H. *Movies, Censorship, and the Law*. Ann Arbor, Michigan: University of Michigan Press, 1966.

Cline, Victor B., editor. *Where Do You Draw the Line?* Provo, Utah: Brigham Young University, 1974.

De Grazia, Edward, and Roger K. Newman. *Banned Films*. New York: R. R. Bowker, 1982.

Devol, Kenneth S., editor. *Mass Media and the Supreme Court*. New York: Hastings House, 1971.

Ernst, Morris L. *The First Freedom*. New York: Macmillan, 1946.

Ernst, Morris L., and Pare Lorentz. *Censored: The Private Life of the Movie*. New York: Jonathan Cape and H. Smith, 1930.

Ernst, Morris L., and Alan U. Schwartz. *Censorship: The Search for the Obscene*. New York: Macmillan, 1964.

Ernst, Morris L., and William Seagle. *To the Pure . . .* New York: Viking Press, 1928.

Gardiner, Harold C. *Catholic Viewpoint on Censorship*. Garden City, New York: Hanover House, 1958.

Griffith, D. W. *The Rise and Fall of Free Speech in America*. Los Angeles: The Author, 1915 (reprinted by Larry Edmunds Book Shop, 1967).

Hunnings, Neville March. *Film Censors and the Law*. London: George Allen & Unwin, 1967.

Inglis, Ruth A. *Freedom of the Movies*. Chicago: University of Chicago Press, 1947.

Miles, William E. *Damn It!* Evanston, Illinois: Regency, 1963.

Phelps, Guy. *Film Censorship*. London: Victor Gollancz, 1975.

Randall, Richard S. *Censorship of the Movies*. Madison, Wisconsin: University of Wisconsin Press, 1968.

Roeburt, John. *The Wicked and the Banned*. New York: Macfadden, 1963.

Schumach, Murray. *The Face on the Cutting Room Floor*. New York: William Morrow, 1964.

Vizzard, Jack. *See No Evil*. New York: Simon and Schuster, 1970.

Wistrich, Enid. *"I Don't Mind the Sex It's the Violence": Film Censorship Explored*. London: Marion Boyars, 1978.

RESOURCES

Papers: New York State Archives (New York State Censorship Board records); Ohio Historical Society (Ohio State Censorship Board records).

CENTAUR FILM COMPANY. David Horsley decided to become a film manufacturer after he lost a few hundred dollars when he opened a small motion picture theatre in 1907. With former Biograph* player Charles Gorman, Horsley, who believed he could make better films than any manufacturer except for Biograph and Pathé*, prepared to shoot his first film early in 1908 at a building Horsley owned in Bayonne, New Jersey (where he constructed an open-air stage). When his cameraman decided not to jeopardize his own career, Horsley (who had no previous experience in filmmaking) decided to shoot the film himself. Knowing that the Motion Picture Patents Company* was forming, Horsley would not wait the eight to nine weeks that it would take for a camera to be sent from England, and so he decided to design his own camera.

His company, the Centaur Film Manufacturing Company, later shortened to the Centaur Film Company, was located at 900 Broadway in Bayonne. It released its first film, *A Cowboy Escapade*, on September 19, 1908, but since this was a few weeks after the Kalem Company* released its first film, Kalem, and not Centaur, was selected to be a member of the Motion Picture Patents Company, while Centaur achieved the distinction of becoming the first independent company. Horsley discontinued production until Ludwig G. B. Erb bought a half interest in the company. After production recommenced, the partners quarreled and Horsley purchased Erb's interest. Erb subsequently formed the Crystal Film Company*.

Centaur went out of existence in 1910 as Horsley's new company, the Nestor Film Company, also located at 900 Broadway, Bayonne, was formed with his brother William. A series based on the "Mutt and Jeff" comic strip, and another series with the comic villain "Desperate Desmond," were among its earliest productions. Players included Violet and Claire Mersereau, Dorothy Davenport, Alice Davenport, and cowboy Art Acord. Al E. Christie was Nestor's chief of production.

In October 1911, Nestor became the first motion picture company to locate in Hollywood, when it rented a building at Sunset Boulevard and Gower Street. By 1912 most of Nestor's films were being produced in Los Angeles, and it was the first producer to bring three companies to California. Thomas Ricketts directed the dramas, Milton Fahrney the Westerns*, and Al Christie the comedies.

Nestor released through the Motion Picture Distributing and Sales Company*, the distribution company for the independents formed in April 1910 to compete with the Motion Picture Patents Company*. When Universal* was formed, Nestor began releasing through that company. Because of a fight for control of Nestor with Universal, in which Horsley had stock, Horsley returned to Bayonne in 1913 and erected a new studio at Avenue E and East 43 Street, where the Centaur productions resumed, with the company now being called the Centaur Film Company. In 1914, Horsley proclaimed that the feature film had seen its day, and, although Centaur produced a six-reel version of *Il Trovatore*, it began to specialize in one-reel comedies under the "Ace" brand. Chester Beecroft was general manager of Centaur in 1915. The "Nestor" brand, which had become part of Universal, ceased to exist in 1919.

BIBLIOGRAPHY

"Centaur's New Building Well Equipped," *The Moving Picture World*, March 7, 1914, p. 1239.

"David Horsley, 'How the First Independent Started,' " *The Moving Picture World*, March 10, 1917, pp. 1518–1519.

"Picture Personalities: David Horsley," *The Moving Picture World*, July 2, 1910, p. 117.

von Harleman, G. P., "Motion Picture Studios of California," *The Moving Picture World*, March 10, 1917, pp. 1601–1602.

CENTRAL CASTING CORPORATION. Following a study by the Russell Sage Foundation, the major Hollywood producers comprising the Association of Motion Picture Producers decided to establish their own organization to provide extras for their films. Central Casting Corporation was established on December 4, 1925, with the purchase of the Screen Service Agency, one of the largest of the independent casting agencies. No "bit" players, only extras, were handled by Central Casting, which required that individuals register with them and check on a daily basis if work was available. Central Casting was entirely funded by the Association of Motion Picture Producers (later Association of Motion Picture & Television Producers), of which it was a wholly owned subsidiary, and extras were not required to pay commissions.

Central Casting Corporation was able to provide any type of extra—man, woman, child, or handicapped—and through the forties extras were divided by Central Casting into four distinct types: "atmosphere," character," "specialized," and "dress." Despite the small percentage of extras who actually found employment in the industry, the numbers registered with Central Casting were substantial. In 1929, 17,541 were registered; in 1935, 15,000; in 1946, 5,500; but by 1976 only 2,200 were on register. From 1929 onward, Central Casting published a Call Bureau Cast Service sheet for each feature, providing invaluable information as to the "bit" and extra players in such films. In 1975, the Call Bureau Cast Service became the Actors Agency Directory.

Initially located at 5504 Hollywood Boulevard, at the intersection with Western Avenue, Central Casting moved in the sixties to 8480 Beverly Boulevard. In 1976, Central Casting ceased to be a service for the studios and was sold to Production Payments, Inc.

BIBLIOGRAPHY
Facts about Extra Work. Hollywood, California: Central Casting, August 1, 1936.
Herbert, Ray, "Want to Act? Maybe This'll Dissuade You," *Los Angeles Times*, June 10, 1957, pp. 1, 9.
MacCulloch, Campbell. *Motion Picture "Extra" Work*. Hollywood, California: Central Casting, 1935.

CENTURY COMEDIES. Formed in 1917 and active through the mid-twenties, Century Comedies was operated by two brothers, Julius and Abe Stern, with a studio at 6100 Sunset Boulevard (at the southwest corner of Sunset and Gower Street). Century Comedies were two reels in length; featured the Century Dog, Baby Peggy, Harry Sweet, and Charles Dorety; and were released by Universal*. The Sterns also operated the Great Western Producing Company.
BIBLIOGRAPHY
Cary, Diana Serra. *Hollywood's Children*. Boston: Houghton Mifflin, 1979.

CHADWICK PICTURES CORPORATION. Active from 1924 to 1928, Chadwick Pictures Corporation was an independent producer of feature films, founded by I. E. Chadwick. The company's best-known film was *The Wizard of Oz* (1925), starring Larry Semon, Dorothy Dwan, and Oliver Hardy.

CHAPLIN STUDIOS. The Chaplin Studios occupied a five-acre site bounded on three sides by De Longpre Avenue, La Brea Avenue, and Sunset Boulevard, with a postal address of 1416 N. La Brea Avenue in Hollywood. Ground breaking for the new studios took place in November 1917, and Chaplin made his first film there, *A Dog's Life*, in 1918. The following Chaplin films were shot at the studio: *The Bond* (1918), *Shoulder Arms* (1918), *Sunnyside* (1919), *A Day's Pleasure* (1919), *The Kid* (1921), *The Idle Class* (1921), *Pay Day* (1922), *The Pilgrim* (1923), *A Woman of Paris* (1923), *The Gold Rush* (1925), *The Circus* (1928), *City Lights* (1931), *Modern Times* (1936), *The Great Dictator* (1940), *Monsieur Verdoux* (1947), and *Limelight* (1952).

The studio was designed in the style of an English village and built for a reported sum of $35,000. At one corner of the studio, at the junction of Sunset and La Brea, stood the McClelan Mansion, which was occupied by Chaplin's brother Sydney. This house was later demolished and on the site stands a Safeway supermarket.

Chaplin sold his studios in September 1953 to the New York real estate company of Weber & Knapp for $650,000. The company announced plans to demolish the studio but instead leased it, in December 1953, to Kling Studios of Chicago for television production. In 1958, Red Skelton's Van Bernard Productions acquired the lot, and in 1962 it was purchased by CBS, Inc., as a production facility for Paisano Productions' television series "Perry Mason." Finally, in August 1966, the present owners, Herb Alpert and Jerry Moss' A

& M Record Company and Tijuana Brass Enterprises, Inc., purchased the studios. The Chaplin Studio was declared a Historic-Cultural Monument by the Los Angeles Cultural Heritage Board on February 5, 1969.

CHARIOT FILM COMPANY. The Chariot Film Company, with offices at 110 West 40 Street, New York, released its first production, the four reel *The God of Vengeance*, in April 1914. Alex Yokel was the president and general manager of the company, which planned to release one film every three weeks.
BIBLIOGRAPHY
"Chariot Film Company Enters the Arena," *The Moving Picture World*, April 11, 1914, p. 225.

CHARLES E. BLANEY FEATURE PLAY COMPANY. See BLANEY-SPOONER FEATURE FILM COMPANY

CHARLES K. HARRIS FEATURE FILM COMPANY. A company which produced films based on the songs of Charles K. Harris, the Charles K. Harris Feature Film Company was incorporated in New York on February 10, 1915. It released with the World Film Corporation*. Charles K. Harris was one of the directors of the company, and among the players who appeared in its films were Edwin August, Grace Washburn, and Muriel Ostriche.

CHASE-PARK-CITRON. See INTERNATIONAL CREATIVE MANAGEMENT, INC.

CHAS. K. FELDMAN'S GROUP PRODUCTIONS. Group Productions was formed in the mid-forties by Charles K. Feldman to produce a small series of quality features, including *Uncle Harry* (1945), *The Red Pony* (1949), *The Glass Menagerie* (1950), *A Streetcar Named Desire* (1951), and *The Seven Year Itch* (1955), released through various distributors. All Group Productions properties were sold in 1955 to 20th Century-Fox* for a reported $1 million. Feldman (who died in 1968 at the age of sixty-three) was also president of Famous Artists Corporation, a talent agency which he formed in 1932 and whose clients included Tyrone Power, Kirk Douglas, Max Steiner, Salvador Dali, John Wayne, Lauren Bacall, George Stevens, Ava Gardner, and Charles Boyer. (The agency was sold in 1962 to Ashley-Steiner and became Ashley-Famous.)

CHATEAU MARMONT. See THE GARDEN OF ALLAH

CHESTERFIELD MOTION PICTURE CORPORATION. A low-budget producer, Chesterfield Motion Picture Corporation was active from circa 1925 to 1936. Films were initially shot on the Universal* lot, and, in the thirties, at what became Republic Pictures Corporation* in Studio City. George R. Batcheller was president of the corporation, whose best-known director—under contract in the early thirties—was Richard Thorpe. In the thirties, Chesterfield was associated with Invincible Pictures Corporation (whose president was Maury Cohen).

CHICAGO INTERNATIONAL FILM FESTIVAL. First held November 4–11, 1965, the Chicago International Film Festival remains under the directorship of Michael Kutza, Jr. It is a competitive festival, held each November, offering a Golden Hugo for best film, with a Silver and Bronze Hugo for runners-up; there are also awards for Best First Feature, Best Actor, Best Actress, and a Special Jury Prize.

Address: 415 North Dearborn Street, Chicago, Ill. 60610.

CHILD LABOR LAWS. Current child labor laws within the motion picture industry govern the number of hours a minor may work, the times during which he or she may work, and the schooling to be provided by the production company. (Schooling is handled by Studio Teachers, Local No. 884 of IATSE*.) Such laws date back to 1927 when an informal agreement was worked out between teachers' groups and the State Labor Commission governing the use of children in films from both a safety and a morality viewpoint. The question of the use of children in films became a major public issue with the deaths of two children and actor Vic Morrow on the set of *The Twilight Zone* on July 23, 1982; the two children were working during hours when the employment of minors in film production was forbidden.

The best known of child labor laws concerns the holding in trust of a minor's earnings until he or she gains maturity. On April 11, 1938, former child star Jackie Coogan filed suit against his mother and stepfather to recover his earnings dating back to the early twenties. Coogan was successful in his suit, but it transpired that the bulk of the money had already been spent. As a result, the State Assembly in Sacramento, California, passed a Child Actor's Bill, commonly known as "The Coogan Act," under Section 36 of the California Civil Code. The bill gave the court authority to approve all contracts between minors and the entertainment industry and provided that at least one-half of the minor's earnings had to be paid by the studio or other employer directly into a trust fund established for the minor's benefit. Deanna Durbin was the first child star to become subject to the new bill.

BIBLIOGRAPHY

Cary, Diana Serra. *Hollywood's Children*. Boston: Houghton Mifflin, 1979.
Silverberg, Herbert T., "Status of Minors in Hollywood," *Daily Variety*, October 24, 1938, p. 74.
Zierold, Norman J. *The Child Stars*. New York: Coward-McCann, 1965.

CHILD STARS. Just as the American public has been fascinated by the image of the child-woman, as exemplified by Mary Pickford, Mary Miles Minter, Audrey Hepburn, and others, so has it had a long and lasting appreciation of child stars, beginning in the early teens. The box office appeal of children reached its zenith between 1915 and 1917, when films featured Ida and Ella Mackenzie, Viola Dana, Billy Jacobs, Clara Horton, Baby Marie Osborne, Thelma Salter, and many other children. The Thanhouser Film Corporation* had a veritable stable of child performers, including Leland Benham; Helen Badgley, billed as the Thanhouser Kidlet; Marie Eline, known as the Thanhouser Kid; and Marion and Madeline Fairbanks, the Thanhouser Twins. Jane and Katherine Lee first came to the public's attention in *A Daughter of the Gods* (1916). They joined Fine Arts* and were featured, along with Charles Spofford, Francis Carpenter, and Virginia Lee Corbin, in *Let Katie Do It* (1916). From Fine Arts, the children moved over as a group to the Fox Film Corporation*, where they were billed as the Fox Kiddies and featured in a series of films, most based on fairy tales, directed by Sidney and Chester Franklin.

Jackie Coogan achieved stardom with his performance in the title role of Charle Chaplin's *The Kid* (1921). Producer Sol Lesser helped advance his career, and Lesser is also responsible for the success of another child star of the twenties, Baby Peggy (Montgomery). In 1922, Hal Roach introduced the "Our Gang" series*.

The thirties saw a new wave of child stars, including dramatic actor Freddie Bartholomew, who was featured in *David Copperfield* (1934) and *Little Lord Fauntleroy* (1937); Mickey Rooney and Judy Garland, who were teamed in a series of M-G-M* musicals; Shirley Temple, who became the biggest box office star at 20th Century-Fox*; Deanna Durbin, who helped save Universal* from bankruptcy with her cheery musicals; boy soprano Bobby Breen; Jackie Cooper, who made a name for himself in *Skippy* (1930) and *The Champ* (1931); Jane Withers, who was 20th Century-Fox's other major child star; Gloria Jean, whom Universal introduced as a second Deanna Durbin; Baby LeRoy, who infuriated W. C. Fields; Bonita Granville, who starred as Nancy Drew; as well as many others.

Margaret O'Brien, Peggy Ann Garner, and Claude Jarman, Jr., were the best of the forties child stars, all of them featured as dramatic rather than musical performers. In more recent years, Tatum O'Neal won an Academy Award for Best Supporting Actress for her work in *Paper Moon* (1973). Ricky Schroder followed in the footsteps of Jackie Cooper in a 1979 remake of *The Champ*, and that same year Justin Henry was nominated for an Oscar, for Best Supporting Actor, for his work in *Kramer vs. Kramer*.

In 1935, the Academy of Motion Picture Arts and Sciences presented a miniature statuette to Shirley Temple, "in grateful recognition of her outstanding contribution to screen entertainment during the year 1934." Beginning with the 1938 awards year, the Academy presented Special Awards to child performers: Deanna Durbin and Mickey Rooney (1938), Judy Garland (1939), Margaret O'Brien (1944), Peggy Ann Garner (1945), Claude Jarman, Jr. (1946), Ivan Jandl (1948), Bobby Driscoll (1949), Jon Whiteley and Vincent Winter (1954), and Hayley Mills (1960).

BIBLIOGRAPHY
Best, Marc. *Those Endearing Young Charms*. New York: A. S. Barnes, 1971.
————. *Their Hearts Were Young and Gay*. New York: A. S. Barnes, 1975.
Cary, Diana Serra. *Hollywood's Children*. Boston: Houghton Mifflin, 1979.
Darvi, Andrea. *Pretty Babies*. New York: McGraw-Hill, 1983.
Maltin, Leonard, editor. *Hollywood Kids*. New York: Popular Library, 1978.
Moore, Dick. *Twinkle, Twinkle, Little Star*. New York: Harper & Row, 1984.
Slide, Anthony. "Child Stars," in *Aspects of American Film History prior to 1920*.
    Metuchen, New Jersey: Scarecrow Press, 1978, pp. 16–25.
Zierold, Norman J. *The Child Stars*. New York: Coward-McCann, 1965.

CHRISTIE FILM COMPANY. Al E. Christie (1886–1951), who was earlier the head of production at the Nestor Film Company, along with his brother Charles leased the old Nestor studio, at Sunset Boulevard and Gower Street, from the Quality Pictures Corporation* on January 1, 1916, and formed the Christie Film Company, to produce comedies for release through Universal* under the "Nestor" brand. Al was president and director of production, and Charles was the general manager. In May 1916, Fred L. Porter became the vice-president and secretary.

In July 1916, Christie severed his connection with Universal and began offering his weekly release to independent exchanges on the open market. Christie doubled its output in October 1916 by adding director Horace G. Davey. Among the players at Christie were Billie Rhodes, Dorothy Devore, Stella Adams, Eddie Barry, and Harry Ham. Laura La Plante and Betty Compson were two major stars of the twenties who made their screen debuts in Christie comedies.

In April 1918, Christie began releasing its comedies with First National*, and, in 1920, Educational began to distribute the films.

Christie turned to feature-length production in the twenties, notably with two versions of *Charley's Aunt*. The first, in 1925, starred Syd Chaplin, and the second, in 1930, featured Charlie Ruggles. The relationship with Educational continued, and, when Christie ceased to be an independent producer, he worked for Educational as a producer of its musical and comedy shorts. Al Christie retired in the late thirties.

BIBLIOGRAPHY
"Al Christie's Comedy Checkerboard," *Photoplay*, May 1925, p. 81.
Christie, Al E. *The Elements of Situation Comedy*. Los Angeles: Palmer Photoplay
    Corporation, 1920.
Weir, Hugh S., "Al Christie's Recipe for a Successful Movie Picture Company," *Moving
    Picture Weekly*, July 24, 1915, p. 46.

CINECOLOR. Introduced in 1932, and a descendent of Prizma Color* and Multicolor, Cinecolor utilized a bipack system of photography, in which two negatives were run through the camera, emulsion to emulsion, and exposed simultaneously. One negative recorded the red-orange portion of the spectrum and the other the blue-green. Prints were made on duplitized positive film with an emulsion coated on both sides—one toned blue-green, the other red-orange. Because it was less expensive than Technicolor* and did not require the three-strip Technicolor camera, Cinecolor was very popular with low-budget feature producers and with producers of short subjects. A similar two-color system, Trucolor, was developed by Consolidated Film Industries* for Republic Pictures*. All of these two-color systems were superseded by Eastman Color*.

CINEMA CORPORATION OF AMERICA. See PRODUCERS DISTRIBUTING CORPORATION

CINEMA EDUCATIONAL GUILD. See COMMUNISM

CINEMASCOPE. A widescreen process that utilizes an anamorphic camera and projector lens—and needs only one camera and projector—CinemaScope was introduced by 20th Century-Fox* with *The Robe*, which opened at the Roxy Theatre*, New York, on September 16, 1953. The CinemaScope lens, which was manufactured in the United States by Bausch & Lomb, was the invention of the Frenchman Henri Chrétien and dates back to 1927. The British Rank Organization had an option on the use of the lens, but when that option expired, it was taken up by 20th Century-Fox, which saw CinemaScope as a solution to its falling profits brought on, in part, by television.

Wholly owned by 20th Century-Fox, the CinemaScope process was subsequently licensed to M-G-M* in March 1953. Warner Bros.* had come up with an anamorphic lens similar to CinemaScope, which it initially called WarnerSuperScope and RKO* introduced its system, SuperScope. However, late in 1953, Warner Bros. abandoned its widescreen process and signed a license agreement with 20th Century-Fox. By the end of 1953, every major studio—with the exception of Paramount* which had its VistaVision* process—was licensed to use CinemaScope. All CinemaScope productions of 1953 were in stereophonic sound, but by 1954 20th Century-Fox had commenced producing prints with monaural soundtracks for those theatres not equipped for stereo. By November 1, 1954, it was reported that some 9,000 theatres in the United States and Canada were able to screen CinemaScope prints.

To improve the quality of its 35mm release prints, 20th Century-Fox introduced CinemaScope 55 in 1956, which utilized a film in the camera 55mm wide. The first film to be shot in CinemaScope 55 was *Carousel*, but the process was abandoned by 20th Century-Fox after *The King and I* (1956).

In 1953, Henri Chrétien, Earl Sponable, Sol Halprin, Lorin Grignon, Herbert Bragg, and Carl Faulkner of the 20th Century-Fox studios received a Class I Scientific or Technical Award (Oscar statuette) "for creating, developing and engineering the equipment, processes, and techniques known as CinemaScope." 20th Century-Fox utilized CinemaScope for all its features through 1967.

BIBLIOGRAPHY
Barr, Charles, "CinemaScope: Before and After," *Film Quarterly*, Summer 1963, pp. 4–24.
Belton, John, "CinemaScope: The Elements of Technology," *The Velvet Light Trap*, no. 21, Summer 1985, pp. 35–43.
Benford, James R., "The CinemaScope Optical System," *Journal of the SMPTE*, January 1954, pp. 64–70.
Geddes, Henry, "Discovering CinemaScope," *Journal of the British Film Academy*, Winter 1954, pp. 9–11.
Kimball, Ward, "Cartooning in CinemaScope," *Films in Review*, March 1954, pp. 118–119.
Shamroy, Leon, "Shooting in CinemaScope," *Films in Review*, May 1953, pp. 226–228.
Southall, Derek J., "Twentieth Century-Fox Presents a CinemaScope Picture," *Focus on Film*, no. 31, November 1978, pp. 8–26, 47.

CINEMA VERITÉ. See DOCUMENTARIES

CINEMIRACLE. Developed by National Theatres, Cinemiracle was similar to Cinerama*. It utilized three projectors and three cameras, with the right and left cameras photographing their images through mirrors. The "joins" between the three strips of film were eliminated through the use of "vignetting" in the cameras and in the laboratory printing. The right and left hand projectors also used mirrors, and the three projectors could be placed in the same booth, unlike Cinerama which required three separate booths. The seven-track stereophonic sound was heard through five speakers placed behind the deeply curved screen and two speakers to the right and left of the auditorium. Both the Roxy* in New York and Grauman's Chinese Theatre in Hollywood were refurbished for the premiere of the one and only feature to be shot in Cinemiracle, *Windjammer*. The world premiere of *Windjammer* took place at Grauman's Chinese Theatre on April 8, 1958, with the Roxy opening following a day later.

BIBLIOGRAPHY
"Cinemiracle with 'Windjammer' Opens Big, Wide View of the World," *The Film Daily*, April 7, 1958, pp. 5–13.
Smith, P. Stanley, "The Cinemiracle Camera and Its Development," *American Cinematographer*, February 1958, pp. 100–101, 118–119.
Zunser, Jesse, "Cinemiracle," *Cue*, April 5, 1958, p. 12.

CINERAMA. Cinerama gave the effect of reality to a presentation by utilizing three synchronized projectors showing the three 35mm images, slightly overlapping, on a wide, curved screen, made up of 1,100 vertical strips of perforated tape. To add to the effect, the system also utilized multitrack stereophonic sound. Theatres screening Cinerama were required to install special projectors (each of which required a separate projectionist) and a new screen. The Cinerama camera unit utilized three films and three 27mm lenses set at 48 degree angles to each other, with the left lens filming the right hand side of the picture and the right lens filming the left. To project Cinerama, the complete film—at least up to a break or intermission—needed to be loaded on one single reel, each for three projectors, and projected at one-and-a-half times the normal speed to allow for the increased size of the film frame.

The process was invented by Fred Waller (1886–1954) and was first seen at the 1937 New York World's Fair, where it was known as Vitarama. Waller explained Cinerama as quoted in the *Journal of the British Film Academy* (Autumn 1954) as "the medium of subjective participation, the only true 'I am a camera' system. Every single scene, every single shot must be conceived *within* the medium; the audience must be brought into the picture. The Cinerama screen is not a mirror of life, but life itself, and is an extension of the physical world, with the spectator at the centre of it." The patent on the Cinerama process was controlled by Vitarama Corporation, jointly owned by Waller and Laurance Rockefeller. The process was exploited by Cinerama, Inc. (formerly Cinerama Corporation), formed by Lowell Thomas and others and which remained in existence as a distribution company, often financially troubled, through the present.

The first Cinerama presentation, *This Is Cinerama*, opened at the Broadway Theatre, New York, on September 30, 1952, and caused such a sensation that even *The New York Times* covered the event as a front-page news story. Eventually problems with the overlapping image of the three projectors and the cost of installation of the special equipment led to Cinerama's being presented, using a single projector, with a single 70mm* film.

BIBLIOGRAPHY

"Cinerama—the Broad Picture," *Fortune*, January 1953, pp. 92–93, 144–146, 148, 150.
Halas, John, "Discovering Cinerama," *Journal of the British Film Academy*, Autumn
    1954, pp. 2–6.

CITY ISLAND. See RYNO FILM COMPANY, INC.

C.K.Y. FILM CORPORATION. The C.K.Y. Film Corporation was formed in August 1917 to market and distribute the films of popular star Clara Kimball Young (1890–1960).

CLEVELAND. See JUVENILE FILM COMPANY

CLIFFSIDE, NEW JERSEY. See JESTER COMEDY COMPANY and SERIAL FILM COMPANY

CLUNE STUDIO. See TEC-ART STUDIO

CODE. See PRODUCTION CODE

COLLECTIVE FILM PRODUCERS, INC. Collective Film Producers, Inc., was formed in the summer of 1937 by Roman Rebush and Edgar G. Ulmer as both a producer and distributor of Yiddish films. Its first production and release was *Green Fields* (1937), directed by Ulmer.

COLONIAL MOTION PICTURE CORPORATION. The Colonial Motion Picture Corporation was formed late in 1913 after having secured the rights to the writings of various novelists. James D. Law was the president, and Frederick S. Dudley was vice-president and general manager of the company. Its first production, the nine reel *Seats of the Mighty*, written by Sir Gilbert Parker, was directed by T. Hayes Hunter and starred Millicent Evans, Lionel Barrymore, and Lois Meredith. It was released by World Film Corporation*. In 1915, Colonial began producing "Cameo" brand comedies featuring Harry Kelley.

COLORADO MOTION PICTURE COMPANY. The Colorado Motion Picture Company began production in October 1913 and was located at 1444 Stuart Street in Denver. It specialized in military and Western* films. Otis B. Thayer was the company's first director, until he left, late in 1914, to go to the Pike's Peak Film Company*. In March 1914, Colorado built a new studio in Canon City, Colorado. It was a regular contributor to Warner's Features, Inc.

COLORADO SPRINGS, COLORADO. See PIKE'S PEAK FILM COMPANY

COLORIZATION. Colorization is the generic term used to describe a computerized process that transforms black-and-white films into color; it was developed by Ralph Weinger, an electronics engineer, in 1978. Weinger's process is used by Color Systems Technology of Los Angeles. An electronic scanner breaks down each frame of film into 525,000 dots. An art director examines the first and last frames of each scene and determines the color for each object in the frame. A computer then colorizes the scene, selecting the colors by comparing each frame with the one preceding it. A similar system is also utilized by Colorization, Inc., a subsidiary of Hal Roach Studios, Inc.*

Film and television distributors are particularly interested in the process, believing it will give new life to black-and-white subjects, for which it is hard to find playing time on television. The process will also, from a legal viewpoint, create new films that can be recopyrighted, providing additional copyright protection for the films' owners. However, most creative people within the industry have denounced colorization as a form of vandalization of films that were shot and meant to be seen only in black-and-white.

BIBLIOGRAPHY

Armstrong, Scott, "Now They're Using Computers to Color Black-and-White Movies," *Christian Science Monitor*, October 16, 1984, pp. 25, 27.

Bierbaum, Tom, " 'Topper' 1st off the Block Using Colorization Process," *Daily Variety*, April 19, 1985, p. 6.

Elmer-DeWitt, Phillip, "Play It Again, This Time in Color," *Time*, October 8, 1984, p. 83.

Maurer, Joseph, "Color Spectography: Film of a Different Color," *Emmy Magazine*, May/June 1985, pp. 60, 62.

COLUMBIA LICENSED MOTION PICTURES. See POWERS COMPANY

COLUMBIA PICTURES CORPORATION (TEENS). See METRO PICTURES CORPORATION

COLUMBIA PICTURES INDUSTRIES, INC. A humble yet spirited company, Columbia Pictures Industries, Inc., was virtually the only "poverty row" studio to transform its image and become a major corporation, thanks entirely to the vigor of its co-founder Harry Cohn (1891–1958). It was Cohn who personally supervised all studio production and who was responsible for signing Columbia's best-known director, Frank Capra (born 1897). Capra was active at Columbia from the late twenties through the late thirties, and his films for the studio included *That Certain Thing* (1928), *Platinum Blonde* (1931), *Lady for a Day* (1933), *It Happened One Night* (1934), *Mr. Deeds Goes to Town* (1936), *Lost Horizon* (1937), and *Mr. Smith Goes to Washington* (1939).

Aside from the Capra features, Columbia produced some of the best screwball comedies* of the thirties, including *Twentieth Century* (1934), *Theodora Goes Wild* (1936), *The Awful Truth* (1937), and *His Girl Friday* (1939). Grace Moore was one of Columbia's first major stars, followed by Rita Hayworth, Kim Novak, William Holden, Glenn Ford, and Judy Holliday. Among the "classic" Columbia features were *Gilda* (1946), *The Jolson Story* (1946), *The Lady from Shanghai* (1948), *Jolson Sings Again* (1949), *All the King's Men* (1949), *Born Yesterday* (1950), *On the Waterfront* (1955), *The Bridge on the River Kwai* (1957), *Lawrence of Arabia* (1962), *A Man for all Seasons* (1966), and *Guess Who's Coming to Dinner* (1968). Columbia also released the first group of major youth-oriented quality features, such as *Easy Rider* (1969), *Five Easy Pieces* (1970), and *The Last Picture Show* (1971).

Columbia was founded in 1922 by Harry Cohn, Joe Brandt, and Jack Cohn as C.B.C. Film Sales Corporation, which produced cheap Westerns*, comedies starring the Hall Room Boys, and the Screen Snapshots series on Hollywood, which Columbia continued to produce through 1958. C.B.C. changed its name when Columbia Pictures was incorporated on January 10, 1924. *More To Be Pitied Than Scorned* is usually referred to as Columbia's first feature. In fact, this six-reel melodrama, directed by Edward Le Saint and starring Rosemary Theby, was a Waldorf Production, produced by Harry Cohn and released by C.B.C. in 1922. Arguably the first Columbia feature is *Yesterday's Wife*; directed by Le Saint and starring Irene Rich, it was produced by Columbia but released by C.B.C. in August 1923. The first major Columbia feature is generally considered to have been *Blood Ship*, directed by George B. Seitz and starring Hobart Bosworth; it opened at the Roxy Theatre* in 1927.

Following Cohn's death, Leo Jaffe maintained a link with Columbia's past; he had joined the studio in 1930, becoming its president in 1967, president of Columbia Pictures Industries in 1969, and chairman of the board in 1973.

Columbia was the first of the major studios to become actively involved in television. It formed Screen Gems in 1952 to produce programs for television and to distribute the studio's product to the new medium. In 1968, Columbia Pictures Corporation was reorganized as Columbia Pictures Industries, Inc. It weathered a major scandal when David Begelman (who had been appointed president of its Motion Picture Division as of September 4, 1973) resigned in 1978, after admitting that he had embezzled $61,000 from the studio. In 1982, the studio was acquired by Coca-Cola Co. as part of its entertainment division, and a year later Frank Price, the company's chief executive officer since 1979, was replaced by Guy McElwaine. That same year Columbia enjoyed two major box office hits with *Tootsie* and *Ghandi*.

In 1972, Columbia left its original studios at Sunset Boulevard and Gower Street in Hollywood to share the newly named The Burbank Studios (TBS)* with Warner Bros.* It has close ties with Tri-Star* and Rastar*. Aside from its own productions, Columbia also releases the films of Johnny Carson's The Carson Film Company, of the Richard Pryor Company, and of Jane Fonda's Jayne Development Corporation. The studio also has a separate division, Triumph Films,* for the release of quality foreign films. Columbia's trademark has always been the lady with the torch, although her look has changed considerably through the years; the emphasis today is more on the light from the torch than on the Columbia lady herself.

Address: Columbia Plaza, Burbank, Calif. 91505.

BIBLIOGRAPHY

Buscombe, Edward, "Notes on Columbia Pictures Corporation," *Screen*, vol. XVI, no. 3, Autumn 1975, pp. 65–82.

Landro, Laura, "Parent and Partners Help Columbia Have Fun at the Movies," *The Wall Street Journal*, December 6, 1984, pp. 1, 18.

Larkin, Rochelle. *Hail Columbia*. New Rochelle, New York: Arlington House, 1975.

McClintick, David. *Indecent Exposure*. New York: William Morrow, 1982.

Pogache, Mark, "On Studios: Columbia Pictures," *On Location*, July 1983, pp. 99–102.

Zito, Stephen, "Columbia Pictures: From Corned Beef and Cabbage to Caviar," *American Film Institute Report*, July 1971, pp. 4–5.

———, "Columbia Pictures: From Corned Beef and Cabbage to Caviar—Part II," *American Film Institute Report*, October 1971, pp. 9–11.

RESOURCES

Films: Library of Congress (preservation materials and some reference prints); UCLA Film Archives (35mm nitrate prints of selected titles).

Still Photographs: American Film Institute.

COMBINED PHOTOPLAY PRODUCERS, INC. See UNITED FILM SERVICE

COMET PRODUCTIONS, INC. Established in 1945 by Mary Pickford (she was its president) as a production company, releasing through United Artists, for her husband Charles "Buddy" Rogers (he was vice-president), Comet Productions was responsible for a handful of minor features beginning with *Little*

Iodine (1946). Rogers produced but did not star in any of the Comet features, which included *Susie Steps Out* (1946), *Stork Bites Man* (1947), and *Sleep My Love* (1948). Although inactive, the company remained in existence through the sixties. A related production company, also controlled by Pickford and Rogers, during this same period, was Triangle Productions, Inc.

COMING ATTRACTION TRAILERS. See TRAILERS

COMIQUE FILM CORPORATION. The Comique Film Corporation was created by Joseph M. Schenck in the spring of 1917 to produce the films of Roscoe "Fatty" Arbuckle and Buster Keaton, for release through Paramount*. The first comedy, *The Butcher Boy*, was released on April 23, 1917, and the last, *The Garage*, on January 11, 1920. The first films were shot at the studios of the Norma Talmadge Film Corporation at 318 East 48 Street, New York. Comique later moved to the Balboa* studios in Long Beach, California, and finally to the Diando* studios in Glendale.

COMMAND PERFORMANCE. See HOLLYWOOD VICTORY COMMITTEE

COMMERICAL ADVERTISING BUREAU. See VITAGRAPH COMPANY OF AMERICA

COMMITTEE FOR THE FIRST AMENDMENT. See COMMUNISM

COMMUNISM. The spectre of Communists infiltrating the film industry is one that has led to extraordinary efforts by government and private individuals to stifle freedom of speech and to purge anyone with even the slightest hint of left-wing leanings.

Communists were active in Hollywood in the thirties in organizations such as the Hollywood Anti-Nazi League* and the Motion Picture Democratic Committee* and in the formation of the Screen Writers Guild. To young men and women in the entertainment industry during the grim days of the depression, communism sparked a social consciousness that was lacking in much of American society. As early as September 16, 1933, *Variety* carried the headline "Pinks Plan to Stalinize Studios." Just as the studios worked vigorously against Upton Sinclair's campaign for governorship of California—with its motto "End Poverty in California" (EPIC)—so did many intellectuals within the industry actively support this socialistic candidate.

The Spanish Civil War galvanized many left-wingers and Communists within the film industry. The Motion Picture Artists Committee was formed by Lewis Milestone, Gale Sondergaard, Luise Rainer, John Garfield, Fredric March, and others to aid Republican Spain. Joris Ivens' documentary *The Spanish Earth*

(1937) was funded by many within the Hollywood community, including John Cromwell, Fredric March, Paul Muni, Frank Tuttle, and James Cagney.

The signing of a nonaggression pact between Hitler and Stalin in August 1939 temporarily destroyed whatever popularity communism might have had within the film community. It was not until the Nazi invasion of the Soviet Union that communism once more found favor within the film industry. In 1943, Goldwyn* produced *The North Star*, scripted by Lillian Hellman and directed by the Russian-born Lewis Milestone; M-G-M* produced *Song of Russia*; and Warner Bros.* filmed *Mission to Moscow*, based on the book by the former American ambassador to the Soviet Union, Joseph E. Davies.

Active organization against communism from within the film industry began in the mid-forties, with the formation of the Motion Picture Alliance for the Preservation of American Ideals* by such right-wingers as King Vidor, Clarence Brown, Walt Disney, and Gary Cooper. Screenwriter John Lee Mahin announced that the Alliance would "turn off the faucets which dripped red water into film scripts." As early as 1944, the Alliance urged a congressional investigation of communism in the film industry.

Attacks on Communists within the industry were seen by many as a way of bringing the film unions, particularly the Conference of Studio Unions*, into line.

On May 7, 1947, the House Un-American Activities Committee (HUAC), under the chairmanship of J. Parnell Thomas, held closed hearings in Los Angeles, at which Robert Taylor, Adolphe Menjou, Leo McCarey, and others told of "Communist subversion" within the industry. Initially, the studio heads were uncooperative in their dealings with the Committee, but their attitudes changed in September 1947 when subpoenas were issued to forty-seven members of the film community, ordering their appearance at hearings in Washington, D.C.

Among the "unfriendly" group of nineteen witnesses were Donald Ogden Stewart, Larry Parks, Dalton Trumbo, and Edward Dmytryk. To defend the rights of these witnesses, the Committee for the First Amendment—which did not permit membership by Communists—was formed by Philip Dunne, William Wyler, and John Huston, a group which held its first meeting at Ira Gershwin's home. Sadly, the Committee and public opinion went against the unfriendly witnesses. Ten who refused to answer the Committee's questions became known as "The Hollywood Ten."* They were denied employment in the industry and subsequently served jail sentences for their belief in the First Amendment.

What became of the Hollywood Ten was only the beginning as far as the search for Communists within the film industry was concerned. The House Un-American Activities Committee, now under the chairmanship of John S. Wood and spurred on by the anti-Communist campaigns of Senator Joseph McCarthy, issued more subpoenas. Guilds and unions demanded loyalty oaths from their members. The Screen Actors Guild* refused to defend one of its members, Gale Sondergaard, against blacklisting. Larry Parks was forced to apologize publicly for his political beliefs. Lucille Ball was able to persuade the Committee and the public that she had only registered as a Communist in 1936 to please her grandfather.

As a result of the HUAC hearings, held through 1953, many within the film industry were blacklisted. Others were forced to find employment abroad or in the New York theatre. Organizations such as Myron C. Fagan's Cinema Educational Guild reminded the public of those film personalities with supposedly Communist backgrounds. Gossip columnist Hedda Hopper made sure that her readers never forgot who was a loyal American and who was not. A publication called *Red Channels*, produced by American Business Consultants, was available to motion picture and television executives, listing the names of Communists within the community. Blacklisting was always subtle, and never did any executive admit to its existence. It was not until 1960, when Otto Preminger and Kirk Douglas began to employ openly those who had been branded as Communists, that the blacklist period in the American film industry came to a close.

The political beliefs of film personalities have never since been that important to film audiences except during the Vietnam War, when the activities of actress Jane Fonda created a considerable outcry. Perhaps symbolic of the laissez-faire attitude of the film industry toward communism is Paramount's financing of the 1981 film, *Reds*, directed by and starring Warren Beatty, which glorified the life of American Communist John Reed.

BIBLIOGRAPHY

Belfrage, Cedric. *The American Inquisition 1945–1960*. Indianapolis: Bobbs-Merrill, 1973.

Bentley, Eric, editor. *Thirty Years of Treason*. New York: Viking Press, 1971.

Ceplair, Larry, and Steven Englund. *The Inquisition in Hollywood*. Garden City, New York: Anchor Press/Doubleday, 1980.

Cogley, John. *Report on Blacklisting, I: The Movies*. New York: The Fund for the Republic, 1956.

Donner, Frank J. *The Un-Americans*. New York: Ballantine Books, 1961.

Fagan, Myron C. *Red Treason in Hollywood!* Hollywood, California: Cinema Educational Guild, 1949.

————. *Documentation of the Red Stars in Hollywood*. Hollywood, California: Cinema Educational Guild, 1950.

Faulk, John Henry. *Fear on Trial*. New York: Simon and Schuster, 1964.

Kanfer, Stefan. *A Journal of the Plague Years*. New York: Atheneum, 1973.

McWilliams, Carey. *Witch Hunt*. Boston: Little, Brown, 1950.

Miller, Merle. *The Judges and the Judged*. Garden City, New York: Doubleday, 1952.

Navasky, Victor S. *Naming Names*. New York: Viking Press, 1980.

Red Channels. New York: American Business Consultants, 1950.

Taylor, Telford. *Grand Inquest*. New York: Ballantine Books, 1955.

Trumbo, Dalton. *The Time of the Toad*. New York: Harper & Row, 1972.

Vaughn, Robert. *Only Victims*. New York: G. P. Putnam's Sons, 1972.

COMPO. COMPO (the Council of Motion Picture Organizations), which remained active through the seventies, was formed in Washington, D.C., in December 1949, by the Conference Committee of the Motion Picture Industry to "plan, organize and supervise a comprehensive, continuous public relations program representing the maximum coordination of all member organizations, such program to include not only projects in the general public relations field, but also those which affect better box office, those which pertain more particularly to the relationship of the 238,000 people in the motion picture industry to one another, and those which are related to discriminatory taxation and restrictive regulations, and to conduct the necessary basic research prerequisite to the initiation and fulfillment of such a program.'' Funding was from payment by exhibitors and distributors of ten cents on each $100 of film rentals. Among the ten founding organizations were Variety Clubs, International; Allied States Association; Motion Picture Association of America*; and the Committee of Trade Press Publishers.

A similar organization, ACE (American Congress of Exhibitors), was formed in 1958, with its concerns being the sale of pre–1948 films to television, pay television, producer-distributor-exhibitor relations, industry-government relations, ways and means of increasing production, and industry research. COMPO worked with ACE as an industry spokesperson, in fighting censorship and in developments in the public relations field.

COMPOSERS. See MUSIC

COMPUTER ANIMATION. In his book, *Computers for Animation*, Stan Hayward writes, ''The field of computer graphics and animation is a no man's land somewhere between visual arts and data processing.'' It has also been described as a new art form, with obvious relevance in the area of special effects*. Computer animation provides for new styles of computer-generated images and offers a cost-efficient method of producing animated films. It involves the transfer of artwork to a computer, a process known as ''digitising'' (in other words, converting the artwork to binary digital form). The drawings must be translated into numbers, which can be done automatically through a scanning device. The computer can subsequently change the size, color, speed, and movement of the drawings. It can also complement or change the voice and other sounds to be utilized.

BIBLIOGRAPHY

Beckerman, Howard, ''Animation Kit: Computer Animation,'' *Filmmakers Newsletter*, February 1978, pp. 53–54.
Catmull, Edwin E., ''New Frontiers in Computer Animation,'' *American Cinematographer*, October 1979, pp. 1000–1003, 1049–1053.
Harden, Fred, ''The Computer in Animation,'' *Cinema Papers*, November-December 1981, pp. 470–477.
Hayward, Stan. *Computers for Animation*. London and Boston: Focal Press, 1984.
McKenna, Sherry, ''The Future of Computer Generated Animation,'' *On Location*, January 1982, pp. 78–87, 90–91.

CONCORDE PICTURES CORPORATION. When he sold New World Pictures*, Roger Corman had agreed not to become involved in film distribution except with his own films. However, following an out-of-court settlement with New World, Corman and his wife, Julie, formed Concorde Pictures Corporation as a cooperative distributorship to handle Corman's own films and those produced by others willing to share distribution costs. Concorde was organized in March 1985, and its first release, in May 1985, was *Streetwalkin'*, which marked a directorial debut for Joan Freeman.

The settlement with New World also gave Corman and Concorde distribution rights to all New World features produced and/or distributed by Corman, a library of 120 titles. Additionally, Concorde distributes features produced by Corman's other company, New Horizon Pictures Corporation. In July 1985, Concorde and Cinema Group formed a new organization, Concorde/Cinema Group, an independent distribution alliance with announced plans to release between fifteen and twenty features a year.

Address: 2218 West Olive Avenue, Burbank, Calif. 91506.

BIBLIOGRAPHY

"Corman Launches Concorde Pictures Co-op Distrib Outfit," *Variety*, March 27, 1985, pp. 5, 106.

Crosby, Joan, "Roger and Julie Corman Form Concorde Pictures," *Drama-Logue*, April 18, 1985, pp. 1, 20.

Klein, Richard, "Roger Corman's Concorde, Cinema Group Join to Form New Distribution Alliance," *Daily Variety*, July 18, 1985, pp. 1, 30.

CONDOR PICTURES. See VAN BEUREN CORPORATION

CONEY ISLAND. See RELIANCE MOTION PICTURE COMPANY AND MAJESTIC MOTION PICTURE COMPANY

CONFERENCE OF STUDIO UNIONS. In 1941, militant trade unionist Herb Sorrell began organizing locals in Hollywood which were not members of the then-discredited IATSE*. Following a successful 1941 strike against the Walt Disney Studios*, the Conference of Studio Unions (CSU) was formed by Sorrell, including office workers, publicists, set decorators, painters, cartoonists, and laboratory technicians. The producers, however, preferred to deal with IATSE, and a violent, thirty-week strike broke out in the spring of 1945. It reached its peak on October 5, 1945, during a violent confrontation outside the Warner Bros.* studios in Burbank, which became known as "The Battle of Warner Bros." Fire hoses were turned on the demonstrators and pickets, the police threw tear gas grenades, and Warner Bros. executives hurled whatever was at hand at the pickets from the studio rooftop. Eventually, that same year, the producers, IATSE, and the Conference of Studio Unions came to an agreement, known as "The Treaty of Beverly Hills." A year later, violence again broke out as the producers and IATSE tried to "lock out" CSU members from studios. IATSE's Roy Brewer denounced the CSU as a Communist organization, and he was aided

in his efforts by the new president of the Screen Actors Guild*, Ronald Reagan. The Teamsters Local 399 also turned against the CSU, and, by 1947, the Conference of Studio Unions was left with only a handful of members.
RESOURCES
Papers: University of California at Los Angeles (papers of Herb Sorrell).

CONSENT DECREE. Prior to 1940, five major studios—M-G-M*, Paramount*, RKO*, 20th Century-Fox*, and Warner Bros.*—effectively controlled the film industry, being producers, distributors, and exhibitors. With ownership of the theatres in which their product was to be shown, these five studios were blatantly in violation of American antitrust laws. The first consent decree was signed between the studios and the Justice Department in November 1940, and under it the five major producers agreed to end blind bidding* and to modify their block booking* activities. The decree was filed in Federal District Court for the Southern District of New York and expired on November 20, 1943, at which time the studios asked for drastic changes in the decree, and the matter dragged on through the legal system for most of the decade.

In the meantime, in 1946, the Justice Department filed suit, again in New York, against Paramount Pictures. The decree of December 1946 basically confirmed the 1940 decree but did not require, as the government had asked, that the studios divest themselves of their theatre chains. However, on appeal to the Supreme Court, in 1948, such divestiture was ordered, and the five independent theatre chains so created were prohibited from acquiring additional theatres if such acquisitions would restrain free trade, and they were given until the early fifties to separate their production and distribution arms from exhibition. Naturally, the studios fought against the consent decree, and it was not until October 16, 1960, that the Supreme Court refused to reconsider the decisions rendered against Loew's Inc. (M-G-M), Warner Bros., and 20th Century-Fox.

With theatre chains freed of restraint, there was an immediate increase in independent film production. Although some theatre chains have since become involved in film production—notably Stanley Warner Corp.* with Cinerama* and National General Corp.*—the Justice Department has effectively ruled against any major changes in the consent decree when they were requested in 1971 and 1984.
BIBLIOGRAPHY
Conant, Michael. *Antitrust in the Motion Picture Industry*. Berkeley, California: University of California Press, 1960.
———, "The Paramount Decrees Reconsidered," in Tino Balio, editor, *The American Film Industry*. Madison, Wisconsin: University of Wisconsin Press, 1985, pp. 537–573.
Mayer, Arthur L., "Dissent with Consent Decree," *Variety*, January 9, 1957, p. 25.

CONSOLIDATED FILM CORPORATION. The Consolidated Film Corporation was formed in June 1916 to produce the sixteen-part serial *The Crimson Stain Mystery*, which Metro Pictures Corporation* distributed. O. E. Goebel of the St. Louis Motion Picture Company was the president, and Ludwig

G. B. Erb, owner of the Erbograph Company*, was also involved. Maurice Costello and Ethel Grandin were the serial's stars, with Albert Payson Terhune as scenarist and T. Hayes Hunter as director.

CONSOLIDATED FILM INDUSTRIES. Consolidated Film Industries began as a film-processing laboratory circa 1924. It was acquired by Herbert J. Yates (1880–1966), best known as the head of Republic Pictures*, who had begun his film career by acquiring Hedwig Film Laboratories and Republic Film Laboratories in the teens. In the twenties, Consolidated acquired two New York laboratories, Erbograph and Craftsman. Its long-time head, for thirty-three years, was Sidney Solow.

The laboratory claims to have been the first to process film for television and the first to produce a kinescope on the West Coast. It continued its expansion by acquiring Paramount Laboratory in New York in 1950; in 1971, it acquired Acme Videotape and Film Laboratories, and a year later acquired Glen Glenn Sound*. It remains a division of Republic Corporation.

Address: 959 Seward Street, Hollywood, Calif. 90038.

CONSOLIDATED NATIONAL FILM EXCHANGES. See TODDY PICTURES COMPANY

CONTINENTAL DISTRIBUTING. See WALTER READE ORGANIZATION

CONTINENTAL FEATURE FILM COMPANY. See MUTUAL FILM CORPORATION

CONTINENTAL PRODUCING COMPANY. Continental Producing Company was formed in June 1916 and began production on the twelve-reel film *The Spirit of '76*. President Robert Goldstein, formerly the head of a West Coast theatrical costume company and an associate of D. W. Griffith, wrote the scenario with George L. Hutchin, a co-organizer of the company, and sold large blocks of stock to finance the production. Frank Montgomery, assisted by Carl Leviness, directed a company of actors, which included Jane Novak, Doris Pawn, Lottie Crews, Adda Gleason, and Howard Gaye, at the old Rolin Studio on Santa Monica Boulevard.

The completed film, which contained scenes depicting the massacre of American settlers by British soldiers at Cherry Valley, Pennsylvania, before the Revolutionary War, portrayed atrocities such as English soldiers stabbing a baby with a bayonet and stabbing an inoffensive Quaker. When the film received its premiere in Chicago in 1917, the city's mayor objected to such scenes and they were removed. When the film had its Los Angeles premiere on November 27, 1917, with the earlier deleted scenes restored, the film was seized and Goldstein was arrested for violation of the Espionage Act, for seeking to arouse enmity against the British, America's wartime ally. During the trial, it was asserted that the majority of the company's stockholders were German. On April 15, 1918, Goldstein was found guilty of violating two counts of the Espionage Act and was sentenced to ten years in a federal penitentiary and fined $5,000.

BIBLIOGRAPHY

"Another Big Producing Firm," *The Moving Picture World*, June 24, 1916, p. 2220.

"Goldstein Is Found Guilty," *The Moving Picture World*, May 11, 1918, p. 865.

Slide, Anthony, "The Spirit of '76," *Films in Review*, January 1976, pp. 1–4.

"THE COOGAN ACT." See CHILD LABOR LAWS

COPYRIGHT. Prior to 1912, motion pictures were not referred to in copyright legislation. The 1912 copyright act gave motion pictures copyright protection for 28 years, after which the copyright could be renewed for a further 28-year period. The Copyright Act of 1976 (which went into effect on January 1, 1978) gave motion pictures copyright for 75 years from the first publication of the work, or 100 years from its creation, if the work was "made for hire." Where the motion picture was not a "work for hire," the copyright lasts for the life of the author plus 50 years. The 1976 Copyright Act was not retrospective. It did not affect any works that had already fallen into the public domain through failure to copyright or to renew copyright. It requires that those motion pictures in their first 28 years of copyright protection must be renewed to gain further protection of 28 years, plus 19 years, giving a total of 75 years if the motion picture is a work "made for hire" (as is virtually always the case with motion pictures). The new law also requires that a copyright notice, consisting of the symbol © or the word copyright or the abbreviation copr., the year of first publication, and the name of the copyright owners, be placed on all publicly distributed copies of the motion picture. Full information as to copyright procedure is given in Circular R45, available at no charge from the Library of Congress Copyright Office.

The copyright laws also provide that copies of motion pictures be deposited with the Library of Congress, but from 1912 to 1942 the Library did not enforce this as part of the copyright process. However, the Library does now request the deposit of one copy of all important motion pictures, and such copies may be viewed on the premises of the Library of Congress at no charge.

Many films are no longer protected by copyright, in other words they are part of the public domain, because their distributors or producers either failed to copyright the films in the first place or failed to renew such copyrights. This is particularly true of films from minor producers and films produced abroad. Occasionally, a major studio will forget to renew a copyright, but in many cases the copyright has not been renewed because the producer's rights to the literary or musical materials used in the film were limited to a certain number of years. Although a film is in the public domain, it may well be that underlying literary or musical rights in the film are still subject to copyright protection. Further, the copyright status of a film applies to the United States only and may be, and usually is, considerably different in Europe or Canada.

The only "safe" way to check the copyright status of a specific film is through a copyright search at the Library of Congress. 7 Arts Press has published *Film Superlist: 20,000 Motion Pictures in the Public Domain* and *Film Superlist for 1940–1949*, which is a reprint of three volumes of the Library of Congress Copyright Catalogs (1894–1949), marked with renewals of copyright where appropriate.

Address: Register of Copyrights, Library of Congress, Washington, D.C. 20559.

BIBLIOGRAPHY

Hurst, Walter E., and William Storm Hale. *Film Superlist for 1940–1949*. Hollywood, California: 7 Arts Press, 1982.

Minus, Johnny, and William Storm Hale. *Film Superlist: 20,000 Motion Pictures in the Public Domain*. Hollywood, California: 7 Arts Press, 1973.

Strong, William S. *The Copyright Book*. Cambridge, Massachusetts: MIT Press, 1984.

COQUILLE FILM COMPANY. René Plaisetty, a director who left France to produce films in the United States because of the First World War, contracted with Pathé Freres to make films for them in this country. He formed the Coquille Film Company in New Orleans in January 1915, built a glass-enclosed studio, and released three- and five-reel films under the brand name "Nola." Leatrice Joy Zeidler, later known as Leatrice Joy, called at that time "a social favorite of New Orleans," was the leading lady. In December 1915, the company became known as the Nola Film Company. Captain William J. Hannon was the president and general manager, Walter Morton was the director, Norton Travis was the cameraman, and William Morgan Hannon was the scenario editor and assistant director. Leatrice Joy continued as the star, along with Madelyn Nichols. Its films were released through the Associated Service. In September 1917, the Diamond Film Company took over the Nola plant.

BIBLIOGRAPHY

"New Southern Film Company," *The Moving Picture World*, January 30, 1915, p. 651.

CORONADO, CALIFORNIA. See LUBIN MANUFACTURING COMPANY

CORRIGANVILLE. A 1,611-acre ranch, on Highway 118 near Chatsworth on the outskirts of Los Angeles, Corriganville was so named by Western actor Ray "Crash" Corrigan (1903–1976), who purchased the property in 1937 for $11,354. Corriganville was utilized for innumerable Westerns and television series. The property was sold, as part of a divorce settlement by Corrigan, in 1964 for $2.5 million. The following year, Bob Hope acquired the property and renamed it Hopetown. The ranch's continued use as a film location was halted a year later, and, in November 1979, fire destroyed the last of the standing sets. From 1948 onward, Corriganville was also open to the public as a Western-style amusement park. The property was acquired for real estate development in 1985.

COSMOFOTOFILM COMPANY. The Cosmofotofilm Company began operations in 1914 as an importer of films from England. Paul H. Cromelin was its head. Cosmofotofilm Company was the sole American distributor of films from the London Film Company, which at that time employed two American producer/directors Harold Shaw and George Loane Tucker.

COSMOPOLITAN PRODUCTIONS. William Randolph Hearst's personal production company, Cosmopolitan Productions was formed in 1918 to produce the features of his mistress, actress Marion Davies. All of Davies' films from *Cecilia of the Pink Roses* (1918) through her last feature, *Ever Since Eve* (1937), were Cosmopolitan Productions. In addition to Cosmopolitan, Hearst also owned International Film Service Company, which produced the 1918 Marion Davies feature, *Beatrice Fairfax*, and whose best-known film was *Humoresque* (1920), starring Alma Rubens.

In 1918, Cosmopolitan Productions were released by Graphic Films*. From 1918 to 1919, they were released by Select. Paramount* released the productions from 1919 to 1922. In 1923, they were Goldwyn* releases. From 1924 to 1934, the films were released by M-G-M*, and, finally, from 1935 to 1937 by Warner Bros.* In addition to the Marion Davies features, Cosmopolitan also produced a number of other major features, including *Enchantment* (1921), *The Valley of Silent Men* (1922), *The Temptress* (1926), *Our Dancing Daughters* (1928), *White Shadows in the South Seas* (1928), *The Big House* (1930), *Gabriel over the White House* (1933), and *Oil for the Lamps of China* (1935).
BIBLIOGRAPHY
Guiles, Fred Lawrence. *Marion Davies*. New York: McGraw-Hill, 1972.

COSTUME DESIGN. By the twenties women were freed from corsets and high necklines; they (for virtually the first time in Western civilization) wore their hair bobbed, their hemlines to the knee, their waists at their hips; they were flat-chested; and they occasionally wore slacks. These changes were due in part to the single greatest disseminator of women's fashion, the motion picture, which reached far more women than the theatre or fashion magazines ever had.

Until the early twenties, when studios began to hire costume designers, leading actors and actresses were generally responsible for their own wardrobes, and a trip for a high-fashion film wardrobe to New York or Paris made for good publicity in the fan magazines. The cost could be nearly bankrupting for the likes of Rudolph Valentino, Mae Murray, or Gloria Swanson (who spent about $125,000 per year).

Very specialized wardrobe departments eventually evolved around the basic steps of costuming a film: (1) read the script and prepare a wardrobe plot with breakdown sheets for each scene in order to determine the number and type of costumes needed (plus duplicates for wear and tear); (2) research the subject as needed, such as for historical or contemporary fashion trends; (3) sketch costumes and select fabrics (or purchase costumes) based on the characters' figure types, color schemes, and line, with consideration to how they will look within the set and with other players; (4) obtain approval from the stars, producer, director, and art director; (5) have the costumes sewn, rented, or bought; (6) arrange for fittings, alterations, and special requirements, like ageing; (7) have wardrobe tests (stills) made; (8) assist stars in dressing appropriately and on time; (9) remain on the set to ensure continuity and in case of emergencies; and (10) maintain the costumes—organize, launder, repair. As Edith Head said, a designer is like "a combination of psychiatrist, artist, fashion designer, dressmaker, pincushion, historian, nursemaid, and purchasing agent."

Many great designers made their names in the twenties, but not all could adapt to changing fashions and filmmaking techniques. Howard Greer (1886–1964) began at Paramount* in 1923 and hired Travis Banton (1894–1958) and Edith Head (1907–1981) soon thereafter. Adrian was hired by set and costume designer Natacha Rambova (Mrs. Rudolph Valentino) (1897–1966) in 1925.

Howard Greer designed for Paramount's leading actresses in the twenties, particularly Gloria Swanson and Pola Negri. He opened his own salon in 1927 and eventually left film work, as would many future film designers. Travis Banton began as an assistant to Howard Greer, then managed Edith Head and the rest of the wardrobe department until 1937, when he left to freelance in film and fashion design. Banton's costumes were often simple but elegant, with the greatest attention paid to detail and quality fabric, lavished with beading and furs. The images and careers of Marlene Dietrich, Carole Lombard, Mae West, and Claudette Colbert were enhanced by his costumes.

Edith Head's most important asset was flexibility—in designing for men or women in films of any genre and working well with the cast, crew, and management. Her credits included the sarong for Dorothy Lamour in the "Road" films, Audrey Hepburn in *Roman Holiday* (1953) and *Sabrina* (1954), Grace Kelly in *To Catch a Thief* (1955), and hundreds of other impressive films over her career of more than fifty years.

Adrian's costumes were more theatrical, Banton's more classic. Adrian was M-G-M's* designer through the Golden Age of the thirties; he left in 1942 and went on to an equally successful career as a dress designer and manufacturer. His best-known costumes were for Joan Crawford (large lapels and padded shoulders), Norma Shearer, Jean Harlow, and the film *The Wizard of Oz* (1939); though he is best remembered for his exotic costumes for Greta Garbo.

Orry-Kelly (1897–1964) of Warner Bros.* was considered one of the best designers of the thirties, along with Adrian and Travis Banton. Kelly's costumes were notably worn by Bette Davis, Kay Francis, and Dolores Del Rio in the thirties; though his credits are impressive through the early sixties.

Despite the Second World War, fabric scarcities, and less emphasis on glamour—in order to set an example to the filmgoing public—film fan magazines and newspapers frequently publicized Hollywood as a world style center since Paris was occupied through the first half of the decade. Since the twenties, films had tremendously influenced fashion around the world, and manufacturers and retail stores were eager for the lucrative tie-ins.

Adrian left M-G-M in 1942 and was replaced by Irene (1901–1962), an established Los Angeles fashion designer with a following of film stars. Irene specialized in suits and evening gowns and thus delegated period films to her able assistants Barbara Karinska and Walter Plunkett and musicals to Helen Rose and Irene Sharaff. Karinska and Sharaff were already acclaimed theatrical designers, and Sharaff continued to design famously for numerous Broadway-inspired films, including *The King and I* (1956), *Can Can* (1960), *West Side Story* (1961), and for Barbra Streisand in *Funny Girl* (1968) and *Hello, Dolly!* (1969). Plunkett had been RKO's chief designer in the thirties and was most famously associated with *Gone with the Wind* (1939); he continued on with impressive M-G-M films as their chief period costume designer through the sixties. Rose succeeded Irene as chief designer in 1950, designing for most of the films with Grace Kelly, Elizabeth Taylor, Esther Williams, and Lana Turner. She opened her own salon in 1958 and retired from M-G-M, but not film design, in 1966.

Jean Louis (born 1907) was Columbia's* talented chief designer from 1944 to 1958 and for Universal* from 1959 to 1968; he is best known for Rita Hayworth's costumes, particularly in *Gilda* (1946). He has continued to design for films and his own fashion line.

20th Century-Fox* enjoyed its heyday with escapist musicals in the forties for the likes of Betty Grable, Alice Faye, and Carmen Miranda. Succeeding Gwen Wakeling (born 1901), Charles Le Maire (1898–1985) was wardrobe director and designer (especially for Betty Grable) from 1943 to 1959, and in the forties he supervised such accomplished designers as Orry-Kelly, Rene Hubert (born 1899), Bonnie Cashin (born 1915), Yvonne Wood (born 1914), Kay Nelson, William Travilla, Renie, and Herschel. Nearly all of these designers continued at film design through the sixties.

Alongside these designers and others like Edith Head, Helen Rose, Walter Plunkett, and Irene Sharaff, the new generation of designers for the sixties and seventies included Bob Mackie (*Funny Lady*, 1974), Thea Van Runkle (*Bonnie and Clyde*, 1967; *Mame*, 1973), Anthea Sylbert (*Chinatown*, 1974), and Theoni Aldredge (*The Great Gatsby*, 1973).

Talented designers continue on in Hollywood, virtually none on a contract basis. With each decade, films seem to be less glamorous and the costumes increasingly mundane. Contemporary low-budget films are often costumed much the same as in the early days of filmmaking—a costumer purchases the costumes, perhaps supplementing the wardrobe with a few original costumes.

The performing arts consistently influence fashion, though television seems to have surpassed motion pictures in popularity. The television shows costumed by Bob Mackie and big-budget soap operas that have adopted high-fashion for publicity and merchandising techniques are consistently popular, though neither contemporary television nor films satisfy the public's fashion quest as in the Golden Days.

BIBLIOGRAPHY

Bailey, Margaret J. *Those Glorious Glamour Years*. Secaucus, New Jersey: Citadel Press, 1982.

Chierichetti, David. *Hollywood Costume Design*. New York: Harmony Books, 1976.

Greer, Howard. *Designing Male*. New York: G. P. Putnam's Sons, 1951.

Head, Edith, and Paddy Calistro. *Edith Head's Hollywood*. New York: E. P. Dutton, 1983.

LaVine, Robert W. *In a Glamorous Fashion*. New York: Charles Scribner's Sons, 1980.

Leese, Elizabeth. *Costume Design in the Movies*. Isle of Wight, England: BCW, 1976.

Mackie, Bob, with Gerry Bremer. *Dressing for Glamour*. New York: A & W, 1979.

Prichard, Susan Perez. *Film Costume: An Annotated Bibliography*. Metuchen, New Jersey: Scarecrow Press, 1981.

Rose, Helen. *Just Make Them Beautiful*. Santa Monica, California: Dennis-Landman, 1976.

Sharaff, Irene. *Broadway & Hollywood*. New York: Van Nostrand Reinhold, 1976.

COSTUME DESIGNERS GUILD. All major Los Angeles–based costume designers are members of the Costume Designers Guild, which was formed in 1953 and became a recognized negotiating body with its 1976 joining of IATSE*. It is IATSE Local 892. The Costume Designers Guild should not be confused with Motion Picture Costumers, which is IATSE Local 705, nor with IATSE Local 829, which takes care of the interests of New York–based costumers.

Address: 14724 Ventura Boulevard, Penthouse, Sherman Oaks, Calif. 91403.

COUNCIL OF MOTION PICTURE ORGANIZATIONS. See COMPO

COUNCIL ON INTERNATIONAL NONTHEATRICAL EVENTS. A nonprofit organization, the Council on International Nontheatrical Events (CINE) selects and enters films and television programs of a nongovernmental, documentary nature in international film festivals. Films submitted to and selected by CINE are awarded Golden Eagles. Films are initially judged on a regional level before being submitted for final selection by CINE's board of directors.

The Council on International Nontheatrical Events was created on October 25, 1957, at a conference of the National Education Association's Department of Audiovisual Instruction. According to *Film/AV News* (May-June 1958), "The Council was formed for the purpose of setting up machinery for choosing and screening non-theatrical, non-governmental motion pictures to be shown at selected film festivals all over the world." Once highly regarded, with winning films regularly announced in *Film News* and other similar periodicals, CINE has, in recent years, been branded too conservative in its selections, and most major

American documentaries are no longer submitted, with their producers finding it easier to submit their films directly to the festivals involved.

Address: 1201 Sixteenth Street, N.W., Washington, D.C. 20036.

COYTESVILLE, NEW JERSEY. See KALEM COMPANY, INC.

CRAFTSMAN LABORATORY. See CONSOLIDATED FILM INDUSTRIES

CREST PICTURE COMPANY. The Crest Picture Company, controlled by Colorado capitalists C. F. Rickey and B. W. Davies, began production in June 1917 for the states rights* market. Judge Lyman Henry, who wrote its first film, *The Chosen Prince*, an eight-reel biblical subject, was also the company's president. William V. Mong was director-general. The company, which produced at Monrovia, California, went out of business in 1920.

CRIME DOES NOT PAY. A series of two-reel short subjects which concluded with proof of the basic premise that "Crime Does Not Pay," these films were produced by M-G-M* from 1935 to 1947. The first was *Buried Loot* and the last *Luckiest Guy in the World*.

BIBLIOGRAPHY

Maltin, Leonard. *The Great Movie Shorts.* New York: Crown, 1972.

CROWN CITY FILM MANUFACTURING COMPANY. Prominent Pasadena, California, businessmen formed the Crown City Film Manufacturing Company in October 1914. Located at 40 West Mountain Street in Pasadena, the company produced comedies under the "Thistle" brand, one of which was a two-reeler about the Pasadena Tournament of Roses, and dramas under the "Paragon" brand. Bruce Mitchell directed Allan Fralick, Rena Rogers, and Ralph McComas in the comedies, while Donald MacDonald directed Dorothy Davenport, Joe Singleton, and Lee Hill in the dramas. Anthony W. Coldeway was the studio manager and scenario editor. The company released on the Kriterion* program.

CROWN INTERNATIONAL PICTURES. Founded in 1959 by Newton P. "Red" Jacobs, Crown International Pictures is an independent distributor which has also produced an average of three or four films a year. Crown specializes in exploitation features, such as *Chain Gang Women* (1971), *The Pom Pom Girls* (1976), *Hustler Squad* (1978), *Coach* (1978), *Dracula's Dog* (1979), and *Satan's Slave* (1979), but it has also released Mae West's last film, *Sextette* (1978), and the critically successful British feature *McVicar* (1981). According to *Boxoffice* (October 15, 1973), Crown is "known for its tailor-made campaigns for individual pictures and trendsetting concepts." Mark Tenser took over as president of the company in 1974 and, in 1985, announced that Crown would be spending $40 million in the next two years on distribution, production, and marketing.

Address: 292 South La Cienega Boulevard, Beverly Hills, Calif. 90211.

BIBLIOGRAPHY

Auerbach, Alexander, "Growth Gives Added Sparkle to Crown," *Boxoffice*, April 1983, pp. 8–9.

CRYSTAL FILM COMPANY. The Crystal Film Company, formed in the latter part of 1912 by Ludwig G. B. Erb to be a producer of weekly split-reel comedies for the Universal* program, was located at Wendover and Park avenues, New York. Pearl White starred in the comedies, the first two of which, *The Girl in the Next Room* and *The Man from the North Pole*, were released on October 6, 1912. Crystal later added dramas but discontinued them in 1914. Joseph A. Golden was the company's first director, and Vivian Prescott and Charles De Forrest appeared in later Crystal films.

At the end of 1914, Crystal severed its connections with Universal and became part of the United Motion Picture Producers, Inc., formed by Erb to provide a daily service of one- and two-reel films to the United Film Service*. Crystal began at this time making one-reel comedies with De Forrest under the "Superba" brand. H. M. "Ben" Goetz was the general manager until April 1915.

When the United Film Service failed in June 1915, Crystal joined a new combination of producers, the Combined Photoplay Producers, Inc., of which Erb was also president. Standard Photoplay Distributors, Inc., handled the product of the new combination. Crystal films were later released on the states rights* market by the Triumph Film Corporation. On October 8, 1917, Joseph A. Golden, previously the company's vice-president, succeeded Julius Steger as president. Crystal ended operations in June 1919.

CUB. See DAVID HORSLEY PRODUCTIONS

CULVER CITY STUDIOS. See LAIRD INTERNATIONAL STUDIOS

D

DANUBIA PICTURES, INC. Danubia Pictures, Inc., was the major, if not the exclusive, distributor of Hungarian-produced films in the United States from 1934 to 1940. The company, which was located at 729 Seventh Avenue, New York, was headed by Eugene J. Lang. It was revived after the Second World War and remained active through the sixties, distributing both Hungarian and Soviet films.

DARMOUR PRODUCTIONS. See MAJESTIC PICTURES CORPORATION

DAVID HORSLEY PRODUCTIONS. In July 1914, pioneer producer David Horsley, whose Centaur Film Company was said to be the first independent production company created after the formation of the Motion Picture Patents Company*, declared that the feature film had had its day. He announced that his nearly completed studio and factory in Bayonne, New Jersey, would produce seven one-reel comedies per week.

In October 1914, Horsley became the first producer invited to join the licensed group distributing through General Film Company since its formation. The invitation came after Pathé* Freres severed its connection with the Company. After a competition to select the name of Horsley's new brand of films, "MinA" was selected, a name which stood for "Made in America." Horsley advertised the invention of a new double exposure camera which made two exposures and produced two separate negatives at once, which was to be used in MinA productions. Circus clown Harry La Pearl was MinA's first leading comedian.

About this time, Horsley acquired the Bostock animals together with their London trainer Harry Tudor, which were sold because of the war. The subsequent Bostock Jungle and Film Company animal pictures were made at Horsley's new studios located at Main and Washington streets in Los Angeles. Other Horsley brands included Ace, of which Milton H. Fahrney was director-in-chief, and Cub. Horsley was also the producer of various serials.

In July 1915, Horsley cancelled his contract to release with General Film Company, and contracted to release with the Mutual Film Corporation*. At that time, the brand name of MinA was retained by the General Film Company.
BIBLIOGRAPHY
"Horsley in Licensed Group," *The Moving Picture World*, October 3, 1914, p. 71.
"Horsley's Animal Studios," *The Moving Picture World*, July 10, 1915, pp. 253–254.
"Horsley's Big Plans," *The New York Dramatic Mirror*, July 8, 1914, p. 24.
"Horsley's Camera Used for MinA Pictures," *The Motion Picture News*, February 6, 1915, p. 36.
"MinA Film Here," *The New York Dramatic Mirror*, December 16, 1914, p. 40.

DAVID MILES, INC. David Miles, formerly the managing director of the Kinemacolor Company of America*, and a director for Biograph*, formed his own company, variously called David Miles, Inc., David Miles Corporation, and David Miles Production Company, with T. Hayes Hunter in August 1914. Miles directed a stock company of actors he had worked with previously, including Linda Arvidson Griffith, John G. Brammall, and Charles Perley in one-reel comedies. Charles Fleming also directed. David Miles, Inc., released two films per week through Sawyer, Inc.*, until Miles died in 1915.

DE FOREST PHONOFILM. Responsible for the audion tube, a key invention in the development of the sound motion picture, Dr. Lee De Forest created a sound-on-film system, the Phonofilm. Through the De Forest Phonofilm Corporation, founded in November 1922, Dr. De Forest exploited his invention, presenting the first public performance of his films before the New York Electrical Society on April 12, 1923. Among the celebrities who appeared in De Forest Phonofilms were Eddie Cantor, DeWolf Hopper, and Fannie Ward; Calvin Coolidge appeared in what is probably the first sound newsreel, produced by De Forest, in 1924. Phonofilms were also produced and marketed in England and Australia.

The system was not commercially successful because it required the installation of new projection equipment, and the subjects were only one reel or less in length. From the mid-twenties onward, De Forest's invention was successfully advanced by two former associates of his, E. I. Sponable and Theodore Case, and the sound-on-film system which they developed became Fox Movietone.
BIBLIOGRAPHY
Carneal, Georgette. *A Conqueror of Space*. New York: Horace Liveright, 1930.
De Forest, Lee, "Pioneering in Talking Pictures," *American Cinematographer*, April 1941, pp. 164, 201–202.
Geduld, Harry. *The Birth of the Talkies*. Bloomington, Indiana: Indiana University Press, 1975.
Griggs, I. C., "De Forest Phonofilms (Australia) Ltd.," *Cinema Papers*, June-July 1976, pp. 16–20, 91.
"Pictures That Talk," *Photoplay*, July 1924, p. 78.
RESOURCES
Films: Library of Congress.

DEITRICH-BECK, INC. Theodore C. Deitrich and Arthur F. Beck formed Deitrich-Beck, Inc., in July 1919 to produce four to six films a year from the novels of Louis Joseph Vance. Doris Kenyon was the star. Deitrich, the president and production manager, had been the president of De Luxe Pictures, Inc.*, for which Kenyon was also starred, and the publicity director of the International Film Service*. Beck, the secretary, treasurer, and business manager, had been the treasurer of Artco Productions, Inc.* The first film of the company was *The Bandbox*, directed by Roy William Neill. The company released through the W. W. Hodkinson Corporation.*
BIBLIOGRAPHY
"New Producing Company Organized," *The Moving Picture World*, July 12, 1919, p. 192.

DeLUXE LABORATORIES, INC. A wholly owned subsidary of 20th Century-Fox, DeLuxe Laboratories, Inc., claims to be one of the three largest processing laboratories in the world. Founded in the mid-teens in Fort Lee, New Jersey, DeLuxe was, for many years, a New York–based laboratory—located at 850 Tenth Avenue—with a Hollywood branch at 1546 North Argyle Street. DeLuxe Color or "Color by DeLuxe" on a film's credits indicates that the production is actually in Eastman Color, but the film was processed by DeLuxe Laboratories.
   Address: 1377 North Serrano Avenue, Hollywood, Calif. 90027.

DE LUXE PICTURES, INC. Theodore H. Deitrich, the publicity director of the International Film Service*, formed De Luxe Pictures, Inc., on November 1, 1917, and became its president and general manager. With offices at 516 Fifth Avenue, New York, the company planned to produce four to eight features a year starring Doris Kenyon. Its first film, *The Street of Seven Stars*, was directed by John B. O'Brien and released through the William Sherry Feature Film Company.
BIBLIOGRAPHY
"Deitrich Forms New Company," *The Moving Picture World*, December 8, 1917, p. 1506.

DeMILLE FOUNDATION FOR POLITICAL FREEDOM. In 1944, Cecil B. DeMille was informed by the American Federation of Radio Artists (AFRA), to which he belonged, that he must, along with all other members, pay one dollar to help fight a California ballot proposition which provided that no man should be required to belong to a union in order to work to support his family. DeMille decided to support the proposition, refused to pay the one dollar, and was suspended by AFRA, resulting in his being unable to work in radio, with which AFRA had a closed-shop contract.
   Dropped as host of *Lux Radio Theatre*, DeMille received many letters of support on his stand. These, along with financial contributions, led to his forming the DeMille Foundation for Political Freedom, which fought for the right to work in some sixteen states. Incorporated in September 1945, the DeMille

Foundation for Political Freedom had as its trustees DeMille, Neil McCarthy, and Sidney Biddell. William M. Jeffers was the first chairman of the board, succeeded by Y. Frank Freeman. The DeMille Foundation for Political Freedom was dissolved in February 1959.

BIBLIOGRAPHY
Hayne, Donald, editor. *The Autobiography of Cecil B. DeMille*. Englewood Cliffs, New
    Jersey: Prentice-Hall, 1959.

DEMOCRACY FILM COMPANY. The Democracy Film Company was incorporated in June 1919 by prominent blacks in California. It planned to make a patriotic feature to show the part that black Americans had played in the First World War and to eliminate racial prejudice. Captain Leslie T. Peacocke, a white American, was signed to write and supervise the film, for which the E & R Studio* near Eastlake Park, Los Angeles, was leased.

BIBLIOGRAPHY
"Democracy Film Company Is All-Negro Organization," *The Moving Picture World*,
    June 7, 1919, p. 1491.

DENVER. See COLORADO MOTION PICTURE COMPANY

DIANDO FILM COMPANY. The Diando Film Company began making five-reel features for Pathé* in December 1917. It had two producing companies at that time, one featuring the child star Baby Marie Osborne, the other featuring Bryant Washburn. W.A.S. Douglas was the president, and L. T. Osborne, Baby Marie's father, was vice-president. In 1918, Diando produced the serial *The Wolf-Faced Man*, starring George Larkin and directed by Stuart Paton, for Pathé release. The company went out of business in 1919.

DIES COMMITTEE INVESTIGATION. The Dies Committee, or the House Un-American Activities Committee, as it was formally known, began its investigations in 1938. Congressman Martin Dies first announced that he would hold hearings in Hollywood in September 1938 to investigate the participation in Communist activities by members of the film industry. In particular, he was attacking the Anti-Nazi League and its members as being, at best, stooges for the Communists. The Anti-Nazi League led the opposition to these hearings in Hollywood, and they were cancelled with an explanation of a "lack of funds and time."

Perhaps assuming that Dies was no longer interested in Hollywood after this retreat, the congressman was feted at a luncheon at 20th Century-Fox* in August 1939, where he spoke to the leaders of the industry (including, among others, Louis B. Mayer, Harry and Jack Warner, Y. Frank Freeman, and Sam Goldwyn) and warned them about subversive elements. Nothing had changed, however, and, in November, Dies was urging the House to re-fund the Committee in order to investigate the charges that Communists were being financially assisted by Hollywood radicals.

These charges were set down in a report and on December 27, 1939, *Daily Variety* reported that the Committee was split as to releasing the report which was supposed to name prominent members of the film industry with Communist ties. Since there had been no investigation of the charges, members of the Committee were reluctant to release it, but Dies pushed to have it released anyway and used the conditions described in the Report as justification for the House to extend the life of the Committee (which was to expire on January 3, 1940) and to fund it for another two years.

This Report was the basis for an article by Dies, which was published in the February issue of *Liberty* magazine. Dies charged that there were forty-two or forty-three prominent members of the Hollywood community who were Communists or Red sympathizers and blamed them for the propaganda appearing in *Juarez, Blockade,* and *Fury.* This article again provoked a reaction from the industry, and *Daily Variety* editorialized on February 9, 1940, that the charges were not new and that the industry would welcome any honest investigation. *The Hollywood Reporter* reacted more cholerically and attacked Dies' motives, charging that there had been no investigation, only one investigator who had a shady past and may have used his position for shakedowns. Finally, a mass meeting was held on February 21, 1940, at which the Committee's motives were attacked by Donald Ogden Stewart, Mary McCall, and Dorothy Parker, among others.

Once again there was a retreat by Dies, and, in June 1940, he announced that the Committee had decided to postpone the Hollywood investigation because of the political situation. Yet hearings were held in Beaumont, Texas, in July, and a former member of the Communist party named forty-two members of the industry as "active in promotion of communism." (This witness, John L. Leech, later testified before a Los Angeles Grand Jury in August and named people, such as Humphrey Bogart, James Cagney, and Fredric March, whom Dies himself stated were not Communists or tied to communism*.)

As before, the Dies Committee did nothing with the information it received, except to use it to argue for money and extension of its life, and on February 23, 1941, the House re-funded the Committee for fifteen months. Yet, if the Dies Committee was basically just bluster, its attacks led to a climate where investigations of Hollywood were acceptable (the Los Angeles Grand Jury in August 1940 and the California Legislature in 1941) and it showed how easily attacks against communism in the industry could be launched with almost no evidence. That was a lesson which a later chairman of the Committee took to heart.

BIBLIOGRAPHY

"Cagney, Others Cleared in Dies Statement," *Daily Variety*, August 21, 1940, p. 4.
Ceplair, Larry, and Steven Englund. *The Inquisition in Hollywood: Politics in the Film Community, 1930–1960.* Garden City, New York: Anchor Press/Doubleday, 1980.

"Dies the Politician," *The Hollywood Reporter*, February 12, 1940, pp. 1, 4.

"Fite [*sic*] Looms on Pic Red Charges," *Daily Variety*, December 27, 1939, pp. 1, 4.

"42 Filmites Aiding Reds Named before Dies Body," *Daily Variety*, July 18, 1940, pp. 1, 4.

Rosten, Leo C. *Hollywood: The Movie Colony, the Movie Makers.* New York: Harcourt, Brace, 1941.

DIRECTORS FILM CORPORATION. See RAMO FILMS, INC.

DIRECTORS GUILD OF AMERICA, INC. The Directors Guild of America, Inc., was organized as the Screen Directors Guild Incorporated on January 16, 1936, to represent the interests of some seventy-five directors. A year later, assistant directors were admitted to the Guild, which had become recognized as a bargaining agent after a strike threat and which signed its first agreement with the Hollywood producers in May 1939. The first contract covering television direction was signed in 1950.

In 1960, the Screen Directors Guild Incorporated merged with the Radio and Television Directors Guild (formed in 1947) and became the Directors Guild of America. That same year the Guild established a pension plan. In 1963, Assistant Directors IATSE* Local 161 (formed in New York in 1944) merged with the Guild, a year later the Unit Production Managers became part of the Guild, and, in 1965, the Screen Directors International Guild (formed on the East Coast in 1957) merged with the Directors Guild.

The Guild presents annual awards, notable among which are the D. W. Griffith Award (first presented to Cecil B. DeMille in 1953) and the Frank Capra Achievement Award (presented to an assistant director or unit production manager, and first given to Emmett Emerson in 1980). Presidents of the Directors Guild of America have been: King Vidor (1936–1938), Frank Capra (1939–1941), George Stevens (1941–1943), Mark Sandrich (1943–1944), John Cromwell (1944–1946), George Stevens (1946–1948), George Marshall (1948–1950), Joseph L. Mankiewicz (1950–1951), George Sidney (1951–1959), Frank Capra (1960–1961), George Sidney (1961–1967), Delbert Mann (1967–1971), Robert Wise (1971–1975), Robert B. Aldrich (1975–1979), George Schaefer (1979–1981), Jud Taylor (1981–1983), and Gilbert Cates (1983 to present).

Addresses: 7950 Sunset Boulevard, Los Angeles, Calif. 90046; 520 North Michigan Avenue, Suite 436, Chicago, Ill. 60611; 111 West 57 Street, New York, N.Y. 10019.

DISCINA INTERNATIONAL FILMS CORP. The American branch of André Paulvé's French company, Discina International Films Corp., distributed all of its sister company's productions, including Jean Cocteau's *Beauty and the Beast* (1947) and *Orpheus* (1950), as well as other foreign-language films, mainly French. The company was active in the forties and fifties.

DISNEYLAND. See WALT DISNEY PRODUCTIONS

DIVISION OF FILMS. See UNITED STATES GOVERNMENT COMMITTEE ON PUBLIC INFORMATION: DIVISION OF FILMS

DIXIE FILM EXCHANGE. See TODDY PICTURES COMPANY

"DR. KILDARE" SERIES. Produced by M-G-M* and set in the mythical Blair Hospital, the "Dr. Kildare" series starred Lew Ayres in the title role, with Lionel Barrymore as the crotchety Dr. Leonard Gillespie. Samuel S. Hinds and Emma Dunn portrayed James Kildare's parents, and Alma Kruger and Nell Craig were featured as nurses. The series had its origins in a 1937 Paramount feature, *Internes Can't Take Money*, in which Joel McCrea portrayed James Kildare, a character created by Max Brand. Lew Ayres and Lionel Barrymore were starred in nine M-G-M Dr. Kildare features: *Young Dr. Kildare* (1938), *Calling Dr. Kildare* (1939), *The Secret of Dr. Kildare* (1939), *Dr. Kildare's Strangest Case* (1940), *Dr. Kildare Goes Home* (1940), *Dr. Kildare's Crisis* (1940), *The People vs. Dr. Kildare* (1941), *Dr. Kildare's Wedding Day* (1941), and *Dr. Kildare's Victory* (1942). When America entered the Second World War, Lew Ayres registered as a conscientious objector, and the studio, fearing adverse public reaction, hastily dropped the Kildare character, continuing the series for six more features with Lionel Barrymore as the lone star.
BIBLIOGRAPHY
Zinman, David. *Saturday Afternoon at the Bijou.* New Rochelle, New York: Arlington House, 1973.

DOCUMENTARIES. The term "documentary" is used to refer to a factual film, of any length, dealing with actual events or people. Film documentaries have their origins in both newsreels* and the actuality subjects shot in the 1890s by the earliest filmmakers. The word was first used by John Grierson in a review of *Moana* in a 1926 issue of the *New York Sun* and comes from the French "documentaire," first used in the January 1924 issue of *Cinéopse*.

Although documentary features were not uncommon in the teens, the father of the American documentary is generally considered to have been Robert Flaherty (1884–1951), who made *Moana* and whose other films included *Nanook of the North* (1922), *Man of Aran* (1934), *The Land* (1942), and *Louisiana Story* (1948). The leader of the documentary film movement is the man who coined the word, John Grierson (1898–1972), who was active in his native Britain, founded the National Film Board of Canada, and produced some documentaries in the United States for his company, The World Today, Inc., in the mid-forties.

Some of the best American documentaries were those sponsored by the U.S. government in the late thirties and through the Second World War, including *The Plow That Broke the Plains* (1936), *The River* (1937), *The City* (1939), *The Forgotten Village* (1941), *The Battle of Midway* (1942), *Prelude to War* (1943),

The Battle of Russia (1943), *The Memphis Belle* (1944), *The Fighting Lady* (1944), and *The Battle of San Pietro* (1945).

Prior to the Second World War, documentaries were shot in 35mm, but by the fifties 16mm* was the medium used by most documentary filmmakers. Because of its lightweight portability, 16mm allowed filmmakers to get closer to their subjects and to document their lives more feasibly on a daily basis. This led to the "cinema verité" movement of the sixties, which has its origins in Soviet cinema, but which was pioneered in the United States by Richard Leacock, D. A. Pennebaker, Albert and David Maysles, and Haskell Wexler.

Although the Academy of Motion Picture Arts and Sciences* has given Academy Awards for Best Short Subjects since 1931–1932 (short subjects which would usually include a novelty subject and might well be considered a documentary), it was not until 1941 that it gave three special awards in the documentary category, to *Churchill's Island* (produced by the National Film Board of Canada), to Rey Scott (for *Kukan*, his documentary on China), and to the British Ministry of Information (for *Target for Tonight*). The categories of best Documentary Feature and Short Subject were not introduced by the Academy until 1964, when the winners were *Jacques-Yves Cousteau's World without Sun* (feature) and *Nine from Little Rock* (short subject). *See also* Frontier Films, March of Time, Motion Picture Society for the Americas, National Film and Photo League, and "Why We Fight" Series.

BIBLIOGRAPHY

Barnouw, Erik. *Documentary*. New York: Oxford University Press, 1974.
Barsam, Richard Meram. *Nonfiction Film*. New York: E. P. Dutton, 1973.
Hardy, Forsyth, editor. *Grierson on Documentary*. Berkeley, California: University of California Press, 1966.
Jacobs, Lewis, editor. *The Documentary Tradition*. New York: W. W. Norton, 1971.
MacCann, Richard Dyer. *The People's Films*. New York: Hastings House, 1973.
Rotha, Paul. *Documentary Film*. London: Faber and Faber, 1936.

DOLBY SOUND. The patented Dolby sound system both enhances the sound and reduces the level of "hiss" on the soundtrack, the "hiss" being inherent to all magnetic tape recording. The system was developed by Ray Dolby as a noise reduction system for the recording industry in 1965. It was first commercially used in the motion picture industry by Stanley Kubrick for *A Clockwork Orange* (1971). Later, Dolby developed a four-channel stereo-optical track, which also utilized its noise reduction system. However, use of the Dolby system did require the installation of a special decoding device in theatres. The use of Dolby on 35mm stereo-optic release prints of *Star Wars* (1977) encouraged theatres to install the equipment, and, as of October 1984, some 6,000 U.S. theatres were equipped to screen Dolby sound. The Dolby sound system is available in theatres in some forty-five countries, and the majority of American films are today released with the potential of Dolby sound.

Address: Dolby Laboratories, Inc., 731 Sansome Street, San Francisco, Calif. 94111.

BIBLIOGRAPHY
Barry, David, "Let's Hear It for Dolby Sound," *Los Angeles Times*, Calendar Section, April 30, 1978, p. 40.
Stetter, Elmar, "Sound Becoming More Important as Integral Part of Motion Pics," *Variety*, January 12, 1983, pp. 147–148.

"DOMINO" BRAND. See NEW YORK MOTION PICTURE COMPANY

DOUGLASS NATURAL COLOR FILM COMPANY, LTD., OF SAN RAFAEL, CALIFORNIA. Leon F. Douglass, one of the patentees of the Victor Talking Machine, developed a color process for motion picture films which had its first public exhibition at the Wurlitzer Fine Hall in New York on February 12, 1918. According to Douglass' company, the Douglass Natural Color Film Company, Ltd., of San Rafael, California, the invention, which involved a small device that could be attached to any camera, could reproduce every hue, shade, and tint of nature. The projection of the films did not involve the use of a rotary colored shutter, as did previous attempts to make color films. According to contemporaneous news items, the attached device to the camera gave several color values to the negative. A positive print then was made by a chemical process. The films, which were projected at a speed of twenty-four frames per second, also were reputed to give a stereoscopic effect. The first exhibition included shots of the sunset, a rainbow, a forest fire, and Nevada Falls. Reviews commented on the brilliant reds and greens obtained. In May 1918, after a public showing at the Kinema Theatre in Los Angeles, W. W. Hodkinson* announced plans to distribute shorts made by the company, among which was *Cupid Angling*, starring Ruth Roland.
BIBLIOGRAPHY
"Douglass Color Process," *The Moving Picture World*, March 2, 1918, p. 1231.

DRACO FILM COMPANY, INC. The Draco Film Company, Inc., began producing early in 1915 with George L. Sargent as chief director and releasing through Mutual Film Corporation*. In December 1915, a company named Dra-Ko Film Company, which may have been the same as Draco, produced a five-reel feature, *The York State Follies*, which was released on the Premier program. J. Snyder was the general manager, and Joseph A. Richmond was the director of the studio at Tappan, New York.

DRA-KO FILM COMPANY. See DRACO FILM COMPANY, INC.

DRAMATIC FEATURE FILM COMPANY. Frank J. Baum and Francis Power were the co-presidents of the Dramatic Feature Film Company, which filmed its first production, *The Little Grey Nun of Belgium*, starring Cathrine Countiss, at the Oz Studio in Hollywood in April 1915. David Proctor was the leading man and Francis Power the film's director. *The Little Grey Nun of Belgium* was released on the Alliance program.

DRIVE-IN THEATRES. The concept of a drive-in theatre can be traced back to 1911 when David S. Hulfish in *The Motion Picture Cyclopedia* first mooted the idea for an open-air movie theatre or airdrome. The first drive-in theatre per se was opened by Richard M. Hollingshead, Jr., in Camden, New Jersey, on June 6, 1933, with a capacity for 400 cars. Hollingshead opened a second drive-in, on Pico Boulevard, Los Angeles, in July of the following year.

Drive-in theatres gradually gained in number. In 1948, there were 743; in 1949, 1,000; in 1956, 5,000. The number of drive-in theatres in the United States reached an all-time high in 1961, with a total of 6,000. By 1969, the number was reduced to 3,700, and in 1985 there were only 2,800. As the number of regular movie theatres diminished in the forties and fifties, the number of drive-ins increased. The success of the drive-in theatre had much to do with the baby boom after the Second World War; drive-in theatres provided cheap entertainment for large families, all members of which could fit into one vehicle. The decline in the number of drive-in theatres can be linked to the increased value of real estate and the increase in ''R''- and ''X''-rated films, which most local authorities barred drive-in theatres from screening.

In *Boxoffice* (May 1984), Dr. Bruce A. Austin wrote, ''The drive-in has been credited with providing an exhibition outlet for the product of smaller, independent film producers and distributors. It also proved to be the means for drawing back to the movies the 'lost audience' of the 1950s. Today, the drive-in is the only form of moviegoing for many patrons, and a few industry observers suggest that, at least in warm weather locales, it will survive and prosper as an alternative to the pay TV competition in the home.''

Among the stranger versions of the drive-in was a ''fly-in, drive-in'' theatre, opened in June 1948 at Asbury Park, New Jersey, which could accommodate 500 cars and 25 planes from an adjoining airstrip. The largest drive-in ever to open was one at Copiague, New York, with a capacity for 2,500 cars.

BIBLIOGRAPHY

Austin, Bruce A., ''Portrait of a Contemporary Drive-In,'' *Boxoffice*, May 1984, pp. 33–38.

Clarke, Gerald, ''Dark Clouds over the Drive-Ins,'' *Time*, August 8, 1983, p. 64.

''The Colossal Drive-In,'' *Newsweek*, July 22, 1957, pp. 85–87.

Geist, William E., ''Drive-In Movie: An Innovation Hits 50 and Passes Its Prime,'' *The New York Times*, June 7, 1983, pp. B1, B5.

Mayerson, Donald J., ''A Night at the Drive-In,'' *Cue*, July 4, 1970, p. 11.

Ornstein, William, ''Growth of the Roofless Theatre,'' *Variety*, January 5, 1949, p. 30.

''The Roof's the Sky and Sky Is Drive-In Limit,'' *Motion Picture Herald*, July 17, 1948, pp. 13, 16.

Schneck, Dale, ''America's Oldest Drive-In Theatre,'' *Boxoffice*, September 1983, pp. 122–123.

Taylor, Frank J., ''Big Boom in Outdoor Movies,'' *The Saturday Evening Post*, September 15, 1956, pp. 31, 100–102.

DROID WORKS. See LUCASFILM, LTD.

DU ART FILM LABORATORIES, INC. Founded in 1922, Du Art Film Laboratories, Inc., is a major New York organization, providing full-service 16mm* and 35mm* black-and-white and color film processing. It specializes in the Frame Count Cueing System, which minimizes the handling of negative film; offers a computer program whereby the work print can be conformed with the original negative in the camera of an optical printer; and is noted for the blow-up of 16mm to 35mm film, utilizing a computerized cueing and timing system.

Address: 245 West 55 Street, New York, N.Y. 10019.

DUBBING. Dubbing, in its most primitive form, is as old as the sound film. Both Bobby Gordon, who played Al Jolson as a child, and Warner Oland, who played Jolson's father, in *The Jazz Singer* (1927) were dubbed. Joan Barry dubbed the dialogue for Anny Ondra in Alfred Hitchcock's first talkie, *Blackmail* (1929). There was nothing technically complex about this earliest of dubbing; the "dubbers" simply stood out of camera range in front of a microphone and spoke the dialogue or sang the songs as the players on camera mouthed the words.

Dubbing was particularly prevalent in the American film industry as nonsinging actors and actresses were cast in musical roles. Anita Ellis sang for Rita Hayworth in *Gilda* (1946) and other films. Jo Ann Greer sang for Hayworth in *Miss Sadie Thompson* (1953), *Pal Joey* (1957), and *Affair in Trinidad* (1952). Other singers who have dubbed for Rita Hayworth include Nan Wynn and Martha Mears. Annette Warren sang for Ava Gardner in *Show Boat* (1951). Mary Martin sang for Margaret Sullavan in *The Shopworn Angel* (1938). Buddy Clark sang for Jack Haley in *Wake Up and Live* (1937). Allan Jones sang for Dennis Morgan in *The Great Ziegfeld* (1936). Pat Friday sang for Lynn Bari in *Sun Valley Serenade* (1941) and *Orchestra Wives* (1942). Trudi Erwin sang for Lana Turner in *The Merry Widow* (1952) and for Kim Novak in *Pal Joey* (1957). Mario Lanza sang for Edmund Purdom in *The Student Prince* (1954). In *South Pacific* (1958), Giorgio Tozzi sang for Rossano Brazzi, Bill Lee for John Kerr, and Muriel Lee for Juanita Hall. Marni Nixon sang for Audrey Hepburn in *My Fair Lady* (1964), for Deborah Kerr in *The King and I* (1956), and for Natalie Wood in *West Side Story* (1961). One of the most often quoted and amusing of all dubbings is that of Andy Williams for Lauren Bacall in *To Have and Have Not* (1944).

Another aspect of dubbing is that of dubbing one actor's voice for another when the film is released in another country where a different language is spoken. Most films are dubbed in either the country of origin or in London, although in recent years more and more films are being dubbed in New York for American release. Dubbing of foreign language films is done by either one of two methods: by having the actors read the band of dialogue which appears at the bottom of the screen or by "looping," which means that the scene to be dubbed is run over and over again until the actors and director are happy with the synchronization.

The use of dubbing rather than subtitles for foreign language films in the United States became increasingly popular in the late fifties. Most purists objected strongly to dubbing, but it had a staunch supporter in critic Bosley Crowther who wrote an impassioned editorial in *The New York Times* (August 7, 1960) titled "Subtitles Must Go!"

Only in Italy is dubbing standard practice for all film production. No attempt is made to achieve perfect sound as the scene is filmed, and only a "wild" or "guide" track is made. All the dialogue is recorded later in a dubbing studio.

BIBLIOGRAPHY

Anderson, Archie A., "The Voice behind the Body," *New York*, February 4, 1980, p. 76.

Gabriel, Jack P., and Stanley Kauffmann, "Films: To Dub or Not to Dub," *Theatre Arts*, October 1961, pp. 20–21, 74–76.

Garisto, Leslie, "Dubbing Is Booming," *The New York Times*, Arts Section, August 29, 1982, pp. 1, 23.

Kaufman, Hank, "Nobody Dubs It Better," *Attenzione*, May 1984, pp. 34–38.

Kreuger, Miles, "Dubbers to the Stars," *High Fidelity*, July 1972, pp. 49–54.

Wolf, William, "Film Voices Anonymous," *Cue*, August 6, 1966, p. 10.

Zucker, Ralph, "In Defense of Dubbing," *Motion Picture Herald*, July 6, 1966, pp. 5–6.

DUDLEY MOTION PICTURE MANUFACTURING COMPANY. M. B. Dudley was the president of the Dudley Motion Picture Manufacturing Company, which produced Western* dramas at its studio in Redlands, California. In September 1916, the company arranged to release one five- or six-reel feature a month with Unity Sales Corporation. The company was reorganized in November 1916.

DUQUESNE AMUSEMENT SUPPLY COMPANY. See WARNER BROS. PICTURES, INC.

DYREDA ART FILM CORPORATION. Frank L. Dyer, the former president of Thomas A. Edison, Inc.*, and of the General Film Company, J. Parker Read, Jr., and J. Searle Dawley combined the first two letters of their last names to form the name of their new production company, the Dyreda Art Film Corporation, formed in October 1914. Dyer was president, Read vice-president and treasurer, and Dawley, a director since 1907 with Edison and Famous Players Film Company, was given full charge of production. The company leased from the Mutual Film Corporation* the studio erected on the Clara Morris estate on the Hudson by the Reliance Company for D. W. Griffith. Dyreda's first two productions were *One of Millions*, with Laura Sawyer and Robert Broderick, and *In the Name of the Prince of Peace*, an antiwar subject. Dyreda released its product with World Film Corporation* from October 1914 until April 1915. In December 1914,

World purchased the rights to two Charles K. Harris songs, "Always in the Way" and "Break the News to Mother," and contracted with Dyreda to produce them. After April 1915, Dyreda released exclusively with the Metro Film Corporation*. In May 1915, its studios were located at 3 West 61 Street, New York. On May 27, 1915, the B. A. Rolfe organization, which was owned in part by Metro, purchased Dyreda. C. M. Maddox of Rolfe became the general manager of the new company.

BIBLIOGRAPHY

"Dyreda—New Producing Company," *The Moving Picture World*, October 3, 1914, p. 69.

E

EACO FILMS, INC. Edwin August and Edward E. Anderson, the brother of Gilbert M. "Broncho Billy" Anderson, formed Eaco Films, Inc., in September 1914. August supervised the production of three reels per week, which included two-reelers in which he played the lead, one-reel comedies with Hal August, and Westerns* with Edward Piel. With offices in the World Tower Building in New York, Eaco used the Pathé* studios in Jersey City and filmed on location in Bermuda and Florida. David Santarelli was the company cameraman and supervised the laboratory work. Eaco's first film, which was released by Apex Film Corporation, was *Below the Dead Line*. In October 1914, Eaco produced its first three-reel production, *The Millionaire Detective*, released by the Strand Film Company, which had secured exclusive rights to Eaco's films. In December 1914, August left Eaco to join the Kinetophote Film Corporation*.

BIBLIOGRAPHY

"Edwin August a Manufacturer," *The Moving Picture World*, September 26, 1914, p. 1786.

EAGLE FEATURE FILM COMPANY. The Eagle Feature Film Company was located at 5 East 14 Street, New York. It produced the four-reel feature *Hawkshaw, the Detective*, in July 1913. Charles Streamer was the company's manager.

EAGLE FILM MANUFACTURING AND PRODUCING COMPANY. The Eagle Film Manufacturing and Producing Company, formed in late 1915, was located at 109 North Dearborn Street in Chicago. William J. Dunn was the general manager and director of the company, which produced *The Adventures of Duffy*, a comedy detective series, and the six-reel feature, *The Pirates of the Sky*. In June 1916, the company relocated to Jacksonville, Florida*, and changed its name to the Eagle Film Company. It produced comedies released through

Unity Sales Corporation*, including the "Tweedledum and Tweedledee" series. Fernandez Perez was the featured comedian. In August 1918, the Jacksonville plant was purchased by a hardware company after Eagle went into bankruptcy.

EAGLE-LION FILMS, INC. The name Eagle-Lion was first introduced by British film magnate J. Arthur Rank, in February 1944, as a worldwide distributor of British films. However, the name was subsequently taken by Arthur Krim and Robert Young (a railroad magnate) for a production company, which had its basis in P.R.C.*, and which was officially formed on April 24, 1946. (The British Eagle-Lion became part of Rank's General Film Distributors but was still utilized in some countries for several years.) Bryan Foy became the new company's production chief, and Eagle-Lion's first film was the Kenny Delmar comedy vehicle, *It's a Joke, Son* (1947).

Although it was little more than a "B" movie* producer, Eagle-Lion's films were quite well regarded critically, particularly those directed by Anthony Mann. Writing of Eagle-Lion's crime melodramas, Don Miller has commented, "Its influence was felt long after the organization had ceased to function, but particularly during the early part of the fifties. Eventually, this influence predominated in American television crime shows, for better or worse." In 1950, Eagle-Lion merged with Film Classics to become Eagle-Lion Classics, and the following year production ceased and the company's product was taken over by the new United Artists* organization.

BIBLIOGRAPHY

Miller, Don, "Eagle-Lion: The Violent Years," *Focus on Film*, no. 31, November 1978, pp. 27–38.

E. & R. JUNGLE FILM COMPANY. See JUNGLE FILM COMPANY

EARL OWENSBY STUDIOS. See E. O. CORP.

EASTERN FILM COMPANY. The Eastern Film Company, a Providence, Rhode Island, production company, was organized in September 1915 by three men from Providence: Elwood F. Bostwick, who became the general manager, Frederick S. Peck, the president and one of the wealthiest men in New England and vice-president of the National Exchange Bank of Providence, and Benjamin L. Cook. The company capitalized at $300,000 and had no stock for sale. It produced under the "Pelican" brand four one-reel films per week, in addition to two-reel comedies and two five-reel features per month. Directors for Eastern included Frederick Esmelton, Lambert Hillyer, George Lessy, Hamilton Crane, Dan Mason, Charles Pitt, and Allen Crolius. Eastern's first film was *Peaceful Valley*, with Frederick Burton, which was followed by *Next*, with Helen Lowell, and *The Red Petticoat*, with John Bunny's brother George, all produced in 1915.

BIBLIOGRAPHY

"New Producing Company," *The Moving Picture World*, September 4, 1915, p. 1624.

EASTMAN COLOR. Eastman color negative and color print film was introduced by Eastman Kodak* in 1950; in 1952, the company received an Academy Award (Scientific or Technical Award, Class I) for the film. The new film was immediately successful and in effect became the industry standard, particularly when the Technicolor* three-strip process became obsolete in the mid-fifties. Unfortunately, the new Eastman color film does not have the stability of Technicolor dye transfer prints and many prints and negatives have faded, resulting in an outcry in the early eighties from filmmakers and archivists. In response, Eastman Kodak introduced a new "low fade" film stock. Virtually every film today is photographed in Eastman color, despite the use of such patented names as Metrocolor, Warnercolor, and Color by De Luxe*. As Technicolor has not printed any original Technicolor dye transfer prints outside of China since 1975, all films presently identified as in Technicolor are in fact printed on Eastman color film but by the Technicolor Corporation.

EASTMAN KODAK COMPANY. The Eastman Kodak Company was formed as the Eastman Dry Plate Company by George Eastman (1854–1932) and Henry A. Strong on January 1, 1881. It became the Eastman Dry Plate and Film Company in 1884, the Eastman Company in 1889, and the Eastman Kodak Company in 1892. The present company was organized in 1901. The company's name is synonymous with film and with still cameras. It introduced the first transparent roll film in 1889; the first acetate* film in 1908; 16mm* film in 1923; x-ray film in 1924; 16mm Kodacolor film in 1928; 8mm* film and cameras in 1932; 35mm* microfilm in 1934; Kodachrome film in 1935; its first 16mm sound-on-film projector, the Kodascope, in 1937; acetate film for general use in the motion picture industry in 1948; and Super 8mm* in 1965. Its trademarks are Kodak, Eastman, Recordak, Brownie, Kodachrome, Instamatic, Ektaprint, Colorburst, and Kodel.

The name "Kodak" was invented by George Eastman in 1888. He wanted a short word that could be spelled and pronounced simply in any language, and after studying many combinations of letters, he selected a word which began and ended with his favorite letter, "K."

Address: Rochester, N.Y. 14650.

BIBLIOGRAPHY

Eastman Kodak. *Eastman Professional Motion Picture Films*. Rochester, New York: Eastman Kodak Company, 1982.

———. *The Book of Film Care*. Rochester, New York: Eastman Kodak Company, 1983.

———. *Eastman Kodak Company: A Brief History*. Rochester, New York: Eastman Kodak Company, 1983.

Simmons, Dr. Norwood L., "Kodak: Innovator behind the Scenes," *Movie/TV Marketing*, March 1970, pp. 9–13.

Smith, Frederick James, "The Man behind the Films—George Eastman," *Motion Picture Magazine*, September 1918, pp. 79–81, 128.

Solbert, O. N. *George Eastman*. Rochester, New York: Eastman Kodak Company, n.d. (reprinted from the November 1953 issue of *Image*).

EAVES COSTUME CO. For many years advertised as "the largest manufacturers of theatrical costumes in the East," the New York–based Eaves Costume Co. provided the costumes for virtually all of the silent films produced in and around the city, including D. W. Griffith's *Way Down East* (1920), *Orphans of the Storm* (1921), *One Exciting Night* (1922), and *The White Rose* (1923); Marion Davies' *When Knighthood Was in Flower* (1922) and *Little Old New York* (1923); Rudolph Valentino's *Monsieur Beaucaire* (1924); George Arliss' *Disraeli* (1921); John Barrymore's *Dr. Jekyll and Mr. Hyde* (1920); Norma Talmadge's *Smilin' Through* (1922); and William Fox's *If I Were King* (1920) and *Over the Hill* (1920). The company later became the Eaves-Brooks Costume Company, and its historical collection of costumes was donated to the Astoria* Motion Picture and Television Foundation.

EBONY PICTURES CORPORATION. Ebony Pictures Corporation of Chicago began releasing films with the General Film Company on April 15, 1918. It made one-reel slapstick comedies with all-black casts. L. J. Pollard was the president and general manager of the company and Bob Horner its scenario editor. In May 1918, the company of 150 persons, which had previously filmed at Oshkosh, Wisconsin, obtained lakefront property on which to erect a studio at Fort du Lac, Wisconsin. Ralph Phillips and Charles N. David directed for the company. Actors included Sam Robinson, Yvonne Junior, Samuel Jacks, and Mattie Edwards. In July 1918, casts comprised of both black and white actors began appearing in Ebony productions. After a short hiatus, the company resumed production in September 1919, producing its first two-reel film, which starred Samuel Jacks, surrounded by a white cast. Late in 1919, Ebony made a six-reel dramatic feature, dealing with spiritualism and titled *Do the Dead Talk?* The company went out of existence in 1922 largely, one suspects, because of opposition from black newspapers which objected to this white-owned company's depiction of blacks and its exploitation of black audiences.

The best known of Ebony comedies was *Spying the Spy* (1918), which is preserved in the National Film Collection at the Library of Congress.

BIBLIOGRAPHY

Sampson, Henry T. *Blacks in Black and White*. Metuchen, New Jersey: Scarecrow Press, 1977.

ECLAIR COMPANY. Charles Jourjon, the president of the Eclair Company in Paris, came to the United States to open the company's American branch in Fort Lee, New Jersey*, in the fall of 1911, in order to "give the trade an American picture made the Eclair way." This meant, Jourjon specified, using American players and French cameramen and technicians trained in Paris. A factory and two glass studios, designed by French experts, were erected, each with the capacity for shooting four scenes simultaneously. Harry Raver, formerly with circus, carnival, and other motion picture enterprises, was business manager of the American branch. Jules Brulatour was the political and financial advisor;

M. Maire, the chief cameraman; C. DeMoos, in charge of the technical end of the plant; Lawrence McGill, George Le Soir, and Joseph Smiley were the directors; Will S. Rising was the scenarist; and Wray Physioc was the scenic artist. The first American-made film was the two-reel *Hands across the Sea in '76*, released November 7, 1911.

Eclair began releasing with the Universal Film Manufacturing Company at its inception in 1912. In November 1913, Eclair sent Webster Cullison to establish a permanent western branch of Eclair in Tucson, Arizona, with a company of twenty-three. A studio and plant were set up there, and, after a disastrous fire at the Fort Lee plant in March 1914 (which destroyed Eclair's laboratory), the entire American producing force was sent to Tucson.

After the fire, some of the Eclair company stayed in Fort Lee and joined the newly created Peerless Feature Film Company, which Brulatour headed. Eclair began releasing with Warner's Features, and, late in 1914, formed Features Ideal, Inc., sometimes called the Ideal Company of Hollywood, as its Hollywood branch. Robert Levy was the general manager; the three directors were Frank Beal, Webster Cullison, and Carl Levinus; and the players included Dolly and George Larkin, Edna Payne, and Fred Hearn. Other players of note who appeared in Eclair's American films were Barbara Tennant, Fred Truesdell, Alec B. Francis, Muriel Ostriche, Clara Horton, and John Adolfi. Other cameramen included René Guissart and Lucien Andriot. Ben Carré was an Eclair scenic artist. Maurice Tourneur came to the United States in 1914 to direct at Eclair's Fort Lee plant.

BIBLIOGRAPHY

"American Eclair Studio," *The Moving Picture World*, October 7, 1911, pp. 24–25.

"Charles Jourjon, 'Concerning Eclair Enterprises,' " *The Moving Picture World*, July 11, 1914, p. 207.

"Cullison Is New Managing Director of Eclair Productions," *The Universal Weekly*, August 22, 1914, pp. 8–9.

ECLECTIC FILM COMPANY. The Eclectic Film Company, located at 110 West 40 Street, New York, began distributing European films in the United States early in 1913 with the two-reel *Lucretia Borgia*. In April 1913, the company distributed the twelve-reel *Les Miserables*, followed by *The Mysteries of Paris*. In mid–1914, it jointly produced the Pearl White serial *The Perils of Pauline*, whose story was presented in the Hearst newspapers, with Pathé* Freres. Compared to the usual twenty-five to thirty made for most previous serials, 147 prints of the serial were struck, so that exhibitions across the country could be coordinated with the newspaper stories. In January 1915, the staffs of Eclectic and Pathé Freres were combined under a new name, Pathé Exchange, Inc.

BIBLIOGRAPHY

"Expediting Service," *The Moving Picture World*, July 11, 1914, p. 284.

"First Eclectic Film," *The New York Dramatic Mirror*, January 15, 1913, p. 60.

EDISON MANUFACTURING COMPANY. The Edison Manufacturing Company, also known as Thomas A. Edison, Inc., has its origins in the primitive films photographed by Edison's associates in the Black Maria studio at Edison's laboratory in West Orange, New Jersey, built in 1891. Here Edison's associate, W.K.L. Dickson, produced the first films to be copyrighted—in 1893. The first public performance of Edison films, under the name of Edison Vitascope, took place at Koster and Bial's Music Hall, Herald Square, New York, on April 23, 1896.

Although Thomas Edison himself took little, if any, interest in film production, his company flourished, and, in 1908, the Edison Company erected a new studio at 2826 Decatur Avenue, Bedford Park, the Bronx, New York. The new studio replaced a makeshift studio at 41 East 21 Street, New York, where Edwin S. Porter (1869–1941) had been in charge of production and had produced and directed some of the first, and certainly most important, narrative films, including *The Great Train Robbery* and *Life of an American Fireman*, both released in 1903. It was Porter's associate, J. Searle Dawley, who directed D. W. Griffith's first screen appearance, in the 1907 Edison short, *Rescued from an Eagle's Nest*.

A fire at the Edison studio on March 27, 1914, caused extensive damage, and for a while the company was forced to utilize the 11 East 14 Street studios of the Biograph Company*.

Among the players making up the Edison stock company were Viola Dana, Mary Fuller, Charles Ogle, Mabel Trunnelle, Marc McDermott, Gertrude McCoy, Bessie Learn, and Herbert Prior. Charles Ogle was the star of Edison's 1910 production of *Frankenstein*, and Mary Fuller was featured in the first serial*, Edison's *What Happened to Mary?* (1912).

As the most important member of the Motion Picture Patents Company*, the Edison Company enjoyed considerable success from 1908 through 1912, but as the power of the Patents Group dissipated, and as Edison failed to embark on an adequate production schedule for feature-length films, the company lost its importance. The last Edison production was *The Unbeliever*, directed by Alan Crosland in 1918.

BIBLIOGRAPHY

Crosland, Alan, "How Edison's 'Black Maria' Grew," *Motography*, April 22, 1916, pp. 911–914.

Dickson, Antonia, and W.K.L. *Edison's Invention of the Kineto-Phonograph*. Los Angeles: Pueblo Press, 1939.

———. *History of the Kinetograph, Kinetoscope and Kineto-Phonograph*. New York: Arno Press, 1970.

"Edisonia," *Exhibitors' Times*, August 30, 1913, pp. 1, 4.

"Edison Pictures and Players," *The New York Dramatic Mirror*, January 31, 1912, p. 54.

"Edison Progress," *The Moving Picture World*, December 11, 1909, pp. 833–835.

Harrison, Louis Reeves, "Studio Saunterings," *The Moving Picture World*, April 13, 1913, pp. 127–131.

Hendricks, Gordon. *The Edison Motion Picture Myth*. Berkeley, California: University of California Press, 1961.

Spehr, Paul C., "Edison Films in the Library of Congress," *The Quarterly Journal of the Library of Congress*, January 1975, pp. 34–50.

Svejda, George J. *The Black Maria Site Study*. Washington, D.C.: Office of Archeology and Historic Preservation, 1969.

RESOURCES

Papers: Edison National Historic Site; Museum of Modern Art (scripts).

EDISON VITAGRAPH COMPANY. See VITAGRAPH COMPANY OF AMERICA

EDITING. Editing is the art and craft of joining together the various pieces of film shot by the cinematographer into a lucid, dramatic, and emotional whole. Some directors work closely with the editor selecting each shot and deciding exactly where a cut should take place, while others recognize the editor's expertise and leave many of the decisions to him or her. Similarly, some directors shoot a minimum of footage which virtually prevents the editor from making creative decisions, while other directors shoot excessive footage to give the editor tremendous choice and variety.

The Soviet theorist and director V. I. Pudovkin has argued that editing is the one crucial and creative act in film production. Certainly the editor can, at times, save a film that might otherwise be mediocre. He can also add much to a film's dramatic or emotional impact. Edwin S. Porter was, arguably, the first filmmaker to recognize the importance of editing, but it was D. W. Griffith who displayed the first true understanding of editing as a creative tool with *The Birth of a Nation* (1915) and *Intolerance* (1916).

During much of the silent era, film editors were called simply cutters, who, using little more than their own two eyes and a pair of scissors, would, literally, cut the film into shape. Although the art of editing is an American invention, it was the Russians who recognized it as such. Many editors, including Dorothy Arzner, Edward Dmytryk, and Robert Wise, were able to make a successful transition to directing. The British David Lean continued both to edit and direct his features up to and including *A Passage to India* (1984).

Editing includes both the cutting of the picture and the soundtrack, and, in recent years, the work of sound effects editors has come to be recognized as a separate craft. Editors work with a "work print" made specifically for editing purposes. Once the "work print" has been cut, it is turned over to a negative cutter, responsible for matching the work of the editor on the "work print" with the camera negative.

Academy Awards for Best Film Editing have been given since 1934. The first winner was Conrad Nervig for his work on *Eskimo*.

BIBLIOGRAPHY

Dmytryk, Edward. *On Film Editing*. Boston: Focal Press, 1984.

Hollyn, Norman. *The Film Editing Room Handbook*. New York: Arco, 1984.

Reisz, Karel, and Gavin Millar. *The Technique of Film Editing*. New York: Hastings House, 1968.

Robertson, Joseph F. *The Magic of Film Editing*. Blue Summit Ridge, Pennsylvania: TAB Books, 1983.

Rosenblum, Ralph, and Robert Karen. *When the Shooting Stops . . . the Cutting Begins*. New York: Viking Press, 1979.

Walter, Ernest. *The Technique of the Film Cutting Room*. New York: Hastings House, 1973.

EDITROID. See LUCASFILM, LTD.

EDUCATIONAL PICTURES, INC. The Educational Films Corporation claimed to have begun operations in 1914 as a distributor of short educational and entertainment subjects. In the 1918–1919 season, it released three films per week, in weekly series, including Robert C. Bruce's *Scenics of Adventure in the Northwest*; Raymond L. Ditmars' *The Living Book of Nature*; George D. Wright's *Mexico Today*; Dwight L. Elmendorf's foreign travel pictures; E. M. Newman's Far East films, *Newman Travels*; and cartoons featuring Happy Hooligan and Tad's Silk Hat Harry, made by Gregory La Cava (who later became a leading comedy director).

George A. Skinner was the president and Earl Wooldrige Hammons (1882–1962) was the vice-president and general manager of Educational, which had fifteen exchanges* across the country. By the twenties, Educational was releasing many series of comedies, and by the end of the decade it was the major independent distributor of short subjects. Lloyd Hamilton and Lupino Lane were the company's leading comedians.

In 1927, Educational reorganized to produce under the new Educational Pictures, Inc., name and distributed through Educational Film Exchanges, Inc. Hammons was the president, Jack White was director-general, and E. H. Allen was general manager.

In the thirties, Educational set up its production headquarters at the Astoria Studios*, and its short subjects featured comedy greats on the way down, such as Buster Keaton and Harry Langdon, and would-be film comedians, such as Danny Kaye, Bert Lahr, Joe Cook, Tom Patricola, and Tom Howard. Educational's short subjects were never of a particularly high quality; film historian Leonard Maltin has written that "Educational films almost always looked cheap, even though they were made in most cases by seasoned veterans." Educational, with its familiar trademark of Aladdin's lamp and its slogan, "The Spice of the Program," disappeared in 1940.

BIBLIOGRAPHY

"Educational Enthusiastic," *The Moving Picture World*, March 26, 1927, p. 384.

"Educational Films Branching Out," *The Moving Picture World*, August 31, 1918, p. 1244.

"Educational to Enlarge Program," *Motion Picture News*, October 18, 1919, p. 2996.

Maltin, Leonard, "The Spice of the Programme," *The Silent Picture*, no. 15, Summer 1972, pp. 19–25.

———. *The Great Movie Shorts*. New York: Crown, 1972.

"Putting Sugar on the Pill," *Photoplay*, June 1919, pp. 90, 93.

EDWARD SMALL PRODUCTIONS, INC. Edward Small's (1891–1977) first involvement with the film industry was as head of his own talent agency, the Edward Small Agency, which he opened in 1924, and which later became the Small Agency and the Small-Landau Agency. Small became an independent producer in the mid-twenties, and, in 1932, organized Reliance Pictures, Inc., with Harry M. Goetz, a company responsible for *I Cover the Waterfront* (1933), *The Count of Monte Cristo* (1934), and several other features. Reliance advertised itself as "Producers of Box-Office Entertainment for United Artists Release."

Edward Small Productions, Inc., was formed in 1938, initially to produce five features for United Artists release, commencing with *The Duke of West Point* (1938). Among the company's films were *The Corsican Brothers* (1941), *Up in Mabel's Room* (1944), *Getting Gertie's Garter* (1945), *Valentino* (1951), *Lorna Doone* (1951), and *Monkey on My Back* (1957). Small's last feature was *The Christine Jorgensen Story* (1970). Aside from Edward Small Productions, the producer also had a television production company, Television Productions of America, Inc., organized in 1953.

RESOURCES

Papers: University of Southern California.

8mm. The first 8mm cameras, projectors, and film were introduced by Eastman Kodak* in 1932. It was intended primarily for amateur, or home, use, but by the sixties was also used for teaching and other educational purposes. With the introduction of Super 8mm*, standard 8mm—as it came to be known—was gradually phased out. 8mm in width, standard 8mm film has perforations down one side of the film only, with eighty frames to one foot of film.

Eastman Kodak introduced an 8mm magazine Cine-Kodak camera in 1940, with the low-priced Brownie 8mm movie camera appearing on the scene in 1951 (followed a year later by the 8mm Brownie projector).

BIBLIOGRAPHY

Callenbach, Ernest, "The State of 8," *Film Quarterly*, Summer 1966, pp. 36–39.

Film News, February 1966, special issue devoted to 8mm.

Provisor, Henry. *8mm/16mm Movie-Making*. New York: Amphoto, 1970.

ELECTRICAL RESEARCH PRODUCTS, INC. A major name in the design, improvement, sale, and service of sound equipment during the pioneering years of the sound motion picture, Electrical Research Products, Inc. (ERPI) was a subsidiary of the Western Electric Company. It published a newsletter, *The Erpigram*, conducted and coordinated much of the research into sound on film and sound on disc on behalf of Western Electric and the Bell Telephone System, and was the recipient of five Scientific or Technical Awards from the Academy of Motion Picture Arts and Sciences between 1930/1931 and 1935. Western Electric discontinued the division in the summer of 1937, but ERPI continued as a licensor and recipient of royalties from equipment covered by ERPI patents.

ELECTRONOVISION. Developed by H. W. (Bill) Sargent, and hailed in 1964 as a major effort to bring stageplays direct to film audiences, Electronovision utilized multiple cameras to "film" electronically a stage production with only available light. The images were transmitted to a monitoring board and converted to the correct size and shape for projection by Theatrofilm. The first production to be shot in Electronovision was Richard Burton's *Hamlet* (1964). It was followed by *The TAMI Show* (1964) and *Harlow* (1965). Electronovision's combination of film and television techniques failed to achieve an adequate audience—despite the low cost of production—and, by the middle of 1965, Sargent's company, Electronovision, Inc., was in financial difficulty.

BIBLIOGRAPHY

Scheuer, Philip K., "Hollywood's Newest Threat," *Los Angeles Times*, Calendar Section, November 1, 1964, pp. 1, 35.

EMBASSY COMMUNICATIONS. Embassy Communications was formed after Norman Lear and Jerry Parenchio purchased Avco Embassy Pictures Corporation on November 30, 1981, for a reported $25 million. Avco Embassy had begun life as Joseph E. Levine's Embassy Pictures Corporation in the late fifties. Under Levine (born 1905), Embassy was noted for the American release of such foreign films as *Divorce—Italian Style* (1962), *8 1/2* (1963), and *Marriage Italian Style* (1964) and for *Long Day's Journey into Night* (1962), *The Carpetbaggers* (1964), *Harlow* (1965), *John F. Kennedy: Years of Lightning, Days of Drums* (1966), *The Oscar* (1966), *The Producers* (1967), and *The Graduate* (1967).

Avco Corp. acquired Embassy in 1968, and Joseph E. Levine left the company to form his own independent organization, in 1974. Tom Laughlin tried to purchase the new company, Avco Embassy, early in 1981, but considered the asking price too high. It was subsequently acquired by Lear and Parenchio, who controlled the television production companies of Tandem and T.A.T. Communications, and the television syndication organization, P.I.T.S. (which stands for "Pie in the Sky"). Embassy Communication's theatrical film division, Embassy Pictures, released the Ingmar Bergman feature *Fanny and Alexander*, in 1983. Embassy Television continued to handle the former Tandem productions, "The Jeffersons," "One Day at a Time," "The Facts of Life," "Silver Spoons," and "Diff'rent Strokes." Embassy Home Entertainment handles home videotape sales of Embassy's own films, as well as feature films controlled by Janus and the Samuel Goldwyn Company*. Embassy moved its production activities to the Universal* lot in May 1982, while maintaining corporate offices in Century City. In June 1985, the Coca-Cola Company announced plans to acquire Embassy for $485 million. Subsequently, Embassy was acquired by Dino De Laurentiis in late September 1985.

Address: 1901 Avenue of the Stars, Los Angeles, Calif. 90067.

BIBLIOGRAPHY

Harmetz, Aljean, "Lear Plans 8 to 10 Films a Year from His New Embassy Studio," *The New York Times*, January 20, 1982, p. C19.

Kaminsky, Ralph, "Avco's Capra 'Very Bullish' on Future, Will Keep Costs 'Lean,' " *The Film Journal*, September 21, 1981, pp. 7, 24.

Kerr, James R., "Billions Make a Nice Cushion," *Variety*, November 13, 1968, p. 31.

Pogache, Mark, "Embassy Communications," *On Location*, February 1984, pp. 156–157.

Pollock, Dale, "A New Team Gives a New Look to Embassy Communications," *Los Angeles Times*, Calendar Section, January 20, 1982, pp. 1, 4.

EMBASSY PICTURES CORPORATION. See EMBASSY COMMUNICATIONS

EMERALD PRODUCTIONS. See FILMAKERS, INC.

EMINENT AUTHORS PICTURES, INC. See GOLDWYN PICTURES CORPORATION

EMPIRE FEATURE FILM COMPANY. See MONROVIA FEATURE FILM COMPANY

ENTERPRISE PRODUCTIONS, INC. Formed by David Loew and Charles Einfeld on February 14, 1946, Enterprise Productions, Inc., was located at the California Studios* and was responsible for more than a dozen memorable features, beginning with *Ramrod*, directed by Andre de Toth in 1947; that same year, de Toth also directed *The Other Love* for Enterprise. Lewis Milestone directed a comedy, *No Minor Vices* (1948), for Enterprise, and he also directed for the company its most prestigious feature, *Arch of Triumph* (1948), an adaptation of the Erich Maria Remarque novel, starring Charles Boyer and Ingrid Bergman, which proved such a disaster at the box office—it had cost a reported $4 million to produce—that Enterprise was forced to cease operations in September 1948. David Lewis served as vice-president and as producer for the Enterprise features, which were released through United Artists. In 1951, the Bank of America, which had put up much of the money for the Enterprise operation, foreclosed its mortgages on eight of the Enterprise pictures, which eventually were released to television through the new Republic Pictures*.

BIBLIOGRAPHY

"Einfeld and Loew Form Enterprise," *Motion Picture Herald*, March 9, 1946, p. 26.

E. O. CORP. E. O. Corp. is a production company founded by Earl Owensby in 1974 with a studio facility in Shelby, North Carolina, which is the largest outside of Los Angeles. An extraordinary figure in non-Hollywood film production, Owensby has been called "the Cecil B. DeMille of North Carolina," producing and starring in a group of features beginning with *Challenge* (1974), which have found audiences outside of the usual Hollywood exhibition and distribution field. Aside from E. O. Corp., Owensby formed a distribution company, Maverick Pictures International, which he sold to McCoy Industries International in 1980.

Address: P.O. Box 184, Shelby, N.C. 28150.

BIBLIOGRAPHY

Auerbach, Alexander, "Earl Owensby Stepping Out from behind Country Boy Image," *Boxoffice*, June 1981, pp. 12, 15.

Bergman, Andrew, "A Very Minor Movie Mogul," *Esquire*, November 1980, pp. 82–87.

Honeycutt, Kirk, "Maverick of the Movies—Regional Filmmakers," *The New York Times*, November 9, 1980, pp. D1, D23.

McCarthy, Todd, "Earl Owensby Undertaking $5 Mil Expansion of His North Carolina Studio," *Daily Variety*, May 26, 1981, pp. 1, 11.

Owensby, Earl, "Grass Roots, Grits and Now, BIG TIME," *Daily Variety*, June 15, 1977, p. 36.

———, "North Carolina's 'Hollywood'; Producer Acts as His Own Star; 11 Films to Date, None in Red," *Variety*, January 3, 1979, p. 36.

EQUITABLE MOTION PICTURE CORPORATION. See WORLD FILM CORPORATION

EQUITY PICTURES CORPORATION. A New York–based distributor of independent productions from 1919 to 1924, Equity Pictures Corporation was chiefly associated with the films of actress Clara Kimball Young, produced by Harry Garson at his Garson Studios (located at 1845 Glendale Avenue in Los Angeles). Among the Garson-produced features released by Equity and starring Young were *Eyes of Youth* (1919), *The Forbidden Woman* (1920), *For the Soul of Rafael* (1920), *Mid-Channel* (1920), *Whispering Devils* (1920), *Hush* (1920), *Charge It* (1921), *Straight from Paris* (1921), *What No Man Knows* (1921), and *The Worldly Madonna* (1922). The first is the best known of the group because of the performance by one of Clara Kimball Young's featured players, Rudolph Valentino.

ERBOGRAPH COMPANY. The Erbograph Company, headed by Ludwig G. B. Erb, was formed in 1916 and released its productions through Art Dramas, Inc.* In April 1917, it added a second company, headed by Marion Swayne with Joseph Levering as director. Erbograph closed down that same year.

ERBOGRAPH LABORATORY. See CONSOLIDATED FILM INDUSTRIES

ERPI. See ELECTRICAL RESEARCH PRODUCTS, INC.

ESSANAY FILM MANUFACTURING COMPANY. The Essanay Film Manufacturing Company was incorporated on February 5, 1907, by George K. Spoor and G. M. Anderson, with the company's name being composed of the first letters of their names. Anderson, born Max Aronson, was a vaudeville performer, who, after appearing as a train robber in Edison's *The Great Train Robbery* in 1903, continued acting in dramatic films made by Vitagraph* and Selig*. Spoor, a proprietor of the Kinodrome Circuit, which showed motion pictures in the Orpheum vaudeville theatres of the West, and the growing National Film Renting Company, which rented the films his circuit showed, needed more productions to meet growing demands for them. Essanay's first production, *An Awful Skate, or The Hobo on Rollers*, was announced in *The Moving Picture World* on July 27, 1907. Essanay's first plant was located at 501 Wells Street in Chicago. According to Robert Grau (in *The Theatre of Science*), Essanay was the first company to turn out 1,000-foot films. On September 8, 1909, Anderson, his cameraman Jesse J. Robbins, and a company of players left Chicago to go West. Along the way, they filmed Essanay's first film shot in the West, *The Best Man Wins*. After stopping in Denver, El Paso, and Santa Barbara, the company settled in Niles, California, near Oakland, where it produced a series of "Broncho Billy" Westerns* starring G. M. Anderson for the next seven years.

Essanay was a member of the Motion Picture Patents Company* and its films were released by the General Film Company. In 1915, it joined with Vitagraph, Lubin*, and Selig to form V-L-S-E* to release longer pictures.

Early in 1910, J. Warren Kerrigan made his debut in motion pictures under the Essanay brand. Kerrigan and most of Essanay's staff and players went to the independent American Film Manufacturing Company* in October 1910, a company which began to copy Essanay's successful formula of producing comedies, dramas, and Westerns. Francis X. Bushman began his motion picture career with Essanay in 1911, and Beverly Bayne followed the next year. William F. "Buffalo Bill" Cody signed with Essanay in 1913 to appear in films depicting the pioneer days of the West. On January 2, 1915, Essanay announced that it had signed Charles Chaplin, but Spoor let the comedian go to Mutual* after his contract had run out in 1916. Shortly thereafter, Spoor bought out Anderson, and, although he hired Max Linder to make films in 1917, the company declined. Late in 1918 it stopped production, and in mid–1919 Victor Kremer purchased the Essanay negatives and prints and began reissuing them.

BIBLIOGRAPHY

"Essanay Chaplin Comedies," *The Moving Picture World*, July 10, 1915, p. 238.
"The Essanay Company Out West," *The Moving Picture World*, December 4, 1909, pp. 801–802.

"Essanay's New Studio," *The Moving Picture World*, March 4, 1916, p. 1452.

"Essanay's Western Plant," *The Moving Picture World*, July 10, 1915, pp. 237–238.

Parsons, Louella O., "The Essanay Days," *Theatre Arts*, July 1951, pp. 33, 96.

"Some Prominent Essanay Players," *The Moving Picture World*, July 11, 1914, pp. 234–235.

Spoor, George K., "Remarkable Growth of Motion Picture Industry," *The Moving Picture World*, July 11, 1914, p. 191.

EXACTUS PHOTO-FILM CORPORATION. Incorporated on August 28, 1914, the Exactus Photo-Film Corporation of Palo Alto, California, would appear to be the first film company organized solely for the production of educational subjects. Its president was Thomas Kimmwood Peters and the company boasted a number of educators as consultants. Its films received two gold medals and one bronze medal at the 1915 Panama-Pacific International Exposition. However, by 1916, the company had auctioned off its assets, and its remaining property was taken over by the Palo Alto Film Company (organized in 1915).
RESOURCES
Papers: Stanford University.

EXCELSIOR FEATURE FILM COMPANY, INC. Excelsior Feature Film Company, Inc., began production in April 1914 at its Lake Placid, New York, studio. Harry Handworth was the company director and Gordon de Maine its leading man. Other actors included Octavia Handworth, Tom Tempest, and William A. Williams, who was also the company's vice-president. Excelsior's first film was *The Toil of Mammon*. It distributed with Alco Film Corporation* as of August 25, 1914, but as of October 10, 1914, it released through the Alliance Films Corporation*. Handworth resigned in January 1915.
BIBLIOGRAPHY
"A New Film Organization," *The Moving Picture World*, April 11, 1914, p. 199.

EXCHANGES. Exchanges take their name from their primary function which is to supply exhibitors with a continuing change of films. In the early years of the film industry, exhibitors acquired their films directly from the producer, but it soon became necessary to set up exchanges on a local level, from which exhibitors could obtain features or shorts. There have always been two types of exchanges, those operated by the producers and those independently owned. Prior to 1910, there were less than a dozen exchanges operating in the United States, but by 1930 there were more than 500, with the biggest increase taking place between 1914 and 1924 (during which time 72 percent of all the exchanges operating in the United States by 1929 came into existence).

EXCLUSIVE SUPPLY CORPORATION. Exclusive Film Corporation, located at 220 West 42 Street, New York, was formed in May 1913 when the Film Supply Corporation of America, which distributed films associated with the Mutual Film Corporation*, was disbanded. Herbert Blaché, with interests in

Blaché-American, Solax*, and the U.S. Amusement Company, was the president; I. C. Oes, the president of Great Northern Special Feature Film Company* and the American representative of Nordisk Film Company, was Exclusive's vice-president. Harry R. Raver, the president and general manager of All-Star Feature Company* and with an interest in the Itala Film Company of America*, was the secretary and treasurer; Joseph R. Miles, the president of the Films Lloyd Company and an officer in Great Northern, was the general manager. By July 1914, the company's name had changed to Exclusive Supply Corporation. It was opposed to the "forced program" (whereby theatres were forced to book complete programs as a package) and while it distributed mainly shorts at the beginning, by July 1914, it was handling features by All-Star Feature Company, Blaché-American, F.R.A., Gaumont*, Great Northern, Itala, Lewis Pennant, Ramo*, Solax, and Films Lloyd. It released five features weekly to the states rights* market. Although it planned to increase to handling seven pictures per week, and intended in the future to deal directly with exhibitors, Exclusive went out of business in October 1914.

EXHIBITORS' MUTUAL DISTRIBUTING CORPORATION. See MUTUAL FILM CORPORATION

EXPLOITATION FILMS.
Exploitation films is a term used to describe productions which exploit a popular social phenomenon. Such films are almost as old as the motion picture itself and can be dated back at least to 1913 when the Universal* feature *Traffic in Souls* exploited the then current public interest in "white slavery." There is no rule as to what is or is not an exploitation film, and certainly what one critic labels as such may not be so called by another. Low-budget horror films, such as *Night of the Living Dead* (1969) and *Texas Chainsaw Massacre* (1974), are generally considered to be exploitation films.

Low budgets and low production values are common among most exploitation films. Bad taste as evidenced in *Pink Flamingos* (1974) can also be the mark of an exploitation film. A subgenre is sex exploitation films, which are not hardcore pornographic in content but are mildly salacious, or softcore, dealing with usually taboo subjects, such as lesbianism or prostitution. The features of erotic film producer Russ Meyer can easily be classified as sex exploitive, dealing as they do with drug abuse and sexual perversion (for example, *Beyond the Valley of the Dolls*, 1970). Films which go beyond exploitation to "camp," such as *Myra Breckinridge* (1970), are outside of the genre.

One major group of exploitation films from the late forties and early fifties were those dealing with the dangers of communism*, such as Republic Pictures' *The Red Menace* (1949), which claimed to be performing a public service, but which was produced purely for the profit of its maker. Indeed, it might well be argued that any American feature with a social message is an exploitation film in that it exploits its audience for the financial benefit of its producer.

BIBLIOGRAPHY

Karr, Katherine, ''The Long Square-Up: Exploitation Trends in the Silent Film,'' *Journal of Popular Film*, vol. III, no. 2, Spring 1974, pp. 107–128.

Taylor, John Russell, ''Beyond the Taste Barrier,'' *Sight and Sound*, Winter 1976/77, pp. 37–39.

EXTRAS. See CENTRAL CASTING CORPORATION and SCREEN EXTRAS GUILD

F

FAIRFAX, CALIFORNIA. See UNITED KEANOGRAPH FILM MANUFACTURING COMPANY

THE "FALCON" SERIES. Based on a character created by Michael Arlen, the "Falcon" series began with *The Gay Falcon* (1941), featuring George Sanders as the dashing hero, Gay Falcon. Sanders continued to play the Falcon in *A Date with the Falcon* (1941) and *The Falcon Takes Over* (1942), but, in *The Falcon's Brother* (1942), he is assassinated by Nazi agents and the role is, literally, taken over by Sanders' brother, Tom Conway (alias Tom Lawrence). As the Falcon, Tom Conway was featured in nine more features, beginning with *The Falcon Strikes Back* (1943) and ending with *The Falcon's Adventure* (1946). Those first thirteen Falcon features were produced by RKO; the remaining three—*The Devil's Cargo* (1948), *Appointment with Murder* (1948), and *Search for Danger* (1949)— were produced by Falcon Productions, released by Film Classics, and starred John Calvert as the Falcon.

BIBLIOGRAPHY

Zinman, David. *Saturday Afternoon at the Bijou.* New Rochelle, New York: Arlington House, 1973.

FAMOUS ARTISTS CORPORATION. See CHAS. K. FELDMAN'S GROUP PRODUCTIONS

FAMOUS ATTRACTIONS CORPORATION. See PREFERRED PICTURES

FAMOUS PLAYERS FILM COMPANY. See PARAMOUNT PICTURES, INC.

FAMOUS PLAYERS-LASKY FILM CORPORATION. See PARAMOUNT PICTURES, INC.

FANTASOUND. Experiments with Fantasound began in 1937, and the process was successfully utilized for Walt Disney's *Fantasia* (1941). The process was explained by Edward R. Kellogg in *The Journal of the Society of Motion Picture and Television Engineers* (August 1955):

> The animated picture was designed specifically for the music, which was taken from great classics. In the initial orchestral recordings many microphones and separate recording channels were used. Recordings were selected or mixed in the re-recording to obtain desired effects such as predominance in turn of various orchestral groups (strings, brass, etc.). Sound and picture were on separate films. The final sound film carried three 200-mil push-pull variable area soundtracks, and three superimposed variable amplitude control tones on a fourth track. The theater equipment consisted of three loudspeakers at the sides and back of the auditorium. The latter could be brought into operation by relays responsive to notches in the edge of the film. They were used effectively for various sound effects and for the music of a large chorus. Abundant sound power and volume range were employed, the volume range being readily obtained by use of the control tracks.

As an early form of stereophonic sound, Fantasound was both a critical and commercial success, but the cost of installation plus America's entry into the Second World War hindered its later use.

BIBLIOGRAPHY
Garity, William E., and J.N.A. Hawkins, "Fantasound," *Journal of the Society of Motion Picture and Television Engineers*, August 1941, pp. 127–146.

FAVORITE PLAYERS FILM COMPANY. Carlyle Blackwell formed the Favorite Players Film Company in August 1914 to produce films starring himself, to be distributed by Alco Film Corporation*. William Desmond Taylor was in charge of production at its new studio in Edendale, California. As of October 10, 1914, Favorite Players released through Alliance Films Corporation*. Its first release was *The Key to Yesterday*, with Edna Mayo. The company disbanded in April 1915 when Blackwell went to the Jesse L. Lasky Feature Play Company.

FBO. See RKO RADIO PICTURES, INC.

FEATURE PRODUCTIONS, INC. See ART CINEMA CORPORATION

FEATURES AND SHORTS. See SHORTS AND FEATURES

FEDERAL FEATURE FILMS CORPORATION. Federal Feature Films Corporation of New York was said to have the largest motion picture studio in the world when it became affiliated with Metro Pictures Corporation* in September 1915. The studio was located at Rocky Glen, Pennsylvania, between Scranton and Wilkes-Barre. Arthur Jans was the company's president, and Merritt Crawford was secretary. The company made productions to sell to small exhibitors before the Metro takeover. It was reorganized in January 1917.

FICTION PICTURES, INC. Fiction Pictures, Inc., was a short-lived producing company of 1915, which was formed by novelist Louis Joseph Vance after he came to Los Angeles to help with the preparation of a series that Universal* was producing from his works. Vance engaged Wilfred Lucas as his director-general, Gilbert Warrenton as his cameraman, and he put together a company which included Cleo Madison, Joe King, and Edward Sloman. Its first film, Vance's *The Spanish Jade*, starred Betty Bellairs. Fiction's studio was located first in Glendale and later at Melrose Avenue and Bronson Street in Hollywood. In June 1915, Fiction went out of business and sold its studio to the Famous Players Film Company.

5TH AVENUE PLAYHOUSE GROUP. See ART HOUSES

FILM ADVISORY BOARD, INC. The Film Advisory Board, Inc., was incorporated on July 19, 1975, when Elayne Blythe broke away from the Southern California Motion Picture Council*, of which she had been president for eleven years. The Film Advisory Board (FAB) presents monthly awards to films, television programs, and individuals that promote family entertainment.

Address: 7080 Hollywood Boulevard, Suite 312, Hollywood, Calif. 90028.

FILMAKERS, INC. An independent production company, noted for its low-budget features dealing with social issues, Filmakers, Inc., was organized in 1949 by producer Collier Young and his then wife—they were divorced in 1951—Ida Lupino. The company had previously been known as Emerald Productions, which was responsible for one feature, *Not Wanted* (1949), which gave Lupino her first opportunity to direct. Filmakers produced five features, directed by Lupino: *Never Fear* (1950), *Outrage* (1950), *Hard, Fast and Beautiful* (1951), *The Hitchhiker* (1953), and *The Bigamist* (1954). It also produced *Private Hell* (1954), starring Ida Lupino, and *Mad at the World* (1955).

FILM ALLIANCE OF THE U.S., INC. See TRANS-LUX CORPORATION

FILM AND PHOTO LEAGUE. See NATIONAL FILM AND PHOTO LEAGUE

FILMARTE THEATRE, NEW YORK. See LENAUER INTERNATIONAL FILMS, INC.

FILM ASSOCIATES. See ART HOUSES

FILM AUDIENCES FOR DEMOCRACY. See FILMS FOR DEMOCRACY

FILM BOOKING OFFICE OF AMERICA. See RKO RADIO PICTURES, INC.

FILM CLASSICS. See EAGLE-LION FILMS, INC.

FILM CLEARING HOUSE. See INDEPENDENT SALES CORPORATION

FILMEX. Filmex, the name by which the Los Angeles International Film Exposition is best known, was created by George Cukor, Philip Chamberlin, and Gary Essert and was first held, under the last's directorship, November 4–14, 1971. A noncompetitive festival for features and shorts, Filmex has never had a permanent home; the first exposition was held at the Chinese Theatre in Hollywood, and the majority of times it has been held at the two Plitt Century Plaza Theatres in Century City.

Gary Essert's flamboyant and often abrasive manner aroused much controversy, and, finally, in the summer of 1983, he resigned from Filmex amid much rancor. He was replaced by Suzanne McCormick, as executive director, and Ken Wlaschin, as artistic director. Following his departure from Filmex, Essert announced plans for an American Cinematheque in Los Angeles, which would be housed at the Pan Pacific Auditorium and include three theatres, a bookstore, study and information facilities, and an exhibition area.

Address: P.O. Box 1739, Hollywood, Calif. 90028.

THE FILM FUND. The Film Fund was formed in 1977 by three men with inherited wealth—David Crocker, George Pillsbury, and Obie Benz—and by filmmaker Barbara Kopple, who was enjoying financial success from her documentary feature, *Harlan County U.S.A.* (1977). According to its then director, Terry Lawler, in an interview with the *Los Angeles Times* (January 14, 1982), the purpose of the Film Fund was "to create a mechanism and a staff through which people can support independent, social issue films, films that can be used by groups organizing for social change."

A service organization for filmmakers and community groups, the Film Fund is best known for its grants to socially aware documentaries. In 1978, it selected the first 22 projects for funding, out of 420 applications. The Film Fund also publishes the quarterly *News from the Film Fund*, providing useful information not only on the activities of the Fund but also on new socially aware films and on festivals of interest to the independent filmmaker.

Address: 80 East 11 Street, New York, N.Y. 10003.

FILM MARKET, INC. Film Market, Inc., was a brokerage company formed by Robert W. Priest, in August 1918, to handle productions from independent producers. Its offices were located in the Times Building, New York.

FILM MUTUAL BENEFIT GUILD. See ART HOUSES

FILM NOIR. *Film noir* was first used as a critical term in France in the fifties and became established after the publication, in 1955, of *Panorama du Film Noir Americain* by Raymond Borde and Etienne Chaumeton. The term was used to designate a group of films that was different from the usual crime and gangster films, both visually and structurally. Visually, the high-key lighting used in most Hollywood* films was replaced by a repeated use of low-key lighting so that the screen was often literally in the dark. Structurally, the redemptive elements of the gangster and crime film—the police win; the city is cleaned up; the gangster dies—are replaced by a narrative in which no one is able to win, especially not the hero.

The visual style of these films was derived from the German expressionist films and was a blend of chiaroscuro, unusual camera angles, and extreme close-ups. This type of style worked to compress space and give the viewer a disorienting view of the action. It also helped establish a mood in which the characters in the film were trapped by the encroaching darkness and the extreme close-ups, without there being any place to escape.

This mood was intensified by the narrative structure of *film noir*, in which the straight-ahead drive of the classic gangster film (from rise to fall) is replaced by a twisting, retrogressive narrative. Flashbacks become crucial for *film noir*, as a mood of hopelessness and fatality is established by beginning the film with the protagonist defeated (*The Killers*), on the run (*Out of the Past*), or, in the most extreme case, dead but still moving (*D.O.A.*) and then flashing back to see how this state was brought about.

Since the films which make up *film noir* do not have the thematic coherence of Westerns* or gangster films*, there has been an argument as to whether *film noir* is a genre or not. If the films do not have common themes, they do share a common perception of the world and of life, a view in which life is nasty and bleak and where there is no escape through the blackness of death.

Films of the genre date, basically, from 1945 to 1957, with Orson Welles' *Touch of Evil* (1958) arguably the last film of the genre.

BIBLIOGRAPHY

Hirsch, Foster. *The Dark Side of the Screen: Film Noir*. San Diego: A. S. Barnes, 1981.

Karimi, A. M. *Toward a Definition of the American Film Noir (1941–1949)*. New York: Arno Press, 1976.

Ottoson, Robert. *A Reference Guide to the American Film Noir (1940–1958)*. Metuchen, New Jersey: Scarecrow Press, 1981.

Selby, Spender. *Dark City: The Film Noir*. Jefferson, North Carolina: McFarland, 1984.
Tuska, Jon. *Dark Cinema: American Film Noir in Cultural Perspective*. Westport, Connecticut: Greenwood Press, 1984.

FILM SECURITY OFFICE. See MOTION PICTURE ASSOCIATION OF AMERICA

FILM SERVICE ASSOCIATION. See MOTION PICTURE PATENTS COMPANY

FILMS FOR DEMOCRACY. A group sponsored by Walter Wanger, Dudley Nichols, Marc Connelly, Sherwood Anderson, Fritz Lang, and Fredric March, Films for Democracy was founded in 1938. In 1939, it merged with Film Audiences to become Film Audiences for Democracy. Films for Democracy was cited as a Communist front organization in the report of the Special Committee on Un-American Activities, March 29, 1944.

FILMS INCORPORATED. Films Incorporated is the largest nontheatrical (or 16mm*) film distributor in the United States, with more than 10,000 features listed in its catalog as of 1985. It includes the former independent 16mm film libraries of Audio Brandon (which began in 1924 as Ideal Film Centers and was consolidated by Macmillan, Inc., in the sixties with the merger of Audio Film Center and Brandon Films, Inc.), Janus Films (a prestigious distributor noted for its classic foreign-language and British features), and Texture Films (which specializes in short subjects and films for children).

The company was founded in 1927 by Orton Hicks as Home Film Libraries, Incorporated, the first major distributor of 16mm films for home use. Paramount* was the first major studio to allow 16mm distribution of its films by the company, followed in 1936 by Universal* and in 1941 by 20th Century-Fox* (whose films continue to be distributed by Films Incorporated). On May 1, 1938, Home Film Libraries, Incorporated, was acquired by Eric Haight and the name changed to Films Incorporated. Films Incorporated was subsequently purchased by Encyclopedia Films in 1951. In 1956, it acquired 16mm, nontheatrical rights, in perpetuity, to all pre–1948 RKO* features, including such classics as *King Kong* and *Citizen Kane*. On May 1, 1968—exactly thirty years after the company became Films Incorporated—it was acquired by Charles Benton, who continues to head the organization.

Among Films Incorporated's other activities have been the 1975 launching of educational sound filmstrips called "Moviestrips," the 1976 publication of *Rediscovering the American Cinema* catalogs, and its first major entry into the field of 35mm distribution in 1978 with a retrospective devoted to 20th Century-Fox.

Films Incorporated is now a division of Charles Benton's Public Media Incorporated, created in 1968. Public Media also controlled Lionheart Television

International, a worldwide television distribution company, which represents both the British Broadcasting Corporation and the Australian Broadcasting Commission in the United States, which was taken over by the BBC in 1986. It was founded on May 1, 1981, with the dissolution of Time-Life Films*, which had previously distributed BBC product in the United States. Also part of the Public Media "family" is Quartet Films (which merged with Films Incorporated in 1979, which distributes quality features and foreign-language films theatrically in the United States.

Address: 1144 Wilmette Avenue, Wilmette, Ill. 60091.

FILMS MADE FOR TELEVISION. The first feature-length film made specifically for television was *The Three Musketeers*, produced by Hal Roach, Jr., in 1950, and seen on CBS under the sponsorship of Magnavox, which paid $25,000 for all rights to the production. A few weeks later, Peter N. Rathvon produced *The Pharmacist's Mate*, directed by Irving Pichel and starring Gene Raymond and Brian Donlevy, which was hailed as the most expensive single film to be made for television. It cost the sponsor, Schlitz Beer, $30,000.

According to Alvin H. Marill, in his definitive reference work, *Movies Made for Television*, the first feature to be produced for television and which heralded the advent of the made-for-television movie on a regular basis was *See How They Run*, directed by John Lowell Rich; starring John Forsythe, Senta Berger, and Jane Wyatt; produced by Universal; and aired on NBC on October 7, 1964.

The made-for-television film may be one feature or a feature-length episode in a mini-series. "It quickly has caught up with its bigger [theatrical] brother," writes Marill, "in its approach to virtually any subject, limited on the network merely by 'viewer sensibilities' and other considerations and guidelines that eliminate nudity, profanity and explicit mayhem." An average of 120 features are now produced annually strictly for television, although some are also released theatrically overseas. Because made-for-television films rise to a climax at a commercial break, their theatrical release is often precluded because the transition from one segment to the next without a break can often seem jarring. Some made-for-television features have, however, received a theatrical release in the United States, notably *Brian's Song* (1972), *Duel* (1983), and *My Sweet Charlie* (1970). There have even been one or two made-for-television films—such as *Warning Shot* (1967) and *Scott Joplin* (1976)—which received a theatrical release prior to their television debut.

Although directors of made-for-television features tend to be a breed unto themselves, some have been able to make the transition to theatrical features, notably James L. Brooks. Similarly, a few respected directors of theatrical features have later worked in television, particularly George Cukor with *Love Among the Ruins* (1975) and *The Corn Is Green* (1979) and Nicholas Meyer with *The Day After* (1983).

One of the best, continuing sources for information on made-for-television films is the monthly column, "The Television Scene," in *Films in Review*.

BIBLIOGRAPHY
Allen, Tom, "The Semi-Precious Age of TV Movies," *Film Comment*, July-August 1979, pp. 21–23, 47.
Champlin, Charles, "TV: The End of the Beginning," *American Film*, October 1975, pp. 60–63.
McGilligan, Patrick, "Movies Are Better Than Ever—on Television," *American Film*, March 1980, pp. 50–54.
Marill, Alvin H. *Movies Made for Television*. New York: New York Zoetrope, 1984.
Menaker, Daniel, "Television Apposite Reactions," *Film Comment*, July-August 1980, pp. 76–77.

FILM SOCIETY OF LINCOLN CENTER. Best known for its sponsorship of the New York Film Festival*, the Film Society of Lincoln Center also sponsors the "Movies for Kids" and "Movies in the Park" programs. Since 1972 it has presented the New Directors/New Films series in cooperation with the Museum of Modern Art, and that same year began its annual tribute to "Film Artists of Distinction," with a salute to Charles Chaplin. Other honorees have included Claudette Colbert, Laurence Olivier, Fred Astaire, George Cukor, Bob Hope, John Huston, and Billy Wilder. The Film Society of Lincoln Center is also the publisher—from 1974—of *Film Comment* magazine.

Address: 140 West 65 Street, New York, N.Y. 10023.

FILMS OF BUSINESS CORPORATION. The Films of Business Corporation was a producer of industrial films formed in January 1918. Camilla Donworth was the president and Charles Charlton the vice-president. Its first films were produced for the H. J. Heinz Company.

FILMS ON TELEVISION. In the September 29, 1948, edition of *The Hollywood Reporter*, Eugene F. McDonald, Jr., president of Zenith Radio Corporation, predicted that "television will soon be using motion pictures for more than half of its programs and commercials." However, the initial reaction of the film industry toward television was a totally negative one. Without dissension, the major studios refused to allow their features to be aired on television; further, the companies refused to permit contract stars and technicians to work in the new medium.

In 1948, Film Classics released twenty-four features produced by the British filmmaker Alexander Korda to Los Angeles station KTLA, which was the first major sale of feature films to television and which heralded increased sales of foreign films to independent stations. (That same year, KTLA screened Vittorio de Sica's 1946 Italian feature, *Shoeshine*.) Television was to herald the demise of the "B" movie*, and it is perhaps not unsurprising that it was the smaller independent producers that specialized in "B" pictures, such as Republic*, that were the first to make their product available to television.

In July 1951, Roy Rogers was able to obtain a temporary injunction preventing the sale of his Republic* features to television, and, at the same time, the various guilds and unions were fighting television sales, demanding additional, supplemental fees from the producers. However, beginning with a November 25, 1952, ruling against the writers, the courts ruled unanimously that those involved in the original production of the films had no control over them.

Universal-International was the first major company to allow its players to work in television, and it was quickly followed by RKO*, Paramount*, M-G-M*, and Columbia*. Producers began to realize the promotional potential of television when CBS, on April 13, 1952, had Edward R. Murrow take viewers behind the scenes of the making of Goldwyn's *Hans Christian Andersen*. Eventually, a 1952 antitrust suit filed by various television companies against the major studios forced the release of feature films to television.

Sales of films to television were initially limited to pre–1948 titles, but following a January 1960 strike by actors, which led to a guarantee that they should share in television sales of films made after January 31, 1960, the studios, beginning with Warner Bros.*, started to release post–August 1948 features to television.

The cutting of films for television for both space and censorship* reasons did not become a problem until the late sixties. Both Otto Preminger (with regard to his 1966 feature, *Anatomy of a Murder*) and George Stevens (with regard to his 1965 feature, *A Place in the Sun*) brought unsuccessful lawsuits against the cutting of their films for television. Alfred Hitchcock was able to work out a special contract with NBC to prevent the editing of *Rear Window* for its 1966 and 1967 network screenings. In 1985, Warren Beatty was able to prevent ABC from screening his film *Reds* except in the version and at the length in which the film was theatrically released in the United States.

According to the Guinness book of *Movie Facts and Feats* (Sterling, 1980), the first film to be shown on television was *The Bride* (1929), experimentally transmitted from the Baird Television Studios in London on August 19, 1929. The first feature-length film to be shown on television was *Police Patrol* (1925), transmitted in six daily episodes by W2XCD of Passaic, New Jersey, April 6–11, 1931. The first feature film to receive its premiere on television was *African Journey* (1947), broadcast on WNBT-New York on January 1, 1948.

In recent years, television has taken to retitling feature films to imply that they have been made for television. For example, *Sometimes a Great Notion* (1971) was aired on television as *Never Give an Inch*, *Bloodbrothers* (1978) as *Fathers and Sons*, *September 30, 1955* (1978) as *24 Hours of the Rebel*, and *Hurricane* (1979) as *Forbidden Paradise*.

The most famous film to be aired on television was, of course, *Gone with the Wind*, which was first shown on Japanese television in 1975. Its first American airing was on Home Box Office, on June 14, 1976. *Gone with the Wind* was first seen on network television, in two parts, on NBC, on November 7 and 8, 1976. It was subsequently aired on CBS in 1979, 1981, 1983, and 1984, and was seen again on Japanese television in 1979.

BIBLIOGRAPHY
Brown, Saul, "How Television Cuts the Bleep Out of Shows," *TV Guide*, May 5, 1973, pp. 6–10.
Canby, Vincent, "Major Films on TV Emerging as Vital Problem for Two Industries," *Motion Picture Herald*, January 19, 1957, pp. 13, 17.
Champlin, Charles, "TV Off and Running in High-Paying Movie Stakes," *Los Angeles Times*, Calendar Section, September 5, 1965, p. 10.
Kael, Pauline, "Movies on Television," *The New Yorker*, June 3, 1967, pp. 120–134.
Maltin, Leonard, "The 75 Best and 25 Worst Movies on TV," *Esquire*, December 1968, pp. 148–149, 266–272.
———, "Show It Again, Sam," *TV Guide*, March 31, 1973, pp. 20–23.
———, editor. *TV Movies*. New York: New American Library, 1985.
Markfield, Wallace, " 'Play It Again, Sam'—And Again," *The Saturday Evening Post*, April 22, 1967, pp. 72–78.
Sarris, Andrew, "The Primal Screen," *The Village Voice*, July 10, 1984, p. 43.
Scheuer, Steven H. *Movies on TV*. New York: Bantam Books, 1983.
Shain, Sam, "Movies Ruling Television's Roost," *Motion Picture Exhibitor*, October 18, 1967, pp. 8, 19.
Spilker, Eric, "The Movies You Don't See on Television," *TV Guide*, April 9, 1966, pp. 6–8.

FILM SUPPLY COMPANY OF AMERICA. See MOTION PICTURE DISTRIBUTING AND SALES COMPANY

FILMUSIC COMPANY. Filmusic Company was formed in 1918 to produce music rolls that could be synchronously connected to a motion picture projector. A demonstration in Los Angeles of the apparatus, arranged under the auspices of Jesse L. Lasky, Cecil B. DeMille, Thomas H. Ince, H. D. Davis, Robert Brunton, Reginald Barker, and Raymond B. West, attracted 600 people. An electric device called a "synchron-o-meter" kept the music in sync with the picture, and two rolls of music were required for each reel of film. Filmusic had a factory at 1729 Highland Avenue in Hollywood, where it produced master rolls from which copies were produced. It was claimed that the Filmusic rolls could be played on any mechanical musical instrument. The invention won two gold medals at the 1915 Panama Pacific Exposition. C. P. Bradshaw was president and general manager of Filmusic, and W. A. Bishop was director of musical production.

BIBLIOGRAPHY
"Filmusic Company Makes Its Bow," *The Moving Picture World*, June 8, 1918, p. 1420.

FILMWAYS, INC. See ORION PICTURES CORPORATION

FINE ARTS CORPORATION. Fine Arts Corporation came into existence on September 4, 1915, when Harry E. Aitken announced that the films to be supervised by D. W. Griffith for release by Aitken's Triangle Film Corporation* would be known as Fine Arts productions. The Fine Arts Corporation studios were located at 4500 Sunset Boulevard in Hollywood, a site which had previously been designated as the Reliance-Majestic Studios and from which D. W. Griffith had directed *The Birth of a Nation*. The company also operated an East Coast studio—formerly the Reliance Studios—at 537 Riverdale Avenue in Yonkers.

Players under contract to Fine Arts included Douglas Fairbanks, DeWolf Hopper, Lillian and Dorothy Gish, Margery Wilson, Mae Marsh, Robert Harron, Elmer Clifton, Wilfred Lucas, and Owen Moore. Directors included Eddie Dillon, W. Christy Cabanne, Paul Powell, Lloyd Ingraham, Jack Conway, Allan Dwan, Sidney and Chester Franklin, and John Emerson. Frank Woods was in charge of the studio. D. W. Griffith was credited as supervisor of all Fine Arts productions, but his role in most of the productions appears to have been minimal at most, as much of the time Fine Arts was in existence Griffith was shooting *Intolerance*. The first Fine Arts film was *The Lamb*, released on November 7, 1915, directed by W. Christy Cabanne and starring Douglas Fairbanks and Seena Owen.

A major event in Fine Arts history came with the signing of Sir Herbert Beerbohm Tree in 1915 to star in a film version of *Macbeth*, released in 1916, with Constance Collier as Lady Macbeth, and directed by John Emerson. When D. W. Griffith resigned from Fine Arts, in March 1917, most of the directors and players followed suit—Douglas Fairbanks had already left for Paramount*—and all future Fine Arts productions were taken over by Thomas H. Ince. The last film to be shot at the Los Angeles Fine Arts studio was *Madame Bo-Peep*, directed by Chester Withey and starring Seena Owen.

By 1921, the Fine Arts Studios had become the Arthur H. Gooden rental studios, and in the later years the complex was utilized as an annex by Columbia Pictures.*

BIBLIOGRAPHY

Duncan, Robert C., "The Fine Arts Studio," *Picture Play*, September 1916, pp. 88–94.

Slide, Anthony. *The Kindergarten of the Movies: A History of the Fine Arts Company*. Metuchen, New Jersey: Scarecrow Press, 1980.

FIRES. Because of its use of nitrate film* and because most movie sets are built of wood, the film industry has suffered more than its share of fires. The first major studio fire took place at the Thanhouser Film Corporation* studios in New Rochelle at 1:30 P.M. on January 13, 1913. The fire created so much publicity that the company produced a short film exploiting the event titled *When the Studio Burned*. The remaining sets—except for one church—on the Inceville* site were destroyed by fire in 1924. That same year, on July 8, a fire caused $175,000 worth of damage at the Hal Roach Studios* in Culver City.

A $200,000 fire took place at the 20th Century-Fox studio on January 25, 1937. Damage totaling $350,000 was caused at the Metro-Goldwyn-Mayer* backlot on November 24, 1940, when fire destroyed storage buildings which held, among other things, many of the props brought over from China for the filming of *The Good Earth* (1937). Two years later, a second fire, on October

14, 1942, caused $100,000 worth of damage at M-G-M. On July 19, 1945, fire swept part of the Universal* backlot causing $250,000 worth of damage and destroying a number of Western sets and seventy "ancient wagons and vehicles."

On May 16, 1952, a fire destroyed eight acres of sets and caused some $1.5 million worth of damage at the Warner Bros.* studio in Burbank. The studios of Samuel Goldwyn, Inc.*, were the site of a number of fires, beginning with two small ones in 1972. A $1 million fire hit the lot in May 1974, followed by a $3 million fire in December 1975, and a much smaller fire in June 1976.

The worst motion picture–related theatre fire took place at the Charity Bazaar in Paris on May 4, 1897. The 1926 edition of *Film Daily Year Book* lists some twenty film-related fires in America, which occurred between October 1924 and September 1925. The worst occurred at Fort Lee, New Jersey, where a nitrate fire claimed two lives and injured many on February 7, 1925. Silent film star Martha Mansfield was burned to death on November 20, 1923, when the dress she was wearing caught fire during the production of *The Warrens of Virginia*.

FIRST ARTISTS PRODUCTION COMPANY, LTD. First Artists Production Company, Ltd., was the first major production company to be created by film industry principals since United Artists* in 1919. It was formed by Barbra Streisand, Sidney Poitier, and Paul Newman in June 1969 as a Delaware company with production offices in both New York and Los Angeles. Steve McQueen joined the company in 1971, and a year later he was followed by Dustin Hoffman. The first president of First Artists was Patrick Kelley, followed in 1973 by Jay Kanter, in 1975 by Phil Feldman, and in 1980 by Erwin E. Holly.

Despite the favorable critical reception of the majority of First Artists films, the company never generated sufficient income for a healthy cash flow. By 1979, it was in severe financial difficulties and involved in a stormy legal suit with Dustin Hoffman. Despite reported assets of $24 million—along with 201 employees—in 1979, the company could not continue, and, in 1982, it merged with the Australian-based Mascot Industries, Inc.

Among First Artists productions were *Pocket Money* (1971), *The Getaway* (1972), *Up the Sandbox* (1972), *The Life and Times of Judge Roy Bean* (1972), *A Warm December* (1973), *Uptown Saturday Night* (1974), *The Drowning Pool* (1975), *A Star Is Born* (1976), *Straight Time* (1978), *Agatha* (1979), *The Main Event* (1979), *Tom Horn* (1980), and *An Enemy of the People* (1981).

BIBLIOGRAPHY

Hollie, Pamela G., "First Artists—Star-Crossed Child of the 1960's," *The New York Times*, December 23, 1979, p. F3.

Marks, Marlene Adler, "First Artists on the Rocks," *Los Angeles Magazine*, October 1979, pp. 180–185, 286–288.

FIRST NATIONAL PICTURES, INC. First National Pictures, Inc., was created as a circuit of independent exhibitors under the initial title of First National Exhibitors Circuit, Inc., on April 25, 1917. Thomas L. Tally and J. D. Williams were the two men responsible for its formation, and they were joined by twenty-five other founding exhibitors, including Frederick Dahnken of the Turner and Dahnken Circuit in San Francisco, Harry O. Schwalbe of Philadelphia, John H. Kunsky of Detroit, S. L. Rothapfel of New York, Nathan H. Gordon of Boston, Tom Saxe of Milwaukee, and Earl H. Hulsey of Dallas.

Because of problems involved in obtaining films from producers, the high cost of rental, block booking*, and the inferior quality of some prints, these exhibitors decided to pool their purchasing power and to obtain films directly from the stars and directors. Its original motto was "The Good Guys Get, by Getting Together." One of the first features the new circuit was able to obtain directly was the Warner Bros.* production of *My Four Years in Germany* (1918). First National's biggest coup was the signing of a million-dollar contract with Charlie Chaplin, whereby the comedian made six films for the new organization: *A Dog's Life* (1918), *Shoulder Arms* (1918), *Sunnyside* (1919), *A Day's Pleasure* (1919), *The Kid* (1920), and *The Pilgrim* (1922).

Adolph Zukor of Paramount* tried various means to cripple the First National organization, which he saw as a very real threat to his organization. The organization reformed as Associated First National Pictures Incorporated and Associated First National Theatres Incorporated. It was able to sign contracts with Norma and Constance Talmadge, Marshall Neilan, Allan Dwan, Maurice Tourneur, J. Parker Reade, Jr., Frank Borzage, and others. In 1921, First National imported the German feature *Du Barry*, retitled it *Passion*, and successfully launched it in the United States, while at the same time creating American careers for its director Ernst Lubitsch and its star Pola Negri.

By 1922, First National decided that it needed to create its own production organization and opened studios in Burbank, California. Two years later, the company took over the former American Biograph* studios in New York but, by 1926, had consolidated production on the West Coast.

In 1928, First National was acquired by Warner Bros. through the latter's obtaining control of the Stanley Company, a theatre circuit which was a majority stockholder in First National. Warner Bros. moved its studio facilities to Burbank, although as part of the acquisition agreement certain Warner Bros. films were called "First National Pictures." Warner Bros. films were later designated as First National productions well into the forties, and the First National name appeared on some Warner Bros. films as late as 1956.

BIBLIOGRAPHY

Einfeld, S. Charles, "The History of First National," *Variety*, June 25, 1930, p. 28.

"First National Exchange Armoured," *The Moving Picture World*, October 27, 1917, p. 513.

"First National Issues Handsome Booklet," *The Moving Picture World*, May 4, 1918, p. 705.

"FNEC of New York at 507 5th Ave.," *The Moving Picture World*, March 23, 1918, p. 1669.

Jobes, Gertrude. *Motion Picture Empire*. Hamden, Connecticut: Archon Books, 1966.

FISHER'S COSTUME HOUSE. See WESTERN COSTUME CO.

FITZPATRICK TRAVELTALKS. Familiarly known as "The Voice of the Globe," and with his famous phrase, "and so we say farewell," James A. Fitzpatrick (1902–1980) produced and narrated some 222 of his Traveltalks for M-G-M*, beginning with *Land of the Maharajas* in 1931 and ending with *Life on the Thames* (1950). Fitzpatrick formed Fitzpatrick Pictures in 1924 to produce short subjects* on European personalities, English poets, and American statesmen. Probably the best-known series of silent shorts which he produced was "The Music Masters," devoted to the lives of great composers, which he reissued as sound films with added musical scores.
BIBLIOGRAPHY
Fitzpatrick, James A., as told to Helen Colton, "After a Million Miles," *Holiday*, August 1946, p. 97.
Meehan, Thomas, "Those Old Movie Travelogues, or, 'As the Sun Sinks Slowly in the West, We Bid Farewell,' " *The New York Times*, Section 10, Travel and Resorts, November 28, 1971, pp. 1, 15.

FLAMINGO FILM COMPANY. The Flamingo Film Company was formed in October 1914 as the result of an alliance between the distribution company Sawyer, Inc.*, Chartered Theaters Corporation, and the stock exchange house of Gilbert Elliott & Company. Flamingo planned to produce two- and three-reel comedies and five-reel dramatic features. Fred Mace was in charge of production, and Roy McCardell and Elaine Sterne wrote for the company. Frederick Upham Adams was the president, A. H. Sawyer was the secretary, and A. H. Hallett was the vice-president and general manager. Offices were in the Meece Building at 48th Street and Broadway, New York.

Flamingo's first release was the four-reel comedy *Without Hope*, starring Marguerite Loveridge. The company released its product with Sawyer, Inc., until February 1915 when Sawyer left Flamingo and it began releasing with World Film Corporation*. In 1915, Flamingo made the farce series "The Feats of Felix" with Charles Mason, directed by J. A. Murphy and shot at the Imperial Studio on New York's East 48 Street.
BIBLIOGRAPHY
"Flamingo Company Organizes," *The Moving Picture World*, October 31, 1914, p. 618.

FLORIDA. During the formative years of the American motion picture industry, numerous location and studio sites across the country were used by the Motion Picture Patents Company* and independent production companies for the making of their films. Although the financial and distribution centers of the emerging American film business were quickly centered in New York and Chicago, a variety of economic, technological, and political factors worked to promote the diffusion of production to warm-weather areas such as Florida and California.

Even as early as the 1898 Spanish-American War, primitive newsreels were being lensed in Florida military staging areas such as Tampa. But it was surging viewer demand for more and better movies a full decade later that precipitated ongoing use of Florida locales. The box office success of Kalem's* initial "Florida Series" shot in Jacksonville and St. Augustine in the 1908–1909 season proved critical not only in encouraging Kalem to return regularly to the state but also in furthering interest in the region by other production companies.

Five basic factors worked to Florida's advantage when the state was compared with other filmmaking alternatives in the pre–First World War period:

1. Pioneer filmmakers working in the South considered the mild winter weather, lush subtropical views, high concentrations of "actinic" sunshine which reproduced well on the cumbersome orthochromatic film stocks then in use, and the static-free climate (unlike that above the northern "frost line" where films were often ruined) as pragmatic considerations favoring selection of Florida before advances in lighting made indoor studio shooting cost-effective.

2. Producers could save time and money as well as ease transport of actors, crews, and props by traveling to Florida cities such as Jacksonville, Tampa, and Miami via convenient rail and shipping connections to the Northeast.

3. Particularly in Jacksonville, inexpensive labor costs and the emergence of an ongoing local industry with cadres of trained support helped establish the state for a time as an attractive film center.

4. Land costs in Florida remained underpriced until the mid-twenties, encouraging planning for a host of movie cities modeled loosely on Universal City in California.

5. Civic leaders, local chambers of commerce, and newspapers in the state generally supported the industry and provided important liaison with moviemakers working in Florida. Unfortunately, much of this boosterism was misdirected into a number of highly speculative schemes which in the end hampered consistent efforts to retain the industry.

Prior to American entry into the First World War, Florida (like California) nevertheless underwent tremendous growth. Many leading figures ranging from D. W. Griffith to Oliver Hardy worked in Florida. As early as 1912, so many movie troupes were attracted to Jacksonville that the area became known as the "World's Winter Film Capital." Over the next few years, interest had increased to the point that more than thirty film companies operated in Jacksonville alone on a regular or semiregular basis, with other filmmakers also active throughout the state.

During the mid-teens, when disenchanted filmmakers in California threatened to move elsewhere unless high prices and governmental restrictions were lifted, business and civic leaders in Jacksonville embarked on a bold campaign to lure them to Florida. In this sense the state could be described as "a rival to Hollywood," although many of the studio organizations in Florida also maintained plants in Los Angeles and New York.

The defeat in a bitter 1917 primary election of J.E.T. Bowden, Jacksonville's mayor and a strong proponent of the motion picture industry, hampered future development of the city and state as a film colony at a time when strong leadership was needed to maintain earlier momentum. As the industry underwent restructuring and adapted to technological advances, the importance of the smaller producers commonly attracted to Florida declined proportionately. This further undercut efforts to build Florida and marks the clear rise of Hollywood as the preeminent American and world motion picture center. Other factors also worked to close many local studios:

1. Failures among the former Motion Picture Patents Company member firms (which had played an important early role in making Jacksonville a vibrant film center) cost the city a stable core of facilities formerly contributing hundreds of thousands of dollars annually to the community.

2. Unexpected eastern coal shortages shut down many businesses and hurt the industry.

3. Decline of the two-reel comedy from a staple to lesser importance on playbills undercut local production.

4. Imposition of a British War Tax closed foreign markets important to some of Florida's more marginal producers.

5. Unwillingness of local banks to play much of a role in the financing of pictures limited development, unlike California where the Bank of Italy (later Bank of America) led in underwriting the industry.

6. Price gouging by Florida merchants irritated producers.

7. A deadly post–First World War influenza epidemic nationally closed theatres and bankrupted many filmmakers dependent on continuous cash flow.

8. Compromise tax, zoning, and social agreements made in Los Angeles ended talk of moving to a new "movie mecca" until frictions resurfaced in the depression.

Unlike California, Florida's indigenous film industry remained diffuse and without centralization (particularly after the fall of Jacksonville). The cities in the state were in effect competing against each other as they were against California. None of the widely advertised studio developments of the twenties, such as Miami Studios and Sun City, were able to break out from this parochialism and become an important national force.

Contributing to the failure was the lack of an assured marketing outlet for most of the independently produced films made in Florida once the major chains were bought up by the big studios, as well as the changing conditions wrought by the industry's conversion to sound at the end of the decade. Innovative approaches such as a location service proposed in the twenties by self-styled movie promoter Harry A. Kelly for a time received widespread trade comment and support, but the unwillingness of Floridians to provide long-term assistance to legitimate enterprises ultimately contributed to the image of unprofessionalism which still continues (unfairly) to haunt the state. Thus, Florida remained dependent on imported outside producing organizations as the source of its movie base, rather than successfully creating a genuine alternative to Hollywood.

During the worst years of the depression, the state moved to adopt tax credits for filmmakers establishing local studios. Even though literally thousands of pictures—many of them excellent—have been shot in-state, the history of Florida as a film center from the late teens through the forties is essentially a dreary story of stock fraud, studio failure, and overoptimistic hopes. Buster Keaton, for example, was persuaded to work in St. Petersburg for an independent production company called Sun Haven Studios, which had earlier produced three quickie films. Despite Keaton's initial enthusiasm (he even formed his own Florida production organization called the Flamingo Film Company), the former silent star succumbed to heat and insect swarms before aborting the project. Several important film companies did set up shop, the most notable being the (Dave and Max) Fleischer Studios which relocated in Miami in the late thirties after a bitter labor strike in New York threatened to cripple their output. Their Florida-made *Mr. Bug Goes to Town* (1941, also known as *Hoppity Goes to Town*) is the first full-length animated film based on an original story.

Throughout the forties and fifties, the formula of palms, cypresses, beaches, and ocean—aided by sporadic promotional efforts endorsed by new gubernatorial administrations—continued to attract films ranging from *Moon Over Miami* (1941) to *Creature from the Black Lagoon* (1954). By the sixties, the local industry had begun rebuilding with the aid of television. Jackie Gleason moved his show to Miami Beach and others followed. Series such as "Surfside 6" (ABC, 1960–1962); "Miami Undercover" (syndicated, 1961); "Tallahassee 7000," with Walter Matthau in the leading role as a Florida sheriff's investigator (syndicated, 1961); "Flipper" (NBC, 1964–1968); "I Dream of Jeannie" (1965–1970); "Gentle Ben" (CBS, 1967–1969); "Caribe" (ABC, 1975); and "Miami Vice" (NBC, 1984–) all helped reestablish a reliable film-television base.

Recognizing previous deficiencies, in 1974, the legislature finally approved funding for a Florida Motion Picture and Television Bureau (with a 1985 budget of $500,000). For more than a decade, the office has acted to promote Florida and serve industry needs by providing information, cutting red tape, scouting locations, holding down fees, and coordinating movie and television productions with local governments. Both Metro Dade (Greater Miami) and Jacksonville now have similar bureaus. Florida also is a right-to-work state ("lower wages") and boasts relatively inexpensive hotels. At the same time, local unions streamlined their contracts and aggressively promoted their expertise. These public efforts have begun to prove themselves effective.

More needs to be done to educate local business leaders to the importance of film-television work and industry figures about the state's capabilities. Unfortunately, Florida's reputation is still tarnished as a "get-rich-quick," fly-by-night fraud center—particularly once stories surfaced about movie money-laundering schemes funded by investors linked to alleged cocaine, heroin, and marijuana "drug" bankers as with *Scarface* (1983). Pornography is also a factor—classics such as *Deep Throat* (1972) and *Devil in Miss Jones* (1973) opted for South

Florida locales and, in the eighties, FBI investigators reportedly tied local organized crime figures to that aspect of the industry.

These negative images can be overcome. What is still lacking is readily available legitimate local financing, plus a solid infrastructure of producers, directors, writers, editors, and other technical support workers. While many filmmakers make a living in-state, most major motion pictures and television shows continue to be shot with out-of-state crews and produced by non-Florida investors. Changes in federal tax shelter regulations undercut some film packages. Bob Clark, producer of the popular *Porky's* movie series, for example, is a native of Broward County but was forced to go to Canada to get financing for investors who tripled their money. Even though some excellent lab facilities exist, almost no post-production feature work is done in-state. Daily footage shot in Florida is usually sent for processing and editing to California or New York. In-state industry leaders want to encourage more all-Florida productions with locally written scripts, financing, locales, talent, post-production work, and distribution.

While all is not necessarily rosy, Florida's film industry today is once again undergoing a surge. The state vies with Texas in ranking third in total film/video production. Many big-budget films, such as *Cocoon* (1985), continue to be made on location in the state. Miami is also developing a reputation as a Latin film center with a number of pictures in Spanish already produced there. In combined economic terms, this means that millions of dollars annually enter Florida's economy directly and indirectly from production of theatrical and made-for-television features, television commercials (up to 600 a year), series program episodes and specials, documentaries, and sponsored business films. Gross budgets in 1984 totaled $187 million for thirty-five major and a number of lesser Florida shoots, compared to only $12.5 million in 1974.

Thus, the future looks positive. Professional organizations are working with the Motion Picture and Television Bureau in organizing seminars, sponsoring the state's $158,000 film student internship program, and supporting technical film and television education at colleges such as Florida State University. Burt Reynolds (*Stick*, 1985) is co-financing with the legislature and local citizens the construction of a $9.5 million stage and video production center called The Theatre, Inc., in Sarasota. Walt Disney* and M-G-M* recently announced plans to build a joint $300 million studio and tourist attraction adjacent to Disney World in Orlando. MCA* has also said it plans to erect a similar complex in the area. Whether visionary Floridians such as Governor Bob Graham ever reach their goal of supplanting Hollywood to make Florida "the Number One site for filmmaking in the nation by the year 2000" is questionable. But there is no doubt that by shooting for the stars, Florida is once again an important contemporary motion picture and television industry force.

BIBLIOGRAPHY

Craig, James C., "Jacksonville—World Film Capital," *Papers of the Jacksonville Historical Society*, vol. III, 1954, pp. 117–127.
Florida Golden Pages. North Miami Beach, Florida: Florida Golden Pages, 1978 to present.

Gill, Samuel A. *Stills Identification List of Photographs Relating to the Early Moving Picture Production, Jacksonville, Florida*. Tallahassee, Florida: Florida State Photographic Archives, 1974.

Kimball, Burt. *The Development of the Television Film Industry in Dade County, Florida*. Masters Thesis, University of Florida, 1969.

Nelson, Richard Alan, "Movie Mecca of the South: Jacksonville, Florida, as an Early Rival to Hollywood," *Journal of Popular Film and Television*, vol. VIII, no. 3, Fall 1980, pp. 38–51.

———. *Florida and the American Motion Picture Industry, 1898–1980*. New York: Garland, 1983.

———, "Palm Trees, Public Relations, and Promoters: Boosting Southeast Florida as a Motion Picture Empire, 1910–1930," *Florida Historical Quarterly*, vol. LXI, no. 4, April 1983, pp. 383–403.

———, "Before Laurel: Oliver Hardy and the Vim Comedy Company, A Studio Biography," in Bruce A. Austin, editor, *Current Research in Film: Audience, Economics and Law*. Norwood, New Jersey: Ablex, 1986.

Reed, Julia, "Shooting for the Stars—Some Players Missing in Florida Film-Making Setting," *Orlando Sentinel*, "Central Florida Business" Section, July 8–14, 1985, pp. 1, 12–13.

FLUSHING, NEW YORK. See KNICKERBOCKER STAR FEATURES

FLYING A. See AMERICAN FILM MANUFACTURING COMPANY

FORDART PRODUCTIONS. Fordart Productions was formed by Francis Ford (1882–1953), in April 1918, to produce films for the states rights* market. *Berlin via America* was the first film which it produced. The company had offices in New York and leased space at the Christie Studios* in Hollywood. Fordart planned to make six features a year plus a series of one- and two-reel shorts. Edna Emerson was Ford's leading lady and Elsie Van Name his scenario writer.

FOREIGN PRESS ASSOCIATION OF HOLLYWOOD. See HOLLYWOOD FOREIGN PRESS ASSOCIATION, INC.

FORT DU LAC, WISCONSIN. See EBONY PICTURES CORPORATION

FORT LEE. With its close proximity to New York City, Fort Lee, New Jersey, offered a variety of scenery for early filmmakers, notably the Palisades on the Hudson River and the many types of country settings. D. W. Griffith made a number of films in the neighborhood for the American Biograph Company*. Indeed, by 1910, one trade paper was complaining of the relentless use by filmmakers of the "Jersey scenery." In the early teens, the town became a major center of filmmaking as various studios were built: Champion, Eclair*, Willat, Peerless/World, Paragon, and Solax*. These studios were utilized by many of the major producers, including William Fox*, Metro Pictures Corporation*, and

Goldwyn*. Among the stars who worked at the Fort Lee studios on a regular basis were Theda Bara, Ethel Barrymore, Alice Brady, June Caprice, Ethel Clayton, Madge Evans, Geraldine Farrar, Elsie Ferguson, Pauline Frederick, Madge Kennedy, Mabel Normand, Olga Petrova, Pearl White, and Clara Kimball Young.

BIBLIOGRAPHY

Altomara, Rita Ecke. *Hollywood on the Palisades*. New York: Garland, 1983.
Spehr, Paul C. *The Movies Begin*. Newark, New Jersey: The Newark Museum, 1977.

FOUR STAR PRODUCTIONS. See ARTCO PRODUCTIONS, INC.

FOX CARTHAY CIRCLE THEATRE. See CARTHAY CIRCLE THEATRE

FOX FILM CORPORATION. Although the Fox Film Corporation was officially incorporated on February 1, 1915, the company's roots stretch back to 1904. In that year, William Fox (1879–1952), a New York City exhibitor who bought his first theatre in 1903, began the Greater New York Film Rental Company to distribute films. The company prospered, and, after surviving a legal battle with the General Film Company (settled in Fox's favor in 1912), William Fox decided to go into production and changed the name of his company in 1913 to Box Office Attractions Film Rental Company. At first, Fox used the Balboa Amusement Producing Company* to supply the films but soon began to produce films by himself, beginning with his first feature, *Life's Shop Window*, in 1914. In 1915, the name of the company was changed to represent its increased activities.

In 1914, the company made its first film in Los Angeles and, in 1915, decided to establish a permanent studio in California. Fox leased the old Selig* studio in Edendale until its own studio, at Sunset Boulevard and Western Avenue, opened in 1916. In 1919, offices were opened in Paris, Rome, Berlin, London, and Dublin to distribute Fox films and to aid in the making of newsreels (as *Fox News* was established that same year).

Buoyed by profits and the need to compete with Adolph Zukor's Paramount Pictures* and the other major studios, the company began to expand in several ways during the twenties. In 1924, Fox owned twenty-four theatres in New York City, New Jersey, Chicago, Oakland, and Detroit. In 1925, West Coast Theatres was acquired and the Fox Theatre Corporation was incorporated in November 1925. In 1927, the Roxy Theatre* was purchased by William Fox, and, in March 1929, he acquired majority control of Loew's, Inc., for some $50 million.

At the same time the company was acquiring theatres, it was also building a new studio in Los Angeles. Construction began on the Westwood Studio (now part of Century City) in 1924, and it was officially dedicated in October 1928. At the same time, the company was making plans for the introduction of sound motion pictures. In July 1925, the rights to the Case-Sponable system were purchased and the system renamed Movietone. This system was later buttressed by the purchase, in July 1927, of the U.S. rights to the German Tri-Ergon patents.

In order to pay for this expansion and experimentation, Fox Film Corporation went public in 1925 with an offering of one million shares. This did not provide enough money for all the acquisitions that William Fox wanted to make, and so, in 1929, in order to purchase Loew's, Inc., he borrowed over $40 million from AT&T, two banks, and his New York investment house, Halsey, Stuart & Co. Loew's was bought, but antitrust questions raised by the government prevented Fox from taking control of the company. Additionally, William Fox was injured in an automobile accident in July 1929, and by the time he had recovered from his injuries the stock market had started to slide and the loans he had taken out to purchase Loew's were becoming due. With no one willing to loan him any money, William Fox was forced out of the company in 1930 by AT&T and Halsey, Stuart & Co. The new president was Harley Clarke, president of General Theatres Equipment Corporation, which took control of Fox in April 1930.

Under Clarke's leadership the company began to lose a great deal of money. From a profit of $8 million in 1930, the company reported losses of $2 million in 1931 and $9.5 million in 1932. After a year as president, Harley Clarke was followed by Edward R. Tinker, who, also after only one year, was followed by Sidney R. Kent. In March 1933, a stockholder filed suit to have the company put into receivership, and, on April 1, 1933, the company was reorganized. Finances did not improve very much and, on May 29, 1935, a merger with Twentieth Century Pictures* was announced. On August 15, 1935, the name of the company was officially changed to 20th Century-Fox Film Corporation*.

BIBLIOGRAPHY

Allvine, Glendon. *The Greatest Fox of Them All*. New York: Lyle Stuart, 1969.
Sinclair, Upton. *Upton Sinclair Presents William Fox*. Los Angeles: The Author, 1933.
Thomas, Tony, and Aubrey Solomon. *The Films of 20th Century-Fox*. Secaucus, New Jersey: Citadel Press, 1979.

RESOURCES

Film: Museum of Modern Art; UCLA Film Archives.
Still Photographs: University of California at Los Angeles.

FOX GRANDEUR. See GRANDEUR

FOX-MOVIETONE NEWS. See NEWSREELS

FOX NEWS. See NEWSREELS

FOX WEST COAST THEATRES CORPORATION. The best known of the 20th Century-Fox–owned theatre chains dating back to the twenties, Fox West Coast Theatres Corporation was a subsidiary of National Theatres Corporation. Other subsidiaries of National Theatres Corporation (which was, in turn, a wholly owned subsidiary of 20th Century-Fox*) were Evergreen State Amusement Corporation, Fox Intermountain Theatres, Fox Michigan Corporation, Fox Midwest Amusement Corporation, Fox Philadelphia Building, Inc., and Fox Wisconsin Amusement Corporation. Following the consent decree*, the 549 theatres owned by National Theatres Corporation in 1951 were transferred to the ownership of the newly formed National Theatres, Inc.

FRANK A. KEENEY PICTURES CORPORATION. Frank A. Keeney, formerly a theatrical promoter and owner of a string of vaudeville houses in various eastern cities, was the head and sole financial backer for Frank A. Keeney Pictures Corporation, which was founded in January 1918 to produce films starring Catherine Calvert. James Kirkwood was the director and Benjamin S. Kutler the scenario editor. It used the Pathé* studios in the Bronx at Park Avenue and 134 Street, and its offices were in the Putnam Building at 1493 Broadway. The William L. Sherry Service* distributed its films, the first of which was *A Romance of the Underworld*.
BIBLIOGRAPHY
"Frank A. Keeney," *The Moving Picture World*, January 12, 1918, p. 247.

FRAZEE FILMS PRODUCTIONS. Edwin A. Frazee, formerly a director with Keystone and Fox*, formed Frazee Films Productions in July 1918 to exploit the trick methods of cinematography that he had developed and perfected, including underwater photography at low cost on a stage. Frazee had a studio in the Boyle Heights section of Los Angeles, and his first film, *The Haunted House*, was distributed by Ernest Shipman.

FREDERICK DOUGLASS FILM COMPANY. The Frederick Douglass Film Company, an early black production company located in Jersey City, New Jersey, was created to present blacks in positive, successful roles, in contrast to the depictions of them in *The Birth of a Nation*. Traverse Sprague was the company's director. Its first production, *The Colored American Winning His Suit*, which received its premiere in Jersey City on July 14, 1916, in six reels, later cut to four, was criticized for its lack of technical expertise. It produced the three-reel *The Scapegoat* in 1917, from a story by Paul Lawrence Dunbar, and a documentary about black soldiers during the First World War, but it soon ended operations because of financial problems and inability to get bookings for its films.

FRENCH RESEARCH FOUNDATION. The French Research Foundation was founded in Hollywood by actor Charles Boyer (1897–1978). It opened on October 15, 1940, to provide film producers with research materials and documentation for features dealing with the work of the French "underground" during the Second World War. Later, it served as a research center for anyone in the film industry requiring general information on France and French customs. The Foundation received its first screen credit on the 1948 Lewis Milestone production of *Arch of Triumph*.

FROHMAN AMUSEMENT CORPORATION. Gustave Frohman, the brother of stage impresarios Daniel and Charles Frohman, followed his brothers into the world of film when he established the Frohman Amusement Corporation, in November 1914, with William L. Sherrill and S. H. Boynton. Its policy was to produce only original scenarios, preferably non-slapstick comedies. George Irving was the director, Ralph Dean the technical director, Jacques Monteron the cameraman, and Frank Norcross the manager of the studio which the company leased and which had formerly belonged to the Gene Gauntier Players. Its first film was *The Fairy and the Waif*, starring Mary Miles Minter. Frohman distributed through World Film Corporation*.

By October 1916, Frohman himself was no longer involved in the company, and Sherrill became its president. The company went out of business in 1920.

"FRONTIER" BRAND. See ST. LOUIS MOTION PICTURE COMPANY

FRONTIER FILMS. Frontier Films was formed in March 1937 as a nonprofit production company, with its origins in the Nykino Collective and the New York branch of the National Film and Photo League*. It was concerned with the production of documentaries* with a left-wing viewpoint, and its original members included Paul Strand, Leo Hurwitz, Ralph Steiner, Willard Van Dyke, Lionel Berman, Ben Maddow, Sidney Meyers, Irving Lerner, and Jay Leyda. The organization's films were funded by liberal and left-wing sympathizers. Its best-known production was the feature-length *Native Land* (1942); its other films were *Heart of Spain* (1937), *China Strikes Back* (1937), *People of the Cumberland* (1938), *Return to Life* (1938), *History and Romance of Transportation* (1939), and *White Flood* (1940).

Ralph Steiner and Willard Van Dyke left Frontier Films early in 1938 to form American Documentary Films, which produced the classic documentary *The City* (1939). Frontier Films was disbanded in 1941, and, as Russell Campbell notes in *Cinema Strikes Back*, "The Depression decade was over, and it would be many years before committed, left-wing filmmaking collectives like Frontier Films would be seen again in America."

BIBLIOGRAPHY

Alexander, William, "Frontier Films, 1936–1941: The Aesthetics of Impact," *Cinema Journal*, vol. XV, no. 1, Fall 1975, pp. 16–28.

Campbell, Russell. *Cinema Strikes Back*. Ann Arbor, Michigan: UMI Research Press, 1982.

FUJIYAMA FEATURE FILM COMPANY. The Fujiyama Feature Film Company was formed in Los Angeles, in October 1916, to produce a series of Japanese films for release in the United States. It planned to build a studio in Redlands, California, and to send a company of actors to film in Japan. Mrs. E. L. Greer was the head of the company.

G

THE GANGSTER FILM. A very American film genre, the gangster film is generally dated from 1912 when D. W. Griffith directed *Musketeers of Pig Alley*. The Modern Story of Griffith's *Intolerance* (1916) depicted gangsterism at work in an American city. Arguably the best silent film with a gangster theme was Josef von Sternberg's *Underworld* (1927), starring George Bancroft as a mobster and Evelyn Brent as his moll. The first all-talking Vitaphone* feature, *Lights of New York* (1928) introduced many of the cliches that have come to be associated with the genre; Warner Bros.*, which produced the feature, became the studio most associated with the gangster film in the thirties and forties, through films such as *The Public Enemy* (1931), *Little Caesar* (1931), *G-Men* (1935), *The Petrified Forest* (1936), *Angels with Dirty Faces* (1938), *The Roaring Twenties* (1939), *Key Largo* (1948), and *White Heat* (1949). Many of these films featured Edward G. Robinson, James Cagney, and Humphrey Bogart, the studio's best-known exponents of the gangster genre. Other major gangster melodramas of the period included Rouben Mamoulian's *City Streets* (1931) and Howard Hawks' *Scarface: The Shame of a Nation* (1932).

Gangsters have been shown in a favorable light in Frank Capra's *Lady for a Day* (1933) and *Pocketful of Miracles* (1961). The musical *Guys and Dolls* (1955) was concerned with gangsters. The British have tried to emulate the American gangster feature with *No Orchids for Miss Blandish* (1948), *Night and the City* (1950), and *The Lavender Hill Mob* (1950).

Real-life gangsters have been portrayed in many films. Mickey Rooney played Baby Face Nelson in the 1957 film of the same title. Al Capone was portrayed by Rod Steiger in the 1959 film of the same name, by Neville Brand in *The George Raft Story* (1961) and in the television series "The Untouchables," by Jason Robards in *The St. Valentine's Day Massacre* (1967), and by Ben Gazzara in *Capone* (1975). John Ericson played "Pretty Boy" Floyd in the 1959 film of that title; Fabian played the gangster in *A Bullet for Pretty Boy* (1970). Ma Barker was portrayed by Shelley Winters in *Bloody Mama* (1970). Bonnie Parker and Clyde Barrow were played by Dorothy Provine and Jack Hogan in *The*

Bonnie Parker Story (1958) and by Faye Dunaway and Warren Beatty in *Bonnie and Clyde* (1967). Dillinger was portrayed by Lawrence Tierney in *Dillinger* (1945), by Nick Adams in *Young Dillinger* (1965), and by Warren Oates in *Dillinger* (1973). Charles Bronson was *Machine Gun Kelly* (1958) and Ray Danton played the title role in *The Rise and Fall of Legs Diamond* (1959).

More recent gangster films have concentrated on the Mafia, notably in Francis Ford Coppola's *The Godfather* (1972) and *The Godfather Part II* (1974), as well as in *The Sicilian Connection* (1973) and *Mafia Junction* (1973). Coppola's *The Cotton Club* (1984) indicates that the gangster film is far from dead in the American cinema.

BIBLIOGRAPHY

Lee, Raymond, and B. C. Van Hecke. *Gangsters and Hoodlums*. New York: A. S. Barnes, 1971.

McArthur, Colin. *Underworld U.S.A.* New York: Viking Press, 1972.

Parish, James Robert, and Michael R. Pitts. *The Great Gangster Pictures*. Metuchen, New Jersey: Scarecrow Press, 1976.

Rosow, Eugene. *Born to Lose*. New York: Oxford University Press, 1978.

THE GARDEN OF ALLAH. One of the best-known hotels among many of the literary and intellectual film communities, the Garden of Allah was a favorite of F. Scott Fitzgerald, Dorothy Parker, Robert Benchley, Errol Flynn, Orson Welles, and others. The modern Hollywood equivalent is the Chateau Marmont, across Sunset Boulevard and slightly to the west of the site of the Garden of Allah, which opened in 1929 as an apartment hotel.

The Garden of Allah was a hotel with twenty-five bungalows, which had formerly been the home of Alla Nazimova, at 8152 Sunset Boulevard in Hollywood. The Garden of Allah opened in January 1927 and was demolished in 1959. A bank presently occupies the site, but there is a miniature of the Garden of Allah on display in its forecourt. The Garden of Allah was recreated by Herman Wouk, as Rainbow's End, in his novel *Youngblood Hawke*.

BIBLIOGRAPHY

Graham, Sheilah. *The Garden of Allah*. New York: Crown, 1970.

Link, Tom, "The Last Days of Hollywood's Rowdiest Watering Hole," *Los Angeles*, August 1979, pp. 100–103.

GARSON STUDIOS. See EQUITY PICTURES CORPORATION

GASPARCOLOR. A three-color process, Gasparcolor required the printing of the three negatives directly in their appropriate colors. The colored emulsions were coated on the film, with the magenta and yellow layers on one side and the blue-green layer on the other. Unlike Technicolor*, Gasparcolor prints could be developed at any standard black-and-white laboratory. Developed prior to the Second World War in Europe by Dr. Bela Gaspar, the color system became known to American audiences through George Pal's Puppetoons*. In 1941,

Colorfilm Laboratory in Burbank began the processing of Gasparcolor in the United States, and, in 1955, Eastman Kodak* obtained a license to utilize Gasparcolor patent nos. 2,344,084 and 2,312, 543.

BIBLIOGRAPHY

Klein, Adrian, "The Gasparcolor Process," *The Journal of the Association of Cine-Technicians*, February 1936, pp. 83–84.

Wyckoff, Alvin, "Gasparcolor Comes to Hollywood," *American Cinematographer*, November 1941, pp. 510–511.

THE GAUMONT ANIMATED WEEKLY. See NEWSREELS

GAUMONT COMPANY. The American branch of the Gaumont Company, which brought over films made by the parent company in France, released its first film made in the United States, *The Faithful Servitor*, on September 15, 1913. Herbert Blaché was at the time Gaumont's vice-president and American representative. It distributed through the Exclusive Supply Corporation*, of which Blaché was president. In January 1915, Gaumont began producing one-reel comedies under the "Empress" brand, featuring Marion Swayne, Joseph Levering, and Arthur Hill and released through the United Film Service.

By October 1915, Gaumont was releasing its entire output with the Mutual Film Corporation*. At that time, it produced Rialto Star Features and Casino Star Comedies in Flushing, New York, and Jacksonville, Florida. Directors for Gaumont included Richard Garrick, William F. Haddock, and Edwin Middleton. In April 1918, after a period of inactivity, Gaumont began to produce features for the states rights* market at its Flushing studio.

BIBLIOGRAPHY

"First American Gaumont," *The New York Dramatic Mirror*, September 10, 1913, p. 27.

"Foreign Films in the American Market," *The New York Dramatic Mirror*, February 12, 1913, p. 29.

GAYETY COMEDIES, INC. A minor production company, active in 1919 and 1920, Gayety Comedies, Inc., produced short subjects featuring comedian George Ovey. It was based in Los Angeles.

G.C.C. THEATRES, INC. See GENERAL CINEMA CORPORATION

GENERAL CINEMA CORPORATION. General Cinema Corporation controls some 1,134 theatre screens, chiefly in suburban shopping malls. It is also involved in various diversified operations, notably as the country's largest independent bottler of Pepsi-Cola products. Its revenue in 1984 was $916 million.

The corporation was founded in 1922 by Philip Smith, a former Pathé* film salesman, with the acquisition of the National Theatre in Boston. The economic depression forced Smith to dispose of most of the more than twenty theatres he controlled in the twenties, and, by 1933, he had only three theatres in his company. However, Smith took the major step of becoming involved in the drive-in theatre* movement and by the outbreak of the Second World War controlled more than half of the drive-in theatres operational in the United States. In 1947, the company began moving away from drive-in theatres and into the acquisition of theatres in shopping malls. In 1960, the company made its first public offering and changed its name from General Drive-In Corporation to General Cinema Corporation. Philip Smith died in 1961, and the corporation was taken over by his son, Richard A. Smith, who serves as chief executive officer. General Cinema Corporation tried, unsuccessfully, to become involved in film production in 1979, when it attempted to acquire 20 percent of the stock of Columbia Pictures*. The corporation's theatre holdings are operated by a subdivision called G.C.C. Theatres, Inc.

Address: G.C.C. Theatres, Inc., 27 Boylston Street, Chestnut Hill, Mass. 02167.

BIBLIOGRAPHY

Harris, Kathryn, "General Cinema More Wall St. Than Hollywood," *Los Angeles Times*, Business Section, August 11, 1985, pp. 1, 5–6.

GENERAL FILM COMPANY. See MOTION PICTURE PATENTS COMPANY

GENERAL SERVICE STUDIOS. See HOLLYWOOD GENERAL STUDIOS

GEORGE KLEINE OPTICAL COMPANY. A manufacturer of optical equipment, lenses, cameras, projectors, and films, the George Kleine Optical Company was incorporated in Chicago in 1907. It was founded by George Kleine (1864–1931). Kleine (pronounced Cline-ee) was one of the founders of the Kalem Company* and of the Motion Picture Patents Company*; in 1910, he sold his company to the General Film Company arm of the Patents Company but retained the majority of the stock in the company, of which he was vice-president and later president.

George Kleine was best known for the importation of foreign films, such as *Quo Vadis*, *Othello*, and *The Last Days of Pompeii*, all of which were brought from Italy in 1913. In 1919, he released *Deliverance*, starring Helen Keller in her only feature-film appearance. From 1919 onward, Kleine operated as an individual rather than a company. In the early twenties he served as chairman of the board of Ritz-Carlton Pictures and was active in the field of educational films.

BIBLIOGRAPHY

Horwitz, Rita, and Harriet Harrison. *The George Kleine Collection of Early Motion Pictures in the Library of Congress: A Catalog*. Washington, D.C.: Library of Congress, 1980.

RESOURCES

Films and Papers: Library of Congress.

GLASS SHOT. Glass shot is the term used to describe a type of special effect* whereby a portion of a scene is painted on glass. Years ago, the glass was positioned in front of the camera and the sequence was filmed with the scene on the glass becoming part of the overall shot. Today, the painting on glass is done following the live-action scene in the studio but utilizing the same negative. Theoretically, it is impossible to tell where the live-action scene and the glass shot join. By utilizing a scene painted on glass, the necessity of building expensive sets is eliminated. A related term is matte shot, for which a portion of the frame is matted out to permit the later insertion of another shot.

BIBLIOGRAPHY

Levitan, Eli L. *An Alphabetical Guide to Motion Picture, Television and Videotape Production.* New York: McGraw-Hill, 1970.

GLEN ALDEN CORP. See RKO THEATRES CORPORATION and STANLEY WARNER CORPORATION

GLENDALE, CALIFORNIA. See LIBERTY MOTION PICTURE COMPANY

GLENDALE, LONG ISLAND. See MIRROR FILMS, INC.

GLEN GLENN SOUND COMPANY, INC. A familiar name in all areas of sound recording for both film and television, Glen Glenn Sound Company, Inc., was founded in 1937 by Harry Eckles and Glen Glenn (1908–1960). The company, which is now a division of Republic Corporation, moved to a new sound center in 1983; this new center has served as post-production headquarters for such major features as *Star Trek—The Motion Picture*, *Raiders of the Lost Ark*, *Indiana Jones and the Temple of Doom*, *Under the Volcano*, and *Purple Rain*.

Address: 900 North Seward Street, Hollywood, Calif. 90038.

BIBLIOGRAPHY

"Glen Glenn a 'Resounding' Success Brought Up to Date," *On Location*, June 1985, pp. 184–185.

GLOBE PRODUCTIONS. See SOUNDIES

"GOLD DIGGERS" SERIES. The "Gold Diggers" series was Warner Bros.* most popular group of musicals* in the thirties. Warner Bros. produced the first film, titled simply *The Gold Diggers*, in 1923; it was based on the 1919 Avery Hopwood play of the same title, as was Warner Bros. 1929 remake, titled *Gold Diggers of Broadway*.

There were three musicals in the thirties: *The Gold Diggers of 1933*, *The Gold Diggers of 1935*, and *The Gold Diggers of 1937*. All three starred Dick Powell and are best remembered for their musical numbers staged by Busby Berkeley. Additionally, Warner Bros. filmed *Gold Diggers in Paris* (1938), starring Rudy Vallee and again with musical numbers by Busby Berkeley.

GOLDEN STATE MOTION PICTURE COMPANY OF CALIFORNIA.

The Golden State Motion Picture Company of California was a production company of 1913. James K. Hackett, after starring in *The Prisoner of Zenda* for the Famous Players Film Company, directed himself as Jean Val Jean in *The Bishop's Candlesticks* for Golden State. Ernest Shipman and H. M. Russell were associated with the company. In July 1913, it produced *One Hundred Years of Mormonism* for the states rights* market.

BIBLIOGRAPHY

"Another Hackett Film," *The New York Dramatic Mirror*, July 2, 1913, p. 26.

GOLDWYN PICTURES CORPORATION.

Goldwyn Pictures Corporation was the first production company to bear the name of Samuel Goldwyn (1882–1974), although he had earlier been associated with the Jesse L. Lasky Motion Picture Company (of which he was treasurer and general manager). It was founded in December 1916 by Samuel Goldfish and Edgar and Archibald Selwyn; Goldwyn adopted the name of the company as his own in 1918. The Goldwyn Corporation continued the concept introduced earlier by Adolph Zukor of utilizing famous names from the theatrical world for its productions. Placed under contract were playwrights such as Bayard Veiller, Avery Hopwood, and Margaret Mayo; actresses such as Madge Kennedy, Maxine Elliott, and Jane Cowl; and opera singers Mary Garden and Geraldine Farrar. Of the group only Farrar and Kennedy proved to have any popularity with filmgoers, as the former had already shown when she was under contract to Famous Players-Lasky. One other stage personality who began what was to be a successful film career under Goldwyn was Will Rogers.

Realizing the need for recognized film personalities, Goldwyn placed under contract Mabel Normand and Mae Marsh, but neither proved particularly successful under the producer's guidance. Equally unsuccessful was Eminent Authors Pictures, Inc., introduced by Goldwyn in 1919, whereby popular writers, including Rex Beach, Gertrude Atherton, Gouverneur Morris, Rupert Hughes, and Mary Roberts Rinehart, would adapt their works for the screen. Because the eminent authors resolutely refused to understand film technique, the experiment proved a failure, although it did lead to Goldwyn's producing one superior feature, *The Penalty* (1920), starring Lon Chaney and based on a story by Gouverneur Morris.

In 1922, Goldwyn was removed as president of his company by a vote of the stockholders. Goldwyn Pictures Corporation merged with Metro Pictures Corporation* and Louis B. Mayer's independent production company to form Metro-Goldwyn-Mayer*, with Goldwyn's Culver City studios becoming the studios for the new organization. In 1924, Goldwyn formed a new company, Samuel Goldwyn, Inc.*

BIBLIOGRAPHY

Goldwyn, Sam. *Behind the Screen*. New York: George H. Doran, 1923.

"Goldwyn Gets Big Playwrights," *The Moving Picture World*, December 30, 1916, p. 1943.

"Goldwyn Pictures Enters Field," *The Moving Picture World*, December 16, 1916, p. 1627.

Hughes, Rupert, "Early Days in the Movies," *The Saturday Evening Post*, April 6, 1935, pp. 18–19, 37, 39–40, 43–44; and April 13, 1935, pp. 30–31, 118, 120–123.

"Life Inside the Goldwyn Gate," *Photoplay*, July 1922, pp. 38–39.

GOTHAM FILM COMPANY. The Gotham Film Company was incorporated on April 24, 1915, to produce and distribute its own and other companies' productions. It had a studio at 237 Lafayette Street in New York and offices at 1600 Broadway. Its first production, *The Man Who Beat Dan Dolan*, starred former lightweight boxing champion Willie Ritchie. Gotham soon contracted with Reel Photoplay Company to release its product on the Gotham program, with Reel's first production being *Love and the Pennant*, featuring baseball star Mike Donlin. Marshall W. Taggart was the president of Gotham.

"GOWER GULCH." "Gower Gulch" was the nickname given to the area at the junction of Gower Street and Sunset Boulevard in Hollywood, where "cowboys" would gather both to socialize and to look for work in the film industry of the twenties. They gathered there much as Chicanos are drawn in the eighties to the intersection of Sepulveda and Pico boulevards in Los Angeles, seeking elusive employment. At the junction of Gower and Sunset stood the Century Studios, where many "B"* Western* productions were filmed, but by the thirties most Western production was centered in the San Fernando Valley.

BIBLIOGRAPHY
Cary, Diana Serra. *The Hollywood Posse*. Boston: Houghton Mifflin, 1975.

GRANDEUR. Grandeur, also known as Fox Grandeur, was a widescreen system, utilizing 70mm* film, with a frame size 48mm by 22.5mm and a soundtrack 10mm wide. It was first exhibited at the Gaiety Theatre, New York, on September 17, 1929, with a scenic short on Niagara Falls, a Grandeur version of Fox Movietone News, and the feature *Fox Movietone Follies of 1929*. The system was developed by the Fox Film Corporation in association with Harley L. Clarke and his company, General Theatres Equipment, Inc. It was utilized for two further features, *Happy Days* (1929) and *The Big Trail* (1930), but due to the cost to theatres of installing new projectors and new screens (at a time when theatre owners had been forced to meet the cost of new sound equipment), it was not successful.

BIBLIOGRAPHY
Vischer, Peter, "Fox Grandeur Films Make New History at First Public Show," *Exhibitors Herald-World*, September 28, 1929, p. 19.

GRAND NATIONAL FILMS, INC. Grand National Films, Inc., was organized on April 16, 1936, by former Pathé* executives and with Pathé financing. Its major coup, in the summer of 1936, was the signing of James Cagney, who was involved in a contract dispute with Warner Bros.* and who starred in two films for Grand National, *Great Guy* (1936) and *Something to Sing About* (1937). The company's first president was Edward L. Alperson and its first feature was *Devil on Horseback* (1936). Grand National began operations on the RKO-Pathé lot in Culver City but, in April 1937, took over the Educational Studios lot at 7250 Santa Monica Boulevard in Hollywood.

In 1938, Grand National was the subject of bankruptcy proceedings and reorganized as Grand National Pictures, Inc., with E. W. Hammons as the new president. Following continued financial problems, the company collapsed in 1940 and its assets were auctioned off on February 28–29 and March 27, 1940. Grand National's trademark was always a clock tower with the company name on its face. It had no financial interest in the British production company, Grand National Pictures, Ltd.

BIBLIOGRAPHY
Fernett, Gene. *Poverty Row*. Satellite Beach, Florida: Coral Reef Publications, 1973.
Robison, Robert J., "A Short History of Grand National Pictures," *The Films of Yesteryear*, July 1977, entire issue.

GRAND NATIONAL PICTURES, INC. See GRAND NATIONAL FILMS, INC.

GRANTWOOD, NEW JERSEY. See LIFE PHOTO FILM CORPORATION

GRAPHIC FILM CORPORATION. After leaving Ivan Film Productions, Inc.*, which he founded and named after himself, Ivan Abramson formed a new company, Graphic Film Corporation, on December 3, 1917, and became its president and director-general. Its first production was *Moral Suicide*, starring John Mason and Anna Luther. Gail Kane and Tallulah Bankhead also appeared in Graphic films. The company, whose offices were located at 729 Seventh Avenue, New York, existed until 1922.

BIBLIOGRAPHY
"Ivan Abramson Creates Own Firm," *The Moving Picture World*, December 22, 1917, p. 1812.

GRAUMAN'S THEATRES. Sidney Patrick Grauman (1879–1950) was, undoubtedly, Hollywood's best-known showman. He was noted for the prologues which accompanied feature films at his theatres from the late teens through the mid-thirties and for the handprints and footprints of the stars in the forecourt of his Chinese Theatre.

He began his theatrical career in the Yukon in the late 1890s. Prior to the San Francisco earthquake, he had opened the Unique Theatre there, and, immediately following the earthquake and fire, he opened a tent theatre, called the Canvas Theatre. Grauman opened a number of theatres in northern California and one in New York, and, by 1915, he was hailed as "one of the liveliest exhibitors on the Pacific Coast."

Sid Grauman opened his first Los Angeles theatre, the Million Dollar, on February 1, 1918, with the William S. Hart feature, *The Silent Man*. In 1919, he acquired the Rialto Theatre, also in downtown Los Angeles, and reopened it, on November 20, 1919, with the Gloria Swanson/Cecil B. DeMille film, *Male and Female*. A third downtown theatre, the Metropolitan, opened on January 26, 1923. These three theatres were all acquired, in 1924, by Paramount*.

The first of Grauman's two Hollywood theatres, the Egyptian, opened on October 18, 1922, with the premiere of *Robin Hood*, starring Douglas Fairbanks. The Egyptian was also the site of the first dual premiere—on May 14, 1926— of the Mary Pickford vehicle, *Sparrows*, and the Douglas Fairbanks feature, *The Black Pirate*. On October 27, 1926, Hollywood was introduced to the first commercial use of sound in a feature film, at the Egyptian, with the West Coast premiere of *Don Juan*, starring John Barrymore. The Chinese Theatre, located as is the Egyptian on Hollywood Boulevard, opened on May 19, 1927, with the world premiere of Cecil B. DeMille's *King of Kings*. The current owners of the Chinese, Mann Theatres*, opened two additional, adjacent theatres, the Chinese I and II on April 12, 1979.

BIBLIOGRAPHY
Beardsley, Charles. *Hollywood's Master Showman*. New York: Cornwall Books, 1983.

GREAT AUTHORS' PICTURES, INC. Benjamin Hampton and George H. Perry formed Great Authors' Pictures, Inc., in February 1919, to produce adaptations of works by well-known authors. Its first production, *The Westerners*, was produced at the Robert Brunton Studios in Hollywood. The company made note of the fact that it would use no stars in its productions. The W. W. Hodkinson Corporation* distributed Great Authors' Pictures through Pathé exchanges*.

BIBLIOGRAPHY
"Hampton and Perry Form Great Authors' Pictures, Inc.," *The Moving Picture World*, February 22, 1919, p. 1020.

"GREATER BRAY PICTOGRAPHS." See BRAY STUDIOS, INC.

GREATER NEW YORK FILM RENTAL COMPANY. See FOX FILM CORPORATION

GREAT NORTHERN FILM COMPANY. The Great Northern Film Company, located in Copenhagen, Denmark, claimed that it was the first concern to introduce a feature-length film in the United States when it released the three-reel *Temptations of a Great City* in the early spring of 1911. O. Olsen was the president, and Ingvald C. Oes was the American representative. In 1913, its product was distributed in the United States by Universal*. Charles (Feature) Abrams was the company's American manager at that time. In 1914, it released its product through the Exclusive Supply Corporation*. In 1915, it produced a series called "Polar Bear Features," which were selected to meet the demands of the American public.

BIBLIOGRAPHY
Bergsten, Bebe. *The Great Dane and the Great Northern Film Company*. Los Angeles: Locare Research Group, 1973.

GREAT WESTERN PRODUCING COMPANY. See CENTURY COMEDIES

GREENAWAY PRODUCTIONS. See RAMPART PRODUCTIONS, INC.

GROSSES. A film's gross is the amount it accrues in rentals from individual theatres or theatre chains. A theatre's gross is the amount it accrues in box office receipts. Each year, *International Motion Picture Almanac* publishes a listing, from 1942, of U.S. box office receipts in relation to personal consumption expenditures. Each January, in its anniversary issue, *Variety* publishes a listing of the "Big Rental Films" of the previous year and a listing of the "All-Time Film Rental Champs," with total rentals for every film included.

GROSSMONT, CALIFORNIA. See MONROVIA FEATURE FILM COMPANY

GROUP PRODUCTIONS. See CHAS. K. FELDMAN'S GROUP PRODUCTIONS

GULF + WESTERN INDUSTRIES, INC. Gulf + Western Industries, Inc., was founded in 1958 by Charles G. Bludhorn (who died in 1983 at the age of fifty-six) and began life as a small Michigan-based auto parts company. Today, it is a major U.S. conglomerate, whose Entertainment and Communication Group controls Madison Square Garden, Paramount Pictures* (which it acquired in 1966), *Esquire* magazine, and the publishing houses of Simon and Schuster and Prentice-Hall.

Address: 1 Gulf + Western Plaza, New York, N.Y. 10023.

H

HALLMARK PICTURES CORPORATION. In September 1919, the Hallmark Pictures Corporation was formed, representing a merger of Frank B. Hall's enterprises, which included Film Clearing House, Independent Sales Corporation, Film Finance Corporation, Hobart Henley Productions, Inc., and Charles Miller Productions, Inc. Hallmark planned to release twenty-six films per year in its "Famous Directors' Pictures" series, which were to be booked by exhibitors on one contract, allowing the exhibitor to view the film before booking and to cancel the contract after two pictures. Hallmark also planned to release twelve films from the British-American Finance Corporation and twelve special features per year. Its first release was the serial *The Trail of the Octopus*. Hallmark took over Triangle* Distributing Corporation in 1920, and was itself taken over by Robertson-Cole* at the end of the same year.

BIBLIOGRAPHY

"Hallmark Merges Hall's Interests," *The Moving Picture World*, September 6, 1919, p. 1500.

HALLMARK PRODUCTIONS, INC. Hallmark Productions, Inc., was organized in 1945 by veteran Ohio showman Kroger Babb (who died in 1980 at the age of seventy-three) to produce and release exploitation films*, features which he described as "Triple-E Presentations: Enlightenment, Education, Entertainment." Hallmark's first release was *Mom and Dad*, filmed by Babb's Hygenic Productions, which dealt, among other things, with childbirth, and was screened before segregated male and female audiences. In 1948, Hallmark filmed a version of the Passion Play, *Prince of Peace*, in Lawton, Oklahoma. Other Hallmark productions—dates for which are obscure—included *Half-Way to Hell*, *One Too Many*, *Monika: The Story of a Bad Girl*, *She Shoulda Said No*, and *Walk the Walk*. Hallmark also released in 1972, a German version of *Uncle Tom's Cabin*. The company's headquarters were initially located in Wilmington, Ohio, but Hallmark eventually moved to Los Angeles.

BIBLIOGRAPHY
Turan, Kenneth, "You've Got to Tell 'Em to Sell 'Em Said Kroger Babb, and Did He Sell 'Em," *The Washington Post*, August 1, 1977, pp. B1, B3.

HAL ROACH STUDIOS, INC. Hal Roach (born 1892) entered the film industry in 1912 and by 1915 had formed his own company, the Rolin Film Company, with a partner, Dan Linthicum, to produce Harold Lloyd one-reel comedies under the series name of "Phun-Philms." In 1919, Roach formed Hal Roach Studios and built his own production facility at 8822 West Washington Boulevard in Culver City. Here, Roach produced the comedies that made him a household name, with a stable of stars that included Harold Lloyd, Laurel and Hardy, Charley Chase, Our Gang, Thelma Todd and Patsy Kelly, and Will Rogers.

As historian Leonard Maltin has commented, "Probably no producer's work has brought the world more laughter than that of movie producer Hal Roach." However, the Hal Roach Studios were responsible not only for comedy shorts and features but also for feature-length dramas, such as *Captain Fury* (1939), *Of Mice and Men* (1939), and *One Million Years B.C.* (1940).

During the Second World War, the Hal Roach Studios were leased to the U.S. government for the production of training films and became known as Fort Roach. Hal Roach appeared to lose interest in film production after the war, and his studios were rented out for the shooting of features such as *Joan of Arc* (1948). The studios became the first major production center to become actively involved in television production in 1948, and among the series filmed there were "My Little Margie," "The Life of Riley," "Oh Susannah," and "Amos 'n' Andy."

Hal Roach entered semi-retirement in 1955, and his studios were taken over by his son, Hal Roach, Jr. (1921–1972). In May 1958, Roach's stock was acquired by the Scranton Corporation, and a year later—in April 1959—the studio was closed when Scranton asked for federal receivership. On December 20, 1962, the fifteen-acre studios were sold, for $1,326,000, to Ponty-Fenmore Realty Fund, which renamed them the Landmark Studios and promised that they would be renovated. However, the contents of the studio were put up for public auction on August 1, 1963, and in September of the same year the studios were demolished.

When the original company was reorganized, following its bankruptcy, it became Hal Roach Studios, Inc., a Toronto-based organization with which Hal Roach had no association. The new company co-produced *The Groundstar Conspiracy* (1972), *Starship Invasions* (1978), and *Children of the Corn* (1984), among other films, and is chiefly involved in the exploitation of the colorization* process.

Address: 1600 North Fairfax Avenue, Hollywood, Calif. 90046.

BIBLIOGRAPHY
Everson, William K. *The Films of Hal Roach*. New York: Museum of Modern Art, 1971.
Slide, Anthony, "Hal Roach on Film Comedy: An Interview," *The Silent Picture*, no. 6, Spring 1970, pp. 3–7.

RESOURCES
Films: Library of Congress.
Papers: University of Southern California (financial records).

"HAM AND BUD" SERIES. See KALEM COMPANY, INC

HANNA-BARBERA PRODUCTIONS. Hanna-Barbera Productions was formed in 1957 by William Hanna (born 1911) and Joseph Barbera (born 1905). The two men had joined M-G-M* in 1937 and are generally considered the creative force behind that studio's "Tom and Jerry" cartoons. Before setting up their own animated production company, Hanna and Barbera had, in 1955, become joint heads of the cartoon department at M-G-M.

Hanna-Barbera claims to be the "world's largest producer of family entertainment" for television, with its highly successful animated and live-action series and specials. Among its best-known series are "Huckleberry Hound" (1958–1962), "Yogi Bear" (1960–1962), "The Flintstones" (1960–1966 and 1979–1980), "Shazzam" (1967–1968), "The Smurfs" (1981 to present), and "Pac-Man" (1982–1984). Its features and movies for television included *A Man Called Flintstone* (1966), *Charlotte's Web* (1973), *The Gathering* (1977), and *Heidi's Song* (1982). The company's animated subjects are chiefly known for their inexpensive methods of production, which usually ignore the details to be found in cartoons from Hollywood's golden age of animation*. Hanna-Barbera's first television series was "Ruff and Ready," aired on NBC from 1957 to 1960. In December 1967, the company was acquired by Taft Broadcasting Company, but Hanna and Barbera remain with the company, with Barbera as president and Hanna as senior vice-president.

Address: 3400 Cahuenga Boulevard, Hollywood, Calif. 90068.
BIBLIOGRAPHY
Lenberg, Jeff. "Hanna and Barbera," in *The Great Cartoon Directors*. Jefferson, North Carolina: McFarland, 1983.

HARMAN-ISING. Hugh Harman (1903–1982) and Rudolf Ising (1903–) first became partners in 1923 in Kansas City, where earlier Harman had worked for the young Walt Disney. It was Disney who brought the pair to Los Angeles, where, in 1929, Harman-Ising was formed to produce animated shorts for release through Warner Bros.* The first cartoon from the new company was *Sinkin' in the Bathtub* (1930), featuring Bosko. For Warner Bros., Harman-Ising created "Looney Tunes" and "Merrie Melodies," which became the studio's best-known cartoon series. In 1934, Harman-Ising left Warner Bros. for M-G-M* for which they worked as independent producers until 1938, when the Harman-Ising unit became a wholly owned M-G-M company. In 1941, Harman formed Hugh Harman Productions, and Ising became involved in government film production. As late as 1958, Harman-Ising was revived and signed a co-production agreement with the Toei Motion Picture Company of Japan.

BIBLIOGRAPHY
McCaskill, Marney, "Harman-Ising," in *The Film Daily Cavalcade*. New York: The
    Film Daily, 1939, p. 302.

HARRY RAVER, INC. See RAVER FILM CORPORATION

HAWORTH PICTURES CORPORATION. See ROBERTSON-COLE
COMPANY

HEARST-METROTONE NEWS. See NEWSREELS

HEARST-PATHÉ NEWS. See NEWSREELS

THE HEARST-SELIG NEWS PICTORIAL. See NEWSREELS

HECHT-HILL-LANCASTER. Hecht-Hill-Lancaster was one of the major
independent film production companies of the late fifties, founded in December
1956 by producer Harold Hecht, screenwriter-director James Hill, and actor Burt
Lancaster, as an extension of the former Hecht-Lancaster company, founded a
couple of years earlier. In *The New York Times* (January 6, 1958), Thomas M.
Pryor wrote, "Its principal assets are ownership in film negatives, ownership of
literary properties and the fact that it has first call on Mr. Lancaster's services
as an actor." Throughout its life, Lancaster also worked independently of the
company. Hecht and Hill did not, but, in the spring of 1959, all three partners
began to take on personal projects outside of their corporate productions, and
by the summer of that same year Hecht-Hill-Lancaster had been effectively
dismantled as a production operation. With headquarters in Beverly Hills,
California, the company released its features through United Artists*, among
which were *Sweet Smell of Success* (1957), *Run Silent, Run Deep* (1958), *Separate
Tables* (1958), *The Devil's Disciple* (1959), and *Take a Giant Step* (1959).

HECHT-LANCASTER. See HECHT-HILL-LANCASTER

HECTOR FILM CORPORATION. Formed in mid–1914 by Hector J.
Streyckmans, the Hector Film Corporation made five-reel features, starring Beulah
Poynter and directed by Wray Physioc.

HEDWIG FILM LABORATORIES. See CONSOLIDATED FILM
INDUSTRIES

HIRLICOLOR. Hirlicolor was a two-color process, which did not require
additional lighting during the shooting process and which could be developed
at any color film laboratory, patented by Hollywood producer and entrepreneur
George Hirliman in 1936. Hirliman was associated with Consolidated Film
Industries* and his color process was later called Magnacolor.

BIBLIOGRAPHY
"Hirliman to Patent a New Color Process," *Motion Picture Herald*, March 28, 1936, p. 66.

HISTORICAL FILM COMPANY. The Historical Film Company was a production company located in New York and London, which was formed, in April 1913, to produce three- and four-reel historical scenarios written by Edward S. Ellis for the open market and states rights* exchanges. Eustache Hale Bennett was the general manager and Garfield Thompson the director. The New York offices were located at One Madison Avenue and the studio was on East 23 Street. In addition to producing features, Historical planned to make educational films with eastern universities, government films, and industrial subjects.

HOLLAND FILM MANUFACTURING COMPANY. The Holland Film Manufacturing Company, located at 105 Lawrence Avenue in the Roxbury district of Boston, claimed to be the first motion picture production company in the city. Organized in October 1914 by Herbert B. Holland, the company acquired the services of director William F. Haddock, formerly with Edison*, Eclair*, and All-Star*, who produced the one-reel *Mary Jane's Burglar*, written by and starring Maude Fealy. In February 1915, the company went bankrupt, and its assets, including the above-mentioned film and five others, were sold at public auction.

BIBLIOGRAPHY
"Maude Fealy Starring for Hub Company," *The Moving Picture World*, October 24, 1914, p. 469.

HOLLYWOOD. The July 1927 issue of *Hi-Hat*, published "for the Hollywood Country Gentleman," came up with a number of still applicable definitions for Hollywood: "Not a place but a mental assumption. . . . Hollywood isn't a place; it's a condition of mind. . . . Hollywood isn't a town. It's a national obsession."

Hollywood came into existence in 1886, when Harvey Wilcox purchased a tract of land, which his wife named Hollywood because she liked the sound of it. There are no woods and no holly in Hollywood. The community first became known as the residence of French-born painter Paul DeLongpre (who moved there in 1901). Hollywood became a city in 1903, but it was annexed by Los Angeles in 1910. The Hollywood Hotel (1902–1956), which lent its name to Louella Parsons' popular radio program, was the city's best-known landmark; other notable Hollywood institutions include the Hollywood Bowl (which opened in 1920), the Brown Derby (1929–1985), Grauman's Chinese Theatre*, and the Griffith Park Observatory (opened 1935).

Despite being synonymous with the motion picture industry, Hollywood had only three major studios ever located in its geographic area—Columbia*, Paramount*, and RKO*—and, today, only Paramount remains. However, many smaller independent and rental studios were, and continue to be, situated in Hollywood.

Today, Hollywood consists of 1,700 acres, bounded, approximately, by Western Avenue, La Brea Avenue, Franklin Avenue, and Santa Monica Boulevard. The postal code for the Hollywood post office is 90028. It has a population of 140,000, many of whom are foreign-born and can be defined as low-earning, working class. The community has declined in recent years and has become increasingly known for prostitution—both female and male—drug-related crimes, and as a basically unsafe neighborhood.

Hollywood's Santa Claus Parade, held the first Sunday after Thanksgiving, is widely televised. Hollywood is the home of three major legitimate theatres—the Pantages (opened as a movie theatre, June 4, 1930), the Henry Fonda, and the Huntington Hartford—and of two major hotels—the Holiday Inn and the Hollywood Roosevelt. (Former important Hollywood hotels were the Plaza, the Knickerbocker, and the Christie.) Its major thoroughfare, Hollywood Boulevard—famous for the Hollywood Walk of Fame*—was initially known as Prospect Avenue. Aside from Grauman's theatres, the most historically important of film theatres in Hollywood is the Warner Theatre, on Hollywood Boulevard, which opened on April 26, 1928, with *Glorious Betsy*, and has a seating capacity of 2,742; it is now a triplex.

BIBLIOGRAPHY

Cini, Zelda, and Bob Crane. *Hollywood, Land and Legend.* Westport, Connecticut: Arlington House, 1980.

Lamparski, Richard. *Lamparski's Hidden Hollywood.* New York: Simon and Schuster, 1981.

Palmer, Edwin O. *History of Hollywood.* Los Angeles: Arthur H. Cawston, 1937.

Torrence, Bruce. *Hollywood: The First 100 Years.* Hollywood, California: Hollywood Chamber of Commerce, 1979.

HOLLYWOOD ANTI-NAZI LEAGUE. The Hollywood Anti-Nazi League came about as a result of the efforts of Prince Hubestus zu Loewenstein, the former leader of the German Center party, who hosted a dinner in Hollywood in April of 1936, at which plans for the League were formulated by Dorothy Parker, Donald Ogden Stewart, Fritz Lang, Fredric March, and Oscar Hammerstein. The League was officially organized on July 23, 1936. It fought fascism through rallies, demonstrations, and picketing of the German consulate. In the late thirties, the Hollywood Anti-Nazi League was denounced as a communist front organization by the Dies Committee*. It was dissolved when the United States entered the Second World War.

BIBLIOGRAPHY

Ceplair, Larry, and Steven Englund. *The Inquisition in Hollywood.* Garden City, New York: Anchor Press/Doubleday, 1980.

HOLLYWOOD CANTEEN. Inspired by New York's Stage Door Canteen and co-founded by Bette Davis, John Garfield, J. K. (Spike) Wallace, and Carroll Hollister, the Hollywood Canteen was a "home away from home" for servicemen during the Second World War. There, the stars entertained, provided meals, washed dishes, and contributed in any way possible toward the well-being of the men and women in uniforms. Only two major Hollywood stars—Charlie Chaplin and Greta Garbo—failed to participate. The Hollywood Canteen opened, in a building which had formerly been a little theatre and a livery stable, at 1451 North Cahuenga Boulevard, in Hollywood, on October 17, 1942. It closed on November 22, 1945. Warner Bros.* produced the 1944 feature *Hollywood Canteen* to raise funds for the organization's work.

Following its closure, the Hollywood Canteen Foundation was established to supervise and distribute the large amount of money which the Canteen had accrued. The Foundation continues its charitable work through the present, and the Hollywood Canteen continues to exist, to a certain extent, as the Bob Hope USO (at 1641 Ivar Avenue in Hollywood). The building which housed the Hollywood Canteen was demolished in 1966.

HOLLYWOOD CO-ORDINATING COMMITTEE. See HOLLYWOOD VICTORY COMMITTEE

HOLLYWOOD FOREIGN CORRESPONDENTS ASSOCIATION. See HOLLYWOOD FOREIGN PRESS ASSOCIATION, INC.

HOLLYWOOD FOREIGN PRESS ASSOCIATION, INC. The Hollywood Foreign Press Association, Inc., was formed in October 1943 as the Hollywood Foreign Correspondents Association, with William Mooring as its first president. The Association presented its first awards in 1944 and two years later introduced the Golden Globes, the name by which its awards ceremony became known. In 1950, a disagreement broke out within the organization, and it split into two, the Hollywood Foreign Correspondents Association and the Foreign Press Association of Hollywood. The former continued to present the Golden Globes, while the latter awarded Henriettas, named after its president, Henry Gris.

The two groups rejoined in October of 1955, and the new Hollywood Foreign Press Association was created. It is an organization of professional journalists and photographers who cover Hollywood film and television production for various foreign publications. The membership, which never drops or increases much beyond seventy-five, is open to anyone who can document their work as a foreign-film correspondent. The organization has been embroiled in considerable controversy through the years, both in terms of the makeup of its membership and the presentation of its awards.

Address: 292 South La Cienega Boulevard, Suite 316, Los Angeles, Calif. 90211.

BIBLIOGRAPHY
Borie, Marcia, "Golden Globes Growth Great," *The Hollywood Reporter*, January 30, 1976, p. 28.
Grant, Lee, "Foreign Press: See How They Work," *Los Angeles Times*, Calendar Section, January 25, 1981, pp. 1, 6–7.
Nugent, John Peer, "And in the Category 'Most Curious Awards Show,' the Winner Is . . . ," *Los Angeles*, January 1978, pp. 60–68.

HOLLYWOOD GENERAL STUDIOS. A studio with many names, Hollywood General Studios was built in the spring of 1919 by architect John Jasper (who was also responsible for the Chaplin Studios*) as a "unitized" studio. In other words, it offered office space and a production space for four filmmaking units. The first producers to move on to the lot were Marshall Neilan and Hunt Stromberg, followed, in 1921, by Harold Lloyd.

Al Christie acquired the studio in 1925 and renamed it the Hollywood Metropolitan Studios. Also in the twenties, Howard Hughes moved his production company to the lot. When Al Christie's company went into receivership, following the Wall Street crash, the studio was taken over, in 1932, by Eastern Service (a division of Electrical Research Products*) and renamed General Service Studios. It was utilized as a rental studio by both Paramount* and United Artists*, and among those filming there were Walter Wanger, Edward Small*, Mae West, Bing Crosby, and Gary Cooper.

In 1947, the studio changed hands again, when it was purchased by James and George Nasser and renamed the Hollywood General Studios. Several production companies, including United Artists, Benedict Bogeaus, James Cagney, Sam Bischoff, Hunt Stromberg, Charles R. Rogers, Golden Productions, and Hopalong Cassidy Productions, remained on the lot. In 1978, Glenn Speidel and Ellison Miles, with their Esquire Holding Co., purchased the lot, and, in 1980, it changed hands again, when Francis Ford Coppola took over Speidel's mortgage and renamed the studio Zoetrope*.

At a bankruptcy auction in 1984, the studio was purchased for $12.3 million by Canadian investor Jack Singer, who set up his office in Harold Lloyd's original studio bungalow. Singer, at the suggestion of film historian Marc Wanamaker, renamed the lot Hollywood Studio Center. One of the oldest tenants on the lot is George Burns, who has maintained an office there since the early fifties and in whose honor, in 1979, Stage One was dedicated as the George Burns Stage. Originally 15 acres, the studio now occupies some 10.5 acres.

Address: 1040 North Las Palmas Avenue, Hollywood, Calif. 90038.

BIBLIOGRAPHY
Farley, Ellen, "Canadian Investor Turns to Films," *Los Angeles Times*, Business Section, May 14, 1984, pp. 1, 5.

HOLLYWOOD METROPOLITAN STUDIOS. See HOLLYWOOD GENERAL STUDIOS

HOLLYWOOD MUSEUM. A museum devoted to the history of film and television and located in Hollywood has long been a dream of many in the industry. Through the enthusiasm of Sol Lesser, the Los Angeles County Board of Supervisors unanimously voted to create such a museum on June 16, 1959. The Board appointed an interim commission, headed by Lesser, and approved a site for the museum across from the Hollywood Bowl on Highland Avenue. Groundbreaking for the new museum took place on October 20, 1963, with Rosalind Russell, Jack L. Warner, Walt Disney, and Gene Autry among the celebrities present.

In the meantime, the County of Los Angeles began acquiring property standing on the proposed museum site through the expediency of condemnation. One of the homes condemned was that of a former marine, Steve E. Anthony, located at 6655 Alta Loma Terrace. Anthony fought the county, first with legal action and eventually by refusal to move. The former marine's fight created a considerable amount of negative publicity for the museum, particularly when the house was seized on April 13, 1964, as Anthony and approximately 100 demonstrators battled with police.

In December 1964, the Board of Supervisors froze funding for the museum amidst criticism that the museum was a private institution and should not be funded with taxpayers' money. Sol Lesser urged, unsuccessfully, that the film and television industry raise the $5 million needed, and, ultimately, in August 1965, resigned as chairman of the commission.

The site for the museum became a parking lot for the Hollywood Bowl, and the many artifacts collected were housed by the Los Angeles City Recreation and Parks Department in Lincoln Heights Jail. The city refused to return donations and insisted that all artifacts could be displayed only in a museum situated in the geographic area of Hollywood. Many plans for a new Hollywood Museum were formulated by Debbie Reynolds, the Hollywood Chamber of Commerce, Jane Withers, and others, but to no avail. In 1981, the city agreed that all paper materials donated to the Museum should be given on a twenty-five-year loan to the Academy of Motion Picture Arts and Sciences*, the American Film Institute, the University of California at Los Angeles, and the University of Southern California.

From 1984 to 1986, a privately funded Hollywood Museum, chiefly utilizing costumes from the John LeBold collection, was opened on Hollywood Boulevard.

BIBLIOGRAPHY

Elvenstar, Diane, "The Hollywood Museum Fades to Black," *Los Angeles Magazine*, September 1981, pp. 148–156.

Luft, Herbert G., "Hollywood's Museum," *Films in Review*, February 1962, pp. 65–70.

Miller, Jonathan, "A Museum for Hollywood: At Long Last?" *Los Angeles Times*, Calendar Section, September 23, 1984, pp. 18–22.

"HOLLYWOOD ON PARADE" SERIES. Produced by Louis Lewyn for Paramount Pictures* during 1932 and 1933, the "Hollywood on Parade" series of one-reel shorts featured Paramount contract stars in brief comedy sketches or musical numbers. For example, No. A–2 (1932) in the series includes Gary Cooper at breakfast with a chimpanzee; No. A–6 (1932) features Charlie Chaplin and Paulette Goddard and a golfing routine with former silent star Viola Dana and Bing Crosby; No. B–11 (1933) includes Clara Bow (who wrote the title song for the series) as well as J. Stuart Blackton, who introduces a handful of former stars from his Vitagraph Company*. No. A–5 (1932) is of particular interest because it includes what would appear to be Maurice Chevalier's screen test, in which he sings "Louise."

THE "HOLLYWOOD" SIGN. The "Hollywood" sign is probably the best known and most enduring of Hollywood landmarks. It was erected in 1923, at which time it read "Hollywoodland," to promote a real estate development on Beechwood Canyon. The sign was placed on land that was originally owned by Mack Sennett (and is now owned by the City of Los Angeles) on top of Mount Lee. It cost $21,000 to build, with each letter thirty feet wide and fifty feet tall, and each of the letters was studded with twenty-watt electric light bulbs.

Stage actress Peg Entwistle, who had come to Hollywood with an RKO* contract, committed suicide by jumping from the "H" of the sign on September 16, 1932. Maintenance of the sign was ended in 1939, and it was severely damaged by vandals. After threats from the city that it would be demolished, the sign was restored by the Hollywood Chamber of Commerce in 1949, at which time it was shortened to read simply "Hollywood." Vandalism continued to plague the sign, as did the ravages of the weather. It was declared a Historic-Cultural Monument in 1973. Eventually, through private donations, a new "Hollywood" sign was erected and officially unveiled on November 11, 1978.

BIBLIOGRAPHY

Reed, Rochelle, "Hollywood Has a New Act," *California*, November 1977, pp. 94–99, 106–107, 111.

Robinson, C. E., and Bruce T. Torrence. *The Hollywood Sign*. Hollywood, California: First Federal Savings and Loan Association of Hollywood, 1976.

Simross, Lynn, "Hullywood [*sic*] Sign Broken—and Broke," *Los Angeles Times*, part IV, December 28, 1977, pp. 1, 6.

HOLLYWOOD STUDIO CENTER. See HOLLYWOOD GENERAL STUDIOS

HOLLYWOOD STUDIO CLUB. The Hollywood Studio Club was founded in 1916, at the suggestion of librarian Eleanor Jones, by the Young Women's Christian Association (YWCA) to provide low-cost housing for young women trying to enter the film industry. It was originally located at 6129 Carlos Avenue in Hollywood. A new building, at 1215 Lodi Place, was erected in 1926, with funds raised by Mrs. Cecil B. DeMille and others. Sponsored by the Motion Picture Producers Association and run by the YWCA, the Club was organized along the lines of a sorority house. By 1953, a reported 8,000 women had been residents there, among them were Marilyn Monroe, Barbara Hale, Donna Reed, Helen Jerome Eddy, Evelyn Keyes, Linda Darnell, and ZaSu Pitts. The Club closed in February 1971.

BIBLIOGRAPHY
Crivello, Kirk, "The Hollywood Studio Club," *Film Fan Monthly*, no. 127, January 1972, pp. 25–29.
"The Hollywood Studio Club," *Pageant*, October 1946, pp. 120–125.
Muir, Jean, "Boardinghouse of Broken Hearts," *The Saturday Evening Post*, September 19, 1953, pp. 41, 135–138.
Simross, Lynn, "Studio Club Closes Doors on Memories," *Los Angeles Times*, View Section, February 9, 1975, pp. 1, 18–20.
Smith, Bradley, "Gateway to Glamor," *Collier's*, March 9, 1946, pp. 22–23.

THE HOLLYWOOD TEN. The Hollywood Ten were Alvah Bessie (1904–1985), Herbert Biberman (1900–1971), Lester Cole (1905–1985), Edward Dmytryk (1908–), Ring Lardner, Jr. (1915–), John Howard Lawson (1894–1977), Albert Maltz (1908–1985), Samuel Ornitz (1891–1957), Adrian Scott (1912–1973), and Dalton Trumbo (1905–1976). The majority of these writers or directors were minor figures in the film industry who achieved a fame that would not have been theirs had not history placed them in a unique and tragic position. The Hollywood Ten were also dubbed the Unfriendly Ten, and it was Billy Wilder who joked, "of the Unfriendly Ten, only two had any talent, the other eight were just unfriendly."

These men, along with Bertolt Brecht, appeared before the House Un-American Activities Committee in the fall of 1947. All refused to answer questions concerning Communist affiliations put to them by the Committee. Brecht fled the country the day following his inquest, but the remaining ten were voted in contempt by Congress on November 24, 1947. They were tried in federal court the following year and found guilty, with each being sentenced to a year in jail and a thousand-dollar fine. In the spring of 1950, the U.S. Supreme Court refused to review the convictions, and the ten went to prison (although Dmytryk later agreed to cooperate with the Committee and was released prior to serving his entire sentence). The wives of the Hollywood Ten published a four-page pamphlet titled *For Justice and Peace*, and Gale Sondergaard (Biberman's wife) and Albert Maltz published a fourteen-page pamphlet, *On the Eve of Prison*.

With the exception of Dmytryk, the group was blacklisted by the film community and could gain work only by utilizing pseudonyms. The best known of such pseudonyms was "Robert Rich," used by Dalton Trumbo, under which he won an Academy Award for Best Screenplay for *The Brave One* (1956). *See also* Communism.

BIBLIOGRAPHY
Cole, Lester. *Hollywood Red*. Palo Alto, California: Ramparts Press, 1982.
Keerdoja, Eileen, "After the Blacklist," *Newsweek*, January 24, 1977, p. 10.
Navasky, Victor S. *Naming Names*. New York: Viking Press, 1980.
Trumbo, Dalton. *The Time of the Toad*. New York: Harper & Row, 1972.

HOLLYWOOD VICTORY COMMITTEE. Organized on December 10, 1941, with its New York affiliate called the United Theatrical War Activities Committee, the Hollywood Victory Committee was responsible for sending out screen personalities to bond drives, to entertain the troops at USO-camp shows and on the front lines, and for other morale-boosting purposes. During the Second World War, the Committee arranged for 56,037 free appearances by 4,147 individuals at 7,700 events. The Hollywood Victory Committee provided stars to perform on *Command Performance*, a short-wave radio transcription broadcast over eighteen international stations each Sunday; it also provided celebrities for similar shows, such as *Mail Call, Anchors Aweigh, Soldiers with Wings, Yarns for Yanks, Main Street U.S.A.*, and *America Speaks*. Personal appearances by stars were also arranged throughout America for charity drives on behalf of the Red Cross, USO, Community Chests, and the relief activities of the United Nations.

The Hollywood Victory Committee's most ambitious venture took place in September 1942, when, on behalf of the U.S. Treasury Department, screen personalities traveled some 21,000 miles to attend bond rallies in 368 cities, raising more than $206 million. This particular campaign, called "Stars over America," also took celebrities to Canada to assist in its Victory Bond Drive and female stars to various cities to participate in "Women at War Week."

At the war's close, the Hollywood Victory Committee became the Hollywood Co-ordinating Committee concerned with coordinating appearances by screen personalities at charitable and other events.

HOLLYWOOD WALK OF FAME. The Hollywood Walk of Fame extends along Hollywood Boulevard from Gower to Sycamore and along Vine Street from Sunset to Yucca. It is a gray terrazzo sidewalk, in which are embedded coral stars bearing the names of personalities from the worlds of film, television, radio, and the recording industry. A different symbol is utilized for each aspect of the entertainment industry, and many celebrities have more than one star if they have been involved in more than one area of entertainment.

The concept of a Walk of Fame was first proposed by E. M. Stuart, then head of the Hollywood Chamber of Commerce, in 1953. It was part of the 1956 Hollywood beautification project, but ground breaking did not take place until February 8, 1960, with civic dignitaries and Linda Darnell, Gigi Perreau, Francis X. Bushman, and Charles Coburn in attendance. The Hollywood Walk of Fame, with 1,500 personalities represented, was officially dedicated on November 23, 1960.

The project was immediately the subject of controversy with its refusal to name a "star" in honor of Charlie Chaplin, an ommission that was not corrected until 1972—the Chaplin "star" is at 6751 Hollywood Boulevard. The Hollywood Walk of Fame continues to be criticized for its failure to honor many pioneers of the industry and for its blatant commercialism in terms of demanding $3,000 from a sponsor and approval by an unidentified committee of the Hollywood Chamber of Commerce. Generally, if a star is unwilling to appear at the unveiling of his "star," then the committee will not honor that personality.

A number of names in the Hollywood Walk of Fame are misspelled. Many have been defaced. And there is one "star" for a "Maurice Diller," whom no one has been able to identify—it is generally assumed that the "star" is actually in honor of the Swedish director, Mauritz Stiller.

BIBLIOGRAPHY

Border, Hi. *Hollywood Star Walk*. Los Angeles: Hi Enterprises, 1984.

HOLLYWOOD WRITERS' MOBILIZATION. Consisting of representatives of the Screen Writers Guild, Radio Writers Guild, Screen Publicists Guild, Screen Readers Guild, Screen Cartoonists Guild, American Newspaper Guild, Independent Publicists, and the Song Writers Protective Association, the Hollywood Writers' Mobilization was established during the Second World War to provide scripts and other written materials for government and war-related productions—motion picture or radio—at no charge. In October 1945, in association with the University of California, the Hollywood Writers' Mobilization established *The Hollywood Quarterly*, which was to become *Film Quarterly*.

HOME FILM LIBRARIES, INCORPORATED. See FILMS INCORPORATED

HORROR FILMS. The horror film had its beginning in the French and German cinemas. One of the first, and certainly the best known, American "horror" films—the term is used loosely—is Edison's 1910 production of *Frankenstein*, starring Charles Ogle. D. W. Griffith adapted Edgar Allan Poe's *The Tell-Tale Heart* as *The Avenging Conscience* (1914), but the director's only other venture into the horror genre was *One Exciting Night* (1922).

Lon Chaney (1883–1930) was the chief acting exponent of the horror genre in the silent era, beginning with *The Hunchback of Notre Dame* (1923) and *The Phantom of the Opera* (1925) at Universal* and continuing at M-G-M* with *The Unholy Three* (1925), *The Black Bird* (1926), *London After Midnight* (1927), and *The Unholy Three* (1930), among others. Chaney's best-known director was Tod Browning (1882–1962), and, aside from the Chaney features, Browning was responsible for *Freaks* (1932), *Mark of the Vampire* (1935), *The Devil Doll* (1936), and, of course, *Dracula* (1931), starring Bela Lugosi in a recreation of his stage role.

Director Paul Leni brought the Germanic vision of horror to the United States with *The Cat and the Canary* (1927), *The Man Who Laughs* (1928), and *The*

Last Warning (1929). Other American films that illustrated a German influence included *The Bat* (1926) and *The Bat Whispers* (1931), both directed by Roland West.

No studio is more associated with the horror genre than Universal*. James Whale (1896–1957) directed three classic horror films there: *Frankenstein* (1931), *The Invisible Man* (1933), and *The Bride of Frankenstein* (1935). The first and last featured Boris Karloff, who is to the sound horror film what Lon Chaney was to the genre in the silent era. Boris Karloff (1887–1969) includes among his American horror films *The Mask of Fu Manchu* (1932), *The Mummy* (1932), *The Black Cat* (1934), *The Raven* (1935), *The Walking Dead* (1936), *Son of Frankenstein* (1939), *Tower of London* (1939), *House of Frankenstein* (1944), *Bedlam* (1946), *Frankenstein 1970* (1958), *The Raven* (1963), and *Mad Monster Party* (1967).

The Universal horror features continued into the forties and fifties, with Lon Chaney, Jr., appearing as the Son of Dracula, the Mummy, and the Wolf Man. By the early fifties, Universal was no longer taking the genre too seriously, with titles such as *Abbott and Costello Meet Frankenstein* (1948), *Abbott and Costello Meet the Invisible Man* (1951), and *Abbott and Costello Go to Mars* (1953). However, honorable mention should be made of some Universal features of the fifties: *It Came from Outer Space* (1953), *Creature from the Black Lagoon* (1954), *Revenge of the Creature* (1955), *The Incredible Shrinking Man* (1957), and *Curse of the Undead* (1959).

Paramount's one major contribution to the horror genre in the thirties was *Dr. Jekyll and Mr. Hyde* (1931), directed by Rouben Mamoulian and starring Fredric March in the title role. Robert Louis Stevenson's novel has been filmed many times: in 1912, by Thanhouser* with James Cruze in the title role; in 1913, by Universal with King Baggot in the title role; in 1920, by Famous Players-Lasky with John Barrymore in the title role; and in 1941, by M-G-M* with Spencer Tracy in the title role, to mention a few.

Other horror films of the thirties worth noting were two directed by Michael Curtiz at Warner Bros*: *Doctor X* (1932) and *The Mystery of the Wax Museum* (1933), both of which were filmed in two-strip Technicolor* and starred Lionel Atwill and Fay Wray. *White Zombie* (1932), featuring Bela Lugosi and Madge Bellamy, has a considerable cult following, as does another feature, also directed by Victor Halperin, *Supernatural* (1933). Halperin tried unsuccessfully to repeat the popularity of *White Zombie* with *Revolt of the Zombies* (1936). A far more memorable production dealing with the "living dead" is Jacques Tourneur's *I Walked with a Zombie* (1943).

The "living dead" was the subject of George Romero's *Night of the Living Dead* (1969). It heralded a new era of explicit and graphic horror films which were to replace films such as Alfred Hitchcock's *Psycho* (1960), which terrified without showing the viewer a knife actually slashing human flesh. Graphic horror films of a more recent vintage are exemplified by the "Halloween" series, which commenced with *Halloween* (1978), and the "Friday the 13th" series, which began with *Friday the 13th* (1980).

BIBLIOGRAPHY

Butler, Ivan. *The Horror Film*. New York: A. S. Barnes, 1967.

Clarens, Carlos. *An Illustrated History of the Horror Films*. New York: G. P. Putnam's Sons, 1967.

Dettman, Bruce. *The Horror Factory*. New York: Gordon Press, 1976.

Drake, Douglas. *Horror!* New York: Macmillan, 1966.

Everson, William K. *Classics of the Horror Film*. Secaucus, New Jersey: Citadel Press, 1974.

Gifford, Denis. *A Pictorial History of Horror Movies*. New York: Hamlyn, 1973.

Glut, Douglas F. *The Dracula Book*. Metuchen, New Jersey: Scarecrow Press, 1975.

―――. *The Frankenstein Catalog*. Jefferson, North Carolina: McFarland, 1984.

Pitts, Michael R. *Horror Film Stars*. Jefferson, North Carolina: McFarland, 1981.

Willis, Donald C. *Horror and Science Fiction Films: A Checklist*. Metuchen, New Jersey: Scarecrow Press, 1972.

―――. *Horror and Science Fiction Films: A Checklist II*. Metuchen, New Jersey: Scarecrow Press, 1982.

―――. *Horror and Science Fiction Films: A Checklist III*. Metuchen, New Jersey: Scarecrow Press, 1984.

HOTEX FILM MANUFACTURING COMPANY. King Vidor, John Boggs, and Ed Sedgwick formed this short-lived company of 1914, located in Texas, which produced two one-reel comedies directed by Sedgwick. Although Vidor succeeded in contracting with Sawyer, Inc.*, in October 1914, to release the comedies, when Sawyer went bankrupt shortly thereafter, the prints, negatives, and royalties were never retrieved. The company produced a film starring Vidor's wife, Florence, about the manufacture and marketing of sugar, before its disbandment when the Vidors left Galveston.

BIBLIOGRAPHY

"Hotel [*sic*] Will Release through Sawyer," *The Moving Picture World*, October 17, 1914, p. 315.

Vidor, King. *A Tree Is a Tree*. New York: Harcourt, Brace, 1952.

HUGH HARMAN PRODUCTIONS. See HARMAN-ISING

HUMANOLOGY FILM PRODUCING COMPANY. The Humanology Film Producing Company of Medford, Massachusetts, produced films in 1913, released by United Film Service*. Jack Rose was the president, and Reginald Wright Kaufmann was hired to write scenarios for the company.

HYGENIC PRODUCTIONS. See HALLMARK PRODUCTIONS, INC.

I

IATSE. See INTERNATIONAL ALLIANCE OF THEATRICAL STAGE EMPLOYES AND MOVING PICTURE MACHINE OPERATORS OF THE UNITED STATES AND CANADA

IDEAL PICTURES CORPORATION. Founded in 1920, Ideal Pictures Corporation was, by the late forties, the largest 16mm* film distributor in the United States. It was also active in the field of 16mm equipment, visual aids, and 16mm and 35mm projection services. With headquarters in Chicago, Ideal had exchanges throughout the United States—twenty-seven in 1957. At one time or another, Ideal was the official distributor for P.R.C.*, RKO*, United Artists*, Universal*, Warner Bros.*, and Allied Artists*. It was one of the largest nontheatrical distributors of black films, having some forty titles in distribution in 1950.

In June 1949, Ideal was acquired by *Esquire* magazine. It remained active through the seventies, although in its last years it operated chiefly as a television distributor.

IMAX. Imax—short for "maximum image"—was developed for Expo 70 in Osaka, Japan. It is a sophisticated widescreen system, which utilizes 70mm* film fed through the camera horizontally and, therefore, ten times the width of 35mm* film. The projector uses a rolling loop movement to advance the film horizontally. The latter was invented by P.R.W. Jones, and the former by William C. Shaw. The Imax system was developed in Canada, as was a similar system, Omnimax, which is designed for use on a domed theatre screen, rather than a curved screen as is Imax. Omnimax was introduced to the United States at the Reuben H. Fleet Space Theater in San Diego in 1973.

Address: Imax Systems Corporation, 36 Isabella Street, Toronto, Ontario, Canada M4Y 1N1.

BIBLIOGRAPHY
Jones, P.R.W., "The Rolling Loop—a New Concept of Film Transport," *Journal of the SMPTE*, January 1968, pp. 21–23.
Shaw, William C., "New Large-Screen and Multi-Image Motion-Picture System," *Journal of the SMPTE*, September 1970, pp. 782–787.

IMP. See UNIVERSAL PICTURES

INCE CULVER CITY STUDIOS. See LAIRD INTERNATIONAL STUDIOS

INCEVILLE. The Miller Bros. 101 Ranch, situated where Sunset Boulevard joins the ocean in Los Angeles, became known as Inceville when it was taken over by pioneer producer Thomas H. Ince (1882–1924) late in 1911. The rugged terrain was used not only for the production of Westerns but also for shooting all types of films. Numerous standing sets were built, many directly on the beach.

The following description of the lot appeared in the October 9, 1915, edition of *The Moving Picture World*:

> Like many of the Western studios, the establishment is made up of a confusion of frame buildings, small and large, each additional structure marking the expansion of the company's business. It has a main stage 175 × 220 feet; a new glass stage 360 × 160 and two auxiliary stages 50 × 80 feet; an administrative building, a restaurant, a commissary, a wardrobe building, a property building, a scene building, 200 dressing rooms, an arsenal where weapons, ammunition and explosives are kept, a power house furnishing light for stages and buildings, a reservoir furnishing fresh water, six stables and corrals and a number of other structures. In addition to the inexhaustible supply of natural settings for exteriors, Inceville has a Spanish Mission, a Dutch village with a genuine canal, old windmill, etc., a Japanese village with jinrikshaws, an Irish village, a Canadian village, an East Indian street and a Sioux camp.

When Ince moved his operation to Culver City in 1915, Inceville continued to be used to a lesser extent until 1922. A 1924 fire destroyed the remaining standing sets except for one church.

BIBLIOGRAPHY
Duncan, Robert C., "The Ince Studios," *Picture Play*, March 1, 1916, pp. 26–39.
"Ince to Move to Culver City," *The Moving Picture World*, October 9, 1915, p. 272.

INDEPENDENT FILM ARTS GUILD. See ART HOUSES

INDEPENDENT MOTION PICTURE COMPANY. See UNIVERSAL PICTURES

INDEPENDENT PRODUCTIONS CORPORATION. Independent Productions Corporation was founded in 1951 by Herbert Biberman, along with Paul Jarrico and Simon Lazarus, after Biberman had served time in a federal penitentiary for contempt of Congress as a member of the Hollywood Ten*. It announced plans for various films, including one on Paul Robeson, one on the trial of Helen Johnson, and a feature on the life of Frederick Douglass titled *The House on Cedar Hill*. The company actually made only one film, *Salt of the Earth*, about the striking miners of New Mexico, which eventually was shown publicly, in 1954, but never gained a commercial release because of the blacklisting of Biberman by the film industry.

INDEPENDENT SALES CORPORATION. The Independent Sales Corporation began December 1, 1918, as a booking organization distinct from producers and exchange organizations. With a New York headquarters and salesmen in every territory of the country, Independent Sales, headed by Frank G. Hall, contracted with Film Clearing House, Inc., to handle the physical distribution of its films. Film Clearing House, incorporated on May 6, 1918, by Colonel Julian Ruppert, a brewer and the owner of the New York Yankees, was formed to eliminate the overhead costs of many exchanges by doing the shipping portion of distribution and leaving the sales end to the individual distributors utilizing their own services. Distributors housed their sales staff in Film Clearing House offices and were able to operate at much lower costs because they did not have to provide the overhead necessary physically to ship the films. One of the organizers of Film Clearing House, William M. Seabury, was the vice-president of Independent Sales, and Frank G. Hall was Film Clearing House's supervising director. After Film Clearing House bought and remodeled the Kleine* exchanges, it contracted to handle films of Blackton Productions, Bacon-Backer*, and the William L. Sherry Service*. Although Independent Sales was not a producer, it did at times put up cash advances on finished negatives and financed printing and advertising. In September 1919, Independent Sales and Film Clearing House merged with other of Frank G. Hall's interests to form Hallmark Pictures Corporation*.
BIBLIOGRAPHY
"Independent Company to Direct Film Salesmen," *The Moving Picture World*, December 7, 1918, p. 1103.
"Ruppert Plans a Film Clearing House," *The Moving Picture World*, June 29, 1918, p. 1822.

INDIANAPOLIS. See CAPITAL FILM COMPANY

INDUSTRIAL FILM COMPANY. The Industrial Film Company, said to be the first company to specialize in making and distributing films for industrial exploitation, commercial education, advertising, and historical recording, was organized in December 1909 in Chicago by Carl Laemmle, Watterson R. Rothacker, and R. H. Cochrane. Rothacker, who was subsequently in the trade paper field, became president, succeeding Laemmle in 1913, when Laemmle sold his stock and left to concentrate his efforts with the Universal Film Manufacturing Company*. Some of the companies for which Industrial produced films included H. J. Heinz Company, du Pont Powder Company, Postum Cereal Company, Winchester Repeating Arms Company, Northern Pacific Railway Company, Imperial Oil Company, and the U.S. Brewers Association. In addition, Industrial made a film for the state of Michigan, showing its natural resources and industrial activities, for the Panama-Pacific Exposition of 1915 and a film of Vernon and Irene Castle dancing on the Orpheum vaudeville circuit. In mid–1916, Industrial was succeeded by the Rothacker Film Manufacturing Company, located at Diversey Parkway and Ward Street in Chicago.

BIBLIOGRAPHY

"Laemmle Sells Stock," *The New York Dramatic Mirror*, September 24, 1913, p. 35.
"The Rothacker Film Manufacturing Company," *The Moving Picture World*, June 3, 1916, p. 1720.
"Watterson R. Rothacker," *The Moving Picture World*, December 5, 1914, p. 1370.

INDUSTRIAL FILMS AND POSTER SERVICE. See UNITED PRODUCTIONS OF AMERICA

INDUSTRIAL LIGHT & MAGIC. See LUCASFILM, LTD.

IN-FLIGHT MOVIES. According to the Guinness record book of *Movie Facts and Feats*, the first in-flight movie was *The Lost World* (1925), shown on a scheduled Imperial Airways flight from London to the Continent in April 1925. The first American in-flight film presentation was of a Universal newsreel and two short subjects shown on a transcontinental Air Transport, Inc., Ford transport aircraft on October 8, 1929.

There is a documentary record of a screening of the 1928 Harold Lloyd feature, *Speedy*, on an American passenger plane, possibly a TAT (later TWA) flight from Los Angeles to New York on an unspecified date but presumably within a year or two of *Speedy*'s release. According to the *Motion Picture Herald*, the documentary feature *Baboona* was previewed on board a plane in December 1934. The film's producers, Mr. and Mrs. Martin Johnson, announced they were equipping one of their planes with a sound projector in order to screen the film for African natives in the summer of 1935. At the same time, Captain Eddie Rickenbacker announced, "The big transatlantic flying boats and the long distance cross-country planes will be equipped with movies before long."

TWA was the first airline to begin regular in-flight movie presentations on July 19, 1961, with the screening of *By Love Possessed*, on a regular flight between New York and Los Angeles. The film was seen by first-class passengers only.

BIBLIOGRAPHY

"Regular Film Fare Seen for Airliners," *Motion Picture Herald*, January 12, 1935, p. 24.

INSPIRATION PICTURES, INC. A major producer from 1921 to 1931, Inspiration Pictures, Inc., was founded by Charles H. Duell (its first president) and J. Boyce Smith, Jr. (its first vice-president). Walter Camp, Jr., became president in the mid-twenties. Releasing through United Artists*, First National*, or Paramount*, Inspiration rightly boasted that its films were "always on the best programs." Richard Barthelmess was the company's first major star, in *Tol'able David* (1921), followed by *The Fighting Blade* (1923), *The Enchanted Cottage* (1924), *Soul-Fire* (1925), and other features. Dorothy Gish was also under contract to Inspiration, appearing in *The Bright Shawl* (1923), *Fury* (1923), and *The Beautiful City* (1925). She also co-starred with her sister, Lillian, in *Romola* (1925), and it was Inspiration that sent Lillian to Italy to make *The White Sister* (1923). Director Henry King spent most of the twenties directing at Inspiration, where he made ten features, from *Tol'able David* in 1921 to *Hell Harbor* in 1930.

INTER-CONTINENT FILM COMPANY. The Inter-Continent Film Company began in January 1914 as the American distributor for the Verafilm Company of Rome as well as two Copenhagen-based companies. It planned to produce one feature per month and a series of educational films to export to Japan and China. F. Baske Yamado, a Japanese-American artist, was hired to supervise these productions. Offices for Inter-Continent were in the World's Tower Building at 110–112 West 40 Street, New York.

BIBLIOGRAPHY

"Inter-Continent Film Company Begins," *The Moving Picture World*, January 10, 1914, p. 177.

INTERNATIONAL ALLIANCE OF THEATRICAL STAGE EMPLOYES [sic] AND MOVING PICTURE MACHINE OPERATORS OF THE UNITED STATES AND CANADA. Commonly known as IATSE, the International Alliance of Theatrical Stage Employes and Moving Picture Machine Operators of the United States and Canada was organized on July 17, 1893, as the International Alliance of Theatrical Stage Employes. It affiliated as an international union on October 1, 1902, and affiliated with the American Federation of Labor and Congress of Industrial Organizations on December 5, 1955.

IATSE, along with the United Brotherhood of Carpenters and Joiners, the International Brotherhood of Electrical Workers, the International Brotherhood of Painters and Paperhangers, and the American Federation of Musicians, was one of the signatories to the first Hollywood film industry recognition of unions, the so-called Studio Basic Agreement, which was signed by nine major producers on November 29, 1926. The Studio Basic Agreement divided work in the industry between various crafts, but with the coming of sound, and resultant new technology and new jobs, jurisdictional disputes broke out. A bitter dispute evolved in the late thirties and early forties between IATSE and the Congress of Industrial Organizations (CIO) and the Conference of Studio Unions*, throughout much of which IATSE branded the last two as Communist front organizations. It was not until 1947 that IATSE finally consolidated its control over film industry labor matters.

The following are the various film-related locals within IATSE: Local I, Stagehands, New York; Local 30, Office & Professional Employees; Local 33, Stagehands; Local 44, Propmen; Local 52, Studio Mechanics; Local 80, Grips; Local 150, Projectionists; Local 161, Script Supervisors, New York; Local 165, Studio Projectionists; Local 174, Studio Secretaries and Office Workers; Local 306, New York Projectionists; Local 644 and Local 659, Photographers; Local 683, Film Technicians; Local 685, Sound, Cinetechnicians & TV Engineers; Local 695 Sound Technicians; Local 702, Motion Picture Laboratory Technicians; Local 705, Motion Picture Costumers; Local 706, Makeup-Hair Stylists; Local 717, Production Office Coordinators & Accounting; Local 720 Stagehands; Local 727, Laborers; Local 728, Studio Electrical Lighting Technicians; Local 729, Set Painters; Local 755, Plasterers; Local 764, Theatrical Wardrobe; Local 767, Motion Picture First Aid Employees; Local 768, Theatrical Wardrobe Attendants; Local 771, Film Editors, New York; Local 776, Editors; Local 780, Laboratory Technicians, Chicago; Local 789, Cinetechnicians; Local 798, Make-up Artists & Hairstylists, New York; Local 816, Scenic & Title Artists; Local 818, Publicists Guild of America; Local 829, United Scenic Artists; Local 839 and 841, Motion Picture Screen Cartoonists; Local 847, Set Designers & Model Makers; Local 854, Story Analysts; Local 871, Script Supervisors; Local 876, Art Directors; Local 892, Costume Designers.

Address: 1515 Broadway, New York, N.Y. 10036.

BIBLIOGRAPHY

Ross, Murray. *Stars and Strikes: Unionization of Hollywood.* New York: Columbia University Press, 1941.

————, "Labor Relations in Hollywood," in Thorsten Sellin, editor, *The Annals of the American Academy of Political and Social Science: The Motion Picture Industry.* Philadelphia: The American Academy of Political and Social Science, 1947, pp. 58–64.

INTERNATIONAL ANIMATED FILM ASSOCIATION. See ASIFA

INTERNATIONAL CREATIVE MANAGEMENT, INC. One of the largest of the Hollywood agents, representing individuals in all areas of film and television production, International Creative Management (ICM), Inc., was created in 1975 with the merger of Creative Management Associates and International Famous Agency. Creative Management Associates had an antecedent in General Amusements Corporation. International Creative Management is a subsidiary of Josephson International (formerly Marvin Josephson Associates, Inc.). In the summer of 1984, it assimilated Chase-Park Citron, which had been formed in 1962 and acquired by Josephson in 1973. In 1985, International Creative Management acquired ATI Equities, Inc., a talent agency which represents many contemporary music groups. Aside from its agency activities, ICM also markets films and represents television programs in syndication.

Addresses: 40 West 57th Street, New York, N.Y. 10019; 8899 Beverly Boulevard, Los Angeles, Calif. 90048.

INTERNATIONAL FILM SERVICE, INC. William Randolph Hearst formed the International Film Service, Inc., which was incorporated on December 3, 1914, following the success of the serial*, *The Perils of Pauline*, whose story appeared in the Hearst newspapers. After sponsoring subsequent serials, *The Exploits of Elaine, The Goddess*, and *The Adventures of Wallingford*, International became more directly involved in the production and distribution of the serials *The Mysteries of Myra, Beatrice Fairfax*, and *Patria* and began production of the Hearst-International News Pictorial, an antecedent to the Hearst-Selig and Hearst-Vitagraph newsreels. In April 1916, Hearst opened exchanges in cities where the Hearst papers were the strongest, and through them he released his own newsreels*, serials, cartoons, and feature productions. Hearst was the president and Edward A. McManus was the general manager. On January 1, 1917, International began distributing its product through the Pathé* exchanges and it combined its newsreel with that of Pathé to form the Hearst-Pathé News. In March 1919, International began releasing with the Famous Players-Lasky Corporation. It remained in existence through 1922.
BIBLIOGRAPHY
"Hearst Opens Exchanges," *The Moving Picture World*, April 8, 1916, p. 230.

INTERNATIONAL MOTION PICTURE ASSOCIATION. See MOTION PICTURE EXHIBITORS' LEAGUE OF AMERICA

THE INTERNATIONAL NEWSREEL. See NEWSREELS

INTERNATIONAL PHOTOPLAY CORPORATION. Based in Chicago, with John Wojtalewicz as president, the International Photoplay Corporation was active in the late teens and early twenties producing a series of one- and two-reel comedies, featuring Art Bates and Lou Tops.

INTERNATIONAL PICTURES. See UNIVERSAL PICTURES

INTER-OCEAN FILM CORPORATION. Active in the teens and twenties as a distributor of and agent for American films abroad, the Inter-Ocean Film Corporation was organized by Paul H. Cromelin. According to the 1921 edition of the *Motion Picture Studio Directory*, "In the efficient execution of foreign film transactions, the American producer needs the co-operation of an export organization equipped with the necessary resources, facilities and experience to render a genuine foreign service—profitably. The tireless efforts of Paul H. Cromelin to bring into being just such an organization has been amply rewarded."

INTERSTATE FEATURE FILM COMPANY. The Interstate Feature Film Company, with headquarters in Middletown, Connecticut, was formed in April 1915 by New England businessmen to produce two feature films per month. Kenneth MacDougall was the vice-president and general manager. Its first feature, the four-reel *Bulldogs of the Trail*, starred leading lady Snyder Shields. Interstate released with the Picture Playhouse Film Company*.
BIBLIOGRAPHY
"Interstate Feature Film Company Founded," *The Moving Picture World*, April 17, 1915, p. 370.

INVINCIBLE PICTURES CORPORATION. See CHESTERFIELD MOTION PICTURE CORPORATION

ITALA FILM COMPANY OF AMERICA. The Itala Film Company of America was organized in July 1915 by Harry R. Raver to produce in America an eight-reel film with "Maciste," the character created by Gabrielle D'Annunzio in the earlier Italian success, *Cabiria*. Ernest Pagano, who played the role in *Cabiria*, continued in subsequent productions. Agnes L. Bain was the company's scenarist.
BIBLIOGRAPHY
"Itala Company's Plans," *The Moving Picture World*, July 31, 1915, p. 800.

ITHACA, NEW YORK. See WHARTON, INC.

IVAN FILM PRODUCTIONS, INC. Ivan Abramson (1872–1934), formerly the manager of the largest traveling opera organization and a manager of Yiddish theatre stars, founded Ivan Film Productions, in 1914, and acted as director-general and writer for the company. Some of his films included *Forbidden Fruit*, *A Fool's Paradise*, *Concealed Truth*, and *The Immortal Flame*. His best-known production was probably *Enlighten Thy Daughter* (1917). When Abramson left the company late in 1917 and formed the Graphic Film Corporation*, I. E. Chadwick became the new head, and Ivan continued production with F. J. Grandon and Edmund Lawrence as directors.
BIBLIOGRAPHY
"Ivan Abramson, Master Craftsman," *The Moving Picture World*, March 4, 1916, p. 1455.

IVERSON RANCH. Located in the Chatsworth area of the San Fernando Valley, on the outskirts of Los Angeles, the Iverson Ranch has been used as a location site for more than 2,000 films from 1912 onward. According to the *New York Herald Tribune* (September 10, 1950), the ranch "offers ten different types of location sites, including jungle, mountain, desert, and open range, and they are so isolated from one another that five companies can be shooting without conflicting with one another." In particular, the 600-acre ranch offered rock formations and rugged scenery making it an ideal venue for Westerns*. The ranch was founded by Karl Iverson and purchased by Bob Sherman, in 1982, from Iverson's son, Joe. Among the films shot in part at the Iverson Ranch were *Tell It to the Marines* (1927), *Noah's Ark* (1929), *Morocco* (1930), *The Lives of a Bengal Lancer* (1935), *Trail of the Lonesome Pine* (1936), *Wee Willie Winkie* (1937), *The Flying Deuces* (1939), *Stagecoach* (1939), and *Cattle Queen of Montana* (1954). It has also been used in the production of many television series.

BIBLIOGRAPHY

Sherman, Robert G. *Quiet on the Set!* Chatsworth, California: Sherway Publishing Company, 1984.

J

J.A.C. See ZODIAK FILM MANUFACTURING COMPANY

JACK WRATHER PICTURES, INC. See WRATHER CORPORATION

JAM HANDY ORGANIZATION. Active from the thirties through the seventies, the Jam Handy Organization was a major producer of educational, training, industrial, and other types of nontheatrical films. Jamison Handy was president of the company, which had headquarters in Detroit and branch offices in New York, Chicago, and Hollywood.

JANS PRODUCTIONS, INC. Founded in 1920 by Herman F. Jans, Jans Productions, Inc., remained active through 1926 as a minor producer of society dramas and melodramas.

JAPANESE-AMERICAN FILM COMPANY. Claiming to be the first company in the United States to be owned, controlled, and operated by Japanese, the Japanese-American Film Company was formed in October 1914 by Japanese businessmen, after existing for the previous two years in Japan as a producer of commercial, educational, and industrial features. The company had a stock company of forty actors and actresses from Japan. Its first production, *The Oath of the Sword*, was said to have treated Japanese themes and customs with fidelity. It was distributed by Sawyer, Inc.* The company planned to make dramatic films part of the year in Japan and also in Hawaii. K. Numamoto was the president, Tomi Morri and Hisa Numa were the leading players, and Kohano Akashi and Jack Y. Abbe also acted in the company.
BIBLIOGRAPHY
"Japanese-American Film Company," *The Moving Picture World*, October 17, 1914, p. 314.

JAPANESE PHOTOPLAYERS' CLUB OF LOS ANGELES. The Japanese Photoplayers' Club of Los Angeles was organized, in October 1917, to see that its members did not appear in films reflecting badly upon the Japanese people. Members were asked to use their influence to urge producers to portray the Japanese race in a dignified manner. Sessue Hayakawa and Frank Tokanaga were the club's leaders.

JASPER HOLLYWOOD STUDIOS. See HOLLYWOOD GENERAL STUDIOS

JENSEN-FARLEY PICTURES, INC. The distribution company of Jensen-Farley Pictures, Inc., was formed in 1981 by Raylan Jensen and Clair Farley with the purchase of Taft International Pictures, Inc., a subsidiary of Taft Broadcasting. Taft International Pictures had been created, in 1980, with the acquisition of the library of Sunn Classics, which was well known for its marketing of such exploitation features as *In Search of Noah's Ark* (1977), *Chariots of the Gods* (1974), and *The Outer Space Connection* (1975). At the time of its acquisition by Taft, Sunn Classics had a library of twenty-two features and fifty-seven television productions. Sunn Classics had its origins in American National Enterprises, formed in Salt Lake City in 1966 by Robert Crosier. The company became Sunn Classics in 1971, when it was acquired by the Schick Razor Company.

Address: 556 East 200 South, Salt Lake City, Utah 84102.
BIBLIOGRAPHY
Hollinger, Hy, ''Jensen Farley Pictures Wants to Fill Niche Once Held by Avco and Filmways,'' *Daily Variety*, November 18, 1982, pp. 1, 22.

JERRY FAIRBANKS PRODUCTIONS. A production house dating back to the thirties, Jerry Fairbanks Productions is best known for three series of short subjects which it produced for Paramount: *Popular Science* (1935–1949), *Unusual Occupations* (1937–1949), and *Speaking of Animals* (1941–1949). In more recent years, the company has been involved in television production. Subsidiary companies are Western Audio Visual Enterprises and Yukon Pictures, Inc.

Address: 826 North Cole Avenue, Hollywood, Calif. 90038.

JERSEY CITY, NEW JERSEY. See FREDERICK DOUGLASS FILM COMPANY and PATHÉ

JESSE D. HAMPTON FEATURE CORP. See ROBERTSON-COLE COMPANY

JESTER COMEDY COMPANY. William Steiner formed the Jester Comedy Company, in December 1917, to make two-reel comedies starring the European Fernandez Perez as the character "Twede-Dan." The Jester studios were located in Cliffside, New Jersey, and its first production was titled *The Recruit*. William A. Seiter was the company's director.

JEWEL PRODUCTIONS, INC. With the slogan "It's a Jewel" to advertise its films, Jewel Productions, Inc., was formed on August 26, 1917, to release "the biggest and best special features," which it would purchase with outright cash. It released approximately one film per month. Harry M. Berman, formerly with Artcraft, was the head of the New York exchange, while Leon J. Bamburger was the general supervisor for all the exchanges. Some films that Jewel released include *Come Through* and *The Heart of Humanity*, both purchased from Universal*. In June 1919, Jewel consolidated its offices with those of Universal, and "Jewel" became a brand name for certain Universal releases.
BIBLIOGRAPHY
"Jewel Productions, Inc.," *The Moving Picture World*, August 25, 1917, p. 1206.

JOEL PRODUCTIONS. See THE BRYNA COMPANY

JOSEPH BURSTYN, INC. Although Joseph Burstyn died in 1953 at the age of fifty-three, the company that bears his name continues in operation as one of the best known and most highly respected of importers and distributors of foreign films. Burstyn entered film distribution in 1930 with the feature *A Jew at War*. He organized his company in 1935 and the following year joined forces with Arthur Mayer to form Arthur Mayer & Joseph Burstyn, Inc., which remained in existence until September 1949 when Burstyn bought out his partner. Although the company did distribute some American features, such as *The Little Fugitive* (1953), Burstyn is more closely associated with the original American release of classic foreign-language films, such as *The New Gulliver*, *Open City*, *Paisan*, *The Bicycle Thief*, and, of course, *The Miracle*, which involved Burstyn in a lengthy and successful fight against film censorship.

Address: 301 West 53 Street, New York, N.Y. 10019.
BIBLIOGRAPHY
Mitgang, Herbert, "Transatlantic 'Miracle' Man," *Park East*, August 1952, pp. 32–36.

JUNGLE FILM COMPANY. The Jungle Film Company, located at Eastlake Park in Los Angeles, was formed in July 1914 to make only wild animal films. It was often referred to as the E. & R., Jungle Film Company, after its owners J. S. Edwards and John Rounan. Paul Machette was the company director, and Irvin Willatt was the head of the camera department. Its best-known films were a series of more than forty one-reel comedies featuring chimpanzees Sally and Napoleon (who were married on stage, as part of a vaudeville act, at the Pantages Theatre, Los Angeles, on December 25, 1913).

BIBLIOGRAPHY

"Napoleon and Sally, the Only Chimpanzees in Motion Pictures Have Romped through Forty E. & R. Comedies," *Motion Picture News Studio Directory*, October 21, 1916, p. 9.

JUNO FILMS. See LOPERT FILMS DISTRIBUTING COMPANY

JUVENILE FILM COMPANY. The Juvenile Film Company, located in Cleveland, was formed in 1915 to produce children's films. James A. Fitz-Patrick—formerly a reporter, acting student, and instructor of child actors—directed, wrote, and acted in the films which featured child performers Janethal and Joseph Monahan in leading roles.

BIBLIOGRAPHY

"Fitz-Patrick with Juvenile Film Company," *The Moving Picture World*, March 4, 1916, p. 1454.

K

KALEM COMPANY, INC. The Kalem Company, Inc., was organized early in 1907 by George Kleine, Samuel Long, and Frank Marion, who created the name from the first letters of their last names. Kleine, the president, was the owner of the Kleine Optical Company of Chicago, which handled films from leading foreign manufacturers as well as projection machines. Long, the vice-president, was formerly the superintendent of the Biograph* factory. Marion, Kalem's secretary and treasurer, was formerly in charge of the Biograph studio and responsible for selling the company's films. Kalem's first production, *A Runaway Sleighbelle*, was directed by Sidney Olcott, who had earlier been associated with Marion at Biograph. The early Kalem films contained subtitles in the form of cartoons drawn by a newspaper artist. Its studio and headquarters were at 131 West 24 Street, New York.

According to Kalem's general manager, William Wright, Marion created a stock company early in Kalem's history, and this may have been the first such motion picture stock company. Wright also claimed that Kalem was the first producer to exploit the names of its players.

After Kalem produced *Ben-Hur* in a one-reel version late in 1907, it was sued by the publishers of the book, the author's estate, and the producers of the stage production in what was the first case dealing with the right to make motion pictures from dramatic or literary sources. A few years later, the U.S. Supreme Court handed down a decision against Kalem, which established the precedent that rights to properties must be obtained by companies prior to the properties being made into films.

Kalem joined the Motion Picture Patents Company* and released its films on the General Film Company program. Olcott made Westerns* in Coytesville, New Jersey, and then, in the fall of 1908, went with a company of twelve players to Jacksonville, Florida, and secured an estate complete with a mansion, cabins, wharf, boats, and a grove. Kalem's first Florida film, *A Florida Feud, or Love in the Everglades*, was released in December 1908. Later films shot in Florida* included Civil War dramas sympathetic to the South.

Sidney Olcott, of Irish descent, took a small company to Ireland in August 1910. Included were Gene Gauntier, who, in addition to being the leading lady, was also the company's scenarist; Robert Vignola; and cameraman George K. Hollister. The company settled in Beaufort, County Kerry, and returned there the following year with a larger company. After Olcott and Gauntier left Kalem, in 1912, to form the Gene Gauntier Feature Players, they continued to return to Beaufort.

Olcott, Gauntier, Vignola, Jack Clarke, and others traveled to Palestine in the fall of 1912 to film the six-reel *From the Manger to the Cross*, which William Wright claimed to be the first film, other than topical subjects, of that length. Although the film was very successful, Kalem refused to continue producing long films and preferred to go out of business once the industry norm was the feature film, rather than take the risks that feature production involved.

Director Kenean Buell took a company of players to the West Coast with William Wright. They established a studio at Verdugo Canyon, Glendale, on December 11, 1910. Included in the company were Alice Joyce, Mr. and Mrs. George Melford, and Jane Wolfe. Early in 1911, Carlyle Blackwell and William H. West joined the Glendale studio, which produced a one-reel Western every week. Later in 1911, P. C. Hartigan opened a Kalem studio in Santa Monica, at which worked Ruth Roland, Marin Sais, Ed Coxen, and Marshall Neilan, who assisted Hartigan and later became the Santa Monica company's chief director. George Melford took over chief directing chores at the Glendale studio when Buell replaced Olcott in Jacksonville, taking with him Miriam Cooper, Anna Q. Nilsson, Guy Coombs, and Hal Clements. In 1913, Carlyle Blackwell became chief director at the new Kalem studios in Hollywood. Neilan joined him and initiated the "Ham and Bud" comedy series, featuring Lloyd Hamilton and Bud Duncan. J. P. McGowan went West shortly thereafter and produced *The Hazards of Helen* serial, starring Helen Holmes. Later, Helen Gibson was featured in the railroad series.

In 1915, Kalem made a series of three-reel "Broadway Favorites" released with General, at a new studio in Cliffside, New Jersey. In 1916, Kalem ended production. Early in 1919, Vitagraph* purchased Kalem's properties, films, and laboratory equipment, as William Wright became associated with Vitagraph. Later that same year, it was announced that Kalem's films would be reissued.

BIBLIOGRAPHY

Blaisdell, George, "Mecca of the Motion Picture," *The Moving Picture World*, July 10, 1915, p. 218.

Condon, Mabel, "Hot Chocolate and Reminiscences at Nine of the Morning," *Photoplay*, January 1915, pp. 69–72.

Gauntier, Gene. *Blazing the Trail*. Manuscript in the files of the Museum of Modern Art, December 16, 1928.

"Kalem Company (Inc.)," *The Moving Picture World*, June 8, 1907, p. 223.

"Kalem Players Combine in Search for Picturesque Locations," *Motion Picture News*, March 31, 1917, p. 2021.

"Kalem Railroad Films Have Seven Years' History," *Motion Picture News*, January 8, 1916, p. 81.

"Kalem's Achievements as Pioneer," *The Moving Picture World*, March 10, 1917, pp. 1504–1505.

Slide, Anthony, "The Kalem Serial Queens," *The Silent Picture*, no. 1, Winter 1968–69, pp. 8–11.

————. "The O'Kalems," in *Aspects of American Film History prior to 1920*. Metuchen, New Jersey: Scarecrow Press, 1978, pp. 87–97.

K & R FILM COMPANY. The K & R Film Company was formed in April 1915 by R. R. Roberts, Pierce Kingsley, and Frances Kell. Kingsley wrote and starred in its first production, *Silver Threads among the Gold*. Leon Victor was the general manager of the company, which had offices in the Putnam Building at 1493 Broadway, New York.

KAUFMAN ASTORIA STUDIOS. See Astoria Studios

K.C. BOOKING COMPANY. See KINETOPHOTE FILM CORPORATION

KELLUM TALKING PICTURES. Similar to Edison's Kinetophone*, Kellum Talking Pictures was developed in Los Angeles by Orlando E. Kellum in 1913. Kellum recorded the action and sound simultaneously, utilizing a device to synchronize the recording phonograph and the camera. Electrical impulses from a commutator connected to the phonograph turntable were sent by wires to a series of electromagnets in the synchronizing device used for either the camera or the projector. The electromagnets were linked by pistons to a crankshaft which rotated the projector mechanism in exact synchronization with the phonograph.

Although not particularly successful from a commercial standpoint, Kellum Talking Pictures were important because the process was utilized by D. W. Griffith for his 1921 feature, *Dream Street*, which included a title song performed by leading man Ralph Graves and an introduction by the director. Accompanying *Dream Street* at its initial screenings in New York, Brooklyn, and Chicago were a series of short subjects produced by Kellum, with such personalities as labor leader Samuel Gompers, the Van Eps Trio, Sam Moore and His Singing Saw, and singer Ruby Norton.

BIBLIOGRAPHY

Hoffman, Hugh, "A New Talking Picture Device," *The Moving Picture World*, November 1, 1913, p. 483.

KENNEDY FEATURES, INC. Aubrey M. Kennedy formed Kennedy Features, Inc., early in 1914 to produce one three- to five-reel feature, starring English tragedienne Constance Crawley and Arthur Maude, every two weeks. Kennedy was vice-president and general manager, while Irving C. Ackerman was the president. Offices for the company were located in the World's Tower Building at 110 West 40 Street in New York. The name of the cinematographer, William

F. Alder, was given equal prominence in the main titles of its films as those of the director and scenarist. Its films were shot on the Pacific Coast and released through the Criterion Feature Film Manufacturing Company. Its first productions were *The Bride of Lammermoor* and *Mary Magdalen*, both three-reel features.
BIBLIOGRAPHY
"New Picture Concern," *The Moving Picture World*, January 17, 1914, p. 300.

KEYSTONE FILM COMPANY. The Keystone Film Company, formed in 1912 by former Biograph* player and comedy director Mack Sennett (1880–1960) and the owners of the New York Motion Picture Company, Adam Kessel, Jr., and Charles O. Baumann, released its first two films, *Cohen Collects a Debt* and *The Water Nymph*, on September 23, 1912, and continued to release a weekly split-reel on Mondays on the Mutual* program. Its offices were located at 150 East 14 Street, New York.

Mabel Normand, Fred Mace, Ford Sterling, and Sennett were featured in the comedies, which Sennett directed. Productions were, at first, shot at Fort Lee, New Jersey*, and in September 1912 the company went West and settled at the old Bison studio in Edendale, California. The demand for Keystone comedies grew, and soon Mabel Normand began directing a second company. Charles Chaplin made his motion picture debut in Keystone's *Making a Living* early in 1914. Before he left the company at the end of that year, Chaplin had developed his Tramp character and was directing and writing his own films, in addition to starring in them. On November 14, 1914, the feature-length *Tillie's Punctured Romance*, featuring Mabel Normand, Marie Dressler, and Chaplin, was released, and it was a huge success.

In 1915, Keystone, along with D. W. Griffith's and Thomas H. Ince's companies, formed the Triangle Film Corporation*. At that time Keystone was comprised of three production companies. In 1917, Keystone began releasing with Paramount*. That same year Keystone officially went out of existence, although it might be argued that it continued until Mack Sennett Productions went bankrupt in 1933. (In 1928, Sennett moved to new studios in Studio City, California, studios which later became known as Republic*.)

Other featured players in Keystone comedies were Raymond Hitchcock, Wallace Beery, Roscoe "Fatty" Arbuckle, Ben Turpin, Dot Farley, Louise Fazenda, Phyllis Haver, Chester Conklin, Alice Davenport, and Mack Swain.
BIBLIOGRAPHY
Bartlett, Randolph, "Why Aren't We Killed?" *Photoplay*, April 1916, pp. 81–84.
Lahue, Kalton C. *Mack Sennett's Keystone*. South Brunswick, New Jersey: A. S. Barnes, 1971.
———, and Terry Brewer. *Kops and Custards*. Norman, Oklahoma: University of Oklahoma Press, 1967.
"The Psychology of a Laugh," *The Moving Picture World*, July 10, 1915, p. 236.
Todd, Stanley W., "Putting the Key in Keystone," *Motion Picture Classic*, November 1917, pp. 27–31.
"Where Laughs Are Made," *The Moving Picture World*, July 10, 1915, pp. 233–236.

KILLIAM SHOWS, INC. Killiam Shows, Inc., is possibly the best-known supplier of silent film footage to television. It was formed by Paul Killiam, who, in 1946, opened the Old Knick Music Hall on New York's Second Avenue and included as part of the entertainment early silent films. Killiam began acquiring rights to early films, including the Biograph* and Edison* productions, and the films of D. W. Griffith. He was involved in the restoration of many films in cooperation with the Museum of Modern Art. Killiam was first seen on television, on a regular basis, on CBS in 1952 with *The Paul Killiam Show*, which utilized Edison films strictly for laugh value. His first major television series (produced in collaboration with Saul Turrell) was *Movie Museum* (1954–1955). It was followed by *Silents Please* (released nontheatrically as *The History of the Motion Picture*), which Killiam again produced in collaboration with Saul Turrell and which consisted of thirty-nine thirty-minute programs. Killiam Shows began screening silent films in their entirety on television with the series *The Silent Years*, first seen on PBS. Killiam Shows was also involved in *The Legend of Valentino* (1961) and *The Great Chase* (1962).

Address: 6 East 39 Street, New York, N.Y. 10016.

KINEMACOLOR. Kinemacolor, the earliest commercially successful natural color film process, was a two-color additive system, involving photography through a red-orange and a blue-green gelatin filter and projection through filters of the same colors at thirty-two frames per second. It was invented by Edward R. Turner and F. Marshall Lee and exploited by American Charles Urban (1867–1942). The first Kinemacolor demonstration was given in London on May 1, 1908, and it was in the United Kingdom that the process gained popularity. Its greatest success came with the filming of the 1911 *Delhi Durbar*. Kinemacolor was first exhibited in the United States, at New York's Madison Square Garden, on December 11, 1909; the Kinemacolor Company of America was established in 1910, and, by 1913, Kinemacolor had reached the height of its American popularity. By the mid-teens, the process had been discarded, largely because of complaints from the audience that the color hurt its eyes.

BIBLIOGRAPHY
Allbee, Burton H., "Impressions of Kinemacolor Films," *The Moving Picture World*, December 25, 1909, pp. 915–916.

"All Eyes Are on Kinemacolor," *Motography*, July 12, 1913, p. 6.

Brown, Theodore, "My Impressions of 'Kinemacolor,' " *The Moving Picture World*, May 28, 1910, p. 886.

Harrison, Louis Reeves, "Sauntering with Kinemacolor," *The Moving Picture World*, February 15, 1913, pp. 661–662.

Thomas, D. B. *The First Colour Motion Pictures*. London: Her Majesty's Stationery Office, 1969.

KINEMACOLOR COMPANY OF AMERICA. Following the 1909 New York presentation of Kinemacolor films, Gilbert H. Aymar, a businessman from Allentown, Pennsylvania, secured an exclusive option on the equipment. With James K. Bowen, Aymar formed the Kinemacolor Company of America in April

1910, with offices in Allentown. By July 1911, the company's offices had moved to 145 West 45 Street, New York, and J. J. Murdock had become the general manager.

In May 1912, the company, then headed by Henry J. Brock, hired Thomas L. Cochrane to superintend the organization of a plant and stock company to produce dramatic and comedy films with the Kinemacolor process. Since the films had to be taken by sunlight, it was appropriate that among the first pictures planned were a travel series to be taken by Alfred G. Gosden of various national parks, called "See America First," and films of U.S. naval battleships. Brock engaged David Miles as the head of Kinemacolor's dramatic production units. Miles worked with three companies at Kinemacolor's Whitestone, Long Island, plant, and on location throughout the eastern states.

In the fall of 1912, he formed three more companies of seventy people and took one to the Grand Canyon and the remaining two to Hollywood, where they moved into a studio at 4500 Sunset Boulevard, previously the Revier Laboratories and later the Fine Arts* studio. Some of those going East were leading lady Linda Arvidson Griffith, Mabel Van Buren, Stella Razetto, Clara Bracy, Ruby Ross, Ethel Davis, Gaston Bell, Charles Fleming, Jack Brammell, Charles Haydon, Guy Oliver, Robert Broderick, Murdock McQuarrie, and Mahlon Hamilton. Frank Woods also directed with the Hollywood company, and Lee Dougherty was the scenario editor. William Haddock directed the company in New York. Lillian Russell was engaged for two weeks at the end of 1912.

Although Kinemacolor obtained a license from the Motion Picture Patents Company* in August 1913, permitting it to install its service in any licensed theatre, the company was failing because of the high cost of the process and the limited number of theatres equipped to exhibit it.

Its Hollywood studio closed in June 1913. Miles returned to New York with director Charles Fleming, Gaston Bell, Jack Brammell, Charles Perley, Guy Oliver, and Linda Griffith, while other members stayed in California, joining other companies. In October 1913, Kinemacolor built a studio at Lowville, New York, near the St. Lawrence River. Also in October, Miles left the company for Biograph* and took most of the stock company with him. Theodore Marston replaced Miles and formed a new company. In November 1913, Kinemacolor formed the Weber-Fields-Kinemacolor Company to make comedies with the famous vaudeville team. Roy McCardell was hired to write scenarios. Rumors circulated that the Kinemacolor plant at Whitestone would again be used for production and that it would make a five-reel feature, but, by 1915, Kinemacolor was effectively dead.

BIBLIOGRAPHY

"Demonstration of Kinemacolor," *The Moving Picture World*, August 6, 1910, pp. 291–292.

"Kinemacolor Closed," *The New York Dramatic Mirror*, June 11, 1913, p. 25.

"Kinemacolor Company Branches Out," *The Moving Picture World*, May 26, 1912, p. 716.

"Kinemacolor Company Now Releasing," *The Moving Picture World*, October 12, 1912, p. 231.
"Kinemacolor in America," *The Moving Picture World*, April 16, 1910, p. 605.

KINETOGRAPH AND KINETOSCOPE. The Kinetograph is the name of Thomas Alvah Edison's first practical motion picture camera, developed by Edison employee W.K.L. Dickson, in principle if not in practical form, in 1891 and patented in 1893. Film photographed by the Kinetograph was first viewed on a peep-show device called a Kinetoscope, a coin-operated machine inside a wooden box. The first commercial presentation of motion pictures in the United States took place in a kinetoscope parlor at 1155 Broadway, New York, on April 14, 1894.

These first films, known as Kinetoscopic records, were produced at a studio built of wood and tar paper at Edison's West Orange laboratory and nicknamed by the inventor's staff as the "Black Maria." (The "Black Maria" presently on view at the Edison National Historic Site in Orange, New Jersey, is a recreation.) The first film to be copyrighted, on January 7, 1894, was *Edison Kinetoscopic Record of a Sneeze*, which showed Edison employee Fred Ott sneezing.

BIBLIOGRAPHY
Hendricks, Gordon. *The Edison Motion Picture Myth.* Berkeley, California: University of California Press, 1961.

KINETOGRAPH COMPANY. The Kinetograph Company was organized by J. J. Kennedy, of the Biograph Company*, and P. L. Waters, former general manager of General Film Company, early in 1913. It obtained a license from the Motion Picture Patents Company* to lease licensed pictures and established distribution offices in New York, Atlanta, and New Orleans. It began distribution on February 9, 1913, but went out of business two months later following a dispute over the distribution rights to the Detective Burns film *Exposure of the Land Swindlers*. All of Kinetograph's stock and assets were sold to General Film Company.

BIBLIOGRAPHY
"Kinetograph Company Quits Business," *The Moving Picture World*, April 26, 1913, p. 359.

KINETOPHONE. The concept of combining a phonograph with a film projector and thus creating synchronized sound motion pictures was conceived by Thomas Edison in 1887. His assistant, W.K.L. Dickson, worked on the project, which was called a Kineto-Phonograph, and by 1895 may have come up with a workable machine. The project was subsequently shelved until 1911, when Edison's staff developed a method of amplification which permitted the phonograph recorder to pick up sounds from a distance of more than twenty feet. Following various modifications, the Kinetophone—one of the first commercial sound film projects— was launched in 1913. The films that were screened in vaudeville houses rather than motion picture theatres were released by the American Talking-Picture

Company, which also leased the projection-sound machines and which was formed by B. F. Keith and E. F. Albee's United Booking Offices of America. Kinetophone films were seen spasmodically during 1913 and 1914 but were not successful, largely because of problems with keeping the phonograph record in synchronization with the film and because the performers in the films were minor entertainers and audiences had little reason for paying to see such performers on film when, for the same amount of money, they could see vaudeville headliners in person.

BIBLIOGRAPHY

Rogoff, Rosalind, "Edison's Dream: A Brief History of the Kinetophone," *Cinema Journal*, vol. XV, no. 2, Spring 1976, pp. 58–68.

Shifrin, Art, "The Trouble with Kinetophone," *American Cinematographer*, September 1983, pp. 50–54, 115–125.

RESOURCES

Films: Library of Congress; Museum of Modern Art.

Papers: Edison National Historic Site.

KINETOPHOTE FILM CORPORATION. The Kinetophote Film Corporation and the K. C. Booking Company, Inc., were established in November 1914 to work in conjunction with one another in the release of American and foreign-made films in the United States. Offices for both companies were at 126–133 West 46 Street, New York. Ira H. Simmons was the general manager of Kinetophote. Some of its releases included films from the Ambrosia Company of Italy and the Hollandia Film Company.

BIBLIOGRAPHY

"Tips from Kinetophone," *The Moving Picture World*, November 7, 1914, p. 800.

KING-BEE FILMS CORPORATION. Louis B. Burstein, one of the organizers of the New York Motion Picture Company* and the Reliance Stock Company, formed King-Bee Films in 1917 to make Billy West comedies. Its studio was located in Jacksonville, Florida. Other players in the films included Ethel Gibson and Oliver Hardy.

KING BROS. PRODUCTIONS, INC. See KING INTERNATIONAL CORPORATION

KING INTERNATIONAL CORPORATION. On April 15, 1942, three brothers, Frank, Maurice (who died in 1977), and Herman King organized King Bros. Productions as a low-budget production company, whose best-known features were *Gun Crazy/Deadly Is the Female* (1950), *The Brave One* (1956), and *Return of the Gunfighter* (1966). The name of the company was changed to King International Corporation in 1970.

Address: 124 Lasky Drive, Beverly Hills, Calif. 90212.

KINNEY NATIONAL SERVICES, INC. See WARNER BROS. PICTURES, INC. and WARNER COMMUNICATIONS INC.

KINOGRAMS. See NEWSREELS

KINO INTERNATIONAL CORPORATION. Kino International was formed, as a Denver-based corporation, by William Pence in 1975. At that time, it handled the 35mm distribution of Janus Films and some productions from Samuel Goldwyn*, Walter Wanger, and RKO*. The company was acquired in 1977 by Donald Krim (who had earlier created the Classics Division of United Artists), and he added the libraries of Charles Chaplin, Alexander Korda, David O. Selznick, Harold Lloyd, and Grove Press. In 1982, Kino acquired Walter Reade's Continental Films Library, along with some Samuel Bronston productions and George Stevens' *Giant*. The following year, Kino released the "restored" versions of the Louise Brooks/G. W. Pabst features, *Pandora's Box* and *Diary of a Lost Girl*. In 1984, it announced worldwide distribution of a restored version of Erich von Stroheim's unfinished 1928 feature, *Queen Kelly*, starring Gloria Swanson.

Address: 250 West 57 Street, Suite 314, New York, N.Y. 10019.

KLEINE-EDISON FEATURE SERVICE. The Kleine-Edison Feature Service began operations in June 1915 to distribute features produced by the two member companies of the Motion Picture Patents Company*. It claimed to have abolished the advance deposit system. Beginning September 2, 1916, the Kleine-Edison-Selig-Essanay Service replaced the previous company and released its members' products through the George Kleine* exchanges.

BIBLIOGRAPHY

"Kleine-Edison Merger Formed," *The Moving Picture World*, July 24, 1915, p. 626.

KNICKERBOCKER STAR FEATURES. Knickerbocker Star Features began producing three-reel pictures in May 1915 for release every other Wednesday with the General Film Company service. Stanner E. V. Taylor was the head of the directorial staff. Players making Knickerbocker films included Ralph Stuart, Alice Brady, J. Forbes Robertson, Mary Nash, Lenore Ulrich, Florence Rockwell, Walter Hampden, and Marion Leonard (Taylor's wife). Knickerbocker had a studio in Flushing, New York. In February 1917, the company went out of business, and the Balboa Amusement Producing Company* began producing Knickerbocker Star Features for General's program.

BIBLIOGRAPHY

"Knickerbocker Star Features Successful," *The Moving Picture World*, September 25, 1915, p. 2189.

KRITERION FILM CORPORATION. The Kriterion Film Corporation was incorporated in November 1914 by H. F. Rhatigan, E. H. Reilly, and C. H. Ayres as a successor to the Mica Film Company. With offices at the Mecca Building, 1600 Broadway, New York, Kriterion began, in January 1915, releasing films of West Coast companies Crown City Film Manufacturing Company*, Navajo Film Manufacturing Company*, Monarch Producing Company*, Alhambra Motion Picture Company*, Robin's Photoplays, Inc., Santa Barbara Motion Picture Company*, Liberty Feature Film Company*, and the Nash Motion Picture Company, Inc.*

Its projected releasing output was to be twenty-one reels per week, including six one-reel subjects and six two-reelers. Aubrey M. Kennedy, the general manager of the Santa Barbara Motion Picture Company, was general representative of the company and had complete authority over the productions of the companies associated with Kriterion. Although each producing company had its own scenario department, Kriterion retained "cooperative jurisdiction" over scenarios and all matters pertaining to each company. Also, the laboratories for the companies were on the East Coast.

The financial difficulties of Kriterion were reported as early as January 1915; the companies associated with Kriterion complained that they could not pay their actors' and employees' back salaries. In May 1915, the Alhambra Motion Picture Company and four minor creditors made an application for receivership of Kriterion, which was accepted. The Associated Film Service Corporation began releasing the product of most of Kriterion's former producing companies in October 1915. Although news items in August 1915 announced that the new Kriterion Sales Company was in the process of reforming the old Kriterion program, the effort never materialized.

BIBLIOGRAPHY

"Kriterion to Release January First," *The Moving Picture World*, November 21, 1914, p. 1052.

L

LACLEDE WESTERN FEATURES. See LLOYD FILMS, INC.

THE LADD COMPANY. The Ladd Company was formed in 1979 as a "mini studio" when Alan Ladd, Jr., left as president of 20th Century-Fox*. Two other Fox employees joined Ladd in the creation of the new company: Jay Kanter and Gareth Wigan. For his logo, Ladd selected a spreading and luxuriantly green oak tree. The Ladd Company was financed in part by Warner Bros.*, with which it had an exclusive distribution deal from 1979 to 1984, and on whose Burbank Studios* lot the company made its headquarters. Sandy Lieberson served as London head of the Ladd Company until the British office was closed in January 1984, and it was Lieberson who was responsible for bringing *Chariots of Fire* (1981) to Ladd's attention. The Ladd Company acquired American rights to the feature, which was released through Warner Bros. *Chariots of Fire* and *Police Academy* (1984) were the only two major "hits" of the Ladd Company, although *The Right Stuff* (1983) enjoyed limited success.

Address: 4000 Warner Boulevard, Burbank, Calif. 91522.

BIBLIOGRAPHY

Waters, Harry F., "The Ladd Co's Wrong Stuff," *Newsweek*, December 12, 1983, p. 88.

LAEMMLE FILM SERVICE. See UNIVERSAL PICTURES

LAEMMLE THEATRES. The Laemmle Theatre chain is a small, Los Angeles–based operation with little more than a dozen theatres, specializing in foreign-language films. It is important because of its location in the American film production capital and because so many shorts* and documentaries* nominated for Academy Award consideration rely on Laemmle theatres for eligibility screenings. (The Academy Awards rules are such that most shorts and documentaries must play seven consecutive days in the Los Angeles area to be eligible for consideration.) *Screen International* (August 27, 1983) described the

Laemmle theatres as "the most respected art and foreign film houses in the U.S."

The chain was founded by Max Laemmle, a distant nephew of Carl Laemmle, who became an American exhibitor in 1939. He acquired the first of his theatres, the Los Feliz, in 1947, and it became the flagship for his chain. As of 1984, the Laemmle Theatre chain consisted of the Music Hall in Beverly Hills; the Town & Country Cinemas 1, 2, and 3 in Encino; the Continental and Los Feliz in Hollywood; the Esquire in Pasadena; the Monica 4-plex in Santa Monica; and the Royal and the Westland 1 & 2 in West Los Angeles.

Address: 11523 Santa Monica Boulevard, Los Angeles, Calif. 90025.

BIBLIOGRAPHY

"Max Laemmle: Laemmle Theatres," *Los Angeles*, March 1981, p. 181.

Thomas, Kevin, "Cultivating the Foreign Film Market," *Los Angeles Times*, Calendar Section, December 30, 1979, pp. 31–32.

Williams, Dick, "Max Laemmle Devotee of Both Movies and Art," *Los Angeles Mirror*, July 29, 1961, pp. 2, 4.

LAIRD INTERNATIONAL STUDIOS. One of the oldest—as late as 1986, a glass-topped stage dating from the late teens still stands on the lot—and the most familiar of all American studio lots, the Laird International Studios opened in 1919 as the new studios, on Washington Boulevard in Culver City, California, of producer Thomas H. Ince. Some of the first films to be shot there were *Behind the Door* (1920) and *Homer Comes Home* (1920). In 1925, following Ince's unexpected death, the studios were acquired by Cecil B. DeMille and utilized for the production of features for Producers Distributing Corporation*. In 1928, DeMille disposed of his interest in the studio and it became the Pathé* Studios, becoming the RKO-Pathé Studios, in 1930, with the merger of the two companies. Among the major RKO* productions filmed on the lot were *What Price Hollywood* (1932), *A Bill of Divorcement* (1932), *King Kong* (1933), *The Informer* (1935), *Top Hat* (1935), and *Citizen Kane* (1941). The first three-strip Technicolor* feature, *Becky Sharp*, was shot there.

In 1935, while still used by RKO, the studio was leased by David O. Selznick and the name was changed to the Selznick International Studios. The colonial-style administration building at the front of the studio, and built by Thomas H. Ince in 1919, became the trademark for Selznick International Pictures*. Here Selznick filmed many of his greatest productions, beginning with *Little Lord Fauntleroy* (1936) and including *The Garden of Allah* (1936), *A Star Is Born* (1937), *Rebecca* (1940), *Spellbound* (1945), *Duel in the Sun* (1946), and *Portrait of Jennie* (1948). The sets from *King of Kings* (1927) and *King Kong* were burned by Selznick for the burning-of-Atlanta sequence from *Gone with the Wind* (1939).

With RKO's demise, the studios were taken over by Desilu Productions and utilized for a number of independent features and television programs, with 20th Century-Fox* filming a number of productions there. Perfect Film and Chemical acquired the lot in 1968; in 1969, it was purchased by OSF Industries, Ltd., and, in 1970, renamed the Culver City Studios. Laird International purchased the lot in December 1977 and renamed it Laird International Studios.

Address: 9336 West Washington Boulevard, Culver City, Calif. 90230.

LAKE PLACID, NEW YORK. See EXCELSIOR FEATURE FILM COMPANY, INC.

LASALIDA FILMS, INC. Lasalida Films, Inc. (the name means "light of the sun"), was formed in April 1917 to produce eight films a year starring the four-year-old Baby Marie Osborne. The films were to be released by the Pathé* Exchange. W.A.S. Douglas, formerly with Pathé, was the vice-president and general manager of the company, which used the David Horsley* studio in Los Angeles. Lasalida's first films were *When Baby Forgot* and *Miss Captain Kidd*. The company went out of existence at the end of 1917 when the Diando Film Company* was formed by Douglas and Baby Marie's father to produce her films.
BIBLIOGRAPHY
"Lasalida Films, Inc. Formed," *The Moving Picture World*, April 14, 1917, p. 259.

LA SALLE FILM COMPANY. The La Salle Film Company released one-reel comedies on the Mutual* program in 1917. Marion De La Parelle was the company's director, with King Vidor as co-director and scenarist. Studios for the company were initially located in Hollywood and later in Culver City.

"THE LASKY BARN." "The Lasky Barn" originally stood approximately at the junction of Hollywood Boulevard and Vine Street in Hollywood and is purportedly where Cecil B. DeMille and Oscar Apfel began shooting *The Squaw Man* in Hollywood in December 1913. (*The Squaw Man* is erroneously considered to have been the first feature-length film to be shot in Hollywood.) The building is called "The Lasky Barn" because Jesse L. Lasky was one of the producers of *The Squaw Man* and the creative genius behind Paramount Pictures*, whose first studio was located next to the barn.

When Paramount moved to its present location, the barn also moved—in 1927. The barn was utilized by Paramount as a gymnasium for many years and was also used as part of the set for the "Bonanza" television series. On December 26, 1956, it was declared California Historical Landmark No. 554. Paramount gave the barn to the Hollywood Historic Trust in October 1979, and the building was moved to a temporary site adjacent to the Palace Theatre on Vine Street. During the night of November 11, 1982, the barn was moved to its permanent site in the parking lot of the Hollywood Bowl, where it opened as the Hollywood Studio Museum in November 1985.

The history of the barn is clouded in mystery and most historians agree that the present building was almost entirely rebuilt—it is a wooden structure—in the thirties or forties.

BIBLIOGRAPHY
Simross, Lynn, "Hollywood's Film Museum to Break Ground," *Los Angeles Times*,
    part V, November 11, 1982, pp. 1, 30, 32–33.

LAUGH-O-GRAMS. See WALT DISNEY PRODUCTIONS

LEE-BRADFORD CORPORATION. The Lee-Bradford Corporation
(sometimes known as Artlee) was a minor distributor of independent productions
of the twenties, formed by Arthur A. Lee, the company's president, and F. G.
Bradford, its vice-president. None of the more than thirty features released by
this New York–based organization are memorable.

LEGION OF DECENCY. See NATIONAL LEGION OF DECENCY

LENAUER INTERNATIONAL FILMS, INC. Active from 1935 to 1940,
Lenauer International Films, Inc., was formed by Jean H. Lenauer (who died
in 1983 at the age of 79) to distribute foreign-language films, mainly French,
in the United States. Contrary to published reports at the time of Lenauer's death,
he did not initially distribute such classic French films as *La Grande Illusion* or
Carnival in Flanders, but, rather, he distributed lesser features such as Sacha
Guitry's *Pearls of the Crown* (1937). Lenauer also leased the Filmarte Theatre
at 202 West 58 Street in New York and made it the East Coast home of the best
in foreign-language films. Lenauer appeared as the waiter in the critically acclaimed
1981 feature *My Dinner with Andre*.

LEWIS J. SELZNICK PRODUCTIONS, INC. Lewis J. Selznick Productions,
Inc., was incorporated early in April 1916 after Selznick left his position as
vice-president and general manager of the World Film Corporation* and created
the Clara Kimball Young Corporation with World's leading star. World was not
the only party upset at the new development. Young's husband, James, sued
Selznick for alienation of his wife's affection, a charge which Selznick dismissed
by stating that the troubles with their marriage started long before he became
interested in Clara Kimball Young's artistic success. Young herself, later in
1917, sued Selznick for having himself elected president of her company and
then creating his own company to distribute her films, thus taking both creative
control and financial rewards from her.
    Selznick Productions soon released films from the Herbert Brenon Film
Corporation, of which Selznick was half owner and which produced films starring
Nazimova; the Kitty Gordon Company; and the Norma Talmadge Film
Corporation. Selznick's distributing company opened franchise exchanges* in
every major city. He owned 50 percent of the individual exchange, and the local
owners, such as Stanley Mastbaum in Philadelphia and Harry Garson in Detroit,
owned the other 50 percent. Other stars releasing with Selznick included Constance
Talmadge and Dorothy Gish.

In August 1917, Adolph Zukor secretly bought 50 percent of the company and offered the use of the Lasky Studio in Hollywood for production, with the result that Selznick still presided over the company, but its new name, Select Pictures Corporation, took Selznick's name away from public attention.

Select continued to release films of Young and the Talmadge Sisters and also those of Alice Brady and Marion Davies. Arthur S. Kane was the general manager.

In January 1919, the Selznick name appeared on marquees again when Lewis' son Myron organized Selznick Pictures Corporation and began producing films starring Olive Thomas. Myron, who for several months previous had been studio manager of the Norma Talmadge Film Corporation, was backed financially by his mother. Myron's brother Howard was his assistant, and brother David was the treasurer. Eugene O'Brien became Myron's second star in films directed by Ralph Ince, and Elsie Janis was also featured in the company's films.

On April 10, 1919, Lewis J. Selznick bought Zukor's half of Select for over $1 million, giving Zukor and Famous Players a profit of more than $500,000. In May 1919, David Selznick, then known as David J. Selznick, became the New England manager of Select. Select went bankrupt in 1923.

BIBLIOGRAPHY

"Lewis J. Selznick Now Sole Owner of Select," *The Moving Picture World*, April 19, 1919, p. 340.

"Selznick Branches Out," *The Moving Picture World*, April 8, 1916, p. 272.

"Selznick Pictures a Family Affair," *The Moving Picture World*, March 15, 1919, p. 1477.

"Selznick Pictures Again in Field," *The Moving Picture World*, January 18, 1919, p. 316.

LIBERTY FILM COMPANY. The Liberty Film Company of San Mateo, California, began releasing its films early in 1915 with Kriterion*. By June 1915, it released with the Associated Service. S. Lindblom was the president.

LIBERTY FILMS, INC. Liberty Films, Inc., was an independent production company, formed, in 1946, by Frank Capra (who served as president), William Wyler, George Stevens, and Sam Briskin. Its offices were located on the RKO* lot, at 780 North Gower Street, in Hollywood, with Marian Spitzer serving as head of the Story Department and Lou Smith as Publicity Department head. The company produced only one feature, Frank Capra's *It's a Wonderful Life* (1946); *State of the Union* was made as a Liberty Film but released as an "M-G-M Picture." Financial troubles forced the sale of Liberty Films to Paramount* in 1947.

LIBERTY MOTION PICTURE COMPANY. The Liberty Motion Picture Company was formed in July 1914 to make one four-reel feature per week and one- and two-reel comedies at regular intervals. Its studio was in Germantown, Pennsylvania. John Oxford was the president and Howard G. Bobb the general manager and vice-president. It distributed its films through Sawyer, Inc.* In November 1914, the company reorganized, backed by a group of Alaskan millionaires. Now located in San Mateo and Glendale, California, it made comedy-dramas released by Kriterion*. Marguerite Clayton, Mona Darkfeather, and True Boardman made films for Liberty. In December 1914, a receiver was appointed for the company.

BIBLIOGRAPHY

"A Big New Enterprise," *The Moving Picture World*, July 18, 1914, pp. 438–439.
"New Liberty Film Company," *The Moving Picture World*, November 28, 1914, p. 1213.

LIFE PHOTO FILM CORPORATION. The Life Photo Film Corporation was organized sometime in 1913 or 1914 and released its first film, *The Baker's Daughter*, in mid–1914. Edward M. Roskam was the president, and Jesse J. Goldburg was the secretary and general manager of the company, whose studio and laboratory were in Grantwood, New Jersey. It began releasing to the states rights* market; then, in late 1914, aligned itself with the Alco Film Corporation*; withdrew from Alco at the end of 1914 because, it complained, Alco failed to live up to the terms of its contract; and, in April 1915, began releasing through Paramount*.

An allied concern of Life Photo was the Commercial Motion Pictures Company, Inc., which in October 1913 filmed the World's Championship baseball series and the Army-Navy football game and made the films available for exhibition in nearby cities the same night as the events.

Roskam was also the president of Commercial, which had a factory at 102 West 101 Street, New York. In mid–1915, Roskam and his vice-president, Leonard Abrahams, resigned at the request of the stockholders of both Life Photo and Commercial. In the reorganization, Bernard Loewenthal became president, while Goldburg remained secretary and general manager. Life Photo, with a substantial increase in capital, increased production, planning by September 1915 to release one five-reel feature every week. It planned to make adaptations of stage successes, but the company disbanded in 1916; at the end of that year it sold, outright, negatives for eight films to the Twentieth Century Film Company.

BIBLIOGRAPHY

"Life Photo Corporation Reorganized," *The Moving Picture World*, June 5, 1915, p. 1583.

LINCOLN AND PARKER FILM COMPANY. The Lincoln and Parker Film Company of Worcester, Massachusetts, with Thomas Edison's son, Charles, on its board of directors, gained control of the Edison* Studio and plant at 2826 Decatur Avenue, New York, and over one million feet of negatives released prior to the arrangement Edison made to distribute its films through the George Kleine* system. Thomas Edison was to act as a consulting editor to the new company, which also planned to produce films. It was active in the late teens.

LINCOLN MOTION PICTURE COMPANY. The Lincoln Motion Picture Company, the first film company to be black-owned and managed, was formed in 1916 by actor Noble M. Johnson and his brother George P., an Omaha mailman. Noble, the president and star, ran Lincoln's studio in Los Angeles, while George—still employed by the post office—distributed the films in Omaha. By 1917, when the company incorporated with capitalization of $75,000, it had created its own exchange and had press agents working for it in the black ghettos of many major American cities.

Lincoln's first release, in 1916, the two-reel *The Realization of a Negro's Ambition*, showed the black hero overcoming discrimination through his own ambition. Its second film, *The Trooper of Troop K*, also released in 1916, portrayed the redemption of a black soldier, "Shiftless Joe," during the Mexican-American War. During the First World War Lincoln produced newsfilms of black sports and Western scenes. In 1920, when Noble Johnson left to continue with Universal*, Clarence Brooks, Lincoln's secretary, starred in *A Man's Duty*. In 1921, Booker T. Washington, Jr., appeared in a "bit" role in *By Right of Birth*, a film about racism and the situation of a black "passing" for white. Lincoln's last film was a documentary about the black 10th Cavalry at Fort Huachuca, Arizona. In 1923, Lincoln, which had always struggled to survive in an all-white industry, disbanded.

BIBLIOGRAPHY

Sampson, Henry T. *Blacks in Black and White*. Metuchen, New Jersey: Scarecrow Press, 1977.

LIONHEART TELEVISION INTERNATIONAL. See FILMS INCORPO-RATED.

LIPPERT PICTURES. Lippert Pictures (also known as Lippert Productions) was the distributor/producer of the films of Robert L. Lippert (1909–1976), self-styled "King of the Bs," who specialized in low-budget features, costing an average of $75,000 each. Lippert began his film career as a theatre owner in 1942. Between 1944 and 1966, he produced some 342 films, half of which were released through Lippert Pictures before the producer signed a distribution deal with 20th Century-Fox*. Lippert's best-known production was *The Fly* (1958), and his last was *The Last Shot You Hear* (1969). Following his retirement from film production, Lippert reactivated Lippert Theatres and returned to film exhibition. Other companies controlled by Lippert included Screen Guild Productions (created in the forties), Screen Art Pictures (formed in 1954), and Regal Films (created in the late fifties).

BIBLIOGRAPHY

Smith, Gerald K., "An Interview with Bob Lippert," *International Photographer*, January 1972, pp. 16–20.

LITTLE RASCALS. See "OUR GANG" SERIES

L-KO MOTION PICTURE COMPANY, INC. Henry M. "Pathe" Lehrman was the head of the L-KO (meaning Lehrman—Knock Out) Motion Picture Company, Inc., which began production on July 14, 1914. Its average output of three reels of comedy per week was released on the Universal* program. Directors included Lehrman, David Kirkland, Harry Edwards, John B. Blystone, and Harry Matthews (who made children's films). Players included Billie Ritchie, Louise Orth, Harry Gribbin, Reggie Morris, Hank Mann, Charles Winninger, and Gertrude Selby. The L-KO studio was located at Sunset Boulevard and Gower Street in Hollywood, and Victor Heerman was its manager and Joe Morgan the head cameraman. L-KO ceased production in 1919.

LLOYD FILMS, INC. Lloyd Films, Inc., formed late in 1913, was the distributor of the three-reel "Laclede Western Features," released semimonthly. *The Pale-Faced Squaw* was its first release. Offices for the company were located in the Candler Building at 220 West 42 Street in New York, and Charles (Feature) Abrams was the general manager.
BIBLIOGRAPHY
"Abrams Handling Lloyd Films," *The New York Dramatic Mirror*, December 3, 1913,
      p. 31.

LOBBY CARDS. As the name suggests, lobby cards were created to promote films in theatre lobbies. They came into being in 1913, and the earliest known lobby cards were produced, in sets of four, by Universal. The early lobby cards were in shades of black and white or brown and white; color lobby cards did not appear until 1917. All lobby cards are a standard size of eleven inches by fourteen inches. There is no documentation as to why this size was adopted, but it is, perhaps, connected to the fact that eight lobby cards take up as much space as a one-sheet poster, and the size makes for easy shipping with the poster.

The standard number of lobby cards to a set is eight, with one being a title card. There were exceptions; between 1919 and 1921, the Goldwyn Company* produced nine lobby cards to a set, and, in the twenties, Universal* produced sets of sixteen lobby cards for their major productions. In the thirties, studios issued sets of four lobby cards for shorts and serial* releases.
BIBLIOGRAPHY
Kobal, John, and V. A. Wilson. *Foyer Pleasure: The Golden Age of Cinema Lobby
      Cards*. N.p.: Album Press, 1982.
Slide, Anthony. *A Collector's Guide to Movie Memorabilia*. Des Moines, Iowa: Wallace-
      Homestead, 1983.

LOCALS, IATSE. See INTERNATIONAL ALLIANCE OF THEATRICAL STAGE EMPLOYEES AND MOVING PICTURE MACHINE OPERATORS OF THE UNITED STATES AND CANADA

LOEW'S, INC. See METRO-GOLDWYN-MAYER

LOEW'S THEATRES. See METRO-GOLDWYN-MAYER

LONE STAR FILM CORPORATION. See MUTUAL FILM CORPORATION

LONE STAR PRODUCTIONS. Formed in 1933 by Paul W. Malvern and located at 9336 West Washington Boulevard in Culver City, Lone Star Productions is best known for the series of sixteen Western features, starring John Wayne, beginning with *Riders of Destiny* (1933), that it produced between 1933 and 1935. The company also produced a number of minor features before it merged with Republic Pictures*.

It should not be confused with Lone Star International Pictures, a distributor that began operations in Texas in 1977. The best-known release of the Texas-based operation was *The Children of Sanchez* (1978).

LOPERT FILMS DISTRIBUTING COMPANY. Lopert Films Distributing Company was formed in 1950, with Ilya Lopert (1906–1971) as president and Robert Dowling (whose company, City Investing, financially controlled the organization) as board chairman. The company was initially associated with Alexander Korda; its aim was to distribute quality British, Italian, and Hollywood product, and among Lopert's first releases in the United States were *Tales of Hoffman* (1951) and *Cry, the Beloved Country* (1952). In 1959, Lopert became a wholly owned, but autonomous, subsidiary of United Artists*, with the purpose of distributing films—such as the productions of the British Rank Organization—which did not fit into the United Artists schedule. In the thirties, Ilya Lopert had operated Pax Films and Juno Films, both of which distributed quality foreign productions in the United States.

LORIMAR PRODUCTIONS. Founded in 1968 by Lee Rich and Merv Adelson, Lorimar Productions became a highly successful producer of such television series as "Dallas," "Knots Landing," "The Blue Knight," "Falcon Crest," and "The Waltons." It entered film production in 1976 with *Twilight's Last Gleaming*. In 1977, the company created Lorimar Distribution International to handle foreign distribution of its product. A year later it moved from the Burbank Studios*, where it had made its home, to the Culver City lot of M-G-M*. In 1979, Lorimar acquired Allied Artists*. A private company, owned by Rich, Adelson, and Irwin Molasky, Lorimar Productions went public in 1981; in 1983, it merged with the New York advertising agency of Kenyon & Eckhardt. On May 20, 1984, the *Los Angeles Times* reported that Lorimar had assets of $307.5 million, with 1,130 employees. In October 1985, it merged with Telepictures to become Lorimar-Telepictures.

Lorimar retreated from film production in 1983, with Lee Rich telling *The New York Times* (May 2, 1983) that Lorimar was "basically a television company."

Among the feature films it produced were *The Choirboys* (1977), *Who Is Killing the Great Chefs of Europe?* (1978), *The Fish That Saved Pittsburgh* (1979), *Cruising* (1980), *The Big Red One* (1980), *The Postman Always Rings Twice* (1981), *Second Hand Hearts* (1981), and *S.O.B.* (1981).

Address: 3970 Overland Avenue, Culver City, Calif. 90230.

LOS ANGELES INTERNATIONAL FILM EXPOSITION. See FILMEX

"LOST FILMS." "Lost films" is a term used to describe those films that are no longer known to be extant from the period prior to 1950 when films were processed on nitrate* film stock and subject to deterioration. These films may also be "lost" thanks to carelessness on the part of their original producers or distributors.

In 1970, the Museum of Modern Art published a book on the subject of lost films, among which it listed *Confessions of a Queen* (1925), *Gentlemen Prefer Blondes* (1928), *The Enemy* (1927), *The Drag Net* (1928), *The Case of Lena Smith* (1929), *Merton of the Movies* (1924), *The Divine Woman* (1928), *The Queen of Sheba* (1921), *The Patriot* (1928), and *Tess of the D'Urbevilles* (1924). Since publication of this book, some of the films included—such as *Fazil* (1928)— have been rediscovered, and, as is so often the case with eagerly sought lost films, they are far from the masterpieces that scholars and historians had thought them to be. A similar listing of lost films has been prepared by the American Film Institute* and includes *Angel of Contention* (1914), *London after Midnight* (1927), *The Man from Blankleys* (1930), *Madame Sans-Gene* (1925), *That Royle Girl* (1925), *Cleopatra* (1917), *The Young Rajah* (1922), *The Four Devils* (1928), and *The Aryan* (1916).

BIBLIOGRAPHY

Carey, Gary. *Lost Films*. New York: The Museum of Modern Art, 1970.

LOWVILLE, NEW YORK. See KINEMACOLOR COMPANY OF AMERICA

LUBIN MANUFACTURING COMPANY. Sigmund (sometimes spelled Siegmund) Lubin, a traveling peddler of jewelry, spectacles, and novelties, from Breslau, Germany, settled in Philadelphia and pursued an interest in lenses and photography that culminated in his association with C. Francis Jenkins to produce cameras, film printing machines, and projectors (the second model of which, manufactured in 1896, was the first projector ever advertised for sale). In 1897, Lubin produced his first film, which he remembered as being of a horse eating hay. Lubin purchased a chain of theatres in Philadelphia, and, later, these, along with others he had acquired in eastern Pennsylvania, were taken over by Stanley V. Mastbaum, who used them as the basis for the Stanley Company.

In 1897, Lubin restaged and filmed the heavyweight championship fight between James Corbett and Bob Fitzsimmons, using two Pennsylvania railwaymen. In 1899, he followed with a re-enactment of the Jeffries-Fitzsimmons fight. After the 1898 filming of the German *Passion Play* proved successful, Lubin produced his own version, modeled after the earlier one, in a Philadelphia backyard. In 1904, he remade Edwin S. Porter's *The Great Bank Robbery* as *The Bold Bank Robbery*.

Although Lubin stopped making films in 1898 because of an Edison* lawsuit against him, his company later joined the Motion Picture Patents Company*, releasing through the General Film Company. Lubin opened the largest glass-enclosed studio in the country in March 1912 in the heart of Philadelphia, which could accommodate four producing companies working at the same time.

In August 1912, Lubin bought the 500-acre estate of brewer John Betz. Located in the Philadelphia suburb of Betzwood, on the Schuylkill River adjoining Valley Forge Park, the estate provided a variety of natural settings and was the site for Lubin's new studio and plant. A fire in June 1914 at the film storage vault in Lubin's plant destroyed the company's early negatives and prints.

In the winter of 1909–1910, Lubin sent a company South, to film in Nassau and Florida, headed by A. D. Hotaling. Lubin had a plant in Jacksonville, Florida, which opened in 1913. Captain Wilbert Melville took a company of players to the West and Southwest United States, in 1913, and established a studio at 4550 Pasadena Avenue, Los Angeles, in 1915. Leon D. Kent and C. C. Miller were directors of the one-, two-, three-, and six-reel pictures made there. Also in 1915, Romaine Fielding headed a Lubin company located in Phoenix, Arizona, and a studio at Coronado, near San Diego, opened in August 1915.

In April 1915, Lubin joined with Vitagraph*, Selig*, and Essanay* to form V-L-S-E* to distribute feature films. August 1916 saw the beginning of the end for Lubin, as the company was absorbed by Vitagraph. In February 1918, the Betzwood plant was purchased by the newly organized Betzwood Film Company*, of which Lubin's son-in-law and general manager, Ira M. Lowry, became the general manager.

Players of note who appeared in Lubin films included Ethel Clayton, Arthur Johnson, Lottie Briscoe, Harry Myers, Rosemary Theby, Ormi Hawley, Edwin Carewe, Billie Reeves, and Frank Borzage, who began his film career as an actor with the company.

BIBLIOGRAPHY

"Betzwood on the Perkiomen," *Motography*, August 23, 1913, pp. 121–122.

Bush, W. Stephen, "Betzwood, the Great," *The Moving Picture World*, July 11, 1914, pp. 274–275.

————, "A Day with Siegmund Lubin," *The Moving Picture World*, July 11, 1914, pp. 209–210.

Eckhardt, Joseph P., and Linda Kowall. *Peddler of Dreams*. Philadelphia: National Museum of American Jewish History, 1984.

"Get Off at Lubin," *The Moving Picture World*, September 13, 1913, pp. 1159–1160.

Harrison, Louis Reeves, "Studio Saunterings," *The Moving Picture World*, March 30, 1912, pp. 1142–1144.

"Lost to Film History," *The New York Dramatic Mirror*, July 8, 1914, p. 21.

"Lubin," *The Moving Picture World*, November 6, 1909, p. 641.

"Lubin Progress," *The Moving Picture World*, February 5, 1910, p. 174.
"Lubin West Coast Plant," *The Moving Picture World*, July 10, 1915, p. 246.
"New Plant of Lubin Manufacturing Company," *The Moving Picture World*, March 26, 1910, p. 473.
"Sigmund Lubin Talks," *Exhibitors' Times*, September 27, 1913, p. 11.
"S. Lubin, Philosopher," *The Moving Picture World*, March 1, 1913, p. 877.
"Studio Efficiency," *The Moving Picture World*, August 9, 1913, p. 624.

LUCASFILM, LTD. Lucasfilm, Ltd., is the empirical organization of filmmaker George Lucas (born 1945), formed in 1972, and housed on a 3,000-acre ranch—Skywalker Ranch—in Marin County, northern California. Lucasfilm, Ltd., is the producer of the *Star Wars* series and of other features, including *Raiders of the Lost Ark* (1981).

The organization has a number of divisions, the best known of which is its special effects arm, Industrial Light & Magic, responsible for the special effects on films such as *Star Trek II*, *Poltergeist*, and *E.T. The Extra-Terrestrial* (all released in 1982). Its Research and Development Division is known as Sprocket Systems. In partnership with 20th Century-Fox Music, Lucasfilm operates the music publishing houses of Bantha Music and Tusken Music. The Droid Works (located at 3855 Lankershim Boulevard, North Hollywood, Calif. 91604–3417) is described in publicity as "the first fully integrated electronic post-production system, picture and sound." Among the equipment introduced by Lucasfilm is the THX Motion Picture Loudspeaker System, developed by chief audio engineer Tomlinson Holman in 1983, which enhances the quality of theatre sound; Pixar, a computer graphics machine; and EditDroid, an automated editor, introduced in 1984. In 1985, Lucas announced plans to "spin off" Droid Works and Pixar as two separate companies.

Address: P.O. Box 2009, San Rafael, Calif. 94902.

BIBLIOGRAPHY
Miranker, C. W., "Lucasfilm Spins Off High-Tech Creations," *San Francisco Examiner*, Business Section, March 24, 1985, pp. 1, 12.
Pollock, Dale. *Skywalking: The Life and Films of George Lucas*. New York: Harmony Books, 1983.

LUNA FILMS. See ALBUQUERQUE FILM MANUFACTURING COMPANY, INC.

M

MACMILLAN FILMS. See FILMS INCORPORATED

MAGNACOLOR. See HIRLICOLOR

MAGNA PICTURES CORPORATION. See TODD-AO

MAIL CALL. See HOLLYWOOD VICTORY COMMITTEE

MAIN STREET U.S.A. See HOLLYWOOD VICTORY COMMITTEE

MAJESTIC MOTION PICTURE COMPANY. See RELIANCE MOTION PICTURE COMPANY AND MAJESTIC MOTION PICTURE COMPANY

MAJESTIC PICTURES CORPORATION. Active from 1932 to 1935, Majestic Pictures Corporation promised a number of screen versions of current literary successes, including *My Life* by Isadora Duncan, but in reality its films were, as its 1934 advertising proclaimed, "action type of productions in keeping with the pulse of box office demand." Among Majestic's better known "B" features were *The Vampire Bat* (1933), *Gun Law* (1933), *The World Gone Mad* (1933), and *The Scarlet Letter* (1934).

Larry Darmour (1895–1942) was in charge of production, and following Majestic's demise he created Darmour Productions, which was responsible for a number of "B" pictures released through Columbia*, including *Under Suspicion* (1937), *Crime Takes a Holiday* (1938), *Fugitive at Large* (1939), and *Ellery Queen, Master Detective* (1940).

MAJOR 16mm PRODUCTIONS. See 16mm

MANDARIN FILM COMPANY. The Mandarin Film Company, located in Oakland, California, was the only Chinese film production company in the United States at the time of its formation in 1917. Marion E. Wong was the president of the company and the star of its first production, *The Curse of Quon Qwon*, some of which was filmed in China. The company strove to make films dealing with Chinese subjects with accurate details and settings. It had its own studio, constructed, it was stated, according to Chinese ideas.

BIBLIOGRAPHY

"Marion E. Wong, Chinese Film Producer," *The Moving Picture World*, July 7, 1917, p. 63.

MANN THEATRES CORPORATION. Founded by Ted Mann as a small Minnesota theatre chain, Mann Theatres Corporation grew with Mann's spring 1973 acquisition of the 266 theatres of the National General* chain. Mann created considerable furor by changing the name of the chain's flagship theatre, Grauman's Chinese Theatre, in Hollywood, to Mann's Chinese Theatre. With Ted Mann Productions, Mann has also been involved in the production of such films as *Buster and Billie* (1974), *Lifeguard* (1976), and *Brubaker* (1980).

Address: Suite 301, 9200 Sunset Boulevard, Los Angeles, Calif. 90069.

MANSON INTERNATIONAL. Founded in 1953 by Edmund Goldman and Sam Nathanson and incorporated ten years later, Manson International was, initially, a distributor of foreign films in the United States. In 1975, it began to concentrate on the marketing of independent films abroad and became one of the first Los Angeles–based international film sales agencies.

Address: 11355 Olympic Boulevard, Suite 500, Los Angeles, Calif. 90064.

MAPO. See WALT DISNEY PRODUCTIONS

MARCH OF TIME. A type of newsreel* that mixed factual footage with staged material, as in a television docudrama, March of Time was sponsored by *Time* magazine, ran approximately twenty minutes, and was narrated by Westbrook Van Voorhis. It was based on a radio series of the same name, first broadcast by CBS in 1931, and was very much the brainchild of one man, Louis de Rochemont, who produced the series until the summer of 1943, when he resigned and was succeeded by his brother, Richard.

The first episode of March of Time was released on February 1, 1935, and consisted of six items, "Saionji," "Speakeasy Street," "Belisha Beacons," "Moe Buchsbaum," "Fred Perkins," and "Metropolitan Opera." Later episodes were limited to two or three items until 1938, when March of Time featured only one story thereafter. The last March of Time, "Formosa—Island of Promise," was released in August 1951. From 1935 to 1942, March of Time was released by RKO* and from thereafter by 20th Century-Fox*. When RKO ceased to distribute March of Time, it began releasing a similar series, "This Is America," produced by Frederick Ullman, Jr., narrated by Dwight Weist, and seen from 1942 to 1951.

Among the better known March of Time issues were *Inside Nazi Germany* (1938), *The Movies March On!* (1939), *Mr. and Mrs. America* (1942), *Show Business at War* (1943), and *Is Everybody Listening?* (1947). 16mm* editions of March of Time, called Forum editions, were released, chiefly for classroom use, from 1944 onward. Some of these Forum editions had different titles from the original March of Time releases; for example, *Is Everybody Listening?* was released in a Forum edition as *Radio Broadcasting Today*.

The March of Time staff was also responsible for four feature films: *The Ramparts We Watch* (1940), *The Story of the Vatican* (1941), *We Are the Marines* (1942), and *The Golden Twenties* (1950).

BIBLIOGRAPHY

Bohn, Thomas W., and Lawrence W. Lichty, "The March of Time: News as Drama," *Journal of Popular Film*, vol. II, no. 4, Fall 1973, pp. 373–387.

Cook, Bruce, "Whatever Happened to Westbrook Van Voorhis?" *American Film*, March 1977, pp. 25–29.

Fielding, Raymond. *The March of Time, 1935–1951.* New York: Oxford University Press, 1978.

"Time Flickers Out: Notes on the Passing of the March of Time," *Quarterly of Film, Radio and Television*, Summer 1957, p. 354.

RESOURCES

Films: National Archives (reference prints and outtakes); Museum of Modern Art (reference prints).

Papers: National Archives (production files); University of Wyoming (Louis de Rochemont papers).

MARINE FILM COMPANY OF LOS ANGELES. The Marine Film Company, located at the old Kalem* studios in Hollywood, was organized in mid–1917. M. Phillip Hansen was the general manager, and Henry Otto was the director of the company. Frances Burnham was the leading lady, and Tyrone Power starred in Marine's first production, the six-reel *Lorelei of the Sea*.

BIBLIOGRAPHY

"Tyrone Power Signs with Marine," *The Moving Picture World*, June 30, 1917, p. 2106.

MASCOT PICTURES CORPORATION. Founded in 1927 by Nat Levine (1899-), Mascot Pictures Corporation is one of the "poverty row" studios remembered with affection by film buffs for its serials, including three—*Shadow of the Eagle* (1932), *The Hurricane Express* (1932), and *The Three Musketeers* (1933)—starring John Wayne. Other Mascot serials included *King of the Kongo* (1929), *The Vanishing Legion* (1931), *The Last of the Mohicans* (1932), *The Lost Jungle* (1934), and *The Fighting Marines* (1935). The company did not commence producing features until the early thirties, and probably the most important of the group was *Harmony Lane* (1935), directed by Joseph Santley and starring Douglass Montgomery, Evelyn Venable, and Adrienne Ames. Players under contract to Mascot included Yakima Canutt, John Wayne, Joe Bonomo, and animal stars Rin-Tin-Tin, Jr., and Rex the Horse.

On January 10, 1935, Mascot moved from cramped production offices in Hollywood to the former Mack Sennett Studios in Studio City. The company was merged with Monogram* and Consolidated Laboratories to form Republic Pictures* and Levine stayed on as president of the new company. However, in February 1937, Nat Levine resigned from Republic, and Mascot was no more.

BIBLIOGRAPHY

Tuska, Jon. *The Vanishing Legion: A History of Mascot Pictures 1927–1935*. Jefferson, North Carolina: McFarland, 1982.

MASQUERS CLUB. The Masquers Club was founded as a theatrical social club by eight Broadway actors—George Read, Robert Edeson, Fred Esmelton, Alphonse Ethier, Ned Sparks, John Sainpolis, Warner Baxter, and Robert Schable—in 1925. It was located, initially, on Yucca Street in Hollywood but moved, in 1927, to Antonio Moreno's former home at 1765 North Sycamore Avenue, Hollywood, where it remained until declining income forced the sale and demolition of the property in 1985. Subsequently, the Masquers moved to the Variety Arts Center in downtown Los Angeles.

The Masquers, whose president was always known as the Harlequin, produced many stage plays through the years, including annual public revels and a 1950 production of *What Price Glory?*, directed by John Ford and starring John Wayne and Maureen O'Hara. The Masquers also produced a series of two-reel comedies in the early thirties.

Address: Variety Arts Center, 940 South Figueroa Street, Los Angeles, Calif. 90015.

BIBLIOGRAPHY

Scott, Tony, "Founded on Laughter and Love, Masquers Keep Young in Spirit and Enthusiasm in Outlook," *Daily Variety*, October 31, 1972, pp. 46–47, 54, 150.
———, "Readying for 50th Anni, Masquers Have Happy Memories of the Past, Apprehensive Hope for Future," *Daily Variety*, April 25, 1975, pp. 3, 10.

MASTERCRAFT PHOTO-PLAY CORPORATION. The Mastercraft Photo-Play Corporation was formed in January 1918, with its first production being the antisocialistic *The One Woman*, written by Thomas Dixon. Mastercraft had a studio in Boston and planned to open one in California. F. Eugene Farnsworth was the president, and Isaac Wolper, a Bostonian, was the vice-president and general manager.

BIBLIOGRAPHY

"Mastercraft Forming Producing Corporation," *The Moving Picture World*, January 26, 1918, p. 491.

MASTER PICTURES CORPORATION. See BALBOA AMUSEMENT PRODUCING COMPANY

MASTERPIECE FILM MANUFACTURING COMPANY. Masterpiece Film Manufacturing Company, a production organization of 1914, made films starring Max Figman, his wife Lolita Robinson, and Al W. Filson. M. De La Parelle and Figman directed from scenarios by Elliott J. Clawson. It released with Reliance Film Corporation. Although it purchased the Loftus Feature Studio at 1339 Gordon Street in Hollywood in December 1914, the company disbanded early in 1915 after the completion of its third film, *Jack Chanty*.

BIBLIOGRAPHY

"Masterpiece Film Men," *The Moving Picture World*, October 10, 1914, p. 171.

MAVERICK PICTURES INTERNATIONAL. See E. O. CORP.

MAYFLOWER PHOTOPLAY CORPORATION. The Mayflower Photoplay Corporation was formed in mid–1919 to produce Allan Dwan and Emile Chautard productions, which were released by Realart Pictures Corporation. Isaac Wolper was the president of Mayflower, and its first production was Dwan's *Soldiers of Fortune* (1919).

MCA, INC. The entertainment conglomerate which controls Universal*, MCA, Inc., has been frequently referred to as the "octopus" of the film industry. It was created, as Music Corporation of America, as a booking agency for dance bands in Chicago in 1924 by Jules Stein to help finance his medical training. In 1936, the corporation had grown in stature, and Stein hired Lew Wasserman (who was to become MCA's president in 1946 and now serves as chairman of the board).

Following MCA's takeover of Universal, the Justice Department intensified its investigation of the corporation, arguing that with its major television production company, Revue, and with its control of 1,400 top entertainers through its talent agency, MCA had restrained trade in violation of the Sherman Antitrust Act between 1952 and 1961. On October 18, 1962, a consent decree was signed whereby MCA agreed to divest itself of its talent agency business, but it was permitted to continue to control Universal Pictures, Revue Productions, Inc., and Decca Records and to remain as parent company of Colorado Savings and Loan Association.

As of 1985, MCA's principal subsidiaries and divisions were Universal Pictures, Universal Television, Universal City Studio Tours and Amphitheatre, Merchandising Corporation of America, MCA Records, MCA Music, MCA Home Video, Spencer Gifts Inc., G. P. Putnam's Sons, and Yosemite Park and Curry Co.

Address: 100 Universal City Plaza, Universal City, Calif. 91608.

BIBLIOGRAPHY

Gottschalk, Earl C., Jr., "If It's Show Business, Chances Are MCA Inc. Is Deeply Involved in It," *The Wall Street Journal*, July 10, 1973, pp. 1, 18.

Moldea, Dan E., and Jeff Goldberg, "The Deal's the Thing," *Reader*, November 2, 1984, pp. 1, 8–14.

MEDFORD, MASSACHUSETTS. See HUMANOLOGY FILM PRODUCING COMPANY

MÉLIÈS MANUFACTURING COMPANY. The films of Georges Méliès, who began producing in France in 1896, were distributed in the United States by the Biograph Company* until February 1904. Georges sent his brother, Gaston, to New York, in November 1902, because of the rampant duping of his films. Gaston set up an office at 204 East 38 Street, New York, to distribute his brother's films, to which he gave what was perhaps the first brand name in film history, "Star Films," and perhaps the first trademark. Gaston Méliès joined the Motion Picture Patents Company* and contracted to release one reel per week on the American market. To help his brother meet this quota, Gaston formed a production company, the Melies Manufacturing Company, in September 1908, with a capitalization of $75,000. The American company had its headquarters in the Criterion Theatre, Chicago.

Gaston and his son Paul took the company to Fort Lee, New Jersey*, where they produced their first film, *The Stolen Wireless*, released October 13, 1909. Early in 1910, Gaston took his company to San Antonio, Texas, and set up the Star Film Ranch there to make Westerns*. The first, *Cyclone Pete's Matrimony*, was released on April 7, 1910. The company was directed by William Haddock, the cameraman was William Paley, and the players included leads Francis and Edith Storey, William Clifford, Mildred Bracken, Anne Nichols, and Daniel Reulos. Gaston occasionally played small parts.

In May 1911, the company, then called the "American Wildwest," traveled to Sulphur Mountain Springs, California. In June 1911, it opened a studio in Santa Paula, California, where it produced one and one-half reels per week, at that time the entire output released by Melies. After making over 130 films between 1910 and 1912, Gaston traveled to the South Seas and Asia, making films as he went, but due to the poor condition that the films were in when they arrived in the United States, he was forced to close down the company, in 1913, and sold it to Vitagraph*.

BIBLIOGRAPHY

Dowling, Paul H., "He's Sixteen Years Ahead of All War Photographers," *Photoplay*, March 1917, p. 122.

Hammond, Paul. *Marvellous Méliès*. New York: St. Martin's Press, 1975.

McInroy, Patrick, "The American Méliès," *Sight and Sound*, Autumn 1979, pp. 250–254.

"Méliès Notes," *The Moving Picture World*, March 26, 1910, p. 472.
"The New Addition to the Licensed Releases. Méliès Film Takes High Rank," *The Moving Picture World*, October 23, 1909, p. 561.

MENTOR PICTURES, INC. Incorporated in December 1932, Mentor Pictures, Inc., was formed to import scientific, educational, novelty, and feature films from Europe.

MERIT FILMS. See SACK AMUSEMENT ENTERPRISES

METRO-GOLDWYN-MAYER, INC. With its trademark of a roaring lion and its logo, "Ars Gratia Artis," Metro-Goldwyn-Mayer (M-G-M) has symbolized quality film production for more than fifty years. It was the company's proud boast that it had more stars than there were in heaven, a far from outrageous claim when one recalls that under contract to the studio, at one time or another, were Greta Garbo, Norma Shearer, Jean Harlow, Joan Crawford, Katharine Hepburn, Clark Gable, Spencer Tracy, Lon Chaney, Elizabeth Taylor, the Marx Brothers, Judy Garland, Mickey Rooney, John Gilbert, Ramon Novarro, Jeanette MacDonald and Nelson Eddy, Greer Garson, and Gene Kelly. The prestige of its stars was matched by its directors—George Cukor, Clarence Brown, King Vidor, Tod Browning, Vincente Minnelli, and so on—and its films, including *Greed* (1924), *The Merry Widow* (1925), *The Big Parade* (1925), *Ben-Hur* (1926), *Grand Hotel* (1932), *Mutiny on the Bounty* (1935), *David Copperfield* (1935), *Goodbye, Mr. Chips* (1939), *The Wizard of Oz* (1939), *Mrs. Miniver* (1942), *Easter Parade* (1948), *Singin' in the Rain* (1952), *Seven Brides for Seven Brothers* (1954), *Gigi* (1958), *Ben-Hur* (1959), and *2001: A Space Odyssey* (1968).

Metro-Goldwyn-Mayer's parent company, Loew's, Inc., had been formed as a theatre circuit by Marcus Loew. To assure a steady flow of product to his theatres, Loew acquired the Metro Pictures Corporation* in 1919, and the new Loew's, Inc., was organized on October 18, 1919. Loew increased the stature of Metro with the acquisition of new stars and by bringing in independent producer Louis B. Mayer (1885–1957). Nicholas Schenck, Loew's right-hand man, arranged for the company to acquire the ailing Goldwyn Pictures Corporation* and to take over Mayer's independent production company. The new organization, Metro-Goldwyn-Mayer, was created on May 17, 1924, with studios that had formerly belonged to Goldwyn in Culver City.

To supervise production, M-G-M selected Mayer's vice-president Irving G. Thalberg (1899–1936), who is generally considered to have been responsible for the prestige of the company's productions. He never accepted credit on any of the films that he personally supervised, among which were *He Who Gets Slapped* (1924), *Flesh and the Devil* (1927), *The Crowd* (1928), *Anna Christie* (1930), *Freaks* (1932), *The Barretts of Wimpole Street* (1934), *A Night at the Opera* (1935), *Mutiny on the Bounty* (1935), *Romeo and Juliet* (1936), and *The*

Good Earth (1937). Following Thalberg's early death, the Academy of Motion Picture Arts and Sciences* created the Irving G. Thalberg Memorial Award (first given in 1937 to Darryl F. Zanuck) "for the most consistent high level of production achievement by an individual producer." M-G-M honored Thalberg by naming its new office building, at the entrance to the lot, in his memory.

By the mid-thirties, M-G-M had some 4,000 employees under contract. There were 23 sound stages on the 117-acre lot. Its reported assets in 1939 were $144 million. Aside from its features, the studio produced short subjects, such as the Pete Smith Specialties, the "Crime Does Not Pay" series*, Tom and Jerry cartoons, and the comedies of Robert Benchley. It also released the Hal Roach Studios* output, and its best-known independent release is, of course, *Gone with the Wind* (1939), produced by David O. Selznick.

In 1937, M-G-M established a British production company with headquarters at Denham Studios, under the management of Ben Goetz and with Michael Balcon in charge of production. Here M-G-M produced *The Citadel* (1938) and *Goodbye, Mr. Chips* (1939).

As with other major studios, M-G-M faced problems in the late forties, brought on in part by the introduction of television and by declining theatre attendance. In need of a new production head, Mayer selected Dore Schary (1905–1980), who had earlier been associated with RKO*, and who was also admired by Loew's president, Nicholas Schenck, who had succeeded to the title following the death of Marcus Loew in 1926.

In 1951, following a bitter dispute between Mayer and Schenck, the former was forced to resign and was replaced by Dore Schary. Schary introduced more serious subjects to M-G-M's production schedule, beginning in 1949 with *Intruder in the Dust* and in 1950 with *The Asphalt Jungle*, but he quickly found himself in dispute with the right-wing element in Hollywood, led by gossip columnist Hedda Hopper, who accused the producer of being either too liberal, communistic, or both. At the same time, Schary was faced with the breakup of the company's theatre and production/distribution holdings following the governmental consent decree*. Loew's, Inc., continued as the parent company of M-G-M, the producer, and the distributor, but a new theatre holding company, Loew's Theatres, was formed on September 1, 1954, to control the 130 houses remaining under the company's control in the United States and Canada.

Dore Schary was fired as studio head in 1956. Meanwhile, there were extensive changes at the corporate level. Arthur Loew succeeded Nicholas Schenck as president in 1955, but a year later he was succeeded by Joseph Vogel, who successfully fended off a challenge from Stanley Meyer. Robert O'Brien was appointed president in 1963, followed by James Polk, Jr., in 1969, and then by James T. Aubrey, Jr., who was backed by M-G-M's new majority stockholder, Kirk Kerkorian.

Under Aubrey's presidency, much of the M-G-M backlot was sold off for real estate development. Aubrey disposed of M-G-M's British studios at Borehamwood, of theatres outside of the United States, and of MGM Records.

In May 1970, the David S. Weisz Company held a public auction of M-G-M's collection of costumes and props. Eventually, in October 1973, Aubrey withdrew the studio from distribution, announcing that forthwith its films would be released by United Artists*.

Following Aubrey's resignation on October 31, 1973, Frank E. Rosenfelt became president, and the company once again prospered, thanks in part to its nonfilm activities such as the MGM Grand Hotel in Las Vegas. In 1981, M-G-M acquired United Artists*, and, in 1983, a new company, MGM/UA Entertainment was formed. MGM/UA was acquired early in 1986 by Ted Turner. United Artists was sold off to Kirk Kerkorian, and MGM/UA was disbanded.

Address: 10202 West Washington Boulevard, Culver City, Calif. 90230.

BIBLIOGRAPHY
Brown, Peter Harry, and Pamela Ann Brown. *The MGM Girls*. New York: St. Martin's Press, 1983.
Carey, Gary. *All the Stars in Heaven*. New York: E. P. Dutton, 1981.
Crowther, Bosley. *The Lion's Share*. New York: E. P. Dutton, 1957.
Eames, John Douglas. *The MGM Story*. New York: Crown, 1975.
Hughes, Emmet John, "M-G-M: War among the Lion Tamers," *Fortune*, August 1957, pp. 98–103, 206, 208, 210, 212, 214, 216.
Knox, Donald. *The Magic Factory*. New York: Praeger, 1973.
"Loew's Inc.," *Fortune*, August 1939, pp. 25–31, 104–106, 114.
Marx, Samuel. *Mayer and Thalberg: The Make-Believe Saints*. New York: Random House, 1975.
Parish, James Robert. *The MGM Stock Company*. New Rochelle, New York: Arlington House, 1973.
———. *The Best of MGM*. Westport, Connecticut: Arlington House, 1981.
Sheehan, Robert, "The Cliff-Hanger at M.G.M.," *Fortune*, October 1957, pp. 134–135, 278, 280, 283.
RESOURCES
Films: George Eastman House (preservation materials and some reference prints).
Still Photographs: Academy of Motion Picture Arts and Sciences.

METRO PICTURES CORPORATION. The forerunner of M-G-M*, Metro Pictures Corporation was incorporated on March 5, 1915, with Richard Rowland as president of the new company. It had its origins in the Alco Film Corporation*, formed a year earlier by Al Lichtman and W. H. Seeley, which served as a distributor for various producers, notably All-Star Feature Corporation. Metro also began as a distributor for the films of the Dyreda Art Film Corporation*, Popular Plays and Players*, Rolfe Photoplays, Inc.*, Quality Pictures Corporation*, and Columbia Pictures Corporation. The first release, on March 29, 1915, of the new company was *Satan Sanderson*. Within a year of its founding, Metro had become an important producer/distributor, with stars such as Francis X. Bushman, Mary Miles Minter, and Olga Petrova under contract. It was able to persuade Mr. and Mrs. Sidney Drew to leave Vitagraph* and become Metro stars. Its studios, formerly the Quality Studios, were located at

6300 Romaine Street in Hollywood, and from there, in the late teens, it produced a series of what it described as big-budget, quality features, under the brand name of Screen Classics, Inc.

Despite an average of more than sixty features a year, Metro suffered a number of financial reversals, brought on in part by the tremendous amount of money it was willing to pay for screen rights to novels such as *The Four Horsemen of the Apocalypse*, which it acquired in 1919. In 1920, Metro stock was acquired by Loews, Inc.*, the first step in the transformation of the company to Metro-Goldwyn-Mayer.

BIBLIOGRAPHY

"Metro Controls Productions," *The Moving Picture World*, March 20, 1915, p. 1745.
"Metro Plans Many Elaborate Productions," *The Moving Picture World*, August 12, 1916, p. 1086.
"Metro's First Birthday," *The Moving Picture World*, April 8, 1916, p. 237.
"Metros in the Making," *The Moving Picture World*, October 21, 1916, p. 411.
"Metro under Full Steam," *The Moving Picture World*, April 24, 1915, p. 562.
Schmidt, Jackson, "On the Road to MGM: A History of Metro Pictures Corporation, 1915–1920," *The Velvet Light Trap*, no. 19, 1982, pp. 46–52.

METROPOLITAN FILM COMPANY. The Metropolitan Film Company was organized in February 1914 to import and manufacture multireel features. Hans Bartsch was the president and H. J. Streyckmans was the sales manager. Its first release was the five-reel *The Money God*, and its offices were located in the World's Tower Building in New York.

METROPOLITAN STUDIOS. See HOLLYWOOD GENERAL STUDIOS

METROPOLITAN THEATRES CORPORATION. Metropolitan Theatres Corporation came into being when Joseph Corwin purchased the Broadway and Metropolitan Theatres in Los Angeles in 1923. Corwin's son, Sherrill, built the chain into what was once the largest in southern California, and the corporation is presently headed by Joseph Corwin's grandson, Bruce. Its primary importance is as the operator of the great movie palaces in downtown Los Angeles, the Orpheum, the Los Angeles, the Million Dollar, and the United Artists. Metropolitan is also noted for its ownership and renovation of the Spanish-style Arlington Theatre in Santa Barbara. On August 9, 1963, the chain screened its first Spanish-language feature, and within a short space of time all its downtown Los Angeles theatres were exclusively running Spanish-language films.

Address: 8727 West Third Street, Los Angeles, Calif. 90069.

BIBLIOGRAPHY

Auerbach, Alexander, "Metropolitan Theatres—A Tradition of Service," *Boxoffice*, August 1983, pp. 14–15.

METROSCOPIX. See THREE-DIMENSIONAL FILMS

M-G-M. See METRO-GOLDWYN-MAYER, INC., and MGM/UA ENTERTAINMENT CO.

M-G-M CAMERA 65. See PANAVISION, INC.

MGM/UA ENTERTAINMENT CO. In July 1981, Metro-Goldwyn-Mayer* acquired United Artists*, and, in 1983, the two companies were merged as a new company called MGM/UA Entertainment Co. At the same time, three other divisions—MGM/UA Home Entertainment, MGM/UA Classics, and MGM/UA Television Group—were formed. The administration of the new company was consolidated on the M-G-M lot. With a library of some 8,500 films, MGM/UA Entertainment Co. has, unquestionably, the finest assets of any American production or distribution company. Ted Turner acquired MGM/UA early in 1986, sold off the United Artists half to Kirk Kerkorian, and disbanded the company. *See also* Metro Pictures Corporation.

MICHEAUX FILM CORPORATION. The best known of all black-owned independent film companies, the Micheaux Film Corporation was formed in 1918 as the Micheaux Film and Book Corporation by Oscar Micheaux (1884–1951). The Corporation's first production was an adaptation of Micheaux's novel, *The Homesteader* (1918). Micheaux remained active as a producer through 1940, and among his other features were *Within Our Gates* (1920), *Son of Satan* (1924), *A Daughter of the Congo* (1930), *Temptation* (1936), *God's Stepchildren* (1939), and *The Notorious Elinor* (1940).
BIBLIOGRAPHY
"Hollywood in the Bronx," *Time*, January 29, 1940, p. 67.
Sampson, Henry T. *Blacks in Black and White*. Metuchen, New Jersey: Scarecrow Press, 1977.

MIDDLETOWN, CONNECTICUT. See INTERSTATE FEATURE FILM COMPANY

MILLION DOLLAR PICTURES. See TODDY PICTURES COMPANY

MINA. See DAVID HORSLEY PRODUCTIONS

THE MIRISCH CORPORATION. The Mirisch Corporation was formed in 1957 by three brothers, Harold (who died in 1968), Walter, and Marvin Mirisch. It was based on the Samuel Goldwyn* studio lot, and its productions were released through United Artists*. In 1968, the Corporation changed its name to Mirisch Productions, Inc., and sold its first twenty features to United Artists.

This group of Mirisch productions consisted of *Sinful Davey* (1969), *How to Succeed in Business without Really Trying* (1967), *In the Heat of the Night* (1967), *Hour of the Gun* (1967), *Fitzwilly* (1967), *Hawaii* (1966), *The Fortune Cookie* (1966), *Return of the Seven* (1966), *What Did You Do in the War, Daddy?* (1966), *The Russians Are Coming, the Russians Are Coming* (1966), *Cast a Giant Shadow* (1966), *The Satan Bug* (1965), *The Hallelujah Trail* (1965), *A Rage to Live* (1965), *Return from the Ashes* (1965), *The Pink Panther* (1964), *633 Squadron* (1964), *A Shot in the Dark* (1964), *Kiss Me, Stupid* (1964), and *The Great Escape* (1963).

The Mirisch brothers—who soon changed the name of their company back to the Mirisch Corporation—continued to release through United Artists, with later titles including *Fiddler on the Roof* (1971), *The Private Life of Sherlock Holmes* (1970), *The Party* (1968), *The Thomas Crown Affair* (1968), *Gaily, Gaily* (1969), and *The Landlord* (1970). In 1974, the brothers signed an exclusive distribution deal with Universal* and moved to the Universal lot; their first release through their new partner was *Midway* (1976). A new distribution deal with United Artists was signed in 1981, but the Mirisch Corporation also continued to release through Universal and remained on the Universal lot.

Address: 100 Universal City Plaza, Universal City, Calif. 91608.

MIRROR FILMS, INC. Mirror Films, Inc., was formed in October 1915 with capitalization of $2.5 million and the expressed purpose of being not so much a theatrical enterprise as a commercial one. Stating ''We intend to look upon film . . . as so much canned product,'' Mirror, whose president was Clifford B. Harmon and treasurer was Frank S. Hastings, hired Hector J. Streychkmans to build its studio from a casino and dance hall located at Woodhaven and Myrtle streets in Glendale, Long Island, and to be its studio manager. Captain Harry L. Lambart, formerly one of Vitagraph's directors, was appointed director-general. Mirror's offices were located at 16 East 42 Street, New York.

BIBLIOGRAPHY
''Lambart Forms New Company,'' *The Moving Picture World*, October 9, 1915, p. 276.

MITTENTHAL FILM COMPANY, INC. The Mittenthal Film Company, Inc., was organized in May 1913 by the Mittenthal brothers, to produce ''Mittenthal Features,'' which were released by Warner's Features, Inc. Theodore Marston was the president and William Winter Jefferson was a principal actor of the company, which used the Pilot* studio in Yonkers, New York. The offices of the company were located at 1402 Broadway, New York, and its productions included *The Human Bloodhound* and *The Prison Needle*. In December 1914, it began producing single-reel films, under the brand name of ''Starlight,'' which were released by United Film Company*, an antecedent to Warner Bros.* Mittenthal ended production in 1916.

BIBLIOGRAPHY
''Share Pilot Studio,'' *The New York Dramatic Mirror*, May 21, 1913, p. 25.

MOHAWK FILM COMPANY. The Mohawk Film Company was a short-lived production company of 1914. Although it arranged at its formation to make twelve features, *Heart of Oak*, written and directed by Wray Physioc, which was distributed by Paramount*, was its only production. During a suit hearing in August 1914, officers Henry Morris, Harry Sterling Goldman, and Ben Levy stated that no more production by the company was being contemplated.

MOLE-RICHARDSON CO. Founded in Hollywood in 1927 by Peter Mole, Mole-Richardson Co. is the best-known manufacturer of studio lighting and power equipment.

Address: 937 North Sycamore Avenue, Hollywood, Calif. 90038.

MONARCH PRODUCING COMPANY. Harry Harvey, formerly with Solax*, Nestor, Broncho, and Frontier, was the managing director of the Monarch Producing Company, which was formed in November 1914 and released on the Kriterion program.

MONOGRAM PRODUCTIONS, INC. "Monogram spoke quickly, simply, in the language of the filmgoer and captured, at times, the spirit of the population, with sentiment in their Westerns, with interest and intrigue in their mysteries, and with defiance in their urban comedies and dramas," wrote Tim Onosko in *The Velvet Light Trap* (Summer 1972). As a "B"* picture producer, Monogram Productions, Inc., was relatively important, almost on a par with Republic*, with which it merged briefly.

The origin of the company dates back to January 1924, when W. Ray Johnston, in collaboration with a number of independent exhibitors, formed Rayart Productions as a low-budget film production company releasing films—a reported annual schedule of twenty-four silent Westerns—to exhibitors who had formed themselves into a cooperative. Rayart was reorganized in 1930 as Monogram Productions, with Johnston as president and Trem Carr as head of production. The first films were produced in 1931. During 1931–1932, the company produced some twenty-eight features, increasing to thirty-two in 1932–1933. In 1932, Monogram signed a distribution deal with the British Pathé company, whereby the latter released Monogram's product in the United Kingdom and Monogram released British Pathé features in the United States. By 1932, Monogram was producing thirty-six features a year and by the forties was producing an average of fifty titles.

When Republic Pictures was formed in 1935, it took over the Monogram exchanges, and Johnston became the new company's first president. However, in 1937, Johnston left Republic and revived Monogram as a separate production entity. When Johnston became chairman of the board in 1946, Stephen Broidy became president, and he is generally credited with increasing the quality of Monogram's films. In November 1946, Broidy created Allied Artists* as a totally owned subsidiary of Monogram, and that company's name appeared on

Monogram's better features. In 1953, the Monogram name was dropped completely, and the company became Allied Artists.

The first Monogram films were shot at the studio located at 6048 Sunset Boulevard. Later, the company moved to the General Services Studio at 1040 North Las Palmas and the Talisman Studios* at 4516 Sunset Boulevard. After revival of operations in 1937, Monogram rented space at Universal*, with its final home being at 4376 Sunset Drive (which is now KCET). Monogram produced a number of series films, including those featuring the Cisco Kid (with Duncan Renaldo), Charlie Chan (with Sidney Toler), Kitty O'Day, Detective (with Jean Parker), Saddle Pals (with Jimmy Wakeley and Dennis Moore), Bomba, Jiggs and Maggie, Snuffy Smith, Joe Palooka, Mr. Wong, the High Schoolers, and Renfrew of the Royal Mounted. The best known of the Monogram series films were those starring Leo Gorcey and Huntz Hall, initially known as the East Side Kids and later as the Bowery Boys (and which had started life at Goldwyn* as the Dead End Kids). The company's first grade "A" feature is generally considered to have been *Silver Skates* (1942), starring Belita.

BIBLIOGRAPHY

Fernett, Gene. *Poverty Row*. Satellite Beach, Florida: Coral Reef Publications, 1973.
Lifton, Louis S., "Monogram Pictures," in *The Film Daily Cavalcade*. New York: The Film Daily, 1939, pp. 156–164.
Onosko, Tim, "Monogram: Its Rise and Fall in the Forties," *The Velvet Light Trap*, no. 5, Summer 1972, pp. 5–9.

RESOURCES

Films (16mm reference prints only, 1931–1946): Wisconsin Center for Film and Theatre Research.

MONOPOL FILM COMPANY. When the Monopol Film Company engaged Marion Leonard, in 1912, for $1,000 a week, which may have been the largest salary any player received at that time, the company had been in existence for a few years and had produced over thirty dramas. Its offices were at 145 West 45 Street, New York. Al Lichtman was an early manager of Monopol and, when Leonard signed, Isadore Bernstein, formerly a publicist for Republic and Yankee, left the International Feature Film Company to become general manager.

Stanner E. V. Taylor took the company to Los Angeles, where he directed three-reel features starring Marion Leonard, including *As in a Looking Glass*, *Carmen*, and *The Dead Secret*. In June 1913, Bernstein left Monopol to manage Universal's West Coast studio. At this time, Monopol released the six-reel *The Seed of the Father*, which it claimed to be the first film of that length to be written from an original story. In September 1913, a receiver was ordered for Monopol, after creditor P. A. Powers filed an involuntary petition in bankruptcy against the company.

BIBLIOGRAPHY

"Marion Leonard Joins Monopol Company," *The Moving Picture World*, December 7, 1912, p. 988.

MONROVIA. See CREST PICTURE COMPANY

MONROVIA FEATURE FILM COMPANY. The Monrovia Feature Film Company arranged to build a $200,000 plant in Monrovia, California, in 1916, which, besides a stage and studio, would include an amusement park, zoo, pool, and picnic grounds. The area was to be laid out like Universal City, and the company planned to charge twenty-five cents admission, with an additional fee for bathing. Officers of the company included R. M. Francisco, president; C. D. Holmes, vice-president; and Edward L. Grafton, a member of the board of directors, who was president of the Grafton Film Publishing Company, which released Monrovia's product. Monrovia produced two ten-reel features, *The Argonauts of California* and *The Daughter of the Don*, directed by Henry Kabierske, a former director of pageants. In September 1916, Kabierske formed the Empire Feature Film Company, which planned to use Monrovia's studios. With three ten-reel spectacles planned, including one titled *The Ten Commandments*, Empire, in December 1916, purchased forty acres at Murray Hill, near Grossmont in the San Diego area of California. Monrovia was declared bankrupt in October 1917.

MOTION PICTURE ALLIANCE FOR THE PRESERVATION OF AMERICAN IDEALS. An anti-Communist group formed in 1944, the Motion Picture Alliance for the Preservation of American Ideals declared itself to be a believer in the American way of life, "in sharp revolt against a rising tide of Communism*, Fascism, and kindred beliefs." It opposed those organizations that had previously chosen to speak out against fascism on behalf of the film industry and which the Alliance labeled as Communist fronts: the Hollywood Anti-Nazi League*, the Hollywood League for Democratic Action, the Motion Picture Democratic Committee*, the Hollywood Theatre Alliance, the Hollywood Unit of the League against War and Fascism, and the American Peace Mobilization, which was earlier known as the Emergency Peace Committee. Founders of the Motion Picture Alliance included Sam Wood, King Vidor, Victor Fleming, Norman Taurog, Walt Disney, Clarence Brown, Harold S. Bucquet, and Jack Conway.

The Motion Picture Alliance quickly ran into opposition from the Screen Writers Guild, which branded it as "a subversive and dangerous organization which comforts the enemy." Nonetheless, the Alliance gained in strength, thanks to the House Un-American Activities Committee hearings. By 1950, when its president was John Wayne, the Motion Picture Alliance was demanding that the City of Los Angeles register all Communist sympathizers and that the Hollywood Ten* not be released until they agreed to respond to questions from a congressional committee. It published a monthly newsletter, *The Vigil*, which documented the work of anyone within the film industry who might have displayed pro-Communist sympathies.

MOTION PICTURE AND TELEVISION FUND. The Motion Picture and Television Fund is a charitable organization, supported entirely by the film and television industries through donations, deductions from payrolls, memorial gifts, and special events. Based on the premise that the film and television industries help their own, the Fund provides financial and medical assistance to anyone in need. It also maintains a facility in Woodland Hills, California, consisting of residential cottages, a hospital, and a residential "lodge" for those not totally capable of caring for themselves. The forty-one-acre facility also includes the Douglas Fairbanks Lounge, the Y. Frank Freeman Library, the Louis B. Mayer Memorial Theatre, and the John Ford nondenominational chapel. The Fund's expenditures in 1985 exceeded $21 million, with financial aid to 3,300, medical aid to 4,600, and personal services aid to 4,800.

The Fund came into being on August 4, 1921, as the Motion Picture Branch of the Actors Fund of America. It was incorporated as the Motion Picture Relief Fund on December 31, 1924, and held its first annual meeting on June 30, 1925. Ground was broken for the Woodland Hills facility in 1941, with funding raised through the Screen Guild radio program. The Fund's Woodland Hills headquarters were officially opened on September 27, 1942.

Any industry member with more than twenty years of service is eligible to retire to the facility, along with his or her spouse. No preference is shown as to the member's occupation within the industry. All personal assets and income, such as Social Security, are placed in an account administered by the Fund. When and if the assets are exhausted and income does not meet the monthly costs of the member's residency, the Fund makes up the difference. After death, any monies remaining in the personal account become part of the resident's estate and are disposed of according to the terms of the individual's will.

Address: 23450 Calabasas Road, Woodland Hills, Calif. 91364.

BIBLIOGRAPHY

Erlich, Cindy, "The Last Reel," *Rolling Stone*, December 16, 1976, pp. 67–71.

Jaynes, Gregory, "In California: A Place for Curtain Calls," *Time*, February 7, 1983, pp. 8–9.

Johnson, Sharon, "A Retirement Home That Retains a Bit of Hollywood Dazzle," *The New York Times*, June 2, 1979, p. 24.

Michaelson, Judith, "Where They Live the Last Picture Show," *Los Angeles Times*, Calendar Section, August 26, 1983, pp. 30–31.

Scott, Tony, "We Take Care of Our Own," *Daily Variety*, October 27, 1981, pp. 12–16, 35, 42, 46, 56.

MOTION PICTURE ARTISTS COMMITTEE. The Motion Picture Artists Committee was founded in 1937 to aid the Republican cause in the Spanish Civil War and to oppose fascism generally. Its organizers included Gale Sondergaard, Dashiell Hammett, Donald Ogden Stewart, Dudley Nichols, John Ford, John Garfield, Luise Rainer, Paul Muni, Fredric March, Melvyn Douglas, Lewis Milestone, and Lester Cole. The Motion Picture Artists Committee was denounced as a pro-Communist front organization by the Dies Committee*.

MOTION PICTURE ASSOCIATION OF AMERICA. The Motion Picture Association of America (MPAA) was formed in 1922 as the Motion Picture Producers and Distributors of America (MPPDA) to serve as a liaison between the industry and the public, to defend the industry against censorship (demands for which were becoming increasingly vocal following various scandals which rocked the film industry at that time), and to safeguard the producers against various demands from labor groups. To head the new group, the various producers—Marcus Loew, Lewis J. Selznick, William Fox, Carl Laemmle, Adolph Zukor, to name a few—making up the new organization selected Will H. Hays, who had served as chairman of the 1920 Republican National Committee and who was subsequently awarded with the position of postmaster general in President Warren G. Harding's administration.

Hays opened offices in New York and Hollywood and selected as his associates Governor Carl Milliken of Maine and attorneys Charles Pettijohn and Gabriel Hess. He summed up the aims of the organization: "To foster the common interests of those engaged in the motion picture industry in the United States, by establishing and maintaining the highest possible moral and artistic standards in motion picture production, by developing the education as well as the entertainment value and general usefulness of the motion picture, by diffusing accurate and reliable information with reference to the industry, by reforming abuses relative to the industry, by securing freedom from unjust or unlawful exactions, and by other lawful and proper means."

The MPPDA spoke out against a censorship bill in Massachusetts and organized its repeal in 1922. Hays addressed civic groups such as the Boy Scouts of America and the Daughters of the American Revolution. The MPPDA argued against the negative depiction of Mexicans in American films. It arranged for the registration of all bona fide film correspondents, and, in 1927, it formulated what was to become the Production Code*.

Will Hays retired and was succeeded by Eric Johnston in 1945, at which time the Motion Picture Producers and Distributors of America became the Motion Picture Association of America. At the same time, the Foreign Department of the MPPDA, which had handled the sale and distribution of American films abroad, was renamed the Motion Picture Export Association, described by Jack Valenti as "the only U.S. enterprise that negotiates on its own with foreign governments." Jack Valenti succeeded Johnston as the Association's president in 1966.

One additional, recent activity of the MPAA had been the cracking down, through its Film Security Office, on film and video piracy both in the United States and abroad.

Address: 522 Fifth Avenue, New York, N.Y. 10036; 1600 Eye Street, N.W., Washington, D.C.; 8480 Beverly Boulevard, Los Angeles, Calif. 90048.

BIBLIOGRAPHY

"The More Things Change . . . A Trilogy," *Journal of the Screen Producers Guild*, September 1966, pp. 14–20.
Shearer, Lloyd, "The House That Hays Built," *Tricolor*, April 1945, pp. 57–61.

————, "The House That Hays Built Part II," *Tricolor*, May 1945, pp. 50–55.
Valenti, Jack, "The 'Foreign Service' of the Motion Picture Association of America,"
    Journal of the Producers Guild of America, March 1968, p. 22.

MOTION PICTURE BOARD OF TRADE OF AMERICA. The Motion Picture
Board of Trade of America was organized in 1915 to provide an organization
in which all branches of the film industry could be represented, to deal with
problems concerning the industry as a whole and to help settle disputes within
the industry. The president was J. Stuart Blackton; Carl Laemmle, the
manufacturers' vice-president; Nicholas Power, the supply vice-president; John
R. Freuler, the exchanges* vice-president; F. J. Rembusch, the exhibitors' vice-
president; W. Stephen Bush, the publication vice-president; W. R. Rothacker,
the miscellaneous [*sic*] vice-president; E. A. McManus, the secretary; and Joseph
W. Engel, the treasurer. In October 1915, D. W. Griffith became the first producer
invited to join. The group received government recognition in 1916, when it
met with President Woodrow Wilson, but that same year it disbanded and was
replaced by the National Association of the Motion Picture Industry*, after
various members quit because exhibitors were given only two out of the ten
positions on the board.
BIBLIOGRAPHY
Bush, W. Stephen, "Motion Picture Board of Trade of America," *The Moving Picture
    World*, September 25, 1915, p. 2156.

**MOTION PICTURE COMMITTEE COOPERATING FOR NATIONAL
DEFENSE.** See WAR ACTIVITIES COMMITTEE

MOTION PICTURE DEMOCRATIC COMMITTEE. The Motion Picture
Democratic Committee (MPDC) was organized in June 1938 to support radical
Democrat Culbert Olsen in his California gubernatorial campaign. Among its
leading members were Philip Dunne, Dudley Nichols, Allen Rivkin, Nat Perrin,
and Dashiell Hammett, who served as chairman. The Committee produced a
film titled *California Speaks*. Perhaps surprisingly, in view of his pro-socialist
politics, Olsen won.
BIBLIOGRAPHY
Ceplair, Larry, and Steven Englund. *The Inquisition in Hollywood*. Garden City, New
    York: Anchor Press/Doubleday, 1980.

MOTION PICTURE DIRECTORS ASSOCIATION. A fraternal organization,
the Motion Picture Directors Association was incorporated first in Los Angeles
on June 18, 1915. (A New York branch was incorporated on January 2, 1917.)
The Association was neither a union nor a business organization; it had four
aims: "to maintain the honor and dignity of the profession; to improve the moral,
social, and intellectual standing of all persons connected with the motion picture
producing business; to cultivate social intercourse among its members; to aid
and assist all worthy distressed members."

Between 1924 and 1927, the Association published a journal titled *The Director* and later *The Motion Picture Director*. At one time, virtually every director in the industry was a member of the Association, but at its demise, in the early thirties, membership was comprised largely of "old-timers."

The following is a list of the Association's founding members: Charles W. Giblyn, Murdock J. MacQuarrie, Travers Vale, Burton King, Jay Hunt, Edward J. Le Saint, Al Christie, J. Farrell MacDonald, Henry McRae, Joseph De Grasse, Reginald Barker, Del Henderson, John O'Brien, George Morgan, William Robert Daly, Leo W. Youngsworth, Raymond B. West, Edward Dillon, Robert Z. Leonard, George Beban, Jack J. Clark, Francis Ford, Allen Curtis, Frank Lloyd, and Tom Mix.

MOTION PICTURE DISTRIBUTING AND SALES COMPANY. The Motion Picture Distributing and Sales Company was formed in April 1910, primarily by two independent companies, the New York Motion Picture Company* and the Independent Motion Picture Company, under the auspices of the National Independent Motion Picture Alliance, to control the output of independent films by releasing to the exchanges all independent productions through one company. While some independent producers agreed immediately to the formation, others, including Nestor, Thanhouser*, Eclair*, Capitol, Great Northern*, and Lux, formed their own alliance, the Associated Independent Manufacturers, distrusting the intentions of the companies heading the Sales Company.

After an agreement was reached in July 1910, whereby the Associated Independent Manufacturers would be fairly represented with the Sales Company, the combined group of independents had an association through which over twenty-one reels of film a week were to be released and which represented the product of Eclair, IMP, Nestor, Yankee, Bison, Kinograph, Lux, Powers*, Thanhouser, Ambrosio, Atlas, Champion, Electragraff, Motograph, Centaur*, Cines, Film d'Art, Defender, Capitol, Carson, Columbia, Great Northern, and Itala. The member companies sold their product directly to the Sales Company, which then dealt with the exchanges. Carl Laemmle was the president, P. A. Powers the vice-president, Charles O. Baumann the treasurer, and Herbert Miles the secretary. Also on the board were William Steiner, William Swanson, and J. J. Murdock. The Sales Company also spent over $300,000 representing the independents in court over litigation brought against them by the Motion Picture Patents Company*.

The Sales Company, by acquiring the rights to the Bianchi camera, owned by the Columbia Phonograph Company, hoped to have a licensing company similar to that of the Motion Picture Patents Company, but the camera was found to be impractical and the patents did not offer the protection promised by Columbia. Later, the Sales Company added other manufacturers to its group, including Solax*, Reliance*, Rex, and Gaumont*.

The Sales Company came to an end in mid–1912, when the ranks of the independents split into two groups. The Film Supply Company of America announced its formation on May 14, 1912, as the releasing agency for Thanhouser, Gaumont, American*, Great Northern, Reliance, Eclair, Solax, Majestic, Lux, and Comet. In addition, the Mutual Film Corporation* was formed as a group of exchanges to handle the product of these companies. Harry E. Aitken was the organizer of both companies. Around the same time, Universal* was formed by the companies remaining in the Sales Company, including IMP, the New York Motion Picture Company, Powers, Rex, Champion, Republic*, and Nestor.

BIBLIOGRAPHY

"Alliance Executive Committee in Session. Projected Sales Co. Seeks to Regulate the Business of the Independents," *The Moving Picture World*, April 2, 1910, p. 549.
"Break in Ranks of Sales Company," *The Moving Picture World*, May 25, 1912, p. 707.
"The Motion Picture Distributing and Sales Company," *The Moving Picture World*, April 16, 1910, p. 595.

MOTION PICTURE EXHIBITORS' LEAGUE OF AMERICA. The Motion Picture Exhibitors' League of America, the first national exhibitors' organization, was formed at a convention in Cleveland in August 1911, due to the efforts of M. A. Neff of Cincinnati, the president of the Exhibitors' League of Ohio. In December 1909, Neff began to push for a national trade organization because of the rental exchanges' indifference to the needs of the exhibitors. The Exhibitors' League was formed in part to protect exhibitors anywhere in the country from restrictive local legislation that would be hard to fight without a national organization. Various state exhibitors' organizations existed prior to the formation of the League and continued to function during its existence, sometimes causing conflicts regarding the control and jurisdiction of the national organization.

Neff was elected president of the August 1911 convention and was reelected in 1912 (by which time the League had branches in fourteen states) and 1913. The International Motion Picture Association formed as a seceding group at the July 1913 convention in New York and elected Charles H. Phillips of Milwaukee as its president. At the Exhibitors' League convention of 1914 in Dayton, Neff withdrew his nomination for reelection, and the new president, M. F. Pearce of Baltimore, effected a reconciliation with the other group.

In August 1917, another split of exhibitors occurred when Lee A. Ochs, the publisher of the new trade paper *Exhibitors' Trade Review*, which called itself the official journal of the League, was reelected president of the organization. Delegates, led by a group from Indiana, complained at the convention in Chicago that Ochs had packed the convention with stockholders of *Exhibitors' Trade Review*, in order to get himself reelected, and that the League's distribution of voting power favored the big cities. They formed the American Exhibitors' Association, but after a year, during which Ochs resigned from the presidency, William A. Brady, the president of the National Association of the Motion Picture Industry*, succeeded in bringing the two groups together. The resulting new national exhibitors' organization, called the National Association of the Motion Picture Industry, Exhibitors' Branch, was incorporated on September 13, 1918.

In 1920, the Motion Picture Theatre Owners of America became the dominant exhibitors' group, with a membership of ten to twelve thousand. Led by its president, Sydney S. Cohen, and its counsel, James J. Walker (later mayor of New York), it strove to fight the wave of theatre takeovers by producers and distributors and was especially fearful of Adolph Zukor and his famous Players-Lasky Corporation.

BIBLIOGRAPHY

"Exhibitors Form National League," *The Moving Picture World*, August 19, 1911, pp. 440–443.

"Factions Get Together in Chicago," *The Moving Picture World*, September 21, 1918, pp. 1691–1695, 1727–1733.

"The Motion Picture Exhibitors' League of America: How It Came into Being Told by President Neff," *The Moving Picture World*, August 17, 1912, pp. 621–623.

"Motion Picture Exhibitors' League of Greater New York Goes on Record in Favor of a National Convention of Exhibitors," *The Moving Picture World*, April 8, 1911, p. 153.

"Principles of American Association Stated," *The Moving Picture World*, August 11, 1917, p. 916.

MOTION PICTURE EXPORT ASSOCIATION. See MOTION PICTURE ASSOCIATION OF AMERICA

MOTION PICTURE GUILD. See ART HOUSES

MOTION PICTURE MOTHERS, INC. A charitable organization comprised of the mothers of film personalities, Motion Picture Mothers, Inc., was formed on June 14, 1939, by Marie Brown. The group was initially involved in a variety of fund-raising activities but has for many years devoted itself to raising money for the Motion Picture and Television Fund*.

Address: c/o Motion Picture and Television Fund, 23450 Calabasas Road, Woodland Hills, Calif. 91364.

BIBLIOGRAPHY

Hendrix, Kathleen, "Mothers of Stars on Memory Lane," *Los Angeles Times*, part V, June 29, 1975, pp. 1, 16–17.

Simon, Al, and Jules Levine, "Mothers of the Stars, Inc.," *Collier's*, December 23, 1944, pp. 18–19, 43.

MOTION PICTURE PATENTS COMPANY. The Motion Picture Patents Company was a monopolistic organization, incorporated in New Jersey on September 9, 1908, which controlled the various patents held by Thomas Edison, the American Mutoscope and Biograph Company*, E. H. Amet, Francis Jenkins, and others, and which sought to license all film production, distribution, and exhibition. Its membership comprised the following manufacturers and importers of films: Biograph Company, Edison Manufacturing Company*, Essanay Film Manufacturing Company*, Gaumont Company* (but limited to its talking pictures only), Kalem Company*, George Kleine*, Lubin Manufacturing Company*, Gaston Méliès, Pathé* Freres, Selig Polyscope Company*, and Vitagraph Company of America*. It also licensed the following manufacturers of moving picture machines: American Moving Picture Machine Co., Armat Moving Picture Co., Edengraph Manufacturing Co., Edison Manufacturing Co., Enterprise Optical Company, Gaumont Company, Lubin Manufacturing Company, Pathé Freres, Nicholas Power Company, Eberhard Schneider, Selig Polyscope Company, George K. Spoor Company, and Vitagraph Company of America. Additionally, it granted licenses to such showmen as Burton Holmes*, Lyman H. Howe, and Fred Niblo, permitting them to import films provided they paid a royalty to the Company.

The Motion Picture Patents Company has its origins in the United Film Service Protective Association, formed November 16, 1907, and the Film Service Association, formed February 8, 1908. The failure of the American Mutoscope and Biograph Company, with its important patents, to join these organizations led to the formation of the new company.

Initially, the Company licensed various film exchanges but, in April 1910, attempted to take them over through the creation of the General Film Company. (The Motion Picture Patents Company resolutely maintained that it did not control the General Film Company, pointing out that the two groups shared only two of the same directors.) The activities of the Motion Picture Patents Group were vigorously fought by independent producers/distributors such as Carl Laemmle and William Fox*, with the latter instituting a suit under the Sherman Antitrust Act. The Motion Picture Patents Company fought back through legal action of its own, occasionally resorting to violence in its efforts to halt the independents.

Although the Company lost the suit in 1915—and an appeal was dismissed in 1918—it was as much doomed from its lack of a clear-cut policy as regards feature-length films, which were becoming increasingly popular in the early teens, from the public interest in film personalities; from the failure of the individual member-producers to support the Company's policies; and from a strong anti-Semitic bias. *Variety* (December 31, 1920) succinctly summed up the reason for the Motion Picture Patent Company or Film Trust's failure:

> Put in a word, it was a matter of morale on the part of the principal men in the "trust." They were, for one thing, frenzied with money being deluged upon them; they would not take a long distance view of their interests, and they would not be subject to mutual counsel. Above all things, they were selfishly concerned with their own individual gains, jealous of each other, and imbued with the idea that their astounding success was the fruits of their own acumen rather than mostly an accident of circumstance.
>
> If the Patents Co., or more properly speaking, the General Film Co., in the days of its greatest height of power, had had the foresight to accept into its circle the best of outside enterprise and business and artistic career, which all the time was striving for admittance, they probably would have established their huge amalgamation on a firm and permanent basis.

Aside from licensing films, the Motion Picture Patents Company also published a trade paper*, *The Film Index*, and established the first "fan" magazine in 1911, *The Motion Picture Story Magazine* (later *Motion Picture*). Its refusal to sell the former, in 1910, to *The Moving Picture World* led to its being boycotted by that trade paper, another nail in the Company's coffin.

BIBLIOGRAPHY

Cassady, Ralph. *Monopoly in Motion Picture Production and Distribution: 1908–1915*. Los Angeles: Bureau of Business and Economic Research, University of California, 1959 (reprinted from *Southern California Law Review*, vol. XXXII, no. 4, 1959).

"General Film Company Is in No Danger of Receiver," *The Moving Picture World*, July 1, 1916, p. 64.

"The Motion Picture Patents Company and Its Work: A Retrospect and Appreciation," *The Moving Picture World*, July 17, 1909, pp. 81–84.

Thomas, Jeanne, "The Decay of the Motion Picture Patents Company," *Cinema Journal*, vol. X, no. 2, Spring 1971, pp. 34–40.

MOTION PICTURE PRODUCERS AND DISTRIBUTORS OF AMERICA. See MOTION PICTURE ASSOCIATION OF AMERICA

MOTION PICTURE PUBLICISTS ASSOCIATION. See PUBLICISTS GUILD OF AMERICA

MOTION PICTURE RELIEF FUND. See MOTION PICTURE AND TELEVISION FUND

MOTION PICTURE SOCIETY FOR THE AMERICAS. Formed by the War Activities Committee* and the Office of the Coordinator of Inter-American Affairs, the Motion Picture Society for the Americas was concerned, during the Second World War, with increasing understanding and knowledge between the two Americas. South American specialists were available to offer guidance to Hollywood producers in their depiction of Latin American life and society. 16mm* projectors and films (in Spanish and Portuguese) were available for screenings in South America. Various U.S. government agencies in cooperation with the film industry produced short subjects for South American audiences, dealing with hygiene, food, sanitation, and child nutrition. The idea, of course, was to foster a pro-American attitude in South America, rather than a pro-axis feeling apparent in some Latin American countries. The work of the Motion Picture Society for the Americas was suspended in March 1946, and its work— on a more limited scale—was taken over by the Motion Picture Association of America*.

MOUNT VERNON, NEW YORK. See ALL-STAR FEATURE COMPANY

MOVIELAB, INC. Opened in 1936, Movielab, Inc., was a major East and West Coast laboratory, handling 35mm*, 16mm*, and Super 8mm*. Its Hollywood laboratory (at 6823 Santa Monica Boulevard) had previously been known as Pathé, Perfect, and Berkey. In June 1969, Movielab acquired the Berkey-Pathé Laboratories. The laboratory operation was closed in July 1984, at which time Movielab's processing equipment was acquired by Technicolor* (against whom, in 1974, Movielab had filed an antitrust suit, which was settled out of court). Movielab continues to operate Movielab Video (formed in 1982) and Movielab Theatre Services.

Address: 619 West 54 Street, New York, N.Y. 10019.

MOVIESTRIPS. See FILMS INCORPORATED

MOVIETIME, U.S.A. Sponsored by the Council of Motion Picture Organizations (COMPO*), Movietime U.S.A. was a public relations project project "to bring the story of Hollywood to the 'grass roots' of America." Stars (such as Greer Garson and Vera-Ellen), directors (such as Archie Mayo), and industry personnel (such as Carey Wilson and Irving Asher) were sent out on various regional tours. Celebrating the Golden Anniversary of the Motion Picture Theatre, there were twenty-nine tours in 1951 and nine in 1952. Movietime U.S.A. came into existence in October 1951 and suspended operations in March 1953.

MOVIOLA. Although Moviola is often used to refer to any type of equipment used for viewing and editing motion picture film—the word appears in *Webster's New World Dictionary*—Moviola is, in fact, a corporate name for a specific type of editing equipment, a name registered with the U.S. Patent Office.

The Moviola and the Moviola Manufacturing Company were created by Dutch-born Iwan Serrurier, who received his first patent in April 1919. After modifying his editing equipment for use on an editing table, Serrurier sold the first Moviola Editing Machine to the Douglas Fairbanks Studio in the fall of 1924. The Mitchell Camera Company built twelve more machines for Serrurier, and the first of these, now called Moviola Midgets, was sold to M-G-M* in November 1924. With the advent of sound, Moviolas became standard equipment in the film industry, utilized for editing and synchronizing separate sound and film tracks. Moviola added a film brake to its equipment in 1936, enabling the editor to stop the film immediately without the risk of damage due to the abruptness of the halt. The Moviola Company began manufacturing rewinders in 1930 and projectors in 1931.

In the 1979 awards year—presented in 1980—the Academy of Motion Picture Arts and Sciences* presented an Award of Merit, in the form of an Oscar, "to Mark Serrurier for the progressive development of the Moviola from the 1924 invention of his father, Iwan Serrurier, to the present Series 20 sophisticated film editing equipment. The Moviola has evolved from the 1924 Midget to the complex machine necessary for the array of picture and sound formats currently employed in motion picture production. It has kept pace effectively to meet the demands of motion picture technology.'' The Moviola Corporation is now known as Magnasync-Moviola Corporation, a subsidiary of the Craig Corporation.

Address: Magnasync-Moviola Corporation, 5539 Riverton Avenue, North Hollywood, Calif. 91601.

BIBLIOGRAPHY

Lehrman, Harry, "Forty Years of the Moviola," *Film World and AV News*, May 1965, p. 208.

"Moviola's New Editing Console," *American Cinematographer*, December 1970, pp. 1194–1195, 1230–1231.

Serrurier, Mark, "The Origins of the Moviola," *The Cinemeditor*, Winter 1965, pp. 5–7.

MPAA. See MOTION PICTURE ASSOCIATION OF AMERICA

MPDC. See MOTION PICTURE DEMOCRATIC COMMITTEE

MPDDA. See MOTION PICTURE ASSOCIATION OF AMERICA

MULBERY SQUARE PRODUCTIONS, INC. Formed in January 1971 by Joe Camp (its president) and James Nicodemus (who is no longer associated with the company) as a producer of television commercials, Mulbery Square Productions, Inc., has gained a reputation for its family features starring Benji, beginning with a film of the same name which received its world premiere in Dallas on May 24, 1974. Other Mulbery Square features were *Hawps!* (1976), *For the Love of Benji* (1977), and *Oh Heavenly Dog* (1980).

Address: 10300 North Central Expressway, Suite 120, Dallas, Texas 73374.

BIBLIOGRAPHY

"Southerners," *Southern Living*, August 1976, pp. 148–149.

MUSIC. Music has always been an integral part of the motion picture. There was no such thing as a silent film, for—from 1896 onward—all films had musical accompaniment of some sort, be it a piano, an organ, or a full orchestra. "Moving pictures and music are inseparable," wrote Paul Evert Denton in *The Moving Picture World* (April 23, 1916). Cue sheets would be provided by distributors for some silent films—as early as 1910 the Edison Company* published on a regular basis lists of musical themes suitable for use with its films—while it was not uncommon for scores to be specially composed or arranged for silent features.

Perhaps the earliest example of music specially composed for a film is Camille Saint-Saëns' score for the one-reel French Pathé* production of *L'Assassinat du Duc de Guise/The Assassination of the Duke of Guise* (1907). In Europe, serious composers, such as Arthur Honneger and Edmund Meisel, composed film scores during the silent era.

Among the many original scores composed or compiled for American silent features were one by Walter Cleveland Simon for *Arrah-na-Pogue* (1911); one by Joseph Carl Breil for *The Birth of a Nation* (1915), which replaced an even earlier score for the same film by Carli Elinor; one by Victor Schertzinger for *Robin Hood* (1922); one by Hugo Riesenfeld for *The Covered Wagon* (1923); and by Mortimer Wilson for *The Thief of Bagdad* (1924). Two of the busiest of silent film music composers/arrangers were David Mendoza and William Axt, who were responsible for *The Big Parade* (1925), *Ben-Hur* (1926), and *Don Juan* (1926), among many others.

Most important silent features had theme songs, several of which became popular hits. Erno Rapée and Lew Pollack wrote the theme song of "Diane" from *7th Heaven* (1927), L. Wolfe Gilbert and Mabel Wayne wrote "Ramona" for the 1928 film of the same name, and Erno Rapée composed "Charmaine" for *What Price Glory* (1926).

With the coming of sound, Hollywood producers gained total control of film music. No longer would the choice, in many cases, be left to local musicians. At the same time, film music gained a new respectability. Some producers used stock music by anonymous composers, but generally film composers were acknowledged, with many becoming associated with an individual studio. Herbert Stothart and Bronislau Kaper were with M-G-M*, Roy Webb with RKO*, Erich Wolfgang Korngold with Warner Bros.*, Cy Feuer with Republic*, and Alfred Newman with 20th Century-Fox*. Among the "serious" composers who contributed film scores were Hanns Eisler, Ernest Torch, and Aaron Copland.

Some composers were associated with a particular production or a group of films. Marvin Hatley is remembered as the composer of the Laurel and Hardy theme music; Bernard Herrmann's name is associated with *Citizen Kane* (1941) and scores for some of Hitchcock's films; Erich Wolfgang Korngold with the lush scores of Warner Bros. adventure films such as *The Adventures of Robin Hood* (1938) and *The Sea Hawk* (1940); David Raksin with the theme song from *Laura* (1944); Miklos Rozsa and Max Steiner with lush, romantic scores; and Ernest Gold with the theme from *Exodus* (1960). The best known of contemporary composers is John Williams, thanks to his instantly recognizable scores for *Jaws* (1975), *Star Wars* (1977), *E. T. The Extra-Terrestrial* (1982), and *Return of the Jedi* (1983). Other contemporary composers with high reputations among their peers are Leonard Rosenman, Jerry Goldsmith, Giorgio Moroder, and Bill Conti, successors to such memorable earlier film composers as John Green, Ray Heindorf, Morris Stoloff, Franz Waxman, and Victor Young.

Academy Awards for Best Music Scores have been given since 1934, when the winner was the Columbia Studio Music Department (Louis Silvers, head) for *One Night of Love*. The award points up the early practice of crediting music departments or their heads for film scores, rather than the actual composers or arrangers.

BIBLIOGRAPHY

Eisler, Hanns. *Composing for the Films*. New York: Oxford University Press, 1947.

Evans, Mark. *Soundtrack: The Music of the Movies*. New York: Hopkinson and Blake, 1975.

Faulkner, Robert S. *Hollywood Studio Musicians*. Chicago: Aldine Atherton, 1971.

Hofmann, Charles. *Sounds for Silents*. New York: DBS Publications, 1970.

Huntley, John. *The Technique of Film Music*. New York: Hastings House, 1957.

Limbacher, James L. *Film Music from Violins to Video*. Metuchen, New Jersey: Scarecrow Press, 1974.

———. *Keeping Score: Film Music 1972–1979*. Metuchen, New Jersey: Scarecrow Press, 1981.

London, Kurt. *Film Music*. London: Faber & Faber, 1936.

McCarty, Clifford. *Film Composers in America*. Glendale, California: John Valentine, 1953.

Meeker, David. *Jazz in the Movies*. New York: Da Capo, 1982.

Thomas, Tony. *Music for the Movies*. New York: A. S. Barnes, 1973.

MUSICALS. "What is a musical?" asked critic John Russell Taylor. "All talking, all singing, all dancing? Well, yes, preferably. But a lot more, and sometimes a lot less. A film musical is, essentially, just that: a film which, in whole or in part, has its shape, its movement, its whole feeling dictated by music."

The musical genre is as old as the sound film itself. *The Jazz Singer* (1927), generally considered the first sound feature, was a musical. The sound era began with all singing, all talking, all dancing revues, such as *Hollywood Revue of 1929* from M-G-M*, *Show of Shows* (1929) from Warner Bros.*, *Paramount on Parade* (1930), and *The King of Jazz* (1930) from Universal*. The first film musical with an original score, by Arthur Freed and Nacio Herb Brown, was *Broadway Melody* (1929) from M-G-M, starring Bessie Love, Charles King, and Anita Page. The first musical in Technicolor* was Warner Bros.' *On with the Show* (1929), starring Betty Compson, Arthur Lake, and Ethel Waters. The first operetta written specially for the screen was Sigmund Romberg and Oscar Hammerstein's *Viennese Nights* (1930), produced by Warner Bros. and starring Vivienne Segal, Alexander Gray, and Walter Pidgeon.

Following the initial enthusiasm for musicals, there was a period in the early thirties when the public turned against the genre. It returned to popularity with Warner Bros.' *42nd Street* (1932), Eddie Cantor's comedy musicals at the Goldwyn* studios, and with the Fred Astaire–Ginger Rogers musicals at RKO*, the first of which (although the two were not its stars) being *Flying Down to Rio* (1933). Maurice Chevalier was Paramount's musical star of the early thirties, usually partnered by Jeanette MacDonald, who moved over to M-G-M to co-star with Nelson Eddy in a series of operettas from the mid-thirties through the mid-forties. At Warner Bros., the "Gold Diggers" series* was popular, thanks largely to the winsome charm of Ruby Keeler and Dick Powell and the extravagant routines choreographed by Busby Berkeley.

Shirley Temple was 20th Century-Fox's first musical star, to be followed by Alice Faye and Betty Grable. Deanna Durbin was responsible for a new form of musical, which embraced serious music for dramatic effect, at Universal, in features such as *100 Men and a Girl* (1937). M-G-M had introduced the "Broadway Melody" series with the 1929 feature of that name; it continued the series with the Broadway Melodies of 1936, 1938, and 1940. Also at M-G-M, Eleanor Powell became the leading exponent of tap dancing (with strong competition from Ann Miller at Columbia*). Judy Garland starred in *The Wizard of Oz* (1939) and was co-featured with Mickey Rooney in a delightful series of musical comedies, such as *Babes in Arms* (1939) and *Strike Up the Band* (1940). Gene Kelly came into his own at M-G-M in the forties, while Mario Lanza dominated the musical scene at the studio in the early fifties, during which period M-G-M's female musical stars included Kathryn Grayson and Betty Hutton. The fifties also saw lyricist Arthur Freed consolidating his reputation as the studio's greatest musical producer with films such as *Annie Get Your Gun* (1950), *An American in Paris* (1951), *Singin' in the Rain* (1952), *The Band Wagon* (1953), *Silk Stockings* (1957), and *Gigi* (1958).

There were five screen versions of Richard Rodgers and Oscar Hammerstein II stage musicals: *Oklahoma!* (1955), *Carousel* (1956), *The King and I* (1956), *South Pacific* (1958), and *Flower Drum Song* (1961).

All-black musicals have failed to make much of an impact, with the best known being *Cabin in the Sky* (1943), *Stormy Weather* (1943), *Carmen Jones* (1954), *Porgy and Bess* (1959), and *The Wiz* (1978). A more enduring subgenre has been that of the biographical musical, which can be devoted to entertainers as with *The Helen Morgan Story* (1957), *The Jolson Story* (1946) and *Jolson Sings Again* (1949), *Yankee Doodle Dandy* (1942), and *The Story of Vernon and Irene Castle* (1939); to band leaders as with *The Glenn Miller Story* (1954); and to composers, as with the highly fanciful Richard Rodgers and Lorenz Hart biography, *Words and Music* (1948).

"Modern" musicals can embrace the strictly entertainment values of their predecessors, as with *The Music Man* (1962), *Mary Poppins* (1964), *The Sound of Music* (1965), *Camelot* (1967), and *Hello, Dolly!* (1969), and can also be new and original, as was evidenced by *West Side Story* (1961) and *All That Jazz* (1979).

Only nine musicals have won Academy Awards for Best Picture: *Broadway Melody* (1929), *The Great Ziegfeld* (1936), *An American in Paris* (1951), *Gigi* (1958), *West Side Story* (1961), *My Fair Lady* (1964), *The Sound of Music* (1965), *Oliver!* (1968), and *Amadeus* (1984).

BIBLIOGRAPHY

Green, Stanley. *Encyclopaedia of the Musical Film*. New York: Oxford University Press, 1981.

Kreuger, Miles. *The Movie Musical*. New York: Dover, 1975.

Mordden, Ethan. *The Hollywood Musical*. New York: St. Martin's Press, 1981.
Taylor, John Russell, and Arthur Jackson. *The Hollywood Musical*. New York: McGraw-Hill, 1971.

MUTUAL FILM CORPORATION. The Mutual Film Corporation was organized in March 1912 as an independent exchange system to function in a manner similar to that of the General Film Company. Harry E. Aitken, Mutual's president, who later in 1912 formed the Film Supply Company of America as an alliance of independent film manufacturers to challenge the Carl Laemmle–controlled Motion Picture Distributing and Sales Company*, and John R. Freuler, Mutual's vice-president, interested financiers Crawford Livingston and Otto Kahn (of Kahn, Loeb, and Company) in the enterprise. With a capitalization of $2.5 million, Mutual eventually succeeded in signing half of the members of the Motion Picture Distributing and Sales Company. Shortly after Mutual's creation, the Universal Film Manufacturing Company was created and it became Mutual's rival independent exchange.

Mutual handled films for Thanhouser*, Gaumont*, American*, Great Northern*, Reliance, Eclair*, Solax*, Majestic, Lux, Comet, and the New York Motion Picture Company*, supervised by Thomas H. Ince, which controlled Kay-Bee, Broncho, and Domino Films. Adam Kessel and Charles O. Baumann, who owned the New York Motion Picture Company and Reliance, formed the Keystone Film Company* in 1912, with Mack Sennett, to produce films for Mutual. In October 1913, Mutual hired D. W. Griffith to be in charge of the amalgamated Reliance-Majestic studio. The next month, Griffith's cameraman, Billy Bitzer, joined Mutual, along with directors Edward Dillon and W. Christy Cabanne, actor Courtenay Foote, and scenarist Frank Woods. Griffith soon established his company at the former Kinemacolor studio at 4500 Sunset Boulevard in Hollywood (when it became known as Fine Arts*).

The Continental Feature Film Company was formed as a subsidiary to Mutual in late 1913, to release features made by Reliance. W. C. Toomey was its manager, and its offices were 219 Sixth Avenue, New York.

In January 1914, Mutual contracted with Pancho Villa for his permission and cooperation regarding the filming of the battles of the Mexican war. According to Terry Ramsaye (in *A Million and One Nights*), Villa was so camera struck that he held off fighting battles until Mutual's camera team was set up, fought during the day rather than at night, and made sure he was always prominent in the picture. Later, Mutual used some of this footage in the fictionalized *The Life of Villa*, which starred Raoul Walsh.

Mutual instituted a series of features called "Mutual Masterpieces" early in 1915. In May 1915, a split between, on one side, Aitken, Kessel and Baumann, and, on the other, Freuler and America's head Samuel S. Hutchinson resulted in Freuler's succeeding Aitken as president. The latter left Mutual, and, two months later, Aitken, Kessel, and Baumann formed the Triangle Film Corporation* to produce the films of D. W. Griffith, Thomas H. Ince, and Mack Sennett.

Freuler appointed J. C. Graham as his general manager and signed David Horsley's Centaur Film Company and the Bostock Jungle and Film Company* to release with Mutual.

On February 26, 1916, Mutual signed Charles Chaplin, for $670,000, to produce comedies for it. His new company, Lone Star Film Corporation, produced twelve films and ended in 1917, when Chaplin signed with First National*. In early 1917, Mutual secured the rights to release the Charles Frohman plays, produced with the Charles Frohman stars by the newly formed Empire All Star Corporation, which was incorporated with $2.5 million capital.

Freuler, who complained that he did not have the backing of his associates to make much needed changes, resigned May 1, 1918, and was replaced by James M. Sheldon. On November 6, 1918, the Affiliated Distributors' Corporation acquired 51 percent of Mutual, which was then losing money at an alarming rate. The Exhibitors' Mutual Distributing Corporation, formed later in 1918, was an outgrowth of Mutual and the Affiliated.

BIBLIOGRAPHY

"Mutual Film Corporation," *The Moving Picture World*, April 6, 1912, p. 34.

"Mutual Withdraws from Film Supply," *The Moving Picture World*, December 12, 1912, p. 1280.

THE MUTUAL WEEKLY. See NEWSREELS

THE NASH MOTION PICTURE COMPANY, INC. Thomas Nash, formerly a producer of one- and two-reel animal films for the Selig Polyscope Company*, formed his own company in mid–1914 and built a studio and zoo in Edendale, California, to make three- to five-reel wild animal features. It released on the Kriterion* program at the beginning, later releasing to the states rights* market.
BIBLIOGRAPHY
"New Wild Animal Company Formed," *The Moving Picture World*, July 4, 1914, p. 87.

NATIONAL ASSOCIATION OF THEATRE OWNERS, INC. The National Association of Theatre Owners (NATO), Inc., came into being on January 1, 1965, with the merger of Theatre Owners of America and the Allied States Association of Motion Picture Exhibitors. According to its constitution, its concerns are the maintenance of a strong, national trade organization; the promotion and protection of interests of motion picture exhibitors; and the cultivation of the highest possible standards in all film industry matters in general and in film exhibition in particular. NATO serves as a spokesperson for all matters affecting exhibitors. It also organizes an annual convention, at which exhibitors can see the latest in products relating to theatre operations, including technical equipment, the latest studio productions, and food and equipment relating to the concessions counter. Also at its convention, NATO presents awards to the stars of the year and the stars of tomorrow and the Sherill C. Corwin Award (named after a former president of NATO) for contributions to theatre exhibition.

Addresses: 1560 Broadway, Suite 714, New York, N.Y. 10036; also regional offices.

NATIONAL ASSOCIATION OF THE MOTION PICTURE INDUSTRY. The National Association of the Motion Picture Industry (NAMPI) was formed in July 1916 as a successor to the Motion Picture Board of Trade of America*. Its objectives were to foster trade and commerce among members, promote business interests of the industry, provide information about the industry, settle difficulties within the industry, and secure freedom from unjust government exactions. The membership represented producers and importers, the Motion Picture Exhibitors' League of America*, manufacturers, dealers and importers of motion picture supplies, distributors, and others connected with the industry. The exhibitors, who wanted a bigger representation on the board of the previous organization, voted to join the National Association of the Motion Picture Industry at its first meeting on July 25, 1916. A few months later, William A. Brady was elected president, Jules Brulatour treasurer, Thomas Furniss the first vice-president, and Adolph Zukor the second vice-president. After the United States entered the First World War in 1917, NAMPI responded to a letter of President Woodrow Wilson and appointed various members to act in conjunction with the various government departments. NAMPI went out of existence when the stronger Motion Picture Producers and Distributors of America, Inc., headed by Will Hays, came into existence early in 1922.

BIBLIOGRAPHY

"Film Men Form Temporary Organization," *The Moving Picture World*, July 22, 1916, p. 612.

"Motion Pictures Mobilized for War," *The Moving Picture World*, August 11, 1917, p. 918.

NATIONAL BOARD OF CENSORSHIP OF MOTION PICTURES. The National Board of Censorship of Motion Pictures, a precursor to the National Board of Review of Motion Pictures*, was formed in October 1909, after an earlier organization, the Board of Censorship, experimented for five months censoring the product of most of the early companies. The Board of Censorship was established by the People's Institute, a New York civic organization, in response to a petition from the Motion Picture Exhibitors of New York State, which financed its operations and had two members on the Board's executive committee. The exhibitors wanted a censorship board to prevent hostility from vigilance groups and to limit the danger of losing exhibitors' licenses as a result of being taken to court—the result of the negative reaction to some of the films that they screened.

The Board's governing body was composed of individuals from nine public-interest bodies, such as the Public Education Association and the City Vigilance League. Dr. George William Knox of the Union Theological Seminary was the chairman. At its formation, the Board had made arrangements with every company in the Motion Picture Patents Company* and a few of the independents to censor its films before they were sent to the exchanges. The Board was opposed to the depiction of crime or violence for its own sake, indecency, and immoral suggestiveness. The Board also emphasized that it would try to encourage the use of motion pictures for educational purposes. It carried no legal weight, and, in its most publicized case, the Board refused to censor D. W. Griffith's *The Birth of a Nation* (1915). In 1916, its name was changed to the National Board of Review of Motion Pictures.

BIBLIOGRAPHY
"An Eloquent Record," *The Moving Picture World*, December 4, 1915, p. 1821.
"The Board of Censorship," *The Moving Picture World*, March 6, 1909, pp. 265–266.
"Censorship of Film Subjects," *The Moving Picture World*, March 20, 1909, p. 325.
"National Board of Censorship of Motion Pictures," *The Moving Picture World*, October
      16, 1909, p. 524.

NATIONAL BOARD OF REVIEW OF MOTION PICTURES, INC. Founded
in 1909 as the National Board of Censorship of Motion Pictures*, the National
Board of Review of Motion Pictures served as a citizens' group concerned with
the evaluation of films. It was initially formed to discourage official censorship
of motion pictures and enjoyed the financial support of the film industry. All
films were submitted to the Board—it became the National Board of Review of
Motion Pictures, Inc., in 1916—for a seal of approval, consisting of the words,
"Passed by the National Board of Review," which would appear on the main
titles. The Board charged a fee, per reel, for the review and approval of each
film.

With the creation of local censorship boards, the National Board of Review's
approval became valueless, and by January 1938 only Providence, Rhode Island,
still required films to carry the Board's seal of approval—and then only for
Sunday screenings.

The National Board of Review is probably better known today for its selection
of "Ten Best Films," which it has undertaken since 1930, with the inclusion—
in more recent years—of citations for Best Actor, Actress, Director, Foreign
Language Film, and so on. It is also noted for its publications: *Film Progress*
(1917–1926), *Exceptional Photoplays* (1920–1925), *Photoplay Guide to Better
Movies* (1924–1926), *National Board of Review Magazine* (1926–1942), *New
Movies* (1942–1949), and *Films in Review* (1950 to present).

Address: P.O. Box 589, New York, N.Y. 10021.

BIBLIOGRAPHY
Fisher, Robert, "Film Censorship and Progressive Reform: The National Board of Cen-
      sorship of Motion Pictures, 1909–1922," *Journal of Popular Film*, vol. IV, no.
      2, 1975, pp. 143–156.
Hochman, Stanley, editor. *From Quasimodo to Scarlett O'Hara: A National Board of
      Review Anthology 1920–1940.* New York: Frederick Ungar, 1982.
"National Board of Review Facing Test on Continuance of Activity," *Motion Picture
      Herald*, January 29, 1938, pp. 16, 18, 28.
Ramsaye, Terry, "Forty Years of the National Board," *Films in Review*, February 1950,
      pp. 23–24.
Warfield, Nancy, "A Film Students Index to the National Board of Review Magazine
      1926–1948," *The Little Film Gazette of N.D.W.*, vol. V, no. 2, December 1974.

NATIONAL CAMERAPHONE COMPANY. The National Cameraphone
Company, an early producer of "talking pictures," began leasing its machines
across the country at the beginning of 1908, after two years of experimentation.
During the company's two-year existence, a number of other processes for

producing talking pictures, including Gaumont's Chronophone, Powers' Fotophone, and the Cinephone, were presented to an interested public, prompting a journalist to predict that "the speaking picture will soon be as common as the moving picture now."

E. E. Norton of Bridgeport, Connecticut, formerly a mechanical engineer with the American Gramophone Company, invented the Cameraphone, a combination of a motion picture projector and the gramophone. The company's factory was located in Bridgeport, at 423 Water Street, and its offices were at 1161 Broadway, New York, where the films were first produced in its "gallery." In May 1908, the company converted a five-story warehouse at 573–579 Eleventh Avenue, New York, into a studio and exhibition hall. Carl Herbert was Cameraphone's general manager.

Although the National Cameraphone Company never lived up to its claim to have perfected synchronization between sound and picture, it did please audiences throughout the country for a short time. Successful exhibitions were reported in Kalamazoo, Michigan; Oakland, California; Pueblo, Colorado; Baltimore, Maryland; Youngstown, Ohio; Helena, Montana; Columbus, Georgia; and New York City. One show consisted of a song, a scene in a Turkish bath, and a dramatic enactment of *The Corsican Brothers*. Another included an impersonation of George M. Cohan.

The company purchased the projectors and gramophones used in the exhibitions from manufacturers and leased them to theatres. The gramophone, which was placed behind the screen, could be turned on and off by the projectionist, to keep the sound reasonably in sync with the picture. Although critics complained that synchronization often was not achieved, and that the sound had a harsh, metallic ring, the company hoped that improvements could be made. However, the Cameraphone Company went out of business by May 1910.

BIBLIOGRAPHY

"The Cameraphone," *The Moving Picture World*, January 16, 1909, p. 71.
"Cameraphone Experiments," *The Moving Picture World*, January 23, 1909, p. 90.
"Cameraphone Hits," *The Moving Picture World*, July 25, 1908, p. 63.
"Cameraphone the Latest Wonder," *The Moving Picture World*, April 25, 1908, pp. 369–370.

NATIONAL CATHOLIC OFFICE FOR MOTION PICTURES. See NATIONAL LEGION OF DECENCY

NATIONAL DRAMA CORPORATION. After the success of *The Birth of a Nation* (1915), Thomas Dixon, author of *The Clansman*, upon which the film was based, formed the National Drama Corporation in 1915, so that he might produce and direct his first film. *The Fall of a Nation* (1916), a warning against disarmament and women's suffrage, was the result. Dixon hired composer Victor Herbert to write the score, which was performed by a sixty-piece orchestra under the direction of Harold Sanford at the film's New York premiere in June 1916 at the Liberty Theatre. After *The Fall of a Nation*, National contracted with Dixon for the rights to his literary output for the next five years. P. D. Gold, Jr., was the president of the company, William R. Perkins the vice-president, Dixon the director-general and treasurer, Bartley Cushing the head producing director, and William C. Thompson and John W. Boyle the cameraman.

NATIONAL FILM AND PHOTO LEAGUE. Radical young filmmakers and film enthusiasts formed the National Film and Photo League (sometimes referred to as the Workers' Film and Photo League and sometimes as simply the Film and Photo League) in 1931. The group included Lewis Jacobs, David Platt, Leo T. Hurwitz, Jay Leyda, Irving Lerner, and Ralph Steiner. It had its origins in the Workers' International Relief, the Workers' Camera League, and the Labor Defender Photo Group.

The League was organized into city groups. It produced a newsreel and documentary shorts; organized protests against anti-Communist Hollywood productions and the screening of pro-Nazi films from Germany; held meetings; and published a magazine, *Film Front*, from 1934–1935. The New York group produced *Albany Hunger March* (1931), *The Strike against Starvation* (1931), *The Fight for the Bonus* (1932), *Hands Off Ethiopia* (1935), among others. From Detroit came *The Ford Massacre* (1932); from Chicago, *The Great Depression* (1934); from Los Angeles, *Tom Mooney Run* (1932) and *Bloody Memorial Day* (1934). Unfortunately, these films gained only very limited screenings, and those chiefly for committed radicals.

By 1937, the National Film and Photo League had basically ceased to exist, although one breakaway group, The Photo League, was still around as late as 1951. Another breakaway group was Nykino, which became the film division of the Theatre of Action and which produced such films as *Pie in the Sky* (1935), *Black Legion* (1936), and *The World Today* (1936). From Nykino emerged Frontier Films*.

BIBLIOGRAPHY

Campbell, Russell. *Cinema Strikes Back*. Ann Arbor, Michigan: UMI Research Press, 1982.
Rosenzweig, Roy, "Working Class Struggles in the Great Depression: The Film Record," *Film Library Quarterly*, vol. XIII, no. 1, 1980, pp. 5–14.
Seltzer, Leo, "Documenting the Depression of the 1930s," *Film Library Quarterly*, vol. XIII, no. 1, 1980, pp. 15–22.

RESOURCES

Films: Museum of Modern Art (16mm reference prints).

NATIONAL FILM CORPORATION OF AMERICA. The National Film Corporation of America was formed in 1915 by comedian "Smiling" Bill Parsons. The following year, Paul Gilmore became associated with the company, which announced plans for a move from Los Angeles to Tampa, Florida, where it was to build a new studio. Despite valid claims by many of the corporation's stockholders as to irregularities in its affairs, National prospered for quite a while. It produced the first "Tarzan" feature, *Tarzan of the Apes* (1918), and two sequels, *The Romance of Tarzan* (1918) and a fifteen-chapter serial*, *The Son of Tarzan* (1920). At its Hollywood studio, at Santa Monica Boulevard and Gower Street, the corporation produced a series of comedies featuring Parsons, his wife Billie Rhodes, Mr. and Mrs. Carter De Haven, and Eddie Flanagan and Neely Edwards as "The Hall Room Boys," as well as dramas with Ann Little, Jack Hoxie, and Henry B. Walthall. Its films were released by Goldwyn*, Pioneer Film Corporation*, and the W. W. Hodkinson Corporation*. Following Parsons' death in 1919, National was acquired by R. E. Frey, who moved the corporation to new studios at 1116 Lodi Street. It lost much of its importance as Frey attempted to make John Bunny's brother, George, into a comedy star. National ceased operations in 1923.

BIBLIOGRAPHY

"National Film Corporation of America," *The Moving Picture World*, July 10, 1915, p. 254.

Nelson, Richard Alan, " 'High Flyer' Movie Finance and the Silver Screen: The Rise and Fall of the National Film Corporation of America," *Film & History*, vol. XIII, no. 4, December 1983, pp. 73–83, 93.

NATIONAL GENERAL CORPORATION. When 20th Century-Fox* was required by the consent decree* to divest itself of its theatre chain, the 549 theatres that it controlled in 1951 became National General Corporation. The number of theatres gradually declined, and in 1973 the remaining 266 were sold to Mann Theatres Corporation*.

NATIONAL LEGION OF DECENCY. The National Legion of Decency (often erroneously referred to as the Legion of Decency) was formed in April 1934 as an agency of the Catholic Bishops of the United States. Its purpose was to assure that motion pictures conformed to the accepted and traditional morality upon which the home and civilization were founded. The Legion rated films into four categories, with the rating undertaken by the Motion Picture Department of the International Federation of Catholic Alumnae: Class A, Section I, Unobjectionable for General Patronage; Class A, Section II, Unobjectionable for Adults; Class B, Objectionable in Part; Class C, Condemned.

An editorial in the Catholic journal *America* (December 13, 1941) pointed out that "the Legion has no legal authority, and wishes none. Its appeal is to the decent citizens in every country, and this, it is confident, will not go unheeded." However, the Legion was the subject of considerable criticism for its ludicrous condemnation of films such as *The Private Life of Henry VIII* (1933), on the grounds that it condoned divorce, and its approval of 120 Nazi films submitted between 1936 and 1937, as well as its refusal to condemn films on the grounds of anti-Semitism.

The National Legion of Decency became the National Catholic Office for

Motion Pictures in January 1966, and the name was again changed, in January 1971, to the U.S. Catholic Conference—Division for Film and Broadcasting. By 1981, films were rated A–1 for General Patronage, A–2 for Adults and Adolescents, A–3 for Adults, and A–4 for Adults with reservations. A new category "O" was added to signify "morally offensive," and, in addition, "recommended," in parenthesis, was placed after some titles.

Address: 1011 First Avenue, New York, N.Y. 10022.

BIBLIOGRAPHY

Facey, Paul W. *The Legion of Decency*. New York: Arno Press, 1974.
"Legion of Decency Exposes Itself," *Film Survey*, August 1938, pp. 1–2, 5–6.
"Legion of Decency Tells How to 'Judge Morality' of Film," *Motion Picture Herald*, November 14, 1936, pp. 35–36.

NATIONAL SCREEN SERVICE. National Screen Service is the country's major provider of promotional materials—such as lobby cards,* still photographs,* posters, and trailers*—to theatres. Through the thirties, the studios produced their own advertising matter. But, in 1940, National Screen Service (which had been in existence since 1919) took over the distribution of such materials for Paramount and RKO, and gradually all the major studios turned over the production and distribution of theatrical advertising matter to National Screen Service (NSS).

The company operates a printing facility in Cleveland, a studio for the production of trailers in London, Advertising Industries for the creation and manufacture of frames and display cases, and Continental Lithograph Corporation for the printing of posters. As of 1984, National Screen Service was servicing some 15,000 theatres. It does not handle advertising material for small distributors, such as New World*, and is licensed to provide materials only to theatres.

Addresses: 1600 Broadway, New York, N.Y. 10019; also offices in Atlanta, Boston, Chicago, Cincinnati, Cleveland, Dallas, Kansas City, Los Angeles, New Orleans, Philadelphia, and Seattle.

BIBLIOGRAPHY

"The NSS Story of Service," *Motion Picture Herald*, March 14, 1959, pp. 18–21.
"The 'Prize Baby' Remembers," *Motion Picture Herald*, November 7, 1959, pp. 16–17.

NATIONAL TELEFILM ASSOCIATES. See REPUBLIC PICTURES CORPORATION (NEW)

NATIONAL THEATRES CORPORATION. See FOX WEST COAST THEATRES CORPORATION

NATIONAL THEATRES, INC. See FOX WEST COAST THEATRES CORPORATION

NATO. See NATIONAL ASSOCIATION OF THEATRE OWNERS, INC.

NATURAL VISION. See THREE-DIMENSIONAL FILMS

NAVAJO FILM MANUFACTURING COMPANY. The Navajo Film Manufacturing Company, formed in late 1914 to make films for the Kriterion* program, erected a studio in Edendale, California. W. H. Bissell was the president, Charles K. French, formerly with Bison, the head of production, and Fred Granville the cameraman. Leading players for Navajo were Wallace MacDonald, Lucille Young, and William Parsons. After Kriterion's demise, Navajo and seven other West Coast companies combined to form the Associated Service to release their films.

NELSON FILM COMPANY. See SMALLWOOD FILM CORPORATION

NESTOR FILM COMPANY. See CENTAUR FILM COMPANY

NEVADA MOTION PICTURE COMPANY. The Nevada Motion Picture Company, organized by wealthy men of Reno, built a studio at 40 West Mountain Street in Pasadena in 1916. Its production of *The Planters*, starring Tyrone Power, was filmed partly in Guatemala. F. W. Manson, a millionaire, was the company's president, and John Ince the production manager. Nevada's studio burned down on March 24, 1917.

NEWHALL RANCH. Less than thirty miles from Hollywood*, the Newhall Ranch, with its 38,000 acres, stretching from Newhall to Simi Valley, is considered the largest and most important location area for Hollywood-produced films and television programs. It offers a variety of scenery, as well as an airstrip, a river, a South American or Asian village, two golf courses, oil wells, a military base, and various standing sets. Founded by Henry Mayo Newhall (1825–1882) in the 1850s, the Newhall Ranch has remained intact largely because Newhall's will forbade the sale of any of his real estate. To supplement the income from oil wells and cattle ranching, the Newhall Ranch has been rented out as a film location from the mid-forties. Among the features filmed there were *Baby Blue Marine* (1976), *Escape from New York* (1981), *Heart like a Wheel* (1983), *Missing in Action* (1984), *Private Benjamin* (1980), *The Best Little Whorehouse in Texas* (1982), *The Pursuit of D. B. Cooper* (1981), and *The Swarm* (1978). It was while *The Twilight Zone* (1984) was being filmed at the Newhall Ranch that actor Vic Morrow and two young children were killed.

Address: The Newhall Land and Farming Company, 23823 Valencia Boulevard, Valencia, Calif. 91355.

NEW HORIZON PICTURES CORPORATION. See CONCORDE PICTURES CORPORATION

NEW LINE CINEMA CORPORATION. Formed in 1967 by Robert Shaye, New Line Cinema Corporation is a specialized New York–based distributor, which first became known for its release of offbeat films for the college market. It later entered film production, with its best-known feature being *Polyester* (1981). New Line also operates a Lecture Bureau.

Address: 575 Fifth Avenue, New York, N.Y. 10018.

"NEW MAJESTIC." See RELIANCE MOTION PICTURE COMPANY AND MAJESTIC MOTION PICTURE COMPANY

NEW ORLEANS. See COQUILLE FILM COMPANY

NEWSREELS. The most succinct description of a newsreel is probably given by Raymond Fielding in his definitive volume *The American Newsreel 1911– 1967*: "a ten-minute potpourri of motion picture news footage, released twice a week to motion picture theaters throughout the country. For more than half a century, from 1911 to 1967, it survived intact and unchanged, during which time it was as predictably a part of every theater's program as the Walt Disney cartoon and the Fitzpatrick travelogue."

The earliest of films were actualities, in themselves a form of newsreel. News events were filmed as early as 1895, and when cameramen were unable to be present the events could easily be faked. Equally, from the earliest years, newsreels have presented a biased view of an event, influenced by the political or social leanings of the newsreel's makers.

The first regular newsreel to be released in the United States was *Pathé's Weekly*, first seen on August 8, 1911, and which later became *Pathé News*, and, in 1947, *Warner-Pathé News*. It was followed in 1912 by *The Gaumont Animated Weekly*. The teens saw the birth of most of the newsreels, including *The Mutual Weekly*, *Kinograms*, *The Hearst-Selig News Pictorial*, *Fox News* (introduced in 1919), and *The Universal Animated Weekly* (which was introduced in 1913 and later became *Universal News*). William Randolph Hearst later was to lend his name to *Hearst-Pathé News* and—in 1927—*Hearst Metrotone News*, which was co-produced with M-G-M*. Hearst had also introduced *The International Newsreel*.

The final group of major newsreels appeared in 1927: *Paramount News*, *Fox-Movietone News*, and the aforementioned *Hearst-Metrotone News*. An all-black newsreel, *All-American News*, was introduced in 1942.

Warner-Pathé News ceased in 1956, followed by *Paramount News* a year later. *Fox-Movietone News* ceased in 1963. *Hearst-Metrotone* produced its last issue in 1967, and, in December of that year, America's last newsreel, *Universal News*, appeared for the final time. The National Archives in Washington, D.C., has the *Universal News*, along with the occasional issues of many silent newsreels. *Fox-Movietone News* is still controlled by 20th Century-Fox. *Pathé News* and

Paramount News are owned by Sherman Grinberg*. *Hearst-Metrotone* was acquired by King Features and has been turned over to the UCLA Film Archives. *See also* March of Time.

BIBLIOGRAPHY
Ballantyne, James, editor. *Researcher's Guide to British Newsreels*. London: British Universities Film & Video Council, 1983.
Fielding, Raymond. *The American Newsreel 1911–1967*. Norman, Oklahoma: University of Oklahoma Press, 1972.

NEW WORLD PICTURES. After leaving American International Pictures*, Roger Corman founded New World Pictures in 1970; he chose the name because he wanted a company that was worldwide in scope, and, in time, New World became America's largest independent producer/distributor. As critic David Chute has commented, New World quickly gained a "reputation for soft-core action pictures and gilt-edged foreign product." New World's first success came with the "Nurse" series of "R"-rated films, beginning with *The Student Nurses* (1970). Its small budgets and short production schedules helped the company enjoy a first year profit of $3.2 million.

Among the directors who began their careers with New World were Andrew Meyer, Stephanie Rothman, Jonathan Kaplan, and Peter Bogdanovich, who both directed and starred in *Targets* (1968) for New World and returned to the company in 1979 to direct *Saint Jack*. Other New World features included *The Harder They Come* (1973), *Big Bad Mama* (1974), *Hollywood Boulevard* (1976, and generally considered to be a parody of New World's production methods), *Eat My Dust!* (1977), *I Never Promised You a Rose Garden* (1977), and *Mutant* (1981). Beginning with *Cries and Whispers* (1973), New World also gained a reputation for the release of outstanding foreign films, with later releases including *Fantastic Planet* (1974), *Amarcord* (1974), *The Story of Adele H* (1975), *Lumière* (1977), *Small Change* (1977), *Dersu Uzala* (1978), *The Tin Drum* (1980), and *Breaker Morant* (1980).

In February 1983, Corman sold the company to Harry E. Sloan, Lawrence E. Kuppin, and Larry A. Thompson for $16.5 million. He subsequently formed a new company, Concorde Pictures Corporation*. According to Robert Rehme, who joined the company in the fall of 1983 as co-owner and chief executive officer, the new New World was "gonna make hit pictures, high concept pictures." However, the first in-house production, *Angel* (1984), bore a striking similarity to the type of films with which New World had been associated under Roger Corman. Angel was followed by *Children of the Corn*, *The Philadelphia Experiment*, and *Body Rock* (all released in 1984).

Address: 1888 Century Park East, Los Angeles, Calif. 90067.

BIBLIOGRAPHY
Caufield, Deborah, "What's New Is Old at the New New World," *Los Angeles Times*, Calendar Section, February 19, 1984, pp. 3–5.
Chute, David, "The New World of Roger Corman," *Film Comment*, March-April 1982, pp. 27–32.

di Franco, J. Philip, editor. *The Movie World of Roger Corman*. New York: Chelsea House, 1979.

Kleiman, Rena, "The B Team," *Stills*, November 1984, pp. 30–32.

Naha, Ed, *The Films of Roger Corman: Brilliance on a Budget*. New York: Arco, 1982.
RESOURCES
Films: UCLA Film Archives (reference prints of films produced and/or released by Roger Corman).

NEW YORK. New York City was the first home of the film industry in the United States. Here D. W. Griffith directed his first shorts at the American Biograph* studios on East 14 Street. Thanks largely to the presence of the Astoria Studios*, filmmaking continued on a moderate scale in New York through the thirties. The revitalization of the Astoria plant in the mid-seventies led to a resurgence of filmmaking in the city, as filmmakers such as Robert De Niro, Martin Scorsese, Sidney Lumet, and Bob Fosse expressed their preference for filmmaking in New York. Among the major features produced in New York in recent years have been *Taxi Driver* (1976), *The Wiz* (1978), *All That Jazz* (1979), *Kramer vs. Kramer* (1979), *Hair* (1979), *Wolfen* (1981), *Arthur* (1981), *They All Laughed* (1981), *Ragtime* (1981), *Raging Bull* (1981), *Tootsie* (1982), *The Verdict* (1982), *Author! Author!* (1982), *The King of Comedy* (1983), and, of course, the films of Woody Allen.

Although the films might have been produced in Hollywood, the streets and landmarks of New York have been immensely popular with filmmakers. Among the "classic" American films with a New York background were *The Crowd* (1928), *Lonesome* (1928), *The Broadway Melody* (1929), *Applause* (1929), *The Struggle* (1931), *King Kong* (1933), *Dead End* (1937), *The Naked City* (1948), *Sorry, Wrong Number* (1948), *On the Town* (1949), *On the Waterfront* (1954), *The Blackboard Jungle* (1955), and *Midnight Cowboy* (1969).

Filmmaking in New York has been avidly encouraged by Mayor Edward Koch, and most filmmaking in the city is coordinated through The Mayor's Office of Film, Theatre & Broadcasting, 110 West 57 Street, New York, N.Y. 10019.
BIBLIOGRAPHY

Haskell, Molly, "Movie Boomtown," *New York*, December 5, 1977, pp. 43–47.

Jacobson, Mark, "New York's Love Affair with the Movies," *New York*, December 29, 1975, pp. 33–44.

Johnson, Hillary, "Hollywood East," *New York*, June 28, 1982, pp. 32–37.

McCourt, James, "City of Your Dreams," *Film Comment*, March-April 1976, pp. 52–54.

Stern, Ellen, "How To Make a Movie in New York," *New York*, December 29, 1976, pp. 55–60.

NEW YORKER FILMS. New Yorker Films takes its name from the New Yorker Theatre on New York's upper East side, films for which Dan Talbot began programming in 1960. Talbot entered film distribution in 1964 when the only way he could screen Bernardo Bertolucci's *Before the Revolution* was by acquiring the U.S. rights. By 1981, Talbot had a library of 200 films from around the world.

Address: 16 West 61 Street, New York, N.Y. 10023.

NEW YORK FILM FESTIVAL. Sponsored by, and always held at, the Lincoln Center for the Performing Arts, the New York Film Festival was first held September 10–19, 1963. It now takes place in either September or October. A noncompetitive festival, the number of films screened at New York is small in comparison with other festivals, but the quality is always very high. The Festival also usually includes several vintage films (often supplied by the Cinémathèque Française). In its formative years, the New York Film Festival was closely linked with the London Film Festival, with both screening the same films and sharing a common director in Richard Roud (who eventually parted with the London Film Festival but remains program director for New York).

Address: Film Society of Lincoln Center, 140 West 65 Street, New York, N.Y. 10023.

NEW YORK MOTION PICTURE COMPANY. The New York Motion Picture Company (NYMPC), one of the first independent production companies formed after the creation of the Motion Picture Patents Company*, was organized by Adam Kessel, Jr., who earlier formed a combination of exchanges* in New York with six or seven exchange owners, and Charles O. Baumann, Kessel's partner and the head of the International Film Exchange, a subexchange created by Kessel. When Kessel was dismissed from the combination for forming the subexchange, he and Baumann created the New York Motion Picture Company to produce films since their supply was stopped. They teamed with cameraman Fred J. Balshofer to make their first film, *Disinherited Son's Loyalty*, released on May 21, 1909. NYMPC's films, known as "Bison" Life Motion Pictures, carried the emblem of a bison in its advertising. The company's first offices were located at 426 Sixth Avenue, New York. It has been called the first to issue multiple-reel weekly releases on a regular program. According to Robert Grau, it was also the first manufacturer to supply exchanges with posters. Later in 1909, NYMPC became the American releasing agent of the Itala* and Ambrosio companies of Italy. In 1910, its offices were in the Lincoln Building at One Union Square, and H. J. Streyckmans was its press agent.

Kessel and Baumann participated in the organization of the Motion Picture Distributing and Sales Company*, the first grouping of independent manufacturers, in April 1910. In April 1912, Kessel and Baumann left the Sales Company and with other manufacturers organized the Universal Film Manufacturing Company, but they left it after six weeks. A few weeks later, they became affiliated with the Mutual Film Corporation*.

In the fall of 1909, a company of seventeen was sent to Los Angeles under the direction of cameraman Fred Balshofer to produce one-reel Bison films. Included in the group were J. Barney Sherry, Charles K. French, Jane Darrell,

Evelyn Graham, William Edwards, William Gibbons, Charles Avery, Charles Inslee, James Youngdeer, and Red Wing. The company established itself in a bungalow and barn in the Edendale suburb, which later became the site of the Keystone* studio.

The Reliance Moving Picture Company*, created by Kessel and Baumann and affiliated with the New York Motion Picture Company, offered its first release in October 1910. Two years after the Edendale company began producing, Kessel and Baumann sent Thomas H. Ince from New York to take over the directing chores. He made only a few films before taking possession of a ranch in the Santa Monica Mountains, which became known as Inceville*. At this time Ince suggested that Kessel and Baumann contract to use the Miller Brothers' 101 Ranch, a popular traveling Wild West show, spending the winter in Los Angeles. After the company left Universal and had to give up the brand names of Bison and Bison 101, for the films made with the Millers Brothers' ranch, it created the new brand names of Kay-Bee and Broncho.

In July 1912, Kessel and Baumann created the Keystone Film Company* with Mack Sennett. In the Spring of 1913, a reorganization created the New York Motion Picture Corporation, with Kessel as president, Baumann as vice-president, Charles Kessel as secretary, Charles J. Hite as treasurer, and Harry E. Aitken as assistant treasurer.

NYMPC created a new brand, "Domino," in September 1913. In 1915, with the creation of the Triangle Film Corporation* and the termination of NYMPC's contract with Mutual, the Ince studios moved to Culver City. Ince formed his own production company to produce Artcraft releases for Famous Players-Lasky Corporation.

Directors working for NYMPC included Ince, Raymond B. West, Reginald Barker, William S. Hart, Lambert Hillyer, Fred Niblo, Victor Schertzinger, Howard Hickman, and Frank Borzage. Players included Louise Glaum, Dustin Farnum, H. B. Warner, Henry Woodruff, Charles Giblyn, Francis Ford, Burton King, Ethel Grandin, Anna Little, Bessie Barriscale, William S. Hart, George Beban, Sessue Hayakawa, Tsura Aoki, Dorothy Dalton, Frank Keenan, Edith Bennett, Charles Ray, and Belle Bennett.

BIBLIOGRAPHY

Balshofer, Fred J., and Arthur C. Miller. *One Reel a Week*. Berkeley, California: University of California Press, 1967.

Blaisdell, George, "New York Motion Picture Company," *The Moving Picture World*, July 10, 1915, p. 233.

"Charles Baumann Goes West," *The Moving Picture World*, August 13, 1910, p. 344.

"C. O. Baumann Talks of Plans," *The Moving Picture World*, September 5, 1914, p. 1349.

Kessel, A., Jr., "When the Field Was Fresh," *The Moving Picture World*, March 10, 1917, pp. 1523–1524.

"New York Motion Picture Company," *The Moving Picture World*, May 15, 1909, p. 632.

von Harleman, G. P., "Motion Picture Studios of California," *The Moving Picture World*, March 10, 1917, pp. 1599–1600.

NICKELODEONS. Nickelodeons were the first theatres in the United States to exhibit films exclusively. As the name suggests, the price of admission was five cents. According to *The Moving Picture World* (November 20, 1907), the first nickelodeon was opened in Pittsburgh by Harris Davis in 1905. By 1908, there were between four and five thousand, and, according to *The Saturday Evening Post*, over two million people, a third of whom were children, attended nickelodeons annually. The heyday of the nickelodeon was from 1908 to 1911, but, by the early teens, the nickelodeon had been supplanted by a more standard type of theatre.

The following description of a typical nickelodeon appeared in the November 23, 1907, edition of the *The Saturday Evening Post*: "The nickelodeon is usually a tiny theatre, containing 199 seats, giving from twelve to eighteen performances a day, seven days a week. Its walls are painted red. The seats are ordinary kitchen chairs, not fastened. The only break in the red color scheme is made by half a dozen signs in black and white, No Smoking, Hats Off, and sometimes, but not always, Stay as Long as You Like."

BIBLIOGRAPHY

"The First Nickelodeon in the States," *The Moving Picture World*, November 20, 1907, p. 629.

Haskin, Frederick J., "The Popular Nickelodeon," *The Moving Picture World*, January 18, 1908, pp. 36–37.

———, "Nickelodeon History," *Views and Film Index*, February 1, 1908, pp. 5, 14.

Patterson, Joseph Medill, "The Nickelodeons," *The Saturday Evening Post*, November 23, 1907, reprinted in *The Moving Picture World*, January 11, 1908, pp. 21–22.

NIGGERS. "Niggers" was a term used in the twenties and thirties to refer to the black boards set up around an open-air set to prevent unnecessary reflection from the lights. The origin of the term is obvious, but it may also date back to the nineteenth century "nigger boards," which were temporary platforms set on the ground for use in open-air productions.

NILES, CALIFORNIA. See ESSANAY FILM MANUFACTURING COMPANY

9.5mm. 9.5mm was developed as a substandard film gauge in 1921 by the French Pathé* Company; a 9.5mm hand-cranked projector was introduced in 1922 and the following year saw the invention of a 9.5mm camera. By the late twenties, 9.5mm had become a popular film gauge for amateur film enthusiasts throughout Europe. Because the sprocket holes appeared between each frame of film, rather than on the sides (as in the better-known substandard gauges of 8mm* and 16mm*), there was a larger picture image and resultant increase in picture quality when the film was projected. Also, Pathé devised a method of notching the film when titles appeared; these notches stopped the projector mechanism for sufficient time to allow the viewer to read the titles and thus saved a considerable amount of film.

Sound was added to 9.5mm in the thirties, and the gauge continued in popularity through the fifties, when the increase in appeal of 8mm heralded the end of 9.5mm as a viable commercial proposition. Despite the demise of the Pathéscope Company, which marketed 9.5mm, there remains a hard-core group of enthusiasts for the gauge, and equipment and films continue to be manufactured. Regardless of its success in Europe, 9.5mm had little impact in the United States.

BIBLIOGRAPHY

Pedler, Garth, "The Silent Picture Guide to 9.5mm," *The Silent Picture*, no. 11/12, Summer-Autumn 1971, unpaged.

———. *The Encyclopedia of 9.5mm Silent Film Releases, Vol. I: 160,000 feet*. South Croydon, England: The Author, 1972.

NITRATE FILM. Although Eastman Kodak* had developed safety film as early as 1908, it was not until 1949, and the introduction of a new, improved safety-based film stock, that nitrate film ceased to be used in commercial motion picture production. (The acetate film* introduced in 1908 proved too brittle and too liable to shrinkage.) Nitrate film had two major drawbacks: it was highly flammable and it would eventually decompose. Its chemical composition is similar to that of guncotton, used in the manufacture of explosives, and nitrate film can burn twenty times as fast as wood, contains sufficient oxygen to continue burning under water, and will self-ignite at 300 degrees or less. Further, burning nitrate film gives off a gas which can form nitric acid in the lungs and lead to death. A major nitrate fire took place at the Ferguson Building, Pittsburgh, in 1909, and a number of fires were attributed to nitrate during a 1949 heatwave in New York.

Nitrate film is chemically unstable and is in a perpetual state of decomposition, which begins with fading of the image, followed by the film becoming sticky, forming bubbles, and eventually turning to a brownish powder. Decomposing nitrate film can also affect other film stored within close proximity to it. If kept at low temperature and humidity, nitrate can be safely stored; some nitrate film from the 1890s is still in excellent condition, while some from the Second World War, made from inferior stock, quickly decomposed. *See also* "Lost Films."

"NOLA" BRAND. See COQUILLE FILM COMPANY

NON-INFLAMMABLE FILM. See ACETATE FILM

NORBIG FILM MANUFACTURING COMPANY. Frank E. North owned all the stock, was the president, and supervised all production at the Norbig Film Manufacturing Company, whose studio was on Allesandro Street in Edendale, between the Selig* and Keystone* studios. Although Norbig did not produce until 1915, it had a functioning laboratory and leased its studio during the previous two years. Norbig made Western and Indian pictures with James Young Deer and Bebe Daniels. In 1916, Harry T. De Vere produced the three-reel drama *Darkness*, starring Margaret Darwin, for Norbig.

NORFOLK, VIRGINIA. See SUBMARINE FILM COMPANY

NORTH CAROLINA FILM CORPORATION. A wholly owned subsidiary of the Dino De Laurentiis Corporation, the North Carolina Film Corporation was formed, as a complete studio complex, in Wilmington, North Carolina, in December 1983. Located on fifteen acres of land, the complex was first used for *Firestarter* (1984). A complete Chinatown street was built at the studio for the production of Michael Cimino's *Year of the Dragon* (1985).

   Address: 1223 North 23 Street, Wilmington, N.C., 28405.

BIBLIOGRAPHY

Wheelock, Julie, and Jack Stahl, "De Laurentiis Sparks Return of Full Scale Filmmaking to North Carolina," *On Location*, June 1985, pp. 186–188.

NYKINO. See NATIONAL FILM AND PHOTO LEAGUE

O

OCCIDENTAL STUDIOS. See ALDRICH STUDIOS

OCEAN FILM CORPORATION. The Ocean Film Corporation was a short-lived company formed in November 1915. James D. Goldburg was the general manager and vice-president and John L. Dudley the president. It planned to make five-reel features to be released to the states rights* market and had no stock company of players. Its offices were at the Candler Building at 220 West 42 Street, New York, and its only production, *Life without Soul*, from Mary Wollstonecraft Shelley's *Frankenstein*, was marketed after its demise by the Raver Film Corporation*.

BIBLIOGRAPHY

"Ocean Film Corporation Formed," *The Moving Picture World*, November 13, 1915, p. 1316.

OFFICIAL FILMS, INC. Based in New York and later New Jersey, Official Films, Inc., was organized in 1939 to produce 16mm* instructional, sponsored, and entertainment shorts for outright sale. It also sold twenty- and thirty-minute edited versions of feature films, Soundies*, and early Charlie Chaplin shorts with music and sound effects. By the forties, the company was also selling films in 8mm*, and, in 1948, listed some 300 titles for sale. Official Films also published a booklet on "The Film Rental Library," indicating to purchasers how they might form their own libraries with films purchased from the company. Official Films remained active through the seventies.

OGDEN PICTURES CORPORATION. The Ogden Pictures Corporation, located at Ogden, Utah, and backed by Ogden capital, claimed to be, at its formation in 1917, the first motion picture studio between Chicago and the West Coast. Albert Scowcroft, a leading Utah businessman, was the president. Lillian Walker was signed to star in Ogden's five-reel comedy-dramas which were to be directed by Harry Revier and written by playwright Aaron Hoffman.

BIBLIOGRAPHY

"Lillian Walker Going to Utah," *The Moving Picture World*, April 7, 1917, p. 82.

OLIVER MOROSCO PHOTOPLAY COMPANY. The Oliver Morosco Photoplay Company was organized on November 9, 1914, with theatrical producer Morosco as president and Frank A. Garbutt, a California sportsman and millionaire who was treasurer of Bosworth, Inc.*, as vice-president. By arrangement with John Cort, who owned a chain of theatres in the West and Northwest, Morosco was to get first call to film Cort's productions and to use his stars. In addition, Morosco's three Los Angeles theatres provided plays and actors for the new company to use.

The Morosco productions were released on the Paramount* program, and the studios were located at 201 North Occidental Boulevard in Los Angeles, studios which were later shared by Pallas Pictures*, a company also releasing with Paramount and which was formed in August 1915. William Desmond Taylor was director of the Morosco films, whose players included Anna Held, Lenore Ulrich, George Beban, Kathlyn Williams, Myrtle Stedman, Fritzi Scheff, Rita Jolivet, Vivian Martin, Constance Collier, Lois Meredith, Elsie Janis, George Fawcett, Cyril Maude, Blanche Ring, Charlotte Greenwood, and Sydney Grant. Although Morosco merged with the Famous Players-Lasky Corporation in October 1916, the name continued to be used through 1923.

BIBLIOGRAPHY

"Morosco and Cort Enter Picture Field," *The Moving Picture World*, November 21, 1914, p. 1093.

"Morosco in Film Field," *The New York Dramatic Mirror*, November 11, 1914, p. 25.

OMNIMAX. See IMAX

OMNI-ZOETROPE. See ZOETROPE

ORION PICTURES CORPORATION. Generally considered a major among contemporary Hollywood companies, Orion Pictures Corporation was formed in January 1978 when five former members of the top management at United Artists*—Arthur Krim, Robert S. Benjamin, Eric Pleskow, William Bernstein, and Mike Medavoy—left following a policy dispute. Krim, who became Orion's president, gave the new company its name—Orion is a five-star constellation. Orion describes itself as "a financing and distribution organization," with close ties to Warner Bros.,* on whose studio lot it was initially located.

In 1982, Orion merged with Filmways, Inc., a production company founded by Martin Ransohoff, which was also involved in magazine and paperback publishing and television syndication, and which had acquired the publishing house of Grosset & Dunlap in 1974. Filmways' distribution arm was Sigma III. Filmways was in financial trouble, brought on, in part, by a March 1979 merger with American International Pictures*.

Among Orion's successes have been the films of Woody Allen, the Dudley

Moore vehicles, *10* (1979) and *Arthur* (1981), the Academy Award–winning *Amadeus* (1984), and the television series "Cagney and Lacy."

Address: 1875 Century Park East, Los Angeles, Calif. 90067.

BIBLIOGRAPHY

Hanson, Steve, "Orion: Looking to the Stars," *Stills*, February 1985, pp. 22–25.

Kilday, Gregg, "Orion: A Humanistic Production," *Los Angeles Times*, part IV, January 5, 1979, pp. 13, 26, 28.

McGilligan, Patrick, "Breaking Away, Mogul Style," *American Film*, June 1980, pp. 28–32.

ORO PICTURES COMPANY, INC. Oro Pictures Company, Inc., was formed in late 1917 and planned to make one six-reel feature per month. H. Grossman was the president and Isadore Bernstein was the production supervisor. Oro, whose motto was "Pictures for the Clean Minded," had offices at 729 Seventh Avenue in New York and took over the plant of Bernstein Productions, Inc., in Los Angeles. Oro's productions included *Loyalty* (1918), *Humility* (1917), and *When Destiny Wills* (1921).

OSHKOSH, WISCONSIN. See EBONY PICTURES CORPORATION

"OUR GANG" SERIES. The most popular of all series featuring children, some 169 "Our Gang" comedy shorts were produced by Hal Roach Studios* between 1922 and 1938, with a final 52 being produced by M-G-M* from 1938 to 1944. The first short in the series, titled *Our Gang*, was released by Pathé* on November 5, 1922; the last, *Tale of a Dog*, was released by M-G-M on April 15, 1944. Among the children featured in the series were Mickey Daniels, Johnny Downs, Joe Cobb, Carl "Alfalfa" Switzer, Jean Darling, Mary Kornman, Spanky McFarland, Darla Hood, Allen "Farina" Hoskins, Bobby "Wheezer" Hutchins, Jackie Cooper, and Matthew "Stymie" Beard. When the films were released to television, Hal Roach was forced to change the series title to "The Little Rascals," as the rights to the title "Our Gang" had been acquired by M-G-M (which had distributed the films from 1927 onward; previously they were distributed by Pathé).

BIBLIOGRAPHY

Maltin, Leonard, and Richard W. Bann. *Our Gang*. New York: Crown, 1977.

OZ FILM MANUFACTURING COMPANY. L. Frank Baum, the creator of the "Oz" books, opened his own production company, the Oz Film Manufacturing Company, in June 1914, to produce films from his books. It had a studio on Santa Monica Boulevard, between Gower and Lodi Streets, in Hollywood, and Baum was the president and general manager. Composer Louis F. Gottschalk, the vice-president and works manager, wrote music and played the piano as the films were being shot. Oz's first film, *The Patchwork Girl of Oz*, was directed by J. Farrell MacDonald and released by Paramount*. After *The Magic Cloak of Oz*, the studio closed temporarily in November 1914, and the Oz players were disbanded. In the spring of 1915, the Oz studio reopened under another brand name, managed by Frank J. Baum, and it released features directed by Francis Powers on the Alliance program.

BIBLIOGRAPHY

Karr, Kathleen. "Oz Lives," in *The American Film Heritage*. Washington, D.C.: Acropolis Books, 1972, pp. 162–167.

"Oz Film Company Starts in Los Angeles," *The Moving Picture World*, June 13, 1914, p. 1531.

P

PALLAS PICTURES, INC. Active from 1915 to 1917, Pallas Pictures, Inc., maintained a studio at 201 North Occidental Boulevard in Los Angeles, which it shared with the Oliver Morosco Photoplay Company*. Its features, which were released on the Paramount* program, were scripted and produced by Julia Crawford Ivers.

PALMER PHOTOPLAY CORPORATION. Active in the late teens and early twenties, the Palmer Photoplay Corporation was formed by Frederick Palmer as a clearinghouse for story materials to be considered for film production and to offer extensive courses, by mail, in screenwriting. There were many such schools of screenwriting operating at this time, but none had the prestige of the Palmer Photoplay Corporation, which boasted an advisory board including Cecil B. DeMille, Lois Weber, Jesse L. Lasky, Thomas H. Ince, and Allan Dwan. The organization published a variety of pamphlets by prominent individuals within the industry, as well as many volumes by Frederick Palmer. Among the latter were *Photoplay Plots and Plot Sources* (1920), *Photoplay Plot Encyclopedia* (1922), *Self-Criticism* (1923), *Technique of the Photoplay* (1924), and *Author's Photoplay Manual* (1924).

PALO ALTO, CALIFORNIA. See EXACTUS PHOTO-FILM CORPORATION

"PANAMA" BRAND. See BALBOA AMUSEMENT PRODUCING COMPANY

PANAVISION, INC. Panavision, Inc., was formed in 1953 by Robert Gottschalk (who was murdered in 1982 at the age of sixty-four). Gottschalk developed the M-G-M Camera 65, which utilized an anamorphic lens* and 65mm film in the camera for a widescreen system. It was first utilized on *Raintree County*, which received its world premiere at the Brown Theatre in Louisville, Kentucky, on

October 2, 1957. *Raintree County* was released in 35mm*, and the system was seen to better advantage in *Ben-Hur* (1959), which was released in 70mm*. In 1972, Gottschalk introduced the Panaflex silent motion picture, followed by the Panaglide floating camera mechanism. In 1978, Gottschalk received a Scientific or Technical Award of Merit (Oscar statuette) "for the concept, design and continuous development of the Panaflex Motion Picture Camera System." Today, Panavision is highly regarded as a leading source of cameras and lenses. Although Gottschalk remained as president of the company, Panavision was sold in 1965 to producer Sy Weintraub, who sold it three years later to Kinney National Service, Inc. (which also owned Warner Bros.*), which, in turn, sold it in 1985 to a consortium headed by Chicago newspaper and department store heir Frederick Field.

Address: 18618 Oxnard Street, Tarzana, Calif. 91356

BIBLIOGRAPHY

Harris, Kathryn, "Panavision Seen as Field's Ticket to Hollywood," *Los Angeles Times*, Business Section, January 24, 1985, pp. 1, 5.

Henderson, Scott, "The Panavision Story," *American Cinematographer*, April 1977, pp. 414–415, 422–423, 432–433.

"Mr. Panavision Speaks Out," *American Cinematographer*, April 1977, pp. 417–418, 424–425, 434–435.

PAPER PRINTS. Prior to 1912, there was no way by which motion picture producers could copyright their films as films with the Library of Congress. Therefore, in order to protect their work, producers deposited motion pictures in the form of paper prints, with the film printed directly on to paper as opposed to celluloid. The first film to be copyrighted—on January 7, 1894—in this fashion was *Edison Kinetoscopic Record of a Sneeze*, a few feet of film recording Fred Ott sneezing made by Thomas Edison's associate, W.K.L. Dickson. Paper prints continued to be deposited for copyright purposes as late as 1916. According to Kemp Niver, "Producers of motion picture films obtained the paper to make the copies of their negatives from various sources. The type that had the best photographic propensities was normal bromide paper cut into strips the same width as the negative and perforated so that a contact print could be made on the same equipment as was used to make the nitrate prints."

Because so few films from the early years of the cinema have survived, the paper print collection offers valuable documentation of this period. The problem of transferring the paper prints back to film was first considered by Carl Louis Gregory of the National Archives in 1943. In 1947, Howard Walls, the first archivist of the Academy of Motion Picture Arts and Sciences*, was able to persuade the Academy to sponsor the project, and Carl Gregory undertook some initial experimentation. The project did not begin in earnest until 1954, when Kemp R. Niver undertook the conversion program with his Los Angeles–based Renovare Film Company. For his work, Niver received a special Academy Award in 1955. Funding was provided by the Academy, the U.S. government and Eastman Kodak*, which donated raw film stock for the project.

Niver's conversion consisted of transferring the films from paper to 16mm* film. Since 1982, the paper print conversion project has been undertaken by the UCLA Film Archives, and for the first time the paper prints have been converted to 35mm* film.

BIBLIOGRAPHY

Niver, Kemp R., "From Film to Paper to Film," *The Quarterly Journal of the Library of Congress*, vol. XXI, no. 4, October 1964, pp. 248–264.

———. *Motion Pictures from the Library of Congress Paper Print Collection 1894–1912*. Berkeley: University of California Press, 1967.

PARAGON. See WORLD FILM CORPORATION

"PARAGON" BRAND. See CROWN CITY FILM MANUFACTURING COMPANY

PARALTA PLAYS, INC. Paralta Plays, Inc., was founded on March 22, 1917, with Carl Anderson as president, Herman Katz as treasurer, Robert T. Kane as vice-president, Nat L. Brown as secretary and general manager, and Herman Fichtenberg as chairman of the board. It announced in *The Moving Picture World* (April 14, 1917) that it would produce films which would be sold to exhibitors for a period of one year, during which time the films could be screened as often as the exhibitor might wish.

Production of Paralta's first film, *A Man's Man*, began at the company's Los Angeles studios on June 4, 1917. Oscar Apfel was the director and J. Warren Kerrigan the star. Other Paralta productions included *Madame Who*, *Within the Cup*, *Carmen of the Klondyke*, *His Robe of Honor*, *Humdrum Brown*, *An Enemy Alien*, and *Shackled*, all released in 1918. The initial Paralta studios were located on the south side of Melrose Avenue in Hollywood, but in the spring of 1918 the company completed the building of a new studio, directly opposite, at Melrose and Van Ness (studios which are now part of Paramount*). Among the stars under contract were Henry B. Walthall, J. Warren Kerrigan, Bessie Barriscale, and Louise Glaum; Paralta's directors included Rex Ingram, Wallace Worsley, Raymond B. West, and Reginald Barker. The company ceased production in the fall of 1918, and its studios were taken over by Robert Brunton.

BIBLIOGRAPHY

"Carl Anderson Produces Splendid Plays," *The Moving Picture World*, April 6, 1918, p. 69.

Slide, Anthony. "The Paralta Company," in *Aspects of American Film History prior to 1920*. Metuchen, New Jersey: Scarecrow Press, 1978, pp. 79–86.

"Work on Paralta Studios Progressing," *The Moving Picture World*, April 13, 1918, p. 256.

PARAMOUNT ACTING SCHOOL. See ASTORIA STUDIOS

PARAMOUNT-BRAY PICTOGRAPH. See BRAY STUDIOS, INC.

PARAMOUNT LABORATORY. See CONSOLIDATED FILM INDUSTRIES

PARAMOUNT NEWS. See NEWSREELS

PARAMOUNT PICTURES, INC. Paramount Pictures, Inc., with its familiar trademark of a snow-capped mountain, surrounded by stars, came into being thanks to three men, of which only one usually receives the credit. Paramount Pictures Corporation was founded, on May 8, 1914, strictly as a distribution organization by W. W. Hodkinson. As a production company, it had its origins in the Famous Players Film Company, incorporated on June 1, 1912, by Adolph Zukor (1873–1976) and in the Jesse L. Lasky Feature Play Company, incorporated on November 26, 1913, by Lasky (1880–1958).

The Famous Players Film Company was responsible for the importation of the French feature *Queen Elizabeth/Les Amours de la Reine Elizabeth* (1912), starring Sarah Bernhardt, the first major film to give the industry respectability and one of the first feature-length productions to be screened in the United States. The Jesse L. Lasky Feature Film Company produced *The Squaw Man* (1914), directed by Cecil B. DeMille and Oscar Apfel, which was the first important feature-length production to be filmed in Hollywood*.

As a distributor, Paramount handled not only the films of Lasky and Famous Players but also those of Bosworth* and Oliver Morosco*. In May 1916, 50 percent of the stock in Paramount was acquired by Zukor and Lasky, and a month later Hodkinson resigned as president of the company (to be succeeded by Hiram Abrams). On June 19, 1916, Famous Players-Lasky Corporation was incorporated, with Zukor as president, but the name Paramount was retained for trade purposes and by the late twenties had become the familiar name to filmgoers. Indeed, the company's slogan was "If It's a Paramount Picture, It's the best show in town."

On July 19, 1916, the company organized Artcraft Pictures Corporation for the release of the films of Mary Pickford, but later the Artcraft name was utilized for any major Paramount release. On May 28, 1919, Realart Pictures Corporation was incorporated to handle lesser Paramount productions. The use of the name ended in July 1922.

Adolph Zukor is the best-known "name" associated with Paramount, and it was he who was responsible for the company's financial success. He built up a theatre chain and tried, unsuccessfully, to give Paramount a monopoly of the film industry. Jesse L. Lasky was the creative force behind the studio, responsible for signing stars such as Mary Pickford, Rudolph Valentino, Geraldine Farrar, Wallace Reid, Pola Negri, Gloria Swanson, and Thomas Meighan; and directors such as Cecil B. DeMille (virtually all of whose career was at Paramount),

Maurice Tourneur, and D. W. Griffith. Both men were able to steer the studio through a series of major scandals in the early twenties, involving the rape and manslaughter charges against Paramount star Roscoe "Fatty" Arbuckle, the murder of Paramount director William Desmond Taylor and the implication in it of contract star Mary Miles Minter, and the death from drug addiction of Paramount leading man Wallace Reid.

The studio suffered a major financial setback in the early thirties through losses from the Paramount-Publix theatre chain, and, in 1933, the company was forced to enter bankruptcy. Jesse L. Lasky was forced out, but under the 1935 reorganization the company re-emerged as Paramount Pictures, Inc., with Adolph Zukor as chairman of the board.

Despite the setbacks, the thirties were arguably Paramount's greatest decade. Its staff of directors was headed by Ernst Lubitsch and included Rouben Mamoulian (who directed the studio's first major artistic sound success in 1929, *Applause*), George Cukor, Norman Taurog, Norman Z. McLeod, Josef von Sternberg, and Mitchell Leisen. Paramount stars of the thirties included Mae West, Jeanette MacDonald, Maurice Chevalier, the Marx Brothers, W. C. Fields, Charlie Ruggles, Marlene Dietrich, Bing Crosby, George Burns and Gracie Allen, Claudette Colbert, and Gary Cooper. The decade ended with Paramount's elevating screenwriter Preston Sturges to director, a move which resulted in some of the greatest screwball comedies* of all time.

Although not as memorable a decade as the thirties, the forties saw Paramount's producing *The Lady Eve* (1941), *Holiday Inn* (1942), *For Whom the Bell Tolls* (1943), *Going My Way* (1944), *The Lost Weekend* (1945), *The Blue Dahlia* (1946), and *The Heiress* (1949). From the fifties, Paramount's best films included *Sunset Boulevard* (1950), *A Place in the Sun* (1951), *The Greatest Show on Earth* (1952), *Roman Holiday* (1953), *The Ten Commandments* (1956), and *Vertigo* (1958). Memorable Paramount features of the sixties and seventies included *Psycho* (1960), *Breakfast at Tiffany's* (1961), *Hud* (1963), *Becket* (1964), *Alfie* (1966), *Rosemary's Baby* (1968), *Love Story* (1970), *The Godfather* (1972), *The Conversation* (1974), *Nashville* (1975), *Marathon Man* (1976), *Saturday Night Fever* (1977), *Heaven Can Wait* (1978), and *Star Trek—The Motion Picture* (1979).

Prior to a major involvement in television production, Paramount sold all rights to its 1929–1949 features to MCA* in 1958. On October 19, 1966, Paramount was acquired by Gulf + Western* and became a wholly owned subsidiary of the Charles Bludhorn conglomerate. By the fifties, the star system* was basically over, and Jerry Lewis and Dean Martin were, arguably, the only two major stars under contract to the studio. Production heads such as Howard W. Koch, Martin Rackin, and Robert Evans tried, with varying degrees of success, to steer Paramount into a new era, with films such as *Ordinary People* (1980), *Raiders of the Lost Ark* (1981), and *Terms of Endearment* (1983).

Aside from the Astoria* studios in New York, and an earlier New York studio on 26 Street (which was destroyed by fire in September 1915), Paramount's studios were in Hollywood, initially at Sunset Boulevard and Vine Street, until 1926, when the company moved to its present location. The famous Paramount Gate, immortalized in *Sunset Boulevard*, is located on Marathon Street. It is no longer used, and the studio has built a new gate on Melrose Avenue.

Addresses: 1 Gulf + Western Plaza, New York, N.Y. 10023; 5555 Melrose Avenue, Los Angeles, Calif. 90038.

BIBLIOGRAPHY

Buchsbaum, J., "Zukor Buys Protection," *Cine-Tracts*, vol. II, nos. 3–4, Summer-Autumn 1979, pp. 49–62.

Daily Variety, Special Paramount Issue, July 26, 1945.

Eames, John Douglas. *The Paramount Story*. New York: Crown, 1985.

Edmonds, I. G., and Reiko Mimura. *Paramount Pictures and the People Who Made Them*. San Diego: A. S. Barnes, 1980.

Halliwell, Leslie. *Mountain of Dreams*. New York: Stonehill Publishing, 1976.

The Hollywood Reporter, Special Paramount Issue, July 27, 1945.

Irwin, Will. *The House That Shadows Built*. Garden City, New York: Doubleday, Doran, 1928.

Lasky, Jesse L., with Don Weldon. *I Blow My Own Horn*. Garden City, New York: Doubleday, 1957.

Luft, Herbert G., "Remembering Adolph Zukor," *Films in Review*, vol. XXVII, no. 10, December 1976, pp. 595–598.

"Paramount," *Fortune*, vol. XV, no. 3, March 1937, pp. 86–96, 194–211.

Parish, James Robert. *The Paramount Pretties*. New Rochelle, New York: Arlington House, 1972.

Taylor, John Russell, "Paramount," *Films and Filming*, June 1984, pp. 7–10, and July 1984, pp. 7–10.

Zukor, Adolph, "Triumph of the Motion Picture," *Theatre*, May 1925, pp. 38, 92.

Zukor, Adolph, with Dale Kramer. *The Public Is Never Wrong*. New York: G. P. Putnam's Sons, 1953.

RESOURCES

Films: Library of Congress (extant Paramount silent features and preservations materials on 1929–1949 titles); UCLA Film Archives (nitrate prints of 1929–1949 features).

Papers: Academy of Motion Picture Arts and Sciences (script materials and pressbooks).

Photographs: Academy of Motion Picture Arts and Sciences.

PARAMOUNT-PUBLIX. See PUBLIX THEATERS CORPORATION

PASADENA. See CROWN CITY FILM MANUFACTURING COMPANY, NEVADA MOTION PICTURE COMPANY, and SIGNAL FILM COMPANY

PASSING PARADE. Also known as *John Nesbitt's Passing Parade*, this series of shorts had its origin in Nesbitt's radio series of the same name and was produced by M-G-M* from 1938 to 1949. One reel in length, each short dealt with a topical subject—sometimes more than one—and was narrated in John Nesbitt's inimitable style.

BIBLIOGRAPHY

Maltin, Leonard. *The Great Movie Shorts*. New York: Crown, 1972.

PATHÉ. Pathé Freres, established in France in 1896 by Charles Pathé with $2,000 in capital, became the largest film company in the world, producing, in addition to motion pictures, cameras and film stock (including a noninflammable film used in most of Pathé's European productions). J. A. Berst, who began working for Pathé as a boy in 1896, was sent to the United States in 1904 with the four-reel film *Passion Play* to develop a market here for Pathé's films. Later, Pathé joined the American trust companies in the Motion Picture Patents Company*. In 1907 or 1908, at Berst's suggestion, Arthur Roussel, the technical head of Pathé's studio at Vincennes, was sent to the United States to build and equip a studio in Bound Brook, New Jersey, which was formerly a cash register factory.

Pathé used the Bound Brook studio to produce weekly releases of Westerns*, comedies, and dramas to suit American tastes. The first American-made film was *The Girl from Arizona*, released on May 16, 1910. Louis J. Gasnier was the director-general of the Bound Brook studio, where the *Pathé Weekly* newsreel, edited by H. C. Hoagland, was also produced. In 1912, Pathé built a new studio at One Congress Street, Jersey City, and this became Pathé's major American studio. Early Pathé stars included Paul Panzer, Pearl White, Octavia Handworth, and Crane Wilbur. In 1912, Pathé sent James Youngdeer to Los Angeles to make films, and, by mid–1914, Pathé's Western company was producing comedies at the Zodiak* studio, under the direction of P. C. Hartigan and featuring Peggy Hart.

In 1914, when General Film Company began releasing the competing *Hearst-Selig Newsreel*, Pathé stopped releasing through General. It sold its American production facilities to Merrill, Lynch & Company, and began its own exchange organization. Its serial, *The Perils of Pauline*, produced in conjunction with the Eclectic Film Company* and the Hearst newspapers, was a great box office success. Pathé and Eclectic followed with further serials, short subjects, and a few features, and late in 1914 combined to form Pathé Exchange, Inc.

As an exchange, Pathé was involved in the productions of a number of companies, including Balboa*, Astra*, Wharton*, and Arrow*. Pathé also released the animated cartoons of J. C. Bray and the "Lonesome Luke" comedies featuring Harold Lloyd, produced by Rolin.

In March 1918, J. A. Berst, who had been the head of Pathé's American branch for most of its existence, resigned as vice-president and general manager. Paul Brunet replaced him, and, in 1919, Pathé moved its headquarters to New York.

The twenties saw Pathé as the distributor of the Hal Roach shorts and features (including the "Our Gang" series*), of Robert Flaherty's *Nanook of the North* (1922), and, from 1923, of the Mack Sennett productions. In 1923 Merrill, Lynch & Company purchased a controlling interest in Pathé, which it retained until October 1926, when it sold such interest to Blair and Company.

In the spring of 1927, Pathé took over Producers Distributing Corporation* and for a short time Cecil B. DeMille, who was involved in the latter company, became a Pathé producer. With the acquisition of Producers Distributing Corporation, Pathé also acquired what became the Laird* studios in Culver City. Joseph P. Kennedy became involved with Pathé in 1928, becoming its chairman of the board the following year. It was Kennedy who was primarily responsible for the sale of Pathé, as a producer and distributor, to RKO* in 1931 (although rights to certain of Pathé's sound features, notably *Holiday*, were sold to Columbia*). Despite the demise of Pathé as a producer/distributor, the company continued to exist and actively financed other production companies and operated a laboratory.

BIBLIOGRAPHY

Blaisdell, George, "Charles Pathé, Film Producer," *The Moving Picture World*, November 14, 1914, pp. 904–905.

"Charles Pathé—World Promoter of the Photoplay," *The Film Index*, January 21, 1911, p. 1.

"The Daddy of Them All," *Photoplay*, April 1918, pp. 61–62.

Everett, Eldon, K., "Frank Leon Smith Remembers the Pathé Serials," *Classic Images*, November 1981, pp. 10–11.

"The Great Works of Pathé Freres," *The Moving Picture World*, March 10, 1917, pp. 1529–1530.

"Pathé Freres," *Views and Film Index*, May 19, 1906, p. 8.

"Pathé's American Film," *The Moving Picture World*, May 14, 1910, p. 777.

"Pathé's American Productions," *The Moving Picture World*, June 18, 1910, p. 1043.

Sadoul, Georges, "Napoleon of the Cinema," *Sight and Sound*, Spring 1958, p. 183.

"25th Anniversary Marks Outstanding Production Schedule of Pathé," *Exhibitors Herald-World*, July 6, 1929, pp. 91, 106.

RESOURCES

Papers: Academy of Motion Picture Arts and Sciences (Pathé Exchange Collection of business and financial records, 1929–1930).

PATHÉ NEWS. See NEWSREELS

PATHÉSCOPE. See 9.5mm

PATHÉ STUDIOS. See LAIRD INTERNATIONAL STUDIOS

PATHÉ'S WEEKLY. See NEWSREELS

PATSY AWARDS. The Patsy Awards were established in 1951 by the American Humane Association to honor Hollywood's animal stars. The first winners were Francis the Talking Mule (First Place); California, the horse (Second Place); Pierre the Chimp (Third Place); Jerry Brown, the horse (Richard C. Craven Award, named after AHA's first western regional director); and Flame, the dog; Lassie; Black Diamond, the horse; and Jackie, the lion (all of whom received Awards of Excellence). From 1958, awards were also given to animals working in television, with Lassie being the first winner. Currently, awards are presented in the Wild Animal Category, the Canine Category, the Special Category (including birds, domestic cats, farm animals, and so on), and the Human/Animal Bond Award (given to production best typifying the bond between animals and people). The American Humane Association also sponsors a "Hall of Fame." "Patsy" stands for "Picture Animal Top Star of the Year."

Address: American Humane Association, P.O. Box 1266, Denver, Colo.

PAX FILMS. See LOPERT FILMS DISTRIBUTING COMPANY

PDC. See PRODUCERS DISTRIBUTING CORPORATION

"PEACEFUL RAFFERTY" SERIES. See ALL-CELTIC FILM COMPANY

PEDIGREED PICTURES, INC. Formed in 1936 by Mrs. Milton Erlanger, Mrs. Sylvester Stern, and Thomas Frelinghuysen, Pedigreed Pictures, Inc., announced plans to produce a series of short subjects on the breeding and care of thoroughbred dogs, for release by Paramount. At least one film, *The Chesapeake Bay Retriever*, was produced in 1936.

PEERLESS FEATURE FILM COMPANY. See WORLD FILM CORPORATION

"PELICAN" BRAND. See EASTERN FILM COMPANY

THE PERMANENT CHARITIES COMMITTEE OF THE ENTERTAIN-MENT INDUSTRIES. Permanent Charities, as The Permanent Charities Committee of the Entertainment Industries is generally known, is the organization through which members of the entertainment industries contribute to various charities, either through pledges or payroll deductions. It has helped establish research into retinitis pigmentosa and makes funds available to charities such as the Kidney Foundation of Southern California, Planned Parenthood, the Sickle Cell Disease Research Foundation, United Way, the Red Cross, and the City of Hope. It was conceived in 1940, when Samuel Goldwyn called a meeting of industry leaders to consider the question of multiple charitable contributions from the various studios. In 1942, Permanent Charities set up its own campaign organization, and in 1968 it merged with the Radio-Television-Recording-Advertising Charities (which had been formed in 1950).

Address: 463 N. La Cienega Boulevard, Los Angeles, Calif. 90048.

PETROVA PICTURE COMPANY. See SUPERPICTURES, INC.

PHOENIX, ARIZONA. See LUBIN MANUFACTURING COMPANY

PHONOFILMS. See DE FOREST PHONOFILM

PHOTO DRAMA PRODUCING COMPANY. The Photo Drama Producing Company of Turin, Italy, established a company in the United States in August 1914, a company which was later owned by George Kleine. Bill Steiner was the general manager, and Pierce Kingsley was hired to direct and to find players and subjects. After filming *After the Ball* and *Prohibition* in the Centaur* studio at Bayonne, New Jersey, Kingsley took the company to Los Angeles. Photo Drama ceased operations in 1924.

PHOTOPLAY. The word "photoplay" was first used to describe a motion picture in the fall of 1910 by the Essanay Company*. Essanay had conducted a newspaper contest "with the object of finding a suitable synonym which would not only be descriptive, but would sum up in one word the spectacular entertainment afforded by picture theatres." The winning word, "photoplay," was contributed by Mr. Edgar Strakosh, and the house organ of the Essanay Company was promptly named *The Photoplay Review*. *Photoplay* was also the title of the motion picture's best-known "fan" magazine, published from 1911 to 1980.

PHOTOPLAY AUTHORS' LEAGUE. The Photoplay Authors' League was formed in 1914 to organize scenarists, story writers, playwrights, writers of fiction whose work had been adapted for films, and story editors to deal with issues of importance to the photoplay writer. Early in its existence, it exposed fake photoplay schools, proposed a copyright bill in favor of photoplays, demanded payment for authors from magazines that printed film plots, and fought for protection for writers treatly unjustly by producing concerns. Frank E. Woods was the president and Richard Harding Davis the vice-president. The Photoplay Authors' League published an official organ, *The Script*, which was edited by William M. Ritchey.

BIBLIOGRAPHY
Wing, William E., "Photoplay Authors' League," *The Moving Picture World*, July 10, 1915, p. 268.

THE PHOTOPLAYERS. A social club similar to the Screen Club*, the Photoplayers was organized in Los Angeles in December 1912 under the initial title of the Reel Club. Fred Mace was elected the first president, and the original membership stood at 150, consisting of producers, directors, actors, trade paper journalists, scenario writers, studio managers, and film importers. The group met at the Gamut Club on South Hope Street in downtown Los Angeles. The Photoplayers would appear to have been disbanded by 1920.

PHOTO PLAY PRODUCTIONS COMPANY. E. K. Lincoln was the president and lead actor of the Photo Play Productions Company, which was founded in April 1914. Frank A. Tichener was the general manager, Edgar Lewis the director, Philip Rosen the cameraman, and Edward Peple the scenarist. Its first production was *The Littlest Rebel*. Photo Play's offices were located in the Candler Building, 220 West 42 Street, New York.

BIBLIOGRAPHY

"Another Feature Company," *The Moving Picture World*, April 25, 1914, p. 531.

PICTURE PLAYHOUSE FILM COMPANY. The Picture Playhouse Film Company began in 1914 as the sole American agent for the films of the Pasquali Company of Turin, Italy. In addition to releasing films from other foreign companies, Picture Playhouse distributed films from the Interstate Feature Film Company. Its offices were at 71 West 23 Street, New York.

PIERROT FILM COMPANY, INC. The Pierrot Film Company, Inc., was formed in mid–1914 to produce one-reel comedies with vaudeville comedian Louis Simon. Edgar Allan Woolf was the scenarist and Charles Marks was the general manager. Later Caryl Fleming appeared in juvenile leads. Pierrot began using the Reliance Studios at Yonkers but later moved to a studio in Tappan, New York. In December 1914, a U.S. district judge enjoined the company from manufacturing, selling, or leasing films made with a camera held to constitute infringement of the patent rights of the Motion Picture Patents Company*.

BIBLIOGRAPHY

"New Company Plans Big Things," *The Moving Picture World*, June 6, 1914, p. 1418.

PIKE'S PEAK FILM COMPANY. The Pike's Peak Film Company, located at the Garden of the Gods studio in Colorado Springs, Colorado, was formed in December 1914. Otis B. Thayer, formerly with Selig*, was the director. George Gebhart and Josephine West were the leading players at the company's inception, and later Gertrude Bonehill starred in two-reel Westerns*, biblical films, and poetic dramas under the "Lariat" brand. Pike's Peak released through the United Film Service* at first, and later it released on the Standard program.

PILOT FILMS CORPORATION. Pilot Films Corporation was formed early in 1913, with Lottie Pickford as one of its stars. Its first production, *The Blacksmith's Story*, was directed by Travers Vail. Later in 1913, it made the four-reel feature *Across the Continent*.

PINE-THOMAS CORPORATION. Pine-Thomas Corporation was formed as an independent producer in 1940 by two former publicists, William C. Thomas and William H. Pine. Based on the Paramount* lot, it produced some eighty-one features for Paramount release, beginning with *Power Dive* (1941). Among its others productions were *Tokyo Rose* (1945), *Caged Fury* (1948), *El Paso*

(1949), *Tripoli* (1950), *Crosswinds* (1951), *Hong Kong* (1951), and *Passage West* (1951). The team broke up with Pine's death in 1955.

All Pine-Thomas productions were low-budget "A" features or Westerns. Its best-known stars were John Payne and Rhonda Fleming. The producers' publicist was A. C. Lyles, who later became an independent producer.

BIBLIOGRAPHY

English, Richard, "Gaudiest Producers in Hollywood," *The Saturday Evening Post*, January 3, 1953, pp. 22, 76–78.

"It's Not Art But...," *Time*, August 6, 1941, pp. 82–84.

Reddy, John, "Hollywood's Double Bills," *Esquire*, June 1945, pp. 64, 140–143.

PIONEER FILM CORPORATION. The Pioneer Feature Film Company, incorporated in March 1915 by Julian Belman, Nathan Hirsch (its president), and Augusta Hirsch, purchased the exchanges of the Cosmo Feature Film Corporation, which Nathan Hirsch had owned since 1912. Pioneer purchased the rights to the Polar Bear features of the Great Northern Film Company*, and the New York State rights to Thomas H. Ince's *Civilization* (1916). In 1918, the company was reorganized and renamed Pioneer Film Corporation. Its policy was to buy negatives of features from independent producers and sell them to the states rights* market. In January 1919, Nathan Hirsch resigned from the company, and M. H. Hoffman merged his releasing company with Pioneer and became its general manager.

PIONEER PICTURES, INC. Pioneer Pictures, Inc., was organized in 1933 by John Hay "Jock" Whitney and his cousin Cornelius Vanderbilt "Sonny" Whitney to produce Technicolor* films for release through RKO*. The Whitneys became enthusiastic about the possibilities of Technicolor thanks to the efforts of producer Merian C. Cooper, who was also instrumental in persuading the Whitneys to purchase a large block of Technicolor stock.

The first Pioneer production was also the first live-action Technicolor short, *La Cucaracha* (1934), produced by Kenneth Macgowan and with color direction by Robert Edmond Jones. It cost $65,000 to produce, compared with $15,000 for the typical two-reel short of the period. *La Cucaracha* was followed by the first three-strip Technicolor feature, *Becky Sharp* (1935), again produced by Kenneth Macgowan and with color design by Robert Edmond Jones, direction by Rouben Mamoulian, and with Miriam Hopkins in the title role. Pioneer Pictures produced only one other film, *The Dancing Pirate* (1936), the first musical feature to be filmed in three-strip Technicolor, starring Steffi Duna, who had also been the star of *La Cucaracha*. *The Dancing Pirate* was not successful, and Pioneer quietly faded from the scene.

BIBLIOGRAPHY

Ayer, Fred, "New Name, New Money, New Notion Given Industry with Jock Whitney," *Motion Picture News*, January 12, 1935, pp. 39–40.

"What? Color in the Movies Again?" *Fortune*, October 1934, pp. 92–97, 161–171.

"Whitney Colors," *Time*, May 27, 1935, pp. 28–34.

P.I.T.S. See EMBASSY COMMUNICATIONS

PIXAR. See LUCASFILM, LTD.

PLANET FILM CORPORATION. The Planet Film Corporation, incorporated in Delaware on March 1, 1916, was formed by Harry B. Raver, its vice-president and general manager, who allied himself with various banking interests. It produced at Raver's studios in Rockville, Long Island, and planned to make one five-reel feature a month from a popular play or book, to be released to states rights* buyers contracting on a yearly basis. It planned to make its profits on its four special eight-reel productions for each year.

BIBLIOGRAPHY

"Raver Forms New Company," *The Moving Picture World*, May 20, 1916, p. 1346.

"PLANET OF THE APES" SERIES. A popular series of five features produced by 20th Century-Fox* and concerned with a world of the future which is governed by apes, the first of the films, *Planet of the Apes*, was based on a novel by Pierre Boulle. For his make-up achievement for this first production, John Chambers received an Honorary Academy Award. The five films in the series were *Planet of the Apes* (1968), *Beneath the Planet of the Apes* (1970), *Escape from the Planet of the Apes* (1971), *Conquest of the Planet of the Apes* (1972), and *Battle for the Planet of the Apes* (1973). Roddy McDowall was featured in all but *Beneath the Planet of the Apes*. Century City, located on the former backlot of 20th Century-Fox, was utilized for the futuristic city of 1991 in *Conquest of the Planet of the Apes*.

PLASTICON. See THREE-DIMENSIONAL FILMS

PLIMPTON EPIC PICTURES, INC. Horace G. Plimpton, formerly in charge of the Edison studios* for some seven years, formed Plimpton Epic Pictures, Inc., in 1915. Its studio was located at 250 Street, between Yonkers and Mount Vernon, in New York, and it released through the Authors' Film Company, which had been formed to distribute films through express companies rather than exchanges. Gertrude McCoy was featured in Plimpton films.

In December 1918, Plimpton-Fischer Photoplays, Inc., was formed, with William J. Reed as president, Horace G. Plimpton as vice-president and general manager, David G. Fischer as the director-general, and Stanley G. Mason as cameraman. It used the Plimpton Epic studios.

PLIMPTON-FISCHER PHOTOPLAYS, INC. See PLIMPTON EPIC PICTURES, INC.

PLITT THEATRES, INC. Plitt Theatres, Inc., the fourth largest chain and the largest privately owned circuit in the United States, came into being in 1978, when Henry G. Plitt, a former ABC executive, along with a group of investors, acquired the theatre chain owned by ABC Television for a reported $45 million. With its largest holding of theatres in California and the Chicago area, Plitt Theatres' flagship is the Century Plaza Theatre in the Century City area of Los Angeles. As of January 1985, it operated 711 theatres. The chain was taken over by the Toronto-based Cineplex Odeon Corp. on November 22, 1985.

In 1985, Plitt Theatres established a $100,000 fellowship at UCLA, to provide grants for students with a desire to enter the field of film exhibition.

Addresses: 2020 Avenue of the Stars, Los Angeles, Calif. 90067; 175 North State Street, Chicago, Ill. 60601.

"POKES AND JABBS" SERIES. See WIZARD MOTION PICTURE CORPORATION

"POLAR BEAR FEATURES." See GREAT NORTHERN FILM COMPANY

POLAROID. See THREE-DIMENSIONAL FILMS

POLYGRAM PICTURES. Polygram Pictures was formed in March 1980, shortly after Neil Bogart quit Casablanca Film Works, which he and Peter Guber founded in 1976 and which was the basis of the new company. Polygram Pictures was a joint venture of N. V. Philips of the Netherlands and Siemens A.G. of West Germany; Guber remained with the company and Gordon Stulberg, formerly with 20th Century-Fox*, was brought in as president. Polygram's best-known productions were probably *An American Werewolf in London* (1981), *Endless Love* (1981), and *Missing* (1983).

Address: 8255 Sunset Boulevard, Los Angeles, Calif. 90046.

POPULAR PLAYS AND PLAYERS COMPANY. Charles O. Baumann formed the Popular Plays and Players Company, incorporated in 1914 for $1 million, to produce high-class features of varying lengths according to the needs of their stories. Directors of the company were Baumann (the president), C. A. "Doc" Willat, A. Butler, Harry J. Cohen (the general manager and treasurer), and L. Lawrence Weber. Offices were at 1600 Broadway, New York. Using the players and facilities of the Lubin Film Manufacturing Company*, Popular Plays and Players produced its first two releases, *Michael Strogoff*, with Jacob P. Adler, and *The Ragged Earl*, with Andrew Mackin and directed by Lloyd B. Carleton. Its subsequent productions were shot at the Willat Studios and Laboratories in Fort Lee, New Jersey*. Olga Petrova was a featured player. The company released first with the Alco Film Corporation* and later with Metro Pictures Corporation*, when Alco went bankrupt. By the end of 1914, Popular Plays and Players had changed from producing features to releasing twenty-eight reels per week of one-, two-, and three-reel films, representing fourteen brands, including Cee-O-Bee, Willat, Niagara, Palisade, Longacre, Canyon, and Continental (all dramas), and Jester, Luna, Owl, Frolic, Gayety, O.K., and Pastime (all comedies). Metro absorbed the company on May 25, 1917.

BIBLIOGRAPHY

"C. O. Baumann Talks of Plans," *The Moving Picture World*, September 5, 1914, p. 1349.

"Popular Plays and Players Company," *The Moving Picture World*, June 6, 1914, p. 1396.

POPULAR SCIENCE. See JERRY FAIRBANKS PRODUCTIONS

POST PICTURES CORPORATION. Founded by Clyde E. Elliott (1885–1959), Post Pictures Corporation was active from 1919 to 1921 in the production of scenic and travelogue shorts under the series titles of Post Travel Pictures, Post Scenics, and Post Nature Pictures. Elliott became known in the thirties and forties for the direction of a number of animal features, including *Bring 'Em Back Alive* (1932).

POVERTY ROW. Poverty Row was the name initially bestowed on the area of Hollywood around Sunset Boulevard and Gower Street, where might be found such once minor producers as Columbia*, whose films were noted for the cheap manner in which they were produced. In time, Poverty Row came to refer not to an area of the city but to a type of production from a minor company, such as Mascot*, Tiffany*, or Grand National*. Among the individuals involved in Poverty Row productions were Nat Levine, Bud Barsky, David Horsley, Edward Finney, Ben Judell, Trem Carr, W. Ray Johnston, and Sig Neufeld. The name Poverty Row was in common usage in the film industry as early as 1924.

BIBLIOGRAPHY

Donnell, Dorothy, "Poverty Row," *Motion Picture Classic*, April 1925, pp. 16–17, 78–79.

Fernett, Gene. *Poverty Row*. Satellite Beach, Florida: Coral Reef Publications, 1973.

POWERS COMPANY. The Powers Company, an early independent manufacturer, began operations in 1909 at a building adapted into a studio at 241 Street and Richardson Avenue, Wakefield, New York. Headed by P. A. "Pat" Powers, who later was a co-founder of the Universal Film Manufacturing Company, the Powers Company, with capital of $250,000, began releasing "Columbia Licensed Motion Pictures" in late 1909, using a non–patent-infringing camera developed by Joseph Bianchi, a recording expert for the Columbia Phonograph Company. Powers was the vice-president of the Motion Picture Distributing and Sales Company*, formed in April 1910, which planned to use the Bianchi camera to license independent manufacturers in a manner similar to that of the Motion Picture Patents Company*. But because the camera proved to be impractical and the patents, held by Columbia, did not offer the protection promised, Powers and the others switched to using infringing equipment and gave up their licensing plan.

Powers changed the name of its releases to "Powers Picture Plays." Joseph Golden was an early Powers director, Ludwig G. B. Erb was its cameraman and technical expert, and Irving Cummings the leading man. In April 1910, the Powers Company came out with talking pictures which it made for the American Fotofone Company. In January 1912, Juliet Shelby, later known as Mary Miles Minter, made *The Nurse*, her first film, for Powers.

Powers became a part of Universal* at its formation. In May 1913, it reincorporated as Powers Photoplays, Inc., and produced in Hollywood, at which time its directors included J. Farrell MacDonald and Harry C. Matthews. It continued production through 1917. In May 1918, the Powers-Cameron Film Company was formed, and it purchased the plant of the Fireproof Film Company in Rochester, New York, to make, among other things, 3-D talking pictures, with the financial backing of Rochester businessmen.

BIBLIOGRAPHY

"P. A. Powers Heads New Rochester Concern," *The Moving Picture World*, May 25, 1918, p. 1125.

"Picture Plays and Their Production: A Visit to the Powers Factory at Wakefield," *The Moving Picture World*, April 23, 1910, pp. 636–637.

"The Powers Company," *The Moving Picture World*, October 2, 1909, p. 444.

"Powers Photoplays Studio," *The New York Dramatic Mirror*, May 21, 1913, p. 25.

"Talking Moving Pictures by the Powers Company," *The Moving Picture World*, April 16, 1910, p. 605.

P.R.C. In the late thirties, producer Ben Judell had formed a couple of independent production companies, Progressive Pictures Corporation and Producers Distributing Corporation (PDC), which had no connection with the earlier Cecil B. DeMille organization of the same name. PDC produced a number of films, notably *Hitler, Beast of Berlin* (1940, retitled for political reasons *Goose Step*). When the company went heavily in debt in 1940, with its major creditor being Pathé Laboratories, the latter decided to reform PDC as P.R.C. (Producers Releasing Corporation), with studios at 6404 Hollywood Boulevard and George Batcheller in charge of production.

One of the company's first productions was *Misbehaving Husbands* (1940), a pathetic comedy featuring two former silent stars, Betty Blythe and Harry Langdon, and which indicated the type of features with which P.R.C. would be associated. Indeed, the company was so denigrated within the industry that it was crudely referred to as "Prick Productions." Aside from cheap melodramas and comedies, P.R.C. produced three Western series, under the guidance of Sigmund Neufeld, "Billy the Kid," "Frontier Marshall," and "Lone Rider." Producing an average of thirty features a year, P.R.C. continued as a production entity through the late forties, when it merged with Eagle-Lion*. However, as a corporate name, P.R.C. existed until 1953, as a subsidiary of Pathé Industries, Inc., a successor to Pathé Laboratories.

BIBLIOGRAPHY

Fernett, Gene. *Poverty Row*. Satellite Beach, Florida: Coral Reef Publications, 1973.

PRE-CINEMA. Pre-Cinema is a term used to describe the various events and discoveries that led to the invention of the motion picture. More specifically, it relates to the invention of the magic lantern, on which a treatise was first published by the Jesuit priest Athanasius Kircher in 1646; to the concept of projection*, which is interrelated to the discovery of concave glass, first discussed in John Baptista Porta's *Natural Magick* (1589); and to the theory of persistence of vision, developed in the early nineteenth century by Peter Mark Roget and Joseph Antoine Ferdinand Plateau. Because of its own importance outside of the development of the motion picture, the invention of photography is not usually discussed as an aspect of pre-cinema.

Magic lanterns and other optical toys from the Victorian era are the most generally known items discussed under the heading of pre-cinema. Indeed, it might be argued that were it not for the popularity of magic lantern entertainments in the mid- through late 1800s, the discovery of the motion picture might not have proceeded so quickly.

Other important events in pre-cinema history include Dr. John Ayrton Paris's invention of the Thaumatrope, William George Horner's invention of the Zoetrope and Emile Reynaud's invention of the Praxinoscope, all of which relate to persistence of vision; Eadweard Muybridge's photographic experiments in the mid–1870s and his invention of the Zoopraxiscope; Alexander Parkes's invention of celluloid in 1855; the Reverend Hannibal Goodwin's perfection of nitro-cellulose film in 1887; and Etienne Jules Marey's experiments with a gun-like photographic camera in 1882.

BIBLIOGRAPHY

Ceram, C. W. *Archaeology of the Cinema*. New York: Harcourt, Brace & World, 1981.
Cook, Olive. *Movement in Two Dimensions*. London: Hutchinson, 1963.
Deslandes, Jacques. *Histoire Comparée du Cinéma: 1826–1896*. Paris: Casterman, 1966.
Quigley, Martin, Jr. *Magic Shadows*. Washington, D.C.: Georgetown University Press, 1948.

PRE-EMINENT FILMS, LTD. Pre-Eminent Films, Ltd., began producing in mid–1915. Its first film, *The Running Fight*, starred Violet Hemming and was directed by James Durkin. W. E. Green was the company's president and general manager.

PREFERRED PICTURES. When B. P. Schulberg (1892–1957) left Famous Players-Lasky in 1920, he formed his own company, Preferred Pictures (also known as Famous Attractions Corporation), with J. G. "Jack" Bachmann (who served as president) and Al Lichtman. The new company's first star was Katharine

MacDonald (with Preferred through 1923), but a more important leading lady with the company was Clara Bow, whom Schulberg spotted in *Down to the Sea in Ships* (1923) and featured in three Preferred features: *Maytime* (1923), *Poisoned Paradise* (1924), and *Capital Punishment* (1925). When Famous Players-Lasky's head, Adolph Zukor, asked Schulberg to return to the studio he did, and Preferred Pictures released its last films in 1926. It should not be confused with a minor company of the same name formed in November 1937 by J. G. Bachmann, Joe Goldberg, and Julius Schlein.

BIBLIOGRAPHY
Schulberg, Budd. *Moving Pictures*. New York: Stein and Day, 1981.

"PREMIER" BRAND. See ST. LOUIS MOTION PICTURE COMPANY

PREMIER COMPANY. The Premier Company made two-reel Westerns released with United Film Service* in 1915. Lillian Hamilton and Fred Church were the leading players, Mr. and Mrs. Al Garcia played supporting roles, and Joseph J. Franz was the director.

PREMO FEATURE FILM COMPANY. The Premo Feature Film Company released its first film, *The Master Hand*, through the World Film Corporation* in August 1915. Nat Goodwin was the film's star.

PREQUELS. "Prequels" is a word coined to describe film sequels that take place prior to the original film. For example, *Another Part of the Forest* (1947) tells of the earlier life of the Hubbard Family from *The Little Foxes* (1941); *The Night Comers* (1971) is the story of Peter Quint and Miss Jessel, who had been seen only as ghosts in *The Innocents* (1961); Robert Redford and Paul Newman starred in *Butch Cassidy and the Sundance Kid* (1969), but Butch and Sundance were seen as younger men, portrayed by Tom Berenger and William Katt, in *Butch and Sundance: The Early Days* (1979).

PREVUES. See TRAILERS

PRIMOGRAF COMPANY. The Primograf Company produced multi-reel films from its studios at 302 East 38 Street in New York in 1914. Irving Billig was the managing director, and its first production was *The Black Cross*, directed by Frank Coygne.

PRINCIPAL PRODUCTIONS, INC. Principal Productions, Inc., also known as Principal Pictures, was the name of Sol Lesser's (1890–1980) production company from 1922 to 1941. For it, he produced the Baby Peggy silent dramas, the Jackie Coogan comedies, the Tarzan features, the Smith Ballew musical

Westerns, and the Bobby Breen musicals, as well as many other features. Associated companies, of which Lesser was also president, were Principal Theatres Corporation of America and Principal Distributing Corporation.

PRIZMA COLOR. A forerunner of Cinecolor*, Magnacolor, and Multicolor, Prizma color was invented by William Van Doren Kelley. It is described by Adrian Cornwell-Clyne in *Colour Cinematography* (London: Chapman and Hall, 1951):

> Negatives were exposed at a speed of 32 pictures per second in a normal camera equipped with a rotating filter carrying the usual two-color taking filters. Prints were made on double-coated film, the alternate frames being selected by a skipping contact printer. One side of the film was toned blue-green by an iron solution, and the opposite side was toned red-orange with uranium. Prizma color was first demonstrated at the Museum of Natural History in New York on February 8, 1917. Its best-known use was in J. Stuart Blackton's production of *The Glorious Adventure*, starring Lady Diana Manners and shot in England in 1921.

Prizma, Inc., began producing a weekly one-reel educational film late in 1918; *Kilauea*, a film about a Hawaiian volcano, was shown at the Rivoli Theatre, New York, the week of December 29, 1918. In November 1919, the company—by then known as Prizma Natural Color Pictures—took over the contract of child actress Madge Evans from the World Film Corporation* and produced two-reel and longer films featuring the actress. H. W. Saulsbury was the president and Carroll H. Dunning the vice-president of the company.

BIBLIOGRAPHY

"How Prizma Films Are Made and Why They Are Practical," *The Moving Picture World*, April 26, 1919, p. 508.

"Prizma to Use Standard Projectors," *The Moving Picture World*, January 11, 1919, p. 190.

PRODUCERS' DISTRIBUTING CORPORATION. Frank G. Hall, an exhibitor in New Jersey, was the president of the Producers' Distributing Corporation, which was formed in September 1918 to furnish exhibitors with twelve special productions a year at the fixed prices of ten dollars, twenty dollars, or thirty dollars a day, depending on the age of the subject, no matter how successful the film became. Franchise holders would sign for all twelve films but could cancel by giving a two-picture notice. The Loew circuit, along with exchanges of Moss, Mastbaum, Keith, and the Ascher Brothers signed with Producers' shortly after its formation. Producers' offices were located at 126–130 West 46 Street, New York. Its first release was *Her Mistake*, featuring Evelyn Nesbit.

PRODUCERS DISTRIBUTING CORPORATION. Formed in 1924 by Jeremiah Milbank, Producers Distributing Corporation (PDC) took over the former Ince Studios in Culver City (Laird International*), and between 1924 and 1927 produced more than 100 features. Cecil B. DeMille joined the corporation in 1925, and, at that time, Cinema Corporation of America was formed as a holding company to control the stock of Producers Distributing Corporation and Cecil B. DeMille Pictures Corporation, with the stock jointly owned by DeMille and Realty and Securities Company.

DeMille was responsible for the Culver City studios, while F. C. Munro (president) and John C. Flinn (vice-president and general manager) were based at the New York office. The corporation published its own house journal, *The Dotted Line*. PDC's features included *The Awful Truth* (1925), *The Coming of Amos* (1925), *Three Faces East* (1926), *White Gold* (1927), and *The Yankee Clipper* (1927), and three films, directed by DeMille: *The Road to Yesterday* (1925), *The Volga Boatman* (1926), and *King of Kings* (1927). The corporation was taken over by Pathé* in 1928.

BIBLIOGRAPHY

Hayne, Donald, editor. *The Autobiography of Cecil B. DeMille*. Englewood Cliffs, New Jersey: Prentice-Hall, 1959.

PRODUCERS FILM COMPANY. Founded by Henry W. Laugenour and based in Oroville, California, Producers Film Company was active in the early twenties in the production of the one-reel "Betty June Comedies."

PRODUCERS GUILD OF AMERICA, INC. In an effect to gain some recognition as the ultimate creator of a motion picture, a group of producers banded together in April 1950 to establish the Screen Producers Guild, whose original objectives were to represent producers in industry matters, to promote the professional interests of members, and to increase the value and importance of the industry. Among the founding members were Buddy Adler, Irwin Allen, Sam Bischoff, Bryan Foy, Edmund Grainger, Joe Pasternak, and Jerry Wald. William Perlberg was the Guild's first president.

Founded initially as little more than a social club, the Guild became a bargaining organization for the producers in their dealings with the studios in 1966. The following year, the Guild changed its name to the Producers Guild of America, Inc. Its efforts to gain recognition as a bargaining agent were never entirely successful, and, in December 1984, the Guild affiliated with the Western Conference of the Teamsters, an action which many viewed as a final endeavor to obtain industrywide contracts from Hollywood studios and to gain recognition as a bargaining agent for *all* producers.

From 1952 to 1977, the Guild published a journal, which examined various aspects of the film and television industries in some detail.

Address: 292 South La Cienega Boulevard, Beverly Hills, Calif. 90211.

PRODUCERS' PROTECTIVE ASSOCIATION. On October 18, 1917, fourteen independent states rights* producers organized the Producers' Protective Association to regulate the states rights field. Directors of the Association were William L. Sherrill, the president; Harry Rapf the vice-president; Jesse J. Goldburg, secretary and treasurer; Leopold Wharton; M. A. Schlesinger, and I. N. Chadwick. The organization was formed because of the unsettled state of business in the states rights market and the doubtful aspect with which banking institutions doing business with states rights producers viewed the present manner of regulating the states rights market. The Association sought to regulate advertising, pass judgment on grievances, institute a central sales exchange, and attempt the complete systemization of states rights production and distribution. Members included the Frohman Amusement Corporation*, Mayfair Film Corporation, Harry Rapf Productions, Ivan Film Productions, Inc.*, Duplex Film Corporation, Crystal Film Corporation, Ogden Pictures Corporation*, and John W. Noble, Inc.

BIBLIOGRAPHY

"Independent Producers Organize," *The Moving Picture World*, September 29, 1917, p. 2013.

"Producers' Protective Association Formed," *The Moving Picture World*, November 3, 1917, p. 714.

PRODUCERS RELEASING CORPORATION. See P.R.C.

PRODUCERS STUDIO. See CALIFORNIA STUDIOS

PRODUCTION CODE. Described as a "moral document," the Production Code encompassed three general principles:

1. No picture shall be produced which will lower the moral standards of those who see it. Hence the sympathy of the audience shall never be thrown to the side of crime, wrongdoing, evil, or sin.

2. Correct standards of life, subject only to the requirements of drama and entertainment, shall be presented.

3. Law, natural or human, shall not be ridiculed, nor shall sympathy be created for its violation.

The Production Code's origins date back to 1927, when Will H. Hays, president of the Motion Picture Producers and Distributors of America (later the Motion Picture Association of America*) formulated a group of directives for producers, consisting of eleven "don'ts" and twenty-six "be carefuls." A more formal "Code to Maintain Social and Community Values" was adopted by the Association and ratified by its board of directors on March 31, 1930. It was not mandatory for producers to adhere to the Code and the majority did not.

However, in the next couple of years, the Motion Picture Producers and Distributors of America came under increasing pressure from the public to adopt a formal code. In 1934, the National Legion of Decency* was created and threatened a Catholic boycott unless some rigid form of internal censorship was imposed on the film industry. Through his publication *Motion Picture Herald*, a leading Catholic layman, Martin Quigley, urged the industry to take action, and he, along with Daniel A. Lord, a Jesuit professor at the University of St. Louis, was largely responsible for drafting the new Production Code. Joseph I. Breen was selected to head the newly created Production Code Administration, which came into being on July 1, 1934.

All producers belonging to the Motion Picture Producers and Distributors of America were obligated to submit scripts and finished films for Code approval. Most independent and foreign productions were also submitted for voluntary approval. An additional Code governing things such as advertising and still photographs* was introduced in 1935. The provisions of the Production Code, initially published in a nineteen-page booklet, could vary from year to year. An up-to-date copy of the Code appeared annually in *International Motion Picture Almanac*.

In the fifties, theatres began screening films that did not have the Code seal of approval. United Artists* released *The Moon Is Blue* (1953) and *The Man with the Golden Arm* (1955) without Code approval, and increasingly important films, such as *Who's Afraid of Virginia Woolf?* (1966) and *Alfie* (1966), were produced whose subject matter precluded approval by the Protection Code Administration. In 1966, the Code was revised and a new heading, "Suggested for Mature Audiences," introduced. Eventually, the Code became obsolete with the introduction—in 1968—of the ratings* system.

BIBLIOGRAPHY

Ramsaye, Terry. *What the Production Code Really Says*. New York: Motion Picture Herald, 1934 (reprinted from the August 11, 1934, issue).

Shurlock, Geoffrey, "The Motion Picture Production Code," in *The Annals of the American Academy of Political and Social Science*. Philadelphia: The American Academy of Political and Social Science, 1947, pp. 140–146.

RESOURCES

Papers: Academy of Motion Picture Arts and Sciences (Review Files of the Production Code Administration).

PROGRESSIVE PICTURES CORPORATION. See P.R.C.

PROJECTION. Projection, one of the crucial elements in motion pictures, is possible as a result of the discovery of "concave glass," first discussed in John Baptista Porta's *Natural Magick* (1589), which permits the projection of objects and forms the basis for Leonardo da Vinci's camera obscura.

Thanks to projection, motion pictures are given the illusion of movement. Film transport is necessary to carry the motion picture from an upper reel, through the projector gate, to a lower reel. The beam from a light source is directed through a condensing lens or a mirror (which can sometimes be adjusted manually to sharpen the image), and motion on the film is synthesized by use of a two-shutter movement, which prevents the eye from perceiving flicker and cuts off the light source during the movement from one frame to the next. The film then moves through a second gate, through which a beam is directed at the sound track, and a photoelectric or a solar cell converts the light waves to sound waves.

Reels of film were one reel (running between eight and eleven minutes) in length, until 1933, when 2,000-foot reels were introduced (which, despite their name, usually hold only 1,700 feet of film). Reel changes, indicated by a visual cue in the right-hand corner of the picture, would be made manually by the projectionist. In order to prevent a break in the presentation, all theatres needed to be equipped with a minimum of two projectors. However, in the seventies, automated projection was introduced whereby the entire feature could be mounted on one single platter—to hold up to 20,000 feet of film—with the lead of the show spliced to the tail, thereby giving a continuous performance. Virtually all theatres are equipped with front projection, although back projection through a translucent screen is occasionally used. *See also* Aspect Ratios.

BIBLIOGRAPHY

The Focal Encyclopedia of Film & Television Techniques. New York: Hastings House, 1969.

Levitan, Eli L., editor. *An Alphabetical Guide to Motion Picture, Television and Videotape Production.* New York: McGraw-Hill, 1970.

PROMOTIONAL FILMS, INC. See ASTOR PICTURES CORPORATION

PROVIDENCE, RHODE ISLAND. See EASTERN FILM COMPANY

PUBLICISTS GUILD OF AMERICA. The negotiating body for various types of publicists working within the industry, the Publicists Guild of America was chartered on July 11, 1955, as IATSE Local 818. It has jurisdiction over the entire country, including New York Publicists Local 872.

The Publicists Guild has its origins in the Screen Publicists Guild, organized on June 2, 1937. Because the original Guild sided with the Conference of Studio Unions*, IATSE chartered the Motion Picture Publicists Association to replace it, but the Screen Publicists Guild was able to organize sufficient support to declare a "closed shop" within the studios in 1950. The Screen Publicists Guild produced a popular radio series in the early fifties and presented annual "Tom-Tom" awards from 1953. The name survives as that of the New York–based Screen Publicists Guild, which is a member of District 65 of the Distributive Workers of America.

The Publicists Guild presents a variety of awards: the Bob Yeager Award (first given in 1977 to Julian Myers), the Les Mason Award (first given in 1965 to Nat James), the Max Weinberg Publicist Showmanship Award (first given in 1982 to Kim Rowley and Margaret Scott), the Motion Picture Showmanship Award (first given in 1964 to Stanley Kramer), the Television Showmanship

Award (first given in 1970 to Kragen-Smothers-Fritz), and the Press Award (first given in 1964 to Don Carle Gillete).

Address: 1427 North La Brea Avenue, Hollywood, Calif. 90028.

PUBLIC MEDIA INCORPORATED. See FILMS INCORPORATED

PUBLIX THEATERS CORPORATION. Also known as the Paramount-Publix theatre circuit, Publix Theaters Corporation has been described by film historian Douglas Gomery as "the most profitable theatre chain in cinema history." It was created by Adolph Zukor in 1925 by the merger of the Balaban & Katz theatres with those owned at that time by Paramount*. At the peak of its importance, in the early thirties, the Publix circuit consisted of some 1,210 theatres in the United States and Canada.

On January 1, 1950, United Paramount Theatres, Inc., was formed to take over all theatre chains, including Publix, owned by Paramount in order to comply with the governmental consent decree*. At that time, Paramount controlled 1,424 theatres under a variety of circuit names, including Arizona Paramount Corporation, Augusta Amusements, Inc., Central States Theatres, Butterfield Circuit, Famous Players Canadian, Florida State Theatres, Georgia Theatre Company, Intermountain Theatres, Interstate Circuit, Inc., Jefferson Amusement Company, Kansas City Operating Company, New England Theatres, Paramount Enterprises, Paramount Pictures Theatres, Tri-States Theatres, and Wilby-Kincey.

BIBLIOGRAPHY

Ayer, Fred, "1,210 Theatres under Paramount's Control," *Motion Picture Herald*, January 5, 1935, pp. 9–12.

Gomery, Douglas. "The Movies Become Big Business: Publix Theatres and the Chain-Store Strategy," in *The American Movie Industry: The Business of Motion Pictures*. Carbondale, Illinois: Southern Illinois University Press, 1982, pp. 104–116.

PUPPETOONS. Puppetoons were a form of animated cartoon created by George Pal (1908–1980) which utilized miniaturized wooden figures instead of drawings. Pal first began making Puppetoons at a studio in Einhoven, the Netherlands, in 1934. The films he made there were advertising shorts for either Philips or Horlicks, with the first Puppetoon being *The Ship of the Ether* (1934) and others including *Ali Baba and the Forty Thieves* (1935), *On Parade* (1936), *What Ho She Bumps* (1937), *The Sleeping Beauty* (1938), *Sky Pirates* (1938), and *Aladdin and the Magic Lamp* (1938).

George Pal came to the United States in 1939 and opened a studio in Santa Monica, California, where he produced his Puppetoons, for release through Paramount*, until 1947. He created the Negro boy Jasper as a favorite Puppetoon character in shorts such as *Jasper and the Watermelons* (1942), *Jasper Goes Fishing* (1943), and *Jasper in a Jam* (1946). The black folk hero, John Henry, was featured in the 1946 Puppetoon *John Henry and the Inky Poo*. In 1943, Pal received a Special Academy Award "for the development of novel methods and techniques in the production of the series of short subjects known as Puppetoons."

BIBLIOGRAPHY

Hickman, Gail Morgan. *The Films of George Pal*. South Brunswick and New York: A. S. Barnes, 1977.

Schepp, Ole, and Fred Kamphuis. *George Pal in Holland 1934–1939*. The Hague: Kleinoffsetdrukkerij Kapsenberg, 1983.

Taylor, Frank J., "Pal of the Puppets," *Collier's*, January 16, 1943, pp. 15, 61.

PURITAN SPECIAL FEATURES COMPANY. Located in Boston, the Puritan Special Features Company produced the 1914 feature *Quincy Adams Sawyer*. Charles F. Atkinson was the company's president.

BIBLIOGRAPHY

"Pictures Stimulate Interest in Play," *The Moving Picture World*, January 10, 1914, p. 153.

PUSSYCAT THEATRES. The best known of adult theatre chains, with theatres throughout California, the Pussycat circuit was formed in 1968 by Vincent Miranda (who died on June 2, 1985, at the age of fifty-two). Miranda had acquired his first theatre, the Lyric, in Huntington Beach, California, in 1961, and to ease his advertising costs began acquiring additional theatres, all of which he managed as "safe," clean theatres for a middle-class white clientele.

Address: 5445 Sunset Boulevard, Los Angeles, Calif. 90027.

PYRAMID PICTURES, INC. Pyramid Pictures, Inc., was formed in mid–1915 to make features, serials, and occasional industrial films under contract to various distributors. Arthur N. Smallwood was the president and general manager, and Pyramid's studio was at Ridgefield Park, New Jersey.

Q

QUALITY PICTURES CORPORATION. Quality Pictures Corporation was organized on March 1, 1915, by Fred J. Balshofer, formerly the head of the original Bison Company. Charles "Feature" Abrams was the company's business manager, and its studios were at the old Nestor plant at Sunset Boulevard and Gower Street in Hollywood. Quality began by producing films featuring Francis X. Bushman and Marguerite Snow, with William Bowman as director and William Alder as cameraman. Beverly Bayne joined Quality soon after release of its first film, *The Second in Command*. The company released on the Metro* program. It fell into other hands in 1916 and continued producing through 1922.

BIBLIOGRAPHY

"Amusement Feast for Public Is Quality's Hope," *Motion Picture News*, September 11, 1915, p. 47.

"Quality Pictures Corporation," *The Moving Picture World*, July 10, 1915, pp. 240–241.

QUARTET FILMS. See FILMS INCORPORATED

R

RADIO AND TELEVISION DIRECTORS GUILD. See DIRECTORS GUILD OF AMERICA, INC.

RADIO CITY MUSIC HALL. The foremost film showplace in the country, designed by Donald Deskey and with seating for 6,200, Radio City Music Hall opened at New York's Rockefeller Center on December 27, 1932, under the direction of S. L. "Roxy" Rothafel. The opening-night program was strictly a vaudeville presentation. The first feature to be screened at the Music Hall was Frank Capra's production of *The Bitter Tea of General Yen*. Increasing financial problems led to the closure of Radio City Music Hall on April 12, 1978, with the feature *Crossed Swords*. However, the Music Hall was saved from demolition thanks to the efforts of various concerned groups and reopened as an entertainment center with occasional live shows and film presentations, on May 31, 1979. The traditional Christmas shows continue to be presented at Radio City, and its famed dancers, the Rockettes, remain in residence, making frequent tours with their precision dance routines, including their specialty, "Parade of the Wooden Soldiers," to the music of Victor Herbert.

Address: 50 Street and Avenue of the Americas, New York, N.Y. 10020.

BIBLIOGRAPHY

Ansen, David, "Radio City Redux," *Time*, June 11, 1979, p. 60.

Francisco, Charles. *The Radio City Music Hall*. New York: E. P. Dutton, 1979.

Morris, Joe Alex, "The Music Hall," *The Saturday Evening Post*, January 11, 1959, pp. 35, 90–92.

Shepard, Richard F., "Radio City Music Hall Returns," *The New York Times*, June 1, 1979, pp. C1, C6.

RESOURCES

Papers: Radio City Music Hall Archives (for description, see Summer 1982 issue of *Broadside*, newsletter of the Theatre Library Association).

RADIO-TELEVISION-RECORDING-ADVERTISING CHARITIES. See THE PERMANENT CHARITIES COMMITTEE OF THE ENTERTAINMENT INDUSTRIES

RALEIGH STUDIOS. See CALIFORNIA STUDIOS

RAMO FILMS, INC. Ramo Films, Inc., began as the brand name of the pictures produced by the Directors Film Corporation in February 1913. It made two releases per week: a split-reel comedy directed by Epes Winthrop Sargent and a dramatic film directed by Wray B. Physioc. Its studios, called Ramo's Perfect Studios, were located at 102 West 101 Street, New York, and it released with the Exclusive Film Corporation. In May 1914, Ramo Films, Inc., was formed as an enlargement of the previous company. Homer H. Snow became director of the company, and C. Lang Cobb, Jr., became chief advisor. Directors during this period included George Gebhart and Will S. Davis, the cameraman was John Arnold, and Pual M. Potter was the scenarist. It moved to a studio in Flushing, Long Island, in August 1914, after the New York Fire Department forced Ramo to leave its previous studio, and, because it planned to confine its activities to the production of features, it got rid of its stock company. However, in 1915, it contracted to make one- and two-reel films under the brand name "Regent" for the United Film Service*. Ramo ceased operations on January 1, 1916.

BIBLIOGRAPHY
"Ramo Films Expanding," *The Moving Picture World*, May 9, 1914, p. 831.
"Ramo Films Soon," *The New York Dramatic Mirror*, February 5, 1913, p. 26.

RAMPART PRODUCTIONS, INC. Rampart Productions, Inc., was an independent production company, headed by William Dozier, which released through Universal-International*. It produced two features in 1948, *Letter from an Unknown Woman* and *You Gotta Stay Happy*, both of which starred Dozier's then wife Joan Fontaine, who was vice-president of Rampart. A third feature, *A Very Remarkable Fellow*, was announced but unproduced. In the sixties, Dozier again had his own independent production company, Greenaway Productions.

RASTAR. Rastar is the umbrella name for four companies created by producer Ray Stark, the earliest of which dates back to 1966: Rastar Films, Rastar Features, Rastar Productions, and Rastar Television (formed in 1981, the best-known series from which is *Ripley's Believe It or Not*). Rastar Productions was acquired by Columbia* in 1974 (although the acquisition did not become generally known until 1978), and Rastar Films was purchased by the same studio in 1980.

Ray Stark serves as chairman of the board of Rastar, which has been responsible for more than fifty popular features, including such Neil Simon titles as *The Goodbye Girl* (1977), *California Suite* (1978), and *The Cheap Detective* (1978), as well as *Funny Girl* (1968), *The Way We Were* (1973), *Funny Lady* (1975),

The Electric Horseman (1979), and *Annie* (1982). In 1983, it was announced that all personally produced Stark films would be known as Ray Stark Productions, while all others would be called Rastar Productions.

Address: Columbia Plaza, Burbank, Calif. 91505.

RATINGS SYSTEM. The system of rating motion pictures was introduced by the Motion Picture Association of America* on November 1, 1968. It is a voluntary service, open to all and generally supported by most producers within the industry. The rating system is sponsored by the Motion Picture Association of America, the International Film Importers & Distributors of America, and the National Association of Theatre Owners*. It is supervised by the Motion Picture Association, and the actual rating is undertaken by a board in Hollywood.* The primary purpose of the rating system is to advise patrons, particularly parents, as to the type of material in a particular film. The Ratings Board is not a censorship board, and its ratings are not intended to indicate the quality or artistry of any motion picture.

There are five categories of ratings. "G" indicates the film is for general audiences of all ages. "PG" indicates that parental guidance is suggested, but all ages can be admitted. Films rated "PG" contain some material which parents may consider too mature for pre-teenagers. "PG–13" (introduced in 1984 after criticism of a number of "PG"-rated films with excessively violent sequences) suggests, but does not require, that children under thirteen be accompanied by a parent or guardian. "R" indicates the film is restricted and that those under seventeen must be accompanied by a parent or adult guardian; the film has an adult theme or treatment. "X" means the film is restricted to those over seventeen. Generally, Hollywood producers are unwilling to have their films rated "X" because of the implication that such films are pornographic in content, although, in fact, the "X" rating can also signify excessive violence. Most adult or pornographic films have self-imposed "X" ratings—they have not been submitted to the Ratings Board.

BIBLIOGRAPHY

"Highlights of the New Voluntary Rating Plan," *Motion Picture Herald*, October 23, 1968, p. 25.

Motion Picture Association of America. *The Motion Picture Code and Rating Program: A System of Self-Regulation*. New York: Motion Picture Association of America, 1968.

Sublett, Scott, " 'Indiana' and 'Gremlins' Stir Up Ratings Squabble," *The Washington Times*, June 22, 1984, pp. 4D–6D.

Tusher, Will, "Censorship's a Horrid Word to Religious Leaders, but on the Other Hand Films Are a Target of Growing Criticism," *Daily Variety*, October 30, 1984, pp. 58, 106, 108, 110, 114, 118.

RAVER FILM CORPORATION. Harry R. Raver, secretary and treasurer of the Itala Film Company of America*, formerly the executive head of the All-Star Feature Company*, general manager of the Eclair Film Company* and the Film Supply Company of America, director of the Motion Picture Distributing and Sales Company, and the man who brought *Cabiria* to the United States from Italy, organized the Raver Film Corporation, of which he was president, in October 1915, after he obtained the rights to produce a number of well-known plays, including a collection of twenty-nine by Augustus Thomas, also formerly associated with All-Star. Raver first used the W. Lindsay Gordon studios on Staten Island, New York, and later moved to Rockville, Long Island. The company's first production was *The Other Girl*, directed by Percy Winter. In February 1916, it took over the exploitation of productions of the Ocean Film Corporation*. Later, under the new name of Harry Raver, Inc., the company released films to the states rights* market through 1921.

BIBLIOGRAPHY
"River [sic] Film Corporation," *The Moving Picture World*, October 15, 1915, p. 589.

RAYART PRODUCTIONS. See MONOGRAM PRODUCTIONS, INC.

RAYBERT PRODUCTIONS. See BBS PRODUCTIONS

R.C.M. PRODUCTIONS. See SOUNDIES

READER, SMITH AND BLACKTON COMBINATION. see VITAGRAPH COMPANY OF AMERICA

REDLANDS, CALIFORNIA. See DUDLEY MOTION PICTURE MANUFACTURING COMPANY and FUJIYAMA FEATURE FILM COMPANY

REEL CLUB. See THE PHOTOPLAYERS

REEL PHOTOPLAY COMPANY. See GOTHAM FILM COMPANY

"REGENT" BRAND. See RAMO FILMS, INC.

REGENT FILM COMPANY, INC. The Regent Film Company, Inc., of which S. L. Warner was the president and general manager, was organized in January 1915 to produce one- and two-reel society dramas under the brand name "Tams" Pictures, starring Irene Tams. It leased the Centaur Studios in Bayonne, New Jersey, with its first release being the two-reel *Rebellious Irene*, directed by Walter Edwin and written by Lawrence McGill. Regent released with the United Film Service*.

THE REGULARS. An informal social club for the younger female members of the film community in the twenties, the Regulars met every Monday night in rotation at a member's home. Among its members were Mary Astor, Margerie Bonner, Priscilla Bonner, Mary Brian, Sue Carol, Virginia Brown Faire, Pauline Garon, Mary Philbin, Esther Ralston, and Jobyna Ralston.
BIBLIOGRAPHY
Slide, Anthony, "The Regulars," *Films in Review*, April 1978, pp. 222–224.

RELIANCE MOTION PICTURE COMPANY AND MAJESTIC MOTION PICTURE COMPANY. Charles O. Baumann and Adam Kessel, Jr., formed the Reliance Motion Picture Company in 1910 at a Coney Island plant. Reliance's first film, *In the Gray of the Dawn*, released October 22, 1910, featured Arthur Johnson, Marion Leonard, Henry B. Walthall, James Kirkwood, Frances Burns, Gertrude Robinson, and Phillips Smalley, many of whom were hired away from the Biograph Company.*

The Majestic Motion Picture Company, formed the first week of September 1911 by Harry E. Aitken, acquired Mary Pickford, her husband Owen Moore, and general manager Thomas D. Cochrane from the IMP Company, while IMP's owner Carl Laemmle was on vacation in Europe. Majestic's offices were located at 145 West 45 Street, New York, and its first film, *The Courting of Mary*, starring Mary Pickford, was released on November 18, 1911, by the Motion Picture Distributing and Sales Company*. The Majestic Company, with Moore and David Miles directing, traveled to California, where its players included Mabel Trunnelle, Herbert Prior, George Loane Tucker, Paul Scardon, and Charles Craig. Its Christmas release, *Little Red Riding Hood*, starred Mary Pickford and was directed by Owen Moore. Pickford left Majestic to return to Biograph in 1912. By January of that same year, Majestic had increased its release schedule to two reels per week.

In October 1911, Baumann sold the Reliance Company to J. C. Graham, who was formerly associated with Aitken in the Western Film Exchange. Both Reliance and Majestic joined the Mutual Film Corporation* upon its formation in 1912. Reliance produced its first three-reeler, *The Man from Outside*, with Irving Cummings, directed by Oscar Apfel, in February 1913. In July 1913, the company acquired the site for a new studio, The Pines, a four-acre estate of actress Clara Morris, overlooking the Hudson River on the Yonkers-Manhattan line at 262 Street and Riverdale Avenue. Later in 1913, Reliance signed D. W. Griffith to be director-in-chief of all its productions, which included those made at the Morris estate, at a studio located at 29 Union Square at the corner of 16 Street and Broadway, New York, and at its newest acquisition, the former Kinemacolor Company* studios at 4500 Sunset Boulevard in Hollywood. Aitken incorporated Reliance for $1 million (apparently it had earlier been part of the Carlton Motion Picture Company) in December 1913. Majestic, at this time, was producing under the name "New Majestic" from its studio at 651 Fairview Avenue, Los Angeles.

In March 1914, Majestic, with directors John Adolfi and Frederick Vroom, joined the Reliance studio at 4500 Sunset Boulevard, which under Griffith's supervision expanded greatly over the next fifteen months. The studio became known as the Reliance-Majestic Studio and remained such until the creation of Fine Arts* in 1915.

BIBLIOGRAPHY

"New Reliance Studio," *The Moving Picture World*, July 26, 1913, p. 433.

"Reliance a Million Dollar Company," *The Moving Picture World*, January 3, 1914, p. 32.

"Reliance-Majestic," *The Moving Picture World*, July 10, 1915, p. 249–250.

"Reliance under New Management," *The Moving Picture World*, October 14, 1911, p. 135.

von Harleman, G. P., "Motion Picture Studios of California," *The Moving Picture World*, March 10, 1917, pp. 1605–1606.

RELIANCE PICTURES, INC. See EDWARD SMALL PRODUCTIONS, INC.

RENFAX FILM COMPANY, INC. The Renfax Film Company, Inc., was organized in January 1914 to make talking pictures illustrating popular songs. Exhibitors who owned a phonograph and who would purchase an attachment to synchronize the phonograph and the projector, could show these novelties, which were released four to a reel. Known vaudeville performers were featured in the films. By the end of its first year, Renfax had opened exchanges in New York; Columbus, Ohio; Chicago; and Pittsburgh. Its main offices were in the World's Tower Building, New York; Arthur M. Hess was the president and treasurer, and DeWitt Fox was the vice-president.

BIBLIOGRAPHY

"Renfax Musical Pictures a Year Old," *The Moving Picture World*, February 6, 1915, p. 833.

"Renfax Talking Pictures," *The Moving Picture World*, January 17, 1914, p. 298.

REOL MOTION PICTURE COMPANY. The Reol Motion Picture Company, an early producer of black films, was owned by Robert J. Levy, a white backer of the Lafayette Players, a Harlem theatre group which appeared in Reol's films. Reol produced at least six features, one of which, *The Call of His People*, was released in 1921.

REPUBLIC DISTRIBUTING CORPORATION. Lewis J. Selznick, the head of Select* Pictures Corporation, took over the entire list of twenty-two exchanges* from the World Film Corporation* and formed the Republic Distributing Corporation, in the fall of 1919, to have no connection with Select. Republic's offices were located at 130 West 46 Street, New York. Although Britton N. Busch was president and general manager, Selznick was in full control in his official role as advisory director. Republic planned to handle the highest grade independent films, including high-class short subjects. The company ended in 1921.

BIBLIOGRAPHY

"Selznick Absorbs a Corporation," *The Moving Picture World*, November 8, 1919, p. 3472.

REPUBLIC FILM LABORATORIES. See CONSOLIDATED FILM INDUSTRIES

REPUBLIC PICTURES CORPORATION. The most important and influential studio in the history of the "B" movie*, Republic Pictures Corporation was also the one studio which made a conscious and at times successful effort to raise its status. Throughout its life, Republic was controlled by only one man, Herbert John Yates (1880–1966), a former executive with the American Tobacco Company who had been involved with various film laboratories, notably Consolidated Film Industries*, from the mid-teens.

Republic's staple product included Westerns and serials (some sixty-six of the latter), and among the best-known stars under contract were Gene Autry, Roy Rogers, John Wayne, and ice skater Vera Hruba Ralston (whom Yates married in 1952). Louella Parsons' daughter, Harriet, began her career as a feature film producer with Republic. From 1937 to 1947, Republic produced the musical revue "Hit Parade" series. In the forties, Yates worked hard to improve Republic's image. Among the directors he placed under contract were such prominent names as Orson Welles, Allan Dwan, Frank Borzage, John Ford, and Ben Hecht, all lured with promises of directorial freedom. Among the "class" features produced by Republic in the late forties and early fifties were *Spectre of the Rose* (1946), *Macbeth* (1948), *Sands of Iwo Jima* (1949), *The Red Pony* (1949), *Rio Grande* (1950), and *The Quiet Man* (1952).

The company was formed on March 29, 1935, when Yates merged Mascot*, Monogram*, and Liberty companies, with headquarters at the former Mascot Studios (earlier the Mack Sennett Studios) at Ventura Boulevard and Radford Avenue in Studio City. Nat Levine, formerly of Mascot, was named first president. Monogram's exchanges were the basis for Republic's distribution setup. After only a few months, M. H. Hoffman withdrew his Liberty Pictures; on August 6, 1936, Trem Carr and Ray Johnston left to reform Monogram, and in 1937 Nat Levine resigned. Yates was left very much in sole command of the company, and its success was entirely to his credit.

Republic prospered, enjoying its most financially successful year in 1946. Its sound department was noted throughout the industry, and, in 1945, Republic received a Special Technical Award from the Academy of Motion Picture Arts and Sciences* "for the building of an outstanding musical scoring auditorium which provides optimum recording conditions and combines all elements of acoustic and engineering design." The studio's profits fell in the fifties, partially because of the increasing popularity of television but also, ironically, because of Yates' promotion of prestige productions which failed to gain an adequate audience and, above all, his promotion of his wife, Vera Hruba Ralston, as a major star.

On July 1, 1959, Yates resigned as Republic's president. Los Angeles industrialist, Victor M. Carter, took over the company, but, for all intents and purposes, Republic had ceased to exist. The studios were leased first to Lippert* and then to CBS*, which purchased them in 1967, renaming the lot CBS Studio Center. (The studios are still utilized by CBS but were acquired in 1984 by Mary Tyler Moore Productions.)

Republic Corporation continues as the parent company of Consolidated Film Industries. In 1984, National Telefilm Associates, which had purchased the library of Republic films in 1967, voted to change its name to Republic and to utilize the Republic logo of the American eagle as its trademark.

BIBLIOGRAPHY

Barbour, Alan G. *Selected Pages from the Republic Reporter 1939–40*. Kew Gardens, New York: Screen Facts, 1975.

Hurst, Richard Maurice. *Republic Studios: Between Poverty Row and the Majors*. Metuchen, New Jersey: Scarecrow Press, 1979.

Mathis, Jack. *Valley of the Cliffhangers*. Northbrook, Illinois: Jack Mathis Advertising, 1975.

O'Connor, Edward, "The Golden Age of Republic Serials," *Screen Facts*, no. 17, 1968, pp. 48–61.

———, "The Golden Age of Republic Serials, Part 2," *Screen Facts*, no. 18, 1968, pp. 20–36.

Swann, Thomas Burnett. *The Heroine or the Horse: Leading Ladies in Republic's Films*. New York: A. S. Barnes, 1977.

Whalen, David B., "Republic Pictures," in *The Film Daily Cavalcade*. New York: The Film Daily, 1939, pp. 176–182.

RESOURCES

Films: UCLA Film Archives (35mm nitrate material and preservation negatives and prints).

Papers: Brigham Young University (film scores); University of California at Los Angeles (scripts, 1935–1955).

REPUBLIC PICTURES CORPORATION (NEW). National Telefilm Associates, formed in 1952, claims to be the world's largest independent distributor of film and television programs. One of its major assets is the entire Republic film library, which it acquired in 1965, along with remake rights and control of the Republic eagle logo. In recognition of the importance of the Republic library, and because it planned to remake some of the Republic titles, National Telefilm Associates changed its name, in December 1984, to Republic Pictures Corporation. The corporation is also involved in nontheatrical distribution and home video sales.

Address: 12636 Beatrice Street, P.O. Box 66930, Los Angeles, Calif. 90066–0930.

RIALTO DE LUXE PRODUCTIONS. Rialto De Luxe Productions was formed early in 1918 to produce one adaptation of a novel or play, five reels or more in length, per month, to be released to the states rights* market by Jesse J. Goldburg. Its first release was *The Unchastened Woman* with Grace Valentine. Rialto, which was located in New York, remained active through 1923.

RIALTO STAR FEATURES. See GAUMONT COMPANY

RIDGEFIELD PARK, NEW JERSEY. See PYRAMID PICTURES, INC.

RKO CENTURY WARNER THEATRES. RKO Century Warner Theatres is a theatre chain with screens, as of 1984, in New York, Connecticut, New Jersey, Ohio, Pennsylvania, and Rhode Island. It is all that remains of two theatre circuit giants, RKO Theatres Corporation* and Stanley Warner Corporation*, both of which were created when the consent decree* forced RKO* and Warner Bros.* to divest themselves of their theatres.

Address: 1585 Broadway, New York, N.Y. 10036.

RKO-PATHÉ STUDIOS. See LAIRD INTERNATIONAL STUDIOS

RKO RADIO PICTURES, INC. One of the smaller of the major Hollywood studios, RKO Radio Pictures, Inc., is best known for the Fred Astaire–Ginger Rogers musicals of the thirties, for *King Kong* (1933), for *Citizen Kane* (1941), and for the Val Lewton low-budget "horror" productions of the early forties. It helped advance the careers of Orson Welles, George Stevens, Katharine Hepburn, Robert Wise, Val Lewton, David O. Selznick, and George Cukor. As Richard B. Jewell wrote in *The RKO Story*, it "generated more than 1000 pictures—some forgettable, some too awful to contemplate, and a handful of the best movies ever made."

RKO, which stands for Radio-Keith-Orpheum, had its origin in the Film Booking Office of America (FBO), which was formed in 1922 from Robertson-Cole* and which produced and released minor, action, melodramatic, and Western features, many starring Yakima Canutt and Strongheart the Dog. The company was acquired in 1926 by Joseph P. Kennedy, but there was little change in the quality of its films. With the coming of sound, David Sarnoff, president of Radio Corporation of America (RCA), joined forces with Kennedy, perceiving FBO as a suitable production company showcase for his RCA Photophone sound system. FBO was merged with the vaudeville circuit of Keith-Albee-Orpheum, which provided the company with theatres in which to screen its product, and, on October 23, 1928, RKO Radio Pictures came into being. Its trademark, seen at the start of each film, was a radio tower perched on top of the world, beaming out the letters "RKO." The company's first film was *Syncopation* (1929), directed by Bert Glennon and starring Fred Waring and His Pennsylvanians.

David O. Selznick became head of production in the autumn of 1931, and to him goes the credit for some of the studio's best early films, including *What Price Hollywood?* (1932), *A Bill of Divorcement* (1932), *The Animal Kingdom* (1932), and *King Kong* (1933). When Selznick left for M-G-M* in 1933, he was replaced by Merian C. Cooper, and when he resigned, a year later, the position was taken over by B. B. Kahane. In 1935, Kahane was replaced by Samuel Briskin, who was, in turn, replaced, in 1938, by Pandro S. Berman. Berman, who had produced many of RKO's successes in the thirties, quit in 1939, and with his departure, a new president, George Schaefer, began bringing freelance talent to the studio and signing "new" names, such as Orson Welles. Although the films produced under the Schaefer regime were of superior quality, many failed to make money, and when Schaefer left in 1942 the company was financially in trouble.

Charles Koerner took over as production head, followed, on his death in 1946, by Peter N. Rathvon and, in 1947, by Dore Schary. In 1948, RKO was acquired by Howard Hughes, whose bad judgment as a producer led to the studio's downfall. He sold the studios in 1955 to General Teleradio, Inc., which was more interested in RKO's library of films for possible television use than in turning out new products. However, under William Dozier's leadership, as head of production, RKO continued to produce features through 1957, with its last film being *The Unholy Wife*, directed by John Farrow and starring Diana Dors. RKO continued to release films, some of which were produced by its British arm, through 1960.

The RKO studio was located at 780 Gower Street in Hollywood. It is now part of the Paramount* studio lot. RKO remains in existence as a corporate entity, RKO General, Inc., which is a division of General Tire.

Address: 129 North Vermont Avenue, Los Angeles, Calif. 90004.

BIBLIOGRAPHY

Haver, Ron, "The Mighty Show Machine," *American Film*, November 1977, pp. 56–61.

———, "RKO Years. Part II," *American Film*, December-January 1978, pp. 28–34.

Jewell, Richard B., with Vernon Harbin. *The RKO Story*. New York: Arlington House, 1982.

Lasky, Betty. *RKO, the Biggest Little Major of Them All*. Englewood Cliffs, New Jersey: Prentice-Hall, 1984.

Parish, James Robert. *The RKO Gals*. New Rochelle, New York: Arlington House, 1974.

"RKO Radio: An Overview," *The Velvet Light Trap*, no. 10, Fall 1973, entire issue.

RESOURCES

Films: Wisconsin Center for Film and Theatre Research (16mm reference prints); Library of Congress (35mm preservation and some reference prints).

Still Photographs: Academy of Motion Picture Arts and Sciences.

RKO THEATRES CORPORATION. When RKO* was required by the consent decree* to divest itself of its theatre chain, the 124 theatres that it controlled in 1948 became RKO Theatres Corporation. The theatres were resold in 1953 to List Industries, which merged with Glen Alden Corp. in 1959. It is now part of the New York–based RKO Century Warner Theatres*.

"ROAD MOVIES." To older filmgoers, the term "road movies" refers to the series of comedy features starring Bing Crosby, Bob Hope, and Dorothy Lamour and produced by Paramount*: *Road to Singapore* (1940), *Road to Zanzibar* (1941), *Road to Morocco* (1942), *Road to Utopia* (1946), *Road to Rio* (1948), and *Road to Bali* (1953). (There was also one final "road" picture, in which Lamour made only a cameo appearance and which was released by United Artists*; that was the 1962 feature *Road to Hong Kong*.)

There is also the new genre of "road movies," of which Mark Williams writes, "Broadly speaking, there are two types of road movie; those that simply pander to car chauvinism, and those that exploit a nation's belief in the freedom that lies across a state line or two, with a car being the means to that end." Among such varied types of "road movies" are *The Grapes of Wrath* (1940), *They Drive by Night* (1940), *Bonnie and Clyde* (1967), *Hells Angels on Wheels* (1967), *Easy Rider* (1969), *Cycle Savages* (1970), *Paper Moon* (1973), *Eat My Dust* (1976), and *Bobby Deerfield* (1977).

BIBLIOGRAPHY

Williams, Mark. *Road Movies*. New York: Proteus, 1982.

ROBERT BRUNTON STUDIOS, INC. Located at 5341–5601 Melrose Avenue in Hollywood, the Robert Brunton Studios, Inc., was one of the major rental studios in the late teens, with seven covered stages, 300,000 props, and thirty acres of land available for exterior scenes. Twenty production companies could operate there at one time. Formerly the home of Paralta, the Brunton Studios became the United Studios in the early twenties and eventually the home of Paramount Pictures*.

ROBERTSON-COLE COMPANY. Robertson-Cole Company was an importer and later producer/distributor out of which came RKO*. Indeed, the RKO studios were the former Robertson-Cole studios, which the company built in 1921 at the junction of Gower Street and Melrose Avenue in Hollywood on 13.5 acres of land which had previously been owned by the Hollywood Cemetery. Robertson-Cole was formed by the English-born Harry F. Robertson and the American Rufus Sidman Cole as an import/export company for which films were a sideline to Rohmer automobiles. Among the first films acquired by the company were *His Birthright* and *The Temple of Dusk*, both produced in 1918 by Haworth Pictures Corporation and starring Sessue Hayakawa. Robertson-Cole continued to distribute Haworth/Hayakawa films through 1920, initially through Exhibitors Mutual Distributing Corp. and later through Robertson-Cole Distributing Corporation. Robertson-Cole also released films produced by B. B. Features (starring Bessie Barriscale and her husband Howard Hickman), National Film Corporation of America*, Jesse D. Hampton Feature Corp. (starring William Desmond), and Brentwood Film Corporation* (starring either ZaSu Pitts or Florence Vidor and directed by King Vidor or Henry Kolker).

After the building of its studio, Robertson-Cole entered production, with its first Hollywood feature being *Kismet*, starring Otis Skinner in a recreation of his famous stage role. (The first Robertson-Cole production was actually *The Wonder Man*, shot at the former Solax* studios in Fort Lee and starring Georges Carpentier.) Both *Kismet* and *The Wonder Man* were released in 1920, with the interior scenes being shot at the Haworth Pictures studios.

In 1922, Robertson-Cole became Film Booking Offices of America (FBO)*, which was the immediate predecessor to RKO.

BIBLIOGRAPHY

Jewell, Richard B., with Vernon Harbin. *The RKO Story*. New York: Arlington House, 1982.

ROCKVILLE, LONG ISLAND. See PLANET FILM CORPORATION and RAVER FILM CORPORATION

ROCKY GLEN, PENNSYLVANIA. See FEDERAL FEATURE FILMS CORPORATION

ROGERS & COWAN, INC. Possibly the best-known public relations company in the United States, Rogers & Cowan, Inc., was founded in 1935 by Henry C. Rogers. Rogers' first major client—in 1939—was Rita Hayworth. In 1945, Rogers joined forces with Warren Cowan, and Rogers & Cowan was created. Among the company's clients have been Audrey Hepburn, Doris Day, Robert Redford, Paul Newman, Kirk Douglas, Shirley MacLaine, Natalie Wood, the Ford Motor Company, and Exxon. In the fifties, Rogers & Cowan was involved in a long-running feud with gossip columnist Hedda Hopper.

Address: 9665 Wilshire Boulevard, Beverly Hills, Calif. 90211.

BIBLIOGRAPHY

Rogers, Henry C. *Walking the Tightrope*. New York: William Morrow, 1980.

" 'Work for the Press' PR Firm's Slogan," *Editor & Publisher*, June 26, 1965, pp. 28, 30.

ROLANDS FEATURE FILM COMPANY. George K. Rolands was the director of films made by the Rolands Feature Film Company, which began in February 1914 to manufacture, import, and export films. Samuel Q. Edelstein was the manager of the company, which was located at 145 West 45 Street, New York, and whose first production was the police thriller *Trapped in the Great Metropolis*. Rolands' 1915 release *The Frank Case*, based on a case still in the courts at that time, was refused approval by the National Board of Review* but was, nevertheless, shown in New York.

BIBLIOGRAPHY

"New Feature Film Company," *The Moving Picture World*, February 7, 1914, p. 687.

ROLFE PHOTOPLAYS, INC. See B. A. ROLFE PHOTOPLAYS, INC.

ROLFE PRODUCTIONS, INC. See B. A. ROLFE PHOTOPLAYS, INC.

ROLIN FILM COMPANY. See HAL ROACH STUDIOS, INC.

ROMAYNE SUPER-FILM COMPANY. H. Y. Romayne was the president of the Romayne Super-Film Company, which was organized in July 1918 to produce five- and six-reel features for the states rights* market without using big names. Betty Burbank was the company's leading actress, Josephine Crowell played supporting roles, and Wyndham Gettins directed. Its first production was *Me und Gott*. Romayne used the David Horsley* studios in Los Angeles, with offices in the Marsh Strong Building, also in the city.

ROTHACKER-ALLER FILM LABORATORIES, INC. One of the major film laboratories of the silent era, with offices in Chicago and New York, the Rothacker-Aller Film Laboratories, Inc., plant opened at 5515 Melrose Avenue in Los Angeles on June 1, 1921. Under the presidency of Watterson R. Rothacker, it could handle up to three million feet of film a week, and among its customers were Mary Pickford, Marshall Neilan, Louis B. Mayer, William S. Hart, and Sessue Hayakawa.

ROTHACKER FILM MANUFACTURING COMPANY. See INDUSTRIAL FILM COMPANY

ROTHAPFEL PICTURES CORPORATION. Samuel L. Rothapfel, formerly the manager of the Strand*, Rialto*, and Rivoli theatres in New York, became a producer in February 1919, when he organized Rothapfel Pictures Corporation to supply exhibitors with complete screen programs, which he called "Rothapfel Unit Programs," containing a feature, shorts, scenics, and music, all related to each other. Frank G. Hall was vice-president, and Hall's distributing organization, the Independent Sales Corporation, handled the productions. Rothapfel himself selected the stories, engaged actors, and supervised the production. The feature in the first "Unit" was *False Gods*, co-directed by Wally Van.
BIBLIOGRAPHY
"Rothapfel's Unit Idea Progressing," *The Moving Picture World*, May 3, 1919, p. 674.
"Samuel Rothapfel, Program Producer," *The Moving Picture World*, February 22, 1919, p. 1048.

ROXY THEATRE. Located at 50 Street and Seventh Avenue in New York, the Roxy Theatre was one of America's greatest movie palaces, advertised as "The Cathedral of the Motion Picture." When it opened on March 11, 1927, with Gloria Swanson's first United Artists* release, *The Love of Sunya*, it was billed as the largest film theatre in the world. With its 5,920 seats it was surpassed only when the Radio City Music Hall* opened. It was named for its first managing director (until 1931), S. L. Rothapfel (1882–1936), and was noted for its lavish stage productions which preceded the feature presentation. The theatre became the venue for New York premieres of Fox* features. Live presentations ceased in February 1960, and a month later—on March 29, 1960—the theatre closed with *The Wind Cannot Read*. It was demolished that same year.

BIBLIOGRAPHY

Marquee, vol. II, no. 1, First Quarter 1979, special issue devoted to the Roxy.

RUBY FEATURE FILM COMPANY. Leon J. Rubenstein was the principal owner of the Ruby Feature Film Company, which was formed early in 1914. Its "twinplex" studio, which it rented to other companies, was located at 217 East 24 Street, New York. Frank Coygne was the director and Julia Kellity the company's star.

BIBLIOGRAPHY

"The Ruby Feature Studio," *The Moving Picture World*, January 24, 1914, p. 423.

RYNO FILM COMPANY, INC. John Noble was the principal director of Ryno Film Company, Inc., a production company formed in February 1913. Its manufacturing plant was located at 189 Terrace Place, City Island, New York. Albert Roscoe was assistant director, Emmett Williams the cameraman, and the players included Julia Bruns, Jane Fernley, and Glenn White.

SACK AMUSEMENT ENTERPRISES. Initially formed in 1920 by Alfred N. Sack, Sack Amusement Enterprises was a major producer/distributor of all-Negro features and shorts, starring and produced for black Americans. The company remained in existence through the seventies. Additionally, Sack organized Merit Films in 1946 as a 16mm subsidiary, Sack Television Enterprises in 1948, and Vogue Films in 1952 as a distributor of foreign art films in the South. He also opened in Dallas—where his various companies had their headquarters—the Coronet Theatre, in 1948, which he claimed to be the first art- and foreign-film theatre in the Southwest.

SAFETY FILM. See ACETATE FILM

ST. AUGUSTINE, FLORIDA. See STELLAR PHOTOPLAY COMPANY

ST. LOUIS MOTION PICTURE COMPANY. The St. Louis Motion Picture Company began in 1913 making Westerns starring George W. "Buck" Conner in "Frontier" brand films for the Universal* program. Gilbert P. Hamilton was the head of the company, and Eugenie Forde and Victoria Forde also appeared in the films. In November 1913, Hamilton and Conner became involved in the newly formed Albuquerque* Motion Picture Company, and by October 1914 O. E. Goebel was president of St. Louis. In January 1915, the "Frontier" brand was replaced by the "Premier" brand, released with the United Film Service*. Its studio at this time was at Santa Paula, outside of Los Angeles. Willis L. Robards and Lillian Hamilton starred in the later productions, which Hal Clements directed and for which his wife Olga Printzlau wrote scenarios.

THE "SAINT" SERIES. Based on the stories by Leslie Charteris, the "Saint" series featured three leading men in the role of Simon Templar (alias the Saint): Louis Hayward, George Sanders, and Hugh Sinclair. Hayward played the Saint in the first film in the series, *The Saint in New York* (1938), and in the last, *The*

Saint's Girl Friday (1954). George Sanders, who is the best-known Saint, played the role in the second through sixth films in the series: *The Saint Strikes Back* (1939), *The Saint in London* (1939), *The Saint's Double Trouble* (1940), *The Saint Takes Over* (1940), and *The Saint in Palm Springs* (1941). Hugh Sinclair played the Saint in two features: *The Saint's Vacation* (1941) and *The Saint Meets the Tiger* (1943). The last was produced by Republic Pictures*. All of the other Saint features were produced by RKO*. The Saint was later played on television by Roger Moore (1967–1969) and by Ian Ogilvy (1978).

BIBLIOGRAPHY

Zinman, David. *Saturday Afternoon at the Bijou*. New Rochelle, New York: Arlington House, 1973.

THE SAMUEL GOLDWYN COMPANY. An independent film and television distributor and producer, founded in 1978 by Samuel Goldwyn, Jr., when his father's estate was settled, the Samuel Goldwyn Company began with a library of 52 classic Goldwyn titles and by 1985 had distribution rights to some 500 films. The Company's chief involvement is in distribution, with only limited interest in production. In 1985, it financed a four-screen theatre complex in west Los Angeles. The first feature to be distributed by Goldwyn on a first-run theatrical basis was the Dutch film *Spetters* in 1981; it was followed by *Gregory's Girl* (1982), *Experience Preferred . . . But Not Essential* (1983), and *Stranger Than Paradise* (1984), among others. The Samuel Goldwyn Company operated out of the former Goldwyn Studios until their sale in 1982, when it moved to Century City.

Addresses: 10203 Santa Monica Boulevard, Los Angeles, Calif. 90067; 527 Madison Avenue, New York, N.Y. 10021.

BIBLIOGRAPHY

Auerbach, Alexander, "Special Treatment for Special Films," *Boxoffice*, November 1981, pp. 52, 54.
Berkowitz, Stan, "Old Studios Never Die," *Los Angeles*, January 1982, pp. 87–96.
Block, Alex Ben, "No Shareholders," *Forbes*, June 3, 1985, p. 228.

SAMUEL GOLDWYN, INC. Following his ouster by the stockholders of the Goldwyn Pictures Corporation*, Samuel Goldwyn (1882–1974) formed a new production company, of which he had absolute control. Samuel Goldwyn, Inc., was to become synonymous with quality entertainment in the years ahead, as Goldwyn displayed an uncanny knack for placing under contract upcoming film stars, such as Vilma Banky, Ronald Colman, Gary Cooper, Eddie Cantor, David Niven, and Danny Kaye. His writers were always of the highest calibre, as were his directors, notably William Wyler, whose association with Goldwyn lasted from 1937 to 1946. Goldwyn's one error in judgment was in signing the Russian-born actress Anna Sten and attempting to build her into a major Hollywood star.

The first feature to bear the words "Samuel Goldwyn Presents" was *The Eternal City* (1923), directed by George Fitzmaurice and starring Lionel Barrymore and Barbara La Marr. Its release led to an action by Goldwyn Pictures Corporation to prevent Goldwyn's use of his name on screen; initially, Goldwyn was required to add ''Not now connected with the Goldwyn Pictures Corporation'' to his main titles, but by private agreement, in 1924, the qualification was no longer sought.

Goldwyn eventually took over the former Mary Pickford–Douglas Fairbanks Studios at 7200 Santa Monica Boulevard, which had become known by the thirties as the United Artists Studios—Goldwyn was a major stockholder in United Artists*. In 1949, Goldwyn lost a bitter fight with Mary Pickford over control of the studio lot, and it was not until after many years of litigation that Goldwyn was able to purchase the studios for $1,920,000, with the name officially changing to the Goldwyn Studios on April 21, 1955.

Goldwyn's second wife, Frances, was very active in the running of the company with her husband, and on her death, in 1976, the studio was left to the Motion Picture and Television Fund*. Later that same year, the lot was sold to Warner Bros.* for $35 million and renamed the Warner Hollywood Studios.

Following Goldwyn's last feature, *Porgy and Bess*, in 1959, the Goldwyn studios were used as a rental lot. It suffered a number of disastrous fires, beginning with two small ones in 1972. The lot was struck by a $1 million fire in May 1974 and a $3 million fire in December 1975. There was also a much smaller fire in June 1976.

The following is a complete list of Goldwyn productions: *The Eternal City* (1923), *Potash and Perlmutter* (1923), *Cytherea* (1924), *Tarnish* (1924), *In Hollywood with Potash and Perlmutter* (1924), *A Thief in Paradise* (1925), *His Supreme Moment* (1925), *The Dark Angel* (1925), *Stella Dallas* (1925), *Partners Again, with Potash and Perlmutter* (1926), *The Winning of Barbara Worth* (1926), *The Night of Love* (1927), *The Magic Flame* (1927), *The Devil Dancer* (1927), *Two Lovers* (1928), *The Awakening* (1928), *The Rescue* (1929), *This Is Heaven* (1929), *Bulldog Drummond* (1929), *Condemned* (1929), *Raffles* (1930), *Whoopee* (1930), *One Heavenly Night* (1930), *The Devil to Pay* (1930), *Street Scene* (1931), *The Unholy Garden* (1931), *Palmy Days* (1931), *Tonight or Never* (1931), *Arrowsmith* (1931), *The Greeks Had a Word for Them* (1932), *Cynara* (1932), *The Kid from Spain* (1932), *The Masquerader* (1933), *Roman Scandals* (1933), *Nana* (1934), *We Live Again* (1934), *Kid Millions* (1934), *The Wedding Night* (1935), *The Dark Angel* (1935), *Barbary Coast* (1935), *Splendor* (1935), *Strike Me Pink* (1936), *These Three* (1936), *Dodsworth* (1936), *Come and Get It* (1936), *Beloved Enemy* (1936), *Woman Chases Man* (1937), *Hurricane* (1937), *Stella Dallas* (1937), *Dead End* (1937), *The Adventures of Marco Polo* (1938), *The Goldwyn Follies* (1938), *The Cowboy and the Lady* (1938), *The Real Glory* (1939), *Wuthering Heights* (1939), *They Shall Have Music* (1939), *Raffles* (1940), *The Westerner* (1940), *The Little Foxes* (1941), *Ball of Fire* (1941), *The Pride of the Yankees* (1942), *They Got Me Covered* (1943), *The North Star* (1943), *Up in Arms* (1944), *The Princess and the Pirate* (1944), *Wonder Man* (1945), *The Kid from Brooklyn* (1946), *The Best Years of Our Lives* (1946), *The Secret Life of Walter Mitty* (1947), *The Bishop's Wife* (1947), *A Song Is Born* (1948),

Enchantment (1948), *Roseanna McCoy* (1949), *My Foolish Heart* (1949), *Our Very Own* (1950), *Edge of Doom* (1950), *I Want You* (1951), *Hans Christian Andersen* (1952), *Guys and Dolls* (1955), and *Porgy and Bess* (1959).

All films up to and including *The Dark Angel* (1925) were released by First National Pictures*. All films from *Stella Dallas* (1925) to *The Westerner* were released by United Artists. All films from *The Little Foxes* to *Hans Christian Andersen* were released by RKO*. *Guys and Dolls* was released by M-G-M and *Porgy and Bess* by Columbia*.

BIBLIOGRAPHY

Easton, Carol. *The Search for Sam Goldwyn: A Biography*. New York: William Morrow, 1976.

Epstein, Lawrence J. *Samuel Goldwyn*. Boston: Twayne, 1981.

Goldwyn, Samuel. *Behind the Screen*. New York: George H. Doran, 1923.

Griffith, Richard. *Samuel Goldwyn: The Producer and His Films*. New York: Museum of Modern Art, 1956.

Johnston, Alva. *The Great Goldwyn*. New York: Random House, 1937.

Marill, Alvin H. *Samuel Goldwyn Presents*. Cranbury, New Jersey: A. S. Barnes, 1976.

Marx, Arthur. *Goldwyn: A Biography of the Man behind the Myth*. New York: W. W. Norton, 1976.

RESOURCES

Papers: Academy of Motion Picture Arts and Sciences (scrapbooks of clippings from later Goldwyn features and still books of sets for various features).

SAN ANTONIO, TEXAS. See MELIES MANUFACTURING COMPANY and SUNSET MOTION PICTURE CORPORATION

SAN FRANCISCO. San Francisco has been featured by name, if not physically, in a number of classic Hollywood features. Perhaps the best known is *San Francisco* (1936), with its title song performed by Jeanette MacDonald. Al Jolson was seen singing at San Francisco's Coffee Dan's in *The Jazz Singer* (1927). *The Maltese Falcon* (1941) is set in San Francisco, with Sam Spade's office located at 111 Sutter Street. Other films with San Francisco locations include *More Pay, Less Work* (1926), *One Way Passage* (1931), *Klondike Annie* (1936), *After the Thin Man* (1936), *Flame of the Barbary Coast* (1945), and *Sudden Fear* (1952).

The first major feature to include scenes actually shot on location in San Francisco was probably *Greed* (1924). As of 1985, major producers with headquarters in San Francisco included John Korty, Francis Ford Coppola with his Zoetrope* Studios, and George Lucas with Lucasfilm* in nearby San Rafael.

BIBLIOGRAPHY

Knowles, Eleanor, "A Late-Movie Buff's Guide to San Francisco," *Passages*, April 1977, pp. 16–17.

SAN MATEO, CALIFORNIA. See LIBERTY MOTION PICTURE COMPANY

SAN RAFAEL, CALIFORNIA. See DOUGLASS NATURAL COLOR FILM COMPANY, LTD., OF SAN RAFAEL, CALIFORNIA

SANTA BARBARA. See AMERICAN FILM MANUFACTURING COMPANY

SANTA BARBARA MOTION PICTURE COMPANY. Dr. Elmer J. Boeske, a prominent Santa Barbara dentist, socialite, polo player, and two-time mayor, organized the Santa Barbara Motion Picture Company in association with other Santa Barbara businessmen. Production commenced on July 29, 1914, with Lorimer Johnston, formerly with American*, as director-general. Johnston brought his best cameraman from American, Roy F. Overbaugh, with him, and Overbaugh, in turn, brought his assistant cameraman, Victor Fleming. Johnston's wife, Caroline Francis Cooke, an actress formerly with Selig*, was the leading lady, while Jack Nelson played opposite her. Jane Scott was the ingenue, Baron Erik von Ritzau was the "heavy," and Harry T. DeVere played character roles. Santa Barbara planned to make four-reel features from well-known novels and plays, with Sawyer* as its initial distributor.

The company's first production, *The Envoy Extraordinary*, was written and directed by Johnston, who left the company soon after, in September 1914. Henry W. Otto, formerly with Selig and American, signed to replace him, but he too left shortly thereafter, to return to American. Cameraman Overbaugh, reminiscing many years later, explained that the reason he and some of the others associated with Santa Barbara left after such short stays was that "the local gentry that put up the money felt that they should be able to get their sons and daughters and wives to play principal parts," and the resulting films were simply no good.

In November 1914, Santa Barbara contracted to release two brands, a comedy and a drama, with the Mica Film Corporation on the Kriterion* program. Aubrey M. Kennedy became the general manager. William Robert Daly directed the dramatic company, headed by Fritzi Brunette, and Bert Angeles directed comedies with Reta Williams. Santa Barbara became the principal producing company for Kriterion, but in June 1915, after the latter's demise, it became part of the Associated Service. Dr. Boeske, at that time, claimed he had lost $25,000 in the year of his ownership.

BIBLIOGRAPHY
"New Producing Company," *The New York Dramatic Mirror*, July 8, 1914, p. 24.

SANTA PAULA, CALIFORNIA. See ST. LOUIS MOTION PICTURE COMPANY

SARATOGA SPRINGS, FLORIDA. See SAWYER, INC.

SAWYER, INC. A. H. Sawyer resigned as the general manager of the Kinemacolor* Company of America and formed Sawyer, Inc., in May 1914, to produce short comedies, no longer than two reels in length, featuring celebrities such as De Wolf Hopper, and to distribute these as well as films from other producers. It used an open-air studio in Asbury Park, New Jersey, and one in

Saratoga Springs, New York, and its offices were located at 1600 Broadway, New York. William H. Rudolph was the general manager. Its first big release was the seven-reel feature *The Lightning Conductor*, with Dustin Farnum, directed by William Elliott.

The distribution wing became known as "Sawyer Film Mart," and among the companies releasing through it were the Santa Barbara Motion Picture Company*, the Liberty Motion Picture Company*, Bosburn Photoplay Company, the Canadian Bioscope Company, Esanja Film Company of Detroit, Trans-Oceanic Films, Ltd., the Japanese-American Film Company*, and the Pheonix Film Company. In December 1914, the company increased its capitalization, changed its name to Sawyer Film Corporation, and began a new policy of purchasing negatives outright and financing production companies releasing through it exclusively. It went out of business in March 1915.

BIBLIOGRAPHY

"Sawyer, Inc., Quarters Superb," *The Moving Picture World*, July 11, 1914, pp. 258–259.

SCENTOVISION. See AROMARAMA AND SMELL-O-VISION

SCIENCE FICTION FILMS. A genre which overlaps into the field of the horror film* and which is generally conceded to have been introduced by French filmmaker Georges Méliès (1861–1938), science fiction was of little interest to American silent filmmakers. Universal and the Williamson Brothers produced a 1916 version of Jules Verne's *20,000 Leagues under the Sea*, and, in 1929, M-G-M* eventually released a screen version of Verne's *The Mysterious Island*. Willis O'Brien provided the special effects* for *The Lost World* (1925). One of the most unusual of silent science fiction films was *The Last Man of Earth* (1924), a Fox* feature directed by J. G. Blystone, with Earle Fox in the title role; it takes place after an epidemic of "masculitis" in 1954 has killed off all men over the age of fourteen.

The first science fiction film from the sound era was *Just Imagine* (1930), one of the few examples of an intentionally funny science fiction subject, with interpolated musical numbers. Also in 1930, Cecil B. DeMille's *Madame Satan* was released; it was not supposed to be funny, but was. In 1933, RKO* released *King Kong*, directed by Merian C. Cooper and Ernest Schoedsack, a classic of the subgenre of monster films which was revived in the fifties with such productions as *The Thing* (1951), *Them!* (1954), *Tarantula* (1956), and *The Fly* (1958). The last was responsible for two sequels, *Return of the Fly* (1959) and *The Curse of the Fly* (1965).

The science fiction genre is very much reminiscent of a comic strip, and nowhere is this more apparent than in the area of serials*, which have frequently utilized science fiction backgrounds. Among the best known of such serials are *The Phantom Empire* (1935), *Flash Gordon* (1936), *Dick Tracy* (1937), *Flash*

Gordon's Trip to Mars (1938), *Buck Rogers* (1939), *Flash Gordon Conquers the Universe* (1940), *Captain Midnight* (1942), *Jack Armstrong* (1947), *King of the Rocket Men* (1949), and *Radar Men from the Moon* (1952).

On a more serious level, science fiction films have dramatized the dangers of nuclear war and the evils that the future may hold with the "Planet of the Apes" series* from 20th Century-Fox* and *On the Beach* (1959). Stanley Kubrick presented a lyrical view of the future in *2001: A Space Odyssey* (1968), a tragically comical one in *Dr. Strangelove or How I Learned to Stop Worrying and Love the Bomb* (1964), and a disturbingly violent view in *A Clockwork Orange* (1971).

Novelist Jules Verne's view of a world of science fiction adventure has continued to appeal to filmmakers, notably with *20,000 Leagues under the Sea* (1954), *Journey to the Center of the Earth* (1959), and *Master of the World* (1961).

With his background in puppet films and special effects, George Pal (1908–1980) was a major figure in science fiction films of the fifties and early sixties. Among his productions were *Destination Moon* (1950), *When Worlds Collide* (1951), *War of the Worlds* (1953), *The Conquest of Space* (1955), *The Time Machine* (1960), and *Atlantis the Lost Continent* (1961). A pupil of Pal's who has a considerable cult following is Ray Harryhausen (born 1920), whose films include *The Beast from 20,000 Fathoms* (1953), *Earth vs. the Flying Saucers* (1956), *The 7th Voyage of Sinbad* (1958), and a dozen other films produced in the United Kingdom.

Prior to 1950, science fiction films were relatively juvenile in appeal—a typical example was *Dr. Cyclops* (1940), with Albert Dekker in the title role of a mad scientist miniaturizing a group of American explorers in the Peruvian jungle. *The Day the Earth Stood Still* (1951) heralded a new era for the genre. Director Robert Wise presented a believable story of an alien from outer space who lands in Washington, D.C., to warn the world of the dangers of nuclear war. Thanks to the lead this film showed, even what might have been an immature feature, *Invasion of the Body Snatchers* (1956) became another frighteningly realistic production dealing with visitors from another planet.

In *The Birds* (1963), Alfred Hitchcock presented a typically terrifying view of a world in which birds take their revenge. Miniaturization—a favorite topic with filmmakers—allowed a group of scientists to explore the human body internally in *Fantastic Voyage* (1966). *Logan's Run* (1976) presented a view of a future world in which no one lived beyond the age of thirty. Equally disturbing glimpses at the world of the future were offered by *Silent Running* (1972), *Westworld* (1973), *Soylent Green* (1973), and *Rollerball* (1975). However, there was also Woody Allen to provide an amusing one in *Sleeper* (1973).

A new era of special effects in science fiction films was heralded in 1977 by *Star Wars*. The eighties saw the production of science fiction films in which the special effects rather than the actors were the stars, as exemplified by *Altered States* (1980), *The Empire Strikes Back* (1980), *Blade Runner* (1982), *E. T. The*

Extra-Terrestrial (1982), *The Thing* (1982), *Tron* (1982), and *Return of the Jedi* (1983). Also worthy of mention are the "James Bond," the "Superman," and the "Star Trek" series.

BIBLIOGRAPHY

Baxter, John. *Science Fiction in the Cinema*. New York: A. S. Barnes, 1970.

Benson, Michael. *Vintage Science Fiction Films, 1896–1949*. Jefferson, North Carolina: McFarland, 1985.

Brosnan, John. *Future Tense*. New York: St. Martin's Press, 1978.

Hardy, Phil. *Science Fiction*. New York: William Morrow, 1984.

Johnson, William, editor. *Focus on the Science Fiction Film*. Englewood Cliffs, New Jersey: Prentice-Hall, 1972.

Parish, James Robert, and Michael R. Pitts. *The Great Science Fiction Pictures*. Metuchen, New Jersey: Scarecrow Press, 1977.

Warren, Bill. *Keep Watching the Skies!* Jefferson, North Carolina: McFarland, 1982.

Wright, Gene. *The Science Fiction Image*. New York: Facts on File, 1983.

SCOPITONE. See SOUNDIES

SCREEN ACTORS GUILD. In March 1933, film producers ordered that all contract players take a 50 percent cut in salaries and that all independent performers take a 20 percent cut. Without an organization to speak on their behalf, the actors had no alternative but to accept the producers' decree. However, this action led six actors—Ralph Morgan, Grant Mitchell, Berton Churchill, Charles Miller, Kenneth Thomson, and Alden Gay Thomson—to meet and conceive of the notion of a Screen Actors Guild, which was officially incorporated on June 30, 1933.

Among the first group of actors to join the Guild were Boris Karloff, C. Aubrey Smith, James Cagney, Groucho Marx, Eddie Cantor, George Raft, Robert Montgomery, Fredric March, Adolphe Menjou, Gary Cooper, Spencer Tracy, Paul Muni, and Miriam Hopkins. The Guild affiliated with the American Federation of Labor in 1935, and, in 1937, following a strike call, the studios officially recognized the Guild's existence.

The Screen Actors Guild (SAG) has more than 44,000 members and is active in both film and television. It negotiates collective bargaining contracts on behalf of its members, provides pension and welfare benefits, regulates relationships between actors and agents, and has branches in Hollywood, New York, Boston, Chicago, and other major cities. The Guild has taken strike action in 1952–1953, 1955, 1960, and 1980. Since its inception, it has published *The Screen Guild Magazine* (first known as *The Screen Player*, 1934–1938), *Official Bulletin of the Screen Actors Guild* (1938–1940), *Screen Actor* (1938–1947), and *Screen Actor* (1959 to present).

Guild presidents have been: Ralph Morgan (1933), Eddie Cantor (1933–1935), Robert Montgomery (1935–1938), Ralph Morgan (1938–1940), Edward Arnold (1940–1942), James Cagney (1942–1944), George Murphy (1944–1946), Robert Montgomery (1946–1947), Ronald Reagan (1947–1952), Walter Pidgeon (1952–

1957), Leon Ames (1957–1958), Howard Keel (1958–1959), Ronald Reagan (1959–1960), George Chandler (1960–1963), Dana Andrews (1963–1965), Charlton Heston (1965–1971), John Gavin (1971–1973), Dennis Weaver (1973–1975), Kathleen Nolan (1975–1979), William Schallert (1979–1981), Edward Asner (1981–1985), and Patty Duke (1985-).

Addresses: 7750 Sunset Boulevard, Hollywood, Calif. 90046; 1700 Broadway, 18th Floor, New York, N.Y. 10019; offices in other major U.S. cities.

BIBLIOGRAPHY

The ABC of the Screen Actors Guild. Hollywood, Calif.: Screen Actors Guild, 1940.

McGilligan, Patrick, "Star Wars," *Films and Filming*, May 1982, pp. 42–43.

Ross, Murray. *Stars and Strikes.* New York: Columbia University Press, 1941.

The Story of the Screen Actors Guild. Hollywood, Calif.: Screen Actors Guild, 1980.

SCREEN CLASSICS, INC. Screen Classics, Inc., was formed in 1918 to release and present features of the highest quality for first-run presentation. Although connected in some manner with Metro*, Screen Classics also handled films made by other producers, with its first two releases being *Revelation*, with Nazimova, and *Lest We Forget*, about the sinking of the Titanic, starring a survivor of the tragedy, Rita Jolivet. Later, Screen Classics marketed a series of Nazimova features. Its offices were at 1476 Broadway, New York.

BIBLIOGRAPHY

"Screen Classics Takes Over Metro Specials," *The Moving Picture World*, April 27, 1918, p. 552.

THE SCREEN CLUB. The Screen Club began in a Broadway café on Labor Day, 1912, with the "triple purpose of unity, advancement, and preservation of the motion picture art, and composed of those allied in the development of the art," which at its inception meant managers, directors, actors, authors, cameramen, and photoplay newspapermen. Those attending the first meeting were Dell Henderson, Lawrence McGill, Pierce Kingsley, Frank Powell, C. A. "Doc" Willat, Herbert Brenon, William E. Shay, King Baggot, William Camp, Frank Russell, H. C. Judson, George F. Blaisdell, Thomas Malloy, P. J. Carroll, and Calder Johnston. By the fourth meeting, on September 14, 1912, the membership, which required a twenty-dollar deposit, had risen to 101.

King Baggot, the first president, was credited with having initiated the idea for the club. John Bunny was the first vice-president. The club, which sought "to raise the industry to the highest status of respectability and dignity," and to eliminate existing evils, served also as a social club, holding annual balls and Thanksgiving dinners. The first clubhouse, located at 163 West 45 Street, New York, contained a library, smoking room, music room, dining hall, café, and meeting hall. The clubhouse acquired the following year was a mansion located at 165 West 47 Street. In 1917, the Club was located at 117 West 45 Street.

James Kirkwood succeeded Baggot as president in 1914, and other presidents included Billy Quirk and Joseph W. Farnham. In later years, Screen Clubs were established in other cities, including San Francisco, Pittsburgh, and Montreal.
BIBLIOGRAPHY
"Screen Club a Winner," *The Moving Picture World*, September 28, 1912, p. 1283.
"The Screen Club Is a Fact," *The Moving Picture World*, September 21, 1912, p. 1163.
"Screen Club Opens Its Door," *The Moving Picture World*, November 23, 1912, p. 778.

SCREEN DIRECTORS GUILD INCORPORATED. See DIRECTORS GUILD OF AMERICA, INC.

SCREEN DIRECTORS INTERNATIONAL GUILD. See DIRECTORS GUILD OF AMERICA, INC.

SCREEN EXTRAS COALITION. See SCREEN EXTRAS GUILD

SCREEN EXTRAS GUILD. An AFL-CIO affiliate, with headquarters in Los Angeles, the Screen Extras Guild (SEG) was formed in 1945 as a breakaway from the Screen Actors Guild (SAG)*. It acts as a negotiating agent with producers regarding appropriate pay for extras, although it has never been able to operate a closed-shop situation as far as the hiring of extras is concerned. It has certainly helped to increase the wage scales for extras; in 1959, a general extra could earn $22.05 for an eight-hour day and a dress extra (one who could provide a suitable wardrobe) could earn $29.04, an increase from $15.56 a day in 1950. By 1965 the daily wage for an extra was $27.31, and by 1976 the average daily wage was $47.50.

Through the years, extras who are members of the Guild have included famous stuntman Richard Talmadge and former silent star Franklin Farnum (who was the Guild's president from 1956 to 1959). In recent years, the Screen Extras Guild has been involved in many internal disputes. In 1980, it commenced talks with the Screen Actors Guild regarding a merger, which the majority of members supported, but which led to the formation of the Screen Extras Coalition, consisting of extras working outside of the union framework. The SEG-SAG merger was overwhelmingly rejected by Screen Actors Guild members in 1984.

Address: 3629 Cahuenga Boulevard, West Hollywood, Calif. 90068.

SCREEN PRODUCERS GUILD. See PRODUCERS GUILD OF AMERICA, INC.

SCREEN PUBLICISTS GUILD. See PUBLICISTS GUILD OF AMERICA

SCREEN WRITERS GUILD. See WRITERS GUILD OF AMERICA

SCREWBALL COMEDY. There is no agreement as to exactly what constitutes a screwball comedy. The term is used, basically, to describe a type of comedy that includes whimsy or the more pleasant aspects of insanity. It is the genre of "daffy" comedies in which the heroes and heroines are "wacky." It emerged from the American depression in the mid-thirties and had its origins, frequently, in stage comedies, particularly those of Philip Barry. The best-known directors associated with screwball comedies were Frank Capra, Leo McCarey, and Preston Sturges, and its better-known stars were Cary Grant and Carole Lombard. Screwball comedies include *My Man Godfrey* (1936), *The Awful Truth* (1937), *Nothing Sacred* (1937), *Bringing Up Baby* (1938), *Holiday* (1938), *You Can't Take It with You* (1938), and *The Lady Eve* (1941). The "Thin Man" series, starring William Powell and Myrna Loy, is a blend of thriller and screwball comedy. The genre lost its popularity in the forties but has, arguably, been revived with features such as Peter Bogdanovich's *What's Up Doc?* (1972).
BIBLIOGRAPHY

Cavell, Stanley. *Pursuits of Happiness*. Cambridge, Massachusetts: Harvard University Press, 1981.

Sarris, Andrew, "The Sex Comedy without Sex," *American Film*, March 1978, pp. 8–15.

Sennett, Ted. *Lunatics and Lovers*. New Rochelle, New York: Arlington House, 1973.

"SEE AMERICA FIRST." See KINEMACOLOR COMPANY OF AMERICA

SELECT FILM BOOKING AGENCY. The Select Film Booking Agency was created early in 1915 by the Famous Players Film Company to exploit and distribute its prestigious film *The Eternal City* and other films which were too long or expensive to be released as program pictures. Select aligned important legitimate and motion picture theatres throughout the country to present its elaborate features, at the minimum admission price of twenty-five cents, for indefinite engagements to be determined by each film's popularity. Adolph Zukor, in announcing the formation of Select, stated that its operation would put motion pictures "on the plane of legitimate theatrical offerings of the most serious type. The adoption of this policy will greatly dignify the public aspects of the trade, as it will now assume every iota of systemization associated with the business methods of the theater." *The Eternal City* opened at Philadelphia's Chestnut Street Opera House. Although Select announced it was ready to release any producer's feature, if it was distinctive enough to warrant its elaborate exploitation, it refused to consider *The Birth of a Nation*, presumably because it was thought that its subject matter would demean the presumably more pristine *The Eternal City*.

BIBLIOGRAPHY
"First Move for Higher Prices," *The Moving Picture World*, February 13, 1915, p. 966.
"Select Film Booking Agency," *The Moving Picture World*, March 20, 1915, p. 1744.

SELECT PICTURES CORPORATION. See LEWIS J. SELZNICK PRODUCTIONS, INC.

SELIG POLYSCOPE COMPANY. William N. Selig, formerly a traveling magician and minstrel show operator, known as the Colonel, formed one of the earliest motion picture companies on April 9, 1896, at 43 Peck Court (later Eighth Street) in Chicago, when he and a partner developed a projector called the Polyscope and a camera, both modeled on drawings of the Lumière camera-projector. First called the Mutoscope & Film Co., the company's name changed after a year to W. N. Selig Co., and finally, six months later, to the Selig Polyscope Company. Selig's first films were slapstick comedies less than fifty feet in length. To avoid the patent suits of the Edison Company*, Selig shot travel films in the Southwest during the first years of the company's operations. In April and May 1901, Selig made films for Armour and Company, of the Chicago stockyards, to document the operations of its slaughterhouse and meat-packing plant. Selig later claimed that this was the first time that motion pictures had been taken by artificial light. In the spring of 1904, Selig produced what he called his "really first" picture, the 700-foot comedy *Humpty Dumpty*. Also in 1904, G. M. Anderson, who was later to found the Essanay Company*, convinced Selig to let him produce Westerns* in western settings.

When Edison brought Selig to court, Philip D. Armour provided free legal representation to Selig, during 1905–1907, in return for prints of the films Selig had previously made, to be used for public relations purposes, because at that time Armour suffered from the attack made on the meat industry by Upton Sinclair in *The Jungle*. Selig joined with Edison and the other trust companies to form the Motion Picture Patents Company* and released its films through the General Film Company.

In September 1907, Selig moved into a new plant at Irving Park Road and Western Avenue, where Thomas S. Nash, who had been with the company since 1907 as an electrician and cameraman, became the general superintendent. Former stage director Francis Boggs was sent west to direct for Selig (in 1911, he was murdered in the Selig Edendale studio by a Japanese gardener). Boggs and his company, which included Thomas Santschi, James L. McGee, James Crosby, Harry Todd, Gene Ward, and Mrs. Boggs, went to California, where, in the early spring of 1908, they shot some scenes for *The Count of Monte Cristo*, thus claiming to be the first motion picture company to shoot a narrative film in the Los Angeles area. By 1909, Boggs had established a permanent company in the West, and he wrote and directed what is claimed to be the first film made completely in Los Angeles, *The Heart of a Race Tout*. The Selig studio in Edendale, on Allesandro Street, constructed in 1909–1910, was managed by

James L. McGee. At this time, Otis Turner wrote and directed the films produced at the Chicago plant.

Selig's first release of 1,000 feet in length was *The Female Highwayman*, made in the fall of 1906. Selig's two-reel *Damon and Pythias*, released in June 1908, may have been the first film of that length produced in the United States. Its *The Coming of Columbus*, made in the fall of 1911 and released May 1912, was claimed to be the first three-reel picture filmed in America. *The Two Orphans* and *Cinderella*, each three-reelers, were produced soon after.

Selig's *Hunting Big Game in Africa*, shot at its Chicago studio with its own animals and released in May 1909, was an early animal picture, which recreated ex-President Theodore Roosevelt's hunting expedition at the time, and enjoyed great success. In 1911, the Selig Jungle Zoo, located opposite Eastlake Park on Mission Road in Los Angeles, was started with a nucleus of animals owned by showman Big Otto, which had been featured in Selig films shot in Jacksonville, Florida. The zoo grew to be the largest collection of wild animals in the world, containing, in 1915, 700 animals and birds on its thirty-two acres. A Glendale studio opened later, and there Tom Mix directed and starred in Westerns. Thomas A. Persons was the supervisor of all of Selig's Western studios.

On December 29, 1913, Selig released the first episode of what is considered to be the first true motion picture serial*, *The Adventures of Kathlyn*, starring Kathlyn Williams. In 1914, the company produced *The Spoilers*, the first screen version of the popular Rex Beach novel.

Selig, along with Vitagraph*, Lubin*, and Essanay*, formed V-L-S-E* in April 1915 to distribute its features. In the next year, the distribution group, K-E-S-E, with Kleine* and Edison replacing Vitagraph and Lubin, was formed to continue distributing features. The Selig Company stopped production in 1918, although Colonel Selig continued to be involved in various film activities through the thirties.

Directors who worked for Selig included Colin Campbell, Tom Mix, Lawrence Marston, Thomas Santschi, George Nicholls, Lloyd Carleton, Marshall Neilan, Jack Le Saint, and Frank Beal. Players included Kathlyn Williams, Thomas Santschi, Tom Mix, Wheeler Oakman, Charles Clary, Hobart Bosworth, Betty Harte, William V. Mong, Al Garcia, Herbert Rawlinson, Bessie Eyton, Nick Cogley, Baby Lilian Wade, Myrtle Stedman, Eugenie Besserer, and Harold Lockwood.

BIBLIOGRAPHY

Blaisdell, George, "Great Selig Enterprise," *The Moving Picture World*, July 10, 1915, pp. 227–228.

Bosworth, Hobart, "The Picture Forty-Niners," *Photoplay*, December 1915, pp. 75–81.

Edwards, Leo, "An Afternoon at the Selig Studio," *Feature Movie Magazine*, April 15, 1915, pp. 34–39, 56–57.

Lahue, Kalton C. *Motion Picture Pioneer: The Selig Polyscope Company*. South Brunswick, New Jersey: A. S. Barnes, 1973.

"Making Selig Pictures," *The Film Index*, November 20, 1909, pp. 4–6.
"The Selig at Edendale," *The Moving Picture World*, July 10, 1915, p. 230.
"Twenty-One Years in the Business," *The Moving Picture World*, May 12, 1917, pp. 948–949.
RESOURCES
Papers: Academy of Motion Picture Arts and Sciences.
Photographs: Academy of Motion Picture Arts and Sciences.

SELZNICK INTERNATIONAL PICTURES. Selznick International Pictures
was formed as an independent production company by David O. Selznick (1902–
1965) in 1935. The company set up office at what is now the Laird International
Studios* in Culver City, utilizing the colonial front of the studios as a trademark.
The first film to be produced by the new organization was *Little Lord Fauntleroy*
(1936), directed by John Cromwell and starring Dolores Costello and Freddie
Bartholomew. It was released by United Artists*, as were the following Selznick
International films: *The Garden of Allah* (1936), *A Star Is Born* (1937), *The
Prisoner of Zenda* (1937), *Nothing Sacred* (1937), *The Adventures of Tom Sawyer*
(1938), *The Young in Heart* (1938), *Made for Each Other* (1939), *Intermezzo*
(1939), and *Rebecca* (1940). The best known of all Selznick International Pictures,
Gone with the Wind (1939), was released by M-G-M*.

Following a legal dispute with United Artists in 1946, Selznick set up his own
distribution company, Selznick Releasing Organization (SRO), through which
he released his final independent productions: *Duel in the Sun* (1947), *The
Paradine Case* (1948), and *Portrait of Jennie* (1949). Prior to a protracted
European trip, Selznick closed down his production company in 1949. With the
exception of *Gone with the Wind*, the rights to all the Selznick independent
productions were eventually acquired by ABC Television.
BIBLIOGRAPHY
Behlmer, Rudy, editor. *Memo from David O. Selznick*. New York: Viking Press, 1972.
Haver, Ronald. *David O. Selznick's Hollywood*. New York: Alfred A. Knopf, 1980.
RESOURCES
Films: University of Texas at Austin (Selznick's personal prints); Museum of Modern
    Art (35mm preservation).
Papers: University of Texas at Austin.

SELZNICK INTERNATIONAL STUDIOS. See LAIRD INTERNATIONAL
STUDIOS

SELZNICK PICTURES CORPORATION. See LEWIS J. SELZNICK
PRODUCTIONS, INC.

SELZNICK RELEASING CORPORATION. See SELZNICK INTER-
NATIONAL PICTURES

SENSURROUND. Sensurround is the trademark of a special effects* system developed by Universal Pictures* in 1974, initially to enhance the tremor sequences in *Earthquake*. The system is one that adds air vibrations (low frequency signals) to the soundtrack of a film during the dubbing process. Special equipment installed in theatres decodes the signals on the soundtrack, triggering a series of audible and subaudible effects, and the vibration of air movement against the bodies and ears of the audience creates the illusion of participation in an event such as an earthquake. Since its introduction, Universal has considerably enhanced the system, and its potential has been realized in features such as *Midway* (1976), *Rollercoaster* (1977), and *Battlestar Galactica* (1979). By 1981, more than 700 theatres had been equipped with the special decoding units, amplifiers and speakers necessary to reproduce the effect of Sensurround, but Universal appears to have no plans for continued use of the system.

BIBLIOGRAPHY

Leonard, Robert, "Recording *Rollercoaster* Sound in Sensurround," *American Cinematographer*, June 1977, pp. 648–649.

SERIAL FILM COMPANY. William Steiner was the supervising director and the head of the Serial Film Company, formed in 1916. Its studio was in Cliffside, New Jersey, and its first production was the serial *The Yellow Menace*, which was released by the Unity Sales Corporation*. Following this, the company made a series of two-reel comedy-dramas about amateur detective Philo Gubb, which was filmed in Jacksonville, Florida. Serial also produced a seven-reel feature directed by Pierce Kingsley.

SERIALS. A genre almost exclusively limited to the United States and France, serials were produced from 1912 to 1956. They were generally cheaply made with shoddy production values, but they enjoyed an appeal that has continued long after the last serial was released. Divided into chapters, serials were intended to hold the interest of their audience from one week's release through the next. Thus, the concept of ending a chapter, or an episode, with a "cliff-hanger" was conceived. Some serials were comprised of self-contained weekly episodes, and these are more correctly identified as series.

The first serial, which was actually a series, was *What Happened to Mary?*, starring Mary Fuller and released by the Edison Company* in 1912. As with many silent serials, it was produced in association with a popular magazine— in this case McClure's *Ladies World*—which published the story concurrently with the serial's release. The first true serial was *The Adventures of Kathlyn*, directed by F. J. Grandon, starring Kathlyn Williams, and produced by the Selig Polyscope Company* for release from 1913 to 1914. *The Adventures of Kathlyn* was released in thirteen episodes; during the silent era there was no uniformity as to the number of episodes to a serial. *The Hazards of Helen*, which the Kalem Company* produced for release from 1914 to 1916, had two leading ladies, first Helen Holmes and later Helen Gibson, and was 119 episodes long. (However, it was not a cliff-hanger serial.) With the coming of sound, serials were limited to either twelve or fifteen episodes. The length of each episode could vary from one to two reels during the silent era, but with the coming of sound it was usual for the first episode to be three reels in length and the remainder to comprise two reels each.

Silent serial stars were usually women. The best known was Pearl White (1889–1938), whose serials included *The Perils of Pauline* (1914), *The Exploits of Elaine* (1915), *The Fatal Ring* (1917), and *Plunder* (1923). Second in popularity to Pearl White was Ruth Roland (1892–1937), whose serials included *The Red Circle* (1915), *Hands Up!* (1918), and *The Adventures of Ruth* (1919). Other silent "serial queens" included Allene Ray, Mollie King, Marie Walcamp, Arline Pretty, and Grace Darmond. The best known of male serial stars were Eddie Polo, Ben Wilson, Harry Houdini, Elmo Lincoln, Joe Bonomo, and William Desmond.

Just as Pathé* was the leading producer of silent serials so was Republic Pictures* during the sound era. As with the silent era, the serials were intended largely for a juvenile audience—for screenings at Saturday afternoon matinees— and plot lines were suitably ludicrous, with no subtle shading in the depiction of heroism and villainy.

Men were more prominent than women in sound serials, with the best-known heroes of the genre having been Reed Howes, Tom Tyler, Johnny Mack Brown, Larry "Buster" Crabbe, Ray "Crash" Corrigan, and Buck Jones. The sound serial also became a refuge for the former silent stars, such as Jack Mulhall. Frequently, their producers would turn to comic-strip heroes, such as Superman or Flash Gordon, for inspiration.

Republic made its last serial in 1955, and the honor of producing the final American serial went to Columbia Pictures* for *Blazing the Overland Trail*, released in the summer of 1956. It was directed by Spencer Gordon Bennet, the best-known name in serial direction.

BIBLIOGRAPHY

Barbour, Alan G. *Days of Thrills and Adventure*. New York, Macmillan, 1970.
———. *Cliffhanger*. New York: A & W, 1977.
Cline, William C. *In the Nick of Time*. Jefferson, North Carolina: McFarland, 1984.
Harmon, Jim, and Donald F. Glut. *The Great Movie Serials*. Garden City, New York: Doubleday, 1972.
Lahue, Kalton C. *Continued Next Week: A History of the Moving Picture Serial*. Norman, Oklahoma: University of Oklahoma Press, 1964.
Landrum, Larry N., and John Nachbar, "The Serials: A Selected Checklist of Published Materials," *Journal of Popular Film*, vol. III, no. 3, Summer 1974, pp. 273–276.
Stedman, Raymond William. *The Serials*. Norman, Oklahoma: University of Oklahoma Press, 1971.
Weiss, Ken, and Ed Goodgold. *To Be Continued*. New York: Crown, 1972.

SEVEN ARTS PRODUCTIONS, LTD. See WARNER BROS. PICTURES, INC.

70mm. The widest film gauge in general use and double the size of the standard 35mm* film gauge, 70mm film currently is used for printing only. It is the basis for most widescreen systems and dates back to the twenties. The film was actually shot on 65mm and printed on 70mm, with the additional 5mm being utilized for the soundtracks (generally six multitrack stereophonic). Special projectors are needed to screen 70mm film and, as of 1985, there were some 600 theatres in the United States so equipped.

With the exception of *Tron* (1982), all U.S. films made after 1970 and released in 70mm were shot in 35mm and blown up, a relatively cheap process compared with shooting in 65mm for 70mm release. Advertising that a film is being screened in 70mm appears to have a positive audience response, and among the many features blown up from 35mm to 70mm were *Star Wars* (1977), *Star Trek—The Motion Picture* (1979), *The Empire Strikes Back* (1980), *Raiders of the Lost Ark* (1981), *Annie* (1982), *The Thing* (1982), and *E. T. The Extra-Terrestrial* (1982).

BIBLIOGRAPHY

Allen, John F., "A 70mm Review," *Box Office*, January 1984, pp. 29–30.

Cohn, Lawrence, "Larger-Than-Life Pix Pay Off," *Daily Variety*, July 28, 1982, pp. 1, 26.

SHERMAN GRINBERG FILM LIBRARIES, INC. The best known stock shot library* in the United States, Sherman Grinberg Film Libraries, Inc., was founded by Grinberg (1928–1982) in 1957, moving to its present Hollywood location in 1965. Suppliers of film footage to all types of films and television programs, the Sherman Grinberg Film Libraries include the Pathé and Paramount newsreel collections, represent the stock footage libraries of 20th Century-Fox* and M-G-M*, and, since 1963, have served as sole representative for the ABC network news.

Grinberg became involved in the film industry in 1950, when he joined 20th Century-Fox as an accountant. His first involvement with stock footage came when he persuaded Darryl F. Zanuck to accept his plan for the marketing of 20th Century-Fox's stock footage. With David Wolper, Grinberg produced the 1961 television series *Biography*, and his other documentary television series included *Greatest Headlines of the Century* (1960), *Sportfolio* (1961), *Battleline* (1964), *Survival* (1965), and the specials *Bogart* (1969) and *Hollywood: The Selznick Years* (1969).

Addresses: 1040 North McCadden Place, Hollywood, Calif. 90038–2486; 630 Ninth Avenue, New York, N.Y. 10036–3787.

SHERPIX. Sherpix was founded by Louis K. Sher, president of the Art Theatre Guild Circuit (established in 1954) in the summer of 1965 to distribute theatrical features of an adult or pornographic nature. The New York–based company quickly became known as America's leading distributor of better class pornographic subjects, such as *A History of the Blue Movie* (1970), *Adultery for Fun and*

Profit (1971), *Meat Rack* (1971), *The Stewardesses* (1969), *Mona* (1970), and *The Nurses* (1972). The company also distributed Alex De Renzy's marijuana documentary, *Weed* (1972); a British lowbrow comedy, *On the Buses* (1972); Arch Oboler's 3-D feature, *The Bubble* (1966); and Andy Warhol's *Lonesome Cowboys* (1968) and *Flesh* (1969). Following Sher's conviction on obscenity charges, in Washington, D.C., in the winter of 1973—charges which were eventually dismissed on appeal in August 1975—Sherpix ceased operations on March 1, 1974.

BIBLIOGRAPHY

MacDonough, Scott, "The Story of Sherpix: Soft-Core, Hard-Core, Encore," *Show*, vol. II, no. 5, July 1971, pp. 18–21.

Verrill, Addison. "Sherpix, Top Nat'l Distrib of Hardcore Pix, Shutting March 1, Will Keep Theatres," *Daily Variety*, January 16, 1974, pp. 1, 19.

———, "Shiffrin Heir to 'Milder' Sherpix," *Variety*, February 20, 1974, p. 5.

SHORTS AND FEATURES. There is no definite ruling as to what constitutes a short film and what a feature-length production. Prior to 1910, all American films were short subjects, but many were featured on a theatre program. Arguably the first American feature-length film was Vitagraph's *The Life of Moses*, released late 1909 and early 1910 in five self-contained reels. Vitagraph* intended that each reel be screened as a separate entity, but many exhibitors chose to show the five reels together at one presentation.

Among the earliest of American feature-length films were *Oliver Twist* (1912), *From the Manger to the Cross* (1912, an American production filmed on location in Palestine), *In the Bishop's Carriage* (1913), *The Count of Monte Cristo* (1913), and *Traffic in Souls* (1913). Cecil B. DeMille's *The Squaw Man* (1914), which was co-directed with Oscar Apfel, is often cited as the first feature-length film to be shot in Hollywood. This is not true, although it is certainly the first major feature-length production to come out of Los Angeles.

The Academy of Motion Picture Arts and Sciences defines any film not more than thirty minutes in running time to be a short subject. The British Board of Trade defines any film running less than forty minutes to be a short subject. Because it is difficult to conceive of a film under one hour in length being a feature, the term "featurette" has been coined to describe films that are too long to be shorts and too short to be features.

SHOWSCAN. Developed by special effects expert Douglas Trumbull in the late seventies and early eighties, Showscan is a revolutionary process that offers the viewer enhanced clarity and dramatic realism with a sensation of three-dimensionality. It involves the shooting of films in 70mm* and their projection at sixty frames per second, as opposed to the normal rate of twenty-four frames per second. Showscan also requires the use of a special projection system. It has yet to be used for any commercial feature film.

Address: Showscan Film Corporation, 4441 W. Airport Freeway, Irving, Tex. 75062.

SHUBERT FILM CORPORATION. See WORLD FILM CORPORATION

SID OLCOTT INTERNATIONAL FEATURES. Sidney Olcott (1872–1949), formerly the director of the Gene Gauntier Feature Players Company, formed his own company in January 1914 to release his "Sidfilms" through Warner's Features. With Valentine Grant as his leading lady, Olcott shot three-reel features in Jacksonville, Florida, until June 1914 and then went to Ireland to shoot. Fred C. "Wid" Gunning, who later founded the trade journal *The Film Daily*, was Olcott's assistant director.
BIBLIOGRAPHY
"New Picture Making Company," *The Moving Picture World*, January 10, 1914, p. 181.

SIGMA III. See ORION PICTURES CORPORATION

SIGNAL FILM COMPANY. The Signal Film Company was formed in October 1915 to produce at the old Western Lubin* studio at 4560 Pasadena Avenue, Pasadena. It produced railroad serials featuring Helen Holmes and nonrailroad dramas, such as the five-reel *The Diamond Runner*, filmed in Honolulu. J. P. McGowan directed the serials and J. Murdock McQuarrie directed the features. S. S. Hutchinson, the president of Signal, was also the president of the American Film Manufacturing Company*. Signal's films were released by the Mutual Film Corporation*, and the company disbanded late in 1917.

SILHOUETTE FILMS. Silhouette films have their origins in eighteenth-century silhouette portraits, in Javanese shadow puppets or Wayangs, and in the Chinese shadow figures. Silhouette films were introduced by Lotte Reiniger (1899–1981) in 1919. The figures were cut out of black paper, with each limb separately cut and joined to another. Backgrounds were cut from black cardboard and from tissue paper. The figures and background were then photographed, using the same principle as with animated films, but utilizing a glass-topped table lit from below.

Lotte Reiniger made her first animated silhouette feature and arguably the first animated feature-length production, *The Adventures of Prince Achmed*, in Germany between 1923 and 1926. Reiniger's work was also featured in the Jean Renoir film *La Marseillaise* (1938).
BIBLIOGRAPHY
Alper, Mara, "Lotte Reiniger," *Film Library Quarterly*, vol. X, nos. 1 and 2, 1977, pp. 40–44.
Reiniger, Lotte. *Shadow Theatres and Shadow Films*. New York: Watson-Guptill, 1970.
White, Eric Walter. *Walking Shadows*. London: Leonard and Virginia Woolf, 1931.
———. *The Little Chimney Sweep*. Bristol, England: White & White, 1936.

SILLY SYMPHONIES. "Silly Symphonies" was a term coined by Walt Disney Productions* to refer to short subjects that combined animation and music in perfect unison, but which did not feature continuing characters (such as Mickey Mouse). The term was first used to describe *Skeleton Dance* in 1928. The first Silly Symphony to be filmed in color, and also the first Disney-animated cartoon shot in Technicolor*, was *Flowers and Trees* (1932). After 1939, Disney did not use the term Silly Symphonies on his cartoons.

BIBLIOGRAPHY

Maltin, Leonard. *The Disney Films*. New York: Crown, 1984.

SIRITZKY INTERNATIONAL PICTURES CORPORATION. Formed by Leon Siritzky and his sons, Sam and Joseph, Siritzky International Pictures Corporation specialized in the distribution of French-language films in the United States from the mid- through late forties. It released for the first time in the United States Marcel Pagnol's Marseilles trilogy, *Marius* (1931), *Fanny* (1932), and *Cesar* (1936), as well as Maurice Tourneur's *Volpone* (1938). Siritzky also managed the Ambassador and Elysee theatres in New York.

16mm. The Eastman Kodak* company introduced 16mm film in 1923 as a film gauge for amateur moviemaking. By the thirties, 16mm was used as an audiovisual aid in educational institutions, churches, hospitals, and prisons. Following their theatrical release, most feature films were released nontheatrically in 16mm. Silent 16mm film has perforations at both edges, while 16mm sound film has only one row of perforations, with the soundtrack printed on the other edge of the film. For bulk printing, 32mm film stock is usually utilized, with the film being slit in two to create two rolls of 16mm film.

Up until fairly recent times, 16mm was not considered suitable for projection before a large audience, although it was utilized for professional filmmaking from the thirties onward, usually in the fields of documentary, educational, instructional, sponsored, and industrial films. Some feature films were shot in 16mm and then blown up to 35mm*. In 1971, a new 16mm frame size, Super 16mm, was introduced, which made available 40 percent more picture image for blow up to the 35mm aspect ratio of 1.75:1. The first feature-length entertainment film to be shot in 16mm is generally considered to have been *Sundown Riders*, filmed in Kodachrome in 1944, by Major 16mm Productions. The film was directed and written by Lambert Hillyer, photographed by Alan Stensvold, and featured Russell Wade, Jay Kirby, and Andy Clyde.

BIBLIOGRAPHY

Happé, L. Bernard. *Basic Motion Picture Technology*. New York: Hastings House, 1975.
Kruse, William F., "The Feature Film in 16mm," *Film News*, September 1966, pp. 6–7.
Offenhauser, William H., Jr. *16mm Sound Motion Pictures*. New York: Interscience, 1949.

Provisor, Henry. *8mm/16mm Movie-Making*. New York: Amphoto, 1970.
Trojan, Judith, and Nadine Covert, compilers. *16mm Distribution*. New York: Educational
   Film Library Association, 1977.

SLAPSTICK COMEDY. Slapstick, also known as "low" or knockabout,
comedy is a comic form that ridicules authority or dignity through physical
humor involving, in its most basic form, a custard pie in the face or a slip on
a banana peel. The origins of American slapstick film comedy lie in turn-of-the-
century European film comedy and in music hall or vaudeville humor. The
greatest name in American slapstick comedy was Mack Sennett (1880–1960),
whose Keystone* comedies contained all of the elements common to slapstick
humor. In his classic piece on "Comedy's Greatest Era" (published in *Life*,
September 3, 1949), critic James Agee wrote, "Mack Sennett made two kinds
of comedy: parody laced with slapstick, and plain slapstick. The parodies were
the unceremonious burial of a century of hamming. . . . The plain slapstick, at
its best, was even better: a profusion of hearty young women in disconcerting
bathing suits, frisking around with a gaggle of insanely incompetent policemen
and of equally certifiable male civilians sporting museum-piece mustaches. All
these people zipped and caromed about the pristine world of the screen as jazzily
as a convention of water bugs."
   The physical humor of slapstick comedy was best suited to the early years of
the silent motion picture. It did not easily make a transition to sound films,
although a 1935 Warner Bros.* short, *Keystone Hotel*, successfully gathered
together all the elements of a good slapstick comedy. The slapstick tradition
continued in such television series as *Laugh-In* (1979) and Stanley Kramer's *It's
a Mad Mad Mad Mad World* (1963).

S.-L. PICTURES CORPORATION. Arthur H. Sawyer and Herbert Lubin,
previously involved together in General Enterprises, Inc., formed S.-L. Pictures
Corporation late in 1918 as both a producer and distributor. S.-L. released the
films of Ralph Ince Film Attractions, and its first such release was *Virtuous Men*,
directed by Ince.
BIBLIOGRAPHY
"New Combination Outline Project," *The Moving Picture World*, November 16, 1918,
   p. 746.

THE SMALL AGENCY. See EDWARD SMALL PRODUCTIONS, INC.

SMALL-LANDAU AGENCY. See EDWARD SMALL PRODUCTIONS, INC.

SMALLWOOD FILM CORPORATION. Arthur N. Smallwood was the
president and general manager of the Smallwood Film Corporation, which in
1913 absorbed the U.S. Film Corporation, with which Smallwood had been
associated since 1908. The U.S. Film Corporation began operations in Cincinnati

and made Westerns*. Later, it opened an office in New York and specialized in industrial, advertising, and educational films. After Smallwood's takeover, the U.S. Film Corporation began making dramatic films for release through Warner's Features. It led an intermittent existence during 1914, opening and closing several times. Finally, J. Arthur Nelson, U.S. Film's vice-president and head of the Nelson Film Company, was arrested early in 1915 for misappropriation of stockholders' funds.

As far as can be ascertained, it was this same Smallwood Film Corporation with which Ray Smallwood became involved in 1914, producing, directing, photographing, and editing one-reel films featuring his wife Ethel Grandin. The brand name "Grandin Films" was incorporated as Grandin Films, Inc., early in 1915. In the beginning, Smallwood worked without studio facilities using a newly developed portable lighting system which could be set up in any room. In April 1915, it used a studio in Cliffside, New Jersey, where society and psychological dramas starring Edwin August and Ruth Blair were produced. L. B. "Pop" Hoadly was in charge of the scenario department, and A. R. Mariner was the technical director. When United Film Service* replaced Warner's Features, Smallwood released through the new organization.

SMELL-O-VISION. See AROMARAMA AND SMELL-O-VISION.

SOCIETY OF MOTION PICTURE AND TELEVISION ART DIRECTORS. A professional society that acts as a bargaining agency, the Society of Motion Picture and Television Art Directors was founded in 1937—the name was changed to include television in January 1968. It is Local 876 of IATSE*. The Society published a journal, *Production Design*, in the fifties.

Address: 14724 Ventura Boulevard, Penthouse, Sherman Oaks, Calif. 91403.

SOCIETY OF MOTION PICTURE AND TELEVISION ENGINEERS. The Society of Motion Picture Engineers was formed on January 24, 1916, in Washington, D.C., by ten motion picture engineers, including C. F. Jenkins, Donald J. Bell, and W. Burton Wescott. The Society's basic aim, which has remained the same through the years, was the standardization of motion picture (and later television) technology and the publication of the research of its members. In the first issue of its publication *Transactions* (July 1916) (now titled *SMPTE Journal*), the Society gave as its goals the "advancement in the theory and practice of motion picture engineering and the allied arts and sciences, the standardization of the mechanisms and practices employed therein, and the maintenance of a high professional standing among its members."

The Society's name was changed to include Television in January 1950. It organizes an annual technical conference, at which papers are read and which includes a major exhibit of current film and television equipment; holds monthly regional meetings; and publishes the monthly *SMPTE Journal*. Membership in the Society of Motion Picture and Television Engineers (SMPTE) is open to qualified members of the film and television industries.

Address: 862 Scarsdale Avenue, Scarsdale, N.Y. 10583.

SOCIETY OF MOTION PICTURE ENGINEERS. See SOCIETY OF MOTION PICTURE AND TELEVISION ENGINEERS

SOCIETY OF OPERATING CAMERAMEN. The Society of Operating Cameramen was formed in 1981 by 120 members of the International Photographers Local 659 of the International Alliance of Theatrical Stage Employes*, as a professional organization concerned with gaining recognition for the craft of operating cameramen. The first president was Bob Marta.

Address: 22704 Ventura Boulevard, Suite 123, Woodland Hills, Calif. 91364.
BIBLIOGRAPHY
"Operating Cameramen Form New Society," *International Photographer*, July 1981, pp. 12, 16.

SOLAX COMPANY. The Solax Company was founded on September 7, 1910, by Madame Alice Guy Blaché, the world's first woman director, in association with her husband, Herbert Blaché, and George A. Magie. Its first release—on October 21, 1910—was *A Child's Sacrifice*. The first Solax studios were located in Flushing, New York, but, in 1912, the company built a new studio complex in Fort Lee, New Jersey*. Alice Guy Blaché directed the more important of the company's productions, including its first major film and its first three-reel feature, *Fra Diavolo*, released on July 12, 1912, and among the players in the Solax stock company were Magda Foy, Billy Quirk, Marion Swayne, Darwin Karr, and Blanche Cornwall. The Solax Company went out of existence in 1914, when Herbert Blaché established Blaché Features and the United States Amusement Company*.
BIBLIOGRAPHY
Blaché, Alice Guy. *The Memoirs of Alice Guy Blaché*. Metuchen, New Jersey: Scarecrow Press, 1986.
Gates, Harvey, "Alice Blaché, a Dominant Figure in Pictures," *The New York Dramatic Mirror*, November 6, 1912, p. 28.
Harrison, Louis Reeves, "Studio Saunterings," *The Moving Picture World*, June 15, 1912, pp. 1007–1011.

SOLDIERS WITH WINGS. See HOLLYWOOD VICTORY COMMITTEE

SONG SLIDES. With the popularity of the nickelodeon* in the early twentieth century, a number of manufacturers—such as the St. Louis (Missouri) Calcium Light Company, DeWitt C. Wheeler, Scott and Van Altena, A. L. Simpson, and Henry B. Ingram—began producing song slides, illustrating the lines of popular "hits" of the day. They were utilized as a vocalist or pianist accompanied the numbers in theatres, with the audiences joining in the chorus. Song slides were not unique to nickelodeons but had been utilized earlier in vaudeville and as part of stereopticon entertainments. They were distributed, for purchase, by film exchanges and were sometimes loaned to nickelodeons by song publishers.

Among the models who appeared in song slides—"live model" slides were generally considered to have been introduced by George H. Thomas, a stage electrician at a Brooklyn theatre—were many future film stars, including Francis X. Bushman, Patricia Collinge, Priscilla Dean, Ethel Grandin, Alice Joyce, Florence La Badie, Anita Stewart, Norma Talmadge, Florence Turner, and Lillian Walker.

BIBLIOGRAPHY

Ripley, John W., "Romance and Joy, Tears and Heartache, and All for a Nickel," *Smithsonian*, March 1982, pp. 77–82.
"Slide Makers Organizing," *The Moving Picture World*, January 4, 1908, pp. 6–7.
"Song Slides: How They Are Produced," *Views and Film Index*, July 28, 1906, p. 10.
"The Song Slide Situation," *Views and Film Index*, March 7, 1908, pp. 13–15.

SONO ART-WORLD WIDE PICTURES, INC. Sono Art-World Wide Pictures, Inc., was a New York–based company, headed first by J. Douglas Watson and later by E. W. Hammons, which was operational from 1929 to 1932. Among the more than thirty features produced by the company, the best known are *The Great Gabbo* (1929), directed by James Cruze and starring Erich von Stroheim as a ventriloquist driven insane through jealous love, and *Reno* (1930), the first sound feature of former serial queen Ruth Roland. The company was not involved with short films and, as far as can be ascertained, had some link with Educational Pictures* and Tiffany Productions*.

SOUND. Film sound can be broken down into three categories—dialogue, music, and sound effects—a typology which corresponds not only to the way in which the film industry traditionally records, edits, and mixes the soundtrack but also to the way in which an audience perceives sound. The soundtrack, though conceived of as a whole, is, in fact, a pastiche of fragments. Hollywood, for example, records dialogue and some sound effects during production, while other sound effects, music, and even some dialogue, which may be dubbed in during a looping session, are recorded in post-production. Moreover, the industry routinely edits dialogue, music, and effects tracks separately, combining them only during the final mix.

If production and post-production practices break down the soundtrack, so too do the processes of perception. Audiences automatically distinguish among the kinds of sounds heard on the soundtrack. The comprehension of dialogue, for instance, depends upon the audience's knowledge of the principles of language in general and of certain language systems in particular; we must possess a certain conceptual ability in order to render words back into things and we must know English, French, German, and so on, depending on the language spoken by the characters in the film. For this reason, we regard dialogue as essentially different from the universal, immediately comprehensible, nonconceptual "languages" of music and sound effects. Viewers, in turn, distinguish the highly organized, rhythmic, and tonal structures of musical underscoring—which are the products of a composer who, like the director, stands outside of the world of the film—from the apparent "noises" produced by characters, objects, or things situated within the world of the film. Filmgoers, in fact, take privilege to certain tracks over others; dialogue, for example, must always (with the notable exception of the films of Robert Altman) be intelligible. Thus, dialogue is universally given precedence over music and effects, which are consequently relegated in terms of viewer attention to a background against which the characters and their stories are displayed. Music, in particular, is associated with "mood," while sound effects contribute to overall "atmosphere." "Mood" and "atmosphere" become attributes, adjectival accompaniments to the main action.

At the same time, it is quite obvious that audiences rarely respond to sound film as if it were nonunified (Jean-Luc Godard's films to the contrary). To some extent, sound editing and mixing practices work to conceal these differences. But what really transforms the heterogeneity of the soundtrack—and, for that matter, the larger heterogeneity that characterizes the total film experience, consisting of the combination of sound and image—into a homogeneity is the all-encompassing unity of narrative, at whose service all the film's different kinds of sounds and images are placed. Even in non-narrative films, audiences construct a "story" that unifies their viewing experience. Thus, Stan Brakhage films become *recountings* of specific events such as childbirth or sensations such as the way light strikes a series of objects.

The opening sequence of *Apocalypse Now* (1979) provides a useful illustration of the way in which commercial cinema manipulates the soundtrack for narrative purposes. The film's sound designer, Walter Murch, described how he mixed certain sound effects to convey to the audience the central character's psychological dilemma. As Captain Willard (Martin Sheen), isolated in his Saigon hotel room, begins to imagine himself back in the jungle on another mission, the sounds of the city—a policeman's traffic whistle, car horns, motorbikes, a fly buzzing against the windowpane—become those of the jungle: the sound of the whistle segues into that of a cricket, the car horns into bird calls, and the fly's buzz into that of a mosquito. Though Willard's body remains in Saigon, his mind is in the jungle.

Film sound, in short, not only helps, through proper sound perspective, to realize the visual space within which the narrative takes place, but it also shapes the audience's perception of events and directs its attention to important details, much as camera movement, editing, and other visual devices do. If the topic of film sound has been neglected by scholars and critics for the past fifty five years, it is partly because the soundtrack has evolved from the pure auditory spectacle which characterized its initial appearance in the transition-to-sound period into a well-integrated component of the narrative. Yet the voice of the soundtrack can still be heard, and its work revealed, if one chooses to listen. *See also* Dolby Sound, Dubbing, Fantasound, Sensurround.

BIBLIOGRAPHY

American Cinematographer, April 1971, special issue on sound.

Cameron, Evan William, editor. *Sound and the Cinema*. Pleasantville, New York: Redgrave, 1980.

"Directors on Sound," *Take One*, vol. VI, no. 2, January 1978, pp. 23–26.

Geduld, Harry M. *The Birth of the Talkies*. Bloomington, Indiana: Indiana University Press, 1975.

Rosenbaum, Jonathan, "Sound Thinking," *Film Comment*, September-October 1978, pp. 38–41.

Sharples, Win, Jr., "The Aesthetics of Film Sound," *Filmmakers Newsletter*, vol. VIII, no. 8, March 1975, pp. 27–32.

Walker, Alexander. *The Shattered Silents*. New York: William Morrow, 1979.

Weis, Elizabeth, and John Belton, editors. *Film Sound*. New York: Columbia University Press, 1985.

SOUNDIES. Soundies was the name given to a film jukebox presentation popular in the early forties. For a nickel, patrons could view a three-minute musical short on a twenty-four-by-eighteen-inch plastic screen. The film was projected by mirrors within the jukebox, called a Panoram, and this required that the film be printed in reverse (the reason why when film collectors purchase Soundies today the titles are always reversed). The musical entertainment might be a novelty number; a jazz number with Hoagy Carmichael, Fats Waller, or Duke Ellington; or a popular favorite performed by a minor celebrity. All-black soundies were produced exclusively for Negro neighborhoods.

Soundies were introduced in 1940 by the Mills Novelty Company of Chicago. The initial films were produced by James Roosevelt's Globe Productions in Hollywood. They were later produced by Minoco Productions, Inc., a Mills subsidiary in New York, and R.C.M. Productions in Hollywood. The initials R.C.M. stood for (James) Roosevelt; (Sam) Coslow, a songwriter whose Cameo Productions was part of R.C.M.; and (Gordon) Mills, the president of the Mills Novelty Company.

Customers could not select individual numbers but had to be content with any one of eight titles in a reel-long program. By 1941, it was reported that more than 4,000 Panoram jukeboxes were in operation. Soundies lost their appeal at the end of the Second World War, and the films became available to private collectors (often offering a unique record of a popular musical personality's performance). In the sixties, a new version of Soundies, titled Scopitone, was introduced.

BIBLIOGRAPHY

"Jimmy's Got It Again," *Look*, November 16, 1940, pp. 12–14.

SOUTHERN CALIFORNIA MOTION PICTURE COUNCIL. Incorporated in 1936, the Southern California Motion Picture Council previews and grades films and television programs for the Parent-Teacher Association (PTA) and church and youth groups. It is not a censorship board but seeks to encourage the production of family entertainment by awarding Golden, Silver, and Bronze halos initially on a monthly and since 1980 on a bimonthly basis. It was involved in a major 1975 dispute with a breakaway organization, the Film Advisory Board*.

Address: 1922 North Western Avenue, Hollywood, Calif. 90027.

THE SOUTH ON FILM. The romantic image of the Old South had appealed to American filmmakers long before D. W. Griffith made *The Birth of a Nation* in 1915. Many of Griffith's earlier films for the American Biograph Company* have southern themes, while the Kalem Company* produced a variety of films concerning Confederate spies, many filmed on location in Florida*. Harriet Beecher Stowe's *Uncle Tom's Cabin* was filmed as early as 1903, and later versions were released in 1909, 1913, 1914, 1918, 1927, and 1965. In 1927, the Duncan Sisters filmed their parody of the classic *Topsy and Eva*.

D. W. Griffith presented a further romanticized view of the South in *A Romance of Happy Valley* (1919) and *The White Rose* (1923). A far more realistic view of southern life was presented by Karl Brown in *Stark Love* (1927), a study of the isolated mountain people of Kentucky, filmed on location in Robbinsville, North Carolina. The rural South was the theme of Henry Hathaway's *The Trail of the Lonesome Pine* (1936). Al Capp is said to have based his character L'il Abner on Henry Fonda's characterization of Dave Tolliver in this film. There have been two versions of *L'il Abner*—in 1940 and 1959—and comic figures of the rural South have been represented by "Sis Hopkins" (first in Kalem* shorts and later by Judy Canova at Republic*) and by Pa and Ma Kettle.

With the coming of sound, the motion picture's view of the South changed little. It was a sentimental land of friendly Negroes, as seen in King Vidor's *Hallelujah* (1929), Paul Sloane's *Hearts in Dixie* (1929), and John Ford's *Judge Priest* (1934), *Steamboat round the Bend* (1935), and *The Sun Shines Bright* (1953). A change in attitude toward the South was first evidenced in *Cabin in the Cotton* (1932), followed by *Jezebel* (1938), *Tobacco Road* (1941), *The Little Foxes* (1941), *The Southerner* (1945), *All the King's Men* (1949), *The Glass Menagerie* (1950), *A Streetcar Named Desire* (1951), *Baby Doll* (1956), *Cat on a Hot Tin Roof* (1958), *The Defiant Ones* (1958), *The Long Hot Summer* (1958), *Suddenly Last Summer* (1959), *Sweet Bird of Youth* (1962), *To Kill a Mockingbird* (1963), and *In the Heat of the Night* (1967).

By the seventies, the South served as a background for crusading cops, as in *Walking Tall* (1973); for a new brand of black women, such as Cicely Tyson in *Sounder* (1972); for womanizers, such as Burt Reynolds in *Smokey and the Bandit* (1977); for political drama, as in *Nashville* (1975); and for unionization, as in *Norma Rae* (1979). At the same time, the old stereotypes were retained in films such as *Mandingo* (1975) and *Drum* (1976), and there can be little question that it is the image of the old, romantic South that remains predominant with filmgoers thanks to *Gone with the Wind* (1939) and, to a lesser extent, *Song of the South* (1947).

BIBLIOGRAPHY

Campbell, Edward D. C., Jr. *The Celluloid South.* Knoxville, Tennessee: University of Tennessee Press, 1981.

French, Warren, editor. *The South and Film.* Jackson, Mississippi: University Press of Mississippi, 1981.

SPEAKING OF ANIMALS. See JERRY FAIRBANKS PRODUCTIONS

SPECIAL EFFECTS. Special effects is a term used to describe a multitude of specialist creative works, from the burning of Chicago in *In Old Chicago* (1938) to the parting of the Red Sea in Cecil B. DeMille's *The Ten Commandments* (1956). It is primarily a visual field, and many times the term special visual effects rather than simply special effects is used. The Academy of Motion Picture Arts and Sciences* has presented Academy Awards for Special Effects or Special Visual Effects since 1938, when a Special Award was given to those responsible for the special photographic and sound effects in Paramount's *Spawn of the North.* Among the films honored by the Academy for their special effects are *The Rains Came* (1939), *The Thief of Bagdad* (1940), *Mighty Joe Young* (1949), *War of the Worlds* (1953), *"tom thumb"* (1958), *Ben-Hur* (1959), *Mary Poppins* (1964), *2001: A Space Odyssey* (1968), *Earthquake* (1974), *Superman* (1978), *Alien* (1979), *The Empire Strikes Back* (1980), *E. T. The Extra-Terrestrial* (1982), *Return of the Jedi* (1983), and *Indiana Jones and the Temple of Doom* (1984).

Because most special effects involve the use of the camera or optical printing by a laboratory, the area of expertise is one that has primarily been held by cinematographers, among whom were Linwood G. Dunn, John P. Fulton, Fred Sersen, and L. B. Abbott.

The earliest film to include a special effect is believed to be Edison's production of *The Execution of Mary, Queen of Scots* (1895), which uses a freeze frame in order to show the decapitation. A freeze frame allows for the stopping of the camera while one object, in this case a dummy, is substituted for another, in this case the actress portraying the Queen. Freeze frames, double exposures, and other similar and simplistic special effects devices were utilized by the French filmmaker Georges Méliès in the early years of the twentieth century. J. Stuart Blackton used the same methods for the production of *Princess Nicotine* (1909) and other early Vitagraph* films. Freeze frame has now come to mean freezing a frame optically for projected effect.

One of the more basic types of special effects is a matte shot, which permits a portion of the frame to be matted out, with another picture substituted for that part of the frame. A similar type of special effect is the glass shot, which involves a painted scene on glass through which the actors are filmed; they thus appear to be within the scene represented on the glass. The glass shot is thought to have originated with Norman Dawn in 1905.

Puppet animation is another form of special effect animation which was utilized in such early films as *The Lost World* (1925), the model prehistoric animals which were created by Willis O'Brien, who had been active in the field from the mid-teens. Willis O'Brien was also involved in the special effects for *King Kong* (1933), which uses animated puppet models, optical printing, miniatures, and other such devices.

Optical printing is a form of special effect undertaken in the laboratory. Rear projection, which first became popular in the early thirties, permits the projection of a scene behind the players, thus allowing them to appear to be riding in a car, traveling on a plane, or whatever. The same effect can also be obtained—many argue more realistically—with front projection. Miniatures have long been used when the building of a full-scale castle or town is obviously impossible. Some films—for example, Cecil B. DeMille's *Cleopatra* (1933)—contained scenes made up of both miniatures and full-scale sets.

The most elaborate and complex of special effects were introduced in the seventies, when electronics and animation were increasingly a part of the special effects field. The new era of special effects was heralded by the films of Steven Spielberg and George Lucas, such as *Star Wars* (1977) and *Close Encounters of the Third Kind* (1977). The seventies also saw new names entering the special effects field such as Carlo Rambaldi, John Dykstra, Richard Edlund, Robert Blalack, H. R. Giger, and Dennis Muren who dominated the Academy Awards nominations for Special Visual Effects. At the same time, a new type of special effect was introduced by Benjamin Burtt, Jr., with his creation of alien creature and robot voices in *Star Wars*. Arguably the end of the old era of special effects and the beginning of the new came in 1976, when the Special Visual Effects Award was shared by *King Kong* and *Logan's Run*, with the winners including "old" names, such as Frank Van Der Veer and L. B. Abbott, and "new" names, represented by Carlo Rambaldi and Matthew Yuricich.

BIBLIOGRAPHY

Abbott, L. B. *Special Effects, Wire, Tape and Rubber Style*. Hollywood, California: American Society of Cinematographers, 1984.

Culhane, John. *Special Effects in the Movies*. New York: Ballantine Books, 1981.

Dunn, Linwood G., and George E. Turner, editors. *The ASC Treasury of Visual Effects*. Hollywood, California: American Society of Cinematographers, 1983.

Fielding, Raymond. *The Technique of Special Effects Cinematography*. New York: Hastings House, 1972.

Finch, Christopher. *Special Effects: Creating Movie Magic*. New York: Abbeville Press, 1984.

Imes, Jack, Jr. *Special Visual Effects*. New York: Van Nostrand Reinhold, 1984.

O'Connor, Jane, and Katy Hall. *Magic in the Movies*. Garden City, New York: Doubleday, 1980.

Perisic, Zoran. *Special Optical Effects*. New York: Focal Press, 1980.

Schechter, Harold, and David Everitt. *Film Tricks*. New York: Harlin Quist, 1980.

SPROCKET SYSTEMS. See LUCASFILM, LTD.

STAMFORD, CONNECTICUT. See AMERICAN CORRESPONDENT FILM COMPANY, INC.

STANDARD PICTURES, INC. See UNITED FILM SERVICE

STANLEY BOOKING CORPORATION OF PHILADELPHIA. The Stanley Booking Corporation of Philadelphia, headed by Stanley and Jules Mastbaum, took over the extensive theatre holdings of Lubin* throughout eastern Pennsylvania. Acting as a "booking combine" for its theatres, Stanley was able to program the theatres and exact a 5 to 10 percent fee above the rental prices. Some exhibitors claimed they were forced into the Booking Corporation, and in 1918 Stanley was ordered by the Federal Trade Commission, in the first order of its kind in the motion picture industry, to cease its unfair methods of competition.

Jules Mastbaum became the president after Stanley's death, and in 1919 the organization was incorporated, with a capitalization of $15 million, as the Stanley Company of America. It fought for an open-booking system, and Adolph Zukor, who served on the Board of Directors, wanted to make the Stanley Company a booking combine for all parts of the country, using the thousands of exhibitors belonging to the First National* Exhibitors Circuit, but the First National exhibitors rejected the idea.

BIBLIOGRAPHY

"Stanley Corporation Is Enjoined," *The Moving Picture World*, September 28, 1918, p. 1869.

STANLEY WARNER CORPORATION. When Warner Bros* was required by the consent decree* to divest itself of its theatre chain, the 436 theatres that it controlled in 1951 became the Stanley Warner Corporation. The latter merged with the Glen Alden Corp. in 1967, which merged the Stanley Warner Corporation with RKO Theatre Corporation and, in 1971, sold the circuit to Cinerama, Inc.*

"STAR" BRAND. See MÉLIÈS MANUFACTURING COMPANY.

STARLIGHT COMEDY COMPANY. See UNITED FILM SERVICE

STARS OVER AMERICA. See HOLLYWOOD VICTORY COMMITTEE

THE STAR SYSTEM. The star system developed as filmgoers began not only to demand to know the names of their favorite actors or actresses but also to patronize those films in which they appeared. It has been suggested that the players did not want their identities known because it would have diminished their importance as stage performers. Such reasoning seems unlikely because almost all players in films had only minimal importance as stage actors or actresses. A far more likely reason is that the early companies feared demands for salary increases if the performers became aware of their newfound prominence.

The first actor to gain recognition in a trade paper, by way of a feature article, was Ben Turpin in the April 3, 1909, issue of *The Moving Picture World*. Florence Turner of the Vitagraph Company* was the first actress to make personal appearances on a regular basis and the first to be featured in a popular newspaper. The Kalem Company* was the first studio to recognize the value of star names and to promote its players through posters and other theatre advertising matter, beginning in January 1910.

The Biograph Company* steadfastly refused to identify its players, and its leading lady, Florence Lawrence, was known simply as ''The Biograph Girl.'' When Carl Laemmle lured Lawrence away from Biograph, he mounted a publicity campaign to the effect that the actress had been killed in a 1910 accident in St. Louis, which he subsequently branded as a deliberate lie planted by his rivals. Florence Lawrence thus became a star in her own right, and the star system was born.

With the formation of his Famous Players Company in 1912, Adolph Zukor recognized the value of star names, in this case from the legitimate stage. However, within a few years, the motion picture industry was to have its own stars, led by Charlie Chaplin, Mary Pickford, and Douglas Fairbanks, all of whom surpassed the popularity of any stage actor and all of whom, coincidentally, had commenced their careers in the theatre. In 1917, it was reported that Fairbanks' salary was $780,000 a year. The formation by Chaplin, Pickford, Fairbanks, and D. W. Griffith of United Artists* in 1919 proved, for once and for all, that the star system had come of age.

The producers also were quick to recognize this fact, and, in the twenties, led by Paramount* and M-G-M*, the various studios began to control the star system. They created stars through their publicity machinery, and they kept such stars under their control through long-term contracts. The studio's control of the system remained in force through the fifties, when television began to create its own stars and when film personalities began to demand larger and larger salaries through the efforts of their talent agents. The breaking point was reached in the early sixties when Elizabeth Taylor made exorbitant demands for her work in *Cleopatra* (1963), which proved a financial disaster for its producer.

As the makeup of the motion picture audiences changed, as the studios had less control over publicity, and as box office success was no longer predicated on who was in a film but rather on a novel storyline or stunning special effects, the star system broke down. The new stars were as much the directors as the actors, with Alfred Hitchcock leading the way for George Lucas, Steven Spielberg, and Francis Ford Coppola. Only a handful of stars, such as Barbra Streisand or Clint Eastwood, could guarantee a film's box office success. It was very much a matter of supply and demand. The supply was still there, but the demand had dried up.

Each year *International Motion Picture Almanac* publishes a listing of the Top Ten Stars of the year, together with a list of previous "money-making stars" from 1933 onward.

BIBLIOGRAPHY

Kindem, Gorham, "Hollywood's Movie Star System: A Historical Overview," in *The American Movie Industry: The Business of Motion Pictures*. Carbondale, Illinois: Southern Illinois University Press, 1982, pp. 79–93.

Slide, Anthony, "The Evolution of the Film Star," *Films in Review*, December 1974, pp. 591–594.

Walker, Alexander. *Stardom: The Hollywood Phenomenon*. New York: Stein and Day, 1970.

STATEN ISLAND, NEW YORK. See ALL-STAR FEATURE COMPANY

STATES RIGHTS. States rights distribution was a system that developed in the days prior to national distribution organizations. In order to distribute a film across the country, an independent producer would lease the rights in the film to independent exchanges in each territory of the United States, with the territory usually being a state (hence the name). The exchanges had the exclusive rights to the film in their territory and then rented the film to exhibitors in the area and handled the physical chores of distribution, such as booking and cleaning prints, collecting rentals, and so on.

This distribution system, while dominant through the teens, was not the most efficient system for producers, for three main reasons: (1) most exchanges were owned by exhibitors and they were not eager to let their competition have films they might be able to use; (2) exchanges handled films from many different producers and could not give much attention to promoting any one film; and (3) there was always the probability of dishonesty by the exchange, either by not reporting rentals (when the film was leased on a percentage basis) or by "bicycling" the print to unlicensed exhibitors and keeping the rentals.

As states rights distribution depended on an industry that was fragmented, it began to disappear when the vertical integration of the industry, begun by Adolph Zukor, became dominant and national distribution systems were formed. Yet, it has never totally disappeared and probably will not as long as there are independent producers around to make films for regional and minority audiences.

BIBLIOGRAPHY

Lewis, Howard T. *The Motion Picture Industry*. New York: D. Van Nostrand, 1933.

Wholesale Distribution/Motion Picture Films. Washington, D.C.: U.S. Department of Commerce, Bureau of the Census, 1932.

STATES RIGHTS DISTRIBUTORS, INC. Sol Lesser headed States Rights Distributors, Inc., which was organized on August 22, 1917, by fifteen distributors representing most of the United States, to purchase the negative rights on pictures in a manner similar to the then recently formed First National* organization.

Each franchise holder was to be taxed a pro-rata share on any film purchased. Louis Haas was the vice-president of the organization, and Louis B. Mayer was the treasurer.

THE STATIC CLUB OF AMERICA. James Crosby, who owned a studio and a laboratory in Los Angeles, was the founder, in 1913, of the Static Club of America, whose membership was limited to active cameramen. Its headquarters were at 406 Court Street, Los Angeles, and Leonard H. Smith was the president in April 1913 and William F. Alder the secretary. In 1915, the Static Club, with a membership of 100, attempted to see that the names of cameramen were included in the credits of films. Its offices at that time were at 1839 Santa Cruz Street, Los Angeles, overlooking Echo Park, and its president was E. G. Ullman. *Static Flashes*, its official weekly paper, was edited by "Captain Jack" Poland, who later became the first editor of *American Cinematographer*, and it ran for about six months before ceasing publication in September 1915.
BIBLIOGRAPHY
Poland, Captain "Jack," "The Static Club," *The Moving Picture World*, July 10, 1915, pp. 272–273.

STEADICAM. Steadicam is the trade name for a lightweight, portable stabilizer for cameras which permits a steady picture image when the camera is in motion. Invented and developed by Garrett Brown—who received an Academy Award in 1977—and marketed by Cinema Products Corporation, Steadicam revolutionized filmmaking in the late seventies. For the first time, a cinematographer—utilizing a 35mm,* 16mm,* or video camera—was able to walk or run and maintain a steady image.
BIBLIOGRAPHY
Brown, Garrett, "The Steadicam and 'The Shining,' " *American Cinematographer*, August 1980, pp. 786–789, 826–827, 850–854.
McDonough, Tom, "The Fabulous Flying Robot Camera," *The Movies*, July 1983, pp. 88–90, 119.

STELLAR PHOTOPLAY COMPANY. Frank J. Carroll, previously with the Selig Polyscope Company*, formed the Stellar Photoplay Company as a production organization late in 1913. Carroll was the president, C. A. "Doc" Willat was vice-president, and William A. McManus was secretary and treasurer. Its first release, the melodrama *Forgiven; or, The Jack of Diamonds*, with Edwin Forsberg and directed by William Robert Daly, was shot at the Ruby Twinplex studio in New York and at St. Augustine. Stellar's offices were in the Candler Building, New York.
BIBLIOGRAPHY
"F. J. Carroll Will Make Pictures," *The Moving Picture World*, January 3, 1914, p. 54.

STERLING CAMERA AND FILM COMPANY. The Sterling Camera and Film Company was formed late in 1913 by Fred J. Balshofer and ceased production in January 1915. Ford Sterling and George Nichols were the featured players in the company's films, released by Universal*, and Robert Thornby directed a company of children for Sterling.

STILLS. Stills is the term used for still photographs of scenes from films used for publicity purposes. Except on the cheapest of productions (which cannot afford a still photographer), stills are posed shots of scenes from the film or production shots showing the cast and crew at work. Frame enlargements from the film itself are only utilized as stills when no still photographer is present. The standard size of a still photograph is eight inches by ten inches, and this has been the standard since the teens. There is no documentation as to when stills, as opposed to frame enlargements, were first used to promote films, but as early as 1907 both the Edison* and Vitagraph* companies were utilizing stills.

Some still photographers became associated with individual studios. Clarence Sinclair Bull and George Hurrell are best known for their work for M-G-M*, while Roman Freulich was Universal's* chief still photographer. These still photographers were also responsible for posed portrait stills of the studio's personalities, both stars and technicians. Prior to the studios' use of an in-house portrait photographer, such Los Angeles photographers as Melbourne Spurr, Lansing Brown, and the houses of Evans, Hartsok, and Witzel would provide portrait stills of the stars.

It is only in recent years that the art of the studio still photographer has come to be recognized, and the value of original still photographs has risen. However, from 1941 to 1947 the Academy of Motion Picture Arts and Sciences* organized exhibits of the work of still photographers and awarded medals to the best.

BIBLIOGRAPHY

Johnston, John LeRoy, "Stillmen Mustn't Stand Still," *International Photographer*, February 1939, pp. 9–12.
Kobal, John. *The Art of the Great Hollywood Portrait Photographers, 1925–1940*. New York: Alfred A. Knopf, 1980.
Slide, Anthony. *A Collector's Guide to Movie Memorabilia*. Des Moines, Iowa: Wallace-Homestead, 1983.
Willinger, L., "Still Please," *International Photographer*, January 1940, pp. 9–11.

STOCK SHOT LIBRARIES. Stock shot libraries provide footage for film or television productions which the producer would either be unwilling to film himself because of cost or time or unable to film because the objects or the events in the stock footage can no longer be duplicated. Stock footage may be in black-and-white or color and can include anything from footage of the 1932 Olympic Games in Los Angeles to a shot of a pride of lions in Kenya. With the preponderance of color films and television programs, color stock footage is the most sought after and utilized, particularly color footage of landmarks or events from the forties and earlier.

It was common practice for studios to operate their own stock footage libraries, in which they deposited surplus footage from their current productions, but it was footage that did not show any identifiable player. If a film was cancelled after certain footage had already been shot, that footage usually finished up in a stock footage library. For example, the film that Orson Welles shot in Brazil for his abortive 1941–1942 project *It's All True* was sold by the studio, RKO*, as stock footage to Paramount*, where it remained for many years until it was deposited in 1985 with the UCLA Film Archives.

The following is a listing of the major New York and Los Angeles stock footage libraries:

Archive Film Productions, Inc., 530 West 25 Street, New York, N.Y. 10001.
Fotosonic Inc., 15 West 46 Street, New York, N.Y. 10036.
Stock Shots To Order, 521 Fifth Avenue, New York, N.Y. 10017.
Stratford International Film Searchers, Inc., 250 West 57 Street, New York, N.Y. 10019.
Telenews Film Corporation, 235 East 46 Street, New York, N.Y. 10019.
Airline Film & T.V. Promotion, Inc., 13246 Weidner Street, Valley Studio, Pacoima, Calif. 91331.
Elmer Dyer Library, 711 North La Jolla Street, Los Angeles, Calif. 90046.
Evco Film Library, 8380 Melrose Avenue, Los Angeles, Calif. 90069.
Galaxy Tape & Film Library, 4121 Redwood Avenue, Los Angeles, Calif. 90066.
Gornick Film Productions, 4200 Camino Real, Los Angeles, Calif. 90065.
H. B. Halicki Productions, 17902 South Vermont Avenue, Los Angeles, Calif. 90248.
Hollywood Newsreel Syndicate, Inc., 1622 North Gower Street, Los Angeles, Calif. 90028.
Larry Dorn Associates, 5550 Wilshire Boulevard, Los Angeles, Calif. 90036.
MacGillvray-Freeman Films, P.O. Box 205, Laguna Beach, Calif. 92677.
Moi Di Sesso & Sons (Animal Film Library), 24233 Old Road, Newhall, Calif. 91321.
Producers Library Service, 7325 Santa Monica Boulevard, West Hollywood, Calif. 90046.
Pyramid Films, 2801 Colorado Avenue, Santa Monica, Calif. 90404.
Sherman Grinberg Film Libraries, Inc.*, 1040 North McCadden Place, Hollywood, Calif. 90038 and 630 Ninth Avenue, New York, N.Y. 10036.
The Stock House, 8271 Melrose Avenue, West Hollywood, Calif. 90046.

Another major source for stock footage is the various newsreel* libraries and film archives such as the Library of Congress, the National Archives, the Museum of Modern Art, and the UCLA Film Archives.

STUDIO BASIC AGREEMENT. See INTERNATIONAL ALLIANCE OF THEATRICAL STAGE EMPLOYES AND MOVING PICTURE MACHINE OPERATORS OF THE UNITED STATES AND CANADA

STUNTS/STUNTMEN. The use of stuntmen to perform dangerous or specialized feats dates back to circa 1908. Although many silent actors and actresses—particularly the comedians—performed their own stunts, stunt doubles were also used when necessary. Richard Talmadge and Harvey Parry doubled for Harold Lloyd. Talmadge doubled for Douglas Fairbanks. Jean de Kay doubled for Norma Phillips in the 1914 Mutual* serial* *Our Mutual Girl*. A number of male stuntmen doubled for Pearl White in her serials. Generally, however, the names of stunt doubles were not publicized, and the industry clung to the myth that stars performed their own stunts.

With the popularity of the "B" Western*, with its frequent and sometimes dangerous action sequences, stuntmen became an established part of the film community. These men called a stunt "a gag," and the doyen of Hollywood stuntmen was Yakima Canutt (born 1895). Canutt was also featured in "B" Westerns (usually as a villain), became noted for his second unit direction work, particularly the chariot race from *Ben-Hur* (1959), and received an Honorary Academy Award in 1966, "for achievements as a stunt man and for developing safety devices to protect stunt men everywhere."

Stunt flying was at its height in the late twenties with *Wings* (1927) and *Hell's Angels* (1930). *The Lost Squadron* (1932) depicted a typical group of stunt flyers, all of whom were members of various flying circuses. Ormer Locklear was the first to become well known as a stunt pilot, and he died in 1920 while filming *The Skywayman*. Probably the best known of all stunt flyers was Dick Grace, who wrote three books on his exploits: *I Am Still Alive* (Rand, McNally, 1931), *Squadron of Death* (The Sun Dial Press, 1937) and *Visibility Unlimited* (Longman's Green, 1950).

As a group, the stuntmen did not become organized until 1962 when the Stuntmen's Association of Motion Pictures (4810 Whitsett Avenue, North Hollywood, Calif. 91607) was formed. A breakaway group, Stunts Unlimited, was created in 1970 by Hal Needham, one of the best known of current stunt people who has been closely associated with Burt Reynolds. Thanks to the 1980 feature film *The Stunt Man*, and to the Lee Majors television series *The Fall Guy*, the public has become increasingly aware of the work of stunt men and women. There is also a Hollywood Stuntmen's Hall of Fame (18450 Seminole Drive, Cabazon, Calif. 92230), which was founded in 1973.

BIBLIOGRAPHY

Baxter, John. *Stunt*. Garden City, New York: Doubleday, 1974.

Canutt, Yakima, with Oliver Drake. *Stunt Man*. New York: Walker, 1979.

Dwiggins, Don. *The Air Devils*. Philadelphia: J. P. Lippincott, 1966.

Farmer, James H. *Broken Wings: Hollywood's Air Crashes*. Missoula, Montana: Pictorial Histories Publishing Company, 1984.

Greenwood, Jim, and Maxine Greenwood. *Stunt Flying in the Movies*. Blue Ridge Summit, Pennsylvania: TAB Books, 1982.

Sullivan, George, and Tim Sullivan. *Stunt People*. New York: Beaufort Books, 1983.

Wise, Arthur, and Derek Ware. *Stunting in the Cinema*. New York: St. Martin's Press, 1973.

SUBMARINE FILM COMPANY. Captain Charles Williamson spent thirty years perfecting his invention, the Williamson Submarine Tube, which his sons, J. Ernest and George M., used to make underwater films for their company called, at various times, the Submarine Film Company and the Williamson Submarine Film Company, of Norfolk, Virginia. Carl Louis Gregory, who had been a cameraman for Edison* and Thanhouser*, and a producer of Mutual's "Princess" pictures, was selected to film the company's productions, which would be released through the Thanhouser Film Company on the Mutual* program. Its first release, *The Terrors of the Deep*, was made in 1914 in the waters off the Bahamas and Bermuda. The film was screened at the Smithsonian Institute, at New York's Museum of Natural History, and at Broadway's Rose Gardens before touring large cities. A company was formed at Universal* early in 1915 to take the films produced by the company throughout the United States with a lecturer. The Williamson brothers' second film, *Twenty Thousand Leagues under the Sea*, shot by Eugene Gaudio, was made in collaboration with Universal. Later in that same year, 1916, the company made *The Submarine Eye*, again in association with Universal, with whom the Williamson brothers were to be connected for some time. In 1917, Harry Houdini signed with the Williamsons to demonstrate on film that he could escape the Williamson Tube without breaking the two-inch-thick glass.

BIBLIOGRAPHY

"Under Water Photography," *The Moving Picture World*, April 25, 1914, p. 497.

SUBTITLES. The word subtitles can be used to refer either to the titles that appear at the bottom of the screen on foreign-language films or to narrative or descriptive titles in silent films. The latter are usually described today as intertitles, but during the silent era they were always called subtitles.

In an average silent feature film, one-fifth of the production consisted of subtitles. Many subtitles in silent films could be quite florid, while others were intelligently witty, and some title writers—such as Ralph Spence—became noted for their humorous titles. Very occasionally, subtitles in silent films were superimposed over the action, but this was most unusual. *The Old Swimmin' Hole* (1921) utilized no subtitles to tell its story but rather explained the action through entries in the diary of the leading man, Charles Ray. The best known of silent films without subtitles was F. W. Muranu's *The Last Laugh*, made in Germany in 1925, which had only one title to explain the "happy ending" tacked on the end of the feature.

The first foreign-language feature to be subtitled in English is believed to have been *Two Hearts in Waltz Time/Zwei Herzen in 3/4 Takt*, produced in Germany in 1930, which was subtitled in the United States by Herman G. Weinberg (1908–1983). Weinberg is the best known of all subtitle writers, with a reported 400 films to his credit. Through the thirties, subtitles on foreign-language films were kept to the minimum, used from time to time to explain the plotline. It was not until the late forties that distributors began providing detailed subtitles for foreign-language features.

BIBLIOGRAPHY
Silent Films
"Artistic Subtitles," *The Moving Picture World*, December 30, 1916, p. 1966.
Bradlet, John W., "On Subtitles," *The Moving Picture World*, February 27, 1909, p. 235.
Bush, Stephen W., "Perfection in Titles," *The Moving Picture World*, October 4, 1913, p. 1261.
Richardson, Dorothy M., "Continuous Performance: Captions," *Close Up*, September 1927, pp. 52–56.
"Why Is a Subtitle?" *The American Cinematographer*, December 15, 1921, p. 12.
Williams, Lawrence, "The Making of Photoplay Titles," *Motion Picture*, March 1919, p. 86.

Foreign-Language Films
Salemson, H. J., "She Walks like a Church," *Action*, November-December 1978, pp. 44–49.

SUNDANCE INSTITUTE. Opened in 1980 by Robert Redford, the Sundance Institute, located in the mountains of Utah, serves to encourage and train serious young directors, producers, writers, and actors, working basically in a laboratory situation each summer. Young filmmakers are encouraged to submit scripts to be made utilizing a Sundance co-production fund, and an average of 400 are received each year. A preliminary reading of the best 50 takes place in October, and the final selection of 7 is made in April. Sundance Institute operates with a reported annual budget of $625,000, with funding provided by Redford, the National Endowment for the Arts, and private foundations and corporations. Robert Redford serves as president, with Sterling VanWagenen as executive director with a board of creative individuals from the film industry.

Address: 19 Exchange Place, Salt Lake City, Utah 84111.

BIBLIOGRAPHY
Greenberg, James, "Sundance Institute Shot in Arm for Indie Prod'n," *Daily Variety*, June 11, 1984, pp. 22, 36.
Lombardi, John, "Redford's Film Lab in the Rockies," *The New York Times Magazine*, October 23, 1983, pp. 48–51, 54, 58–61.
Perry, Gerald, "Sundance," *American Film*, October 1981, pp. 46–51.
Pollock, Dale, "Robert Redford and the Sundance Kids," *Los Angeles Times*, Calendar Section, July 4, 1982, pp. 1, 26, 27, 30, 31, 33.
"Robert Redford's Summer Camp," *Vogue*, February 1984, pp. 114, 116.

SUNN CLASSICS. See JENSEN-FARLEY PICTURES, INC.

SUNSET COMEDY COMPANY. Based in Youngstown, Ohio, the Sunset Comedy Company, under the presidency of H. C. Kunkleman, produced a series of one-reel comedies in the late teens and early twenties, released on a states rights* basis and featuring "Fatty Beilstein" (an obvious copy of Roscoe "Fatty" Arbuckle).

SUNSET MOTION PICTURE COMPANY. The directors and stockholders of the Sunset Motion Picture Company included such distinguished men as U.S. Senator James B. Phelan; Judge B. V. Sargent of the Superior Court; bankers Herbert Fleischhocker and C. L. Smith; J. H. Henry, one of California's wealthiest men; and Charles K. Field, the editor of *Sunset Magazine*, from which the company got its name. Sunset was formed in 1914, with M. E. Cory as general manager, and had offices in the World's Tower Building at 110 West 40 Street, New York. For its first film, *Rescue of the Stefansson Arctic Expedition*, it sent cameraman Fred LeRoy Granville to Kamchatka and Siberia to document the Arctic explorers' expedition.

SUNSET MOTION PICTURE CORPORATION. The Sunset Motion Picture Corporation began producing films on five acres of land and an open-air stage on the outskirts of San Antonio, Texas, in September 1918. Frank Powell directed the company's films, which were released by the W. W. Hodkinson Corporation*.

SUNSHINE COMEDY COMPANY. William Fox was the president and Henry "Pathe" Lehrman was the vice-president and general manager of the Sunshine Comedy Company, formed in March 1917 and also referred to as Sunshine Comedies, Inc. Four companies were put in operation to make two reels of comedy every two weeks. Lehrman supervised all the productions and also directed his own company and one featuring Mildred Lee. David Kirkland directed a company featuring Billie Rhodes, and Noel Smith directed H. I. Symonds. By mid–1919, Hampton Del Ruth had taken over supervision of the company, which included directors Eddie Cline, Roy Del Ruth, Mal St. Clair, Vin Moore, Jack Blystone, and Frank Griffin and stars Chester Conklin, Polly Moran, Slim Summerville, Jack Cooper, Alice Davenport, Laura LaVarnie, and Ethel Teare.
BIBLIOGRAPHY
"Fox Has New Comedy Company," *The Moving Picture World*, March 31, 1917, p. 2130.
"Sunshine Comedies Live Up to Name," *The Moving Picture World*, July 19, 1919, p. 356.

SUNSHINE FILM CORPORATION. See UNITED FILM SERVICE

"SUPERBA" BRAND. See FREDERICK DOUGLASS FILM COMPANY

SUPERBA COMPANY. See UNITED FILM SERVICE

SUPER 8mm. Super 8mm was introduced by the Eastman Kodak Company* in 1965 in the form of Kodachrome II film in an easy-loading cartridge and instamatic movie cameras and projectors. The Super 8mm format provided approximately 50 percent more image area per frame than standard 8mm*. The use of the system was licensed to other manufacturers by Eastman Kodak, and for its development of the format the company received the Albert S. Howell Award from Bell & Howell*. Super 8mm virtually ended the use of standard 8mm, and, in turn, Super 8mm has largely been superceded by the use of videotape. This area of filmmaking was covered from 1972 to 1981 by *Super 8 Filmmaker* magazine.

BIBLIOGRAPHY

Glenn, George D. *Super 8 Handbook*. Indianapolis, Indiana: Howard W. Sams, 1974.

Lipton, Lenny. *The Super 8 Book*. San Francisco: Straight Arrow Books, 1975.

McClain, Bebe Ferrell. *Super 8 Filmmaking from Scratch*. Englewood Cliffs, New Jersey: Prentice-Hall, 1978.

Matzkin, Myron A. *The Super 8 Film Maker's Handbook*. New York: Amphoto, 1976.

SUPERLATIVE PICTURES CORPORATION. Superlative Pictures Corporation, whose formation was announced on June 1, 1917, consisted of two subsidiary producing companies working independently of each other to produce high-class features: Irving Cummings Pictures, Inc., and Lois Meredith Pictures, Inc. Morris F. Tobias was president and Irving Cummings was vice-president. Lois Meredith was the vice-president of her own company and had the privilege of approving any stories before they were accepted for production.

BIBLIOGRAPHY

"Superlative Company Launched," *The Moving Picture World*, June 16, 1917, p. 1793.

SUPERPICTURES, INC. Superpictures, Inc., was incorporated in Delaware in November 1916, with a capitalization of $9 million, to encourage, finance, and distribute films of quality. W. W. Hodkinson, formerly the head of Paramount*, was the president; Frederick L. Collins, the president of McClure Publications, was the vice-president; and Raymond Pawley, of Paramount, was the treasurer. In keeping with Hodkinson's belief that distributors should not produce films, Superpictures planned to pick and choose its releases from the product of the best studios and provide capital to producers to make films of the highest quality. The McClure publications were to publicize Superpictures releases.

Superpictures acquired a substantial interest in Paramount and in the Progressive Motion Picture Company, the Western distributing concern of Paramount. Soon after its inception, Superpictures joined with the Triangle Film Corporation* to form the Triangle Distributing Corporation, which operated twenty-two exchanges* and handled productions of Triangle-Fine Arts, Kay Bee, and Keystone. Hodkinson was the president and general manager of the new concern, whose offices were at 1454 Broadway, New York.

In 1917, the Superpictures Distribution Corporation was formed to distribute films made by the Petrova Picture Company, the star of which was Olga Petrova, a partner with Frederick L. Collins. Ralph Ince directed its productions, beginning with *Daughter of Destiny*, at the Bacon-Backer studio at 230 West 38 Street, New York.

BIBLIOGRAPHY
"Hodkinson to Head Superpictures," *The Moving Picture World*, November 25, 1916,
    p. 1140.

SUPERSCOPE. See CINEMASCOPE

SUPER 16mm. See 16mm

SUPER TECHNIRAMA 70. See TECHNIRAMA

SUTHERLAND STUDIOS. See ALDRICH STUDIOS

SYNCHRONOPHONE MOTION PICTURE COMPANY OF NEW YORK.
The Synchronophone Motion Picture Company of New York was formed early
in 1913 to promote the Synchronophone and the Cinematophone, two talking
picture devices. These were exhibited at Sherwood's Picture Theatre, Fulton
Street, New York.

BIBLIOGRAPHY
"Talking Picture Devices," *The Moving Picture World*, March 29, 1913, p. 1318.

T

TAFT INTERNATIONAL PICTURES. See JENSEN-FARLEY PICTURES, INC.

TALISMAN STUDIOS. Talisman Studios was the name given to the former Fine Arts* studios, with a postal address of 4516 Sunset Boulevard, from 1934 to 1942. From 1935 onward, John F. Meehan held the position of studio manager. The studio had previously been owned from 1932 to 1933 by Bert Kelly, Sam Bischoff, and Bill Saul. During the period that the lot was controlled by Talisman Pictures Corporation, it was used by Monogram*, Crescent Pictures, Benny Zeidman, Jam Handy*, Majestic Pictures*, and Splay Commercials.

BIBLIOGRAPHY

Hearn, Marjorie, "Talisman Studios," in *The Film Daily Cavalcade*. New York: The Film Daily, 1939, p. 281.

TALKING PICTURE EPICS, INC. Formed in 1929 as a New York–based company and with Frank R. Wilson as president, Talking Picture Epics, Inc., was one of the more impressive sounding of the smaller independent producer/distributors from the early years of sound. In an advertisement in the 1931 edition of *The Film Daily Year Book*, it promised "features and short subjects vibrant with strange realities, pulsing with the fascination of nature's wonders and changing moods, and human and animal oddities."

Indeed, its films were unusual. Among the company's feature-length releases (some of which were also released as serials) were *Around the World via Graf Zeppelin* (1929), *Hunting Tigers in India* (1929), *Across the World with Mr. and Mrs. Martin Johnson* (1930), *The Bottom of the World* (1930), *Break-Up* (1930), *South Seas* (1930), *Wild Men of Kalihari* (1930), *Lost Gods* (1930), and *In the South Seas with Mr. and Mrs. Pinchot*. Talking Picture Epics also produced the 1931 "Intimate Interview" series of one-reel shorts, which featured conversations with such Hollywood personalities as James Cagney, Mae Clarke, and Bela Lugosi. The company ceased operations in 1932.

"TAMS" PICTURES. See REGENT FILM COMPANY, INC.

TANDEM. See EMBASSY COMMUNICATIONS

TAPPAN, NEW YORK. See DRACO FILM COMPANY, INC., and PIERROT FILM COMPANY, INC.

T.A.T. COMMUNICATIONS. See EMBASSY COMMUNICATIONS

TEC-ART STUDIO. Located at 5360 Melrose Avenue, Hollywood, at the junctions of Melrose and Bronson Avenue, the Tec Art Studio was one of the major rental studios of the twenties. It was opened in 1913 by William H. Clune (who also operated Clune's Auditorium in downtown Los Angeles), and the first important film to be shot there was *Ramona* (1916). In the early twenties, the studio became known as Tec-Art, and among the films shot there were *Timothy's Quest* (1922), *Soul-Fire* (1925), *Ramona* (1928), *She Goes to War* (1929), *Hell Harbor* (1930), and *Mamba* (1930). Among the sound shorts produced there were the Meglin Kiddie Revues and the "Voice of Hollywood"* series. Although Tec-Art was not known as a producer, all but three of the films in the latter series were copyrighted by the studio. As far as can be ascertained, Tec-Art ceased to exist in 1931. *See also* California Studios.

TECHNICOLOR. The best-known name in the history of color motion pictures, Technicolor has been applied to several different processes since the introduction of the name by Dr. Herbert T. Kalmus (1881–1963). The name Technicolor was chosen by Kalmus, because he, along with other physicists who worked on the invention, were graduates of the Massachusetts Institute of Technology.

The first Technicolor process was an additive one. The camera photographed a pair of images through red and green filters, and when the one strip of film with these two images was projected through red and green filters they merged on the screen. The first and only film to be shot in the additive process by Technicolor was *The Gulf Between*, supervised by C. A. Willat and starring Grace Darmond and Niles Welch, which was filmed in the summer of 1917 in Jacksonville, Florida. A special passenger car was purchased and remodeled by the Technicolor Corporation* to serve as both a laboratory and an office, while the film was being shot on location. *The Gulf Between* was first screened, privately, at New York's Aeolian Hall on September 21, 1917.

Technicolor developed a two-color process utilizing a special camera, which photographed objects in two of the three primary colors—red and green. The camera contained a beam-splitter prism which made red and green exposures on two frames simultaneously, with one of the frames inverted. The film moved through the camera two frames at a time, using twice as much film as with regular black-and-white production. Two prints were made from the negative—

one for each primary color—utilizing stocks of half the normal thickness. These two pieces of film were then cemented together and dyed complementary colors.

The first film to be shot in Technicolor's new two-color process was *The Toll of the Sea*, which was originally intended to be a short subject but which cameraman Ray Rennahan persuaded Technicolor to release as a five-reel feature. Filmed in Santa Monica, California, in 1921, and released in 1922, *The Toll of the Sea* starred Anna May Wong and Kenneth Harlan in a version of *Madame Butterfly*, which was directed by Chester Franklin. The Technicolor process was first utilized for a sequence in a major feature—the exodus of the Israelites from Egypt—in Cecil B. DeMille's *The Ten Commandments* (1923), and was subsequently used in other features. The first interior use of Technicolor was for a sequence in George Fitzmaurice's *Cytherea* (1924). The first major commercial feature to be filmed entirely in two-color Technicolor was Paramount's *Wanderer of the Wasteland* (1924), followed by Douglas Fairbanks' *The Black Pirate* (1926). It was also used for sequences in *The Phantom of the Opera* (1925), *Ben-Hur* (1926) and *The King of Kings* (1927), among others. The first sound feature to be shot entirely in Technicolor—although the sound was limited to music and effects—was *The Viking* (1928). Subsequently, Warner Bros.* utilized Technicolor for many of its early sound features, including *On with the Show* (1929), the first all-Technicolor, all-talking, all-singing, all-dancing production.

In 1928, Technicolor introduced two-color imbibition prints, which did not require two strips of film cemented together, but which could be printed using the imbibition (or dye transfer) process on one strip of film.

The full-color or three-color Technicolor process—utilizing the primary colors of blue, red, and green (which in the printing process became the subtractive primary colors of yellow, cyan, and magenta)—was introduced in1932, following the completion of the building of the first three-strip camera under the direction of J. A. (Joseph Arthur) Ball, who became the company's director of research following the 1932 death of Dr. Leonard T. Troland. As Dr. Kalmus recalled in a December 1938 article

By May 1932, Technicolor had completed the building of its first three-component camera, and had one unit of its plant equipped to handle a moderate amount of three-color printing. The difference between this three-component process and the previous two-component process was truly extraordinary. Not only was the accuracy of tone and color reproduction greatly improved, but definition was markedly better. However, we could not offer the three-component product to one customer without offering it to all, which required many more cameras, and the conversion of much of our plant. To allow time for this and to prove the process beyond any doubt, we sought first to try it out in the cartoon field. But no cartoonist would have it. We were told cartoons were good enough in black-and-white, and that of all the departments of production, cartoons could least afford the added expense. Finally Walt Disney tried it as an experiment on one of his "Silly Symphonies." The first attempt was *Flowers and Trees*, following which Disney contracted for a series.

Flowers and Trees was released in 1932. *La Cucaracha*, the first live-action subject photographed in Technicolor, was released in 1934, and *Becky Sharp*, the first full-length feature to be shot in the Technicolor three-strip process, was released in 1935. *Thunderhead*, the first all-Monopak (Kodachrome converted to Technicolor in the printing process) Technicolor feature, was released in 1944.

Technicolor quickly became the industry standard for color. It was expensive, with Technicolor's providing not only the camera and the cameraman (the best known of which was Ray Rennahan) but also a color consultant in the person of Natalie Kalmus, the divorced wife of the company's founder. As explained by the company, "The credit phrase, Color by Technicolor, is used for motion pictures in color which have been controlled from the developing of the original negative or 'taking' film to the manufacture of the positive release prints by a Technicolor company." The phrase "Print by Technicolor" was utilized to describe release prints made by Technicolor but not necessarily photographed in Technicolor. In 1975, economic reasons forced the demise of imbibition printing by Technicolor, and all films after that date were simply printed by the Technicolor laboratory but generally photographed in Eastman Color*. The only laboratory capable of printing in the original three-strip Technicolor process is the dye transfer processing plant built by Technicolor in Peking in 1979.

BIBLIOGRAPHY

Basten, Fred E. *Glorious Technicolor*. San Diego: A. S. Barnes, 1980.

Behlmer, Rudy, "Technicolor," *Films in Review*, June-July 1964, pp. 333–351.

Kalmus, H. T., "Technicolor Adventures in Cinemaland," *Journal of the Society of Motion Picture Engineers*, December 1938, pp. 564–568.

Kalmus, Natalie, "Color Consciousness," *Journal of the Society of Motion Picture Engineers*, August 1935, pp. 139–147.

Penfield, Cornelia, "Joseph's Coat for the Silver Screen?" *Stage*, July 1936, pp. 49–50.

Taylor, Frank J., "Mr. Technicolor," *The Saturday Evening Post*, October 22, 1949, pp. 26–27, 131–134.

"The Three Color Process," *Academy Technicians Branch Technical Bulletin*, May 31, 1935, special issue.

"What? Color in the Movies Again?" *Fortune*, October 1934, pp. 92–97, 161–171.

TECHNICOLOR CORPORATION. The Technicolor Corporation had its origins in the company of Kalmus, Comstock & Wescott, Inc., founded by Dr. Herbert Thomas Kalmus (1881–1963), Dr. Daniel F. Comstock, and W. Burton Wescott in 1912. This research and development group was approached by a Boston lawyer named William H. Coolidge to investigate a new motion picture projector called the Vanoscope. The trio persuaded Coolidge to invest in the design of a motion picture camera that would photograph color, and, in 1915, Coolidge and C. A. Hight provided the $10,000 necessary to establish the Technicolor Motion Picture Corporation. In 1920, William Travers Jerome replaced Coolidge as Technicolor's principal backer, and that same year Marcus Loew became involved in the corporation.

Wescott left the corporation in 1921, followed in 1925 by Comstock. Initially a Boston corporation, Technicolor began the removal of its headquarters to Hollywood in 1930 with the opening of Plant No. 4 at 1016 North Cole Avenue— a postal address that was later changed to 6311 Romaine Avenue—which was to become the corporation's headquarters. (In 1973, Technicolor moved its laboratory to new premises on the Universal* lot, while maintaining corporate headquarters in Century City.) John Hay Whitney became interested in the Technicolor* process in the early thirties, when he formed Pioneer Pictures* and purchased a considerable amount of Technicolor stock.

A British Technicolor laboratory was established in 1936, with the first British Technicolor feature being *Wings of the Morning* (1937). In 1938, Technicolor's J. Arthur Ball received a Special Academy Award "for his outstanding contributions to the advancement of color in motion picture photography."

As of 1933, the corporation had processed 9 million feet of Technicolor film stock. The amount increased to 80 million feet by 1940 and 125 million by 1943. As of 1956, it was reported that Technicolor had processed some 5 billion feet of film, with 41 million of that footage being used for prints of *Gone with the Wind* (1939).

In May 1947, the U.S. government filed an antitrust suit against both Technicolor and Eastman Kodak*, a suit perhaps prompted by the government's control of a German color process developed by General Analine which was making little headway in the United States thanks to Technicolor's monopoly. A consent decree between Technicolor and the Justice Department was signed in 1950. The increase in the use of Eastman Color* led to Technicolor's diversification with Technirama*, its introduction of 8mm cassette projectors; the creation of a television syndication company, Gold Key Media (which was sold in 1982); and its eventual move into video.

On June 30, 1956, the Technicolor Motion Picture Corporation was renamed Technicolor Corporation. (Technicolor, Inc., was incorporated in New York in 1922.) The Technicolor Corporation was acquired by Patrick J. Frawley, Jr., in 1961, but a stockholders' group, led by producer Harry Saltzman, wrested control away from Frawley in 1970. In 1982, the corporation was acquired by MacAndrews and Forbes Group, Inc., of New York.

Address: 2049 Century Park East, Suite 2400, Los Angeles, Calif. 90067.
RESOURCES
Papers: Academy of Motion Pictures Arts and Sciences (selected items only).

TECHNIRAMA. Developed by the Technicolor Corporation*, Technirama was a widescreen process utilizing an anamorphic lens* and 35mm* film traveling horizontally through the camera (as with VistaVision*), thus, according to Technicolor, photographing approximately 50 percent more of the horizontal dimension. The first film to be shot in Technirama was *The Monte Carlo Story*, which received its premiere at the Reposi Cinema in Turin, Italy, on December 19, 1956. A 70mm* version of Technirama was introduced as Super Technirama 70 with *Spartacus* (1960).

BIBLIOGRAPHY

Mascelli, Joseph V., "Technirama," *International Photographer*, June 1957, pp. 5–8.

TED MANN PRODUCTIONS. See MANN THEATRES CORPORATION

TELEVIEW. See THREE-DIMENSIONAL FILMS

TELEVISION. See FILMS MADE FOR TELEVISION

TELEVISION PRODUCTIONS OF AMERICA, INC. See EDWARD SMALL PRODUCTIONS, INC.

TELLURIDE FILM FESTIVAL. A small yet exclusive—some might say elitist—film festival, the Telluride Film Festival takes place each Labor Day weekend. It is held in the small Victorian mining town of Telluride, with a population of little over 1,000, located some 320 miles southwest of Denver, with Telluride's Sheridan Opera House serving as the focal point of the festival. Because of its location and limited housing facilities, attendance at Telluride remains small and tickets are eagerly sought after. It offers a blend of the best of new and old world cinema.

The Telluride Film Festival was founded in 1974—it was first held from August 30 to September 2 that year—by Bill Pence, and the first celebrity guests were Gloria Swanson, Francis Ford Coppola, and Leni Riefenstahl. Pence's co-directors are Tom Luddy and William K. Everson (who replaced the first co-director James Card).

Address: The National Film Preserve Limited, 110 North Oak Street, Telluride, Colo. 81435.

TERRYTOONS. Terrytoons was organized as an animated film production company in 1930 by Paul Terry (1887–1971), who had commenced his career as an animator in 1915. The best-known series to be produced by Terrytoons was "Mighty Mouse," which was a rodent version of Superman and which, for its first cartoons, had been known as Supermouse. The first of the series, *The Mouse of Tomorrow*, was released by 20th Century-Fox* on October 16, 1942.

Paul Terry sold his company to CBS in 1955, but Terrytoons continued to produce cartoons through the seventies, with one of its best-known later animators being Ralph Bakshi (who became supervising director in 1966). The company was located in New Rochelle, New York, from 1935 through 1972, when it moved to the New York headquarters of Viacom*, which eventually acquired CBS Films, including Terrytoons.

BIBLIOGRAPHY
Klein, I., "On Mighty Mouse," in Gerald Peary and Danny Peary, editors, *The American Animated Cartoon*. New York: E. P. Dutton, 1980, pp. 171–177.
Maltin, Leonard, "Paul Terry and Terrytoons," in *Of Mice and Magic*. New York: McGraw-Hill, 1980, pp. 121–153.
RESOURCES
Paul Terry Papers: Museum of Modern Art.

TEXTURE FILMS. See FILMS INCORPORATED

THANHOUSER FILM CORPORATION. The Thanhouser Film Corporation was formed by theatrical entrepreneur Edwin Thanhouser in 1909, with studios located at Grove and Warren streets and Crescent Avenue in New Rochelle. Thanhouser's first film, *The Actor's Children*, featured Orilla Smith and Yale Boss and was directed by one of Thanhouser's first two contract directors, Barry O'Neil or Lloyd B. Carleton. It was released on March 15, 1910. As the title suggests, Thanhouser often featured children in its films, and among those it had under contract were Helen Badgley (The Thanhouser Kidlet), Marie Eline (The Thanhouser Kid), and Marion and Madeline Fairbanks (The Thanhouser Twins). Other actors under contract included Florence La Badie, Mignon Anderson, Marguerite Snow, James Cruze, and William Russell.

In 1912, Thanhouser opened a winter studio in Jacksonville, Florida, and that same year the company was acquired by a syndicate headed by C. J. Hite. The year 1913 saw the destruction of Thanhouser's New Rochelle studios by fire, the signing of noted stage actress Maude Fealy, and the release of the company's first serial, *The Million Dollar Mystery*. When C. J. Hite was killed in a 1914 automobile accident, Edwin Thanhouser returned as head of the studio. The company had always released its films independently, but in 1916 Pathe* took over the distribution of its product, which, in that year, included the two films in which Jeanne Eagels made her screen debut, *The World and the Woman* and *Fires of Youth*.

Edwin Thanhouser retired in February 1918, and the studio was loaned out to Clara Kimball Young. In 1919, it was sold to Crawford Livingston and Wilbert Shallenberger, and later that same year it was acquired as the site for B. A. Rolfe Productions*.

BIBLIOGRAPHY
"A Day with Thanhouser," *The Moving Picture World*, April 24, 1915, p. 563.
Duncan, Robert C., "Forty-Five Minutes from Broadway," *Picture Play*, January 1917, pp. 90–96.
Harrison, Louis Reeves, "Studio Saunterings," *The Moving Picture World*, July 13, 1912, pp. 123–126.
Photoplay Arts Portfolio of Thanhouser Moving-Picture Stars. New York: Photoplay Arts, 1914.
Slide, Anthony. "The Thanhouser Company," in *Aspects of American Film History prior to 1920*. Metuchen, New Jersey: Scarecrow Press, 1978, pp. 68–78.

Thanhouser, Edwin, "Reminiscences of Picture's Babyhood Days," *The Moving Picture World*, March 10, 1917, pp. 1524–1525.
"Thanhouser Company: A New Film Producer," *The Moving Picture World*, March 12, 1910, p. 374.

THEATRE OWNERS OF AMERICA. See NATIONAL ASSOCIATION OF THEATRE OWNERS, INC.

THEATROVISION. See ELECTRONOVISION

"THE THIN MAN" SERIES. A series of six features produced by M-G-M* between 1934 and 1947, "The Thin Man" starred William Powell and Myrna Loy as the husband-and-wife detective team of Nick and Nora Charles. The first four films in the series, which were noted for their witty dialogue, were directed by W. S. Van Dyke. The characters, which were based on a couple created by Dashiell Hammett, lived in New York, were wealthy socialites, and owned a wire-haired fox terrier named Asta. They were also featured on radio and in a 1957–1959 NBC television series, on which they were played by Peter Lawford and Phyllis Kirk. The following is a complete list of "The Thin Man" films: *The Thin Man* (1934), *After the Thin Man* (1936), *Another Thin Man* (1939), *Shadow of the Thin Man* (1941), *The Thin Man Goes Home* (1944), and *Song of the Thin Man* (1947).

BIBLIOGRAPHY
Zinman, David. *Saturday Afternoon at the Bijou*. New Rochelle, New York: Arlington House, 1973.

35mm. 35mm is the standard gauge used in professional filmmaking and has been such since the 1890s. It is 35mm in width, with four perforations on each side of the film frame and sixteen frames to one foot of film.

THIS IS AMERICA. See MARCH OF TIME

"THISTLE" BRAND. See CROWN FILM MANUFACTURING COMPANY

THOMAS A. EDISON, INC. See EDISON MANUFACTURING COMPANY

THOMAS H. INCE CULVER CITY STUDIOS. See LAIRD INTERNATIONAL STUDIOS

THREE-DIMENSIONAL FILMS. The British film pioneer William Friese-Greene is generally credited with the creation of the first three-dimensional films, although there is little, if any, factual documentation to back up the claim. He utilized the theory behind stereoscopic viewers, popular in Victorian households and whose contemporary equivalent would be the Viewmaster. Images were photographed twice, with the camera being moved 2 1/2 inches for the second photograph. The 2 1/2 inches represented the average distance between the eyes of the viewer, and when the two photographic images were viewed through the stereoscopic device, a three-dimensional effect was obtained. In the late 1890s, Friese-Greene used the same principle but applied it to motion picture film.

Early three-dimensional experiments used what is known as the anaglyphic process, which, simply explained, uses two cameras to photograph the same image. The film representing the left eye is dyed red and the film representing the right eye is dyed green. In processing, these two pieces of film are placed on top of each other, and when viewed through red and green glasses a three-dimensional effect is obtained.

On September 27, 1922, Harry K. Fairall screened the first major 3-D production, a five-reel feature titled *The Power of Love*, starring Barbara Bedford and Noah Beery. William Van Doren Kelley (who invented Prizma Color*) exhibited his 3-D process, known as Plasticon in the fall of 1922, and, some two years later, Frederick Eugene Ives and J. F. Leventhal produced a series of 3-D shorts called Plastigrams. Film pioneer George K. Spoor, who co-founded the Essanay Company*, worked throughout the twenties on a three-dimensional process called Natural Vision and shot at least one feature, *Danger Lights* (1930), and one short, *Campus Sweethearts* (1930), utilizing his system, which, apparently, also boasted widescreen and some form of stereophonic sound.

Slightly different from the anaglyphic process was the Teleview, invented by Laurens Hammond and William F. Cassidy, which required the spectator to view the film through a glass screen fitted with a shutter that operated in synchronization with the shutter on the one projector required for the process. One six-reel feature, *Mars* (also known as *Radio-Mania*, 1923) was filmed in Teleview; directed by Roy William Neill and starring Grant Mitchell and Margaret Irving, it told of an inventor who tried to manufacture a radio to contact Mars and, in his dreams, met a group of Martians.

Abel Gance considered using 3-D for his production of *Napoléon* (1927) but had to content himself instead with a triple-screen effect; most producers during the twenties and thirties displayed little interest in 3-D. The anaglyphic process reappeared in the mid-thirties with a couple of shorts, *Audioskopics* (1936) and *The New Audioskopics* (1938), produced by Pete Smith for M-G-M*. With a budget of $3,000, and using two Bell & Howell* cameras with specially matched Bausch and Lomb lenses, technicians Irving Ries and A. G. Wise, director George Sidney, and Pete Smith produced a parody of the Frankenstein story titled *Third Dimension Murder* (1941), for which the 3-D process was rechristened Metroscopix by M-G-M.

The invention of the polaroid process by Edwin H. Land in 1932 heralded a new era for the three-dimensional film. Using Land's original concept, John A. Norland developed a polarizing three-dimensional film system. Two cameras, representing the human eyes, photograph the object, as in the anaglyphic process. However, two projectors are used to screen the two pieces of film, with polaroid filters in front of each projector lens. One filter passes light waves vibrating vertically, while the other passes light waves vibrating horizontally. The polaroid glasses worn by the viewer operate in a similar fashion, and as each eye sees the image, as in a natural binocular effect, a three-dimensional picture is obtained. Unlike the anaglyphic process, the new polaroid process permitted the use of color film. However, it had one major disadvantage in that two projectors were required, running in precise synchronization, something which many contemporary projections and theatres seem incapable of handling.

The first American film to use the new process was a fifteen-minute short produced by J. A. Norling for the Chrysler Corporation exhibit at the 1939 New York World's Fair. A 3-D feature, *Beggar's Weekend* was produced in Italy in 1936, and two 3-D features were filmed in Germany: *You Can Nearly Touch It* (1937) and *Six Girls Drive into the Weekend* (1939). The Soviets used the polaroid process but did away with the need for glasses by placing a grille of 30,000 copper wires in front of the screen on which the film was projected. The Moscow Cinema was set up for this purpose, and the first Russian 3-D film, *Land of Youth*, filmed partly in color, was screened there in 1941.

It was not until ten years later that the film industry again showed an interest in 3-D, when, in 1951, a three-dimensional abstract short, *Around Is Around*, directed by Norman MacLaren for the National Film Board of Canada, was screened at the annual convention of the Society of Motion Picture and Television Engineers*. A Hollywood entrepreneur, Milton Gunzburg, was the first to realize the dormant commercial potential of 3-D, and in 1952 he and Arch Oboler produced *Bwana Devil*, a shoddy melodrama starring Robert Stack and Barbara Britton. Three-dimensional films were revived in the United Kingdom for the 1951 Festival of Britain; the 1953 British Coronation was filmed in 3-D; and two Italian features, *Beauty to Measure* and *Odessey*, were screened in 3-D. The most important and successful 3-D feature of the fifties was Warner Bros.' *House of Wax* (1953), starring Vincent Price and directed by André de Toth. Other 3-D features included *It Came from Outer Space* (1953), *Man in the Dark* (1953), *Charge at Feather River* (1953), *Creature from the Black Lagoon* (1954), *Kiss Me Kate* (1953), and *Dial M for Murder* (1954), which was not actually seen in 3-D until 1979.

CinemaScope* effectively ended the industry's interest in 3-D until the seventies when there was a minor revival with *The Stewardesses* (1970), *Prison Girls* (1972), *Andy Warhol's Frankenstein* (1974), and a major reissue of *Creature from the Black Lagoon*. The year 1982 marked another return for 3-D with *Friday the 13th Part III*. Murray Lerner produced a seventeen-minute 3-D short, *Journey into the Imagination*, for the Eastman Kodak* Pavilion at the new EPCOT Center at Disney World in Florida, and *Jaws 3-D* (1983) was released. However, the failure of the last at the box office may prove another stumbling block in the continued exploitation of three-dimensional films.

BIBLIOGRAPHY
Connor, Edward, "3-D on the Screen," *Films in Review*, March 1966, pp. 159–174.
Kerbel, Michael, "3-D or Not 3-D," *Film Comment*, November-December 1980, pp. 11–20.
London, Harley W., "3-D: A Brief History," *Boxoffice*, November 1982, pp. 19–22.
Quigley, Martin, Jr. *New Screen Techniques*. New York: Quigley Publishing Company, 1953.
Slide, Anthony, "3-D Back Again and Again and Again," in F. Maurice Speed, editor, *Film Review 1983–84*. London: W. H. Allen, 1983, pp. 17–21.
"Strictly for the Marbles," *Time*, June 8, 1953, pp. 66–74.

THX MOTION PICTURE LOUDSPEAKER SYSTEM. See LUCASFILM, LTD.

TIFFANY FILM CORPORATION. Herbert Brenon left the Universal Film Manufacturing Company in October 1914 to become the head of the Tiffany Film Corporation, which planned to release with the Alco Film Corporation*. Intending to make films that would enjoy long runs on Broadway, Brenon signed Mrs. Leslie Carter to play in the civil war drama *The Heart of Maryland*, in which she had appeared on Broadway and around the country for some 3,500 performances for the previous twenty years. The film was shot at the Oz* studio in Hollywood, with William Shay in the male lead. When it was released by Metro* in March 1915, the film was the first feature to be shown at the New York Hippodrome, the largest theatre in the world seating 5,400. Although Brenon planned to make his next film at Tiffany with actress Nance O'Neil, instead he went to the newly formed Fox Film Corporation, taking O'Neil and Shay with him.

BIBLIOGRAPHY
"Brenon to Produce for Tiffany," *The Moving Picture World*, October 31, 1914, p. 619.

TIFFANY PRODUCTIONS. Incorporated in 1921, Tiffany Productions was a minor film producer, but one that eschewed the types of features—"B" Westerns and the like—that one might expect from such a company. It specialized in society dramas and melodramas, notably *Peacock Alley*, starring Mae Murray, which Tiffany produced both as a silent feature (1922) and as a part-talkie with a Technicolor sequence (1930). From 1927 to 1929, director John Stahl was associated with the company, which became known during that period as Tiffany-Stahl Productions.

The most important of all Tiffany films was *Journey's End* (1930), directed by James Whale; it was the first Anglo-American sound co-production. *Journey's End* brought such prominence to Tiffany that in 1930 an injunction against the use of the name was filed by the jewellers Tiffany and Company. Unfortunately, *Journey's End* also marked the end of quality production at Tiffany, with the exceptions of *Lucky Boy* (1929), a part-talkie starring George Jessel; *The*

Medicine Man (1930), starring Jack Benny; and *Mamba* (1930), a Technicolor feature. In an effort to overcome its financial problems, Tiffany began to turn out the staple of the "B" movie* producers: "B" Westerns, featuring Ken Maynard and Bob Steele, and short subjects such as The Tiffany Talking Chimps series, The Voice of Hollywood*, Paul Hurst comedies, *Al Mannon's Sports Folio, Screen Book of Knowledge, Romance of the Old and New World,* and *Screen Novelties* series. It ceased operations in 1932. (From 1927 onward, Tiffany was located at the former Fine Arts* studio on Sunset Boulevard.)
BIBLIOGRAPHY
Fernett, Gene. *Poverty Row.* Satellite Beach, Florida: Coral Reef Publications, 1973.

TIME-LIFE FILMS, INC. A division of Time, Inc., Time-Life Films, Inc., was formed in 1973 by the merger of Time-Life Films, Time-Life Video, and Time-Life Entertainment. It was chiefly noted for its exclusive distribution of BBC Television productions in the United States, a ten-year partnership which terminated on April 30, 1981. In 1973, the company signed an agreement for the nontheatrical distribution of films produced by the American Film Institute, and that same year it acquired worldwide rights to the Harold Lloyd films. It financed a number of theatrical features: *They All Laughed* (1981), *Loving Couples* (1980), and *Fort Apache, the Bronx* (1981). There was talk early in 1981 of the sale of the company to 20th Century-Fox*, but, in August 1981, its assets were acquired by Columbia Pictures*. The sale became necessary following a loss of some $9 million, after taxes, in 1980.

TINTING AND TONING. Tinting and toning was a popular method of coloring silent films. Tints could be used to indicate changes in mood, while green and blue tints might be utilized for night scenes. By the mid-twenties, tinting and toning was used less frequently, and it virtually disappeared with the coming of sound because of problems in printing the sound track on tinted film stock. (However, tinting is used to advantage in a number of early sound films, notably in two 1932 features, *One Hour with You* and *Bird of Paradise.*)

Tinting involved the dipping of the film in the appropriate colored dye, which gave an overall color to the film stock. Toning involved the conversion of the silver in a black-and-white film through chemical toning. Thus, the black image could be changed to any color, while the white image remained unaffected. Unfortunately, the "tinting" of silent films today is usually handled by copying the original print on to Eastman Color* stock, which captures the essence of the original tinting but loses much of its delicacy and can even slightly change the coloring.
BIBLIOGRAPHY
Eastman Kodak Company. *Tinting and Toning of Eastman Positive Motion Picture Film.* Rochester, New York: Eastman Kodak, 1924.
"Toning and Tinting as an Adjunct to the Picture," *The Moving Picture World,* March 18, 1911, p. 574.

TODD-AO. A widescreen system developed by Dr. Brian O'Brien of the American Optical Company, Todd-AO utilized a single camera, with four lenses, and a single projector. The width of the film in the camera was 65mm, and the width of the projected film was 70mm*. The first film to be shot in Todd-AO was *Oklahoma!*, which received its premiere at the Rivoli Theatre, New York, on October 13, 1955. *Oklahoma!* was released by Magna Pictures Corporation (which also released *South Pacific* in 1958 and *Harlow* in 1965), of which Todd-AO became a wholly owned subsidiary until 1976. The second Todd-AO feature is probably the best known, and that was *Around the World in 80 Days*, produced by the man who gave the system its name, showman Mike Todd, and which received the 1956 Academy Award for Best Picture.

BIBLIOGRAPHY

Rowan, Arthur, "Todd-AO—Newest Wide-Screen System," *American Cinematographer*, October 1954, pp. 494–496, 526.

TODDY PICTURES COMPANY. One of the most important producers of all-black films strictly for black American audiences was Toddy Pictures Company, formed in 1941 by its president Ted Toddy by merging his other companies, Dixie Film Exchange of Atlanta, Million Dollar Pictures, and Consolidated National Film Exchanges. It produced both features and shorts, starring celebrities such as Lena Horne, Joe Louis, Nina Mae McKinney, Ralph Cooper, and Louise Beavers, with a production office at 6406 Sunset Boulevard in Los Angeles, New York headquarters, and film exchanges in Atlanta, Dallas, Chicago, and Los Angeles. In the April 12, 1947, issue of *Motion Picture Herald*, Toddy explained the nature of his product: "Negro audiences do not care for heavy emotional dramas. Their choice in film entertainment is the picture which features light comedy, outdoor adventures, musical comedies with an abundance of singing and dancing, and comedy romances." Toddy Pictures remained in existence through the early seventies.

TONING. See TINTING AND TONING

TOUCHSTONE FILMS. The creation of Touchstone Films was announced by Walt Disney Productions* on February 15, 1984. As explained by Disney president Ron Miller, in the *Walt Disney Exhibitor Newsletter* (March 1984):

> With Touchstone we are making a very clear distinction between classical, customary Disney entertainment for the entire family and our diversification into a wider spectrum of films. The name Walt Disney Pictures on a production will signal that the film is designed as family entertainment, while the Touchstone name will identify those films appealing to other segments of the audience. In effect, Disney is now the only studio to have its own self-imposed, in-house rating system to guide parents in the selection of motion picture viewing for their families.

Touchstone, meaning a test of quality, was selected from some 1,200 suggested names. The first film to be released under the Touchstone banner was *Splash* (1984); it was followed by *Country* (1984) and *Baby . . . Secret of the Lost Legend* (1985).

Address: 500 South Buena Vista Street, Burbank, Calif. 91521

BIBLIOGRAPHY

"Disney Forms Touchstone Banner to Identify Its Non-Family Output," *Variety*, February 22, 1984, pp. 23, 26.

Karp, Alan, "Touchstone Films: Disney's Movies Grow Up," *Boxoffice*, October 1984, pp. 7–8, 12.

TRADE PAPERS. Trade papers are the means by which those within the industry keep abreast of matters relating to all aspects of the motion picture—production, distribution, and exhibition. The oldest surviving and best known of all such papers is *Variety*, which has been published weekly in New York since December 16, 1905. Often referred to as the "Bible of Show Business," *Variety* began life as a publication chiefly concerned with vaudeville, and it was not until the twenties that motion pictures began to take up half of each issue. The earliest of trade papers exclusively devoted to film was *The Film Index*, which was founded as *Views and Film Index* on April 25, 1906, and which ceased publication on July 1, 1911, when it merged with *The Moving Picture World*.

The Moving Picture World is the best known of silent film trade papers to those studying the history of the motion picture. First published on March 9, 1907, it was published as a separate entity until December 31, 1927, when it merged with *Exhibitor's Herald* to become *Exhibitor's Herald World*. In time, the latter, along with the other major trade papers from the silent era—*Motion Picture News* (May 1908–December 27, 1930) and *Motography* (which began life as *The Nickelodeon* in January 1909 and ceased publication on July 13, 1918)—became *Motion Picture Herald*. A Quigley publication, *Motion Picture Herald* was first published January 3, 1931, and ended life May 5, 1973, as *QP Herald*. Quigley Publications was also responsible for the *International Motion Picture Almanac* and for *Motion Picture Daily* (which began life as *Exhibitor's Trade Review* on December 9, 1916).

Certainly the first major and possibly one of the best known of daily trade papers was *The Film Daily*, which began publication as *Wid's Films and Film Folks* in October 1915. *The Film Daily* along with its annual publication, *The Film Daily Year Book*, ceased publication in 1970. Presently, there are two daily trade papers, published five days a week: *The Hollywood Reporter* and *Daily Variety*. Both are published in Hollywood, the former since September 3, 1930, and the latter since September 6, 1933.

BIBLIOGRAPHY

Slide, Anthony. *International Film, Radio, and Television Journals*. Westport, Connecticut: Greenwood Press, 1985.

TRAILERS. Trailers, also known as Coming Attraction Trailers and Prevues, are utilized to ''sell'' a new film to a theatre audience by providing a brief outline of the star or emphasizing the most commercial aspects of the production (that is, its stars, director, or unusual theme). Trailers date back to the early teens when they consisted of nothing more than the film's main title and one or two important scenes. Extensive new artwork to promote a film was not introduced until the twenties.

By the thirties, trailers had become an integral part of a film presentation and remained so through the sixties. Research has indicated that trailers constitute 25 or 35 percent of the motivating force that encourages people to see a film, and as such producers are generally willing to spend between $10,000 and $30,000 on the production of individual trailers. Distributed to theatres by National Screen Service*, trailers are almost always prepared by independent production companies, with M-G-M* being the only studio to have had its own trailer department.

It is almost unprecedented for a film's maker to prepare a trailer, but, in recent years, directors such as Michael Cimino, Francis Ford Coppola, and Paul Schrader have overseen production of trailers promoting their current releases. Some trailers have attained ''classic'' stature, notably the one for *Citizen Kane* (1941), Cecil B. DeMille's lengthy promotional trailer for *The Ten Commandments* (1956), and a number of Alfred Hitchcock's trailers. Among the last, the best known is the trailer for *Rope* (1948), which introduces a character who is dead at the start of the film itself, and Hitchcock's personal tour of the Bates Motel in an eight-minute promotional trailer for *Psycho* (1960). In 1983, John Landis prepared a sixty-minute compilation of Universal trailers for pay television under the title of *Coming Soon*.

The average trailer is two to three minutes in length. Additionally, trailers from ten to ninety seconds are prepared for promotional purposes on television.

BIBLIOGRAPHY

Blair, Iain, ''Film Trailers: Attracting Audiences with Flair,'' *On Location*, January 1983, pp. 39–49.

Fadden, James, ''Trailers: Hollywood's Recreational Vehicle,'' *Back Stage*, August 19, 1983, pp. 5, 8, 10, 18, 29, 38.

Francis, Barbara, ''Movie Trailers: The Lure of the Filmstrip Tease,'' *Los Angeles Times*, Calendar Section, October 7, 1979, p. 7.

Goodwin, Michael, ''The Lost Films of Alfred Hitchcock,'' *New West*, April 1981, pp. 84–87, 142.

Lees, David, and Stan Berkowitz, ''The True Story behind Those 'Coming Attractions' (You'll Laugh! You'll Cry!),'' *Los Angeles*, January 1979, pp. 94–99.

TRANS-LUX CORPORATION. Trans-Lux Corporation was founded in 1920 by Percy N. Furber, who had invented a rear projection screen which made possible the showing of motion pictures in daylight and which formed the basis for the screen utilized for the projection of the ticker tape on the New York Stock Exchange. In the early thirties, Trans-Lux expanded its operations to include the management of newsreel theatres, and the name quickly became synonymous with newsreel* presentations, the Trans-Lux theatres becoming known as "Luxers." The corporation—which changed its name in 1937 from Trans-Lux Daylight Picture Screen Corporation to Trans-Lux Corporation— operated newsreel theatres in New York at 58 Street, 49 Street and Broadway, 60 Street and Madison Avenue, 52 Street and Lexington Avenue, and 85 Street and Madison Avenue.

In time, some of the theatres began screening second-run features in competition with a young man named Harry Brandt (who was president of the Independent Theatre Owners Association, formed in 1933), who persuaded Trans-Lux, in 1939, to form Film Alliance of the U.S., Inc., to import and exhibit films from the United Kingdom and France. The new endeavor was not successful, but Brandt remained associated with Trans-Lux, gaining control of the corporation in the late forties. He transformed the Trans-Lux theatres at 60 Street and Madison Avenue, 52 Street and Lexington Avenue, and 85 Street and Madison Avenue into art houses. In 1955, Trans-Lux Distributing Corporation was created, with its first film being Federico Fellini's *La Strada*.

Trans-Lux operated two exhibits at the 1964 New York World's Fair, which led to the corporation's later involvement with the multimedia attractions, the New York Experience, and the Seaport Experience.

Addresses: 110 Richards Avenue, Norwalk, Conn. 06854; 625 Madison Avenue, New York, N.Y. 10022.

TRIANGLE FILM CORPORATION. Leading figures associated with the Mutual Film Corporation* met in La Junta, California, on July 20, 1915, and created the Triangle Film Corporation, with a capitalization of $5 million, to produce and market films. Harry A. Aitken was the president, Adam Kessel was the treasurer, and producers D. W. Griffith, Thomas H. Ince, and Mack Sennett, along with Charles O. Baumann, were vice-presidents. The company was formed to produce and release multiple-reel films made by the separate companies of the three producers and to lease a chain of first-class theatres in major U.S. cities to exhibit the company's more elaborate productions. Triangle's offices were in the Brokaw Building, Broadway and 42 Street, New York.

Triangle's first release, which on September 23, 1915, opened New York's Knickerbocker Theatre, was composed of *The Lamb*, Douglas Fairbanks' first feature, nominally supervised by D. W. Griffith; *The Iron Strain*, produced by Ince and starring Dustin Farnum; and Keystone's *My Valet*, starring Raymond Hitchcock. Triangle attracted stars from the legitimate stage, vaudeville, and musical comedy to its three production entities: Sir Herbert Beerbohm Tree, Mary Anderson de Navarro, Weber and Fields, DeWolf Hopper, William Collier, Billie Burke, Mario Doro, Elliott Dexter, Texas Guinan, Helen Ware, Jane Grey, Joe Jackson, Eddie Foy, Mary Boland, and Julie Dean.

In late 1916, the Triangle Distributing Corporation, which was jointly owned by the Triangle Film Corporation and Superpictures, Inc.*, was created to handle the productions of Fine Arts*, Kay-Bee, and Keystone*. W. W. Hodkinson was the president and general manager, and Raymond Pawley was the treasurer. Its offices were located at 1454 Broadway. Early in 1917, Allan Dwan became supervising director of Triangle's Yonkers, New York, studios. After Hodkinson left in mid–1917, Stephen A. Lynch gained control. When Griffith, Ince, and Sennett left the organization at the same time, Triangle retained control of the Keystone trademark, and H. O. Davis assumed control of the company.

Paralta* distributed through Triangle for a short period in the latter half of 1917. In September 1917, there was an announcement that Triangle was planning to produce films in India, China, and Buenos Aires, but nothing came of these plans, and a year later the company dismissed its stock company of seventy five. In mid–1919, Goldwyn* purchased the Triangle studio in Culver City.

BIBLIOGRAPHY

"H. E. Aitken Announces Triangle Merger," *Motion Picture News*, March 25, 1916, p. 1767.

"Kessel-Baumann-Aitken," *The Moving Picture World*, July 3, 1915, p. 42.

Lahue, Kalton C. *Dreams for Sale*. South Brunswick, New Jersey: A. S. Barnes, 1971.

Milne, Peter, "The First Knickerbocker Triangle Program," *Motion Picture News*, October 9, 1915, pp. 84–85.

"Triangle Film Incorporated," *The Moving Picture World*, July 31, 1915, p. 824.

"Triangle Opening Announced," *The Moving Picture World*, September 4, 1915, pp. 1622–1623.

"Triangle's Auspicious Opening," *The Moving Picture World*, October 9, 1915, pp. 233–234.

TRIANGLE PRODUCTIONS, INC. See COMET PRODUCTIONS, INC.

TRI-STAR PICTURES. Formed by CBS, Home Box Office, and Columbia Pictures* as a major Hollywood producer/distributor on November 30, 1982, Tri-Star Pictures did not gain its name until May 9, 1983. Prior to that it was known simply by the code name of Nova, a name which could not be retained as it was used by PBS for a science series. Gary Hendler was the company's first president—he resigned in December 1984—and responsible for its first two features, *The Natural* and *Places in the Heart*, both released in 1984. Because of a very limited production schedule in its first year, Tri-Star found it necessary to release a number of independent features during 1984, including *Where the Boys Are*, *Supergirl*, and *Silent Night, Deadly Night*. The company's logo is a white horse.

Address: 711 Fifth Avenue, New York, N.Y. 10022.

BIBLIOGRAPHY

Auerbach, Alexander, "Tri-Star—Triple Clout on Screen," *Boxoffice*, October 1983, p. 9.

Crook, David, "A Case of Intrigue," *Los Angeles Times*, Calendar Section, December 12, 1982, pp. 1, 4–5.

Kilday, Gregg, "How Dare They," *Esquire*, February 1985, pp. 121–125.

Pollock, Dale, "Just What Is This 'Eighth Studio'?" *Los Angeles Times*, Calendar
    Section, December 13, 1982, pp. 1–2.
Salmans, Sandra, "Tri-Star's Bid for Movie Stardom," *The New York Times*, May 13,
    1984, pp. F1, F12-F13.

TRIUMPH FILM CORPORATION. See WORLD FILM CORPORATION

TRIUMPH FILMS. Triumph Films was formed in February 1982 by Columbia Pictures* as a separate corporate entity for the specialized release of foreign and American independent features. Shortly after its creation, Triumph became closely associated with the French Gaumont Company, whose films it distributed in the United States. Charles Schreger was named Triumph's first president—he resigned in 1984—and the company's first release was the German feature *Das Boot* (1982). In November 1985, Triumph Films was totally absorbed by Columbia Pictures' Classics Division (which had been founded in 1971 by Dennis Doph).

Address: Columbia Plaza South, Burbank, Calif. 91505.

BIBLIOGRAPHY

Jacobson, Harlan, "How the Classics Kids Snatched the Foreign Film," *The Village
    Voice*, November 22, 1983, pp. 74–76.

TRUART FILM CORPORATION. Active from the early through mid-twenties, the Truart Film Corporation was a New York–based producer and states rights* distributor, formed by L. A. Young. It had three minor stars under contract: Larry Semon, Elaine Hammerstein, and Richard Talmadge.

TRUCOLOR. See CINECOLOR

TUCSON, ARIZONA. See AL JENNINGS PRODUCTION COMPANY

TUSKEN MUSIC. See LUCASFILM, LTD.

20th CENTURY-FOX FILM CORPORATION. By 1935 the Fox Film Corporation* was in need of new corporate blood, and on May 28 of that year its merger with Twentieth Century Pictures* was announced, with the new company named 20th Century-Fox Film Corporation. Darryl F. Zanuck became vice-president and head of production, Joseph M. Schenck was named chairman of the board, and Sidney Kent continued over from the Fox Film Corporation as president.

Zanuck took over a company with two major stars, Shirley Temple and Will Rogers, but lost the latter in a plane crash the first year of the new studio's existence. Tyrone Power became the company's new major male star, and Zanuck embarked on an ambitious production schedule which included *Lloyds of London* (1936), *Alexander's Ragtime Band* (1938), *Suez* (1938), *In Old Chicago* (1938), *Jesse James* (1939), *Stanley and Livingstone* (1939), and *Drums along the Mohawk*

(1939). Don Ameche played the inventor of the telephone in *The Story of Alexander Graham Bell* (1939) and Stephen Foster in *Swanee River* (1939). Zanuck produced the popular series of Charlie Chan, Mr. Moto, and The Country Doctor, featuring Jean Hersholt and the Dionne Quintuplets. New female stars, such as Alice Faye, Betty Grable, and Sonja Henie, were created.

In the forties, Zanuck produced the commercially and critically unsuccessful biographical feature—one of his favorite genres—*Wilson* (1944), but he was also responsible for such important social dramas as *The Grapes of Wrath* (1940), *Gentleman's Agreement* (1947), and *The Snake Pit* (1948). In the fifties, it was Zanuck and 20th Century-Fox that made Marilyn Monroe a star, in a decade that also saw the company introduce the widescreen system of CinemaScope*.

In 1956, Darryl F. Zanuck left the company he had worked so hard to create, and he was succeeded by Buddy Adler (who died in1960). Spyros Skouras, who had been the head of the studio since 1942, found himself in financial difficulties with *Cleopatra*, the costly Elizabeth Taylor–Richard Burton epic, which was eventually released in 1963. In 1962, Zanuck returned to the studio as its president and with his son, Richard, embarked on a production program that included the highly successful *The Sound of Music* (1965), *Patton* (1970), and *M*A*S*H* (1970) and also the poorly received *Doctor Doolittle* (1967) and *Star!* (1968).

Zanuck resigned as president in 1969, and, after an interim period during which his son ran the company, Dennis C. Stanfill took over in 1971. He became chairman of the board, and Gordon T. Stulberg stepped in as president, to be succeeded in 1975 by Stanfill (who also served as chairman of the board and chief executive officer). That same year Alan Ladd, Jr., became head of production and did much to help the studio's financial position with the *Star Wars* trilogy. In 1981, Alan Hirschfield became chairman of the board, with Sherry Lansing as president, succeeded a year later by Joe Wizan.

Denver oilman Marvin Davis acquired the company in 1981, selling 50 percent of it to Rupert Murdoch in 1985. Alan Hirschfield resigned in October 1984; he was succeeded by Barry Diller, and Lawrence Gordon became president. Rupert Murdoch acquired Davis' half of the company in October 1985 for a reported $325 million, plus real estate.

The 20th Century-Fox studio lot, which had begun life as Movietone City and which was initially part of Westwood before becoming part of the newly developed Century City, was sold to Alcoa Corporation in 1961. The bulk of the backlot was used for the Century City development, with 20th Century-Fox leasing back some sixty-three acres for its production needs. The entrance to the lot is notable for the *Hello, Dolly!* New York street set, constructed in 1968.

Address: 10201 West Pico Boulevard, Los Angeles, Calif. 90035.

BIBLIOGRAPHY

Dunne, John Gregory. *The Studio*. New York: Farrar, Straus & Giroux, 1969.

Parish, James Robert. *The Fox Girls*. New Rochelle, New York: Arlington House, 1971.

Thomas, Tony, and Aubrey Solomon. *The Films of 20th Century Fox*. Secaucus, New Jersey: Citadel Press, 1979.

"20th Century-Fox," *The Hollywood Reporter*, November 13, 1984, special issue.

RESOURCES

Films: Museum of Modern Art (35mm preservation material and some 16mm reference
        prints); UCLA Film Archives (35mm preservation material, 35mm nitrate prints).
Papers: University of California at Los Angeles; University of Southern California.
Still Photographs: University of California at Los Angeles.

TWENTIETH CENTURY PICTURES. When Darryl F. Zanuck resigned as
production head of Warner Bros.* in the spring of 1933, he joined with Joseph
Schenck to form a new company, utilizing $100,000 that Louis B. Mayer had
given to Zanuck in order that Mayer's son-in-law, William Goetz, would be
Zanuck's executive assistant. The company was called Twentieth Century Pictures
at the suggestion of Samuel G. Engel, who supposedly told Zanuck that he had
a name for him that would be good for sixty-seven years.

Twentieth Century Pictures owned no studio and leased space at the United
Artists* lot. The first production was *The Bowery* (1933), directed by Raoul
Walsh and starring Wallace Beery and Fay Wray. The company produced
seventeen further features: *Broadway through a Keyhole* (1933), *Blood Money*
(1933), *Advice to the Lovelorn* (1933), *Gallant Lady* (1934), *Moulin Rouge*
(1934), *The House of Rothschild* (1934), *Looking for Trouble* (1934), *Born to
Be Bad* (1934), *The Affairs of Cellini* (1934), *Bulldog Drummond Strikes Back*
(1934), *The Last Gentleman* (1934), *The Mighty Barnum* (1934), *Clive of India*
(1935), *Folies Bergere* (1935), *Cardinal Richelieu* (1935), *Les Miserables* (1935),
and *The Call of the Wild* (1935). On May 29, 1935, Twentieth Century Pictures
merged with the Fox Film Corporation* to become 20th Century-Fox*.

TWYMAN FILMS, INC. One of the oldest surviving 16mm* distributors,
Twyman Films, Inc., was founded in 1935. The company presently distributes
more than 1,500 feature films—notably the films of Harry Langdon, Buster
Keaton, Douglas Fairbanks, D. W. Griffith, and other personalities—which are
owned by entrepreneur Raymond Rohauer and which were previously available
for rental from Audio-Brandon. Twyman is best known as a nontheatrical film
distributor, but it also is involved in theatrical and television distribution.

Address: Box 605, 4700 Wadsworth Road, Dayton, Ohio 45401.

U

UA. See UNITED ARTISTS CORPORATION

UNION PHOTOPLAY COMPANY. Charles R. Macauley, cartoonist for the *New York Evening World*, was the head of the Union Photoplay Company, which was formed in 1914. It produced *Alice in Wonderland*, followed by a series of half-reel cartoons.

BIBLIOGRAPHY

"Charles R. Macauley Making Pictures," *The Moving Picture World*, October 17, 1914, p. 315.

UNITED ARTISTS CLASSICS. United Artists (UA) Classics was the first division to be established by a major studio to acquire and release "art" or noncommercial films, generally from abroad. United Artists Classics was formed in 1980 from the old UA Classics, established to handle bookings from revival houses for the Warner Bros.* features and shorts controlled by United Artists Corporation*. The first film to be acquired by the newly reorganized division was François Truffaut's *The Last Metro* (1981). As a result of UA's success with its Classics Division, Columbia Pictures* formed Triumph Films*, Universal* created Universal Classics, and 20th Century-Fox* established Twentieth Century Fox International Classics. With the merger between M-G-M* and United Artists, United Artists Classics became MGM/UA Classics.

Address: MGM/UA Classics, 10202 West Washington Boulevard, Culver City, Calif. 90230.

BIBLIOGRAPHY

Springer, Alicia, "Sell It Again, Sam!" *American Film*, March 1983, pp. 50–55.

UNITED ARTISTS COMMUNICATIONS, INC. With three separate divisions, United Artists Eastern Theatres, Inc., United Artists Communications, Inc., and Rowley Division, United Artists Communications, Inc., is the second largest theatre circuit in the United States with a reported 835 screens as of 1980.

Addresses: United Artists Eastern Theatres, Inc., 2545 Hempstead Turnpike, East Meadow, N.Y. 11554; United Artists Communications, Inc., 172 Golden Gate Avenue, San Francisco, Calif. 94102; Rowley Division, 314 South Harwood Street, Dallas, Tex. 75201.

UNITED ARTISTS CORPORATION. The formation of United Artists Corporation (UA) marked the first time that a group of artists rather than businessmen had come together to create a major distribution corporation for their films. The four principals in the new company were Mary Pickford, Douglas Fairbanks, Charles Chaplin, and D. W. Griffith; a fifth, William S. Hart, was involved in the original discussions as to the corporation's formation but later dropped out. On January 15, 1919, United Artists came into being, and Richard A. Rowland, president of Metro Pictures Corporation*, made his famous remark to the effect that "the lunatics have taken charge of the asylum."

United Artists was established to market films produced by its four stockholders, each of whom received 1,000 shares of preferred stock, with an additional 1,000 going to UA's general counsel, William Gibbs McAdoo. The corporation was incorporated on April 17, 1919, with headquarters in New York, and the first feature it released—on September 1, 1919—was Douglas Fairbanks' *His Majesty, the American.*

Despite early financial problems, the company prospered by the mid-twenties. D. W. Griffith left the organization when his contract expired in December 1924, but at the same time Joseph Schenck joined the group as its new chairman of the board. It was Schenck who was instrumental in forming the United Artists Theatre Circuit, Inc., in 1926, a theatre circuit which at last gave the company guaranteed screenings for its releases. To United Artists Schenck brought Norma Talmadge and Gloria Swanson. Rudolph Valentino's *The Eagle* (1925) and *The Son of the Sheik* (1926) were released by United Artists. Samuel Goldwyn agreed, in 1925, to release his productions through the organization, and two years later he became a partner. Howard Hughes and Buster Keaton released their films through United Artists.

With the coming of sound the company faced a crisis. D. W. Griffith had rejoined the group in 1927, but his later films were not particularly successful. Fairbanks and Pickford were in decline, and Chaplin was producing fewer and fewer features. The only major addition to UA's producers was Walt Disney*, who agreed, in 1931, to release his cartoons through the company, followed by the newly formed Twentieth Century Pictures* and Alexander Korda's British-based London Film Productions.

The year 1935 was a crucial one for United Artists. Schenck resigned, Alexander Korda became a partner, and David O. Selznick agreed to release eight features through UA. Walter Wanger Productions was formed in 1936 to release through UA, and that same year A. H. Giannini, chairman of the Bank of America, became the company's new president.

The Second World War heralded the beginning of the end for the old United Artists as its partners fought over the company—there was a particularly bitter dispute between Goldwyn and Pickford over the United Artists Studios in Hollywood, which the former utilized as a production center—and product became scarce, despite UA's release of some of the J. Arthur Rank British productions. In 1950, after three consecutive years of losses of almost a million dollars, Arthur B. Krim and Robert S. Benjamin (of the law firm of Phillips, Nizer, Benjamin & Krim) took over the company, and a new United Artists was created. (Chaplin sold his remaining stock to Krim and Benjamin in 1955, and Mary Pickford followed suit a year later.)

Benjamin and Krim went into partnership with new producers, whose films they were willing to finance partially. In the fifties, United Artists released more than fifty features a year, including such memorable productions as *The African Queen* (1951), *High Noon* (1952), *The Night of the Hunter* (1955), *Marty* (1955), *Witness for the Prosecution* (1957), *Some Like It Hot* (1959), *Exodus* (1960), and *The Apartment* (1960). In 1957, the company acquired the Warner Bros.* library of 800 pre–1950 features and 1,500 shorts and cartoons.

In that same year, United Artists became a public company, and some ten years later 98 percent of its stock was acquired by the TransAmerica Corporation, which continued to run the organization, under the guidance of Benjamin and Krim, as a wholly owned subsidiary. Following a policy dispute with TransAmerica, Krim, Benjamin, and three other top executives left United Artists to form Orion Pictures Corporation* in January 1978. In July 1981, United Artists was acquired by Metro-Goldwyn-Mayer*, and in 1983 the two companies were merged as MGM/UA Entertainment Co.* In 1986, Ted Turner acquired MGM/UA, sold off the United Artists half to Kirk Kerkorian and disbanded the company.

Address: MGM/UA Entertainment Co., 10202 West Washington Boulevard, Culver City, Calif. 90230.

BIBLIOGRAPHY

"All They Say Is: 'See Our Lawyer,' " *Photoplay*, May 1919, pp. 54–55.

Balio, Tino. *United Artists*. Madison, Wisconsin: University of Wisconsin Press, 1976.

————, "Charles Chaplin, Entrepreneur," *Journal of the University Film Association*, vol. XXXI, no. 1, Winter 1979, pp. 11–21.

Mayer, Arthur L., "The Origins of United Artists," *Films in Review*, August-September 1959, pp. 390–399.

North, Christopher, "UA's 35th Birthday," *Films in Review*, April 1954, pp. 165–170.

"United Artists: Final Shooting Script," *Fortune*, December 1940, pp. 99–102.

RESOURCES

Papers: Wisconsin Center for Film and Theater Research (corporate papers, correspondence, financial records, distribution records, and press books).

Still Photographs: Wisconsin Center for Film and Theater Research.

UNITED COSTUME COMPANY. See WESTERN COSTUME CO.

UNITED FILM SERVICE. The United Film Service was a releasing program of Warner's Features, Inc., which began on November 8, 1914. Later, by court order, the name of Warner's Features was changed to the United Film Service. United released sixteen brands of short films, including those made by the

Gaumont Company, Regent Film Company*, Sunshine Film Corporation (which made Juno, Mars, and Magnet single-reel comedies), Colonial Motion Picture Corporation, Pyramid* Film Company, Superba Company (which made one-reel comedies with Edith Thornton, directed by Frank Hutchinson), Starlight Comedy Company (which produced comedies in the Mittenthal brothers' studio in Yonkers with Jimmy Aubrey and Walter Kendig), Lariat Company, Premier Company, and Luna Company. P. A. Powers was the first president of United. Later, J. C. Graham became the president and general manager.

In December 1914, a group of production companies organized to form the United Motion Picture Producers, Inc., to supply the United Film Service with a daily volume of films. The affiliated producers were Albuquerque Film Manufacturing Company*, Crystal Film Company (which produced the Superba brand of comedies), Features Ideal, Gene Gauntier Feature Players Company (which produced two-reel dramas written by and starring Gauntier), Mittenthal Film Company, Inc., Nelson Film Corporation, St. Louis Motion Picture Company, and Smallwood Film Corporation. Ludwig G. B. Erb was the president of the producers group, and Gilbert P. Hamilton, the head of Albuquerque, was the vice-president.

In June 1915, when United went bankrupt, the group of producers organized a new combination called the Combined Photoplay Producers, Inc. Producing companies included were Crystal, Gaumont, Erbograph Company, Ideal Company (which produced dramas from directors Frank Beal, Carl Levinus, and Webster Cullison and starred Edna Payne, George Larkin, and Fred Hearns), Pike's Peak Film Company*, St. Louis, Albuquerque, Grandin Films, Inc., Smallwood, and Mittenthal. Erb was the president. At the same time, A. and H. M. Warner, formerly with Warner's Features, Inc., and Al Lichtman, formerly with Paramount* and Alco*, formed Standard Pictures, Inc., to handle the product of the Combined Photoplay Producers. Standard planned to sell its pictures outright to its exchange connections rather than lease them. Standard signed a contract with the producing organization which gave Standard control of the quality of the films which it handled.

BIBLIOGRAPHY

"New Combination Formed," *The Moving Picture World*, July 3, 1915, p. 43.

"United Motion Picture Producers," *The Moving Picture World*, December 12, 1914, p. 1500.

"United's Affairs Aired in Court," *The Moving Picture World*, August 14, 1915, p. 1140.

"Warner's to Inaugurate New Service," *The Moving Picture World*, November 14, 1914, p. 947.

UNITED FILM SERVICE PROTECTIVE ASSOCIATION. See MOTION PICTURE PATENTS COMPANY

UNITED KEANOGRAPH FILM MANUFACTURING COMPANY. James Keane was the president and general manager of the United Keanograph Film Manufacturing Company of Fairfax, California, which was organized in mid–1914. Keane directed and wrote the five-reel *Money* (1914), his company's first and perhaps only production.

BIBLIOGRAPHY

"New California Producing Co. Formed," *The Moving Picture World*, July 18, 1914, p. 448.

UNITED MOTION PICTURE PRODUCERS, INC. See UNITED FILM SERVICE

UNITED PARAMOUNT THEATRES, INC. When Paramount* was required by the consent decree* to divest itself of its theatre chain, the 1,424 theatres that it controlled in 1949 became United Paramount Theatres, Inc. American Broadcasting Companies, Inc., merged with United Paramount Theatres in 1953, and when ABC decided to leave the theatre circuit business in 1978, the chain was sold to Plitt Theatres*.

UNITED PHOTOPLAYS COMPANY. United Photoplays Company was a Chicago-based producing company of 1915. Although it specialized in topical and educational films, such as *Ming Tombs and Camel Trail into Mongolia* and *Nara, the Cradle of Japanese Art*, United did produce a five-reel dramatic feature, *The Victory of Virtue*, featuring Gerda Holmes and Wilmuth Merkyl, directed by Harry McRae Webster, which was released late in 1915.

UNITED PICTURE THEATRES OF AMERICA, INC. The United Picture Theatres of America, a cooperative to distribute films that were owned, financed, and controlled by exhibitors, commenced operations on March 1, 1918. Lee A. Ochs, United's president, was also the president of the Motion Picture Exhibitors League of America*. C. R. Seelye, former business manager of Pathé*, Vitagraph*, and World*, was United's vice-president. In its first statement to the press, United announced that it planned to "reduce the film rentals by about thirty percent, giving producers a larger and quicker revenue than under the present expensive exchange system." It announced that its method of financing its operations would be to divide the cost of the film negative proportionately among as large a number of exhibitors as it could align. There would be five grades of exhibitors, each paying a different rate of the cost of the negative. Profits would be paid to the exhibitors who were United's stockholders. Early in January 1919, United merged with the World Film Corporation, which was to distribute films made for United by the Peerless Company. At that time there were 1,300 moving picture houses which were members of United, and J. A. Berst was the organization's president.

BIBLIOGRAPHY
"New Company Outlines Working Plans," *The Moving Picture World*, March 16, 1918,
    p. 1496.
"United Picture Theatres Formed," *The Moving Picture World*, March 2, 1918, p. 1219.
"World and United Theatres Merge," *The Moving Picture World*, February 1, 1919,
    p. 599.

UNITED PRODUCTIONS OF AMERICA. United Productions of America was formed in 1945 by a young animator named Stephen Bosustow from an earlier company, Industrial Films and Poster Service. In 1948, Bosustow signed a long-term distribution agreement with Columbia*, and his company's cartoon characters, Gerald McBoing-Boing and Mister Magoo, became two of the most popular with filmgoers, thanks to the quality of the films with their unusual storylines and lack of assembly-line approach. The company was also noted for many of its other cartoons, such as *Magic Flute* (1949), *Man Alive!* (1952), and *The Tell Tale Heart* (1953).

On January 1, 1956, the company changed its name to UPA Pictures, Inc., and around the same time it was sold to Henry G. Saperstein. In 1959, UPA's contract with Columbia ended, but it continued to produce cartoons for television into the sixties.

BIBLIOGRAPHY
Hine, Al, "McBoing-Boing and Magoo," *Holiday*, June 1951, pp. 6, 8–9, 11.
Langsner, Jules, "UPA," *Arts and Architecture*, December 1954, pp. 12–15.
Lee, Walter W., Jr., "UPA," *Pendulum*, Spring 1953, pp. 42–50.
Penney, Ed, "U.P.A. Animated Art," *The Arts*, March 1953, pp. 12–13.

UNITED STATES AMUSEMENT CORPORATION. Herbert Blaché, the president of Blaché Features, Inc., and the Exclusive Supply Corporation*, formed the United States Amusement Corporation in April 1914 to produce large feature films, five or more reels in length, based on well-known novels and plays. Other directors of the company were Madame Alice Blaché, the president of Solax*; Joseph M. Shear; Charles D. Lithgow; Joseph Borries; Henri Menessier; and Jules E. Brulatour. The company used the newly enlarged Blaché studio and laboratory at Fort Lee, New Jersey*, and its first production was Charles Dickens' *The Chimes*, starring Tom Terriss and directed by Terriss and Blaché. Productions of the United States Amusement Corporation were first released by World* and later by Art Dramas, Inc., of which Blaché was treasurer. Madame Blaché began directing the company's films in 1917.

BIBLIOGRAPHY
"Blaché Forms New Company," *The Moving Picture World*, May 2, 1914, p. 653.

UNITED STATES EXHIBITORS' BOOKING CORPORATION. Frank G. Hall and William Oldknow formed the United States Exhibitors' Booking Corporation late in 1917 to buy special productions directly from producers and then, through M. H. Hoffman's Four Square Exchanges, to rent them to exhibitors.

By not selling to territorial buyers, it planned to eliminate the middleman and thus reduce rental fees to exhibitors. Both Hall, the president and general manager, and Oldknow, the secretary and treasurer, had previously been exhibitors. Each production was sold separately, with the organization's first release being Thomas H. Ince's *The Zeppelin's Last Raid* (1918). In June 1918, it terminated its agreement with Foursquare and signed with regional independent exchanges to handle the films that it bought. The company went out of existence early in 1919.

BIBLIOGRAPHY

"Bill Oldknow and Frank Hall Hook Up," *The Moving Picture World*, November 3, 1917, p. 682.

UNITED STATES GOVERNMENT COMMITTEE ON PUBLIC INFORMATION: DIVISION OF FILMS. On September 25, 1917, the Division of Films of the United States Government's Committee on Public Information was established by presidential order. Under the direction of Charles S. Hart, who had been an advertising manager at *Hearst's Magazine*, the Division of Films produced three feature-length propaganda documentaries concerning the First World War: *Pershing's Crusaders* (1918), *America's Answer* (1918), and *Under Four Flags* (1919). The Division also produced the one-reel weekly newsreel *The Official War Review*, released by Pathé Exchange, Inc., which commenced on July 1, 1918, and continued for thirty-one issues.

The Division of Films' Advisory Board of Motion Picture Directors included J. Searle Dawley (who served as chairman), James Vincent (secretary), Maurice Tourneur, Captain E. H. Calvert, Edwin Carewe, Charles Giblyn, Raoul Walsh, Sidney Olcott, George Irving, and Travers Vale. In addition to producing, the Division, with the help of the motion picture industry, succeeded in eliminating German propaganda films from being exhibited in neutral European countries. American producers demanded that their exported films be screened only if the Division's propaganda films be shown with them. Because of the popularity of the American films, furnished at cost, German productions were unwanted. The Committee and its Division of Films were disbanded by an Order of Congress on June 30, 1919.

BIBLIOGRAPHY

Creel, George. *How We Advertised America*. New York: Harper & Brothers, 1920.
"Film Division Names Director Advisers," *The Moving Picture World*, July 20, 1918, p. 363.
"Government Forging Ahead in Picture Making," *The Moving Picture World*, March 2, 1918, p. 1228.
"Hart to Dissolve Division of Films," *The Moving Picture World*, February 22, 1919, p. 1056.
"U.S. Film Division Makes Vast Plans," *Motion Picture News*, June 29, 1918, p. 3863.

UNITED STATES MOTION PICTURE CORPORATION. The United States Motion Picture Corporation built its studio between the Susquehanna River and the Blue Mountains in Wilkes-Barre, Pennsylvania, in August 1915. Fred W. Hermann, a Wilkes-Barre exhibitor, was the company's vice-president, and James O. Walsh was the president. Playwright Daniel L. Hart was the scenario editor and Leatrice Joy the leading woman. The company made single-reel Black Diamond comedies, which were released by Paramount,* and ended operations early in 1918.

BIBLIOGRAPHY

"New Studio in Pennsylvania," *The Moving Picture World*, August 14, 1915, p. 1141.
"Wilkes-Barre Company Enlarging," *The Moving Picture World*, June 30, 1917, p. 2126.

UNITED STUDIOS. See ROBERT BRUNTON STUDIOS, INC.

UNITED THEATRICAL WAR ACTIVITIES COMMITTEE. See HOLLYWOOD VICTORY COMMITTEE

UNITED WORLD FILMS. Recognizing the increasing importance of 16mm film*, Universal* established a wholly owned 16mm division, United World Films, in 1946, in which year it also took over the 16mm Bell & Howell Filmosound Library and Castle Films*. United World Films ceased operations in 1967, becoming Universal 16, which has also now ceased to exist. With no 16mm library of its own, Universal currently rents 16mm prints of a selection of its films through Swank Motion Pictures of St. Louis and Clem Williams Films of Pittsburgh.

UNITY SALES CORPORATION. The distributor Unity Sales Corporation was formed in May 1916, with Andrew J. Cobe as president and general manager. Among the films that it handled were the serial *The Yellow Menace*, starring Edwin Stevens, produced by the Serial Film Company; *My Country First*, produced by the Tom Terriss Film Corporation; and the "Tweedledum and Tweedledee" series, produced by the Eagle Film Company of Jacksonville, Florida. Unity disbanded early in 1917.

BIBLIOGRAPHY

"First Month of Unity Sales," *The Moving Picture World*, June 10, 1916, p. 1892.

THE UNIVERSAL ANIMATED WEEKLY. See NEWSREELS

UNIVERSAL-INTERNATIONAL. See UNIVERSAL PICTURES

UNIVERSAL NEWS. See NEWSREELS

UNIVERSAL PICTURES. For more than one-third of its existence, Universal Pictures was associated with one man, Carl Laemmle (1867–1939), who created a distinctive company and whose films had a definite studio style. He aimed for a studio with a family atmosphere, with himself as the genial "Uncle Carl." A pioneer of the modern film industry, Laemmle began his motion picture career with a nickelodeon*, the White Front Theatre, located at 909 Milwaukee Avenue in Chicago, which he opened on February 24, 1906. With his partner, Robert Cochrane, Laemmle established the Laemmle Film Service, which, by 1909, had become one of the largest film exchanges in the country. When the Motion Picture Patents Company* began questioning his independence, Laemmle fought back by turning to production and, in 1909, formed the IMP (Independent Motion Picture Company). IMP's first film was a one-reel version of Longfellow's "Hiawatha," directed by William V. Ranous and starring Gladys Hulette. A year later, Laemmle was able to lure Florence Lawrence away from the Biograph Company*, of which she was the leading lady. Mary Pickford also worked for a short period as an IMP actress.

On June 8, 1912, Carl Laemmle formed a new organization, Universal, by merging IMP with Pat Powers' Picture Plays, Adam Kessel and Charles Baumann's Bison Life Motion Picture Company, William Swanson's Rex Company, and Nestor and Champion. Legend has it that Laemmle selected the name Universal after seeing it on the side of a truck belonging to Universal Pipe Fittings. The first Universal production was *The Dawn of Netta*, a two-reel short directed by Tom Ricketts.

Universal operated two studios in Los Angeles, one in Edendale and the former Nestor Studios on Sunset Boulevard at Gower Street. Among some of the company's best-known early films were *Traffic in Souls* (1913), *Neptune's Daughter* (1914), and *Damon and Pythias* (1914).

On March 15, 1915, Universal City was opened on the site of the 250-acre Taylor Ranch in the San Fernando Valley; it remains as the present headquarters of Universal, the oldest continuously operating studio in the country and the only city in the world purpose-built as a film studio. It was at Universal City that John Ford made his directorial debut in 1917; Irving Thalberg was studio manager from 1918 to 1923; Erich von Stroheim made the first of his screen masterpieces, *Blind Husbands* (1919) and *Foolish Wives* (1922); and Lon Chaney became a star and made *The Hunchback of Notre Dame* (1923) and *The Phantom of the Opera* (1925).

With the coming of sound, Universal made the obligatory all-talking, all-singing, all-dancing revue, *The King of Jazz* (1930). A year earlier, Carl Laemmle, Jr. (generally known as Junior Laemmle), had been appointed head of production by his father, leading Ogden Nash to comment that "Uncle Carl Laemmle has a very large faemmle." Despite considerable adverse criticism, Junior Laemmle was responsible for many fine films, including *All Quiet on the Western Front* (1930) and a series of classic horror films such as *Dracula* (1931), *Frankenstein* (1932), *The Mummy* (1932), *The Invisible Man* (1933), *The Black Cat* (1934), and *The Bride of Frankenstein* (1935).

Carl Laemmle lost control of the studio in 1936, when it was taken over by Charles Rogers and J. Cheever Cowdin, with the former as head of production. The studio was financially in trouble, but it was saved thanks almost entirely to one child star, Deanna Durbin, who delighted thirties and forties audiences with *Three Smart Girls* (1936), *100 Men and a Girl* (1937), and *First Love* (1939), among others. Cliff Work replaced Charles Rogers in 1938 and embarked on a production schedule that consisted of low-budget, quality features, including a continuing batch of horror subjects, exotic features with Maria Montez, a group of W. C. Fields titles, the Sherlock Holmes series with Basil Rathbone and Nigel Bruce, and the classic Abbott and Costello comedies.

On November 12, 1946, Universal was merged with the independent International Pictures production company to become Universal-International. William Goetz and Leo Spitz took over production, and they introduced a new logo to replace the ultra-modern glass logo, which had, in turn, replaced the original logo of a biplane encircling the world in 1936. A year earlier, Universal became associated with the British producer J. Arthur Rank and began releasing his prestige features in the United States. Low-budget features, such as the "Ma and Pa Kettle" series, formed a prominent part of the new production schedule.

Universal was taken over by Decca Records in 1952, and Edward Muhl became head of production, introducing glamorous Technicolor* features, often directed by Douglas Sirk. In the late fifties, MCA, Inc.*, began acquiring a controlling interest in Decca, and, by 1962, Universal had become part of the MCA empire, headed by Dr. Jules Stein and Lew Wasserman. Universal-International became Universal once again, with a new, modern logo. Celebrities, such as Alfred Hitchcock and Edith Head, were lured to the studio from Paramount*. Universal became the home of such major productions as *The Sting* (1973), *Jaws* (1975), *E. T. The Extraterrestrial* (1982), and the "Airport" series.

As of 1985, Universal occupied some 450 acres of land, with thirty-six sound stages and two administrative buildings, the "Black" and "White" towers. Additionally, two hotels, the Sheraton Universal and the Premiere, were located on the lot, along with several restaurants, the world headquarters of the Getty Oil Company, and a branch of Bank of America. Universal Pictures is a division of Universal City Studios, Inc., which is a subsidiary of MCA, Inc.

Address: Universal City, Calif. 91608.

BIBLIOGRAPHY

Dettman, Bruce. *The Horror Factory*. New York: Gordon Press, 1976.

Edmonds, I. G. *Big U*. Cranbury, New Jersey: A. S. Barnes, 1977.

Fitzgerald, Michael G. *Universal Pictures*. New Rochelle, New York: Arlington House, 1977.

Hirschhorn, Clive. *The Universal Story*. New York: Crown, 1983.

Koszarski, Richard. *Universal Pictures: 65 Years*. New York: The Museum of Modern Art, 1977.

Perry, Jeb H. *Universal Television*. Metuchen, New Jersey: Scarecrow Press, 1983.

RESOURCES

Films: Library of Congress (preservation materials and some reference prints).

UNIVERSAL STUDIOS TOUR. One of the best-known tourist attractions in Los Angeles, and second in popularity only to Disneyland, the new Universal* Studios Tour opened on June 17, 1964. It was intended only as a summertime operation but proved so successful that it continued through the winter months.

The attractions, none of which have anything to do with actual filmmaking, change periodically, but the best known include the *Jaws* shark attack, the Doomed Glacier expedition, the collapsing bridge, the parting of the Red Sea, Conan the Barbarian, Castle Dracula, the Screen Test Theatre, the Western stunt show, and the animal actors stage. Visitors are taken through the tour by tram and get to see some of the stars' dressing rooms and standing sets. In 1964, 39,000 visitors toured the studio, but by 1984 the average admission was 25,000 a day.

Tours of the studio originated in 1915 when Universal City opened. Visitors were permitted to watch filming from bleacher seats built above the dressing rooms and were provided with box lunches. These original tours ended when the coming of sound made visiting the set impracticable.

Address: 100 Universal City Plaza, Universal City, Calif. 91608.

BIBLIOGRAPHY

Harmetz, Aljean, "Why Studio Tour Focuses on Big Films," *The New York Times*, June 25, 1984, p. C11.

Marple, Albert, "A Solution for the 'Movie' Visitor Problem," *Motion Picture Magazine*, March 1916, p. 143.

Scheuer, Philip K., "So You Want to Visit a Studio?" *Los Angeles Times*, Calendar Section, July 19, 1964, p. 3.

Stoddard, Maynard Good, "420 Acres of Make-Believe," *The Saturday Evening Post*, May/June 1984, pp. 62–63, 100–101.

Sutton, Horace, "A Traveler in Flickville," *Saturday Review*, January 9, 1965, pp. 61–62.

UNUSUAL OCCUPATIONS. See JERRY FAIRBANKS PRODUCTIONS

UPA PICTURES, INC. See UNITED PRODUCTIONS OF AMERICA

USA FILM FESTIVAL. The first completely American film festival, the USA Film Festival is held annually on the campus of Southern Methodist University in Dallas, with the films being selected by a group of American film critics. It was first held from March 8 to 14, 1971, under the directorship of L. M. Kit Carson and William Jones. (A year earlier Carson and Jones had organized The Screen Generation Film Festival.) The first director to be honored was George Stevens, and the USA Film Festival has honored one director a year ever since. From 1974, beginning with Gregory Peck, it has also presented a Master Screen Artist Award. From 1980, with a salute to Gene Kelly and the American Musical, it has presented special tributes. Until 1973, the Festival was competitive, but since then it has served as a showcase. In 1981, it expanded its activities to include year-long screenings in the Dallas area.

Address: 8080 North Central Expressway, Suite 650, LB 24, Dallas, Tex. 75206–1806.

U.S. ARMY PICTORIAL CENTER. See ASTORIA STUDIOS

U.S. ARMY PICTORIAL SERVICE. See ASTORIA STUDIOS

U.S. CATHOLIC CONFERENCE—DIVISION OF FILM AND BROADCASTING. See NATIONAL LEGION OF DECENCY

U.S. FILM CORPORATION. See SMALLWOOD FILM CORPORATION

V

VAN BEUREN CORPORATION. In existence from 1928 to 1937, the New York–based Van Beuren Corporation produced a number of features, including *Bring 'Em Back Alive* (1932), but is better known for its short subjects, the Aesops Fables and Tom & Jerry cartoons, Bill Corum Sports Review, the World on Parade, the Struggle to Live, and the Chaplin shorts from the teens released with added music and sound effects. All Van Beuren films were released through RKO*. President of the corporation was Amadee J. Van Beuren, who also owned Condor Pictures during this same period.

VANGUARD FILMS, INC. Vanguard Films was a production company formed by David O. Selznick in 1945, with Daniel T. O'Shea as president. Films, such as *Duel in the Sun* (1946), were advertised as both Selznick* productions and Vanguard productions. The company remained in existence through the late forties.

VENUS FEATURES COMPANY. The Venus Features Company was formed in mid–1913 with a studio in Hollywood. Thomas W. Evans was manager of its productions, the first of which was the three-reel *Sleeping Beauty*, directed by H. C. Matthews. Later, J. Farrell MacDonald began directing three-reel Venus productions, and, in October 1913, Richard Willis was hired to write a series of films for MacDonald to direct.

VIACOM INTERNATIONAL, INC./VIACOM ENTERPRISES. Spun off from CBS, Inc., in 1971, Viacom International, Inc., is a diversified communications and entertainment company, the best-known division of which is Viacom Enterprises, which promotes itself as "the world's leading distributor of television programming."

Viacom distributes films and television programs throughout the world; it also develops programs for cable and network television and for the home video market. It has syndicated three of the best-known comedy series on television,

"I Love Lucy," "The Honeymooners," and "All in the Family." It has also developed Showtime, the pay television movie network. In 1979, Viacom paid $30 million for twenty-eight theatrical features owned by CBS and its defunct subsidiary, Cinema Center Films. That same year, it acquired Sonderling Broadcasting, which controlled one television and eight radio stations. In 1982, the company purchased Video Corporation of America, a major television post-production house.

Address: 1211 Avenue of the Americas, New York, N.Y. 10036.

VICTOR FILM COMPANY. Florence Lawrence, earlier known as "The Biograph Girl," and her husband, Harry Salter, formed the Victor Film Company, located in Fort Lee, New Jersey*, in 1912. Salter directed Lawrence in one-, two-, and three-reel films, with Owen Moore as her leading man. Victor's first film, *Not Like Other Girls*, was released on June 14, 1912. Shortly after its formation, Victor joined the newly organized Universal Film Manufacturing Company, and by 1914 Universal* had absorbed the company. The brand name "Victor" was no longer used after 1917.

VIGILANT PICTURES CORPORATION. See ASTOR PICTURES CORPORATION

VIM COMEDY COMPANY. Vim Comedy Company typified the short-lived expansionist studios of the mid-teen movie boom. By the sheer number of films released (156 one-reelers) as well as the personalities making them, Vim historically is one of the more interesting of the early studios producing comedy shorts. Founded in late 1915 by two flamboyant figures of the early industry, Louis Burstein and Mark Dintenfass, Vim controlled production facilities in both New Jersey and Florida*. Former Lubin*, Sterling, and Wizard* stars, Bob "Pokes" Burns and Walter "Jabbs" Stull continued their pratfall series as headliners with Vim. The new "Pokes and Jabbs" comedies entered the market in November 1915 to replace MinA ("Made in America") films on the General Film Company program, when a dispute between General and MinA head David Horsley led him to disband the company, form other brands, and move his releasing program to Mutual*.

To increase its teamed offerings, Vim also quickly obtained the services of Oliver "Babe" Hardy, another Lubin veteran, to perform opposite diminutive Billy Ruge in a second unit of thirty-five slapstick "Plump and Runt" pictures released in 1916. Surviving films show the series was important in developing Hardy's comedy style critical to his much later teaming with Stan Laurel.

Other regulars at Vim included Harry Myers and Rosemary Theby who specialized in domestic comedies, plus talented performers such as Kate Price, Billy Bletcher, his wife Arline Roberts, ingenue Ethel Burton, and others. Including casts, directors, cameramen, crew, and administrative personnel, the Vim southern studio in Jacksonville (at 740–750 Riverside Drive, where most of the pictures were made) employed nearly fifty people plus extras in 1916, with a regular weekly payroll of approximately $3,800.

A number of expansion companies collapsed in 1917 because of market uncertainties connected with the First World War, but Vim might have continued indefinitely had the two owners not tried to cheat each other. The resulting legal battles ended the partnership, with the bulk of Vim's interests eventually being taken over by the Amber Star Film Corporation, a subsidiary of Eastern Film Corporation of Providence, Rhode Island. Burstein (later Burston) retained control of the former Vim northern studio in Bayonne and used it to make early Billy West comedies under his new King Bee Film Company brand with the help of Hardy and other ex-Vim supporting players before moving everything to Hollywood.

BIBLIOGRAPHY

Nelson, Richard Alan, "Before Laurel: Oliver Hardy and the Vim Company, a Studio Biography," in Bruce A. Austin, editor, *Current Research in Film: Audience, Economics and Law*. Norwood, New Jersey: Ablex Publishing, 1986.

"Scenes at the Vim Studio," *Florida Times-Union* (Jacksonville), January 16, 1916, section 3, p. 5.

Young, Jordan R., "Early Ollie: The Plump and Runt Films," *Pratfall*, vol. I, no. 12, 1975, pp. 3–7.

VISTAVISION. VistaVision was Paramount's answer to the widescreen CinemaScope* system. It utilized a camera through which the 35mm* film traveled horizontally, rather than vertically, with eight sprocket holes per frame (instead of four). This resulted in a negative image with an area three times that of a normal 35mm negative. The film was then processed in a normal way and optically reduced. (At first, in a few key theatres, the films were shown via horizontal projection.)

The VistaVision process received its premiere presentation on April 27, 1954, at New York's Radio City Music Hall*, with *White Christmas*. All major Paramount features of the succeeding few years were shot in VistaVision, and the process was also used for productions from other studios, such as *High Society* (1956) from M-G-M*. For the invention of VistaVision, Paramount Pictures*, Loren L. Ryder, and John R. Bishop received a Class I Scientific or Technical Award (an Oscar statuette) in 1954, and Paramount was also honored with a Class III Award in 1956 for the introduction of a lightweight, horizontal movement VistaVision camera. *One Eyed Jacks* (1961) was the last major feature to be shot in VistaVision.

BIBLIOGRAPHY

Daily, C. R., "New Paramount Lightweight Horizontal-Movement VistaVision Camera," *Journal of the SMPTE*, May 1956, pp. 279–281.

Easey, Bert, "Production in VistaVision," *Journal of the British Film Academy*, Spring 1955, pp. 14–15.

VITAGRAPH COMPANY OF AMERICA. The Vitagraph Company of America was the most important of the early film producers. It was the first to build up a stable of stars, the first to experiment successfully with animated and trick films, the first to film the classics from Shakespeare to Dickens, and the first to use the motion picture for propaganda purposes.

Founded by J. Stuart Blackton (1875–1941) and Albert E. Smith (1875–1958), the Vitagraph Company had its origins in the Reader, Smith and Blackton Combination (formed circa 1894), the Edison Vitagraph Company (formed 1897), the Commercial Advertising Bureau (formed 1897), and the American Vitagraph Company (formed 1898). Associated with Smith and Blackton in those early companies were Ronald A. Reader and William T. "Pop" Rock. In 1898, the company produced two of its most important early films, *The Burglar on the Roof* and *The Battle of Manilla Bay*, both shot at Vitagraph's first studio on the roof of the Morse Building on New York's Nassau Street.

Vitagraph opened its own studio in the Flatbush area of Brooklyn in 1905 and shortly thereafter began building up a stock company of players and directors, including Florence Turner, Maurice Costello, Paul Panzer, Lawrence Trimble (who owned Jean, the Vitagraph Dog), John Bunny (who became the most famous of early screen comedians), and Gladys Hulette (who starred in the 1909 trick film *Princess Nicotine*). Norma and Constance Talmadge began their screen careers at Vitagraph, as did Anita Stewart and Corinne Griffith.

In 1913, Vitagraph established a West Coast Studio at 1438 2nd Street in Santa Monica, California, under the direction of Rollin Sturgeon. Later, the company opened new studios at Prospect and Talmadge Avenues in Hollywood (now the ABC Television Center). From 1914 to 1916, the Criterion Theatre became the Vitagraph Theatre and was the New York showcase for Vitagraph productions. Vitagraph helped Theodore Roosevelt's "preparedness" efforts prior to the American entry into the First World War with the production of *The Battle Cry of Peace* (1915), the first major use of film for propaganda purposes.

In 1915, Vitagraph consolidated its importance by establishing V-L-S-E* to release the feature-length productions of Lubin*, Selig*, Essanay*, and itself. In 1919, it took over what was left of the Kalem Company*.

Blackton left Vitagraph in 1917 to pursue independent production, but he returned to the studio in 1923. By that time Vitagraph had lost much of its importance, thanks to the rise of Paramount* and Metro*, among others, but it still had major stars such as Antonio Moreno, Larry Semon, Alice Calhoun, and Jean Paige under contract and continued to produce important features such as *Black Beauty* (1921), *The Clean Heart* (1924), and *Captain Blood* (1924). However, on April 20, 1925, an agreement was signed with Warner Bros.* for the purchase of the company for $735,000. The Vitagraph name continued to be used as a trademark by Warner Bros. through the fifties.

BIBLIOGRAPHY

Musser, Charles, "American Vitagraph: 1897–1901," *Cinema Journal*, vol. XXII, no. 3, Spring 1983, pp. 4–46.

Slide, Anthony. *The Big V: A History of the Vitagraph Company*. Metuchen, New Jersey: Scarecrow Press, 1976.

Trimble, Marian Blackton. *J. Stuart Blackton: A Personal Biography by His Daughter*. Metuchen, New Jersey: Scarecrow Press, 1985.

RESOURCES

Films: The largest collection of Vitagraph films is held by the National Film Archive, London.

Papers: Princeton University (some corporate papers retained by Warner Bros.); University of California at Los Angeles (papers of Albert E. Smith).

VITAGRAPH-LUBIN-SELIG-ESSANAY, INC. See V-L-S-E

VITAPHONE. Although it was neither the first nor the ultimate sound film system, Vitaphone is possibly the best known, largely because the 1927 Vitaphone feature *The Jazz Singer*, starring Al Jolson, is generally lauded as the feature that gave the motion picture a voice. The Vitaphone sound-on-disc system was created by Western Electric, utilizing the audion tube (invented by Dr. Lee De Forest in 1906 and acquired by Western Electric in 1913) and an electromagnetic phonograph reproducer (invented in 1913 by Western Electric scientists, Dr. Irving B. Crandall and F. W. Kranz). These two inventions were of importance to Western Electric in terms of their value to the Bell Telephone system, but Western Electric also utilized them in the twenties for experimentation into sound-on-film and sound-on-disc motion pictures.

In 1925, Western Electric's Nathan Levinson demonstrated the sound-on-disc process to Sam Warner of Warner Bros.*, which viewed the new invention as a possible solution to its financial problems. Warner Bros. created the Vitaphone Corporation on April 20, 1926, taking the name from its then recently acquired Vitagraph Company of America*. The first Vitaphone shorts were produced at the former Vitagraph studios in Brooklyn, but because of a lack of soundproofing, new studios were created at the Manhattan Opera House on New York's West 34 Street. The first feature to utilize the Vitaphone system was *Don Juan*, starring John Barrymore, which opened at the Warners Theatre, New York, on August 6, 1926. The program also included a series of short subjects, commencing with an address by Will H. Hays, followed by the overture to *Tannhauser* played by the New York Philharmonic, Mischa Elman, Roy Smeck, Marion Talley, Efrem Zimbalist, Giovanni Martinelli, and Anna Case. The first Vitaphone all-talking feature was *Lights of New York*, which received its premiere at the Mark Strand Theatre, New York, on July 6, 1928.

The Vitaphone system discs, manufactured by the Victor Talking Machine Company and later RCA, were recorded at 33 1/3 r.p.m. and were played from the inside out. The sixteen-inch records were the equivalent of one reel of film. The projectionist was required to place the stylus on the disc when he had the picture frame marked "Start" in the gate of the projector. Quite obviously such a system was subject to synchronization problems, and, by the early thirties, Vitaphone was no longer in use and Warner Bros. had joined all other studios in releasing its motion pictures with sound on film.

BIBLIOGRAPHY
Institute of the American Musical, Inc. *The 50th Anniversary of Vitaphone 1926–1976.* New York: The Author, 1976.
"The Vitaphone—Pro and Con," *The Literary Digest*, September 25, 1926, pp. 28–29.
"Vitaphone's Third Anniversary," *Motion Picture News*, August 10, 1929, pp. 531–539, 596.

VITARAMA. See CINERAMA

V-L-S-E. Vitagraph-Lubin-Selig-Essanay, Inc., or V-L-S-E, was incorporated on April 5, 1915, to release features made by the member companies that could not be adequately handled by the exchanges of the General Film Company. The company's creation marked the acceptance by these member companies of the Motion Picture Patents Company* of the importance of longer films, for which independent companies had earlier created a market. Most of the features released by V-L-S-E were five or six reels in length. Albert E. Smith of Vitagraph* was V-L-S-E's president, William N. Selig was treasurer, George K. Spoor of Essanay* was secretary, and Walter W. Irwin was general manager. The company released mostly films based on successful novels or plays, beginning with *The Carpet from Bagdad*. V-L-S-E was dissolved on August 17, 1916, when the Selig* and Essanay companies withdrew and joined the Kleine* and Edison* companies to form the Kleine-Edison-Selig-Essanay Service.

BIBLIOGRAPHY
"Scope of the V-L-S-E," *The Moving Picture World*, May 1, 1915, pp. 703–704.

VOGUE FILMS. See SACK AMUSEMENT ENTERPRISES

VOGUE FILMS, INC. Vogue Films, Inc., also known as the Vogue Motion Picture Company, began producing comedies at the old Lubin* studio at 4560 Pasadena Avenue, Los Angeles, in October 1915. It released on the Mutual program. Samuel S. Hutchinson, the president of the American Film Manufacturing Company*, was also the president of Vogue. In 1916, the company used a studio at the corner of Santa Monica Boulevard and Gower Street in Hollywood and produced two-reel comedies with two companies: Rube Miller directed the Ben Turpin and Gypsy Abbott unit, and R. E. Williamson directed the Patsy McGuire and Lillian Hamilton unit. Vogue disbanded in 1917.

THE VOICE OF HOLLYWOOD. A series of shorts produced by Louis Lewyn for Tiffany* in 1930–1931, the Voice of Hollywood was supposedly presented by a fictitious radio station, S-T-A-R, and featured Hollywood celebrities filmed at official functions and brief items with personalities whose stars were fading. Each short was hosted by a minor celebrity, such as Reginald Denny or Lloyd Hamilton.

BIBLIOGRAPHY

Maltin, Leonard. *The Great Movie Shorts*. New York: Crown, 1972.

WALT DISNEY PRODUCTIONS. Although he was not himself a great animator, Walt Disney (1901–1966) has come to stand for the best in animated art, or at least the best known and the most easily understood. Thanks to Mickey Mouse and Donald Duck, to features such as *Snow White and the Seven Dwarfs* and *Mary Poppins*, and to one of the longest-running of television shows, Walt Disney is a household name. As *The New York Times* reported at Disney's death, he "founded an empire on a mouse," but it was such an empire that it survived and prospered after he was gone thanks largely to the legacy of his films, cartoon characters, and the entertainment enterprises that he created and so successfully promoted.

Walt Disney's company began as Laugh-O-Gram Films, a Kansas City partnership with Ub Iwerks, which produced animated short subjects for the Newman Theatre Company and which was incorporated on May 23, 1922. In the summer of 1923, Walt Disney went to Hollywood and that same year, with his brother Roy, formed the Disney Bros. Studio to produce Alice cartoons, which combined both live action and animation and were distributed by a minor company, M. J. Winkler. Early in 1926, the brothers moved to a new studio on Hyperion Avenue in the Silverlake district of Los Angeles, and the Walt Disney Studio, later Walt Disney Productions, came into being. (When the company outgrew the Hyperion Avenue studios, the brothers purchased land for a new studio, in August 1938, on Buena Vista Street in Burbank.)

In 1929, Walt Disney Productions was incorporated. It was "re-incorporated" in 1938, with its stock shared between Walt and his wife, Lillian, and Roy and his wife, Edna. Stock in Walt Disney Productions was first offered for public sale in April 1940.

The first Mickey Mouse cartoon, *Plane Crazy*, was produced in 1928; the third Mickey Mouse cartoon, also released in 1928, was *Steamboat Willie*, which was Disney's first sound subject. Donald Duck was first seen in *The Wise Little Hen* (1934). In 1932, Walt Disney first used Technicolor*—for *Flowers and Trees*—and from that point onward all of his Silly Symphony* films were in color. The first Disney animated feature was *Snow White and the Seven Dwarfs* (1937); it was followed by *Pinocchio* (1940), *Fantasia* (1940), *The Reluctant Dragon* (1941; it began with live-action sequences starring Robert Benchley), *Bambi* (1942), *Victory through Air Power* (1943), *The Three Caballeros* (1945; it also combined live action), *Make Mine Music* (1946), *Song of the South* (1946; it also combined live action), *Fun and Fancy Free* (1947; it also combined live action), *Melody Time* (1948; it also combined live action), *The Adventures of Ichabod and Mr. Toad* (1949), *Cinderella* (1950), *Alice in Wonderland* (1951), *Peter Pan* (1953), *The Lady and the Tramp* (1955), *Sleeping Beauty* (1959), *One Hundred and One Dalmatians* (1961), *The Sword in the Stone* (1963), *The Jungle Book* (1967), *The Aristocats* (1970), *Robin Hood* (1973), *The Rescuers* (1977), *The Fox and the Hound* (1980), and *Mickey's Christmas Carol* (1983).

The first completely live-action Disney feature was *So Dear to My Heart* (1949). Among the best known of later live-action Disney features were *Treasure Island* (1950), *20,000 Leagues under the Sea* (1954), *Davy Crockett, King of the Wild Frontier* (1955), *Old Yeller* (1957), *Kidnapped* (1960), *Pollyanna* (1960), *The Absent-Minded Professor* (1961), *The Parent Trap* (1961), *The Moon-Spinners* (1964), *Mary Poppins* (1964), *The Happiest Millionaire* (1968), *The Love Bug* (1969), *The Black Hole* (1979), *Tron* (1982), and *Never Cry Wolf* (1983). With *The Living Desert* (1953) Disney also became noted for its "true-life" nature features, which included *The Vanishing Prairie* (1954) and *Perri* (1957). On television, Walt Disney Productions was represented by *Disneyland*, *The Mickey Mouse Club*, *Davy Crockett*, and *Zorro*.

Following Disney's death, the company came under the management of E. Cardon Walker, who had joined the organization in 1938 and who, in 1976, became president and chief executive officer. He was faced with a 1979 defection by a group of Disney animators, led by Don Bluth, who felt that the company's artistic standards had deteriorated. The company also experienced financial problems with some of its new films, notably *Tron*, and increasingly received the bulk of its income from its theme parks, Walt Disney World and Disneyland.

A new president, Ron Miller, introduced major changes—against the wishes of majority shareholder Roy Disney, Walt's nephew, who resigned from the board in April 1984. It was Miller who created the new Touchstone Films* to produce films outside of the normal type of Disney product and who sought to improve the quality of programming on the pay-television service, the Disney Channel.

The Walt Disney name is also synonymous with two entertainment complexes, both of which are unique theme parks, accurately described as world's fairs of the imagination. Disneyland opened as the Magic Kingdom brought to reality on July 17, 1955, in Anaheim, California. Walt Disney had conceived of the idea for such a park as early as 1928. Disneyland features Main Street America, Adventureland, Fantasyland, Frontierland, and Tomorrowland. A similar, but more ambitious, undertaking is Walt Disney World in Florida, which opened on October 23, 1971. Some eleven years later EPCOT, the experimental prototype community of tomorrow, opened as part of Walt Disney World. Both the latter and Disneyland were built by WED Enterprises, founded in 1952, which is described as "the creative laboratory" for Walt Disney Productions. A sister manufacturing and production company to WED is MAPO, named after the most commercially successful Disney film at the time of its formation, *Mary Poppins* (1964).

Address: 500 South Buena Vista Street, Burbank, Calif. 91521.

BIBLIOGRAPHY

Bailey, Adrian. *Walt Disney's World of Fantasy*. New York: Everest House, 1982.

Bain, David, and Bruce Harris. *Mickey Mouse: Fifty Happy Years*. New York: Harmony Books, 1977.

Beard, Richard R. *Walt Disney's EPCOT Center*. New York: Harry N. Abrams, 1982.

Blitz, Marcia. *Donald Duck*. New York: Harmony Books, 1979.

Disney, Walt. *Walt Disney Parade*. New York: Garden City Publishing, 1940.

————. *The Life of Donald Duck*. New York: Random House, 1941.

Feild, Robert D. *The Art of Walt Disney*. New York: Macmillan, 1942.

Finch, Christopher. *The Art of Walt Disney*. New York: Harry N. Abrams, 1973.

————. *Walt Disney's America*. New York: Abbeville Press, 1978.

Maltin, Leonard. *The Disney Films*. New York: Crown, 1984.

Miller, Diane Disney, as told to Pete Martin. *The Story of Walt Disney*. New York: Henry Holt, 1957.

Munsey, Cecil. *Disneyana*. New York: Hawthorn Books, 1974.

Schickel, Richard. *The Disney Version*. New York: Simon and Schuster, 1968.

Shale, Richard. *Donald Duck Grows Up: The Walt Disney Studio during World War II*. Ann Arbor, Michigan: UMI Research Press, 1982.

Shows, Charles. *Walt: Backstage Adventures with Walt Disney*. La Jolla, California: Communication Creativity, 1979.

Thomas, Bob. *Walt Disney: The Art of Animation*. New York: Simon and Schuster, 1958.

————. *Walt Disney: Magician of the Movies*. New York: Grosset & Dunlap, 1966.

Thomas, Frank, and Ollie Johnston. *Disney Animation: The Illusion of Life*. New York: Abbeville Press, 1981.

Treasures of Disney Animation Art. New York: Abbeville Press, 1982.

RESOURCES

Papers: Walt Disney Archives.

Still Photographs: Walt Disney Archives.

WALT DISNEY WORLD. See WALT DISNEY PRODUCTIONS

WALTER READE ORGANIZATION. With its beginnings in a Port Chester, New York, vaudeville house that Walter Reade, Sr., acquired in 1908, the Walter Reade Organization grew from 1946, when Walter Reade, Jr.—who died in 1973 at the age of fifty-six—assumed control of the company. It operated a major theatre circuit, with more than seventy screens by 1970, and was also involved in educational and nontheatrical film distribution, in independent co-production—of features such as *Ulysses* (1967)—and in theatrical distribution through Continental Releasing.

The company merged with Sterling Television in 1961 to become Walter Reade–Sterling, Inc., and in September 1966 adopted the name of the Walter Reade Organization. In 1970, the company sold off its theatrical and television distribution divisions, including Continental Distributing (with the latter's library being acquired in 1982 by Kino International*). In 1977, the Walter Reade Organization filed for reorganization under Chapter XI of the Federal Bankruptcy Act, reorganization which was finally approved by the courts in 1981. By 1984, the organization, which controls such major New York theatres as the Ziegfeld, the Baronet, the Coronet, the Waverly, and the New Yorker, had 41 percent of its stock owned by Columbia Pictures*.

Address: 241 East 34 Street, New York, N.Y. 10016.

WALTER WANGER PRODUCTIONS, INC. Walter Wanger (1894–1968) formed Walter Wanger Productions, Inc., incorporated on July 24, 1936, with funding provided by United Artists* and the Bank of America. Located at what became known as the Samuel Goldwyn Studios in Hollywood, Walter Wanger Productions was responsible for many memorable features, including *You Only Live Once* (1937), *History Is Made at Night* (1937), *Algiers* (1938), *Stagecoach* (1939), *Foreign Correspondent* (1940), and *The Long Voyage Home* (1940). Walter Wanger Productions ceased to exist in November 1941, when it was renamed United Artists Productions, Inc.

WAMPAS BABY STARS. See WESTERN ASSOCIATED MOTION PICTURE ADVERTISERS

WAR ACTIVITIES COMMITTEE. Organized in June 1940, with the fall of France to the Nazis during the Second World War, as the Motion Picture Committee Cooperating for National Defense, the War Activities Committee officially came into being on December 12, 1941. Presidents of thirty-four motion picture organizations formed a national committee to coordinate the activities of seven working divisions. The Theatres Division consisted of 16,486 theatres pledged to screen approved government- or industry-produced trailers and short subjects and to participate in bond drives and scrap drives. The Distributors Division had 352 film exchanges in 31 cities to handle releases of approved films without charge to the government. The Hollywood Division was made up of 30,000 studio workers involved in various war duties. The Newsreel Division consisted of the five major newsreel* companies and March of Time* with the responsibility of filming the war at home and abroad. The Trade Press Division was made up of the entire staff of sixteen trade papers* concerned with the reporting of war activities within the motion picture industry and providing free advertising. The Foreign Managers Division was concerned with the distribution of gifts and appropriate films to the allied forces. The Public Relations Division, as its name suggests, consisted of 1,800 publicity and public relations men promoting the activities of the Committee. The War Activities Committee was liquidated on January 7, 1946.

WAR FILM HEARINGS. A Senate subcommittee was appointed at the instigation of Senator Gerald P. Nye to investigate war propaganda produced by the film industry in the form of films which attacked Nazi Germany and supported the British war effort. Serving on the subcommittee, which began its hearings on September 8, 1941, were five isolationist senators, D. Work Clark (chairman), Homer T. Bone, Charles W. Tobey, C. Wayland Brooks, and Ernest W. McFarland.

The motion picture industry appointed Wendell Wilkie as its spokesman and legal counsel, although the industry needed little support, for the subcommittee was thoroughly castigated as little more than a Nazi tool by all except Father Coughlin. Anti-Semitic comments by the subcommittee regarding Jewish control of the industry were the subject of many editorials. The subcommittee recessed after two weeks of hearings.

WARNER BROS. PICTURES, INC. Although Warner Bros. Pictures was not incorporated until 1923, the history of the four Warner Bros.—Harry, Albert, Sam, and Jack—in the film industry goes back a lot further, to 1907 when the boys opened the Duquesne Amusement Supply Company, with offices in Pittsburgh, Pennsylvania, and Norfolk, Virginia. The company folded in 1909, and three years later Warner Bros. moved to the West Coast, producing its first important feature, *My Four Years in Germany*, in 1918.

In 1925, Warner Bros. acquired the Vitagraph Company*, which gave the brothers a studio in Brooklyn, an additional studio in Hollywood, and Vitagraph's thirty-four exchanges. With *Don Juan* (1926) and *The Jazz Singer* (1927), Warner Bros. pioneered the sound motion picture and also acquired sufficient funding to purchase, in 1929, First National Pictures* and Fox West Coast Theatres*. With the acquisition of First National, Warner Bros. moved to its Burbank Studios*, although it continued for a time to operate the former Vitagraph Studios and its own studios on Sunset Boulevard in Hollywood (which became the home of the independent television station KTLA). (Through the early forties the name First National appeared on many Warner Bros. productions, just as Vitagraph continued to be used as a trademark.)

The thirties may well be considered as Warner Bros.' "golden age," when the studio's name was associated with Busby Berkeley musicals, gangster pictures, social dramas, action spectacles, and soap operas. Among the company's best-known films from this decade were *The Public Enemy* (1931), *Little Caesar* (1931), *I Am a Fugitive from a Chain Gang* (1932), *42nd Street* (1933), *The Story of Louis Pasteur* (1936), *Anthony Adverse* (1936), *The Life of Emile Zola* (1937), *The Adventures of Robin Hood* (1938), and *Dark Victory* (1939). Among the directors under contract were Busby Berkeley, Michael Curtiz, and Mervyn

LeRoy, while the stars under contract included James Cagney, Bette Davis, Olivia de Havilland, Errol Flynn, Paul Muni, Pat O'Brien, Dick Powell, and Edward G. Robinson.

Darryl F. Zanuck, who had been the studio's production chief under Jack L. Warner, resigned in 1933, following the studio's refusal to rescind, on a specified date, the 50 percent pay cuts advocated by the Academy of Motion Picture Arts and Sciences*. Zanuck had been responsible for keeping the studio alive in the twenties, with his Rin-Tin-Tin features, and is generally considered the person to whom credit should go for Warner Bros.' early success. He was replaced by Hal Wallis, who was, in turn, replaced in 1941 by Steve Trilling, who had less authority.

Warner Bros. continued to prosper in the forties, with films such as *The Sea Hawk* (1940), *Sergeant York* (1941), *The Maltese Falcon* (1941), *Kings Row* (1941), *Now, Voyager* (1942), *Yankee Doodle Dandy* (1942), *Casablanca* (1943), *Objective, Burma!* (1945), *Mildred Pierce* (1945), *The Big Sleep* (1946), *Johnny Belinda* (1948), and *White Heat* (1949). The forties also saw the addition of a new Warner Bros. star in Ronald Reagan.

In the fifties, Warner Bros. became involved in television production, but it experienced financial difficulties in the early sixties. In 1956, rights to almost all of the pre–1950 features were sold to Associated Artists, which in turn sold them to United Artists*. In 1966, Seven Arts Productions, Ltd., a Toronto-based company acquired Warner Bros. outright. Warner Bros.–Seven Arts, Ltd., became known chiefly as a television distributor, with not only the Warner Bros. features but also films from 20th Century-Fox*, Allied Artists*, and Universal*. Additionally, Seven Arts operated the record companies of Atlantic, Warner, and Reprise.

On July 9, 1969, the company changed hands again when it was acquired by Kinney National Services, Inc., a New York–based operation previously known for its parking lots and funeral homes. Ted Ashley, of another Kinney-owned company, Ashley-Famous Agency, became the new head of Warner Bros. Kinney subsequently formed Warner Communications, Inc.*, to supervise its entertainment activities, including Warner Bros.

Despite financial problems and a takeover bid by Rupert Murdoch, Warner Bros. entered the eighties in a financially sound position, thanks largely to films such as *Gremlins* and *Tightrope* (both released in 1984), which exemplified the studio's policy of utilizing major talent—in this case Steven Spielberg and Clint Eastwood, respectively—on films with moderate budgets.

Address: 4000 Warner Boulevard, Burbank, Calif. 91522.

BIBLIOGRAPHY

Behlmer, Rudy. *Inside Warner Bros.* New York: Viking Press, 1985.

Freedland, Michael. *The Warner Brothers.* New York: St. Martin's Press, 1983.

Friedwald, Will, and Jerry Beck. *The Warner Brothers Cartoons.* Metuchen, New Jersey: Scarecrow Press, 1981.

Hanson, Steve, ''Warners: Walking the Tightrope,'' *Stills*, May 1985, pp. 64–67.

Higham, Charles. *Warner Brothers*. New York: Charles Scribner's Sons, 1975.

Hirschhorn, Clive. *The Warner Bros. Story*. New York: Crown, 1979.

Jerome, Stuart. *Those Crazy Wonderful Years When We Ran Warner Bros*. Secaucus, New Jersey: Lyle Stuart, 1983.

Meyer, William A. *Warner Brothers Directors*. New Rochelle, New York: Arlington House, 1978.

Roddick, Nick. *A New Deal in Entertainment: Warner Brothers in the 1930s*. London: British Film Institute, 1983.

Sennett, Ted. *Warner Brothers Presents*. New Rochelle, New York: Arlington House, 1971.

Silke, James R. *Here's Looking at You, Kid*. Boston: Little, Brown, 1976.

Warner, Jack L., with Dean Jennings. *My First Hundred Years in Hollywood*. New York: Random House, 1965.

Wilson, Arthur, editor. *The Warner Bros. Golden Anniversary Book*. New York: Film and Venture, 1973.

RESOURCES

Films: Library of Congress (35mm preservation material and some reference prints of pre–1950 titles); UCLA Film Archives (35mm nitrate prints from studio collection); Wisconsin Center for Film and Theater Research (16mm reference prints of pre–1950 titles).

Papers: Princeton University (corporate legal and distribution papers from New York office); University of Southern California (legal, story, and production files, etc., from Burbank Studios).

Still Photographs: George Eastman House; University of Southern California.

WARNER BROS.–SEVEN ARTS, LTD. See WARNER BROS. PICTURES, INC.

WARNER COMMUNICATIONS, INC. Following its 1969 takeover of Warner Bros.*, Kinney National Services, Inc., formed Warner Communications, Inc., to operate its entertainment divisions. Warner Communications, Inc. (WC), was the parent company of the following, some of which have since been sold off: Warner Bros., Warner Bros. Television, Licensing Corporation of America, Panavision*, Warner Bros. Distributing Corporation, David Wolper Productions, Warner Home Video, Warner Books, Warner Publishing Service, Mad Magazine, DC Comics, Warner Amex Cable Communications, Warner Amex Satellite Entertainment Company, Atari, Malibu Grand Prix, Knickerbocker Toys, Warner Bros. Records, Atlantic Records, Elektra Records, Asylum Records, Nonesuch Records, WEA Corporation, WEA International, WEA Manufacturing, Warner Bros. Music Publishing, New York Cosmos Soccer Club, Warner Cosmetics, Warner Theatre Productions, and Franklin Mint.

Address: 75 Rockefeller Plaza, New York, N.Y. 10019.

BIBLIOGRAPHY

Gustafson, Robert, "What's Happening to Our Pix Biz? From Warner Bros. to Warner Communications Inc.," in Tino Balio, editor, *The American Film Industry*. Madison, Wisconsin: University of Wisconsin Press, 1985, pp. 574–602.

WARNER'S FEATURES, INC. See UNITED FILM SERVICE

WARNERSUPERSCOPE. See CINEMASCOPE

WAYNE-FELLOWS PRODUCTIONS. See BATJAC PRODUCTIONS, INC.

WEBER-FIELDS-KINEMACOLOR. See KINEMACOLOR COMPANY OF AMERICA

WED ENTERPRISES. See WALT DISNEY PRODUCTIONS

THE WESTERN. One of the American film industry's favorite genres from the early years of the twentieth century through the fifties, the Western has generated its own stars, writers, and directors. It is the genre of William S. Hart, Tom Mix, Buck Jones, John Wayne, Roy Rogers, Gene Autry, Ken Maynard, George "Gabby" Hayes, and George O'Brien, and of director John Ford, who succinctly summed up his career with the words, "I make Westerns."

Although it was not the first Western, Edwin S. Porter's *The Great Train Robbery* (1903) is usually considered as the starting point for a study of the American Western film. It was pioneer producer Thomas H. Ince who legitimized the genre in the early teens, and it was Broncho Billy Anderson and William S. Hart who created the Western hero. In the twenties, Tom Mix glamorized the image of the West, and Mix's view of the genre was perpetuated by the singing cowboy heroes of the thirties and forties, such as Gene Autry and Roy Rogers, whose films were the staple of Republic Pictures* and who, along with Hopalong (William Boyd) Cassidy, carried the image to radio and television.

The epic Western can be dated back to James Cruze's *The Covered Wagon* (1923) and John Ford's *The Iron Horse* (1924). Raoul Walsh's *In Old Arizona* (1929) was the first sound Western to make effective use of outdoor locations, but it was Raoul Walsh's *The Big Trail* (1930) that was the first epic talkie Western. The most popular Western story is, arguably, *The Virginian*, based on a novel by Owen Wister and a play by Kirke La Shelle, which had been filmed in 1914, 1923, 1929, and 1946. Another favorite stage Western was Edwin Royle's *The Squaw Man*, which Cecil B. DeMille filmed in 1914 (co-directed by Oscar Apfel), 1918, and 1931.

For much of the thirties, the Western was relegated to the level of a "B" movie*, but that changed with John Ford's *Stagecoach* (1939), starring John Wayne and a good example of the brilliant stuntwork of Western veteran Yakima Canutt (who was featured in many "B" Westerns and also served as second unit director on many more). The Western genre prospered in the forties with *Santa Fe Trail* (1940), *Virginia City* (1940), *The Westerner* (1940), *Western Union* (1941), *The Ox-Bow Incident* (1943), *The Outlaw* (1946), *My Darling Clementine* (1946), *Fort Apache* (1948), *Three Godfathers* (1948), *Red River* (1948), and *She Wore a Yellow Ribbon* (1949).

John Ford continued to make his inimitable Westerns into the fifties, with *Wagon Master* (1950) and *Rio Grande* (1950), but a new, more adult Western came on the scene, as represented by Henry King's *The Gunfighter* (1950), Fred Zinnemann's *High Noon* (1952), Fritz Lang's *Rancho Notorious* (1952), Nicholas Ray's *Johnny Guitar* (1954), Anthony Mann's *The Man from Laramie* (1955), Samuel Fuller's *Run of the Arrow* (1956), and Howard Hawks' *Rio Bravo* (1959). Violence became a more prominent aspect of the Western genre with the films of Sam Peckinpah, including *Major Dundee* (1964), *The Wild Bunch* (1969), *The Ballad of Cable Hogue* (1970), and *Pat Garrett and Billy the Kid* (1973).

John Ford continued to direct Westerns into the sixties, with *Sergeant Rutledge* (1960), *Two Rode Together* (1961), *The Man Who Shot Liberty Valance* (1962), and *Cheyenne Autumn* (1964). Other major Westerns of the sixties and seventies included *The Alamo* (1960), *How the West Was Won* (1962), *Cat Ballou* (1965), *El Dorado* (1966), *True Grit* (1969), *Butch Cassidy and the Sundance Kid* (1969), *A Man Called Horse* (1970), *Soldier Blue* (1970), *Rio Lobo* (1971), and the Western spoof *Blazing Saddles* (1974). Elvis Presley became a new-style Western hero in *Flaming Star* (1960) and *Charro!* (1969).

The Western lost its appeal for American filmmakers in the seventies, but the genre continued chiefly in the so-called spaghetti Westerns produced in Italy and Spain, of which Sergio Leone is the best-known director.

Among the most popular Western figures to have been portrayed on film were Billy the Kid (William H. Bonney), Wyatt Earp, the James brothers, and Wild Bill Hickok (James Butler Hickok). Billy the Kid was played by Johnny Mack Brown in *Billy the Kid* (1930), by Roy Rogers in *Billy the Kid Returns* (1938), by Buster Crabbe in *Billy the Kid Wanted* (1941), by Robert Taylor in *Billy the Kid* (1941), by Jack Beutel in *The Outlaw* (1946), by Lash LaRue in *Son of Billy the Kid* (1949), by Paul Newman in *The Left-Handed Gun* (1958), by Michael Pollard in *Dirty Little Billy* (1972), and by Kris Kristofferson in *Pat Garrett and Billy the Kid* (1973).

Wyatt Earp has been played by George O'Brien in *Frontier Marshall* (1934), by Randolph Scott in *Frontier Marshall* (1939), by Richard Dix in *Tombstone— the Town Too Tough to Die* (1942), by Henry Fonda in *My Darling Clementine* (1946), by Joel McCrea in *Wichita* (1955), by Burt Lancaster in *Gunfight at the O.K. Corral* (1957), by James Stewart in *Cheyenne Autumn* (1964), by James Garner in *Hour of the Gun* (1967), and by Harris Yulin in *Doc* (1971).

The James brothers have been featured in more than twenty films, including *Jesse James* (1927), in which Fred Thomson played the title role; *Jesse James* (1939), in which Tyrone Power played the title role and Henry Fonda played Frank James; *Return of Frank James* (1940), in which Henry Fonda played the title role; *Jesse James at Bay* (1941), in which Roy Rogers played the title role; *Jesse James Rides Again* (1947), a serial in which Clayton Moore (better known as the Lone Ranger) played the title role; *The Return of Jesse James* (1950), in which John Ireland played the title role; *Alias Jesse James* (1958), in which Bob Hope played the title role; *Jesse James Meets Frankenstein* (1961), in which

Jack Beutel played James; *I Shot Jesse James* (1949), in which Reed Hadley played James; *Kansas Raiders* (1950), in which Audie Murphy played Jesse James; and *The Long Riders* (1980), in which James Keach played Jesse and Stacy Keach played Frank James.

Wild Bill Hickok has been featured in *Wild Bill Hickok* (1923), *Aces & Eights* (1936), *Great Adventures of Wild Bill Hickok* (1938), *Wild Bill Hickok Rides* (1941), *Prairie Gunsmoke* (1942), *Deadwood '76* (1965), *The Plainsman* (1966), and *The White Buffalo* (1977), among others.

BIBLIOGRAPHY

Eyles, Allen. *The Western.* Cranbury, New Jersey: A. S. Barnes, 1975.

Fenin, George N., and William K. Everson. *The Western.* New York: Grossman, 1973.

French, Philip. *Westerns: Aspects of a Movie Genre.* New York: Viking Press, 1973.

Hardy, Phil. *The Western.* New York: William Morrow, 1983.

Nachbar, John G. *Western Films: An Annotated Critical Bibliography.* New York: Garland, 1975.

Parks, Rita. *The Western Hero in Film and Television.* Ann Arbor, Michigan: UMI Research Press, 1982.

Place, J. A. *The Western Films of John Ford.* Secaucus, New Jersey: Citadel Press, 1974.

Tuska, Jon. *The Filming of the West.* New York: Doubleday, 1976.

WESTERN ASSOCIATED MOTION PICTURE ADVERTISERS. Founded in 1920, the Western Associated Motion Picture Advertisers (WAMPAS) was comprised of professional publicists in the film industry. With less than 20 members in 1920, the organization had grown to more than 100 by 1933. According to an early press release, "The WAMPAS founders were animated by a spirit of fraternity and cooperation. Their aims were both social and professional. Their objectives, as stated in their constitution, which remains unchanged, were to foster comradeship, promote the ethics of the profession, and encourage cooperation among the members."

The best-known activity of the Association was the annual selection of thirteen young actresses with potential star power, an idea that was conceived in 1921 and first undertaken in 1922. Among those actresses selected as WAMPAS Baby Stars were Mary Astor, Joan Blondell, Mary Brian, Dolores Del Rio, Janet Gaynor, Laura La Plante, Bessie Love, Colleen Moore, Karen Morley, Sally Rand, Ginger Rogers, Lupe Velez, Fay Wray, and Loretta Young.

The Association merged with the Writers Club in 1930, but it retained its separate identity. No WAMPAS Baby Stars were selected in 1933, and in 1934 the "stars" included freelance actresses as well as studio contract players. The winners, none of whom achieved any prominence in the industry, were featured in two films, *Kiss and Make Up* and *Young and Beautiful.* The following year, the WAMPAS Baby Stars idea was discarded, and the Western Associated Motion Picture Advertisers disbanded. In 1955 the idea of naming WAMPAS Baby Stars was revived unsuccessfully.

BIBLIOGRAPHY
Uselton, Roi A., "The WAMPAS Baby Stars," *Films in Review*, February 1970, pp. 73–97.

WESTERN AUDIO VISUAL ENTERPRISES. See JERRY FAIRBANKS PRODUCTIONS

WESTERN COSTUME CO. The best-known supplier of film costumes in the world, the Western Costume Co. dates back to the early teens when a former Indian trader named L. L. Burns was asked by Western star William S. Hart to provide authentic costumes for his films. Burns acquired Fisher's Costume House and opened his first company at 7th and Figueroa in downtown Los Angeles. As more Hollywood producers turned to Western Costume to provide clothing, the company moved, in 1924, to a new ten-story building.

Through heavy competition from United Costume Company, created by his former employees, Burns was forced into bankruptcy, and Western Costume Co. was acquired, in 1928, by Dan, Joe, and Ike Greenberg. The Greenberg brothers moved the company in 1932 to its present location in Hollywood. Joe and Abe Schnitzer acquired the company in 1934, and in 1937 a consortium of major Hollywood studios acquired Western, after its competitor, United Costume Company, had been taken over by Warner Bros.* and its assets merged with the studio's wardrobe department. G. B. Howe was named president of the company in 1950, and upon his retirement John Golden, the present president, took over.

Western Costume Co. maintains an inventory of 1 million men's and women's clothes and also houses a research library of 10,000 volumes. On the premises are a laundry and dry cleaning plant, a paint shop, a studio art and metal shop, and a leather shop.

Among the more recent films for which Western Costume Co. has provided costumes—usually for the extras and "bit" players rather than stars, whose costumes were specially designed—are *Spartacus*, *A Star Is Born*, *Star Trek—The Motion Picture*, *Ship of Fools*, *Call Me Madam*, *Airplane*, *Myra Breckenridge*, *Brigadoon*, *Cleopatra*, *Who's Afraid of Virginia Woolf?*, *The King and I*, *West Side Story*, *The Sting*, *Airport*, *Sweet Charity*, *The Alamo*, *Planet of the Apes*, *Jaws*, and *Love Story*. It has also been associated with such television series as "M*A*S*H," "Wagon Train," "Hill Street Blues," "Dragnet," "Ironside," and "Gunsmoke."

Address: 5335 Melrose Avenue, Hollywood, Calif. 90038.

WESTERN ELECTRIC. See VITAPHONE

WESTERN PHOTOPLAYS, INC. Western Photoplays, Inc., began producing for Pathé in mid–1918. Joseph A. Golden and A. Alperstein were the company's officers. Western produced two-reel Westerns* starring Helen Gibson and a serial*, *Wolves of Kultur*, with Leah Baird and Sheldon Lewis, which Golden wrote, produced, and directed. The company went out of business late in 1918, and Astra Film Corporation completed production of the remaining episodes of the serial.

WGA. See WRITERS GUILD OF AMERICA

WHARTON, INC. Theodore W. Wharton, who earlier was scenario editor and studio supervisor for the Edison Company*, established the Kalem Company's first indoor studio and started Pathé* Freres' American studio and became its first director. He went to Ithaca, New York, in the fall of 1912 to produce a football picture for Essanay* and decided to make the city his home. He convinced Essanay to send a company under his direction for the summer of 1913; when he saw that Essanay was not interested in sending one there again, he left the company and formed Wharton, Inc., with his brother Leopold, previously an actor and director with Pathé, and with the assistance of the Ithaca business community.

The company began production on May 1, 1914, using the glass ball cage of Cornell University as a temporary studio. Later in that year, it built its own studio and plant in the city. Wharton, Inc., was a contracting producer for Pathé, for which it made the serials* *The Exploits of Elaine*, *The New Exploits of Elaine*, *The Romance of Elaine* (all starring Pearl White), and *The New Adventures of J. Rufus Wallingford*. Early in 1916, it began producing for other companies and made the serials *Beatrice Fairfax* and *Patria* for the International Film Service*. By the beginning of 1919, Wharton had ceased production.

BIBLIOGRAPHY

Stainton, Walter R., "Pearl White in Ithaca," *Films in Review*, May 1951, pp. 19–25.

"Wharton Incorporated," *The Moving Picture World*, April 18, 1914, p. 349.

"Whartons, of Ithaca, Rest on Oars," *The Moving Picture World*, January 25, 1919, p. 470.

WHITESTONE, LONG ISLAND. See KINEMACOLOR COMPANY OF AMERICA

WHITMAN BENNETT STUDIOS. The home of Whitman Bennett Productions (released through First National* and United Artists*), the Whitman Bennett Studios were the former East Coast studios of Fine Arts*, located at 537 Riverdale Avenue in Yonkers. Operating from 1919 to 1925, the Whitman Bennett Studios were also used by other independent producers.

WHITMAN FEATURES COMPANY. The Whitman Features Company, which began producing in 1914, had Martin J. Faust, formerly with Lubin*, as its director and John William Kellette as its scenario editor. Its productions included the three-reel *His Flesh and Blood* (1914), about recent gang troubles in New

York; the five-reel *Lena Rivers* (1914), starring Violet Horner; and the four-reel *Jane Eyre* (1914). Blinkhorn Photoplays Corporation released Whitman's films to the states rights* market.

"WHY WE FIGHT" SERIES. The most successful and the best-known series of documentaries to be produced by the U.S. government during the Second World War was "Why We Fight," supervised by Major (later Lieutenant-Colonel) Frank Capra. Chief of Staff George C. Marshall placed Capra in charge of the project, and the former Hollywood director set about producing a series of films which blended actuality footage with staged theatrical scenes. There were seven films in the series: *Prelude to War* (1942), *The Nazis Strike* (1942), *Divide and Conquer* (1943), *The Battle of Britain* (1943), *The Battle of Russia* (1943), *The Battle of China* (1944), and *War Comes to America* (1945). Additionally, Capra's unit also created a newsreel, *Army-Navy Screen Magazine*, and produced a number of other documentaries, notably *The Negro Soldier* (1944).
BIBLIOGRAPHY
Barnouw, Erik. *Documentary*. New York: Oxford University Press, 1974.
Capra, Frank. *The Name above the Title*. New York: Macmillan, 1971.
Murphy, William Thomas, "The Method of *Why We Fight*," *The Journal of Popular Film*, vol. I, no. 3, Summer 1972, pp. 185–196.

WIDESCREEN. See ANAMORPHIC LENS, CINEMASCOPE, CINEMIRACLE, CINERAMA, SHOWSCAN, TODD-AO, VISTAVISION

WILKES-BARRE, PENNSYLVANIA. See UNITED STATES MOTION PICTURE CORPORATION

WILLIAM A. BRADY PICTURES PLAYS, INC. See WORLD FILM CORPORATION

WILLIAM L. SHERRY SERVICE. William L. Sherry opened the William L. Sherry Feature Film Company of New York on March 15, 1913, to distribute *The Prisoner of Zenda* and, later, other productions of the Famous Players Film Company and the Jesse L. Lasky Feature Play Company in the state and city of New York. On September 26, 1916, Sherry, formerly vice-president of Paramount*, opened his own offices and exchanges nationwide. In May 1918, the William L. Sherry Service was started to distribute Frank A. Keeney Productions, starring Catherine Calvert, and soon the Service added Edgar Lewis Productions, De Luxe Pictures, Inc.*, and features of Gilbert M. "Broncho Billy" Anderson. In late 1918, Sherry used the physical apparatus of the General Film Company to release his films but, in May 1919, switched to using the Film Clearing House.

WILLIAM MORRIS AGENCY. The oldest talent agency in the world, the William Morris Agency was founded, on New York's 14 Street, by William Morris, Sr., in 1898. It dates from the golden age of vaudeville, when its clients included Will Rogers, Harry Lauder, and Al Jolson. Other famous William Morris clients included James Cagney, Eddie Cantor, Katharine Hepburn, Marilyn Monroe, and Frank Sinatra. As of 1983, there were 150 agents working for the organization, whose best-known employee was Abe Lastfogel, who joined the agency in 1912 and remained with it until his death in 1984 at the age of eighty-six. William Morris, Jr., became president of the agency on the death of his father in 1932 and remained president until 1952.

Addresses: 151 El Camino, Beverly Hills, Calif. 90212; 1350 Avenue of the Americas, New York, N.Y. 10019; also offices in London, Munich, Rome, and Sydney.

BIBLIOGRAPHY

Loynd, Ray, "William Morris Agency Toasts Its 85th Anni in Show-Business," *Daily Variety*, June 3, 1983, pp. 1, 18.

WILLIAMSON SUBMARINE FILM COMPANY. See SUBMARINE FILM COMPANY

WILL ROGERS MEMORIAL FUND. The financial branch of the Will Rogers Memorial Hospital and the Will Rogers Institute, the Will Rogers Memorial Fund has its origins in the National Vaudeville Association (NVA) Lodge at Saranac Lake, New York, which came into being in 1925. Established as a hospital for those suffering from tuberculosis, the NVA Lodge was turned over to the Will Rogers Memorial Commission in 1936. As drugs against and treatment of tuberculosis became standardized, the Will Rogers Memorial Hospital became concerned with pulmonary research and health education, for which the funds are now used. Since the thirties, the film industry has supported the Will Rogers Memorial Fund through radio and motion picture appeals by Hollywood personalities. The Will Rogers Memorial Fund should not be confused with the Will Rogers Memorial in Claremore, Oklahoma, which serves as a repository of Rogers' papers and artifacts.

Address: 785 Mamaroneck Avenue, White Plains, N.Y. 10605.

BIBLIOGRAPHY

Daniels, Bill, "Will Rogers Institute: Caring for Medical Needs of Showbiz," *Daily Variety*, December 3, 1984, pp. 3, 6.

WINCHESTER PICTURES CORPORATION. In existence through the fifties, and with offices at 780 North Gower Street in Hollywood, Winchester Pictures Corporation was the production company of director Howard Hawks (1896–1977)—Winchester was his middle name. It produced Hawks' 1952 feature *The Big Sky* and the 1951 feature *The Thing*, directed by Christian Nyby (probably with uncredited help from Hawks).

WIZARD MOTION PICTURE CORPORATION. The Wizard Motion Picture Corporation was formed in mid–1915 to produce the "Pokes and Jabbs" comedy series starring Bob Burns and Walter Stull as two henpecked husbands. Burns, Stull, and general manager Louis Burstein organized the company, whose films were distributed through the World Comedy Stars Film Corporation*. The company disbanded later in 1915, with Burstein, Burns, and Stull continuing the "Pokes and Jabbs" series for Vim*.

BIBLIOGRAPHY

"Pokes and Jabbs," *The Moving Picture World*, September 11, 1915, p. 1811.

WOMEN FILMMAKERS. Writing in the December 1923 issue of *The Business Woman*, Myrtle Gebhart commented,

> Excluding acting, considering solely the business possibilities, the positions are held by women in the Hollywood studios as typists, stenographers, secretaries to stars and executives, telephone operators, hairdressers, seamstresses, costume designers, milliners, readers, script girls, scenarists, cutters, film retouchers, film splicers and other laboratory work, set designers and set dressers, librarians, artists, title writers, publicity writers, plaster moulder, casting director, musicians, film editors, executives and department managers, directors and producers.

Gebhart ended her article by noting, "We are here, sisters, and we're so stubborn that we're going to make our mark—indeed many of our sisterhood are already making it, and indelibly, too."

There was nothing that unusual about women directors in the American silent film industry. The first female director in the world was Alice Guy, who made her first film for Gaumont in the 1890s, and, with her husband Herbert Blaché, came to the United States in 1907, establishing the Solax Company* and working as a director until 1920. Screenwriters such as Frances Marion, Anita Loos, June Mathis, Beulah Marie Dix, Bess Meredyth, and Lenore Coffee dominated the silent film industry. Frances Marion directed three features—*The Love Light, Just around the Corner*, and *The Song of Love*—between 1921 and 1923, and other female screenwriters who tried their hand at direction included Marguerite Bertsch, Mrs. George Randolph Chester, Julia Crawford Ivers, Marion Fairfax, Jane Murfin, and Elizabeth Pickett.

The most important of all women film directors in America was Lois Weber, whose career extended from the preteens to the early thirties. She was an uncompromising filmmaker, whose productions dealt with social issues such as abortion, birth control, capital punishment, and anti-Semitism. Margery Wilson, one of D. W. Griffith's leading ladies in *Intolerance*, was active as a director in the early twenties. Another D. W. Griffith star, Lillian Gish, directed one feature, *Remodeling Her Husband* (1920). Other actresses who tried their hand at directing included Gene Gauntier, Kathlyn Williams, and Mabel Normand.

At one time or another, nine women directors were at work at Universal*, including Ida May Park, Ruth Ann Baldwin, Grace Cunard, Cleo Madison, and

Ruth Stonehouse. With the death of her husband Wallace Reid in 1923, Dorothy Davenport (better known as Mrs. Wallace Reid) took to production and direction and was to remain active through the fifties. The only American female director to make a successful transition from silent features to talkies was Dorothy Arzner, who began her directorial career in 1927 and made her last feature, *First Comes Courage*, in 1943.

Aside from Arzner, only one other woman directed an American feature in the thirties, and that was Wanda Tuchock, who co-directed *Finishing School* in 1934. Women did not come into their own as directors again until Ida Lupino co-directed *Not Wanted* in 1949. In more recent years, Shirley Clarke came to prominence with *Portrait of Jason* (1967). Stephanie Rothman is noted for her exploitation films*, such as *It's a Bikini World* (1966), *The Student Nurses* (1970), and *Working Girls* (1974). Ruth Orkin co-wrote and co-directed three features with her husband Morris Engel: *The Little Fugitive* (1953), *Lovers and Lollipops* (1956), and *Weddings and Babies* (1958). Elaine May directed *A New Leaf* (1970) and *Heartbreak Kid* (1972). Other American women directors active from the sixties onward included Mary Ellen Bute, Claudia Weill, Martha Coolidge, Nell Cox, Storm de Hirsch, Lynne Littman, Joan Micklin Silver, Joan Rivers, Barbara Kopple, Francine Parker, Faith Hubley, Kathleen Dowdey, Eleanor Gavor, Buffy Queen, Karen Arthur, and Amy Heckerling.

In 1980, the Directors Guild of America* reported that in the previous thirty years only seven women had directed features and only twenty-three women had been employed as directors of prime-time television. Since then the position has improved somewhat, but women have yet to gain the prominence they held in the American film industry during the silent era.

BIBLIOGRAPHY

Heck-Rabi, Louise. *Women Filmmakers: A Critical Reception*. Metuchen, New Jersey: Scarecrow Press, 1984.

Kay, Karyn, and Gerald Peary, editors. *Women and the Cinema*. New York: E. P. Dutton, 1977.

Slide, Anthony. *Early Women Directors*. South Brunswick and New York: A. S. Barnes, 1977.

Smith, Sharon. *Women Who Make Movies*. New York: Hopkinson and Blake, 1975.

WOMEN IN FILM. Women in Film was formed, by twelve women, on March 2, 1973, as a nonprofit organization for professional women in the film industry. Tichi Wilkerson, editor-in-chief of *The Hollywood Reporter*, was the organization's first president. Women in Film organizes workshops, conferences, publishes a newsletter, and, since 1977, has presented Crystal Awards to honor outstanding individuals ''whose professional careers have been distinguished by their excellence, endurance and expansion of the role given women within the entertainment industry.'' (Lucille Ball, Nancy Malone, Eleanor Perry, and Norma Zarky were the first honorees.) Membership in Women in Film requires sponsorship by two current members and is limited to those with three years or more experience in the industry.

Address: 8489 West Third Street, Suite 25, Los Angeles, Calif. 90048.

WOMEN OF THE MOTION PICTURE INDUSTRY. Formed in 1953, Women of the Motion Picture Industry (WOMPI) is a nationwide organization, with chapters in various cities, concerned with community and industry service. It is involved in fund-raising and charitable work and sponsors a room at the Will Rogers Memorial Hospital.

Address: 940 Seventh Street, Santa Monica, Calif. 90403.

WONDERGRAF PRODUCTION COMPANY. Founded by C. H. Gowman in December 1920, and based in Los Angeles, the Wondergraf Production Company produced a series of novelty shorts, under the headings of "Wondergrafs," "Stay-at-Home Tourists," "The Little Players," and "Cameo Playlets."

WORCESTER, MASSACHUSETTS. See LINCOLN AND PARKER FILM COMPANY

WORKERS' FILM AND PHOTO LEAGUE. See NATIONAL FILM AND PHOTO LEAGUE

WORLD COMEDY STARS FILM CORPORATION. The World Comedy Stars Film Corporation was formed early in 1915 by Phil Gleichman to produce one-reel comedies with famous stars of the legitimate and vaudeville stages. Edmund Lawrence, formerly with Kalem*, was the director, William W. Jefferson was associate director, and Mark Swan, Roy McCardell, Paul Arlington, Herbert Hall Winslow, and Robert Broderick were hired to write scenarios. The comedy team of Weber and Fields appeared in *Two of the Bravest* (1915), and other players with the company included Jeff De Angelis, Lulu Glaser, Florence Tempest, Paula Tempest, Katherine Osterman, Richard Carle, and Tom Wise. After distributing a series of "Pokes and Jabbs" comedies made by the Wizard Motion Picture Corporation*, the World Comedy Stars Film Corporation went out of business in August 1915.

BIBLIOGRAPHY

"Gleichman Heads New Company," *The Moving Picture World*, February 6, 1915, p. 806.

"To Make Comedies," *The Moving Picture World*, March 6, 1915, p. 1422.

WORLD FILM CORPORATION. The World Film Corporation was formed on February 16, 1914, when E. Mandelbaum and Philip Gleichman, the founders of the World Special Films Corporation (which the year before had brought to the United States the Italian films *The Last Days of Pompeii* and *Protea* and released two films per month until its demise two days before World's formation) interested Wall Street bankers, W. A. Pratt, Van Horn Ely, and others in their enterprise. G.L.P. Vernon was the president, Mandelbaum the first vice-president, Gleichman the second vice-president, and Britton Busch the secretary and treasurer. World's offices were at 130 West 46 Street.

On June 10, 1914, World and the Shubert Theatrical Company, representing the interests of the William A. Brady, Charles A. Blaney, and Owen Davis enterprises, formed a $3 million corporation to film the theatrical successes of the Shubert Company. The Shubert Film Corporation, which had been formed a few months earlier to produce and distribute Shubert-Brady productions, planned to produce one feature-length film a week, to be released by World.

When Mandelbaum sold his interest in World in mid–1914, the company became incorporated for $2 million, and Lewis J. Selznick became vice-president and general manager in July 1914. In September 1914, Selznick signed Clara Kimball Young and her husband, James, to produce films for the Peerless Feature Film Company, which was formed in July by Jules Brulatour to produce Brady and Blaney plays with former Eclair* players such as Barbara Tennant, Alec B. Francis, and Stanley Walpole. Peerless built a studio at which four companies worked in Fort Lee, New Jersey*. World had by this time secured twenty-four distributing offices throughout the country.

In October 1914, Gleichman left the company. World next formed an alliance with Liebler and Company to produce its big stage successes, including *Alias Jimmy Valentine*. World added the product of the Dyreda Art Film Corporation*, the Colonial Motion Picture Corporation, the California Motion Picture Corporation*, and the Frohman Amusement Corporation* to its releases. At the end of the year, Al Lichtman became the general manager of a Special Attractions Department, which imported *Salambo*, among other films, from Italy.

In May 1915, World took over completely the Shubert Film Corporation, which owned Peerless, which, in turn, owned half of William A. Brady Picture Plays, Inc., earlier having split the ownership with the Shuberts. The Equitable Motion Picture Corporation was formed in June 1915 and incorporated for $2 million to produce two features and two comedies per month, which World would release. Arthur Spiegel was president, Selznick the vice-president, and Isadore Bernstein the technical director. In July 1915, the Wizard Motion Picture Corporation* was formed to release comedies through World. In August 1915, World gained control of the new Paragon studios in Fort Lee, which were to be the largest studios in the East. Maurice Tourneur was the vice-president and general manager of Paragon, which planned to make twenty-four five-reel features a year, plus three to four longer features. The Triumph Film Corporation, a subsidiary of Equitable, came into existence in September 1915 and took over the old Horsley studio in Bayonne, New Jersey. Julius Steger was the president, Joseph Golden was the director-in-chief, and Eve Unsell was in charge of adaptations.

In February 1916, World reorganized again. Arthur Spiegel, who died a few months later, was elected president. Selznick left the company and took World's leading star, Clara Kimball Young, with him and formed Lewis J. Selznick Productions, Inc. World acquired all the stock of Equitable, and William A. Brady assumed active control of World's producing units.

In October 1917, the Famous Players-Lasky Corporation bought the Paragon studio. Brady resigned as head producer in February 1918 and became an independent producer. In January 1919, World, with which Selznick was again associated, merged with the United Picture Theatres of America, Inc. World's distribution system was used for United productions, and Peerless was used to make special productions for United. Later in 1919, the Republic Distributing Corporation, which was controlled by Selznick, took over World's entire list of exchanges.

Directors of note who made films for World included Maurice Tourneur, Albert Capellani, Emile Chautard, Stanner E. V. Taylor, Edwin August, Oscar Apfel, J. Searle Dawley, Edwin Carewe, Romaine Fielding, and O.A.C. Lund. Writers for World included Frances Marion, Joseph Franklin Poland, Clara S. Beranger, Harry O. Hoyt, and Giles R. Warren. World's players included Clara Kimball Young, Alice Brady, Kitty Gordon, Robert Warwick, Carlyle Blackwell, Madge Evans, Vivian Martin, Lillian Russell, Marie Dressler, Doris Kenyon, Edwin August, and Elaine Hammerstein.

BIBLIOGRAPHY

"Selznick Absorbs a Corporation," *The Moving Picture World*, November 8, 1919, p. 3472.

"Shuberts and World Film in Best Deal," *The Moving Picture World*, June 20, 1914, p. 1700.

Spehr, Paul C. *The Movies Begin*. Newark: The Newark Museum, 1977.

"Wall Street Bankers Enter Film Business," *The Moving Picture World*, February 21, 1914, p. 966.

"World and United Theatres Merge," *The Moving Picture World*, February 1, 1919, p. 599.

"World Film Anniversary," *The Moving Picture World*, February 20, 1915, p. 1153.

"World Film Reorganizes," *The Moving Picture World*, February 12, 1916, p. 931.

WORLD'S BEST FILM COMPANY. The World's Best Film Company produced animal pictures in Florida, early in 1913, for release by Universal*. Harold M. Shaw was the company's director.

THE WORLD TODAY, INC. See DOCUMENTARIES

WRATHER CORPORATION. A Beverly Hills–based conglomerate, the Wrather Corporation controls the Queen Mary and the Spruce Goose (two tourist attractions in Long Beach, California); the Disneyland Hotel; television series such as "Lassie," "The Lone Ranger," and "Sergeant Preston of the Yukon"; and films based on these characters as well as other independently produced features. Founded by Jack D. Wrather (1918–1984), the Wrather Corporation has its origins in Jack Wrather Pictures, Inc., formed in 1946. The corporation went public in June 1961.

Address: 270 North Canon Drive, Beverly Hills, Calif. 90210.

WRITERS CLUB. See WRITERS GUILD OF AMERICA

WRITERS GUILD OF AMERICA. The Writers Guild of America (WGA) has its origins in the Writers Club, a social group popular in the twenties for its annual revues and presided over for many years by Rupert Hughes. From the Writers Club, the Screen Writers Guild was organized, as part of the Authors League of America, with 173 charter members. John Howard Lawson was elected the nonprofit organization's first president on April 6, 1933. The Guild was open to all writers and was extremely vocal in its opposition to the Academy of Motion Picture Arts and Sciences*, which it saw as a tool of the producers. The thirties were bitter years for the new Guild as it fought for unionization and recognition by the studios. Its members were blacklisted, accused of being Communists, and it was, at times, split by internal bickering between left- and right-wing elements. (Certainly it is worth noting that the bulk of the members of the Hollywood Ten* were screenwriters.) It was not until the summer of 1938 that the Guild was recognized by the National Labor Relations Board as the collective bargaining agent for writers within the film industry.

In the early fifties, the Guild was once more under attack with regard to Communist infiltration and the refusal of certain members to support the signing of a loyalty oath. At the same time, it was anxious to claim the right to negotiate on behalf of television and radio writers and, during 1953 and 1954, discussed merger with the Radio Writers Guild and the Television Writers of America. In the summer of 1954, a new organization was formed from the Screen Writers Guild called the Writers Guild of America, which quickly gained recognition as the negotiating body for writers in film, radio, and television and which was divided into two national chapters: WGA/East in New York, and WGA/West in Hollywood.

The Writers Guild of America has been involved in four major strike actions against producers: in 1959–1960, in February-June 1973, in April-July 1981, and in March 1985.

It also presents a number of annual awards. The Laurel Award for Screen Writing Achievement was first given in 1953 to Sonya Levien and is for the Guild member who has, in the opinion of the board of directors, "advanced the literature of the motion picture through the years, and who has made outstanding contributions to the profession of the screen writer." The Laurel Award for TV Writing Achievement (now called the Paddy Chayefsky Laurel Award) was first given in 1976 to Rod Serling and honors members in the field of television literature. The Valentine Davies Award, first presented in 1962 to Mary McCall, Jr., is given to the person(s) "whose contribution to the motion picture community has brought dignity and honor to writers everywhere." The Morgan Cox Award, first given in 1970 to Barry Trivers, is presented "to that member or group of members whose vital ideas, continuing efforts and personal sacrifices best exemplify the ideal of service to the Guild which the life of Morgan Cox so fully represented." The previous awards were presented by WGA/West. WGA/East presented three memorial awards: The John Merriam Memorial Award, first given in 1977 to Ralph D. Buglass; the Evelyn F. Burkey Memorial Award, first given in 1978 to Fred Coe; and the Richard B. Jablow Memorial Award, first given in 1978 (in memoriam) to Richard B. Jablow.

Addresses: Writers Guild/West, 8955 Beverly Boulevard, Los Angeles, Calif. 90048; Writers Guild/East, 55 West 57 Street, New York, N.Y. 10019.

BIBLIOGRAPHY

Academy of Motion Picture Arts and Sciences and the Writers Guild of America West. *Who Wrote the Movie and What Else Did He Write?* Los Angeles: The Authors, 1970.

Ceplair, Larry, "The Writers Guild Redeems Itself," *Emmy*, January/February 1983, pp. 6, 44.

Schwartz, Nancy Lynn. *The Hollywood Writers' War.* New York: Alfred A. Knopf, 1982.

W. W. HODKINSON CORPORATION. W. W. Hodkinson, who earlier founded Paramount Pictures Corporation* and was its president until June 1916, formed W. W. Hodkinson Corporation in November 1917 as a distribution company. Hodkinson obtained the use of the General Film Company exchange organization, through which to distribute its product physically, and installed its own salesmen in each of the twenty-eight exchanges. Hodkinson, a longtime advocate of separation of control in the industry between producers, distributors, and exhibitors, maintained that his company was not controlled by producers or exhibitors, but he promulgated a plan whereby, through his company, exhibitors would advance money to producers to make films but would retain no financial interest in the production companies. Later, the exhibitors would acquire the completed films on a percentage basis.

Some of the companies that released through Hodkinson included Paralta*, Artco Productions, Deitrich-Beck*, Great Authors Pictures, Zane Grey Pictures, and companies formed to produce features starring Bessie Barriscale, J. Warren Kerrigan, Henry B. Walthall, Louise Glaum, and Lillian Walker. Although Hodkinson announced, early in 1918, the proposed marketing plan of "Motion Picture Plus"—an invention of the Photo Motion Company of Kansas City, Missouri, which, by exposing pictures sideways on the negative and having images twice as wide as the then present height and the same height as the then present width, promised a widescreen format—there is no indication that the theatres or the public were very interested. At the end of 1918, Hodkinson began to release through Pathé* exchanges. The company lasted until 1924.

BIBLIOGRAPHY

"Hodkinson Comes Back," *The Moving Picture World*, November 10, 1917, p. 843.
"What 'Motion Picture Plus' Is," *The Moving Picture World*, January 12, 1918, p. 214.

RESOURCES

Papers: University of California at Los Angeles (the personal papers of W. W. Hodkinson).

Y

YANKEE FILM COMPANY. The Yankee Film Company, an independent producer, released its first film, *Jeffries on His Ranch*, on June 15, 1910, just before the July 4th Heavyweight Championship fight between ex-champion James J. Jeffries and his successor, Jack Johnson. Afterward, Yankee released one reel every Monday with the Motion Picture Distributing and Sales Company, until December 1910, when it began releasing two films a week. William Steiner was the director-general, and Isadore Bernstein rose from publicity man to become general manager of the company, whose offices were at 344 East 32 Street, New York. Its last film, *The Two Rooms*, was released on November 17, 1911.

BIBLIOGRAPHY

"Growth of the Yankee," *The Moving Picture World*, November 19, 1910, p. 1182.

YARNS FOR YANKS. See HOLLYWOOD VICTORY COMMITTEE

YUKON PICTURES, INC. See JERRY FAIRBANKS PRODUCTIONS

Z

ZION FILMS, INC. Zion Films, Inc., produced the feature *Broken Barriers*, starring Alice Hastings and directed by Charles E. Davenport from the Sholom Aleichem story "Khavah," in 1919. Although it planned to produce a series of Jewish and Russian pictures written by Jewish and Russian authors, Zion's plans never materialized. S. Adler was Zion's president.

BIBLIOGRAPHY

"Zion Company to Produce Russian and Jewish Films," *The Moving Picture World*, April 19, 1919, p. 394.

ZODIAK FILM MANUFACTURING COMPANY. The Zodiak Film Manufacturing Company took over one of the largest and best-equipped studios and laboratories on the West Coast when it purchased, in mid–1914, the J.A.C. plant located at Hill and Court streets in downtown Los Angeles. J. A. Crosby, who formerly was in charge of the technical operations for the Selig Polyscope Company*, New York Motion Picture Company, Reliance Motion Picture Company, and Universal*, began his own studio and laboratory, the J.A.C. Film Manufacturing Company, in 1913, in the old Bradbury mansion on South Hill Street. Companies which used the J.A.C. studios included the Albuquerque Film Manufacturing Company*, Pathé's* Western company, the Nash Motion Picture Company*, Bosworth, Inc.*, and the Famous Players Film Company, which produced many of its Mary Pickford features there. Thomas S. Nash acquired the plant and renamed it Zodiak. Albert S. Ruddell was secretary and general manager of the new company.

BIBLIOGRAPHY

"J.A.C. Film Company," *The New York Dramatic Mirror*, May 28, 1915, p. 26.

ZOETROPE. Impressed by independent producer John Korty's facility in San Francisco, director/producer Francis Ford Coppola (born 1939) created his own independent production company, American Zoetrope, in San Francisco in 1969. The first film of the new company was *The Rain People* (1969), followed by

THX 1138 (1971) and *Apocalypse Now* (1979). Coppola's *The Conversation* (1974) was produced by his Directors Company.

In 1973, Coppola purchased his present headquarters; in 1979, he changed the name of his company to Omni-Zoetrope, and, a year later, he purchased the former Hollywood General Studios*, renaming them the Zoetrope Studios (and dropping the Omni). Coppola planned his new studios to be a state-of-the-art facility, to be run along the lines of the old Hollywood studios. The same year he acquired the studios, he hired Gene Kelly to put together a musical unit, he announced plans for a Performing Arts High School on the lot, and he brought in veteran British director Michael Powell as "Senior Director in Residence." Wim Wenders' *Hammett* was the first film to go into production at the new studio but proved to be plagued with problems and was not released until 1982. It was followed by *One from the Heart* (1982), *The Outsiders* (1983), and *Rumble Fish* (1983). Aside from his own productions, Coppola used his company to sponsor the first screenings of Kevin Brownlow's restoration of Abel Gance's *Napoleon* (1927) and to sponsor the release of new films by foreign directors, such as Akira Kurosawa.

Unfortunately, financial problems forced Coppola to curtail his operations, and, in 1984, the Zoetrope Studios were sold at a bankruptcy auction. Coppola was forced to retrench at his San Francisco headquarters, from where he co-produced *The Cotton Club* (1984).

Address: 917 Kearny Street, San Francisco, Calif. 94123.

BIBLIOGRAPHY

Bock, Audie, "Zoetrope and Apocalypse Now," *American Film*, September 1979, pp. 55–60.

Linck, David, "Zoetrope Takes Cue from Studios of '30s and '40s," *Boxoffice*, May 4, 1980, pp. 1–2, 4.

Myles, Lynda, "The Zoetrope Saga," *Sight and Sound*, Spring 1982, pp. 91–93.

Pollock, Dale, "Has Coppola Won Battle for Studio?" *Los Angeles Times*, Calendar Section, March 5, 1980, pp. 1, 4–5.

Ross, Lillian, "Onwards and Upwards with the Arts," *The New Yorker*, November 8, 1982, pp. 48–87.

ZOOM LENS. Although it is often confused with different kinds of camera movement, the zoom stands in direct opposition to traditional moving shots. In a dolly or trucking shot, for example, the camera moves bodily through space, producing an image that reflects, through changes in perspective and the presence of parallax, the original filming process in which the camera actually traversed a three-dimensional space. A zoom lens, on the other hand, produces the illusion of movement *optically* through continuous changes in the focal length of the lens rather than through actual movement of the camera; it creates an image which progressively alters the original space being photographed, either flattening (by zooming out to the telephoto focal lengths) or elongating it (by zooming in to the wide-angle range of the lens).

Prototypes of the modern zoom lens were developed in the late twenties and the early thirties. The first zoom lenses consisted of two optical elements which moved in relation to one another. They had extremely small apertures for the period (f/11 or f/8) and, though they required a great deal of high key light and the negative required longer development than usual, they possessed good depth of field. Bell & Howell's Cooke Vara Lens (circa 1932) was a three-element lens possessing a slightly larger aperture (f/8 to f/3.5) and a greater range. The elements of the lens were moved in relation to one another mechanically by a series of cams, operated by a crane.

Contemporary zoom lens technology dates from the development of the Zoomar lens by Dr. Frank G. Back in 1946. Unlike the earlier variable focal length lenses, the Zoomar had no cams with which to contend. It was entirely optical, employing four lens elements. Movable lens elements were mounted in a common barrel; manual movement of the barrel to any position in the housing produced a change in image size, creating a zoom effect. The uniqueness of the Zoomar lens related to the lens' aperture or iris diaphragm. In earlier zoom lenses, the iris diaphragm had to be changed each time there was a change in focal length, a procedure which required a complex mechanical linkage between the cams operating the focal length and the aperture. By placing the iris diaphragm *behind* all the movable elements of the lens, the Zoomar eliminated the need for coordinating the changes in focal length with the aperture setting; the aperture was merely set for the shot and remained constant during it.

Initially associated with television and newsreel work, where it enabled continuous coverage of events, such as baseball games, without time-consuming changes by the camera operator of lenses of different, fixed focal lengths to capture action at different distances, the zoom lens quickly became a staple of documentary filmmaking in the late fifties and early sixties and of feature-film production in the sixties and seventies. Filmmakers most frequently associated with innovative use of the zoom included Roberto Rossellini, Michael Snow, Robert Mulligan, Claude Chabrol, Blake Edwards, and Robert Altman.

BIBLIOGRAPHY

Belton, John, "The Bionic Eye: Zoom Esthetics," *Cineaste*, vol. XI, no. 1, Winter 1980–81, pp. 20–27.

Lightman, Herb A., "Some Interesting Facts about Zoom Lenses," *American Cinematographer*, March 1975, pp. 324–325.

Resource Libraries and Institutions

The following libraries or institutions appear under the "Resources" heading as repositories of papers, photographs, or films.

Academy of Motion Picture Arts and Sciences, Margaret Herrick Library, 8949 Wilshire Boulevard, Beverly Hills, Calif. 90211.

American Film Institute, 2021 North Western Avenue, Hollywood, Calif. 90027.

Brigham Young University, Harold B. Lee Library, Provo, Utah 84602.

Edison National Historic Site, Box 126, Orange, N.J. 07051.

George Eastman House (International Museum of Photography at George Eastman House), 900 East Avenue, Rochester, N.Y. 14607.

Historical Society of Long Beach, Rancho Los Alamitos, 6400 Bixby Hill Road, Long Beach, Calif. 90815.

Library of Congress, Washington, D.C. 20540.

Museum of Modern Art, 11 West 53 Street, New York, N.Y. 10019.

National Archives and Records Service, Washington, D.C. 20408.

National Film Archives, 81 Dean Street, London W1V 6AA, England.

New York State Archives, Albany, N.Y. 12230.

Ohio State Historical Society, 1–71 and 17 Avenue, Columbus, Ohio 43211.

Princeton University, Firestone Library, Princeton, N.J. 08544.

Radio City Music Hall Archives, 50 Street and Avenue of the Americas, New York, N.Y. 10020.

Stanford University Libraries, Stanford, Calif. 94305.

UCLA Film Archives, Department of Fine Arts, University of California, Los Angeles, Calif. 90024.

University of California at Los Angeles, 405 Hilgard Avenue, Los Angeles, Calif. 90024.

University of Southern California, Doheny Memorial Library, University Park, Los Angeles, Calif. 90007.

University of Texas, Hoblitzelle Theatre Arts Library, Box 7219, Austin, Tex. 78712.

University of Wyoming, Division of Rare Books and Special Collections, Box 3334, Laramie, Wyo. 82071.

Walt Disney Archives, 500 South Buena Vista Street, Burbank, Calif. 91521.
Wisconsin Center for Film and Theater Research, 816 State Street, Madison, Wis. 53706.

Bibliography

Balio, Tino, editor. *The American Film Industry*. Madison, Wisconsin: University of Wisconsin Press, 1985.

Behlmer, Rudy. *America's Favorite Movies*. New York: Frederick Ungar Publishing, 1982.

Bergman, Andrew. *We're in the Money: Depression America and Its Films*. New York: New York University Press, 1971.

Blum, Daniel. *A Pictorial History of the Silent Screen*. New York: G. P. Putnam's Sons, 1953.

————. *A Pictorial History of the Talkies*. New York: Grosset & Dunlap, 1958.

Bordwell, David, Janet Staiger, and Kristin Thompson. *The Classical American Cinema*. New York: Columbia University Press, 1985.

Brownlow, Kevin. *The Parade's Gone By . . .* New York: Alfred A. Knopf, 1968.

————. *Hollywood: The Pioneers*. New York: Alfred A. Knopf, 1979.

————. *The War, the West and the Wilderness*. New York: Alfred A. Knopf, 1979.

Ceplair, Larry, and Steven Englund. *The Inquisition in Hollywood: Politics in the Film Community 1930–1960*. Garden City, New York: Anchor Press/Doubleday, 1980.

Dooley, Roger. *From Scarface to Scarlet: American Films in the 1930s*. New York: Harcourt Brace Jovanovich, 1981.

Everson, William K. *American Silent Film*. New York: Oxford University Press, 1978.

Farber, Stephen, and Marc Green. *Hollywood Dynasties*. New York: Delilah/Putnam, 1984.

Film Daily Year Book (formerly *Film Year Book* and *Wid's Year Book*). New York: Film Daily, 1919–1969.

Grau, Robert. *The Theatre of Science*. New York: Broadway Publishing Company, 1914.

Green, Abel, and Joe Laurie, Jr. *Show Biz: From Vaude to Video*. New York: Henry Holt, 1951.

Griffith, Mrs. D. W. *When the Movies Were Young*. New York: E. P. Dutton, 1925.

Griffith, Richard, Arthur Mayer, and Eileen Bowser. *The Movies*. New York: Simon and Schuster, 1981.

Hampton, Benjamin B. *A History of the Movies*. New York: Covici, Friede, 1931.

International Motion Picture Almanac (formerly *Motion Picture Almanac*). New York: Quigley Publishing Company, 1930 to present.

Jacobs, Lewis. *The Rise of the American Film: A Critical History*. New York: Harcourt, Brace and Company, 1939.

Jobes, Gertrude. *Motion Picture Empire*. Hamden, Connecticut: Archon Books, 1966.

Jowett, Garth. *Film: The Democratic Art*. Boston: Little, Brown, 1976.

Karr, Kathleen, editor. *The American Film Heritage*. Washington, D.C.: Aeropolis Books, 1972.

Kindem, Gorham, editor. *The American Movie Industry: The Business of Motion Pictures*. Carbondale, Illinois: Southern Illinois University Press, 1982.

Krafsur, Richard, editor. *The American Film Institute Catalog: Feature Films 1961– 1970*. New York: R. R. Bowker, 1971.

Lauritzen, Einar, and Gunnar Lundquist. *American Film Index: 1906–1915*. Stockholm, Sweden: Film-Index, 1976.

———. *American Film Index: 1916–1920*. Stockholm, Sweden: Film-Index, 1984.

McCarthy, Todd, and Charles Flynn, editors. *King of the Bs*. New York: E. P. Dutton, 1975.

Macgowan, Kenneth. *Behind the Screen*. New York: Delacorte Press, 1965.

Monaco, James. *American Film Now*. New York: New York Zoetrope, 1984.

Munden, Kenneth W., editor. *The American Film Institute Catalog: Feature Films 1921– 1930*. New York: R. R. Bowker, 1971.

O'Connor, John E., and Martin A. Jackson. *American History/American Film*. New York: Frederick Ungar Publishing, 1979.

Powdermaker, Hortense. *Hollywood: The Dream Factory*. Boston: Little, Brown, 1951.

Quigley, Martin, Jr., and Richard Gertner. *Films in America: 1929–1969*. New York: Golden Press, 1970.

Ramsaye, Terry. *A Million and One Nights*. New York: Simon and Schuster, 1926.

Rideout, Eric H. *The American Film*. London: The Mitre Press, 1937.

Rosten, Leo C. *Hollywood*. New York: Harcourt, Brace and Company, 1941.

Sklar, Robert. *Movie-Made America*. New York: Random House, 1975.

Slide, Anthony, and Edward Wagenknecht. *Fifty Great American Silent Films: 1912– 1920*. New York: Dover Publications, 1980.

Spears, Jack. *Hollywood: The Golden Era*. New York: A. S. Barnes, 1971.

Spehr, Paul C. *The Movies Begin*. Newark, New Jersey: The Newark Museum, 1977.

Thorp, Margaret Farrand. *America at the Movies*. New Haven, Connecticut: Yale University Press, 1939.

Wagenknecht, Edward. *The Movies in the Age of Innocence*. Norman, Oklahoma: University of Oklahoma Press, 1962.

Index

ABC Motion Pictures, Inc., 1
Abrams, Charles (Feature), 150, 279
Abramson, Ivan, 148, 174
Academy Awards, 2
Academy Foundation, 2–3
Academy of Motion Picture Arts and Sciences, 1–3
Academy of Science Fiction, Fantasy & Horror Films, 3–4
Academy War Film Library. *See* Academy of Motion Picture Arts and Sciences
A.C.E., 10
ACE, 75
"Ace" Brand, 87
Acetate film, 4
Acme Videotape and Film Laboratories, 78
Actophone Company, 4
The Actors Studio, Inc., 4–5
Adams, Frederick Upham, 130
Adelson, Merv, 199
Adler, Buddy, 355
Adler, S., 401
The Adult Film Association of America, 5
AEA. *See* American Exhibitors' Association
Affiliated Distributors' Corporation, 5–6
AFI. *See* American Film Institute
A. H. Features, Inc., 36
AIP. *See* American International Pictures

Aitken, Harry E., 13, 126, 231, 245, 285, 352
Albuquerque Film Manufacturing Company, Inc., 6
Alco Film Corporation, 6–7
Aldrich, Robert, 7
Aldrich Studios, 7
Alexander, Richard, 24
Alhambra Motion Picture Company, 7
Al Jennings Production Company, 7
All-American News, 241
All-Celtic Film Company, 8
Allen, E. H., 108
Alliance Films Corporation, 8
Alliance of Motion Picture and Television Producers, 8
Allied Artists, 9
All-Star Feature Company, 9–10
Alperson, Edward L., 148
Alperstein, A., 387
American Cinema Editors, Inc., 10
American Congress of Exhibitors. *See* COMPO
American Correspondent Film Company, Inc., 10–11
American Documentary Films, 139
American Exhibitors' Association, 11, 222
American Express Films, 15
American Film Institute, 11–13
American Film Manufacturing Company, 13–14

American Film Market, 14–15
American Film Theatre, 15
American Humane Association, 260
American International Pictures, 15–17
American Mutoscope and Biograph Company, 39–40
American Mutoscope Company, 39–40
American Releasing Company, 15
American Society of Cinematographers, 17–18
American Talking-Picture Company, 187
American Woman Film Company, 18
America Speaks, 162
Amkino Corporation, 30
Anamorphic lens, 18
Anchors Aweigh, 162
Anderson, Carl, 255
Anderson, Edward E., 101
Anderson, G. M., 113
"Andy Hardy" series, 18–19
Animation, 19–24
Apogee, Inc., 24
Apollo Pictures, Inc., 24
Argosy Pictures Corporation, 25
Arkoff, Samuel Z., 15, 16
Army-Navy Screen Magazine, 33
Aromarama, 25–26
Arrow Film Corporation, 26
Art Cinema Corporation, 26
Artcolor Pictures Company, 26–27
Artco Productions, Inc., 27
Artcraft Pictures Corporation, 256
Art direction, 27–28
Art Dramas, Inc., 28
Art Film Company, 28–29
Art Finance Corporation, 26
Art houses, 29–30
Arthur H. Gooden Studios, 127
Arthur Mayer & Joseph Burstyn, Inc., 179
Artkino Pictures, Inc., 30
Artlee, 194
Art Theatre Guild Circuit, 311
Asbury Park, New Jersey, 299
ASC. *See* American Society of Cinematographers
Ashley, Ted, 382
Ashley-Famous Agency, 382

ASIFA. *See* Association International du Film d' Animation; International Animated Film Association
Aspect ratios, 30
Associated Cinema Stars, 31
Associated Film Sales Corporation, 31
Associated First National Pictures Incorporated, 129
Associated First National Theatres Incorporated, 129
Associated Motion Picture Advertisers, Inc., 31
Associated Pictures, Inc., 31–32
Associated Producers, Inc., 32
Associates & Aldrich, 7
Association International du Film d'Animation, 30
Association of Motion Picture & Television Producers, 8
Association of Motion Picture Producers, 8
Astoria Motion Picture and Television Center Foundation, 33
Astoria Studios, 32–33
Astor Pictures Corporation, 33
Astra Film Corporation, 33–34
Atkinson, Charles F., 277
Aubrey, James T., Jr., 210
Audio Brandon, 122
Audio Film Center, 122
August, Edwin, 101
Avco Corp., 110
Avco Embassy Pictures Corporation, 110
Aymar, Gilbert H., 185
Ayres, C. H., 190
Aywon Film Corporation, 34
Azteca Films, 34

Babb, Kroger, 151
Bachmann, J.G. "Jack," 269
Backer, George, 35
Bacon, Gerald F., 35
Bacon-Backer Film Corporation, 35
Baker, George, 33
Balaban & Katz, 276

Balboa Amusement Producing Company, 35
Ball, J. A. (Joseph Arthur), 339
Balshofer, Fred J., 279, 328
Bamburger, Leon J., 179
Bank nights, 36
Banner Film Company, 36
Bantha Music, 202
Barbara, Joseph, 153
B. A. Rolfe Photoplays, Inc., 36
Bartsch, Hans, 212
Batcheller, George, 268
Batjac Productions, Inc., 36–37
"The Battle of Warner Bros.," 76
Baum, Frank J., 95
Baum, Frank L., 251
Bauman, Charles O., 184, 244, 266, 285, 352
Bayonne, New Jersey, 59, 87, 262, 284, 371, 394
BBS Productions, 37
Beach movies, 37–38
"Beauty" brand, 14
Beck, Arthur F., 89
Beecroft, Chester, 60
Begelman, David, 71
Bell, Donald H., 38
Bell & Howell, 38–39
Bell Telephone System, 373
Belman, Julian, 264
Benjamin, Robert S., 250, 359
Bennett, Eustache Hale, 155
Benton, Charles, 122
Berman, Harry M., 179
Berman, Pandro S., 290
Bernstein, Isadore, 216, 251, 394, 399
Bernstein, William, 250
Berst, J. A., 259, 361
"Betty June Comedies," 272
Betzwood, Pennsylvania, 39, 201
Betzwood Film Company, 39
Beyfuss, Alexander E., 53
Bianchi, Joseph, 267
Biberman, Herbert, 169
The Big Broadcast series, 39
Billig, Irving, 270
Biograph Company, 39–40
Birns, Jack, 40

Birns & Sawyer, Inc., 40
Bisbee, Arizona, 46
Bischoff, Sam, 337
Bishop, John R., 371
Bishop, W. A., 126
"Bison" Life Motion Pictures, 244
Bissell, W. H., 240
Blaché, Alice, 317
Blaché, Herbert, 28, 114, 143, 317, 362
Black American Cinema Society, 40–41
Black Diamond comedies, 364
Black Filmmakers Hall of Fame, Incorporated, 41
"The Black Maria," 187
Blacks in American film, 40–43, 90, 104, 134, 197, 213, 286, 295, 349
Blackton, J. Stuart, 31, 372
Blackwell, Carlyle, 118
Blackwell, Earl, 56
Blaney, Charles E., 43
Blaney-Spooner Feature Film Company, 43
Blauner, J. Stephen, 37
Blazed Trail Productions, Inc., 43
Blind bidding, 43–44
Block booking, 44
"Blondie" series, 44–45
Bludhorn, Charles G., 150
Blythe, Elaine, 119
"B" movies, 45
B 'n' B Film Corporation, 33
Bobb, Howard G., 195
Bob Hope USO, 157
Boeske, Dr. Elmer J., 299
Bogart, Neil, 266
Boggs, John, 165
Boots and Saddles Pictures, Inc., 54
Border Feature Film Corporation, 46
Boris Thomashefsky Film Company, 46
Bostock Jungle and Film Company, 46
Boston, 155, 206, 277
Bostwick, Elwood F., 102
Bostustow, Stephen, 362
Bosworth, Hobart, 46
Bosworth, Inc., 46–47
Bound Brook, New Jersey, 259
Bowen, James K., 185
Box Office Attractions Company, 47

Boy City Film Corporation, 47–48
Boyer, Charles, 138
Boynton, S. H., 139
Bradford, F. G., 194
Bradshaw, C. P., 126
Brady, William A., 395
Brandon Films, Inc., 122
Brandt, Harry, 352
Brandt, Joe, 70
Bray, J. R., 48
Bray Studios, Inc., 48
Breen, Joseph I., 274
Brenon, Herbert, 347
Brentwood Film Corporation, 48–49
Bridgeport, Connecticut, 236
Briskin, Sam, 195, 290
"Broadway Favorites," 182
Brock, Henry J., 186
Broidy, Stephen, 215
Brown, Garrett, 327
Brown, Judge Willis, 47
Brown, Marie, 223
Brown, Nat L., 255
Brulatour, Jules, 104
Brunet, Paul, 259
Brunton, Robert, 255, 291
The Bryna Company, 49
B. S. Moss Motion Picture Company,
    49–50
Buena Vista Distribution Company, Ltd.,
    50
Bulls Eye Film Corporation, 50
The Burbank Studios, 50
Burns, L. L., 387
Burstein, Louis, 370, 390
Burstyn, Joseph, 179
Burton Holmes Travelogues, 50–51
Busch, Britton N., 286, 394
Butler, A., 266

The Caddo Company, Inc., 53
California Motion Picture Corporation,
    53–54
California Pictures Corporation. See Cali-
    fornia Studios
California Studios, 54
"Cameo" Brand Comedies, 69
Cameo Productions, 320

Camp, Joe, 227
Camp, Walter, Jr., 171
The Cannon Group, Inc., 54–55
Canon City, Colorado, 69
Capital Film Company, 55
Capra, Frank, 195, 389
Cardinal Film Company, 56
Carr, Trem, 215
Carroll, Frank J., 327
Carson, L.M. "Kit," 367
Carter, Victor M., 288
Carthay Circle Theatre, 56
Casablanca Film Works, 266
Casino Star Comedies, 143
Cassidy, William F., 345
Castle, Eugene W., 56
Castle Films, 56
C.B.C. Film Sales Corporation, 70
CBS Studio Center, 288
Celebrity Service, 56–57
Censorship, 57–59
Centaur Film Company, 59–60
Centaur Film Manufacturing Company,
    59
Central Casting Corporation, 60–61
Century Comedies, 61
Chadwick, I. E., 61, 174
Chadwick Pictures Corporation, 61
Champion Film Company, 4
Chaplin, Charles, 61, 232, 358
Chaplin Studios, 61–62
Chariot Film Company, 62
Charles E. Blaney Feature Play Com-
    pany, 43
Charles K. Harris Feature Film Com-
    pany, 62
Charlton, Charles, 124
Chase-Park Citron, 172
Chas. K. Feldman's Group Productions,
    62
Chateau Marmont, 142
Chautard, Emile, 207
Chesterfield Motion Picture Corporation,
    62–63
Chicago, 63, 104, 169, 173, 306, 361
Chicago International Film Festival, 63
Child Labor laws, 63
Child stars, 63–64

Chinese Theatre, Los Angeles, 149
Chrétien, Henri, 66
Christie, Al E., 65
Christie, Charles, 65
Christie Film Company, 65
Cincinnati, 315
CINE. *See* Council on International Non-
    theatrical Events
Cinecolor, 65–66
Cinema Corporation of America, 272
Cinema Educational Guild, 74
CinemaScope, 66–67
Cinemiracle, 67
Cineplex Odeon Corp., 266
Cinerama, 67–68
Cinerama, Inc., 68
City Island, New York, 294
C.K.Y. Film Corporation, 68
Clarke, Harley, 137, 147
Clausson, M. B., 10
Clayton, Mrs. Mayme Agnew, 40
Cleveland, Ohio, 180
Cliffside, New Jersey, 179, 182, 309,
    316
"Clipper" dramas, 14
Clune, William H., 338
Cobe, Andrew J., 8, 364
Cochrane, R. H., 169, 365
Cochrane, Thomas D., 285
Cochrane, Thomas L., 186
Cohen, Harry J., 266
Cohen, Maury, 63
Cohen, Milton L., 50
Cohen, Sydney, 5
Cohn, Harry, 70
Cohn, Jack, 70
Cole, Rufus Sidman, 291
Collective Film Producers, Inc., 68
Collins, Frederick L., 334
Colonial Motion Picture Corporation, 69
Colorado Motion Picture Company, 69
Colorado Springs, Colorado, 263
"Color by DeLuxe," 89
Colorization, 69
Color Systems Technology, 69
"Columbia Licensed Motion Pictures,"
    267
Columbia Phonograph Company, 221

Columbia Pictures Industries, Inc., 70–
    71, 354
Combined Photoplay Producers, Inc., 360
Comet Productions, Inc., 71–72
Coming Attraction Trailers, 351
Comique Film Corporation, 72
Command Performance, 162
Commercial Advertising Bureau, 372
Commercial Motion Pictures Company,
    Inc., 196
Communism, 72–74, 90–92, 161
COMPO, 74–75
Computer Animation, 23, 75
Comstock, Dr. Daniel F., 340
Concorde Pictures Corporation, 75–76
Conference of Studio Unions, 76–77
Consent decree, 77
Consolidated Film Corporation, 77–78
Consolidated Film Industries, 78
Consolidated National Film Exchanges,
    349
Continental Feature Film Company, 231
Continental Producing Company, 78–79
"The Coogan Act," 63
Cook, Benjamin L., 102
Coolidge, William H., 340
Cooper, Merian C., 25, 264, 290
Coppola, Francis Ford, 401
Copyright, 79–80
Coquille Film Company, 80
Corman, Julie, 75
Corman, Roger, 75–76, 242
Corrigan, Ray "Crash," 80
Corriganville, 80
Corwin, Joseph, 212
Corwin, Sherrill, 212
Cory, M. E., 333
Cosmofotofilm Company, 81
Cosmopolitan Productions, 81
Costume design, 81–84
Costume Designers Guild, 84
Council of Motion Picture Organizations.
    See COMPO
Council on International Nontheatrical
    Events, 84–85
Cowdin, J. Cheever, 365
Coytesville, New Jersey, 181
Craft, P. P., 8

Crandall, Irving B., 373
Crawford, Cheryl, 4
Creative Management Associates, 172
Crest Picture Company, 85
"Crime Does Not Pay" series, 85
Cromelin, Paul H., 81, 173
Crosby, J. A., 401
Crosby, James, 327
Crosier, Robert, 178
Crown City Film Manufacturing Company, 85
Crown International Pictures, 85–86
Crystal Awards, 392
Crystal Film Company, 86
CSU. See Conference of Studio Unions
Cub. See David Horsley Productions
"Cub" brand, 87
Culver City Studios, 193
Cummings, Irvin, 334

Danubia Pictures, Inc., 87
Darmour, Larry, 203
Darmour Productions, 203
David Horsley Productions, 87–88
David Miles, Inc., 88
Davies, B. W., 85
Davis, H. O., 353
Davis, Marvis, 355
Dawley, J. Searle, 98
De Forest, Lee, 88, 373
De Forest Phonofilm, 88
Deitrich, Theodore C., 89
Deitrich-Beck, Inc., 89
De Laurentiis, Dino, 111, 248
DeLuxe Laboratories, Inc., 89
De Luxe Pictures, Inc., 89
DeMille, Cecil B., 89–90, 193, 272
"The DeMille Barn," 193
DeMille Foundation for Political Freedom, 89–90
Democracy Film Company, 90
Denver, 69
de Rochemont, Louis, 204
de Rochemont, Richard, 204
Deskey, Donald, 281
Detroit, 177
Dewey, Chris, 54

DGA. See Directors Guild of America, Inc.
Diamond Film Company, 80
Diando Film Company, 90
Dickson, W.K.L., 187
Dies, Martin, 90–92
Dies Committee Investigation, 90–92
Dietrich, Noah, 53
Diller, Barry, 353
Dintenfass, Mark M., 4, 370
Directors Film Corporation, 282
Directors Guild of America, Inc., 92
Discina International Films Corp., 92
Disney, Roy, 377
Disney, Walt, 377
Disneyland, 378
Dittmar, L. J., 26
Dixie Film Exchange, 349
Dixon, Thomas, 236
"Dr. Kildare" series, 93
Documentaries, 93–94
Dolby, Ray, 94
Dolby Sound, 94–95
"Domino" brand, 245
Donworth, Camilla, 124
Doph, Dennis, 354
Dorney, Roger, 24
Douglas, Kirk, 49
Douglas, W.A.S., 90, 193
Douglass, Leon F., 95
Douglass Natural Color Film Company, Ltd., of San Rafael, California, 95
Dowling, Robert, 199
Dozier, William, 282, 290
Draco Film Company, Inc., 95
Dra-Ko Film Company, 95
Dramatic Feature Film Company, 95
Drive-in theatres, 96
The Droid Works, 202
Du Art Film Laboratories, 97
Dubbing, 97–98
Dudley, Frederick S., 69
Dudley, John L., 249
Dudley, M. B., 98
Dudley Motion Picture Manufacturing Company, 98
Duell, Charles H., 171
Dunlap, John, 10

Dunn, William J., 101
Dunning, Carroll H., 271
Duquesne Amusement Supply Company, 381
Dwan, Allan, 32, 207
Dyer, Frank L., 98
Dykstra, John, 24
Dyreda Art Film Corporation, 98–99

Eaco Films, Inc., 101
Eagle Feature Film Company, 101
Eagle Film Manufacturing and Producing Company, 101–2
Eagle-Lion Classics, 102
Eagle-Lion Films, Inc., 102
E. & R. Jungle Film Company, 179
Eastern Film Company, 102
Eastlake Park, Los Angeles, 179
Eastman, George, 103
Eastman Color, 103
Eastman Kodak Company, 103, 109, 333
Eaves-Brooks Costume Company, 104
Eaves Costume Co., 104
Ebony Pictures Corporation, 104
Eckles, Harry, 145
Eclair Company, 104
Eclectic Film Company, 105
Edelstein, Samuel Q., 292
Edendale, California, 118, 184, 233, 240, 245, 247, 306, 365
Edison, Charles, 196
Edison, Thomas A., 106, 187
Edison Manufacturing Company, 106–7
Edison Vitagraph Company, 372
Editing, 107
Educational Films Corporation, 108–9
Educational Pictures, Inc., 108
Edward Small Productions, Inc., 109
Egyptian Theatre, Los Angeles, 149
8mm, 109, 333–34
Einfeld, Charles, 111
Electrical Research Products, Inc., 109–10
Electronovision, 110
Elliott, Clyde E., 267
Ely Landau Organization, 15
Embassy Communications, 110
Emerald Productions, 119

Emerson, Mrs. May Whitney, 18
Eminent Authors Pictures, Inc., 146
Empire Feature Film Company, 217
Engel, Samuel G., 356
Enterprise Productions, Inc., 111
Enterprise Studio, 54
E. O. Corp., 112
EPCOT, 378–79
Equitable Motion Picture Corporation, 394
Equity Pictures Corporation, 112
Erb, Ludwig G.B., 59, 78, 86, 112, 360
Erbograph Company, 112
Erlanger, Mrs. Milton, 261
Erotic Film Awards, 5
ERPI. See Electrical Research Products, Inc.
Essanay Film Manufacturing Company, 113–14
Essert, Gary, 120
Evans, Robert, 257
Evans, Thomas W., 369
Exactus Photo-Film Corporation, 114
Excelsior Feature Film Company, Inc., 114
Exchanges, 114
Exclusive Supply Corporation, 114–15
Exhibitors' Mutual Distributing Corporation, 232
Exploitation Films, 115–16

Fairall, Harry K., 345
Fairbanks, Douglas, 358
Fairbanks, Jerry, 178
Fairfax, California, 361
The "Falcon" series, 117
"Famous Directors' Pictures" series, 151
Famous Players Film Company, 256
Famous Players-Lasky Corporation, 256
Fantasound, 118
Farley, Clair, 178
Farnsworth, F. Eugene, 206
Faust, Martin J., 388
Favorite Players Film Company, 118
FBO. See RKO Radio Pictures, Inc.
"The Feats of Felix" series, 130
Feature Productions, 26
Features Ideal, Inc., 105

Federal Feature Films Corporation, 118
Feldman, Charles K., 62
Feldman, Phil, 128
Fellows, Robert, 36
Fichtenberg, Herman, 255
Fiction Pictures, Inc., 119
5th Avenue Playhouse Group, 29
55th Street Playhouse, New York, 29
Film Advisory Board, Inc., 119
Filmakers, Inc., 119
Film Alliance of the U.S., Inc., 352
Film Art Cinema, Philadelphia, 29
Filmarte Theatre, New York, 194
Film Associates, 29
Film Audiences for Democracy, 122
Film Booking Office of America, 289
Film Classics. See Eagle-Lion Films, Inc.
Filmex, 120
The Film Fund, 120
Film Guild Cinema, New York, 29
Film Market, Inc., 121
Film Mutual Benefit Bureau, 29
Film Noir, 121–22
Film Service Association, 224
Films for Democracy, 122
Films Incorporated, 122–23
Films made for Television, 123–24
Film Society of Lincoln Center, 124
Films of Business Corporation, 124
Films on television, 124–26
Filmusic Company, 126
Filmways, 16, 250
Fine Arts Corporation, 126–27
Fires, 127–28
First Artists Productions Company, Ltd., 128
Firstenberg, Jean, 12
First National Exhibitors Circuit, Inc., 128–29
First National Pictures, Inc., 128–29
Fischer, David G., 265
Fisher's Costume House, 387
Fitzpatrick, James A., 130, 180
Fitzpatrick Pictures, 130
Fitzpatrick Traveltalks, 130
Flamingo Film Company, 130
Flinn, John C., 272

Florida, 130–35. See also individual cities
Flushing, New York, 143, 317
Ford, Francis, 135
Ford, John, 25
Fordart Productions, 135
Fort du Lac, Wisconsin, 104
Fort Lee, New Jersey, 24, 89, 105, 135–36, 184, 208, 266, 317, 362, 370, 394
"Four Star Productions," 27
Fox, DeWitt, 286
Fox, William, 47, 136, 333
Fox Carthay Circle Theatre, 56
Fox Film Corporation, 136–37
Fox Grandeur, 147
Fox-Movietone News, 241
Fox News, 241
Fox West Coast Theatres Corporation, 137–38
Francisco, R. M., 217
Frank A. Keeney Pictures Corporation, 138
Frawley, Patrick J., 341
Frazee, Edwin A., 138
Frazee Films Productions, 138
Frederick Douglass Film Company, 138
Frelinghuysen, Thomas, 261
French Research Foundation, 138–39
Freuler, John R., 13, 231
Frey, R. E, 238
Friedland, Dennis, 54
Frohman, Gustave, 139
Frohman Amusement Corporation, 139
"Frontier" brand, 295
Frontier Films, 139
Fujiyama Feature Film Company, 140
Furber, Percy N., 351

Galveston, Texas, 165
The Gangster film, 141–42
Garbutt, Frank A., 46, 250
The Garden of Allah, 142
Garson, Harry, 112
Garson Studios, 112
Gasnier, Louis J., 33
Gaspar, Dr. Bela, 142
Gasparcolor, 142–43
The Gaumont Animated Weekly, 241

Gaumont Company, 143
Gayety Comedies, Inc., 143
G.C.C. Theatres, Inc., 144
General Amusements Corporation, 172
General Cinema Corporation, 143–44
General Film Company, 224
General Service Studios, 158
General Teleradio, Inc., 290
General Tire, 290
George Kleine Optical Company, 144
Germantown, Pennsylvania, 195
Giannini, A. H., 358
Gibbs, Dwight, 56
Gilmore, Paul, 237
Glass shot, 145
Gleichman, Philip, 393, 394
Glendale, California, 33, 182, 196, 307
Glendale, Long Island, 214
Glen Glenn Sound Company, Inc., 145
Glenn, Glen, 145
Globus, Yoram, 55
Gloversville, New York, 43
Goebel, O. E., 77, 295
Goetz, H.M. "Ben," 86
Goetz, William, 356, 366
Golan, Menahem, 54
Gold, P. D., Jr., 237
Goldberg, Joe, 270
Goldburg, James D., 249
Goldburg, Joseph J., 196, 289
"Gold Diggers" series, 145
Golden, John, 387
Golden, Joseph, 394
Golden, Joseph A., 86, 387
Golden Globes, 158
Golden State Motion Picture Company of
  California, 146
Goldman, Edmund, 204
Goldman, Harry Sterling, 215
Goldstein, Robert, 78–79
Goldwyn, Samuel, 146, 296–98
Goldwyn, Samuel, Jr., 296
Goldwyn Pictures Corporation, 146–47
Gordon, Lawrence, 355
Gotham Film Company, 147
Gottschalk, Louis F., 251
Gottschalk, Robert, 253
Gould, Symon, 29

"Gower Gulch," 147
Gowman, C. H., 393
Grafton, Edward L., 217
Graham, J. C., 285, 360
Grandeur, 147
Grandin Films, Inc., 316
Grand National Films, Inc., 148
Grantwood, New Jersey, 196
Graphic Film Corporation, 148
Grauman, Sidney Patrick, 148–49
Grauman's theatres, 148–49
Great Authors' Pictures, Inc., 149
"Greater Bray Pictographs," 48
Great Northern Film Company, 149–50
Green, W. E., 269
Greenaway Productions, 282
Greene, Walter, 32
Greer, Mrs. E. L., 140
Griffith, D. W., 126, 352, 358
Grinberg, Sherman, 311
Grosses, 150
Grossman, H., 251
Group Productions, 62
Guber, Peter, 266
Gulf + Western Industries, Inc., 150,
  257
Gunzburg, Milton, 346

Hackett, James K., 146
Haight, Eric, 122
Hall, Frank G., 151, 169, 271, 293, 362
Hallett, A. H., 130
Hallmark Pictures Corporation, 151
Hallmark Productions, Inc., 151–52
Hal Roach Studios, Inc., 152–53
"Ham and Bud" series, 182
Hamilton, G. P., 6, 360
Hammond, Laurens, 345
Hammons, Earl Wooldrige, 108, 148,
  318
Hampton, Benjamin, 149
Handsworth, Harry, 114
Handy, Jamison, 177
Hanna, William, 153
Hanna-Barbera Productions, 153
Hannon, Captain William J., 80
Hansen, Phillip M., 205
Harman, Hugh, 153

Harman-Ising, 153–54
Harmon, Clifford B., 214
Harris, Charles K., 62
Harry Raver, Inc., 284
Hart, Charles S., 363
Harvey, Harry, 215
Hastings, Frank S., 214
Hawks, Howard, 390
Hays, Will H., 219, 273
Hearst, William Randolph, 81, 173
Hearst-Metrotone News, 241
Hearst-Pathé News, 241
Hearst-Selig News Pictorial, 241
Hecht, Harold, 154
Hecht-Hill-Lancaster, 154
Hecht-Lancaster, 154
Hector Film Corporation, 154
Hedwig Film Laboratories, 78
Hendler, Gary, 353
Henriettas, 157
Henry, Judge Lyman, 85
Herbert, Carl, 236
Herbert Brenon Film Corporation, 194
Hermann, Fred W., 364
Herrick, Margaret, 2
Hess, Arthur M., 286
Hicks, Orton, 122
Hill, James, 154
Hirlicolor, 154–55
Hirliman, George, 154
Hirsch, Augusta, 264
Hirsch, Nathan, 34, 264
Hirschfield, Alan, 355
Historical Film Company, 155
Hite, Charles J., 13, 245, 343
Hodkinson, W. W., 46, 256, 334, 353, 396
Hoffman, Dustin, 128
Hoffman, M. H., 264
Holland, Herbert B., 155
Holland Film Manufacturing Company, 155
Holly, Erwin E., 128
Hollywood, 155
Hollywood Anti-Nazi League, 156
Hollywood Canteen, 157
Hollywood Foreign Correspondents Association. *See* Hollywood Foreign Press Association, Inc.
Hollywood Foreign Press Association, Inc., 157–58
Hollywood General Studios, 158
Hollywoodland, 160
Hollywood Metropolitan Studios, 158
Hollywood Museum, 159
"Hollywood on Parade" series, 160
The "Hollywood" sign, 160
Hollywood Studio Center, 158
Hollywood Studio Club, 160–61
Hollywood Stuntmen's Hall of Fame, 330
The Hollywood Ten, 161–62
Hollywood Victory Committee, 162
Hollywood Walk of Fame, 162–63
Hollywood Writers' Mobilization, 163
Holmes, Burton, 50–51
Holmes, C. D., 217
Home Film Libraries, Inc., 122
Hope, Bob, 80
Hopetown, 80
Horkheimer, Elwood, 35
Horkheimer, H. M., 35
Horror films, 163–65
Horsley, David, 46, 59, 87–88
Horsley, William, 59
Hotex Film Manufacturing Company, 165
House Un-American Activities Committee, 73–74, 161–62
Howe, G. B., 387
Howell, Albert S., 38
Hughes, Howard, 53, 290
Hughes, Lloyd C., 49
Humanology Film Producing Company, 165
Hutchin, George L., 78
Hutchinson, Samuel S., 13, 313, 374
Hygenic Productions, 151

IATSE. *See* International Alliance of Theatrical Stage Employees and Moving Picture Machine Operators of the United States and Canada
ICM. *See* International Creative Management, Inc.
Ideal Company of Hollywood, 105
Ideal Film Centers, 122

Ideal Pictures Corporation, 167
IMAX, 167–68
IMP, 365
Ince, Ralph, 31
Ince, Thomas H., 32, 168, 192, 352
Inceville, 168
Independent Productions Corporation, 169
Independent Sales Corporation, 169
Indianapolis, Indiana, 55
Industrial Film Company, 169–70
Industrial Light & Magic, 202
In-flight movies, 170
Inspiration Pictures, Inc., 171
Inter-Continent Film Company, 171
International Alliance of Theatrical Stage Employes and Moving Picture Machine Operators of the United States and Canada, 171–72
International Animated Film Association, 30
International Creative Management, Inc., 172–73
International Famous Agency, 172
International Film Arts Guild, 29
International Film Service, Inc., 173
International Motion Picture Association, 222
The International Newsreel, 241
International Photoplay Corporation, 173
International Pictures, 366
Inter-Ocean Film Corporation, 173
Interstate Feature Film Company, 174
"Intimate Interviews" series, 337
Invincible Pictures Corporation, 63
Ising, Rudolf, 153
Itala Film Company of America, 174
Ithaca, New York, 388
Ivan Film Productions, Inc., 174
Iverson, Joe, 175
Iverson, Karl, 175
Iverson Ranch, 174–75
Ives, Frederick Eugene, 345
Iwerks, Ub, 377

J.A.C. Film Manufacturing Company, 401

Jacksonville, Florida, 101, 143, 181, 198, 309, 313, 343, 370
Jacobs, Newton P. "Red," 85
Jaffe, Leo, 70
Jam Handy Organization, 177
Jans, Herman F., 177
Jans Productions, Inc., 177
Janus Films, 122
Japanese-American Film Company, 177
Japanese Photoplayers' Club of Los Angeles, 178
Jarrico, Paul, 169
Jasper, John, 158
Jennings, Al, 7
Jensen, Raylan, 178
Jensen-Farley Pictures, Inc., 178
Jerome, William Travers, 340
Jerry Fairbanks Productions, 178
Jersey City, New Jersey, 33, 138, 259
Jesse L. Lasky Feature Play Company, 256
Jester Comedy Company, 179
Jewel Productions, Inc., 179
Joel Productions, 49
John Nesbitt's Passing Parade, 258
Johnson, George P., 197
Johnson, Noble M., 197
Johnston, Eric, 219
Johnston, W. Ray, 215
Jones, P.R.W., 167
Jones, William, 367
Joseph Burstyn, Inc., 179
Josephson International, 172
Jourjon, Charles, 104
Judell, Ben, 268
Jungle Film Company, 179
Juno Films, 199
Juvenile Film Company, 180

Kabierske, Henry, 217
Kahane, B. B., 290
Kalem Company, Inc., 181–83
Kalmus, Comstock & Westcott, Inc., 340
Kalmus, Dr. Herbert T., 338, 340
K & R Film Company, 183
Kane, Robert T., 255
Kansas City, 377
Kanter, Jay, 128, 191

Karger, Maxwell, 36
Katz, Herman, 255
Kaufman, George S., 33
Kaufman, Reginald Wright, 165
Kaufman Astoria Studios, 33
Kazan, Elia, 4
K. C. Booking Company, Inc., 188
Keane, James, 361
Keeney, Frank A., 138
Kell, Francis, 183
Kelley, Patrick, 128
Kelley, William Van Doren, 271, 345
Kellum, Orlando, 183
Kellum Talking Pictures, 183
Kelly, Bert, 337
Kelly, Harry A., 123
Kennedy, Aubrey M., 183, 190, 299
Kennedy, J. J., 187
Kennedy, Joseph, 260, 289
Kennedy Features, Inc., 183–84
Kent, Sidney R., 137, 354
Kerkorian, Kirk, 210, 211, 213, 359
Kessel, Adam, Jr., 184, 244, 285, 352
Keystone Film Company, 184
Killiam, Paul, 185
Killiam Shows, Inc., 185
Kinemacolor, 185
Kinemacolor Company of America, 185–
87
Kinematograph, 187
Kinematograph Company, 187
Kinetophone, 187–88
Kineto-Phonograph, 187
Kinetophote Film Corporation, 188
Kinetoscope, 187
King, Frank, 188
King, Herman, 188
King, Maurice, 188
King-Bee Films Corporation, 188
King International Corporation, 188–89
Kingsley, Pierce, 183
Kinney National Services, Inc., 254, 382
Kinograms, 241
Kino International Corporation, 189
Klaw & Erlanger, 40
Kleine, George, 144, 181, 189, 262
Kleine-Edison Feature Service, 189
Knickerbocker Star Features, 35, 189

Koch, Howard W., 257
Koerner, Charles, 290
Kranz, F. W., 373
Kremer, Victor, 113
Krim, Arthur, 102, 250, 359
Krim, Donald, 189
Kriterion Film Corporation, 190
Kunkleman, H. C., 332
Kuppin, Lawrence E., 242
Kutza, Michael, Jr., 63

"Laclede Western Features," 198
Ladd, Alan, Jr., 191, 355
The Ladd Company, 191
Laemmle, Carl, 169, 364
Laemmle, Max, 192
Laemmle Film Service, 365
Laemmle Theatres, 191–92
Laird International Studios, 192–93
Lake Placid, New York, 114
Lambart, Captain Harry L., 214
La Mesa, California, 14
Lancaster, Burt, 154
Land, Edwin H., 345
Landau, Ely A., 15
Lang, Eugene J., 87
Langenour, Henry W., 272
Lansing, Sherry, 355
Lasalida Films, Inc., 193
La Salle Film Company, 193
Lasky, Jesse L., 193, 256
"The Lasky Barn," 193
Lastfogel, Abe, 390
Laube, Professor Hans, 25
Laugh-O-Gram Films, 377
Law, James D., 69
Lawrence, Florence, 370
Lazarus, Simon, 169
Lear, Norman, 110
Lee, Arthur A., 194
Lee, F. Marshall, 185
Lee-Bradford Corporation, 194
Legion of Decency, 238–39
Lehrman, Henry M. "Pathe," 198, 333
Lenauer, Jean H., 194
Lenauer International Films, Inc., 194
Lesser, Sol, 9, 270, 326
Leventhal, J. F., 345

Levine, Joseph E., 110
Levine, Nat, 205
Le Vino, Albert S., 26
Levy, Ben, 215
Levy, Robert J., 286
Lewis, David, 111
Lewis J. Selznick Productions, Inc., 194
Lewyn, Louis, 160, 375
Liberty Film Company, 195
Liberty Films, Inc., 195
Liberty Motion Picture Company, 195–96
Library of Congress, 79
Lichtman, Al, 6, 211, 216, 269, 360, 394
Lieberson, Sandy, 191
Life Photo Film Corporation, 196
Lincoln, E. K., 263
Lincoln and Parker Film Company, 196
Lincoln Motion Picture Company, 197
Lindblom, Sadie, 36, 195
Linthicum, Dan, 152
Lippert, Robert L., 197
Lippert Pictures, 197
Little Carnegie Playhouse, New York, 29
Little Picture House, New York, 29
Livingston, Crawford, 343
L-KO Motion Picture Company, Inc., 198
Lloyd Films, Inc., 198
Lobby cards, 198
Loew, Arthur, 209
Loew, David, 111
Loew, Marcus, 209, 340
Loewenthal, Bernard, 196
Loew's Inc., 209
Loew's Theatres, 210
Lone Star Film Corporation, 232
Lone Star International Pictures, 199
Lone Star Productions, 199
Long, Samuel, 181
Long Beach, California, 35, 72
Long Island, New York, 27
Lopert, Ilya, 199
Lopert Films Distributing Company, 199
Lorimar Productions, 199–200
Lorimar-Telepictures, 199–200
Los Angeles International Film Exposition, 120

"Lost films," 200
Lotus Feature Studio, 207
Lowry, Ira M., 39, 201
Lowville, New York, 186
Lubin, Herbert, 31, 315
Lubin, Sigmund, 200
Lubin Manufacturing Company, 200
Lucas, George, 202
Lucasfilm, Ltd., 202
Lupino, Ida, 119
Lynch, Stephen A., 353

Macauley, Charles R., 357
MacDonald, J. Farrell, 18
MacDougall, Kenneth, 174
Machet, Nathan, 29
Maddox, C. M., 99
Maddox, Charles B., 36
Magic lanterns, 269
Mail Call, 162
Main Street U.S.A., 162
Majestic Motion Picture Company, 285–86
Majestic Pictures Corporation, 203
Major 16mm Productions, 314
Malvern, Paul W., 199
Mandarin Film Company, 204
Mandelbaum, E., 393, 394
Mann, Ted, 204
Mann Theatres Corporation, 204
Manson, F. W., 240
Manson International, 204
MAPO, 379
March of Time, 204–5
Marine Film Company of Los Angeles, 205
Marion, Frank, 181
Marston, Theodore, 214
Marvin, Henry Norton, 39
Mascot Industries, Inc., 128
Mascot Pictures Corporation, 205–6
Masquers Club, 206
Mastbaum, Jules, 324
Mastbaum, Stanley V., 200, 324
Mastercraft Photo-Play Corporation, 206
Master Pictures Corporation, 35
Masterpiece Film Manufacturing Company, 207

Matte shot, 322
Maverick Pictures International, 112
Mayer, Arthur, 179
Mayer, Louis B., 209
Mayflower Photoplay Corporation, 207
MCA, Inc., 207–8, 366
McAdoo, William Gibbs, 358
McClune, Grant, 24
McElwaine, Guy, 71
McKinley, Abner, 39
McManus, Edward A., 173
McManus, William A., 327
McNabb, Joe Hector, 38
McQueen, Steve, 128
Medavoy, Mike, 250
Medford, Massachusetts, 165
Méliès, Gaston, 208
Méliès, Georges, 208
Méliès Manufacturing Company, 208–9
Mentor Pictures, Inc., 209
Meredith, Lois, 334
Metro-Goldwyn-Mayer, Inc., 209–11
Metro Pictures Corporation, 211–12
Metropolitan Film Company, 212
Metropolitan Theatre, Los Angeles, 149
Metropolitan Theatres Corporation, 212
M-G-M, 209–11
MGM/UA Entertainment Co., 213
Mica Film Company, 190
Micheaux, Oscar, 213
Micheaux Film Corporation, 213
Middleton, George E., 53
Middletown, Connecticut, 174
Miles, David, 88
Miles, Ellison, 158
Miles, Joseph R., 115
Millbank, Jeremiah, 272
Miller, Alvah, 24
Miller, Ron, 349, 378
Miller, William H., 55
Miller Bros. 101 Ranch, 168
Million Dollar Pictures, 349
Million Dollar Theatre, Los Angeles, 149
Mills Novelty Company, 320
"MinA" Brand, 87–88
Mindlin, Michael, 29
Minoco Productions, Inc., 320
Miranda, Vincent, 277

Mirisch, Harold, 213
Mirisch, Marvin, 213
Mirisch, Walter, 213
Mirisch Corporation, 213–14
Mirisch Productions, Inc., 213
Mirror Films, Inc., 214
Mittenthal Film Company, Inc., 214
Mohawk Film Company, 215
Mole, Peter, 215
Mole-Richardson Co., 215
Monarch Producing Company, 215
Monogram Productions, Inc., 215–16
Monopol Film Company, 216
Monrovia, California, 85, 217
Monrovia Feature Film Company, 217
Morosco, Oliver, 250
Morris, Henry, 215
Morris, William, 390
Moss, Benjamin S., 49
Motion Picture Alliance for the Preservation of American Ideals, 217
Motion Picture and Television Fund, 218
The Motion Picture Artists Committee, 72, 218
Motion Picture Association of America, 219–20
Motion Picture Board of Trade of America, 220
Motion Picture Democratic Committee, 220
Motion Picture Directors Association, 220–21
Motion Picture Distributing and Sales Company, 221–22
Motion Picture Exhibitors' League of America, 222–23
Motion Picture Guild, 29
Motion Picture Mothers, Inc., 223
Motion Picture Patents Company, 223–25
Motion Picture Producers and Distributors of America, 219
Motion Picture Relief Fund, 218
Motion Picture Society for the Americas, 225
Motion Picture Theatre Owners of America, 223
Mount Vernon, New York, 9
Movielab, Inc., 226

Movietime, 136
Movietime, U.S.A., 226
Moviola, 226–27
MPAA. *See* Motion Picture Association of America
MPPDA. *See* Motion Picture Producers and Distributors of America
Muhl, Edward, 366
Mulbery Square Productions, Inc., 227
Munro, F. C., 272
Murdock, J. J., 186
Murdock, Rupert, 355, 382
Music, 227–29
Musicals, 229–31
"The Music Masters" series, 130
"Mustang" Westerns, 14
Mutual Film Corporation, 231–32
The Mutual Weekly, 241

NAMPI. *See* National Association of the Motion Picture Industry
Nash, Thomas, 233, 306, 401
Nash Motion Picture Company, Inc., 233
Nasser, James and George, 158
Nathanson, Sam, 204
National Association of Theatre Owners, Inc., 233
National Association of the Motion Picture Industry, 233–34
National Board of Censorship of Motion Pictures, 234–35
National Board of Review of Motion Pictures, Inc., 235
National Cameraphone Company, 235–36
National Catholic Office for Motion Pictures, 238–39
National Drama Corporation, 236–37
National Film and Photo League, 237
National Film Corporation of America, 237–38
National Film Day, 12
National General Corporation, 238
National Legion of Decency, 238–39
National Screen Service, 239
National Telefilm Associates, 288
National Theatres, Inc., 138
National Theatres Corporation, 137–38

NATO. *See* National Association of Theatre Owners, Inc.
Natural Vision, 345
Navajo Film Manufacturing Company, 240
Neff, N. A., 222
Neilan, Marshall, 32
Nelson, J. Arthur, 316
Nestor Film Company, 59–60
Nevada Motion Picture Company, 240
Newhall Ranch, 240
New Horizon Pictures Corporation, 76
New Line Cinema Corporation, 241
Newman, Paul, 128
New Orleans, 80
New Rochelle, New York, 343
News Parade, 56
Newsreels, 241–42
New World Pictures, 242–43
New York, 243
New Yorker Films, 243–44
New York Film Festival, 244
New York Motion Picture Company, 244–45
New York Security and Trust Company, 39
Nicholson, James H., 15, 16
Nickelodeons, 246
Nicodemus, James, 227
"Niggers," 246
Niles, California, 113
9.5mm, 246–47
Nitrate film, 247
Niver, Kemp, 254–55
Noble, John, 294
Nola Film Company, 80
Norbig Film Manufacturing Company, 247
Norfolk, Virginia, 331
Norling, J. A., 346
North, Frank E., 247
North Carolina Film Corporation, 248
Norton, E. E., 236
NSS. *See* National Screen Service
Numamoto, K., 177
Nye, Senator Gerald P., 381
Nykino Collective, 139

NYMPC. *See* New York Motion Picture
    Company

Oakland, California, 204
O'Brien, Dr. Brian, 349
O'Brien, Robert, 210
Ocean Film Corporation, 249
Ochs, Lee A., 222, 361
Oes, Ingvald C., 115, 149
Official Films, Inc., 249
Ogden Pictures Corporation, 249
O'Hara, Charles J., 8
Olcott, Sidney, 313
Oldknow, William, 362
Oliver Morosco Photoplay Company, 250
Olsen, O., 149
Omnimax, 167
Optical Printing, 323
Orion Pictures Corporation, 250–51
Oro Pictures Company, 251
Oroville, California, 272
Osborne, L. T., 90
"Oscar," 2
O'Shea, Daniel T., 369
Oshkosh, Wisconsin, 104
"Our Gang" series, 251
Owensby, Earl, 112
Oxford, John, 195
Oz Film Manufacturing Company, 251

Pal, George, 276
Pallas Pictures, Inc., 255
Palmer, Frederick, 253
Palmer Photoplay Corporation, 253
Palo Alto, California, 114
Palo Alto Film Company, 114
Panavision, Inc., 253–54
Panoram, 320
Paper prints, 254–55
Paragon Studios, 394–95
Paralta Plays, Inc., 255
Paramount Acting School, 32
Paramount-Bray Pictograph, 48
Paramount News, 241
Paramount Pictures, Inc., 256–58, 371
Paramount-Publix, 276
Parenchio, Jerry, 110
Parrot, Charles, 50

Parsons, "Smiling" Bill, 237
Pasadena, California, 85, 240, 313
Passing Parade, 258
Pathé, 259–60
Pathé News, 241
Patheé's Weekly, 241
Patsy Awards, 260–61
Paulvé, André, 92
Pawley, Raymond, 334, 353
Pax Films, 199
Payne, Herbert, 53
PDC. *See* Producers Distributing
    Corporation
"Peaceful Rafferty" series, 8
Peck, Frederick S., 102
Pedigreed Pictures, Inc., 261
"Pelican" brand, 102
Pence, William, 189, 342
People's Institute, 234
Percy, Charles, 38
The Permanent Charities Committee of
    the Entertainment Industries, 261
Perry, George H., 149
Peters, Thomas Kimmwood, 114
Petrova Picture Company, 334
Pettijohn, Charles C., 5, 11
Philadelphia, 28, 200
Photo Drama Producing Company,
    262
The Photo League, 237
"Photoplay," 262
Photoplay Authors' League, 262
The Photoplayers, 262
Photo Play Productions Company, 263
"Phun-Philms," 152
Pickford, Mary, 71, 358
Picture Playhouse Film Company, 263
Pierrot Film Company, Inc., 267
Pike's Peak Film Company, 263
Pilot Films Corporation, 263
Pine, William H., 263
Pine-Thomas Corporation, 263–64
Pioneer Film Corporation, 264
Pioneer Pictures, Inc., 264
P.I.T.S., 110
Pixar, 202
Planet Film Corporation, 265
"Planet of the Apes," series, 265

Plasticon, 345
Platt, George Foster, 10
Pleskow, Eric, 250
Plimpton, Horace G., 265
Plimpton Epic Pictures, Inc., 265
Plimpton-Fischer Photoplays, Inc., 265
Plitt, Henry G., 266
Plitt Theatres, Inc., 266
Poitier, Sidney, 128
"Pokes and Jabbs" series, 391
"Polar Bear Features," 150
Polk, James, Jr., 210
Pollard, L. J., 104
Polygram Pictures, 266
Popular Plays and Players Company,
    266–67
Popular Science, 178
Porter, Fred L., 65
Post Pictures Corporation, 267
Poverty Row, 267
Power, Francis, 95
Powers, P. A. "Pat," 267, 360
Powers-Cameron Film Company, 268
Powers Company, 267–68
"Powers Picture Plays," 268
P.R.C., 268–69
Pre-Cinema, 269
Pre-Eminent Films, Ltd., 269
Preferred Pictures, 269–70
Premier Company, 270
Premo Feature Film Company, 270
Prequels, 270
Prevues, 351
Price, Frank, 71
Priest, Robert W., 121
Primograf Company, 270
Principal Distributing Corporation, 271
Principal Pictures, 270
Principal Productions, Inc., 270–71
Principal Theatres Corporation of Amer-
    ica, 271
Prizma, Inc., 271
Prizma Color, 271
Prizma Natural Color Pictures, 271
Producers' Distributing Corporation, 271
Producers Distributing Corporation, 268,
    272
Producers Film Company, 272

Producers Guild of America, Inc., 272
Producers' Protective Association, 273
Producers Releasing Corporation, 268
Producers Studios Incorporated, 54
Production Code, 273–74
Production Code Administration, 274
Progressive Pictures Corporation, 268
Protection, 274–75
Promotional Films, Inc., 33
Providence, Rhode Island, 102
Prudential Studios, 54
Publicists Guild of America, 275–76
Public Media Incorporated, 122
Publix Theatres Corporation, 276
Puppet Animation, 323
Puppetoons, 276
Puritan Special Features Company, 277
Pussycat Theatres, 277
Pyramid Pictures, Inc., 277

Quality Pictures Corporation, 279
Quartet Films, 123
Quigley, Martin, 274

Rackin, Martin, 257
Radio and Television Directors Guild, 92
Radio City Music Hall, New York, 281
Radio-Television-Recording-Advertising
    Charities, 261
Rafelson, Robert J., 37
Raleigh Studios, 54
Ralph Ince Film Attractions, 315
Ramo Films, Inc., 282
Rampart Productions, Inc., 282
Rastar, 282–83
Rathvon, Peter N., 290
Ratings system, 283
Raver, Harry, 9–10, 24, 27, 104, 115,
    174, 265, 283–84
Raver Film Corporation, 283–84
Rayart Productions, 215
Raybert, 37
R.C.M. Productions, 320
Read, J. Parker, 98
Reade, Walter, 379–80
Reader, Smith and Blackton Combina-
    tion, 372
Realart Pictures Corporation, 256

Rebush, Roman, 68
Redford, Robert, 332
Redlands, California, 98, 140
Reed, Dr. Donald, 3
Regal Films, 197
"Regent" brand, 282
Regent Film Company, Inc., 284
The Regulars, 285
Rehme, Robert, 242
Reilly, E. H., 190
Reiniger, Lotte, 313
Reliance Motion Picture Company, 285–
    86
Reliant Pictures, Inc., 109
Rembusch, Frank, 5
Renfax Film Company, Inc., 286
Reol Motion Picture Company, 286
Republic Distributing Corporation, 286–
    87
Republic Film Laboratories, 78
Republic Pictures Corporation, 287–88
Republic Pictures Corporation (New),
    288
Research Council, 2
Rhatigan, H. F., 190
Rialto De Luxe Productions, 289
Rialto Star Features, 143
Rialto Theatre, Los Angeles, 149
Rich, Lee, 199
Rickey, C. F., 85
Ridgefield Park, New Jersey, 277
Ries, Irving, 345
Ritz-Carlton Pictures, 144
RKO Century Warner Theatres, 289
RKO-Pathé Studios, 192
RKO Radio Pictures, Inc , 289–90
RKO Theatres Corporation, 290
Roach, Hal, 152, 251
"Road movies," 291
Robert Brunton Studios, Inc., 291
Roberts, R. R., 183
Robertson, Harry F., 291
Robertson-Cole Company, 291–92
Rochester, New York, 268
Rock, William T. "Pop," 372
Rockville, Long Island, 265, 284
Rocky Glen, Pennsylvania, 118
Rogers, Charles, 365

Rogers, Charles "Buddy," 71
Rogers, Henry C., 292
Rogers & Cowan, Inc., 292
Rolands, George K., 292
Rolands Feature Film Company, 292
Rolfe, Benjamin A., 36
Rolin Film Company, 152
Romayne, H. Y., 293
Romayne Super-Film Company, 293
Rose, Jack, 165
Rosenfelt, Frank E., 211
Roskam, Edward S., 196
Rothacker, Watterson R., 169
Rothacker-Aller Film Laboratories, Inc.,
    293
Rothafel, S. L. "Roxy," 281, 293–94
Rothapfel, S. L., 281, 293–94
Rothapfel Pictures Corporation, 293
Roud, Richard, 244
Rowland, Richard, 211
Roxy, Theatre, New York, 293–94
Rubenstein, Leon J., 294
Ruby Feature Film Company, 294
Ruddell, Albert S., 401
Rudsill, H. T., 46
Ryder, Loren L., 371
Ryno Film Company, Inc., 294

Sack, Alfred N., 295
Sack Amusement Enterprises, 295
Safety film, 4
SAG. See Screen Actors Guild
St. Louis Motion Picture Company, 295
The "Saint" series, 295–96
Salter, Harry, 370
Saltzman, Harry, 341
Samuel Goldwyn, Inc., 296–98
The Samuel Goldwyn Company, 296
San Antonio, Texas, 208, 333
San Diego, California, 217
San Francisco, 298
San Juan Capistrano, California, 14
San Mateo, California, 36, 195, 196
San Rafael, California, 53, 95
Santa Barbara, California, 14, 299
Santa Barbara Motion Picture Company,
    299
Santa Monica, California, 182, 372

Santa Paula, California, 208, 295
Saperstein, Henry G., 362
Sargent, George L., 95
Sargent, H. W. (Bill), 110
Saul, Bill, 337
Saulsbury, H. W., 271
Savini, Robert M., 33
Sawyer, Arthur H., 31, 130, 299, 315
Sawyer, Cliff, 40
Sawyer, Inc., 299–300
Sawyer Film Mart, 300
Schaefer, George, 290
Schary, Dore, 210, 290
Schenck, Joseph M., 26, 72, 354, 356, 358
Schenck, Nicholas, 209
Schlank, Ike, 55
Schlein, Julius, 270
Schneider, Berton J., 37
Schreger, Charles, 354
Schulberg, B. P., 32, 269
Science Fiction Films, 300–302
Scopitone, 320
Scowcroft, Albert, 249
Screen Actors Guild, 302–3
Screen Art Pictures, 197
Screen Classics, Inc., 212, 303
The Screen Club, 303–4
Screen Directors Guild Incorporated, 92
Screen Extras Coalition, 304
Screen Extras Guild, 304
Screen Gems, 71
Screen Guild Productions, 197
Screen Producers Guild, 272
Screen Publicists Guild, 275
Screen Service Agency, 60
Screwball comedy, 305
Seabury, William H., 169
Sedgwick, Ed, 165
"See America First" series, 186
Seeley, Walter Hoff, 6, 211
Seelye, C. R., 361
SEG. See Screen Extras Guild
Seitz, George B., 33
Select Film Booking Agency, 305–6
Selig, William N., 306
Selig Polyscope Company, 306–8
Selwyn, Archibald, 9, 146

Selwyn, Edgar, 146
Selznick, David O., 289, 308, 358, 369
Selznick, Lewis J., 194–95, 286, 394
Selznick, Myron, 195
Selznick International Pictures, 308
Selznick International Studios, 192
Selznick Pictures Corporation, 195
Sennett, Mack, 32, 184, 245, 352
Sensurround, 309
Serial Film Company, 309
Serials, 309–10
Serrurier, Iwan, 226
Serrurier, Mark, 226–27
Seven Arts Productions, Ltd., 382
70mm, 311
Shallenberger, W. E., 26, 343
Shaw, Harold, 395
Shaw, William C., 167
Shayne, Robert, 241
Sheehan, Winfield R., 47
Shelby, North Carolina, 112
Sheldon, James M., 232
Shepherd, Robert, 24
Sher, Louis K., 311
Sherman, Bob, 175
Sherman, Harry, 54
Sherman Grinberg Film Libraries, Inc., 311
Sherpix, 311–12
Sherrill, William L., 28, 139
Sherry, William L., 389
Shorts and features, 312
Shourt, William, 24
Showscan, 312
Shubert-Brady Productions, 394
Shubert Film Corporation, 394
Sid Olcott International Features, 313
Sigma III, 250
Signal Film Company, 313
Silhouette Films, 313
Silly Symphonies, 314
Simmons, Ira H., 188
Siritzky, Joseph, 314
Siritzky, Leon, 314
Siritzky, Sam, 314
Siritzky International Pictures Corporation, 314
16mm, 314

Skinner, George A., 108
Skouras, Spyros, 355
Slapstick comedy, 315
Sloan, Harry E., 242
S-L Pictures Corporation, 315
Small, Edward, 109
Small Agency, 109
Small-Landau Agency, 109
Smallwood, Arthur N., 277, 315
Smallwood, Ray, 315
Smallwood Film Corporation, 315–16
Smell-O-Vision, 25–26
Smith, Albert E., 372
Smith, Douglas, 24
Smith, J. Boyce, Jr., 171
Smith, Philip, 143
Smith, Richard A., 144
SMPTE. *See* Society of Motion Picture
    and Television Engineers
Snyder, J., 95
Society of Motion Picture and Television
    Art Directors, 316
Society of Motion Picture and Television
    Engineers, 316–17
Society of Operating Cameramen, 317
Solax Company, 317
Soldiers with Wings, 162
Solow, Sidney, 78
Song slides, 317–18
Sono Art-World Wide Pictures, Inc., 318
Sorrell, Herb, 76
Sound, 318–20
Soundies, 320
Southern California Motion Picture Coun-
    cil, 320–21
The South on film, 321–22
Speaking of Animals, 178
Special effects, 322–23
Speidel, Glenn, 158
Spiegel, Arthur, 394
Spitze, Leo, 366
Spooner, Cecil, 43
Spoor, George K., 113, 345
Stamford, Connecticut, 10
Standard Pictures, Inc., 360
Stanfill, Dennis C., 355
Stanley Booking Corporation of Philadel-
    phia, 324

Stanley Warner Corporation, 324
"Star Films," 208
Stark, Ray, 282
"Starlight" brand, 214
"Stars over America," 162
The Star system, 324–26
Staten Island, New York, 9, 284
States rights, 326
States Rights Distributors, Inc., 326–27
The Static Club of America, 327
Steadicam, 327
Steger, Julius, 86, 394
Stein, Jules, 207, 366
Steiner, William, 179, 309, 399
Stellar Photoplay Company, 327
Sterling Camera and Film Company, 328
Stern, Julius and Abe, 61
Stevens, George, 195
Stevens, George, Jr., 12
Stills, 328
Stock Shot Libraries, 328–29
Stoddard, Brandon, 1
Strakosh, Edgar, 262
Streamer, Charles, 101
Streisand, Barbra, 83, 128, 325
Streyckmans, Hector J., 8, 154, 212, 214
Strong, Henry A., 103
Strong, Ted, 56
Stulberg, Gordon, 266, 355
Stuntmen's Association of Motion Pic-
    tures, 330
Stunts/Stuntmen, 330
Submarine Film Company, 331
Subtitles, 331–32
Sulphur Mountain Springs, Colorado, 208
Sundance Institute, 332
Sun Haven Studios, 133
Sunn Classics, 178
Sunset Comedy Company, 332
Sunset Motion Picture Company, 333
Sunset Motion Picture Corporation, 333
Sunshine Comedies, Inc., 333
Sunshine Comedy Company, 333
Super 8mm, 333–34
Superlative Pictures Corporation, 334
Superpictures, Inc., 334
Sutherland and Occidental Studios, 7

Synchronophone Motion Picture Company of New York, 335

Taft International Pictures, Inc., 178
Taggart, Marshall, 147
Talbot, Dan, 243
Talisman Studios, 337
Talking Picture Epics, Inc., 337
Tally, Thomas L., 128
Tampa, Florida, 237
"Tams" Pictures, 284
Tandem, 110
Tappan, New York, 263
T.A.T. Communications, 110
Taylor, Stanner E.V., 189
TBS, 50
Tec-Art Studio, 54, 338
Technicolor, 264, 338–40
Technicolor Corporation, 340–41
Technirama, 341–42
Ted Mann Productions, 204
Teleview, 345
Television, 123–26
Television Productions of America, Inc., 109
Telluride Film Festival, 342
Tenser, Mark, 85
Terry, Paul, 342
Terrytoons, 342–43
Texture Films, 122
Thalberg, Irving G., 209–10, 365
Thanhouser, Edwin, 343
Thanhouser Film Corporation, 343–44
Theatrofilm, 110
"The Thin Man" series, 344
35mm, 344
"This Is America" series, 205
Thomas, Augustus, 9, 27, 284
Thomas, Lowell, 68
Thomas, William C., 263
Thomas A. Edison, Inc., 106–7
Thomashefsky, Boris, 46
Thompson, Larry A., 242
Three-Dimensional Films, 344–47
THX Motion Picture Loudspeaker System, 202
Tiffany Film Corporation, 347
Tiffany Productions, 347–48, 375

Tiffany-Stahl Productions, 347
Time-Life Films, Inc., 348
Tinker, Edward R., 137
Tinting, 348
Tobias, Morris F., 334
Todd-AO, 349
Toddy, Ted, 349
Toddy Pictures Company, 349
Tombstone, Arizona, 46
"Tom Tom" Awards, 275
Toning, 348
Toomey, W. C., 231
Touchstone Films, 349–50
Tourneur, Maurice, 32
Trade papers, 350
Trailers, 351
TransAmerica Corporation, 359
Trans-Lux Corporation, 351–52
"The Treaty of Beverly Hills," 76
Triangle Film Corporation, 352–53
Triangle Productions, Inc., 72
Tri-Star Pictures, 353
Triumph Film Corporation, 394
Triumph Films, 354
Troland, Dr. Leonard, 339
Truart Film Corporation, 354
Trucolor, 66
Trumbull, Don, 24
Trumbull, Douglas, 312
Tucker, George Loane, 32
Tucson, Arizona, 7, 105
Turner, Edward R., 185
Turner, Ted, 211, 213, 359
Tusken Music, 202
"Tweedledum and Tweedledee" series, 102, 364
20th Century-Fox Film Corporation, 354–56
Twentieth Century Pictures, 356
Twyman Films, Inc., 356

UA, 358–59
Ulmer, Edgar G., 68
Union Photoplay Company, 357
United Artists Classics, 357
United Artists Communications, Inc., 357–58
United Artists Corporation, 358–59

United Costume Company, 387
United Film Service, 359–60
United Film Service Protective Association, 224
United Keanograph Film Manufacturing Company, 361
United Motion Picture Producers, Inc., 360
United Paramount Theatres, Inc., 276, 361
United Photoplays Company, 361
United Picture Theatres of America, Inc., 361–62
United Productions of America, 362
United States Amusement Corporation, 362
United States Exhibitors' Booking Corporation, 362–63
United States Government Committee on Public Information, Division of Films, 363
United States Motion Picture Corporation, 364
United Theatrical War Activities Committee, 162
United World Films, 364
Unity Sales Corporation, 364
The Universal Animated Weekly, 241
Universal City, 365
Universal-International, 366
Universal News, 241
Universal Pictures, 364–67
Universal Studios Tour, 366–67
Unsell, Eve, 394
Unusual Occupations, 178
UPA Pictures, Inc., 362
Urban, Charles, 185
USA Film Festival, 367
U.S. Army Pictorial Center, 32
U.S. Army Pictorial Service, 33
U.S. Catholic Conference, 239

Valenti, Jack, 219
Van Beuren, Amadee, Jr., 369
Van Beuren Corporation, 369
Vance, Louis Joseph, 31, 119
Vanguard Films, Inc., 369
Venus Features Company, 309

Vernon, G.L.P., 394
Viacom Enterprises, 369–70
Viacom International, Inc., 369–70
Victor, Leon, 183
Victor Film Company, 370
Victor Talking Machine Company, 373
Vidor, King, 165
Vigilant Pictures Corporation, 33
Vim Comedy Company, 370–71
VistaVision, 371
Vitagraph Company of America, 372–73
Vitaphone, 373–74
Vitarama Corporation, 68
V-L-S-E, 374
Vogel, Joseph, 210
"Vogue" comedies, 14
Vogue Films, Inc., 374
Vogue Motion Picture Company, 374
The Voice of Hollywood, 375

Wakefield, New York, 267
Waller, Fred, 68
Walsh, James O., 364
Walt Disney Productions, 50, 314, 349, 377–79
Walt Disney World, 378
Walter Reade Organization, 379–80
Walter Reade-Sterling, Inc., 380
Walter Wanger Productions, Inc., 380
WAMPAS Baby Stars, 386–87
Wanger, Walter, 380
War Activities Committee, 380–81
War film hearings, 381
Wardman Park Theatre, Washington, D.C., 29
Warner, Albert, 360, 381
Warner, Harry M., 360, 381
Warner, Jack, 381
Warner, S. L. (Sam), 284, 381
Warner Bros., 373–74, 381–83
Warner Bros.-Seven Arts, Ltd., 382
Warner Communications, Inc., 383
Warner Hollywood Studios, 297
Warner-Pathé News, 241
Warner's Features, Inc., 359
Wasserman, Lew, 207, 366
Waters, P. L., 187
Watson, J. Douglas, 318

Wayne, John, 36
Wayne, Michael, 37
Wayne-Fellows Productions, 36
Weber, L. Lawrence, 266
Weber-Fields-Kinemacolor Company, 186
Weinger, Ralph, 69
Weintraub, Sy, 254
Weiss, Charles, 25
Wells, Jack, 11
Wescott, W. Burton, 340
The Western, 384–86
Western Associated Motion Picture Advertisers, 386–87
Western Costume Co., 387
Western Electric Company, 109, 373
Western Photoplays, Inc., 387–88
West Orange, New Jersey, 106
WGA. See Writers Guild of America
Wharton, Inc., 388
Wharton, Theodore W., 388
White, Jack, 108
Whitestone, Long Island, 186
Whitman Bennett Productions, 388
Whitman Bennett Studios, 388
Whitman Features Company, 388–89
Whitney, Cornelius Vanderbilt "Sonny," 264
Whitney, John Hay "Jock," 264
"Why We Fight" series, 389
Wigan, Gareth, 191
Wilkes-Barre, Pennsylvania, 364
William A. Brady Picture Plays, Inc., 394
William L. Sherry Service, 389
William Morris Agency, 390
Williams, J. D., 128
Williamson, Charles, 331
Williamson, George W., 331
Williamson, J. Ernest, 331
Williamson Submarine Film Company, 331
Willat, C. A. "Doc," 266, 327
Will Rogers Memorial Fund, 390
Wilmington, North Carolina, 248
Winchester Pictures Corporation, 390
Wise, A. G., 345
Wizan, Joe, 355

Wizard Motion Picture Corporation, 391
W. Lindsay Gordon Studios, 284
Wojtalewicz, John, 173
Wolf, Clarence, 39
Wolper, Isaac, 206, 207
Women filmmakers, 391–92
Women in Film, 391–92
Women of the Motion Picture Industry, 393
WOMPI. See Women of the Motion Picture Industry
Wondergraf Production Company, 393
Wong, Marion E., 204
Woods, Frank E., 262
Worcester, Massachusetts, 196
Workers' Film and Photo League, 237
World Comedy Stars Film Corporation, 393
World Film Corporation, 393–95
World's Best Film Company, 395
World Special Films Corporation, 393
Wrather, Jack, 395
Wrather Corporation, 395–96
Wright, William, 181
Writers Club, 396
Writers Guild of America, 396–97
W. W. Hodkinson Corporation, 397
Wyler, William, 195

Yankee Film Company, 399
Yates, Herbert J., 78, 287–88
Yokel, Alex, 62
Yonkers, New York, 214, 263, 388
Young, Collier, 119
Young, L. A., 354
Young, Robert, 102
Youngstown, Ohio, 332

Zanuck, Darryl F., 354, 355, 356
Zanuck, Richard, 355
Zion Films, Inc., 401
Zodiak Film Manufacturing Company, 401
Zoetrope, 401–2
Zoetrope Studios, 158
Zoom lens, 402–3
Zukor, Adolph, 256, 276, 305

About the Author

Anthony Slide has served as associate archivist of the American Film Institute and resident film historian of the Academy of Motion Picture Arts and Sciences. He is the author or editor of more than twenty-five books on the history of popular entertainment, among which are *Early American Cinema* (1970), *The Films of D. W. Griffith* (1975, with Edward Wagenknecht), *Early Women Directors* (1977), *The Vaudevillians* (1981), *A Collector's Guide to Movie Memorabilia* (1983), *A Collector's Guide to TV Memorabilia* (1985), *International Film, Radio, and Television Journals* (1985), the seven-volume *Selected Film Criticism* series, and the three-volume *Selected Theatre Criticism* series. He is also editor of the ''Filmmakers'' series of books, published by the Scarecrow Press, and is active as a lecturer and filmmaker.